Bevis Hillier

Bevis Hillier, formerly editor of *The Connoisseur* and *The Times* Saturday Review, has written over twenty-five books (mainly on art) in addition to the three volumes of his authorized biography of John Betjeman. He is a Fellow of the Royal Society of Literature.

Praise for the three-volume biography

'Utterly compelling . . . Bevis Hillier is the brilliant chef of this orgy'
John Bayley, *London Magazine*

'Magnificent'
Jackie Wullschlager, *Financial Times*

'It's a triumph'
Ferdinand Mount, *The Spectator*

'Bevis Hillier brings his monumental life of John Betjeman to a triumphant conclusion . . . a true work of scholarship, intelligent, generous, sympathetic and often entertaining'
Allan Massie, *Literary Review*

'One of the most difficult parts of the biographer's art is bringing to life the inter-connecting groups of people who move around the subject, to give an idea of their world. Hillier achieves this superbly well . . . Whatever happens to John Betjeman's reputation, he has had the best and most sympathetic biographer he could have wished for'
Artemis Cooper, *Evening Standard*

'There was a wealth of feeling and imagination in [Betjeman's] life, and in Hillier's account it is getting the record it deserves'
John Gross, *Sunday Telegraph*

Works by Bevis Hillier include

The Connoisseur Year Book, 1959 (contributor)
Master Potters of the Industrial Revolution: The Turners of Lane End
Pottery and Porcelain 1700–1914
Art Deco of the 20s and 30s
Posters
Cartoons and Caricatures
The World of Art Deco
Austerity/Binge: Decorative Arts of the 1940s and 50s
A Tonic to the Nation: The Festival of Britain, 1951 (ed., with Mary Banham)
Fougasse
The New Antiques
John Betjeman, *Uncollected Poems* (ed. and introduced)
The Style of the Century
John Betjeman: A Life in Pictures
Young Betjeman
Early English Porcelain
Art Deco Style (with Stephen Escritt)
John Betjeman: New Fame, New Love
Betjeman: The Bonus of Laughter

John Betjeman

The Biography

BEVIS HILLIER

JOHN MURRAY

B BET

First published in Great Britain in 2006 by John Murray (Publishers)
A division of Hodder Headline

2

A CIP catalogue record for this title is available from the British Library

ISBN-13 978-0-7195-6443-7
ISBN-10 0-7195 6443-3

Typeset in 10.75/13 Monotype Bembo by Servis Filmsetting Ltd, Manchester

Printed and bound by Clays Ltd, St Ives plc

Hodder Headline policy is to use papers that are natural, renewable and recyclable products and made from wood grown in sustainable forests. The logging and manufacturing processes are expected to conform to the environmental regulations of the country of origin.

John Murray (Publishers)
338 Euston Road
London NW1 3BH

To Jake and Philippa Davies
with love and gratitude

Item to John Betjeman (the most
Remarkable man of his time in any position)
We leave a Leander tie and Pugin's ghost
And a box of crackers and St Pancras Station
And the *Church of Ireland Gazette* and our confidence
That he will be master of every situation.

W. H. Auden and Louis MacNeice, 'Auden and MacNeice:
Their Last Will and Testament', *Letters from Iceland*, London, 1937

I often met Jerrard Tickell [whose novel about a cow, the 'Venus de Milko',
she was involved in filming], in the Connaught Hotel, where, he said, he
met colleagues during his days in Intelligence. He introduced me to his
friend, John Betjeman; he and Tickell struck me as two very loveable
eccentrics as we sat with our drinks, talking about *Appointment with Venus*.
Betjeman said, 'History must not be written with bias – both sides must be
given, even if there is only one side . . .'

Betty E. Box, *Lifting the Lid: The Autobiography of
Film Producer Betty Box, OBE*, Lewes, Sussex, 2000

Contents

CONTENTS

Illustrations

The author and publishers would like to thank the following for permission to reproduce illustrations: Plates 1, 2, 3, 4, 5, 6 and 7, John Betjeman Archive; 8 and 19, the late John Bowle; 9, Lady Fergusson of Kilkerran; 10, the late Lionel Perry; 11, David Synnott; 12, G. R. Barcley-Smith; 13, 14 and 17, the late Mrs Christopher Sykes; 15, Duncan Andrews Collection; 16, Lady Mary Dunn; 18, the Hon. Mrs Derek Jackson; 22, Mrs Sibyl Harton; 27, Noel Blakiston; 31, Faringdon Estate; 35, Dallas Bower; 36, John Murray Archive; 41 and 42, Mrs Betty Packford; 44, Christopher Loyd; 45, the late Mollie Baring; 46, Candida Lycett Green; 47, 50 and 51, the late Hon. Penelope Betjeman; 48, William Norton; 49, Veronica Sharley; 52, Sotheby's; 53, Jane Bown; 54, Gordon Whiting; 56, The Times © News International; 57, William Westenra and the late Bishop Mervyn Stockwood; 58, 59 and 60, Jonathan Stedall; 61, British Rail.

Preface

In the 1960s, twenty-one, not eighteen, was the age at which one ceased to be a minor – a 'boy' became a 'man'. As the music-hall song had it,

> I've got the key of the door –
> Never been twenty-one before.

I reached twenty-one in 1961, a year that seemed to have some cabbalistic magic to it: it was the only year of the twentieth century which read the same when the figures were turned upside-down. (We must wait more than four thousand years for that to happen again, in 6009.) I was an Oxford undergraduate then, reading history, with A. J. P. Taylor, Alan Bennett and Churchill's biographer (Sir) Martin Gilbert among my tutors.

The year 1961 was a miserable one for John Betjeman: the Euston Arch was demolished, in spite of his efforts to save it. It was also the first year I wrote about him – ten years before I met him – in an article headed 'Oxford Aesthetes' in the undergraduate magazine *Mesopotamia*, a precursor of *Private Eye*. (A copy survives in the Bodleian Library.) I decorated the piece with a caricature of Betjeman, whom I described as 'that lonely batrachian figure on the platform of St Pancras or Euston, clutching an extinct Bradshaw and gazing with bulbous mystic eyes at the iron-and-crystal roof snaking away to infinity and Watford Junction'.

In 1961 I was lucky enough to attend the inaugural lecture of Richard Southern – a leading medievalist – as Chichele Professor of Modern History. Most inaugural lectures consist of expansive pronouncements relieved by some donnish humour. But Southern's lecture was revolutionary. He damned the entire syllabus of the History School and spoke of 'the dull despotism of examination papers – to examine them is slavery'.

He did not disappoint in the humour quotient of his lecture. He spoke of Montague Burrows, who had become the first Chichele Professor of Modern History in 1862.

A naval man by profession, he retired, read the school of Law and Modern
History, set himself up as a coach in the new school, and wrote a book to
teach others what books they should read. Gunnery officer of HMS *Excellent*
in 1852; Professor in 1862! He was immensely surprised: 'Not even my First
Class astonished me more.'

Southern traced the origins of the combined School of Law and
Modern History. It was founded in 1850. Up to then, most would-be historians had taken degrees in the classics, Greek and Latin. 'You might
think', Southern added, 'that historians of England would be gratified at
the academic respectability conferred on their subject by the founding of
the new school' – but E. A. Freeman, Oxford's then Regius Professor of
Modern History, said it was 'an easy school for rich men'.

When it was suggested that the three volumes of my biography of John
Betjeman should be abridged into one volume – to be published in the year
of the poet's centenary – my first thought was similar to Freeman's: is this
going to be just a soft option? I had thought Betjeman was worth three volumes, and my publishers, John Murray (not without some arm-twisting),
kindly allowed me to realize my vision of what the biography should be.

But the answer to my question is: yes! A soft option is precisely what is
intended. It is no reflection on a grand restaurant when somebody feels
that all he wants is a snack – and it is still a pretty substantial snack, even
with all the cuts that have been made. I hope Betjemaniacs will continue
to lap up all that is in my three volumes; but others might fretfully wonder,
'Do I really need to know all this about him?' For them, there is now this
manageable deckchair book.

Most of the reviews of my volumes have been favourable. But John
Gross, while saying he 'enjoyed the book enormously', thought it 'far too
long'. (Craig Brown, by contrast, wished it had gone on for another two
thousand pages.) How long is a biography? I was in the happy position of
being able to interview Betjeman, his wife Penelope and many of their
friends on my tape-recorder. No Johnny-come-lately will be able to do
that: he will have to rely on the art of paraphrase.

I bore in mind, certainly, what Rebecca West wrote at ninety, in reviewing a biography of Somerset Maugham: 'No one has told this man that *you
don't put everything in.*' But, equally, I knew that what I failed to put into
my book would be lost to history; the wells would dry up. I thought that
Betjeman deserved a large canvas – as poet, conservationist, television presenter and a central figure in a circle of fascinating friends. I thought
also of future writers on other subjects who would find in my volumes

material of value to them. Suppose somebody were to research English education in the twentieth century. Betjeman was at two prep schools and a public school and taught in two prep schools: what a goldmine for the researcher, though he or she would need to look elsewhere for insights into state education. An architectural historian wanting to know about the destruction of the Euston Arch or the London Coal Exchange would find not just Betjeman's attempts to prevent those atrocities, but, in each case, a lot of background.

I saw myself as a source as well as a chronicler. Like the Venerable Bede, I knew some of the people I was writing about. At the same time, I always realized that many potential readers – perhaps the majority – would prefer a more compact book which would give them the gist of my volumes between two covers. A skilful abridgement would distil the essential Betjeman. I wrote just now of arm-twisting my publishers. Robert Southey was an indifferent Poet Laureate (see Byron's 'Vision of Judgment'), but his *Nelson* is one of the great biographies. No doubt it could be profitably reduced to a half-Nelson. As they say, Alfa-Romeo is better than no Romeo at all.

When my publishers suggested an abridged version, I did not want, in person, to 'murder my babies', Medea-style. I requested that someone else should do the cutting – and, I have to say, Murray's accepted that idea with some alacrity. I am fortunate that the work was undertaken by Peter James, who copy-edited the last two volumes so adeptly.

When the idea of a compact version of my book was first mooted, I did wonder whether it might be 'an abridge too far'. I even ventured into verse to predict what I thought might be my reaction to the truncated text.

> With worry-lines my brow is ridged
> To see my handiwork abridged –
> My gallon in a pint-pot poured,
> My purple passages ignored;
> My banquet in a tin can squashed,
> My arsenal of notes kiboshed;
> My wine decanted into thimbles,
> My trumpets junked for tinkling cymbals;
> My mighty oak, which scraped the sky,
> Supplanted by a mere *bonsai* . . .

I need not have worried. Peter James has abridged my text most sensitively and cleverly – in fact, superlatively well. In my relief I have added a few lines to my fledgling poem:

I hope this trifle suits your palate.
No man's a hero to his valet –
To his biographer, still less,
Who sees him in complete undress,
Who knows who shared his sheets and pillows
And jots down all his peccadilloes.
JOHN BETJEMAN, I've jotted yours;
But from my story also soars
A figure, not, perhaps, heroic –
More Sybarite, for sure, than Stoic –
And yet a marvel of his time.
He wrote in metre and in rhyme . . .

And there I gave up.

As I write this preface, I am the same age (sixty-five) that John Betjeman was when I first met him in 1971, I knew him for thirteen years, until his death in 1984, that year of Orwellian omen. I wonder what Betjeman would have made of the years since then if he had lived to be one hundred. In 1986 he would have sorrowed at the news of Penelope's death in India. Lady Elizabeth Cavendish would still have been around to love and look after him. He might have managed a few more poems. What fun he would have had at the expense of the ghastly Millennium Dome. If still Poet Laureate, he could have felt obliged to write an ode or odes on Prince William's eighteenth and/or twenty-first birthday/s.

Well, as Betjeman might have muttered at the New Gallery cinema, London, in his days as a 1930s film critic, 'I think this is where I came in . . .' And, as it happens, the New Gallery cinema is where Chapter 1 begins, on the next page.

The Hospital of St Cross, Winchester
November 2005

I

To Highgate

————◦◦◦◦◦————

IN AUGUST 1934, a few days before his twenty-eighth birthday, John Betjeman went to the New Gallery cinema in London for a private viewing of the Gaumont-British film *Little Friend*. He had been film critic of the *Evening Standard* for seven months. The film, directed by Berthold Viertel, starred the fourteen-year-old schoolgirl Nova Pilbeam.

John was impressed by the 'horrifyingly unsentimental' movie. 'I'm not sure that *Little Friend* isn't the best English film I have ever seen,' he wrote. He tended to be liberal with such compliments. Within hours, he knew, the quotable encomium would appear on the New Gallery's billboards, artfully cut – ' "The best English film I have ever seen" – JOHN BETJEMAN, *Evening Standard*.' Perhaps those who had bullied him at school, those who (unlike him) had taken degrees at Oxford or those who had snubbed him when he courted their daughters, would pass by and see what an arbiter he had become.

But there was another reason for John's commendation of *Little Friend*. Its story rang disturbingly true to him, reviving memories of his own childhood.

> Do you remember [he wrote] what it was like to dread the dentist's drill? Do you remember, as a child, being frightened by the villain in the pantomime? Being irritated by your nurse? Hating your cousins? Being made to eat when you felt sick? Being made to 'lie down' when you wanted to get up and kick things?
>
> And do you remember, worst of all, waking from a dream to hear, in the next room, your parents quarrelling?
>
> That is how *Little Friend* will open when it first greets you at the New Gallery on Sunday. A little girl (Nova Pilbeam) wakes up after a nightmare to hear an acrid argument going on between her father and her mother.
>
> The parents protest that nothing is wrong. But their daughter is too clever, as all children are, and too sensitive, as all children are too.

The rows between John's parents, Ernest and Bess Betjemann, reverberate in his poetry. 'They quarrelled all the time,' said Joan Kunzer (*née*

Larkworthy), who knew the family from 1910. In a passage of an early version of *Summoned by Bells* (1960), omitted from the published poem, John – speaking in the person of his father – suggested that relations between his parents had worsened after a second child had died at birth:

> And how house-proud and how baby-proud was she
> When first we knew the next was on the way.
> But oh! how still and ugly stood the pram,
> Disused and blocking up the little hall,
> How shut the tidy drawers of baby clothes
> When the child came, and choked a bit and died
> To leave us only with our one to love.
> Then it was 'us', now it is 'she and I'
> For I am deaf and she is someone else.

One of the things Ernest and Bess quarrelled about was their surname. John's great-grandfather, a London cabinet-maker, spelt his name 'George Betjeman', in stylish copperplate, on the cover of his 'work-book' and in the printed heading of his business invoices. But John's grandfather and father both spelt their names with two 'n's' – Betjemann. The double 'n' suggested German origins. A single 'n', John's mother thought, looked Dutch; and she assured him that his ancestors had come from Holland.

When German products were popular, in the late nineteenth century, it was almost an advantage for the family firm, G. Betjemann & Sons, cabinet-makers, to have a name that looked Teutonic. But during the First World War, when the Battenbergs changed their name to Mountbatten and German traders' windows were shattered, a double 'n' became a liability. Ernest, however, continued to spell his name Betjemann until the end of his life, and his son's birth certificate was in the name of John Betjemann. At Highgate Junior School, which John attended from September 1915 to March 1917, two boys danced round him shouting

> Betjemann's a German spy –
> Shoot him down and let him die:
> Betjemann's a German spy,
> A German spy, a German spy.

During the war his mother decided to drop the second 'n' from the surname. As he grew older he saw no reason why he, too, should not revert to the spelling favoured by his great-grandfather. In a letter of 1927 (when John was twenty-one) his father wrote to him: 'I see you sign as a "one enner". Very cowardly!' But in 1933, for legality's sake, John signed the marriage register 'John Betjemann'.

John always insisted that his ancestors were Dutch and that the founder of the cabinet-making business had come from Holland in the late eighteenth century. Dutchmen had been emigrating to England for centuries, to escape religious persecution and to find work. But it is much more likely that John's family was of German origin. The name is German. A tradition in the family, which after 1914 they did their best to forget, suggested that John's great-great-grandfather, George Betjemann, was born in Bremen in 1764. He was described as a 'sugar baker' on two marriage certificates – his own on his marriage to a London girl, Eleanor Smith, in 1797, and that recording the marriage of his daughter Rebecca to John Merrick, a London cabinet-maker, in 1846.

John Merrick was the son of William Merrick, who had a cabinet-making business in Red Lion Square, London. John Betjeman's great-grandfather, George Betjeman (1798–1887), who was learning the same trade, used to visit the workshops. He fell in love with William Merrick's daughter Mary Anne and married her at St Giles, Cripplegate, on 16 July 1830. So the Betjeman(n) and Merrick families were doubly linked.

William Merrick died intestate in 1836, leaving £7,000, which was divided among his children. One of them, Mary Anne Betjeman, was dead by then, but she had four children: John's grandfather John, George, Polly and Harriott Lucy. Part of the money was invested in the cabinet-making business which their father, George Betjeman, had established at 6 Upper Ashby Street. By the time John Betjemann married, in 1870, the firm had moved to Pentonville Road, where it remained until the liquidation of the company in 1945.

John Betjemann (1835–93), who is mentioned in John's poem 'City', married Hannah Thompson, daughter of Edward John Thompson, a watch-material maker, and his wife Jessica (née Roberts). Like the Betjemanns, the Thompsons were North London people of the lower-middle class. But members of both families had accomplishments some way beyond the do-it-yourself entertainment of the average Victorian home. John's Thompson grandmother wrote gushing verse, and the Betjemann family included Cousin Stanley who belonged to a touring opera company. A Cousin Henry (Betjemann) designed the Betjemann Patent Bedstead Lock.

The best-known member of the family, before John himself became famous through his poetry and his television appearances, was the violinist, conductor and composer Gilbert H. Betjemann (1840–1921), Musician-in-Ordinary to Queen Victoria and King Edward VII. He composed a cantata, 'Song of the Western Men', but he was better known as a conductor of Beecham-like panache. John told Michael Parkinson, in a television interview of 1977: 'Gilbert Betjemann introduced Wagner to Glasgow. They just laughed at it. So he rapped with his baton on the rail and said, "Are you going to listen to this music or are you not? Because if you're not, I shall go home and enjoy a whisky toddy."' John's grandfather, John Betjemann, was a cousin of Gilbert, and as a child John was taken to meet the old musician and his wife, the singer Rose Daffone, in Hillmarton Road, Camden Town, London.

John Betjemann and his wife Hannah had two sons. The elder, John George, was considered a wastrel. So it was left to Ernest, the younger son, to take over the family business as the 'third generation'.

Ernest Betjemann was the kind of man every Victorian headmaster's speech, every boys' magazine, was calculated to produce. When Sarah Bernhardt was asked to fill in 'The quality I most admire in men' in an Edwardian 'Confessions' album, she wrote (not, perhaps, without her tongue in her cheek), 'Uprightness'. Ernest Betjemann was upright. With his sanguine complexion and military bearing, he looked as if he exercised with Indian clubs each morning. He was a cricketer, a footballer, an enthusiastic fisherman and a good shot – the epitome of *mens sana in corpore sano*.

Born in 1872, he was educated at Highbury Park School, at the City of London School and in Switzerland. He entered the family firm in 1899, when the main product was the Betjemann patent tantalus, a metal apparatus for locking away decanters of drink from the servants. The tantalus remained part of Betjemann's manufacture until, towards the outbreak of the Second World War, it became harder to obtain servants than to stop them pilfering the drink. The factory also continued making the goods that George Betjeman had been producing in the 1820s: cabinets, dressing-tables and writing-desks.

In 1902 Ernest married Mabel Bessie Dawson, daughter of James Dawson, a maker of artificial flowers, and his wife Alice (*née* Daniel). In spite of slightly protruding teeth, 'Bess' was considered attractive. A friend who knew her before her marriage described her as 'such a pretty girl, always so gay, clever and amusing'. Both bride and groom had grown up in Highbury, and they were married there at St Saviour's, Aberdeen Park. Perhaps because he felt *dépaysé* in lower Highgate, John half adopted the Highbury of his parents and grandparents as his homeland, at the same time somewhat exaggerating his parents' social standing there:

> These were the streets my parents knew when they loved and won –
> The brougham that crunched the gravel, the laurel-girt paths that wind,
> Geranium-beds for the lawn, Venetian blinds for the sun,

A separate tradesman's entrance, straw in the mews behind,
Just in the four-mile radius where hackney carriages run,
   Solid Italianate houses for the solid commercial mind.

These were the streets they knew; and I, by descent, belong
   To these tall neglected houses divided into flats.
Only the church remains, where carriages used to throng
   And my mother stepped out in flounces and my father stepped out
                                                    in spats
To shadowy stained-glass matins or gas-lit evensong
   And back in a country quiet with doffing of chimney hats.

Ernest and Bess Betjemann's first home after their marriage was 52 Parliament Hill Mansions in north-west London. John, their only child to survive, was born there on 28 August 1906, and christened by the assistant curate of St Anne's, Highgate Rise, on 25 November. After his birth, his mother sent out beribboned cards to her acquaintance. The cards with their fine engraving and pretty bows (blue for a boy) were a *de luxe* trimming characteristic of Bess Betjemann. Like the woman in John's poem 'How to Get On in Society', she liked to have things 'daintily served'.

Parliament Hill Mansions is the kind of building which John was unjustly accused of liking when he began to champion Victorian architecture. It is an undistinguished terracotta block with railed-off balconies, just off the Highgate Road. He did not mention it when he took Valerie Jenkins of the *Evening Standard* on a tour of the 'haunts of his childhood' in 1974. But he rhapsodized then and also in *Summoned by Bells* over 31 West Hill, a more attractive villa to which his parents moved when he was still an infant.

Deeply I loved thee, 31 West Hill! . . .
Here from my eyrie, as the sun went down,
I heard the old North London puff and shunt,
Glad that I did not live in Gospel Oak.

Gospel Oak is just where John *did* live in his earliest years. Parliament Hill Mansions was about as close to Gospel Oak station as it was possible to be.

John gives one vignette of life in Parliament Hill Mansions in *Summoned by Bells* – not early in the poem, as one might expect, but as a 'flashback' to contrast with Ernest Betjemann's unwelcome arrival in Cornwall when John was a disaffected teenager:

That early flat, electrically lit,
Red silk and leather in the dining-room,
Beads round the drawing-room electrolier . . .

Singing in bed, to make the youngster laugh,
Tosti's 'Goodbye', Lord Henry's 'Echo Song' –
And windy walks on Sunday to the Heath,
While dogs were barking round the White Stone Pond.

Bess Betjemann did not intend the family to stay in the Mansions for long. Socially aspiring, she wanted to move up the hill into more genteel Highgate. Marriage to Ernest had dampened her down, but she remained spirited, someone who liked having fun. Her cousin Queenie Avril recalled her as 'a vivid and vital person . . . when I was a gauche young girl and Bess an elegant, lovely and witty young married woman'. Ernest was overbearing but Bess had a mind of her own; before the First World War she was a suffragette and attended Emmeline Pankhurst's meetings. As late as the 1940s John still thought her sharp enough to précis novels for him when he was reviewing books for the *Daily Herald*. But, though she was bright and good-hearted, Bess was a little snobbish and silly. John wrote:

I feared my father, loved my mother more,
And just because of this would criticize,
In my own mind, the artless things she said.

She used the exaggerated language of the society flapper – 'ghastly', 'simply maddening', 'simply charming', 'fearfully common', 'a perfect beast', 'a dream of comfort', 'thrilled to death'. John enjoyed her wit and gaiety, but too often in his childhood she was away from home, pursuing her social life. Mary Bouman, who as a child knew John and his parents, thought John was 'left on his own far too often – rather as Winston Churchill was neglected by Lady Randolph Churchill'.

If Bess Betjemann was like Lady Randolph, then Hannah Wallis had the place in John's life that Mrs Everest had in Churchill's: the comforting, ever-benevolent nanny who was always there when he needed her. ('Perhaps it is the only disinterested affection in the world,' Churchill wrote of the nanny's love for her charge.) Hannah Wallis lived with her daughter in Dongola Road, Philip Lane, Tottenham. 'She was an old-fashioned person, small and dumpy,' John remembered, 'and she wore a black bonnet when we used to take the train to Philip Lane station and walk to . . . Dongola Road.' She listened for hours while John read poetry to her: Bess was fond of recounting how she came home once and found John reading poetry aloud outside the lavatory door 'behind which the old girl had locked herself'. Hannah played draughts with him and always let him win. He teased her and she laughed. 'I exceeded the bounds of decency and decorum and she didn't mind.' She was never angry or fussed. Hannah's imperturbable goodwill even survived a 'fatal Christmas Day' which John evoked in a Christmas broadcast of 1947:

> I woke up early. Heavy on my feet were the presents of my relations, presents of sympathy for an only child. I don't remember what they were. But one of them I do remember. It was one of those pieces of frosted glass in a wooden frame and behind the glass a picture in outline which one was supposed to trace on the glass with a pencil. 'To Master John with love from Hannah Wallis.' I stood up on my bed among the brown paper of the opened parcels. I stood up. I stepped a step. Crack! I had smashed the frosted glass of her present.
>
> Hannah Wallis, you who are now undoubtedly in Heaven, you know now, don't you, that I did not do that on purpose? I remember thinking then that she might think I had smashed it because I did not think it a good enough present and that it looked too cheap among the more expensive ones of my relations. But, as a matter of fact, it was just what I wanted. And now I had smashed it. I remember putting it on a shelf over my bed between some books so as to hide the accident. Guiltily I went down to breakfast.
>
> 'Did you like the slate? It was just what you wanted, wasn't it? The biggest I could get!' Poor people were poor in those days and she must have saved up for it.
>
> 'Oh yes, and thank you very much. It was lovely.' Oh, the guilt, the shame! I did not dare, for fear of hurting her feelings whom I loved so much, – I did not dare to tell her I had smashed it. Yet that evening when my room had been tidied and the presents put away, I found the broken glass and frame put in my waste-paper basket. She must have found it out. But we neither of us ever mentioned it again. I think that cracked glass was the first crack in my heart, the first time I lost ignorance and the first time I realized the overwhelmingly unpleasant things of the world.

John described himself, in *Summoned by Bells*, as 'an only child, deliciously apart'; but he was often pitifully lonely. He treated his teddy bear, Archibald, as a surrogate brother. The loneliness was tinged with an irrational feeling of guilt: he learned about the child who had died, and who might have been so much more to his father's liking than he was. Because of his lack of brothers and sisters, John had no readily accessible standard with which to compare his own behaviour. Was it normal, he wondered, to lock a small girl in the lavatory and to wait outside until she cried? (He played this trick on Hannah Wallis's granddaughter, Hilda.) Did other small boys have a strong desire, as he did, to smash the faces of china dolls?

Hannah Wallis was prepared to put up with all John's eccentricities; but his Calvinist nursemaid, Maud, the dark angel of his childhood, was not. Her sadistic treatment of him is described in *Summoned by Bells*; and she instilled in him a dread of eternal damnation, as he recalled in 'N.W.5 & N.6'. Her frightening prophecies gave him nightmares, including 'a clear vision of the Devil':

> I used to go up in a black lift made of wood. We would arrive at the top where it was blindingly white and I would be in this little wooden lift one side of which was open and showed that we were floating on a limitless white sea. But I was not alone in the lift. Oh no! There rose up from the corner a tall thin-faced man with ram's horns springing out of his forehead. He was the Devil. His horns were outlined black against the sky. He was coming nearer. There was no escape.

In 'N.W.5 & N.6' John suggests that the indoctrination by Maud took place in 1911. This date cannot be relied on with much confidence, as John was rhyming it with 'Heaven'; 1910 and 1912 would not serve. But a 1950 radio talk confirms that the words which made such an impression on him were spoken after the Betjemanns moved to West Hill, Highgate.

> Lying in bed of a late summer evening I remember hearing the bells ring out from St Anne's, Highgate Rise – the church where I was christened . . . Maud, the nurse, was looking out of the open window. Crossed in love, I suppose, and for once fairly gentle with me. I remember asking her if I should go to Heaven. 'You will, but I won't,' she said. I remember recognizing even then that she spoke from her heart about herself. I did not recognize this, at the time, as any sign of grace in Maud.

Moving to 31 West Hill was, literally and metaphorically, going up in the world. The villa is about a mile uphill from Parliament Hill Mansions. Though Highgate stood in a wilderness of suburbs, it had the air of a Middlesex village – and still has, even if the old shops with wooden canopies over the pavement have been painted up and converted into 'galleries'. When John was nostalgic about the Highgate he had known in the reign of Edward VII, he liked to claim that 'At that hill's foot did London then begin / With yellow horse-trams clopping past the planes . . .' The horse-drawn trams were succeeded by electric trams, and to these, also, John had a lifelong attachment.

The Betjemanns' stucco villa was about halfway up the social graph: the ideal vantage-point for gaining a nice sense of English social distinctions. Snobbery is a branch of applied sociology, and in this discipline John proved instinctually adept. Comparisons were to be made even among immediate neighbours. John early realized that:

> we were a lower, lesser world
> Than that remote one of the carriage folk

> Who left their cedars and brown garden walls
> In care of servants.

But he could also tell:

> That we were slightly richer than my friends
> The family next door: we owned a brougham
> And they would envy us our holidays.

The family next door were the Boumans, whose children were, for a while, like a brother and sisters to John. Jan Bouman, the father, was a Dutch journalist, who worked for the Press Association of America in London, Paris, Berlin and The Hague. His wife Ethelwynne came of Scottish and Cumbrian parents, border folk in Northumbria. They had three children: Bill (b. 1907), Mary (b. 1908) and Betty (b. 1909). Mary Bouman recalled John as 'a rather sad little boy'. Tears poured down his face when he could not do his sums in the nursery: 'he found them extraordinarily difficult'. But he was capable, too, of impishness. 'We haven't any paste,' Mary observed when they were cutting out pictures for their scrap books. 'Oh, that doesn't matter,' he said. 'We'll stick them in with marmalade.'

The Bouman children did not go to Byron House, John's first school. But Bill Bouman, a year younger than John, was his best friend and companion, a handsome and popular child, even though a severe attack of scarlet fever had, in Mary's words, 'left something missing'. John used to take Bill out on to Parliament Hill Fields and say, 'We will write poetry.' John would sit on a seat on top of one of the two small hills above Highgate Ponds and wait for inspiration, pencil and paper on his knees. 'What [Bill] did I can't remember,' John later said, 'except that I made him bring pencil and paper too.' 'John is out with Bill,' Ethelwynne Bouman wrote to her husband (then in Holland) in January 1916. 'They walk to Golders Hill Park every morning.'

It seems likely that John engaged in some sexual experiment with Bill Bouman; that Bess Betjemann discovered them and warned John to cool the friendship; and that John later made the incident the subject of his poem 'Narcissus', published in 1966. The poem describes how the poet—narrator would go for walks with his friend 'Bobby',

> And when we just did nothing we were good,
> But when we touched each other we were bad.

The poet's mother said they were 'unwholesome' in their play.

> And then she said I was her precious child,
> And once there was a man called Oscar Wilde.

The narrator is easily identified as John: a delicate only child with a father in trade, a suffragette mother, and a teddy bear to cling to when in trouble. 'Bobby' (Billy) lives near the poet and has sisters. In a radio talk of 1950 John said: 'Bill was, my mother told me "easily led". Perhaps this was why I liked him so much.'

Ethelwynne Bouman, a serenely beautiful and sweet-natured woman, encouraged John's interest in poetry. In 1916, when John was ten, Jan Bouman was posted abroad and his family joined him. 'I did not realize at the time', Mary Bouman said, 'how utterly desolating that was for John. It meant that he lost his "second mother" and his brother and sisters.' John himself said in 1950: 'I think the saddest moment of my life, as numbing as any subsequent loss, was the time when Bill, Mary and Betty left the district . . . The pavements outside our houses on West Hill, the Heath, our little gardens seemed empty for ever.'

In 1922 the Boumans returned to London. In April Bill Bouman wrote to his father, who was in Paris for the Peace Conference: 'I got such a nice surprise one day. It was the day after we had broken up at school and mother came to take us for a walk. I went out of the schoolroom to put on my boots and who should I see but John Betjeman standing next to mother. My breath was taken away when I saw him. We had a nice walk together on the Heath. John is the same old John as when we left [in 1916], as jolly as ever.'

At the top of the hill lived John's 'first and purest love', Peggy Purey-Cust, daughter of Admiral Sir Herbert Purey-Cust. Satchel on back, he used to hurry up West Hill to catch her as she walked to school, accompanied by her nanny. She had fair hair, ice-blue eyes, long pale lashes, freckles and a turned-up nose – 'all my loves since then / Have had a look of Peggy Purey-Cust'. It was in her Georgian home that John experienced the first social snub of his life. Having been invited to tea once ('It seemed a palace after 31') he was never asked again. After the tea he called on Peggy many times, but was always told she was out, away or unwell. When she was sick, he took her *House of the Sleeping Winds, / My* favourite book with whirling art-nouveau / And Walter Crane-ish colour plates' to cheer her up; but it was merely taken in to her.

> Weeks passed and passed . . . and then it was returned.
> O gone for ever, Peggy Purey-Cust!

Another, more brutal, social slight also rankled with John into adult life. Eventually he 'wrote it out of his system' as his growing reputation gave him confidence. 'False Security', written after 1954, apparently exorcized the memory of a children's party in The Grove, Highgate:

Can I forget my delight at the conjuring show?
And wasn't I proud that I was the last to go?
Too overexcited and pleased with myself to know
That the words I heard my hostess's mother employ
To a guest departing, would ever diminish my joy,
I WONDER WHERE JULIA FOUND THAT STRANGE, RATHER
COMMON LITTLE BOY?

John was at least able to walk with Peggy Purey-Cust to his first school, Byron House in Hampstead Lane. (The building has since been demolished.) The school had been set up in 1885 and was run on the Montessori system. Montessorians thought children were more likely to be good when they were happy, and more likely to be happy when they were interested in their work. A large part of the curriculum was handicraft, 'blob-work, weaving, carpentry and art'. Subjects were first approached through practical examples: geometry through folding and cutting up paper of different colours; geography and history through building models; nature-study through walks and the collection of leaves and wild flowers for pressing.

John's earliest poems belong to his Byron House days. Miss Brenda Thompson, who was in his class in 1914, remembered that one day they were asked to write some verse:

> I wrote some lines about bunnies in the snow – John and I were seated side by side and he looked to see what I had written.
>
> He said, 'Oh I like that, did you really make it up yourself?' and I replied that I had read it in a Christmas annual. Had it been any other child in the class I feel sure I would have said indignantly, 'Of course I did' but with John the stark truth was right, and safe, he would not 'split' because he would understand . . .

Brenda Thompson also remembered that when she and another small girl were comparing the lengths of their hair in the playground at Byron House, John, who was present, suddenly exclaimed with great emphasis: 'I'm going to have long hair when I grow up and be a poet.' With his darkening hair, big brown eyes and waxy complexion, at this period he looked less English than Mediterranean – perhaps the soulful child on a 'His First Communion' postcard from Italy or France. On Sundays, his mother dressed him like an expensive doll, in a white coatee and white, buttoned shoes.

There was already in John's character an element of the exhibitionism that shy people sometimes assume to mask or conquer their shyness. Winifred Macdonald, another of his contemporaries at the school, remembered his proclaiming, at a school picnic: 'I had nineteen helpings of pudding yester-day!' The other children were impressed by this, but Miss Griffin, the teacher in charge, replied: 'All I can say, John, is that you are a very greedy little boy!'

John always recalled his days at Byron House as an idyllic time, marred by one act of gratuitous violence, which he could neither understand nor forgive. He described the attack, though disguising the location, in his poem 'Original Sin on the Sussex Coast' (first published in *Time and Tide*, 8 December 1951) and in *Summoned by Bells*; but probably the most reli-able account of the incident is the one he gave in a radio talk of 1950:

> I recollect Jack Drayton [Jack Shakespeare], a dissenting minister's son. He asked me to tea. He was very nice to me. He showed off at tea and made me laugh. Then he grew thick with Willie Dunlop [Willie Buchanan], a fat little boy who even when he was seven looked like the beefy business man he probably now is. Together they waited for me after school one afternoon.
>
> 'You come down Fitzroy Avenue,' they said. I did. But they seemed a bit strange.
>
> 'Stand here,' said Drayton and stood me against a wall. 'You're not to speak to us, see?'
>
> 'Yes.'
>
> 'Promise.'
>
> 'Yes.'
>
> 'Punch him, Willie.' Willie punched. It winded me a bit. I started to blub. They ran away. I had no idea why they suddenly turned nasty. I don't know to this day. Perhaps one of their parents had said, 'You're not to know that horrid little Betjeman boy.'
>
> That happened going home from a kindergarten – Byron House, Highgate. It was an enlightened, happy place. Jack and Willie were its only blots.

When John went on to Highgate Junior School, he found that 'this detestable couple' had got there first. (They were the boys who danced round him shouting 'Betjemann's a German spy'.) He entered the school in September 1915 and stayed for five terms, leaving in March 1917. Sir Anthony Plowman, a fellow pupil of John's at the school, remembered John 'reciting verses of his own composition in the playground, sur-rounded by a ring of small boys . . .' Sir Anthony recalled some of the verses, too, which were prompted by the air raids that marked that period of the First World War:

> On dark nights when the lights are put out
> That is the time when the Zepps are about.

They frighten the people and do so much harm
And set the whole place in a state of alarm.

We shoot them at times and then they come down
But not once in a while do they fall on the town.

★　★　★

So we must shoot them all and bring them to the ground
So that bits of Zeppelin may easily be found.

In a book of 1948, John wrote that Highgate Junior School had been 'a rough place' during his time there. 'I hated that school,' he told his contemporary, Harold Langley. There were bullies among both boys and masters. John especially loathed the headmaster, E. H. Kelly. In *Summoned by Bells* he recalled:

> how Kelly stood us in a ring:
> 'Three sevens, then add eight, and take away
> Twelve; what's the answer?' Hesitation then
> Meant shaking by the shoulders till we cried.

He remembered the shaking again on his Highgate tour with Valerie Jenkins – 'and you would be held down at the foot of this slope, so that boys could take a running jump at your bottom'. Was he exaggerating? Sir Anthony Plowman thought so: 'J.B. was a rather tender plant in those days.'

But Harold Langley recalled Kelly's brutality in a poem he wrote for John in 1954 entitled 'At Highgate Prep. in 1917'. ('I think Kelly ought to have been put in prison,' John wrote in his letter of thanks.) The publication of *Summoned by Bells* prompted further memories of the headmaster's cruelty. N. C. Selway recalled that he had once been given 'twelve of the best' by him. 'I was beaten . . . with a boy called Allwork. His father came to our house late that night to persuade my father to go to the police about it. I was got out of bed and examined, but my father was a strict man and would have no interference with discipline. In these days [1960] there would be questions in the House!'

A master who did not bully John was T. S. Eliot, known as 'the American master', who taught at Highgate Junior for the three terms of 1916. John wrote in a symposium on Eliot:

Some of the cleverer boys from Muswell Hill . . . knew he was a poet. How? I have often wondered, for I cannot imagine him telling them or anyone . . . Anyhow, they persuaded me to lend (or did I present it to him?) a

13

manuscript called *The Best Poems of Betjeman*. I had forgotten the incident until he reminded me of it, in as kind a way as possible, in the early 'thirties. I record this now purely out of self-advertisement, because I think I must be the only contributor to this book of my age who knew him so long ago.

John was never sure about Eliot's reaction to *The Best Poems of Betjeman* (the title is abridged to *The Best of Betjeman* in *Summoned by Bells*, presumably for the sake of the metre):

> That dear good man, with Prufrock in his head
> And Sweeney waiting to be agonized,
> I wonder what he thought? He never says
> When now we meet, across the port and cheese.
> He looks the same as then, long, lean and pale,
> Still with the slow deliberating speech
> And enigmatic answers. At the time
> A boy called Jelly said: 'He thinks they're bad' –
> But he himself is still too kind to say.

John not only 'knew as soon as I could read and write / That I must be a poet'; he was sure he was going to be a famous poet, whose early literary development would be of interest to posterity. *The Best Poems of Betjeman* has not survived: perhaps he did give it to Eliot. But in the Betjeman Archive of the University of Victoria, British Columbia, are two notebooks with covers and title-pages elaborately lettered by John. One, with a cover design mimicking that of a slim 1890s volume published by Elkin Mathews and John Lane, is entitled, in a small box in the top right-hand corner,

BILGE
BY JB

and is dated February 1922, when John was fifteen and at Marlborough college. It contains a fair copy of his poems up to that date. The other book is larger. Its title, in the bulging lettering of Mabel Lucie Attwell, is *Versatile Verse*. In it John again copied out the poems, recording the date at which each was written. The latest was written at fifteen.

Three poems in *Versatile Verse* – 'The Fairies', 'The Silent Pool' and 'The St Enodock Ghost' – were written at the age of eight. 'The Fairies', which is printed in *Summoned by Bells*, was inspired, John indicated, by William Allingham's 'Up the Airy Mountain'. Characteristics of the later Betjeman show up in these novice exercises. 'Our Local Station: By a villager', written at eleven, shows an early talent for assuming other voices and accents for comic effect:

14

I

Our local station be most fine –
  A splendid sight it be
It's on the local railway line
  From Muddleton-on-Sea.

2

We 'ave a little waitin' room
  (The vicar gave the mats)
But the fast express from Muddlecombe
  Keeps shakin' up the rats . . .

5

We 'ave a little garden too
  With plants all fresh and green
And a thing you puts a penny through
  Wot's called a slot machine . . .

The notebooks can be compared to a scientist's record of failed experiments. False scansion, lame rhymes, maudlin sentiment and over-ripe lyricism mar most of the verses; those which are redeemed are usually redeemed by humour.

The poets John read at Highgate Junior School included Henry Wadsworth Longfellow, Thomas Campbell and Edgar Allan Poe. His affectionate derision of Longfellow is made clear in two 1930s poems about Dumbleton Hall, in 'A Literary Discovery' (1952) and in his later poem 'Longfellow's Visit to Venice' ('To be read in a quiet New England accent'). He enjoyed 'Hiawatha's Photographing', Lewis Carroll's parody of Longfellow's 'Hiawatha', and could recite it from memory when in party mood.

That T. S. Eliot taught the ten-year-old Betjeman was a bizarre coincidence which could only have been matched if Verlaine, during his stint as a private schoolmaster in England (an episode mortalized in one of Max Beerbohm's caricatures), had taught the infant Henry Newbolt. But unlike the master–pupil relationship which had developed between Richard Watson Dixon and Gerard Manley Hopkins in Highgate School seventy years before, the encounter between Eliot and John at Highgate Junior School was not fruitful in the younger man's work. Indeed, Lord David Cecil has pointed out that at Oxford John led a reaction against the pervasive influence of Eliot. 'You have no idea', Lord David said, 'how original it was for John to be writing in the style of Tennyson and other Victorians when his friends were all pastiching Eliot.'

John's natural stance would have been anti-Eliot; but because he had known and liked him at an early age, and Eliot had been absorbed into the Betjeman automythology, John continued to feel sympathy for him and to give him as much benefit of his doubts as he could. This was made easier by their like thinking on religion. '[Eliot's] soul's journey', John wrote in 1948, 'travels in the same carriage as mine, the dear old rumbling Church of England which is high, low and broad all at once. I know that we are both "high" and object to certain weaknesses of the system, and that we both regard the Church of England, despite these weaknesses, as *the* Catholic Church of this country.'

As for the poetry, John dwelt not on the differences between Eliot's vision and technique and his own, but on those fragments in which he could find welcome similarities. He liked Eliot's topographical exactitude. John could identify with Eliot when the older poet wrote of 'the wind that sweeps the gloomy hills of London. / Hampstead and Clerkenwell, Campden and Putney, / Highgate, Primrose and Ludgate . . .' These places were of John's own world – and that of Mr Pooter.

John wrote that people must not be misled by the solemnity of Eliot's poetry and criticism, and his serious face, into thinking him an unhumorous person. 'Allow one doomed for ever to be thought a "funny man" to say that Eliot is extremely funny. He has a slow deep humour, subtle and allusive, the sort of humour that appreciates that immortal book *The Diary of a Nobody.*' John also emphasized Eliot's 'exquisite ear for rhythm'. He remembered an old poet of the Nineties complaining to him that Eliot's poetry did not scan. (That was before the publication in 1939 of Eliot's *Old Possum's Book of Practical Cats*, whose metrical ingenuity John thought 'a combination of Gilbert and A. A. Milne'.) But John argued that 'Eliot has rhythms of his own. Each line he writes is a scanning line that could not possibly be mistaken for prose . . . And each line sets off the rhythm of the line that follows it.'

One of the merits claimed for Eliot's verse is that he does not deliver his message to us on a plate: by deliberate obscurantism he forces the reader to prise out the meaning from a welter of symbolism and sophisticated allusion; and it is further claimed that this very act of teasing out the meaning makes its final exposure more rewarding, like the capitulation of a lover who has 'played hard to get'. This was not a theory of poetry to which John ever subscribed.

Because he was certain, from an early age, that his destiny was to be a poet, he began learning his craft before most of his contemporaries. This precocity did not, as might have been expected, put him ahead of them. Beginning so early, he gave himself, in effect, the training of a Victorian poet. The models available to him were nearly all pre-twentieth century. It must have been a shock, when he arrived at Oxford University, to find that his contemporaries were infatuated with Eliot and that they were experimenting enthusiastically with *vers libre*. It was like training for the cavalry as a cadet and then growing into a world of nuclear warfare – only to find that one's old cavalry instructor had become the foremost expert in atom-splitting.

Intellectually, John could be radical, but emotionally he was conservative. The antidote to his permanent sense of insecurity was an accretion of experiences and characters, built into a personal mythology. He reinterpreted his friends and enemies as *dramatis personae* in the masque of his life, and with such consistency that he not only believed in them himself, but was able to impose his version on other people. Least real, and therefore (as in a religion) *most* real and central to the cosmography, was Archibald, his teddy bear:

> I used to wait for hours to see him move,
> Convinced that he could breathe.

The loneliness John suffered as a boy was intensified by his father's deafness and his mother's uncerebral garrulity. In Archibald he found solace when he had been spanked by his 'hateful nurse', Maud, for being late for dinner. 'One dreadful day' Archibald was hidden from him as a punishment:

> Sometimes the desolation of that loss
> Comes back to me and I must go upstairs
> To see him in the sawdust, so to speak,
> Safe and returned to his idolator.

Archibald was taken up to Oxford, and was later immortalized as the teddy bear of Lord Sebastian Flyte in Evelyn Waugh's *Brideshead Revisited*. He also became the hero of John's fable *Archibald and the Strict Baptists*. Once, when John and his wife Penelope had a quarrel in their house at Wantage, Penelope dangled Archibald over a well and threatened to throw him down; John's distress was acute.

In 1950 he summarized what he had learned at Highgate Junior School. 'I learned how to get round people, how to lie, how to show off just enough to attract attention but not so much as to attract unwelcome attention, how to bribe bullies with sweets (four ounces a penny in those days) – and I learned my first lessons in mistrusting my fellow beings.'

Every summer, the Betjemann family escaped from London to Trebetherick in Cornwall. Their first lodgings were in a boarding-house called The Haven, owned by Gordon Larkworthy. Larkworthy's daughter Joan (later Mrs Kunzer) first met John in 1910, when he was four and she was five. 'I can remember to this day the arrival of the Betjemanns,' she recalled. 'I was frightfully quizzy to know who was coming – peering about. The first one I saw was Bess Betjemann. She always bustled about tremendously: John used to walk exactly like her, rather fast. And then this little thing – I can see him now – coming in a white suit, little anxious face, big eyes.'

As a small boy, John did what other small boys do at the seaside: paddled, built dams and sandcastles, climbed cliffs and collected shells. Joan Kunzer said that, though nervous, he forced himself to take a leading part in deeds of daring.

> We went round in such a gang [she remembered] – there must have been fourteen or fifteen of us. We used to do the most appalling things, and it was always John who would volunteer. There was one awful occasion; we had this terrific scheme, we all went out at dead of night, and it was decided that one of the party was to go into St Enodoc's church and pull the bell. Well, who volunteers? John And I have never seen . . . when he came out, I can see his face now, he was so petrified – white and trembling. But he'd *done* it, you see.

At times, John's nerve failed him. Joan Kunzer again recalled:

> We used to have ghastly cricket matches – we were all terribly hearty. Poor John, there weren't enough children one year, and he had to be in one of the teams. And I've never forgotten, we were all sitting round waiting and a figure appeared in rather funny kind of cricketing clothes and he was walking in a very stiff, painful way. So I asked what on earth was the matter. He said: 'I'm covered in newspapers. I'm afraid of being hurt.' He had newspapers rolled round his arms, newspapers rolled round his legs, newspapers padding his chest and stomach, newspapers stuffed down his trousers. He looked like the Michelin Man.

In spite of his lack of *esprit de corps*, John was popular with the other Trebetherick children, because he knew how to make them laugh. Probably his unorthodox cricket pads were worn as much for comic effect as for protection.

John went flower-hunting in Cornwall as he went church-hunting. His quarry might be a cinquefoil flower or a quatrefoil window. As he grew older and his interest in people became predominant, architecture came to mean more to him than flowers. Buildings were the spoors of human beings. Flowers were only interesting insofar as they were chosen by people for their

gardens, houses or costume. Flowers can symbolize, as in the dahlias black-
ening in the forest which represent death at the end of 'The Heart of
Thomas Hardy'. But no *Zeitgeist* inhabits them, as it inhabits architecture.

As John reached adolescence, church architecture was to become his
overriding enthusiasm. The local church of St Enodoc could be easily
reached on foot. It was no architectural masterpiece, but it had a romantic
history. St Enodoc or Caradoc was a Welshman ('What faith was his, that
dim, that Cornish saint, / Small rushlight of a long-forgotten church').
The church had been built in 1430 on the site of the saint's cell. For several generations, the little building, with its bent spire like a crooked
witch's-hat, was almost overwhelmed with sand, and was known locally as
Sinkininney Church. In the early nineteenth century the church was so
deeply buried in sand that, to secure its privileges, a clergyman had to be
lowered through a skylight once a year to hold a 'service'. In 1863 the
church was dug out and restored. The interior of the building was nothing to write home about. It had 'a humble and West Country look'. But
because, like Archibald the teddy bear, or T. S. Eliot, the nondescript little
church was part of his childhood experience, John was prepared to suspend
his critical powers for it.

> So soaked in worship you are loved too well
> For that dispassionate and critic stare
> That I would use beyond the parish bounds
> Biking in high-banked lanes from tower to tower
> On sunny, antiquarian afternoons.

For John, shopping in Padstow, the main town of the area, was excit-
ingly different from trailing behind his mother at Daniel's or the Bon
Marché in Kentish Town. On the slippery quay was a marine store, its
window gleaming with lanterns, brass and ships' compasses. From the
Misses Quintrell, fancy stationers, he bought dialect tales in verse published
by Netherton and Worth of Truro, and model lighthouses of serpentine.
Ernest and Bess took him to see the ancient May Day festival of the hobby
horse (or ''obby 'oss') at Padstow, in which a circular 'horse' covered with
a black tarpaulin was jogged round the town, followed by the townsfolk
singing a pagan hymn. Today it is a lusty and flourishing rite and a tourist
attraction; but in John's childhood the people of Padstow did not trouble
to make much of a show of it. John's imagination was caught by the ritual,
which he was to see re-enacted many times.

The 'obby 'oss festival was a rare instance of something John and his
father could enjoy together. (Edwardian-style music-hall entertainment

would have been another, but Ernest was deaf by the time John could enjoy it.) In golf, too, there was an element of ceremony – the ritual with mashie and niblick – and on the St Enodoc links John wore the prescribed dress: flat cap, jazzy pullovers, plus fours, clocked stockings and mahogany-coloured brogues. It is clear that the beauty of the links' setting gave him more pleasure than the game, though at times he found an almost hearty exhilaration in some unexpected deftness of his. He never became an expert golfer, but the limited proficiency he did gain was a golden asset when he went to Marlborough College. It enabled him to beg off hated team games to play golf on the downs.

Rather as Hilaire Belloc, the doggedly English Frenchman, adopted Sussex as his preserve, stumping over the South downs and composing odes to ale and windmills, John, with his foreign name and ancestry, made his family honorary citizens of north Cornwall. When his father died he had a stone tablet designed for the south wall of St Enodoc's nave. On the plaque was no mention of Highbury or Clerkenwell or Gospel Oak: it was 'Sacred to the memory of Ernest Edward Betjemann of Undertown in this Parish'. When his mother died, John had her buried under the north boundary wall of St Enodoc's churchyard under a slab of Delabole slate. And in a rainswept ceremony of 1984, John too was buried there, under a stone carved with Gothic letters.

2

The Dragon School

J OHN'S RELEASE FROM the terrors of Highgate Junior School came through his parents' friendship with A. E. ('Hum') Lynam and his wife May, who had a cottage called Cliff Bank in Trebetherick. Hum was senior master, and was soon to be headmaster, of the Dragon School, Oxford – also known as 'Lynam's' and 'the O.P.S.' (Oxford Preparatory School). The Lynams' children, Joc and Audrey, were among John's childhood friends.

John arrived at the Dragon School in May 1917 and left in July 1920. The two main boarding houses were School House and Gunga Din. John was in Gunga Din, presided over by Gerald ('Tortoise') Haynes, who earned his nickname both on Lewis Carroll principles ('because he taught us') and because he looked like a tortoise. John's near-contemporary J. P. W. Mallalieu thought Haynes 'glaringly unattractive-looking'. Lanky, with a small head and protruding, bloodshot eyes, Haynes wore baggy grey flannels and a patched brown sports jacket. An expiring Gold Flake cigarette was usually attached to his lower lip. He applied board compasses to the bottom of any boy who failed to prepare his Latin exercises. 'Once, during a prolonged fit of coughing, he swallowed a still smouldering Gold Flake and lost his voice for a fortnight; but he continued to teach effectively with board compasses alone.'

When John arrived at the Dragon School, Hum's elder brother, Charles Cotterill ('Skipper') Lynam, was still headmaster. John remembered 'the dramatic moment at a prize-giving when Skipper threw off his gown and Hum assumed it'. Skipper believed in the virtue of learning Latin and Greek. He also believed in corporal punishment, for 'slackness in school work' even more than for lies or theft. But he was kind to John. 'When I first arrived, like most boys I was miserably homesick and in tears for days. I remember him walking up and down with me along the pavement outside the Lodge with his arm on my shoulder and telling me not to cry and how in some inexplicable way his sympathy brought comfort.'

Hum Lynam, so called because he hummed while doing the rounds of the dormitories to give the boys the chance of *not* being caught out of bed, could be testy or sarcastic; but, like Skipper, he was kind to John.

> Hum was like a father to me [John recalled]. One always knew one could go to him if up the spout, although one never did. There was the feeling that he was there as a protection against injustice. He taught me how to speak in public and how to recite. 'Hands behind your back. Eyes on the clock. Stand at the front of the stage. Now speak up.' Hum's preoccupation with religion and the school services, I realize now, greatly affected me. Here was this great, but never remote and always kind man, interested in religion. There must be something in it.

John thought that he learned most from Hum Lynam when he managed to squeeze in next to the master at school luncheons and ply him with questions about poetry. 'I remember him talking of Swinburne to me one day and recommending "Les Noyades" which was, to say the least, a liberal piece of advice to a private schoolboy. But he knew I would love the sound of the words and miss their meaning . . .'

One of Skipper's most enlightened acts was the admission of girls to the school. Naomi Haldane (later Mitchison) had been a pupil as well as her brother J. B. S. Haldane, the scientist. Among John's contemporaries was Biddy Walsham, who, like the Lynam children, lived in North Oxford and holidayed in Cornwall. She was the daughter of a baronet, Sir John Walsham, and the granddaughter of an admiral, John Warren, and her brother, (Sir) John, also became an admiral. John knew her both at school and in Cornwall, and fell in love with her. In 1976, when *Betjemania*, a revue in which some of John's poems were set to music, was running at Southwark, Audrey Lynam wrote to John that she thought Gay Soper, in the show, was like Biddy Walsham. She added: 'I can see Biddy in our garden at 85 Banbury Road [Oxford] with John [Walsham] beside her, very solemn and his shorts too long . . . Biddy was the girl that you all admired and I thought her grown-up and marvellous.'

John replied:

> You're quite right; now I come to think of it, Gay Soper was very Biddy, one of my first stirrings of heterosexual passion or indeed any sex passion. I was bound to have been there at 85 Banbury Road. I was at all those parties with Biddy and John including his grandmother's (Mrs Warren) at 8 Winchester Road [Oxford] when we had fireworks in the garden . . . Biddy married a very nice fella called Crookshank and had handsome children . . . She was adorable and kind and still is.

John's love for Biddy Walsham was at its height when he was in his late teens in Cornwall, though Mrs Crookshank says he did not reveal it to her at the time.

'Dragons', as the pupils were called, knew few people outside the English middle class. But the First World War did impinge on Oxford slightly. In *Summoned by Bells* John recalled how Skipper would announce, before the morning hymn, 'the latest names of those who'd lost their lives / For King and Country and the Dragon School'. The boys 'did their bit' for the war effort, knitting shapeless string gloves for men in mine-sweepers and sticking allied flags along the Somme on the map.

The curriculum was heavily classical. About half the teaching periods were devoted to Latin and Greek. French was well taught by Tortoise Haynes, whose pupils could ever afterwards distinguish between the French for fish and poison, cousin and cushion, hair and horse. The amount of 'prep' – up to two hours – depended on age and form. It included much memorizing of poetry, particularly of Tennyson's 'Ulysses' and 'Morte d'Arthur'. John learned a lot of poetry by heart and won a prize for recitation. He was composing his own verse too. He contributed a cheeky squib on Hum Lynam and his wife May to the September 1920 issue of the school magazine, *The Draconian*:

> Hum and May went out one day
> On a motor-bike painted vermillion [*sic*]
> Hum was the nut of the latest cut
> And May was the girl on the pillion.

The model for this was the nursery rhyme 'Jack and Jill'. Another nursery rhyme inspired John's 'Ode to a Puppy (By His Mistress)', published in *The Draconian* of April 1920, which began:

> Oh! puppy dear, I sadly fear
> Your waistcoat's at the wash,
> Your cutlet, too, is soaked right through
> With all your lemon squash.

John was noticed at this time by one of the masters, J. B. 'Bruno' Brown. In 1976, living in retirement in Oxford, Brown wrote:

I knew him as a sensitive and far from typical Prep School boy, and little, if at all, interested in games of any sort. However not many boys of thirteen went about with a volume of Charles Dibdin's poems – the author of 'Tom Bowling' – in their pockets, or had already become fascinated by architecture

. . . For this last, Gerald ('Tortoise') Haynes was the great influence: John himself never forgot this, and later dedicated a book to him. (Haynes died in 1944.)

I was a Scot in origin, and at the end of term sing-song (it would be the Easter term of 1920) sang a song in broad Scots, 'A lum hat wantin' a croon'. This apparently struck John, for from then onwards for the next fifty years he affected what he imagined was a Scots accent when we met, and wrote letters in a hybrid Anglo-Scots dialect – full of 'Macs', 'toons', 'och ayes', 'ye' (for you) and so on. He called this extraordinary language 'Skitch'.

John's great friend among the boys was, like him, a rather unusual type in a Prep School – Ronnie Wright. He later became a Roman Catholic priest. I think he died in 1969.

Another friend was Hugh Gaitskell, the future leader of the Labour Party, whom John was to meet again at Oxford University. Gaitskell was five months older than John: the school roll for Christmas Term, 1918, showed that H. Gaitskell of form VIa was aged twelve years eight months, while J. Betjemann of form Va was aged twelve years three months. Gaitskell's parents refused to let him invite John to their home in Onslow Gardens, London, because John's father was 'in trade'. But the two boys sometimes met in London. When Alan Wood wrote an article on Gaitskell for *Picture Post* in 1951, John told him that he remembered seeing Gaitskell 'in the holidays, at the age of twelve, walking about London impeccably dressed with a bowler hat and a stick'. He added that at the time Gaitskell was 'mild and friendly and very correct'. Himself at least emotionally a conservative, John was teasingly implying that Gaitskell, the socialist, had been brought up as a toff. Gaitskell disputed the story about the bowler hat, and riposted that 'by Betjeman's standards, then and since, almost anyone else but Betjeman would have been described as "very correct" '.

John was also on generally friendly terms with another future Labour politician, Per Mallalieu. 'This morning we had a very short service it lasted about three minutes and it had no sermon,' Mallalieu wrote to his mother in 1917. 'Then we went for a walk. I went with a boy called Jhon Betchiman and we told Ghost stories to each other which passed the time very well.' But Mallalieu appears in *Summoned by Bells* as 'Percival Mandeville, the perfect boy . . . / Upright and honourable, good at games' who challenged John to a fight behind the bicycle shed. John got out of the fight by lying, 'My mater's very ill.'

> No need for more –
> His arm around my shoulder comforting:
> 'All right, old chap. Of course I understand.'

Mallalieu did not mention this episode in his autobiography, but he did recall John and Ronald Wright as 'two of the odder boys during my time in a far from even school':

> Betjeman first achieved notice when his father sent him an unusually sophisticated stationary steam engine which inspired me to some pyrotechnical mis-spellings. 'Betgiman's engin was going to-night,' I wrote to my mother, 'and it has go a lovely pump that pumps in water whill the thing is going.' The 'engin' drove a variety of tools including a miniature circular saw on which H. K. Hardy tried to cut his finger nails, spending a week in bandages after . . .
>
> Thereafter Wright and Betjeman specialized in eccentricity . . . on Saturday nights they entertained with ribaldish music-hall songs – words as amended by Betjeman, music as hammered out on the Boys' Room piano by Wright. They also went in for elaborate hoaxes. Once I received a letter on expensive notepaper with a letterhead gravely printed 'The West London Lunatic Asylum' and signed by a physician. The perfectly typed text told me, with regret, that two school friends of mine, Ronald Wright and John Betjeman, had just been admitted to the asylum babbling about somebody called 'P.M.M.P.' 'Having,' wrote the doctor, 'discovered that the correct name is Mallalieu, I thought best to let you know the nature of their illness which is that they imagine themselves to be tea cups and we have to provide large saucers for them to sit in.'

John found himself in competition with both Gaitskell and Mallalieu at the end of Easter Term 1919, when one of the parents, Mr Fitch, established a Speech Prize, open to the whole school. The entrants had to speak for five minutes, proposing or replying to the toast of 'The British Navy' or 'The British Army'. The result was: *1st* P. Mallalieu, *2nd* H. Gaitskell, *3rd* J. Betjemann.

John also performed alongside Gaitskell and Mallalieu in the school plays. His first appearance was as Ruth in Bruno Brown's production of Gilbert and Sullivan's *The Pirates of Penzance* in 1918. Reviewing it in the school magazine, R.E.C.W. wrote: 'A pleasing buxom wench was Ruth who scored a great success in the part of "Maid of all work". Always perfectly self-possessed she enunciated her lines with a clearness which even in that company was remarkable.' Per Mallalieu played 'Edith, one of General Stanley's daughters', and Gaitskell was in the Chorus of Police. In 1920, John took two parts in the school play, *Henry V*: Charles VI of France and the Earl of Cambridge. Frank Sidgwick wrote of Wylie's Henry:

> It was a gallant performance, and I don't think anyone else could have been cast for the part. Except, perhaps, Betjemann. Having beheld him

manufacture, out of two small parts, the Earl of Cambridge and the King of France, two separate, distinct and perfect gems of character-acting, I am not prepared to say that he could not have acted, with equal insight and genius, Henry the Fifth, Fourth, Sixth and Eighth, or Othello, Falstaff, Imogen, Caliban, Hamlet, Juliet's Nurse or Lance *and* his dog Crab.

John's acting success was to be repeated at Marlborough and Oxford, and gives the clue to his later mastery as a television performer. Acting ability – the ability to put oneself in somebody else's shoes – also helped him to understand people of the past, especially the Victorians. And the Victorian poets he read and learned by heart at the Dragon School intensified his feeling for the Victorian age: its heroic, impossible ideals; its pervasive religiosity and lugubrious doubts; the matrix of its hierarchical society. They introduced him to its cruelties, prudery, codes of honour, freaks of humour, passions and self-delusions, its angularities of vision, its generous and wizened souls. In the architecture of North Oxford he read the same themes – the same social hierarchy, from mustard-brick terrace to marble mansion; the same angularities and freaks in gable and campanile, the same religiosity in the Ruskinian Gothic of stained-glass windows, arches and madonnas in niches.

Though he was alive to the beauties of the ancient Oxford of 'dreaming spires', John from the first found that he responded more to the Gothic Revival buildings of North Oxford. North Oxford had come into being in the mid-nineteenth century when dons were at last allowed to marry. John, who had only to see the outside of a building to visualize the inhabitants, was always aware of the dons and their wives in the academic ghetto of North Oxford. In his poem 'Oxford: Sudden Illness at the Bus-stop' he described a don's wife waiting at a bus stop outside her North Oxford house, a rose pinned to her evening velvet.

> From that wide bedroom with its two branched lighting
>   Over her looking-glass, up or down,
> When sugar was short and the world was fighting
>   She first appeared in that velvet gown.

That was precisely when John himself first lived in North Oxford – the latter years of the First World War. He is more commonly regarded as an escapist than as a brutal realist, but after all the idyllic poems about Oxford, John's verses for the first time showed the squalid reality of university life – ill-paid dons, suburban gardens, petty gossip, tinned peas, toothbrushes airing on the windowsill.

His accounts of his days at Lynam's suggest that he gained more from looking at Oxford and the surrounding limestone villages than from his education at the Dragon School. The instrument of liberation was the bicycle. Because the bicycle was a means to an end – visiting churches – John mastered it as he mastered no other sport. 'Most of us could bicycle with our hands in our pockets, slowly zigzagging past the railed-in gardens where tamarisk and forsythia grew; or we would lean against the cream-coloured lamp-posts with their terra-cotta coloured gas-lamps which were placed at infrequent intervals down all the leafy North Oxford roads.'

The Dragon School was in 'the red-brick Anglo-Jackson* part of North Oxford, which only burst into full beauty when the hawthorn and pink may was in flower'. But John preferred the inner North Oxford – Crick Road, Norham Gardens, Norham Road, and 'the magic, winding Canterbury Road, the cottages and stables by North Parade, and those ecclesiastical-looking houses gathered round the northerly spire of St Philip and St James ("Phil-Jim")' – which he found 'more haunting and more daunting'.

Dragons were free to bicycle into the city and look at colleges and churches. John usually went with Ronald Wright, who was the son of 'a barrister of Tractarian opinions and . . . a mother who had recently been converted to Rome'.

> Ronald Hughes Wright, come with me once again
> Bicycling off to churches in the town . . .

Other Dragons collected butterflies or postage stamps; John collected churches. At an age when his friends were excited by Red Admirals or Penny Blacks, he was absorbed by the mystique of church-viewing, which had its own argot:

> Can words express the unexampled thrill
> I first enjoyed in Norm., E.E. and Dec.?[†]
> Norm., crude and round and strong and primitive,
> E.E., so lofty, pointed, fine and pure,
> And Dec. the high perfection of it all,
> Flowingly curvilinear, from which
> The Perp.[‡] showed such a 'lamentable decline'.

---

[*]The term 'Anglo-Jackson' derived from the name of the Oxford architect Sir Thomas Jackson (1835–1924), whose designs included Hertford College's 'Bridge of Sighs'.
[†]Norman, Early English and Decorated.
[‡]Perpendicular.

With Tortoise Haynes, there were bicycle excursions to the village churches near Oxford. Haynes would fix up his huge plate camera and photograph font or pulpit with 'pale grey slides / Of tympana, scratch dials and Norfolk screens'. He had a passion for Norman architecture. 'From him,' John wrote, 'I learned to think that Norman was the only style that mattered, and that Iffley church was far the most interesting building in Oxford or its vicinity.' There were also orchid-hunts in the Wytham Woods, rounders at Oxey mead and belly-flops from punts near Godstow, John was soon to break free from many of Haynes's prejudices, but he remembered him always as a great, natural teacher: 'He was the giver: ours it was to take.' In 1952 John dedicated *First and Last Loves* to the memory of Haynes, 'who first opened my eyes to architecture'.

While John was at the Dragon School, his parents moved to 53 Church Street, Chelsea, a Georgian box almost opposite the mansion where Charles Kingsley had lived. He missed Hannah Wallis, who was given her *congé*. He missed the familiar scenery of Highgate, the hawthorns, the sheep-tracks and the mulch of trodden leaves in autumn. In a part of Chelsea served only by bus, he longed for the Highgate trams, the North London trains and the Underground to Kentish Town. But there was one big compensation: Ronald Wright also lived in Chelsea.

Together the boys explored London – its churches and its suburbs, as far out as the Metroland of 'beechy Bucks'. To mystify other passengers, they sometimes talked 'Loud gibberish in angry argument, / Pretending to be foreign'. On his own, John visited the second-hand bookshops of the Essex Road and the Farringdon Road bookstalls. He bought poetry books, books on churches and Edward Lear's *Views of the Ionian Isles*, the flyleaf inscribed by the artist. He enjoyed the smell of old books, their polished bindings and the armorial bookplates of obscure country squires. Book-collecting was one of the few enthusiasms in which his father encouraged him. He slipped him half-a-crown and said: 'If you must buy books, buy the best.' He also gave him George Godwin's *The Churches of London*, which he inscribed: 'To my dear boy in the hope that his appreciation of all that is beautiful will never fade.'

The move from Highgate to Chelsea was an uprooting and intensified John's loneliness at home. His mother's smart new friends assured her that the Chelsea home was 'simply sweet' as they deposited their wraps and settled down to a game of bridge; but during the school holidays John escaped from the 'poky, dark and cramped' house as often as he could. On Sunday evenings he attended Evening Prayer in different City churches.

A hidden organist sent reedy notes
To flute around the plasterwork. I stood,
And from the sea of pews a single head
With cherries nodding on a black straw hat
Rose in a neighbouring pew. The caretaker?
Or the sole resident parishioner?

Guilt, not just antiquarian interest or religious fervour, drew John to these bleak services. His mother's querulous, self-pitying refrain ran through his mind: 'When I am dead, you will be sorry, John.' He prayed that she would live.

Bess may have neglected John in his early childhood, but now that he was at the Dragon School and away from home more often than she, her love for him became oppressive. The character who represents her in his Oxford playlet 'The Artsenkrafts' tells her son, 'You know I love you more than anything else in the world,' and when he complains of the way his room is constantly tidied up, she bursts into tears 'with very loud sobs'. John writhed under this smothering, blackmailing love. What he felt for Bess in return was strong enough to put him in danger of being a 'mother's boy'. He could not repress it, but did his best to mask it: 'The love that waited underneath, / I kept in check.'

John's relationship with his father was no less fraught. Ernest Betjemann was overjoyed when his first-born was a son. His ambition to perpetuate the Betjemann dynasty was as ardent as Henry VIII's to secure the Tudor succession. Like Henry VIII, he was blessed with a son wise beyond his years, a prodigy with the pen – but a boy unhandy with a gun, a milksop who cut no figure in the trials of physical prowess in which his father excelled. And like Henry VIII, Ernest intended to make sure that his son was fit to succeed him when the time came.

During the First World War, the luxury-goods trade languished. G. Betjemann & Sons made Sopwith propellers and shell cases at as patriotic a cost to the Government as they could afford. In the 1920s business picked up wonderfully. Ernest realized earlier than most traditional manufacturers that some concession must be made to the popular new Art Deco style, then known as 'Jazz Modern' or *moderne*. In *Summoned by Bells* John wrote of goods made in his father's factory 'To shine in Asprey's show-rooms under glass, / A Maharajah's eyeful'.

Ernest Betjemann ran his business on paternalistic lines, but he accepted the welfare responsibilities of being an employer as well as the profits. When George Jones fell ill with nephritis (kidney disease) in 1918 after serving only two years of his apprenticeship, Betjemann paid for him to stay in the London Hospital for fourteen weeks. Betjemann allowed three of the apprentices at a time to go to the Norfolk Broads and stay on his three-berth yacht, moored at Coltishall. 'It was called *Queen of the Broads*,' remembered Albert Dubery, another of the apprentices. 'Mr Ernest had it made partly in the works, from finest Honduras mahogany.' John also used to stay on the yacht, with his father, in the untroubled times before they quarrelled. Recalling those holidays in his 1945 poem 'East Anglian Bathe', John described spartan swims in Horsey Mere, not far from Coltishall.

Ernest Betjemann had one great handicap as an employer: his deafness. You could only speak to him through his 'trumpet', which had a black Moorish silk tube and an ebony mouthpiece. 'If he didn't agree with you,' Albert Dubery said, 'he would snatch the trumpet away.' Brave spirits had been known to seize it back. Bill Hammond, a Betjemann's workman, recalled: 'On one occasion I had a bookcase to do with only two boards of Austrian wainscot oak to use. Mr Ernest came along and said that two panels didn't match and should do. He flung it up the shop, and wouldn't listen to me. So I ran after him, and grabbed hold of the trumpet. Then I put all the boards together and I proved to him that I couldn't get two matching panels out of the boards. And without being too humble, he agreed I'd done the best I could.' Ernest's deafness exacerbated his rows with John. Sometimes he misunderstood what John said, and bridled; John's pert replies seemed the more insolent when bellowed into the speaking-tube.

Ernest's changing fortunes were indicated by his house-moves from Gospel Oak to West Hill to Church Street, Chelsea, and by the standard of his successive motor-cars. In 1974, W. Boddy, who had been editor of *Motor Sport* for forty years, wrote: 'John Betjeman cannot have liked the motor-car very much and I often wonder what he used for travelling about this changing land and looking at old churches . . .' In a reply, John wrote: 'The first motor-car my father had was a Rover Landaulette . . . Then . . . when we moved to Chelsea, [he] bought an Arrol-Johnston . . . Our chauffeur was called John and he knew about cars and steered my father who, being deaf, could never drive a car. After that we sank to an Essex Saloon.'

Like many other manufacturers of luxury goods, Betjemann's suffered from the 1929 Crash: this probably explains why Ernest 'sank to an Essex Saloon'. Percy Threadgill remembered that in the early 1930s the men accepted a 10 per cent cut in wages, and that the factory was put on short time – no Saturday working, and finishing at four o'clock each day. But luckily the firm's palmy days coincided with John's years at Oxford and the setbacks of his early career, so his father was able to bolster his bank-balance when he got into scrapes such as bouncing cheques or a fine for speeding – though Ernest was far from being a fondly indulgent father, and financial first-aid was invariably accompanied by a lecture.

The conflicts started when John was at the Dragon School. The first two surviving letters from Ernest to his son show something of the relationship between them during and just after the First World War. With both letters Ernest enclosed pocket-money. The first, from 53 Church Street, Chelsea, is dated 16 June 1917:

Dear Boy,

Enclosed is £10, hope it sees you through. Mother comes to London Saturday and the operation is on Tuesday.

Macmanus [the Betjemann family doctor] says I *must* lie up for a week, more or less, and rest, Mother doesn't know this, so I shall be glad to see you home after the Exams, and help me out with the numbers of little things to be seen to.

The second letter, of 1 May 1919, suggests that John had offended his father and was now repentant or feigning repentance. It contains the line: 'So pleased you have decided not to be a second-rate chap.'

Until Ernest Betjemann began to realize that John had no intention of entering the family business, relations between them were generally cordial.

> My dear deaf father, how I loved him then
> Before the years of our estrangement came!
> The long calm walks on twilit evenings
> Through Highgate New Town to the cinema . . .

These walks had one by-effect on John that was lasting. On Michael Parkinson's television show in 1973, he said he thought he had developed his eye for architecture because his father, being deaf, had especially developed his eyesight and would always point things out. In his response to architecture, John did not disappoint Ernest; but he was unresponsive where an enthusiastic interest would have given most pleasure – on visits to the Betjemann factory in Pentonville Road. Ernest was showing off the works to his son, but he was also showing off his son to the works.

Master John, the heir-apparent, was not enthralled. As a small boy he amused himself in a desultory way, pretending to be an electric train over the silversmith's uneven floor or pretending to work with old Buckland as he electroplated. The words John chooses to describe the factory processes, in *Summoned by Bells*, suggest the resistance and distaste he felt at the time: the 'whining saws' of the cabinet-makers' shop; the 'scream of tortured wood'; the 'blackened plank / Under the cruel plane'; the 'reeking swabs' of the French polishers. Like someone in an interminable discordant concert looking forward to smoked salmon and champagne in the interval, he waited eagerly for lunch-time, which 'brought me hopes of ginger-beer'. But to obtain that he had to wait for his father, who was among his clerks in the counting-house and greeted him absently with the saintly smile of the deaf. So John was left to his own devices: hours of tedium in the upper rooms – 'One full of ticking clocks, one full of books'.

As John grew older, his father began to prepare him for his succession. But John was no more adept at carpentry under Ernest's instruction than when making model boats at the Dragon School. ' "Not *that* way, boy! When will you ever learn" – / I dug the chisel deep into my hand.' He proved an equal duffer in shooting lessons, forgetting to release the safety-catch when his father shouted at him to shoot a rabbit. His most humiliating shooting recollection was of Hertfordshire, in his poem of that title: trudging with his 'knickerbockered sire' in a syndicated shoot at Buntingford, he fired by mistake into the ground. On the drive home in the Rover Landaulette, through Welwyn, Hatfield and Potter's Bar, he had to suffer his father's recriminations. 'How many times must I explain / The way a boy should hold a gun?'

John could not share his father's interests, but Ernest made at least some attempt to humour John in his. As a letter of 1919 shows, he gave him some encouragement in his verse-writing. However, there was a certain forced jocularity to the encouragement which undermined the kind intention:

> 'And how's our budding bard? Let what you write
> Be funny, John, and be original.'

The jollying-along approach might well embarrass, rather as teasing questions as to 'Who's your little lady-friend, then?' can infect with an adult unease the kind of childhood romance that John wrote about in 'Indoor Games near Newbury' and *Summoned by Bells*. When John and his father visited the Tate Gallery and John was enraptured by Frank Bramley's painting *The Hopeless Dawn*, Ernest suggested he should translate the picture into verse, and gave him the inspiring opening

> Through the humble cottage window
> Streams the early dawn.

John completed the rhyme:

> O'er the tossing bay of Findow
> In the mournful morn.

But a hunt through a gazetteer showed that there was no such place as Findow . . . 'and the poem died'. John's choice of Bramley's painting may have had psychological significance: in *The Hopeless Dawn* a young wife and an old mother gaze out to sea (an angry sea which reminded John of the waves 'in splendid thunder over Greenaway'), knowing that the man of the house is lost and will not return. Wishful thinking?

With both father and son, love was overlaid by resentment and resentment hardened into antagonism. The mutual hostility had causes deeper than John's lack of interest in carpentry or shooting pheasants. It was the inevitable counterpart to his excessive emotional dependence on his mother. Six years after Ernest's death in 1934, John wrote a poem about him – 'On a Portrait of a Deaf Man' – that has an almost vindictive quality. He dwells on his father's fate with a morbid relish that recalls the gloating mortification of the flesh in medieval German paintings of martyrdom:

> He would have liked to say good-bye,
> Shake hands with many friends,
> In Highgate now his finger-bones
> Stick through his finger-ends.

Compare these lines with the exalted *In Memoriam* tone of John's 1945 threnody on Basil, Marquess of Dufferin and Ava, whom he loved.

Later, when remorse had set in, John recalled in his poem 'Norfolk' the happy times he had spent on his father's yacht on the Norfolk Broads, and wondered when and how the rift had grown so deep between them:

> How did the Devil come? When first attack?
> These Norfolk lanes recall lost innocence,
> The years fall off and find me walking back
> Dragging a stick along the wooden fence
> Down this same path, where, forty years ago,
> My father strolled behind me, calm and slow.

3

Marlborough

———⊶⊶⊷———

JOHN CAME TO Marlborough college in September 1920, just after his
fourteenth birthday. He was slim and below the average height, with a
sallow complexion, large, questing eyes – saved from femininity by the
satyric slant of his eyebrows – and full lips which he twisted downwards
when smiling, so as not to expose his buck teeth. A contemporary, Arthur
Byron, remembered John's distinctive hair – 'long, straight, jet-black . . .
almost Chinese in effect'.

The college was less than a century old when John arrived there. All
new boys went into one of the houses reserved for first-year boys: John was
assigned to Upcot in the Bath Road, a house like a small Victorian rectory.
The housemaster was Clement Carter, a Fellow of the Royal Geographical
Society and joint author of *The Marlborough Country*. The portrait-painter
Derek Hill, who was in Upcot some years after John, said of Carter: 'He
was not very human. He was the sort of master who, if you complained of
bullying, would punish you for being a "sneak".'

The 'new bug' at Marlborough had to learn the school slang in his first
few weeks, on pain of beatings. Grey trousers were 'barnes'. The cushion-
cum-bag in which he carried his books was a 'kish' (pronounced kīsh). It
had to be carried under the left arm, with only a quarter of the cushion
sticking out in front. A characteristic word in the Marlborough argot was
'coxy'. Suggestive of 'cocksure' and 'coxcomb', it had roughly the same
meaning as the slang word 'uppity'. Third-termers were given powers of
punishment to curb the coxy. They could make offenders 'turf down basement' – walk down a long flight of stone steps and up again, as many as
ten times.

More slang and etiquette had to be learned by experience and by heart
at mealtimes. A milk-jug was a 'tolly'. The poet Louis MacNeice, a near-
contemporary of John's at the school, got little to eat at his first few meals
because he did not understand the custom of 'rushing': as soon as you
entered hall you were expected to stick a fork in your patty and a spoon in
your porridge, otherwise anyone could 'rush' (appropriate) them.

Dormitory entertainments included two tortures: 'bum-shaving' (two boys in pyjamas or less bent down and the prefect made a swift vertical cut with his cane between them) and 'hot-potting' (tooth-mugs filled with flaming paper were clapped on the victims' buttocks where, when the oxygen was used up, suction held them in place). John devised his own entertainments. In 1967 his contemporary Charles D'Costa wrote to him: 'I wonder if you remember those evenings after lights out in the dormitory when you used to imitate Dr Norwood [the Master of Marlborough] riding up the hill on his bicycle and being spoken to by God and telling God what Marlborough stood for?'

At the end of a boy's first year, there was much fearful speculation about which senior house he would be assigned to. Whichever it was, gloating older boys would assure him that it contained the most fiendish masters and prefects in the school. John would have liked to be in 'C' House, the old Castle Inn building with its panelled rooms and great oak staircase. Instead he was put in 'B2', one of the graceless 1840s buildings by Edward Blore. The furnishings inside were spartan: iron beds in an austere room, and a big communal showerbath opposite a row of lavatories with no doors.

'Marlborough really was the most awful barbarous place,' recalled John's friend John Bowle, 'and it was extraordinary that people were willing to pay large sums to subject their children to it.' But he conceded that the school had some good masters, and an exceptional headmaster in Cyril Norwood. 'The only part of the curriculum that was taken seriously', Bowle added, 'was classics. If you weren't good at Greek and Latin, you were regarded as almost expendable.' Beverley Nichols, who was at the school just before John, wrote that Greek was taught at Marlborough 'as though it were not merely dead but as though it had never lived at all'. John's natural antipathy to the classics, a subject which required a learning by rote of irregular verbs and participles before any literary glories could be discerned, was aggravated by his dislike of the masters who taught the subject. Bowle recalled in 1976:

> John was put through the normal grind of the classical curriculum. He went into the Classical Fifth which was in the charge of a pedantic old gentleman called Emery – quite a benevolent old boy but a complete pedant. Then he went on to the Lower Sixth where he was taken by a man called A. R. Gidney.
>
> Gidney was an Oxford man, with a very icy kind of mind, and a very cutting, sarcastic tongue, and he really lashed John with his sarcastic tongue – cut him up horribly for inaccuracies in grammar; and John has never really forgiven that, you know. He simply hates 'Gidders' still.

John sustained his vendetta against Gidney for over fifty years. In March 1958, when asked to contribute to a series called 'John Bull's Schooldays' in *The Spectator*, he took the opportunity to write a vitriolic open letter to Gidney, disguising him as 'Dear Mr Atkins'. Later that year he told a *Daily Mail* interviewer: 'I was bullied and crushed by a master, and it is immensely gratifying to me to know that the hidebound old prig is still alive and perhaps occasionally reading my name.' In *A Nip in the Air* (1974) he published the poem 'Greek Orthodox' which begins:

> What did I see when first I went to Greece?
> Shades of the Sixth across the Peloponnese.
> Though clear the clean-cut Doric temple shone
> Still droned the voice of Mr Gidney on;
> 'That ὅτι? Can we take its meaning here
> Wholly as interrogative?'

Gidney continued to live in Marlborough until his death in 1978. With his short-cropped white hair and erect bearing, he seemed an affable 'Mr Chips' figure, but it was clear that he had little time for John Betjeman. 'He was in no way distinguished,' he said. 'The only thing I remember about him is that at the beginning of one term, when the form list was being passed round, he said to me: "Please, sir, I can't remember whether my surname is spelt with one 'n' or two." He was posing as usual, you see. So I said: "Make up your mind and let me know when you've decided." The class laughed and seemed to think that was the right reply – which showed what they thought of *him*.'

In *Summoned by Bells*, John listed what to him were the main horrors of life at Marlborough:

> The dread of beatings! Dread of being late!
> And, greatest dread of all, the dread of games!

The school's reputation in games outweighed its reputation in anything else. The official school history was full of Marlburian legends, such as E. E. Kewley, 'famous for his dribbling powers', and F. H. Fox, 'considered by many to be the finest half-back ever turned out by Marlborough'. John was uninterested in rugby or cricket; and he did not find 'exhilarating' (as did Louis MacNeice) the gruelling runs over the downs with a time limit out and back and a caning if you were late either way. One of the few sports that John and his equally games-hating friend John Bowle enjoyed was swimming. Bowle competed for the Brooke Swimming Cup but was defeated by the captain of his house. 'I'm so glad,' he commented in his diary. 'I rather admire the animal physically.' James Robertson Justice, the future film actor, also took part in the diving competition. 'James has an amazing backwards somersault dive which is hugely applauded,' Bowle wrote. 'It is very bad for him. He is temporarily a little popular in his frightful house.' Another future film star, James Mason, was also remembered by John and Bowle in connection with the swimming-pool: he was flung in, dressed in his dinner-jacket, for 'coxiness'.

A pernicious pecking order ran from the Senior Prefect, usually a prize athlete who was *ex officio* editor of the school magazine, down through Upper School captains, minor 'bloods' and juniors to the persecuted fags. MacNeice's and John's descriptions of the institution called Upper School, in *The Strings are False* and *Summoned by Bells*, are so nearly identical in content that the latter might have been a rendering into verse of the former. John wrote:

> There was a building known as Upper School
> (Abolished now, thank God, and all its ways),
> An eighteen-fifty warehouse smelling strong
> Of bat-oil, biscuits, sweat and rotten fruit . . .
> Great were the ranks and privileges there:
> Four captains ruled, selected for their brawn
> And skill at games; and how we reverenced them!
> Twelve friends they chose as brawny as themselves.
> 'Big Fire' we called them; lording it they sat
> In huge armchairs beside the warming flames
> Or played at indoor hockey in the space
> Reserved for them. The rest of us would sit
> Crowded on benches round another grate.

There is also a striking similarity between MacNeice's and John's descriptions of the captains, who arrived slapping the desks with their canes and made the juniors scavenge for apple-cores and paper darts. The captains would throw blank cartridges into the fireplaces, which exploded and blew live coals on to the boys' desks.

The most dreaded disgrace in Upper School was a 'basketing'. A chosen victim ('Perhaps he sported coloured socks too soon, / Perhaps he smarmed his hair with scented oil') was stripped of most of his clothing, smeared with ink, treacle or paint, then hoisted in one of the two big waste-paper baskets. MacNeice describes this ceremony as 'a perfect exhibition of mass sadism' and adds, 'The masters considered this a fine old tradition, and any boy who was basketed was under a cloud for the future. Because the boys have an innate sense of justice, anyone they basket must be really undesirable. Government of the mob, by the mob, and for the mob.' John makes the same point in *Summoned by Bells*:

> 'By the boys, *for* the boys. The boys know best.
> With that rough justice decent schoolboys know.'
> And at the end of term the victim left –
> Never to wear an Old Marlburian tie.

John gave a more detailed and highly dramatized account of the ordeal-by-basket in his contribution to *Little Innocents* (1932), a book of childhood reminiscences edited by his Oxford friend Alan Pryce-Jones. Here, as in *Summoned by Bells*, he recalls how someone told him that he was next for the basket, and how as a result he crept about for three terms afterwards, keeping his books down in a basement where boots were cleaned. Over the years, the story lost nothing in the telling. Lady Longford remembers how 'When John came to stay at Pakenham Hall in 1930 – Evelyn Waugh was there as well and mentions John in his diary – John kept us in fits with stories of going up in the basket at Marlborough. It made your flesh creep in the shadowy great hall at Pakenham. I remember John's saying how when the boy was hoist up in the basket, they threw "darts of sharp pen-knibs" at him.' From merely being lifted on to a table in *Little Innocents*, the wretched victim was 'strung . . . up among the beams' in *Summoned by Bells*. John himself became so identified with the story that some of his contemporaries firmly believed eventually that he had been basketed: his schoolfellow T. C. Worsley states in his autobiography *Flannelled Fool* that 'He [John Betjeman], like many others, paid the supreme penalty of the "basket".' This was denied by John Bowle, who said: 'You mustn't think of John as having been a miserable, persecuted creature at Marlborough: he has always been popular wherever he's been, always had plenty of friends.' And Anthony Blunt (the art historian and spy, who was John's contemporary at Marlborough) explained in 1977: 'He had this marvellous sense of humour, and when the toughs tried to be bloody, he simply laughed in their face: and, as you know, when John Betjeman laughs, it's quite something. They were absolutely routed. In his last year he had a study right down the other end from mine, the narrow court between Upper School and the Museum block – and one would suddenly hear this great hiccough of laughter, very very infectious.'

The school was divided into battle-lines of aesthetes against hearties. The antagonism between them had been a part of Marlborough life for at least half a century, and successive Masters had vainly tried to reconcile the two sides. The masters as well as the boys were divided into two camps on this issue. The old guard, led by Gidney and by the fanatical T. C. G. S. Sandford, housemaster of Bowle's house, faced the younger generation appointed by Norwood as a 'leaven'. Among the latter was Oswald Flecker, a younger brother of James Elroy Flecker, author of the begemmed, exotic play *Hassan*.

Bowle was impressed by Oswald Flecker: 'He was my first experience of the impact of a really brilliant Jewish mind on myself,' he said. John's memory of Flecker was cooler. When, in 1954, *The Spectator* invited him to review the reviewers of his latest collection of poems, *A Few Late Chrysanthemums*, John wrote:

> I have come to dread all but unstinted praise or friendly or constructive criticism from people who write poetry themselves. Perhaps an experience I had when a boy of about fifteen at school may partly account for this morbid fear. I was in a set taught by Mr H. L. O. Flecker, the present headmaster of Christ's Hospital, a brother of the poet, and I showed him a poem I had written about a City church. It was very bad and, for motives no doubt kindly meant, he read out my verses to the set of boys, making fun of each line as he went along. Most boys who write verse must have had similar ragging, if not from masters at least from contemporaries.
>
> But most boys who write poetry do not intend to be poets all their lives. That had always been my intention.

John found much more sympathetic Christopher Hughes, the art master, who took the boys on sketching expeditions into the Wiltshire countryside and gave them old-fashioned instruction in the art of watercolour. Hughes was modern enough to ridicule Landseer – causing John, by natural contrariness, to become fascinated by Victorian art. But Hughes disapproved of Blunt and Ellis Waterhouse (the future art historian), who were full of Cézanne and 'significant form'.

In March 1924 John Hilton, a friend of MacNeice, wrote in his diary: 'There's a new college paper coming out for the first time next Saturday called the "Heretick". It is a very high-brow sort of thing I believe. Blunt's got a lot to do with it. He says it is meant to form a focus for the literary talent in the school.' John Bowle's diary suggests that Matthew Wordsworth (son of the Bishop of Salisbury) was the prime mover of the new magazine: 'Wordsworth is starting a paper. Tonight Betj., Wordsworth, myself, Philip Harding, Ben Bonas and Sam Soames had a tremendous talk in W's study. The project is superb.'

The Heretick was a snook-cocking attack on the athletic faction. It aimed (Anthony Blunt later wrote) 'to express our disapproval of the Establishment generally, of the more out-of-date and pedantic masters, of all forms of organized sport, of the Officers' Training Corps and of all the other features that we hated in school life, not so much the physical discomforts – they were almost taken for granted – but, you might say, the intellectual discomforts of the school'.

On St Valentine's Day 1924, Bowle had his first idea for the cover design which he, as the best artist of the group, had been assigned. It was to be 'a Betjemanesque spirit tormenting a "bourgeois" under a tree; mound, Chapel, R. Football goal etc.'. By early March the paper was far enough advanced for Bowle to note: 'I am too dissatisfied with the cover I have designed to publish it, so I have to design another by Saturday when we meet again.' John Betjeman was now suggesting 'an athlete trampling on an aesthete in a welter of footballs' but 'he spent the afternoon playing golf', Bowle recorded, and could contribute no more to the final editorial meeting as he was in the Classical Fifth and had 'to cope with a deluge of impositions'.

At last on 29 March *The Heretick* appeared. (The title had been suggested by Christopher Hughes, the spelling by Bowle.) Before Hall, it was sold from a classroom. 'Court alive with the orange covers on black suits,' Bowle wrote in his diary. 'A strange silence in Hall, everyone reading it.' It was John Betjeman's first experience of the power of the pen.

Bowle's final cover design showed a scowling 'tough' with a hockey stick, seated on a mound in front of rugby posts, while fauns (perhaps 'Betjemanesque') played pipes and taunted him from the branches of a tree. Under the picture was the magazine's motto: 'Upon Philistia will I Triumph.' John's contributions were a 'Prodigies' Song', a satire on the classical scholars among the boys; a short story entitled 'Death'; and an account of 'Dinner of Old Marlburian Centipede Farmers in Unyamwazi, S.A.'.

The reaction of the school's ruling athletes to the new magazine was no less gratifying for being predictable. It was rumoured that the 'bloods' were going to attack the editors after the end-of-term concert. John Bowle was so alarmed by the threat of vengeance that he obtained a 'squaler' from a boy in college – a stick about a foot long with a lump of lead on the end, traditionally used to kill squirrels in Savernake Forest. Armed with it, he made his way back to his house after the concert, unmolested.

On the last Sunday of term, Dr Norwood preached a sermon and quoted the magazine's motto. If, he said, it meant 'overcoming the Philistine in all of us', it was a good thing; if it was 'an expression of intellectual snobbery', it was *not* a good thing. He took a tolerant stance and reproved the extremists of both camps. The second issue, published in June 1924, contained a poem entitled 'Ye Olde Cottage (Quite Near a Town)' and initialled 'J.B.'. Written in a manner already recognizably 'Betjemanesque', it began:

> The happy haunt of typists, common, pert,
> 'We're in the country now!' they say, and wear
> Tweed clothes, and let the wind disturb their hair,
> And carry ash sticks. 'Don't be silly, Gert!
> Afraid of cows?' 'Oh Elsie, mind my skirt,
> It will get muddy.'

The Heretick was suppressed after this issue because it contained an article by Anthony Blunt on the Wildean theme that there can be no morality in art. Norwood was reluctant to close down the magazine: he, too, opposed the excessive athletic bias of the school. But Blunt's article was thought to be so shocking that a parent wrote to Norwood and threatened to remove his boy from the school if the magazine were not suppressed.

John also contributed to the official school magazine, *The Marlburian*. Most of the verse contributions were under real or pseudonymous initials, and it is sometimes difficult to determine which are by John. The first *Marlburian* poem certainly by him appeared in the issue of 26 March 1923. 'The Scholar', a pastiche of Thomas Moore's 'The Minstrel Boy', was aimed at the classics as taught by old Mr Emery, the Fifth Form master, two of whose favourite phrases, 'You little owl!' and 'You won't get on!' were mocked. These are the last two verses:

> The Scholar gazed with a look of alarm
> And he murmured the wrong translation
> But a volume of Vergil under his arm
> Gave him classical consolation.

> 'For two long terms have I taught this form
> But it brings my proud soul under.
> You won't get on,' did the master storm
> In a classical clap of thunder.

By this time there was a feeling among the senior boys that John, only a third-year boy, was getting above himself, or 'coxy'. Ellis Waterhouse, a daunting Marlborough intellectual but also a rebel who was never made a prefect, decided to take him gently down a peg. He composed a satire of John's more yearning manner and published it in *The Marlburian* over the reversed initials 'B.J.' in the issue of 19 June 1923. John was quick to retaliate. As a reader of *The Marlburian* since 1920, he knew that Waterhouse himself had been responsible for some archaic and derivative effusions, so in his reply (12 July 1923) he reprimanded him for his hypocrisy in denouncing a fault of which he himself had been guilty; and he beat Waterhouse at his own game by making his reply an acrostic of 'WATERHOUSE, E. K.':

LINES INSPIRED BY REVERSED INITIALS

Who art thou, second Calverley,* who hast
   Aspired in nonsense uninspired by skill
To crush extravagance, which once was cast
   E'en from thy mighty pen, no doubt at will,
Revealing youth? As nonsense was the theme
   Happy you were to write of, for the gaze
Of mocking intellectuals, or the dream,
   Unwittingly Swinburnian faults displays.
Spare me! thou slaughterer in bombastic verse;
   England hath need of thee for more – why waste
Elaborate genius on a rhymster worse,
   Knowing we both have written in poor taste?

John's first recorded speech in the School Debating Society was on 30 May 1924, supporting the motion proposed by Bowle 'That in the opinion of this House, progress is a figment of man's imagination'. *The Marlburian* reported: 'Mr Betjemann, eloquently recalling the exhibition of 1851 with scorn, lamented the fact that then, as now, comfort was mistaken for progress. Progress is not control over nature, it is control over self. He railed against the "advantages" science has brought, liquorice, anchovy paste, Wembley [the British Empire Exhibition of 1924 at Wembley] and the *Daily Mirror*. If this is progress we can only look forward to "an eternity of yellow ochre".'

The Marlburian also records the first of John's many conservation campaigns. The issue of 18 February 1925 contained a letter from him to the editor:

Dear Sir,

   The college is not devoid of architectural curiosities, and it possesses one which was the culmination of polite elegance in the eighteenth century. This is the historical grotto in the Mound [an artificial cone of chalk], built by Lady Hertford and referred to by Stephen Duck, the 'thresher poet' of Queen Caroline's court . . . It is rather a desecration to use such a rare rural Establishment as a storehouse for College Potatoes. The 'ruins' in the wilderness have been removed, and the upper grotto has been allowed to tumble to pieces by the absurd proselyte of Mr Ruskin. The one remaining relic can still be saved. Surely we have advanced enough now not to condemn a thing because it is 'artificial'?

   Yours faithfully,

   ALEXANDER POPE

---

*John may have known that Waterhouse's father had been at Cambridge with the Victorian poet John Stuart Calverley.

The letter heralds John's tactics in future conservation battles: his use of ridicule to goad the authorities into taking action, and his tenacity in returning to the charge. He renewed the attack in *The Marlburian* of 25 May 1925: 'In all the debris only one building remained intact, and this was the grotto. But it has not been repaired – so the College lost a fitting monument as the crowd eagerly groped for potatoes strewn about the floor.' That John's campaign to save the grotto was successful, we learn from a letter signed 'G. R. Otto' in *The Marlburian* of 25 October 1925.

This victory was not his only success in his last year at school. On 28 March 1925 he took part in *The Grand Cham's Diamond* by Allan Monkhouse. *The Marlburian* of 28 May reported: 'Betjemann, whose acting was masterly throughout, made a most realistic Mrs Perkins, and carried the whole weight of the play on his shoulders.' On Prize Day he took the part of Lady Teazle in *The School for Scandal*, which was repeated before an audience from Marlborough town on 7 July. (*The Marlburian* of 24 July commented that 'Betjemann's rendering of his part was the best of the evening.')

John was also active in the school's Literary Society. His friend Philip Harding, as secretary of the society, recorded in the minutes on 2 December 1923 that 'a visitor, Mr Betjeman, read a paper on Early Victorian Art and Literature . . . an extremely amusing and enlightening paper which he very aptly illustrated by passing round examples to prove to what artistic depths the Victorians had debased themselves. He also read us several amusing poems for "Young Ladies".' Harding described John as a 'visitor' because John had not yet been elected to the society. He was elected, with Louis MacNeice and Graham Shepard (son of the book illustrator E. H. Shepard), in September 1924.

John and MacNeice regarded each other with mutual wariness, and never became close friends. MacNeice recalled John in his memoirs, *The Strings are False*:

Down the passage from Graham [Shepard]'s study was a door with an inscription above it:

> *Here thou, Great Anna, whom three realms obey,*
> *Dost sometimes counsel take and sometimes tea**

– and inside sat John Betjeman writing nonsense on his typewriter or polishing his leather books with boot-polish. John Betjeman at that time looked like a will-o'-the-wisp with Latin blood in it. His face was the colour of peasoup

---

*From Pope's *Rape of the Lock*.

and his eyes were soupy too and his mouth was always twisting sideways in a mocking smile and he had a slight twist in his speech which added a tang to his mimicries, syncopating the original just as a slightly rippling sheet of water jazzes the things reflected in it. He was a brilliant mimic but also a mine of useless information and a triumphant misfit. I felt ill at ease with him, not understanding his passion for minor poetry and misbegotten ornament . . .

A letter of 1930 from John to his Oxford friend Patrick Balfour shows his dislike of MacNeice, only a few years after they had been together at Marlborough (and at Oxford):

I have not read it yet, but I believe the new School book called 'Out of Step' by Derek Walker Smith (Gollancz) is really by Louis MacNeice – that fucking little Oxford aesthete who lives near Belfast. If so it will be about Marlborough and about me – for I remember someone telling me that MacNeice had written a school story which contained a description of me. Please expose him [in the gossip column Balfour was then writing for the *Daily Sketch*] so that he gets lynched – unless it is a Good Book – but I expect, if it is by this creature, it will be a sexless, complaining affair.

MacNeice's oxymoron 'triumphant misfit' is probably a fair description of John at Marlborough. John seemed almost to have chosen the rôle of misfit – and it was a rôle that suited him. A friendlier observer among his Marlborough contemporaries, Arthur Byron, remembered him as 'the boy who always had to be different from the others'. His hair was suspiciously long, at a time when 'short back and sides' was the rule. To other boys, letter-writing was a penance, 'but John seemed to revel in it and he impressed us all by having large, expensive deep blue writing paper and oversized envelopes which nearly matched the blue 2½d stamps. In 1924 postage was reduced to 2d, but John went on using the blue stamps instead of the orange 2d which aesthetically clashed with his envelopes.' John was unique, too, in his method of evading team games:

'May I half change?' This question, to a house prefect in charge of games, was how a junior boy would ask if he could change his school jacket for a blazer, be excused the compulsory games which he hated, and go off to the Marlborough Downs to play golf. He was the only boy in the house who brought his golf clubs to school. Others had sets at home, but they either enjoyed games, tolerated them or lacked the moral courage to do the same as John Betjeman. John's request was seldom refused.

John's failure to conform did not make him universally unpopular. Chief among his friends in 'B' House was Philip Harding, who entered the school with him in September 1920 and remained a friend until Harding's death in 1972. Harding was born in Dorset, and he introduced John to that county one vacation: the two made a tour of the towns and villages which resulted in John's early poem 'Dorset'. Because John Betjeman and John Bowle were in different houses, they did not meet until both were quite senior in the school. 'I never knew John until I was about sixteen and he was fifteen plus,' Bowle said. 'We met through the art room and we used to spend hours there, drawing and painting. John would improve the occasion by reading poetry aloud to me from *The Oxford Book of English Verse*: he educated me a great deal in those days.'

Through Bowle, John met the blond giant Arthur Elton, who was in the same house as Bowle (Preshute) under the games fiend T. C. G. S. Sandford. Though no good at games, Elton 'was so large that he was left alone'. The heir to a baronetcy, he lived at Clevedon Court in Somerset, to which the body of Tennyson's Arthur Hallam had been brought for burial in 1833. John visited the house in Sir Ambrose Elton's old Ford and admired the 'Eltonware' made by his friend's grandfather, which had a glaze like gilded sun-cracked mud.

On 14 February 1924 Bowle confided to his diary: 'Betj inserted a rhymed valentine into M. . .'s hymn book. There was an immediate and blushing reaction.' In later years John and his friends were candid about the prevalence of homosexual behaviour at Marlborough in their day. In 1973 John wrote to Kingsley Amis, whose new novel *The Riverside Murders* had been reviewed in *The Times* that morning:[*]

> Dear Kingers,
>
> A bloody good review I thought . . . I enjoyed every word of the book including the extremely complicated end, but top for me is the chapter called 'Moments of Delight'. I think it would be very nice if you were to write a school story. No one has done it properly for years. What is so wonderful about your writing about Peter Furneaux, old boy, is that you've entered completely into the unshockable practical mind of Peter and his friend, Reg. That's the way to do it. It's the way Dean Farrar did it in *Eric* and in *St Winifred's*.[†] If you just substitute what really happened, which was quick, practical sex, for drinking whisky, you have got the guilt- and doom-ridden life that I lived as a boarder in the early 1920s . . .

[*]The novel was reviewed by Myrna Blumberg, who wrote: 'Peter Furneaux, of Riverside Villas, near Croydon, is 14, keen on Wodehouse and *The Wizard of Oz*. It is the 1930s, Geraldo's Band days, and though he feels enslaved by hypocritical prohibitions he frees himself of some. "I masturbate and I've done things with other boys and I've *thought* of all sorts of things . . ." he tells his neighbour Mrs Trevelyan while they spend an afternoon in her bed.'
[†]Frederic William Farrar was Master of Marlborough 1871–76 and Dean of Canterbury 1895. He wrote the school novels *Eric, or Little by Little* (1858) and *St Winifred's* (1862).

Anthony Blunt's recollection was that 'There was not much "quick, practical sex", but there were many romantic friendships. John was wildly in love at one stage with a boy in my house [C3] and once asked me to deliver a note to him: but I annoyed him considerably by delivering it too *publicly*.' John Bowle said: 'There were various boys that John found attractive and made a great fuss about. He would come up to you and say, "Ooh, isn't he lovely!" One was a boy called Neville Greene, to whom John applied a line by Lord Alfred Douglas – "Wet green eyes, like a full chalk stream".'

John was not only reading and quoting Lord Alfred Douglas at Marlborough. Ernest Betjemann was scandalized to discover that his son was also corresponding with the former lover of Oscar Wilde.

When I was at Marlborough [John recalled] I discovered that Oscar Wilde was someone one ought not to mention; so naturally he had great attraction for me. And I borrowed from one of the masters a volume containing *Lady Windermere's Fan*. The master seemed rather reluctant to lend it to me – he had a whole set of Oscar in that lovely Methuen edition. Then I discovered that Lord Alfred Douglas was actually still alive. So I wrote to him from Marlborough. He was only too pleased to reply and asked me for a photograph. So I went round to the school's photographers, Roberts, and had myself taken, sideways-on and looking, I hoped, rather like the portrait of Rupert Brooke in that Sidgwick and Jackson edition – of Rupert Brooke with an open shirt – and sent it to him, and it brought a reply at once. He was in Belgium at the time; he was living there with his mother as he had libelled Winston Churchill in some speech he had made, which was published in Aberdeen. He said that Winston Churchill had published a false report of the Battle of Jutland in order to satisfy the Jews. He was madly anti-Semitic. That I didn't know about at the time. He wrote me long letters about Shakespeare. Well, then I bought some of Bosie's [Douglas's] poems. I said how beautiful his poems were, as indeed I thought they were . . .

His letters arrived from Belgium about once a week while I was on holiday in Cornwall. My mother noticed them and must have steamed them open, because one day Nancy Wright, the sister of my friend Ronnie Wright, a fair-haired girl – very pretty but I never thought of sex in those days either with my own or the opposite sex – was invited to stay; and in a rather marked way my mother and Nancy Wright left the room at luncheon and my father took me for a walk up a lane.

You know that he was deaf and could only hear through a speaking tube. And if he didn't want to hear you, he would roll it up and put it in his pocket and he couldn't lip-read very well . . . He said: 'You've been having letters from Lord Alfred Douglas.' I couldn't deny it. 'Do you know what that man is?' I said: 'No.' 'He's a bugger. Do you know what buggers are? Buggers are two men who work themselves up into such a state of mutual admiration that one puts his piss-pipe up the other one's arse. What do you think of that?' And of course I felt absolutely sick, and shattered . . . My father said: 'You're not to write another letter to that man.' And I didn't. And more and more letters came – 'If I don't hear from you again, I shan't write.' My father did not let me see the further letters that arrived. He put them in his safe. After my father's death I gave them to a biographer of Bosie . . . They weren't very interesting.

In *Summoned by Bells* John described his romantic feelings for boys at Marlborough. In the Victorian chapel the Old Marlburian Bishop of London, Dr Winnington Ingram, preached a sermon on Purity – 'When all I worshipped were the athletes, ranged / In the pews opposite,' John wrote. And in his last term at the school, in 1925, John to his surprise was asked to go into town by 'a noisy boy, / One of a gang so mad on motor-cars / That I, the aesthete, hardly noticed him'. Back in college, after the trip into town, they found they had time for a bicycle ride in the summer sun. They rode to Silbury. At the top of Hackpen Hill John's new friend 'sat among the harebells in his shorts, / Hugging his knees till I caught up with him'. Pushing back a lock of hair that kept falling on his face, the boy asked 'Why do you always go about with Black [i.e. Greene]?'

> Here was love
> Too deep for words or touch. The golden downs
> Looked over elm tops islanded in mist,
> And short grass twinkled with blue butterflies.
> Henceforward Marlborough shone.

The new friend was Donovan Chance, of Compton Kinver, Stourbridge. In the 1930s he opened a garage, Friary Motors (agents for Lagonda and Chevrolet) at Old Windsor, Berkshire, and in 1937 he answered a query from John about his Ford.

One summer afternoon on a Cornish holiday far from Marlborough, when he was fifteen or sixteen, John pedalled off to the parish of St Ervan. It was to be a day of Damascus-road revelation. He was coasting along, past lichened stones and buddleia, when he heard the note of a bell from the combe below. Following the sound, he came upon the half-ruined church of St Ervan. A heavy bell hung from an elm tree by the churchyard gate, and by it stood the bearded rector, a gong stick in one hand, a book in the other. He invited John to Evensong and then to a cup of tea in the damp, ramshackle rectory where, evidently, he lived alone. The rector was Wilfred Johnson, minister of St Ervan's for forty years (1915–55). This gaunt bachelor priest made on him an impression he never forgot.

He talked of poetry and Cornish saints;
He kept an apiary and a cow;
He asked me which church service I liked best –
I told him Evensong . . . 'And I suppose
You think religion's mostly singing hymns
And feeling warm and comfortable inside?'
And he was right: most certainly I did.
'Borrow this book and come to tea again.'
With Arthur Machen's *Secret Glory** stuffed
Into my blazer pocket, up the hill
On to St Merryn, down to Padstow Quay
In time for the last ferry back to Rock,
I bicycled – and found Trebetherick
A worldly contrast with my afternoon.

'When John came back to Marlborough the next term,' John Bowle recalled, 'he was full of *The Secret Glory*.' By modern standards the book seems blowsily overwritten, and too didactic, like a Bernard Shaw preface run amok; but it appealed to John powerfully on two fronts. It was suffused with a poetic romanticism, a passionate nostalgia for the old saints, grail-quests, holy wells and holy bells of Celtic Wales, which chimed in perfectly with his interest in primitive Cornish saints. But even more appealing to him than the mystical raptures was the satire that Machen levelled at the British public school system, from which John, when he first read the novel, was suffering in much the same way as its hero, Ambrose Meyrick. Everything John most loathed about Marlborough was savagely guyed – the discipline, the team games, the emphasis on classicism. Machen also satirized the hypocrisy about sex in the near-monastic society of the public schools: 'Suppose . . . a whole society organized on the strict official understanding that . . . breakfast, lunch, dinner and supper are orgies only used by the most wicked and degraded wretches . . . In such a world, I think, you would discover some very striking irregularities in diet.'

When John first read those words, he was already familiar with the 'quick, practical sex' of the Marlborough dormitories. His early relations with girls were slower and less practical. Biddy Walsham and her brother. John (whose parents were usually in China) grew up in Trebetherick with the Adams boys, Ralph, Vasey and Alastair, who lived with their aunt, Elsie MacCorkindale. Of all the adults in Trebetherick, Elsie MacCorkindale was the only one, John felt, who took him at his own estimate. He plucked

*A novel published in 1922.

up his courage and asked if he might borrow her Talbot-Darracq motor-car to take Biddy to a dance. In his fantasy of driving Biddy to the party, he pictured himself braking, switching off the headlights. And if his hand should accidentally touch hers, perhaps the love in him 'would race along to her / On the electron principle?' No-nonsense Scottish Miss MacCorkindale told him it would be more sensible to walk.

> She would explain that I was still a boy.
>   'Was still a boy?' Then what, by God, was this –
> This tender, humble, unrequited love
> For Biddy Walsham?

It is not easy to assess how unhappy John was at Marlborough. Clearly, he enjoyed dramatizing his tribulations there; but the evidence of his con-temporaries, too, suggests an institution closer to a concentration camp than a school. 'Even now,' one of them wrote to him in 1960, 'I tend to wake screaming in the night at the thought of an impending flogging from Sandy [Sandford] or Canning for having gone down three places in form during the week. Has such treatment made men of us?' An Anthony Blunt might decide: 'If this represents the establishment, I shall conspire to destroy the establishment.' (That is the theme of Julian Mitchell's 1982 play *Another Country*.) John's response to the ordeal was to adapt rather than rebel. He used his burgeoning charm and wit to make things easier for himself, while storing up hatred of those he took to be his chief torment-ors. A desire to *épater* sometimes triumphed, but he did not want to make himself so noticeable that he would be put in the basket. As he moved up the school, his schoolfellows became more sophisticated and were better able to appreciate his quiddities, so that the sixth form was a comparatively happy time for him. But he leaves us in no doubt that he was unhappier at Marlborough than he thought he had any right to be. Along with the bullying and the beatings, the poor food and the cold, lack of privacy was one of his main grievances. He liked Blore's 1840s chapel, not just because it was Victorian Gothic and decorated with sensuous Pre-Raphaelite murals by Roddam Spencer-Stanhope, but because it was 'The only place where I could be alone'.

4

Oxford

M AGDALEN COLLEGE, OXFORD, to which John went in the
Michaelmas Term of 1925, was not the most academically distinguished of the colleges: Balliol had not lost the intellectual supremacy
which Benjamin Jowett had wrested for it from Newman's Oriel in the
nineteenth century. Neither was it the most aristocratic: Christ Church
was even more familiar with the clamour Evelyn Waugh described in
Decline and Fall – 'the sound of the English county families baying for
broken glass'. But by common consent Magdalen was and is the most beautiful of the colleges. Standing at the edge of the old city on the bank of the
River Cherwell, it is one of the largest colleges, a congeries of architectural
showpieces: William of Waynflete's slender tower of perfect proportion,
from which the choristers sing their half-pagan anthem on May morning;
echoing medieval cloisters guarded by grotesque gargoyles, some lewdly
embracing; Pugin's Grammar Hall, picturesquely decrepit; the honey-
coloured New Buildings (1703), colonnaded, festooned with wistaria in
summer, and overlooking the deer park. The beauties and comforts of
Magdalen encouraged lotus-eating and languid self-indulgence. The college emblem, the Waynflete lily, symbolized, it was said, the habits of many
of the undergraduates: they toiled not, neither did they spin.

Herbert Warren, who was President of Magdalen when John arrived at
the college, was born at the beginning of the Crimean War. A legendary
snob, he had the arms of De Warenne, to which he was not remotely entitled, set in stained glass in the Founder's Tower. When introducing his
wife, he would say, 'Meet Lady Warren, the daughter of Sir Benjamin
Brodie, Bart.' He was only thirty-one when he became President in 1885.
He set out to change the character of the college. 'Magdalen had been too
much identified with aestheticism, peacocks' feathers and blue china,' he
told the *Isis* in 1929. 'I had been taught at Clifton and by Plato that the cult
of the Muses and the Arts to which I was devoted, should be tempered by
politics and athletics. I encouraged the devotees of these.' In 1911 he was
elected Professor of Poetry.

John owed his admission to Magdalen almost entirely to Warren's personal intervention. He did not go up with a scholarship, as Evelyn Waugh had to Hertford College three years before, or with an exhibition, like his Marlborough friend Philip Harding, also at Hertford. He was to be a commoner, maintained at his father's expense. He had failed the entrance examination twice by May 1925, and it began to look as though he would have to abandon thoughts of Oxford and enter his father's business. But at that date the President of Magdalen had the power to admit anybody he liked to the college. (The privilege was later docked to a statutory fourteen places, and has since been abolished.) Warren fancied himself as a poet, and John seems to have made a good impression by sending him some of his Marlborough verses. By August it had been arranged that he would come up to Magdalen in the next term.

John went up to the University on 8 October 1925. Michaelmas Term began the next day. It was the Oxford of plus fours, verandah suits, violet hair cream, batik or Charvet silk ties and open sports cars; shingled hair and slave bangles for the rare fashionable 'undergraduettes'. In spite of the new jazzy tempo of life for the Bright Young People, some formalities were preserved. Evening dress was still *de rigueur* for dinner. For daytime wear, the extravagantly wide 'Oxford bags' had until recently been the fashion, and some of the more exhibitionist undergraduates still sported them. In one college, it was reported, the servants had orders 'to ignore undergraduates thus attired'. In an article of 1958, 'The Silver Age of Aesthetes', John wrote:

> I came up to the University just as 'Oxford Bags' were going out. I doubt if they had ever come in with the grand sets in which I aspired to move. The year must have been 1925 when still the tales of Harold Acton, Brian Howard and Cyril Connolly lingered and the few aesthetes of that generation who had not been sent down, were staying on for a final year. Most aesthetes belonged to the Liberal Club, to which no Liberals were ever admitted but which was supported, we believed, out of the pocket of Lloyd George. No aesthete was political and the Union was only used for a wash and brush up – whether one was a member or not. Of course I was an aesthete and never played any game for my college and never discovered, nor have yet discovered, where the playing fields of my college were.
>
> The world for me and for many undergraduates was divided into aesthetes and hearties. These divisions overrode all social and college distinctions. True there was one college, Brasenose, which was entirely hearty and dangerous for an aesthete to enter wearing the usual badges of his party – a shantung silk tie, lavender trousers, orange, red or saxe blue shirt. A friend of mine, Michael Dugdale, always entered it limping as he thought the

hearties would be too sporting to attack a fellow athlete. Otherwise one's
college did not matter and one very much despised the sub-men who tried
to whip up college spirit. It was too much like school.

Magdalen was predominantly a college of hearties. President Warren
had been only too successful in de-aestheticizing it. Martyn Skinner, John's
exact contemporary at Magdalen, said: 'I can't remember a single night
when there wasn't a drunken party and somebody breaking glass. It was
riotous. The idea was that you could do what you wanted within college,
within reason, provided you didn't do it outside. You couldn't be drunk in
the streets, but you could be drunk in college. One man got so tight that
he smashed up his *own* rooms without realizing they were his.'

John had no wish to antagonize the athletes. He followed the same strat-
egy as at Marlborough, turning himself into a joke figure whom they
would laugh at rather than persecute. Humphrey Ellis, the future literary
editor of *Punch*, who came up to Magdalen the year after him, recalled:
'One day I noticed a figure in extraordinary clothes standing just inside the
door of the porter's lodge. I asked somebody who it was, and he said, "Oh,
that's John Betjeman, waiting to be hissed by the athletes."'

John entitled his 1958 article 'The Silver Age of Aesthetes' to distinguish
his undergraduate days from those of the preceding Golden Age of
Aesthetes – the age of Harold Acton, Brian Howard and Robert Byron,
who had been at Eton together. Also of the Golden Age were Evelyn
Waugh, John Sutro, Christopher Hollis and Douglas Woodruff, who had
enjoyed such *réclame* at Oxford that they could hardly bear to leave it. They
returned at weekends to add their lustre to parties and salons. John eventually met them all, through Philip Harding's elder brother Archie, who
was a friend at Keble College of Waugh's cousin Claud Cockburn; through
such dons as Maurice Bowra and 'Colonel' Kolkhorst; casually at the
George restaurant; and in the Christ Church rooms of Harold Acton's
younger brother, William.

But in the Michaelmas Term of 1925 he was only just acclimatizing
himself to life in Oxford. It was intoxicating to be free at last of the oppressive authority of home and school, but there were new difficulties to cope
with – such as living within his income, which meant the income his father
chose to allow him. Ernest Betjemann was to pay all John's college bills and
had also agreed that in the first term – the most expensive time for an
undergraduate – he would pay for clothes and accessories up to £18.
Perhaps to propitiate him, John's first clothes list ('I need . . .') included a
golfing cap and golf shoes.

By John's third term, Ernest was beginning to warn him about overspending. He wrote on 13 May 1926: 'I enclose you a cheque for £5, try to keep the provisions and drink bill down a bit, there is a steady upward progress. I don't mean to say at all that you are extravagant.' The reason John's food and drink bill had risen is that he had ceased to take his meals in College Hall after his first term. 'Only sub-men ate in hall,' he later explained. A pleasant but more expensive alternative to eating in hall was to have meals brought over from the kitchens by one's scout. The richer undergraduates often held breakfast, lunch or dinner parties in their rooms, ordering from the chef and butler in advance.

Another alternative to eating in hall was to go to St George's Café-and-Restaurant – 'the George' – at the junction of the Cornmarket and George Street, 'where there was a band consisting of three ladies, and where punkahs, suspended from the ceiling, swayed to and fro, dispelling the smoke of the Egyptian and Balkan cigarettes. Mr Ehrsam, the perfect Swiss hotelier, and his wife kept order, and knew how much credit to allow us.' The George was a domain of aesthetes, including the revenants who could call in there without a special invitation from anybody. The aesthetes who dined at the George were known as 'the Georgeoisie'. John Fernald (another Old Marlburian) recalled that one of their favourite jokes was to discomfit a hearty by staring at him in silence and then, on a prearranged signal, bursting into a chorus of guffaws.

In his first term John was also experiencing the gentle constraints of the Oxford tutorial system. C. S. Lewis was his tutor in English language and literature. One might have expected that these two men – both poets, both Christian apologists – would have been compatible. But though John had already been Summoned by Bells, Lewis had not yet been Surprised by Joy. (It was not until 1929, the year after John left Oxford, that Lewis gave in to his inner spiritual urgings, 'admitted that God is God', knelt on his Magdalen carpet and prayed, 'perhaps that night the most dejected and reluctant convert in all England'.) Their love of English literature, too, might have led to some rapport; but Lewis preferred the oldest gnarled roots of the language, John its most luxuriant Victorian blossoming. The lover of bleak Norse legend and Tolkienesque hobgoblins could not understand the lover of cosy suburbs and garden gnomes. No Underground line connected Middle Earth with Metroland.

In 1925 Lewis was a pugnacious atheist, while John was flirting with Anglo-Catholicism, a persuasion unlikely to appeal to someone who had been brought up by Ulster Protestants. Lord David Cecil, who liked Lewis, said: 'It's one of those great comedy ideas, that John Betjeman should have been Jack Lewis's pupil. The very idea of believing in the Church but at the same time making fun of it, would have been distasteful to him. It was too bewildering, this odd little boy making jokes about the things he [John] claimed to think sacred, and yet with tears in his eyes at a hymn. It was rather shocking to Jack Lewis.'

Lewis's mind was analytic; John's was intuitive, addicted to fantasy and flippant posturing. Lewis favoured the big guns of English literature – Shakespeare, Spenser, Milton. John's taste was for the minor figures – Frederick Locker-Lampson, T. E. Brown, Lord de Tabley. His thesis that Lord Alfred Douglas was greater than Shakespeare did not strike Lewis as an entertaining conceit or as the starting-point for an enjoyable exercise in critical debate: he thought it merely perverse and exasperating – another of Betjeman's silly stratagems for wasting tutorial time. He was not amused when John turned up for his tutorial in carpet slippers. On 27 May 1926 Lewis wrote in his diary:

> Betjeman and [Deric] Valentin came for Old English. Betjeman appeared in a pair of eccentric bedroom slippers and said he hoped I didn't mind them as he had a blister. He seemed so pleased with himself that I couldn't help saying that I should mind them very much myself but that I had no objection to *his* wearing them – a view which I believe surprised him. Both had been very idle over the O.E. and I told them it wouldn't do.

He was again incensed with John on 19 January 1927: 'While in College, I was rung up on the telephone by Betjeman speaking from Moreton-in-Marsh, to say that he hadn't been able to read the Old English, as he was suspected for measles and forbidden to read a book. Probably a lie, but what can one do?' John confirms these suspicions in *Summoned by Bells*:

> I cut tutorials with wild excuse,
> For life was luncheons, luncheons, all the way.

He found Old English an arid subject; and even when Lewis discussed nineteenth-century poetry, there was little common ground. John recalled: 'He ruined Coleridge's "Kubla Khan" for me by wondering whether the pants in the line "As if this earth in fast thick pants were breathing" were woollen or fur.' Lord David Cecil said: 'Jack Lewis had a loud voice and asked John difficult questions which he couldn't answer. John did awfully good imitations of being taught by Lewis. "What's wrong with you, Betjeman, is that you've no *starl*. No sense of *starl*."'

John made one game attempt to lure Lewis into his world, but it was a failure. In his diary for 24 January 1927 Lewis describes how John invited him to a party in his lodgings, then in St Aldate's – 'a very beautiful panelled room looking across to the side of the House [Christ Church]'.

> I found myself pitchforked into a galaxy of super-undergraduates, includ-ing [John] Sparrow of the Nonesuch Press and an absolutely silent and astonishingly ugly person called McNiece [*sic*], of whom Betjeman said afterwards, 'He doesn't say much, but he's a great poet.' It reminded me of the man in Boswell 'who was always thinking of Locke and Newton'. The conversation was chiefly about lace curtains, arts and crafts (which they all dislike), china ornaments, silver versus earthen teapots, architecture, and the strange habits of 'hearties'. The best thing was Betjeman's very curious col-lection of books. Came away with him and back to college to pull him along through Wulfstan until dinner time.

John's other tutor in Magdalen was the Rev. J. M. Thompson, whose friendly interest in him was an antidote to Lewis's spikiness – a dock-leaf, as it were, growing beside the nettle. He prepared John for the History Previous examination, the equivalent of the later 'Prelims'. From the start, John liked and respected this 'shy, kind, amusing man'. Thompson, too, was a poet. His fluent *My Apologia* (1940), a long verse autobiography printed for private circulation, was probably a more immediate inspiration of John's 'The Epic', part of which became *Summoned by Bells*, than Wordsworth's *Prelude*. Thompson had become Dean of Divinity at Magdalen in 1906. As John was obsessed with religious differences in 1925, Thompson had a special fascination for him, because in 1911 he had caused a furore by denying the existence of miracles in his book *Miracles in the New Testament*. The Bishop of Winchester, Visitor of Magdalen, had withdrawn Thompson's licence to exercise a cure of souls in the college. However, Thompson was so popular with his Magdalen colleagues that he was at once re-elected to his tutorial Fellowship.

Martyn Skinner liked Thompson too, but was less impressed by him than John was. 'Thompie was a clergyman but he had lost his faith – had suddenly seen the dark! As our tutor, he was very easily deceived . . . We had the art of filleting a book; and Thompie thought we were very eru-dite – he said so at Collections [the tutor's end-of-term report to the President of Magdalen]. We were not erudite at all, we were just con-men. He was a nice chap – urbane, kindly – but he was no damn good as a tutor. He didn't teach one anything.' John wrote to Skinner in 1960: 'Lewis was my undoing at Magdalen as well as my own temperament. Thompie was a rock of goodness and I loved him.'

In his article 'The Silver Age of Aesthetes', John wrote: 'I went to one lecture when I was at Oxford. That was in my first term, given by T. S. R.

Boase, known as "the popular dean of Hertford", on *Gesta Francorum*.' This was an ironic in-joke: Boase was anything but popular with John and his friends. Like Maurice Bowra he was one of the generation of young dons who had fought in the First World War. He had lost an eye and won the Military Cross. But he was not the tough character that this war record might suggest. He was silkily charming and a touch effete: Bowra called him 'a man of large public virtues and small private parts'.

John's surviving lecture-notes show that in fact he attended more than one of Boase's lectures. That he was not engrossed by them is suggested by marginal notes to the unknown person sitting next to him:

> I love you, yes, I think I do.
> Oh God! that such a thing is true.

And below: 'His name is Prentice. He was at school with Ronald Wright and me. He Scottish – very. Broad accent and pince-nez.' And then: 'Try writing your notes in blank verse – it makes things more interesting.' At this point John began converting the lecture into verse as Boase spoke:

> Seems to dislike ALEXIS and the Greeks
> We must be on our guard against all this.
> The other leaders are conventional
> In their descriptions. And alone are praised
> Friends Boamund and Tancred . . .

Few poets can have attempted this exercise – high-speed versifying, aiming at a moving target.

John's greatest friends among the dons were Boase's enemy Maurice Bowra, Dean of Wadham, and Bowra's enemy 'Colonel' George Kolkhorst, a University lecturer in Spanish. Bowra and Kolkhorst were a kind of contrapuntal Chorus to his life. Only accredited aesthetes were welcome at Kolkhorst's, but Bowra liked to be accepted as 'one of the boys' by the Wadham rowing eight. Kolkhorst giggled; Bowra guffawed. In modern slang, Kolkhorst was 'camp' and Bowra was 'butch'.

Lord Clark wrote that Bowra was 'without question, the strongest influence in my life'. 'You made us what we were,' declared John Sparrow in a valedictory ode. And John Betjeman was:

> certain then,
> As now, that Maurice Bowra's company
> Taught me far more than all my tutors did.

'At the back of his mind,' Clark added, 'were Homer, Pindar, Aeschylus, Dante, Pushkin, Tolstoy, Camoens and St Paul, all read in the originals.'

It was quite possible that John would be frightened by this formidable person, and that Bowra would be added to the growing list of his bogey-men. Why did that not happen? First, although Bowra held an establishment job he was in some respects an anti-establishment figure. Second, vulnerability in others always appealed to John; and, beneath his super-confident exterior, Bowra was vulnerable. He was worried about his appearance. Anthony Powell thought him 'noticeably small, this lack of stature emphasized by a massive head and tiny feet'. A. L. Rowse remembered Bowra's appearing in court on behalf of a Wadham undergraduate who had been found *in flagrante* with a mechanic on the Oxford Canal bank. ' "Stand up, Mr Bowra," said the judge. "I am standing up," said Maurice. Everybody laughed – and Maurice was terrified of being laughed at.'

But what most won John over was that Bowra warmly appreciated *him*. The second Lord Birkenhead recalled in 1958: 'Many years ago, when I was an undergraduate at Oxford, Sir Maurice Bowra remarked to me of John Betjeman, who was then writing such verses as "The 'Varsity Students' Rag" and other juvenilia: "Betjeman has a mind of extraordinary original-ity; there is no one else remotely like him." ' This remark, which was doubt-less intended to get back to John, doubtless did. And though Bowra may have preferred the 'big stuff' of literature, he was wise enough to accept John on his own terms. At their first meeting they discussed minor Victorian poets, as Bowra recalled in his memoirs:

> He was slight and not very tall, and had a wonderfully expressive and mobile face, which changed from moment to moment, and a certain elfin quality. The first time I met him he talked fluently about half-forgotten authors of the nineteenth century – Sir Henry Taylor, Ebenezer Elliott, Philip James Bailey, and Sir Lewis Morris, but this was not done for effect. He was fascin-ated by the Victorian Age and was already exploring its bypaths.

'*This was not done for effect.*' Bowra did not fall into Lewis's disparaging assumption that John's enthusiasm for the minor poets was just a pose. He might challenge John's views – he challenged all his friends' views. But he also encouraged him, taught him not to be embarrassed by his own per-sonality, but to trade on it. At the Bowra salon John also learned 'how not to be a bore':

> And merciless was his remark that touched
> The tender spot if one were showing off.

John became the chief clown in the Bowra circus. 'I thought of him as an entertainer,' Lord David Cecil said, 'an extraordinary entertainer. He would do marvellous turns – sudden parodies, imitations of a radio play, anything – and it all came out spontaneously.' But what struck him most about John was 'his saying he loved a thing, and laughing at it. I mean, it wasn't just a kindly smile at what he loved. He would say: "I love that building, it's so ugly." ' Elizabeth Longford thought this was something else John took from Maurice Bowra, who 'had this famous saying of some girl: "I like her, she smells." ' When a few years later Elizabeth's brother-in-law, Edward Longford, and John performed religious charades in Ireland, dressed in tablecloths as bishop and priest, 'one knew, even in those early days, that John was deadly serious about religion at the same time as laughing at it'. Bowra also influenced John's taste in poetry by his enthusiasm for Yeats and Hardy, who were both still living. Bowra made Yeats almost as popular in the Oxford of the 1920s as Swinburne had been in the 1860s when young men had linked arms and had marched through cloisters chanting the choruses from 'Atalanta in Calydon'.

In Bowra's salon, John made friends who were not only congenial, but influential. Kenneth Clark is a good example. But for the relaxed atmosphere of Bowra's parties, and Bowra's propaganda on John's behalf, John might never have become a friend of this aloof man. Clark was one of the powerful figures who made sure that John's talents were not wasted during the Second World War. Later, Clark was also useful to him as chairman of the Independent Television Authority. Freddy Furneaux (afterwards the second Lord Birkenhead) introduced one of the collections of John's poetry. John Sparrow became Warden of All Souls and wrote the introduction to another. Bowra himself pulled strings to obtain John a job on *The Architectural Review* in 1930.

Some of the undergraduates in Bowra's circle also attended the salon of 'Colonel' George Kolkhorst at 12.30 on Sunday afternoons. Those who did were in danger of being regarded as 'double spies' by both dons; and some remained strictly loyal to only one – for example, Kenneth Clark was a committed Bowra man, and no mention of Kolkhorst is found in his memoirs. At first, Kolkhorst was known as G'ug (the apostrophe, indicated by a little yawn, was supposed to imply deference). But Denis Kincaid and John invested him with a mythical colonelcy in the Portuguese Medical Corps – because he looked wonderfully unlike a colonel. His rooms were at 38 Beaumont Street, near the Ashmolean Museum. In the sitting-room where he received, there were suits of Japanese armour in which, Osbert Lancaster alleged, 'whole families of mice had made their homes'; oriental figures under glass domes; fly-blown *kakemonos*; copies of *The Yellow Book*; a collection of novels of school life; and a photograph of Walter Pater on which Lancaster had scrawled 'Alma Pater'.

The Colonel was a tall, stooping, pampered-looking man. He wore an eye-glass on a black moiré ribbon and hung a lump of sugar round his neck 'to sweeten conversation'. Like Bowra, he had a clear memory of his first meeting with John. In 1956 he wrote to him: 'So you have reached your 50th birthday! Just the other day you were 20, and Paul Wilson [a scholar at Trinity College] brought in a dark young man (an *ephebe* {Socratic all right}) with flashing black eyes and a marked strain of the satirical and a faked-up love of Schopenhauer.'

There was an almost ritual order to events at the Beaumont Street Sunday salons. After a few glasses of sherry or marsala, the junketings began. At a given signal those present would form a circle round the Colonel and sway from side to side, chanting 'The Colonel's drunk! The Colonel's drunk! The room's going round!'. As the pace hotted up, everybody joined in what was regarded as the 'school song', to the tune of 'John Peel':

> D'ye ken Kolkhorst in his art-full parlour,
> Handing out the drinks at his Sunday morning gala?
> Some get sherry and some Marsala –
> With his arts and his crafts in the morning!

The Colonel might be outraged by these antics and expel one of the malefactors, usually Alan Pryce-Jones (who turned up in a bathing-dress one day) or John. If in more mellow mood, he could be persuaded to move into the back room and sing 'Questa o quella' from *Rigoletto* in 'a very juicy tenor' to his own accompaniment on the harmonium. After one party, Kolkhorst climbed with Robert Byron, Billy Clonmore and some other undergraduates to the top of St Mary Magdalen's tower in the Cornmarket, where they sang hymns and began spitting on the people below. 'The Proctors were called,' John wrote, 'and waited at the bottom of the tower for the delinquents to descend, which they eventually did, headed by the Colonel in his white suit. As a graduate of the university and lecturer in Spanish, he was immune from punishment, but the others were fined.' This kind of irresponsibility appealed to John. Maurice Bowra, with all his irreverence for the establishment, would never have behaved in that way.

According to Osbert Lancaster, Kolkhorst's 'very existence was denied by the Dean of Wadham, who held that he was nothing but an intellectual concept thought up by Betjeman'. As contributor to and later editor of the *Cherwell*, John constantly referred to him. The last reference made to Kolkhorst in the magazine was a Beaumont Street witticism of Osbert Lancaster's, quoted in the issue of 8 December 1928: 'The Colonels and the Queens depart.'

John's first friendships in Oxford were made, not in the Bowra and Kolkhorst salons, but in his own college. Magdalen was so large and various that one did not need to venture into the wider university to find agreeable company. One of the first people he met there was Martyn Skinner, who, like Joseph Addison and Oscar Wilde before him, was a Demy (the Magdalen word for a scholar, since scholars had originally received half a Fellow's emolument). At Oxford, Skinner 'went native'. With a small group of friends, he lived a kind of Scholar Gypsy life, in which the gypsy element considerably outweighed the scholarship. He was what would later be called a dropout. John shared his reaction against public school, his love of the countryside and his cavalier attitude to the Oxford syllabus. In later life the two became good friends, and in 1961 John addressed a poem to Skinner, which was published in *High and Low* (1966), but in his undergraduate days John did not want to drop out of Oxford society. He wanted to be at its spinning centre.

His best friend at Magdalen was Lionel Perry, who had an entrée to some of the sets John was most eager to join. Perry, who had come up to Magdalen the year before John, was rich, handsome and witty. With his blond hair and unfading suntan, he was known as 'the Golden Boy'. His year of seniority enabled him to introduce John to some of the previous Oxford generation who belonged to the Golden Age of Aesthetes. In the later part of 1926 Perry shared rooms with John at 142 Walton Street, Oxford. 'Of course he was terrified of the landlady [Perry recalled]. John had this great capacity for making his phobias and guilts very enjoyable conversation for a lot of other people. At Magdalen, his great fear was the head porter, he didn't like going through the Lodge alone. "I daren't go through it. That man hates me."'

Henry Yorke, who came up to Magdalen with John in 1925, had his first novel, *Blindness*, published in 1926 under the pseudonym Henry Green. He had begun it at Eton, where he was secretary of the Eton Society of Arts. He collected Victoriana and was interested in Gothic architecture and the writings of William Beckford; and he and John were further drawn together by their common loathing of C. S. Lewis, who was Yorke's tutor also. Yorke did not finish his course at Oxford, partly because he was so 'irritated and bored' by Lewis, and partly because he wanted to work in his father's Birmingham factory to get copy for another novel.

Another Etonian who became a friend of John's arrived at Magdalen in 1927: Alan Pryce-Jones, the future editor of the *Times Literary Supplement*. Pryce-Jones was a freshman and John a third-year swell when the two first met. Pryce-Jones recalled: 'I was wearing a dressing-gown on my way to the very remote bathroom which one had in those days, about half a mile from one's room in college; and John thought it such a curious dressing-gown – it was kind of cape-shaped – that he suddenly said, "What are you doing wearing that extraordinary garment?" and we made friends from that point.' John drove him to see churches – 'In those days the eighteenth century was his great interest, not the nineteenth.' The first church Pryce-Jones was driven to see, in the open Morris Cowley John by then owned, was St Katherine's, Chiselhampton (1762), on which John was to write a poem in 1952.

Alan Pryce-Jones's father was a colonel at the Duke of York's Headquarters, Chelsea, not far down the King's Road from John in Church Street. So the two undergraduates were able to meet often in the vacations and got to know each other's families. Pryce-Jones's mother Vere took a particular liking to John and asked him to look after her son at Oxford. Osbert Lancaster said it was like asking Satan to chaperone Sin, but a more apt parallel is Lady Marchmain's asking Charles Ryder to watch over Lord Sebastian, in *Brideshead Revisited*. Despite these attentions, in 1928 Pryce-Jones was 'rusticated' for various misdeeds, and his father would not allow him to return. 'The dear boy *has* been stupid!' Vere Pryce-Jones wrote to John. Pryce-Jones obtained a job as assistant editor of *The London Mercury*, and soon persuaded the editor, John Squire, to publish work by John.

Lionel Perry introduced John to Lord Clonmore, son of the seventh Earl of Wicklow: the Perrys and the Wicklows had known each other from far back in Ireland. 'Billy' Clonmore was an ordinand at St Stephen's House in Norham Road, North Oxford. John Bowle said that he 'looked exactly like the Mad Hatter: he *was* the Mad Hatter'. Waugh wrote that 'his extravagances were refined by a slightly antiquated habit 'of speech and infused by a Christian piety that was unique among us . . .' Clonmore was the first real live lord to be numbered among John's friends. He was amusedly aware of this aspect of his appeal to John, and he both teased him about it and encouraged him in his not too vicious kind of snobbery. For years afterwards they sent each other newspaper cuttings and anecdotes about obscure peers.

Through Clonmore, John met Robert Byron, who had been in Clonmore's house at Eton. John's and Byron's undergraduate days overlapped by only one term but Byron was one of the most frequent revenants. He was killed in 1941 when the ship taking him to Egypt as a newspaper special correspondent was torpedoed, so his youthful image remained clear in his Oxford contemporaries' minds and was not overlaid by the palimpsest of an older self. He looked remarkably like Queen Victoria, and he made full use of the resemblance whenever he went to fancy-dress parties. He was a master of spoken and written invective. In his company, Brian Howard wrote, one felt 'like an empty electric battery which has suddenly and mysteriously become recharged'. Probably nobody among the friends John made at Oxford so profoundly influenced his taste and prose style.

A friend of Byron's, and like him a survivor of the Golden Age of Aesthetes, was John ('the Widow') Lloyd, whom Lionel Perry described as 'small, with sparkling black eyes . . . infinitely vivacious, infinitely malicious'. Lloyd knew John less well at Oxford than in later years, when Lloyd composed a pasquinade on him in Gilbertian measure ('I am the very model of a perfect Betjemanian, / I know all the London churches, from R.C. to Sandemanian . . .'). In this, he suggests that he was introduced to John at one of Kolkhorst's Sundays. Both Clonmore and the Widow were decidedly of Kolkhorst's coterie rather than Bowra's.

Lionel Perry had known John Dugdale since the age of thirteen: they had been at school together. It was through his introduction to Dugdale by Perry that John came to stay in his first great English house, for John Dugdale lived at Sezincote, a mansion in Indian style. Its domes, minarets and multifoil arches of golden Stanway stone rise like a mirage from the Gloucestershire countryside between Stow-on-the-Wold and Moreton-in-Marsh, about twenty miles from Oxford. Though John was fascinated by the architecture and the landscape vistas, he was still more interested in the new experience of staying in a great English mansion, and Sezincote became a second home (or a third, if one counts Oxford) to him and to his friends.

John Dugdale shared his mother's political views. He later became a Labour MP and Parliamentary Private Secretary to Clement Attlee. At Oxford, he was already a member of the Labour Club and a friend of Hugh Gaitskell. Lionel Perry was also among Gaitskell's friends in this group of socialites with some kind of a social conscience. John and Gaitskell had not seen each other since they had left the Dragon School (Gaitskell had gone on to Winchester College). They met again at Maurice Bowra's dinner parties.

It was during the General Strike of 1926 that John became aware of Gaitskell as someone more than the usual Oxford aesthete. The Strike impinged on the University as few other public events did. Only the most cloistered of dons or the most butterfly-brained of undergraduates could ignore it. Some undergraduates became strike-breakers, while others saw the crisis as a 'lark', perhaps the chance to realize boyhood dreams of driving a train. A much smaller group of undergraduates gave help to the strikers. Bede Griffiths, who was with John at Magdalen, offered to sell the *Daily Worker* in the streets. Tom Driberg, who had joined the Communist Party during his last year at Lancing, distributed literature from CP headquarters in Covent Garden. He was arrested and interrogated at Scotland Yard. John might easily have become a strike-breaker. Nothing could have been more tempting to him than the prospect of driving a train or a bus. (He achieved both ambitions in the 1960s and 1970s.) But Gaitskell and John Dugdale persuaded him to help the strikers. Gaitskell and Lionel Perry took him to meet G. D. H. Cole and his wife Margaret in Holywell. John was pleased to find that the left-wing Reader in Economics was not just a politico, but something of an aesthete too, a connoisseur of antique glass. With Gaitskell and Perry, John was sent to Didcot in Dugdale's Morris, to take messages for the National Union of Railwaymen. 'I do not recall their having any messages for us to take,' John wrote. 'The gesture, however, was made.' But he lacked any real commitment to the Strike. 'To Hugh and John [Dugdale],' he wrote, 'the General Strike was not the lark it was to me. It was a righteous cause.'

By this date (mid-1926), John had still written no signed article or poem for either the *Isis* or the *Cherwell*, the two undergraduate publications. His first contribution appeared in the *Isis* at the beginning of his second year at Oxford, on 27 October 1926, an article entitled 'Our Lovely Lodging Houses', and a week later his first verse appeared in the magazine, a quatrain on 'Arts and Crafts'. From January 1927 he supplied architectural notes to the *Cherwell*. The issue of 5 February contrasted the 'Edwardo-Victorian baroque' of Cousins Thomas, Chemists, Banbury Road, with the seventeenth-century baroque of Greyfriars, Paradise Street, St Ebbe's. John was learning that odious comparisons are often the most effective form of criticism. He succeeded Bryan Guinness (later Lord Moyne) as editor of the *Cherwell* in May 1927. The change of regime was marked by an immediate stepping-up of the paper's architectural content. 'Go and look at the back quad of the Examination Schools,' the issue of 14 May advised readers. 'It will all count towards your period of purgatory. Its architecture is in the Neo-State-Public-Baths style.'

Shortly after John's editorship ended, the *Cherwell* published 'A 'Varsity Student's Rag', one of the juvenilia which were to have a permanent place in his *Collected Poems*. The announcement read: 'A 'VARSITY STU-DENT'S RAG is the first of a series to be written by Mr Betjeman which will be ultimately comprehended in a new " 'Varsity Students' Song-Book".

These are primarily intended to be sung as curtain-raisers for "shows" on Boat-Race night, but may also be used as "wines" and "cyders".' Unfortunately, this ambitious plan – if plan it was – came to nothing. But 'A 'Varsity Student's Rag' remains (under a slightly altered title) as an enjoyable skit on the rowdy hearties whose idea of fun was a 'rag' at Monico's (Delmonico's), the Troc (Trocadero) or the Grill Room at the Cri (the Criterion Theatre Restaurant), followed by the excitement of smashing up somebody's rooms:

> And then we smash'd up ev'rything, and what was the funniest part
> We smashed some rotten old pictures which were priceless works of art.

On 24 October 1928 one of the best of John's early poems appeared in the *Isis* under the title 'To the Blessed St Aubin'.* (It appears in his *Collected Poems* as 'Hymn' and is based on S. J. Stone's hymn 'The Church's One Foundation'.) He had already sent a copy to his father, who replied: 'Thank you so much for the "Restoration" poem. I think it splendid and have sent copies to Mrs Atkinson and Father Deakin (of St Augustine's, Queen's Gate).' As the last line of the poem, John had written: 'He has renewed the roof.' In returning the typescript, Ernest arrowed 'renewed' and commented: 'Probably unnecessary.' John accepted this technical advice and altered the word to 'restored' in later versions.

The *Cherwell* files show John's growing notoriety as an Oxford figure. The first mention of him is on 13 February 1926 in a review by S. P. B. Mais of the Oxford University Dramatic Society's *Henry IV Part II*: 'J. Betjemann (Magdalen) is to be congratulated on his face. There was true comedy in his Wart as well as in his porter.' John proudly showed this comment to Colonel Kolkhorst, who said *he* liked port and water too – a neat Spoonerism. By the summer term of 1926, John was well established in the Society, the *Cherwell* on 12 June publishing some pen-portraits of 'Personalities in the OUDS', including: 'J. Betjemann – quite a little comedian . . . He is the club naughty little boy. He could be a poet if he took the trouble.'

The Russian Theodore Komisarjewsky came to Oxford in 1927 to produce *King Lear*. John was cast as the Fool – a plum part. But two weeks before he was due to appear in the rôle, he was expelled from the OUDS in disgrace, as Osbert Lancaster recalled:

> It so happened that the *Cherwell*, the less reputable but by far the livelier of
> the two undergraduate magazines, was at that time edited by John Betjeman,

---

* Piers St Aubyn (thus spelt) was a nineteenth-century architect whose restoration of churches John deplored.

who published a cod photograph, with a ribald caption, of the OUDS rehearsing. The club, which in those days took itself very seriously, was furious and both Denys Buckley, the president, and Harman Grisewood, who was playing Lear, insisted on the poet's immediate expulsion. Unluckily this resolute but rather hastily considered move involved a major reshuffle of the cast less than a fortnight before the first night, for Betjeman was playing the Fool, a major rôle which now had to be taken over by John Fernald, who relinquished the part of the Duke of Cornwall to Peter Fleming, until then only the Duke of Cornwall's servant, to enact whom I was now promoted from the anonymous ranks of Goneril's drunken knights.

Colonel Kolkhorst tittered that 'For playing the fool, John has been prevented from playing the Fool.' John was quite unrepentant over the incident. In the *Cherwell* of 26 February he published an apology as impudent as the original spoof: 'WE MUST APOLOGISE to the OUDS for the unfortunate misprint that appeared under the photograph of our office dramatic society the initials of which are O.O.D.S., which were naturally supposed by the printers to stand for a better known dramatic institution, and altered accordingly.' After this piece of calculated cheek, John was soon back on good terms with the ruffled officers of the OUDS. The *Cherwell* reported on 21 May 1927 that 'John Betjeman gave an amusing lunch-party on Tuesday, at which some of the guests were Bryan Guinness, Denys Buckley, and erudite young John Sparrow.' The same issue contained a reference to him, not for the first time, as 'Bishop Betjeman'.

John's religious tendencies continued to be a subject of interest. The *Cherwell*'s editorial of 11 February 1928 observed:

A new paper called *Protest* has been launched upon us. It is the organ, we understand, of Oxford Anglo-Catholicism. Where would Oxford be without ritualism? The picture of undergraduate life of romantic fiction would be incomplete without the cultured enthusiast hurrying Romeward. On Saturday, Mr Betjeman delivered a spirited harangue from a balcony in the High Street which was listened to by several taxi-drivers in supine astonishment.

John's emergence as an undergraduate religious leader surprised those of his friends who remembered him at Marlborough. Though baptized and brought up in the Church of England, he had 'suddenly decided' at Marlborough that he was an atheist, and had refused to be confirmed. Was this part of a rebellion against his parents? Was he influenced by humanist friends such as Anthony Blunt? Or was it just another example of John's inclination to *épater* and be different? Most probably, in a setting where authority seemed to him malign, he was learning to challenge all received opinions. ('Honest doubt' continued to assail him for the rest of his life.) But then he met Father Johnson in Cornwall and was given Machen's *The Secret Glory* 'which suddenly showed me there were the Sacraments, and then I became very interested in ritual and I was first, I suppose, brought to belief by my eyes and ears and nose. The smell of incense, and sight of candles, High Church services, they attracted me and I liked them.'

Ritualism led naturally in the direction of Anglo-Catholicism, and Oxford was the fountainhead of Anglo-Catholicism. The Oxford Movement had begun in the 1830s as an attempt to reassert the authority of the Church. An appeal to historical precedent was accompanied by a new interest in the Middle Ages and their architecture, resulting in the Gothic Revival style in which North Oxford was so rich. The Oxford Movement had split into two main factions: those who 'went over to Rome', and those who, while ritualistic, remained within the Church of England, which they considered an integral part of the Catholic Church. When John first came to Oxford, he worshipped at St Peter-le-Bailey, the church he had liked best when a boy at the Dragon School. But soon he began to attend High Mass at Pusey House, the centre of Anglo-Catholicism, whose Principal was Darwell Stone, white-bearded, donnish and unworldly. When mention was made in Stone's presence of the Dolly Sisters – vaudeville artists of the time – he said he was not familiar with any nuns of that name.

The portrayals of John in the *Cherwell* suggest that his reputation in Oxford was mainly as an Anglo-Catholic, an architectural expert, a socialite, a journalist, an actor and a practical joker. At that time he was not widely regarded as a poet, still less as a good poet. The kind of poetry admired in Oxford was the luxuriant style of the Sitwells, tangled with the deliberate obscurities of Eliot and the literary surrealism of Gertrude Stein. There was less appreciation of John's revamped hymns and music-hall dit-ties, or the Nordic austerities of W. H. Auden, then an undergraduate at Christ Church. The stars among the undergraduate poets of the time were Harold Acton, Peter Quennell, Eric Walter White and Tom Driberg.

John and Acton knew each other quite well. Sir Harold remembered John as he was when he first met him: 'He looked as if he had tumbled out of bed and dressed in a hurry, necktie askew and shoe-laces undone, while a school bell seemed to be tinkling in the distance. A boy scout out of uni-form, with Ruskin as his Baden-Powell.' Peter Quennell's and John's Oxford careers overlapped for only ten days, because on 18 October 1925 Quennell was sent down for the offence, unusual for an Oxford under-graduate of that time, of having sexual relations with a woman in

Maidenhead. But he continued to be published and reviewed in the university magazines, and John heard all about him from Eric Walter White who was at Balliol with Quennell in the academic year 1924–5 and hero-worshipped him. By 1927, however, the best-known undergraduate poet in Oxford was Tom Driberg. One of his works had appeared in the *Cherwell* of 14 May, which was then under John's editorship:

Spring Carol

The latterday compendium
has burst a half, has burst a half,
And winter's deep has come to equal
the supervision of the first.

Destitute, destitute of caramel.
White water comes to take its place.
The fountain burns spasmodically
and (quick, quick Kamchatka swells and streams
                 (quick grace and face
dying dying dying down
'Calm and Free' (*Wordsworth*)
        quite abstract

Despite giving it space in the magazine, John was not taken in by this highfalutin gibberish. On 21 May he published a parody of 'Spring Carol', which indeed he may have written:

Mr Driberg's Next Poem?

An aard-vark, Aaron's-beard aback:
Abacus Abaddon, abaft abandon
Abase, abask.

A, ab, absque, coram, de:
Y, yaffil, yapp:
Zeppelin, zouave, zygote:

Destitute, destitute of meaning –
The Concise Oxford Dictionary comes to take its place:
The beginning and the end –
Between A and Z
    quite obviously %.

But many Oxford intellectuals accepted Driberg at his own estimate of himself. Geoffrey Grigson was taken round to see him in his rooms at Christ Church. 'The black hair, the white face, the nervous insolence, the elegant tailoring – Stendhal might have seen him and modelled upon the sight a young priest, machiavellian and subfuscly burning with ambition . . . No one else, so far as I know, reached the flesh-pots of the *Daily Express* by way of the bare sustenance of *Prufrock* and *The Waste Land.*'

As the first 'William Hickey' of the *Daily Express*, Driberg was able to help publicize the career of the young Betjeman. Later, he had a more valuable rôle in John's life. When John wanted an opinion or a revision of his poetry, it was to Driberg (and John Sparrow) that he turned. In that capacity Driberg served him well: he was a better editor of other people's poetry than of his own.

As John won acceptance by the 'smart set', he did not lose touch with his Marlborough friends – Philip Harding at Hertford, Ben Bonas at Worcester or John Bowle at Balliol. The lustre of Bowle's academic reputation was wearing thin: he was having too good a time. The reckoning came in 1927, when he sat his Finals. Billy Clonmore wrote to John Betjeman on 16 August: 'John Edward got a Third. I hear he nearly got himself ploughed as at the Viva he was asked a question which he thought irrelevant and unfair and answered: "I am not an encyclopaedia." ' Bowle continued to feel a sense of brilliance spurned. His string of grievances became a running joke among his friends: he *would* have taken a First and become a leading don if it had not been for his unsympathetic father, his bad sight, his sexual lusts, and the too lavish hospitality of Ben Bonas. John rehearsed all Bowle's complaints in a long, malicious poem for private circulation – a lament for innocence lost and genius wasted.

At Oxford John met the men who were to be his best friends until their or his death – an inner circle of intimates to which only a few later friends (John and Myfanwy Piper among them) were added. Other Oxford friends, less close, drifted in and out of his life like the subsidiary characters in Anthony Powell's *A Dance to the Music of Time*. Indeed, Powell – who was at Balliol with Bowle – was one such friend. He remembers meeting John only once at Oxford, when they talked about bamboo furniture. The Balliol generation then drawing to an end included Cyril Connolly, grappling ineffectually with the enemies of his promise; Graham Greene, whose now forgotten poetry, published in the *Cherwell* in John's first term, may have influenced John; Patrick Balfour, Lord Kinross's son and heir, one of John's greatest friends; and Pierce Synnott, with whom Bowra and John stayed in Ireland in 1926. Synnott was a dandy and wore cloth-of-gold waistcoats. F. F. ('Sligger') Urquhart, the Dean of Balliol, called him 'a gilded popinjay', but Synnott confounded him by taking a First and went into the Admiralty.

Michael Dugdale had also come up to Balliol with Synnott and Peter Quennell in 1923. A raffish figure (not to be confused with John Dugdale of Sezincote, who was no relation), he is mentioned in *Summoned by Bells* as one of John's companions. Bowle thought he was 'a bad influence' on John: he was an exaggerated aesthete who, in the slang of the day, 'willowed about'. Osbert Lancaster came up to Lincoln College in October 1926 and quickly became a friend of John's: their shared interest in the Victorians was immediately apparent. Lancaster, who for fifty years was to contribute a 'pocket cartoon' to the *Daily Express*, was already an accomplished cartoonist.

At New College, with Hugh Gaitskell and Frank Pakenham, was John Sparrow 'with his cowlick lock of hair / And schoolboy looks', who was to remain one of John's closest friends. Together John and Sparrow edited a magazine called *Oxford Outlook*, to which John contributed (under the pseudonym 'Archibald Dixon') a playlet, 'The Artsenkrafts', satirizing his parents. Richard Crossman, the butt of John's early poem 'The Wykehamist', was also at New College. So was Hamish St Clair-Erskine, son of the Earl of Rosslyn, a socialite with whom John often stayed at the Rosslyns' home in Sussex.

New College was about on a par with Magdalen in the snob-ranking of the Oxford colleges, but *the* college of the smart set was Christ Church. It contained a few poor scholarship boys, including the Cornishman A. L. Rowse and the Welshman Emlyn Williams. But here too were Lord Dunglass (later Sir Alec Douglas-Home and Prime Minister), Quintin Hogg (later Lord Hailsham and Lord Chancellor), the Earl of Rosse, Lord Weymouth (later sixth Marquess of Bath), the Earl of Cardigan, the Earl of Dumfries, Lord Stavordale and the fabulously rich Edward James.

If self-interest had been the motive for John's social climbing, Edward James would have been his best catch. There was probably nobody, throughout his life, who gave him more valuable help when it was most needed − a debt acknowledged in *Summoned by Bells*. Edward James was the son of Mr and Mrs Willie James of West Dean Park, Sussex. King Edward VII was his godfather. His father was of American parentage and his fortune came from copper mines and railways. James may be best known to posterity from the back view of his brilliantined head – in Magritte's portrait of him, *La Reproduction Interdite*. He was to be a leading patron of the surrealists, especially of Magritte and Dalí. Already in the mid-1920s his rooms at Oxford showed something of the eccentric creativity which was manifested in later life in the Gaudí-like concrete towers which he designed and built in the Mexican jungle. The most striking of his four rooms was the drawing-room. There John enjoyed breakfasts of champagne and Virginia ham, swung a censer around to banish the breakfast smells with incense-smoke, 'And talked of Eliot and Wilde'. James had a clear memory of John at Oxford:

> I noticed two things, neither of them very kind. One was that his teeth were sort of greenish – slightly prominent, and not a good colour. He giggled a lot, so the teeth showed a lot. And, as I am very conscious of aesthetic things – I like people to have good looks – I realized very quickly that I was enormously drawn to Betjeman *in spite* of his looks, by his charm and his vitality. And I began to think: 'It's funny, that you should like this fellow, who is not very pretty.'

John persuaded James to put money into the ailing *Cherwell*. The printer was owed a lot of money; James agreed to pay off this debt and, at the beginning of Michaelmas Term 1927, he succeeded John as editor. By nature quarrelsome and easily bored, James held the job for less than a month before 'retiring', but during his brief tenure he published John's 'A 'Varsity Student's Rag' and created a new cover for the magazine, imitating the design of Grinling Gibbons's carving in Queen's College.

James was distantly related to Christopher Sykes, but little love was lost between them. Sykes's impression was that James's protégés often suffered more than they benefited from his patronage:

> He had that meanness which very rich men have. He counted every penny and he suspected people of sponging. I dare say John saw the red light. A trick James had was taking up people who were not well off and giving them a nice, jolly time, taking them out in society. And then they'd say, 'Well, I haven't got the right clothes, I've not got a tail coat,' 'Oh, go and get it on *me*.' And then he'd suspect them of overstepping the bounds, and he would suddenly turn on them and demand repayment of all the money he had spent on them. He tried to do that to Dali, but Dali saw the danger, as John may have done.

Sykes had more respect for John than for Edward James, but even so he regarded him as a bizarre eccentric. 'I remember one thing that was odd about him. When he passed a building he admired, he used to clap.'

Through Edward James, John also met Basil, Marquess of Dufferin and Ava. Dufferin had been with James not only at Eton but earlier, at his 'prison-like' private school, Lockers Park. 'I was told to look after him, because he was a year and a half younger than I,' James recalled, '– but he was so much more intelligent and alive than I was that it ended by him looking after me.' At Oxford, Dufferin might have been an understudy for the Duke of Dorset, the nonpareil undergraduate of Max Beerbohm's *Zuleika Dobson*. Randolph Churchill later wrote: 'Basil Dufferin was the most lovable man I met at Oxford. His liquid spaniel eyes and his beautiful, charming manner, commanded affection. He was the most brilliant of all my contemporaries at Oxford. An undue addiction to drink blighted what might have been a fine political career.' To Edward James, Dufferin seemed 'very Irish':

> He had this round Irish nose, like a sort of Paddy caricature; beautiful brown eyes, very very alive and deep and large; very quiet and reserved, beautiful manners. And I was in love with him. And John was, too. And I suppose we both told him we were. Anyway, he asked us both over to Clandeboye [the Dufferins' family home in Northern Ireland].

Elizabeth Longford also remembered John's attachment to Basil Dufferin: 'John made fun of everything he liked: that was his line. It was he who christened Basil "Little Bloody"; he was always known as "Little Bloody". John adored him, and Basil was brilliantly clever, not little at all, very well grown, extremely handsome, very athletic – but this was John's way of expressing his affection, to give him this funny nickname.' John's mock-Metaphysical poem 'The bluish eyeballs of my love . . .' was a tribute to Dufferin's *beaux yeux*. When Dufferin was killed in Burma at the end of the Second World War, John was middle-aged and the father of two children; yet something of the romantic exaltation of the Oxford friendship survives in his threnody on 'my kind, heavy-lidded companion', written in Oxford where John was working in 1945:

> Stop, oh many bells, stop
>> pouring on roses and creeper
> Your unremembering peal . . .

Two friends made John slightly ashamed of chasing the lords and Croesuses of the smart set. One was Randolph Churchill, who, with his Blenheim Palace connection, was 'smart' enough himself to feel no need of social climbing. In 1969 John recalled:

> So far as Randolph had a set of friends in those days, I suppose it would be with the members of Canterbury Quad in Christ Church, who consisted

chiefly of Edward James, Christopher Sykes and Lord Dumfries. To me, an outsider from Magdalen, these people were the height of fashion, and suddenly with Randolph I realized that my standards were barmy. Randolph was not in the least bit the snob I was. He took them on their own merits, and he took me on mine, which were in those days poetry. He encouraged me to read the stuff out loud at dinner parties, and he insisted on my reading satires I had written, when I was quite sure that the other people round the table did not want to hear them at all. Any table that he was at Randolph dominated. That was how I got a hearing for my verses.

The other friend who gave John qualms about his tuft-hunting was W. H. Auden, who came up to Christ Church at the same time as John arrived at Magdalen. Auden was 'not in the least interested in the grand friends I had made in the House'. This 'tall, milky-skinned and coltish' undergraduate impressed John by his knowledge of poetry – like John he had already read Ebenezer Elliott and Philip Bourke Marston 'and other poets whom I regarded as my special province'. They both loved railways and canals and Bradshaw's timetables. Auden, too, was drawn to the Church of England, and enjoyed visiting churches.

In his *W. H. Auden: The Life of a Poet* (1979), Charles Osborne suggested that John and Auden had slept together at Oxford and that they were discovered in bed by Auden's scout, who had to be bribed £5 to keep quiet about it. This passage appeared in the American edition, published by Harcourt Brace Jovanovich, but John's lawyers secured its removal from the English edition published by Eyre Methuen. Auden himself often described the incident, according to his brother Dr John Auden, adding the punchline: 'It wasn't worth the £5.' Was the story true? Probably: but the episode has to be considered in the context of Oxford sexual *mores* of that time.

It is no exaggeration to say that the majority of John's undergraduate friends at Oxford were homosexual; among them Brian Howard, Patrick Balfour, Robert Byron, John Bowle, Lionel Perry, Michael Dugdale, Gyles Isham, Hamish St Clair-Erskine, Mark Ogilvie-Grant, Edward James and of course Tom Driberg, who made a career of his homosexuality to which his political activities were secondary. Osbert Lancaster pointed out that interest in women in the Oxford of the late 1920s was generally slight. 'Women played a very small part in our lives. There were, it is true, the women's colleges but their inhabitants were for the most part unknown and unregarded and their entertainment, which took the form of morning coffee at the Super, was left by right-thinking men to the scruffier members of the dimmer colleges.' Of course not all male undergraduates were rouged epicenes or uninterested in girls, but the general tenor of undergraduate sex-life was homophile. A. J. P. Taylor (John's exact contemporary) brought a historian's objectivity to the subject when he discussed it in his volume of the *Oxford History of England*: 'The strange one-sexed system of education at public schools and universities had always run to homosexuality. In Victorian times this, though gross, had been sentimental and ostensibly innocent. At the *fin de siècle* it had been consciously wicked. Now [in the 1920s] it was neither innocent nor wicked. It was merely, for a brief period, normal.'

John's name was also linked with the names of other Oxford contemporaries. Lionel Perry remembered that he 'had a crush' on Hugh Gaitskell. 'He would say to him, "Hugh, may I stroke your bottom?" And Hugh would say, "Oh, I suppose so, if you *must*."' The long erotic poems John wrote at this time were about schoolboys. John Bowle said that one of the poems was called 'Bags in Dorm'. Another, entitled 'Going back to Bradfield', was a fantasy about John's sitting opposite a boy on a train and noticing from his luggage labels that he was bound for Bradfield School. In the poem 'John seduces the boy into going in his car to Reading – then off into the woods where an indecency takes place'. Bowle described both poems as 'very indecent and very vivid'.

But there were already signs that John's inclinations were not exclusively homosexual. In February 1926 he attended a party given by an Old Marlburian friend in Cambridge where he was very taken with a 'dark girl'. Another friend who had been at the party wrote: 'Dear Benjy . . . I thought that sooner or later you would go completely mad and get mixed up with some *girl* or other . . .' For a time John courted a waitress from the George restaurant. He took her round churches with him, but gave her up when she performed dance steps in the aisle of Gloucester Cathedral. Another romance was evidently flagging when John wrote to Pierce Synnott, in September 1927: 'My girl has broken my heart – she sent me some hideous etchings in the picturesque style for my birthday – I put them in the waste-paper basket at once.'

In later life John's tastes were predominantly heterosexual, but he liked to speculate about the 'percentage' of homosexuality in people's psychological make-up, including his own. He commented on Edward Heath: 'I never realized what percent he was until I saw him pouring tea.' His own 'percentage' probably remained above the average.

At the beginning of Michaelmas Term 1927 John moved out to The Beeches, Sandfield Road, Headington, but he was by now too enmeshed in Oxford society to become a rustic hermit. By January 1928 he had so often failed 'Divvers' – the Divinity examination all undergraduates then had to sit – that there was talk, at Magdalen, of sending him down. Sir Herbert Warren decided he should be given another chance, but wrote sternly to Ernest, who in turn wrote sternly to John on 22 January:

> I was on the point of replying to Sir Herbert Warren but have not done so. I have re-read his letters through and commend to you the following: . . . 'Of course if you are to give him this great opportunity he must really set himself to work and forgo some of the pleasurable cultivation of his taste which up to now he has been allowed.'

On 2 February he wrote again: 'How are you getting on? and did you pass your "divvers" or "divers" or whatever it is, silence I am afraid denotes that the topic is one best avoided.' He was right: John had failed yet again. This time the college authorities decided that he must be rusticated for a term – temporarily sent down from Oxford to concentrate on his work away from the distractions of parties and acting and undergraduate journalism. He could return in October for one last try.

Maurice Bowra had a theory about John's repeated failure in 'Divvers'. As the examination was 'dishonourably easy', and as no undergraduate was more obsessively interested in religion than John, it followed that 'unconsciously he wished to fail . . . He had no wish to take his finals, for which he had done very little work, and found instinctively a way out.'

On being rusticated, John took himself, as had Evelyn Waugh (and Paul Pennyfeather of *Decline and Fall*) before him, to the scholastic agents Gabbitas-Thring of Sackville Street, London. They were quite prepared to find a job for him even though he had no degree and was uninterested in team sports. But there proved to be a difficulty. John was asked for written testimonials from the President of his college, from the headmaster of his school and from his tutor. When he applied to C. S. Lewis for a testimonial, Lewis told him that he could not say anything in his favour academically. All he could say was that John was 'kindhearted and cheerful'. On the strength of this, John was turned down by the first three schools to which Gabbitas-Thring introduced him. In some desperation, the agency began sending him the details of jobs abroad, including a post to teach English in Krakow, Poland, for 7,600 Polish *zlotys* (about £176) a year. At this point John decided to ditch Lewis's testimonial and to ask for one from his old friend, the Rev. J. M. Thompson – who warmly recommended him. John was soon offered a post as a master at Thorpe House preparatory school, Oval Way, Gerrard's Cross. The salary was £30 a term.

John wrote to Lewis to tell him what was happening and to ask whether he might have his permission to complete the three years at Oxford necessary to qualify for a degree. He took occasion to complain about the testimonial which had lost him three 'decentish' jobs. Lewis now sent him a letter which made John his enemy for life:

Dear Betjemann,

You must write to the Secretary of the Tutorial Board at once, telling him your position, and asking to be allowed to take a pass degree . . .

As to my being 'a stone', I take it we understand each other very well. You called the tune of irony from the first time you met me, and I have never heard you speak of any serious subject without a snigger. It would, there-fore, be odd if you expected to find gushing fountains of emotional sympa-thy flowing from me whenever you chose to *change* the tune. You can't have it both ways, and I am sure that a man of your shrewdness does not really demand that I should keep 'sob-stuff' (is that the right word in your vocabu-lary?) permanently on tap in order to qualify me for appearing alternately as butt and as fairy godfather in your comedy. But you are quite mistaken if you attribute any animosity to me, and, if I am consulted, I shall certainly advise any measures that are necessary in order to enable you to get a degree.

Yours v. sincerely

C. S. Lewis

John kept up the vendetta with Lewis in his published works. The open-ing salvo was fired in *Ghastly Good Taste* (1933): 'Finally, the author is indebted to Mr C. S. Lewis . . . whose jolly personality and encourage-ment to the author in his youth have remained an unfading memory for the author's declining years.' The acknowledgement was left in the 1970 reprint, to pursue Lewis beyond the tomb.

From the 1950s onwards, John received letters from disciples of C. S. Lewis (who had almost as large a following as Tolkien, especially in America) saying, 'I have heard that you do not like C. S. Lewis. Could you please explain why?' John declined these invitations as politely as he declined the several invitations to speak in Slough, the town whose destruction by 'friendly bombs' he had willed in a much quoted poem. But a comprehensive answer to the question exists in the Betjeman Archive of the University of Victoria, British Columbia. It is an eight-page letter which John wrote to Lewis in a cold fury of recrimination on 13 December 1939. With it is an envelope addressed to Lewis at Magdalen College, which has been ripped open. It is possible that John, having purged his feel-ings towards Lewis by 'writing them out', decided that the letter was too savage to send; or it may be that he wanted to make a fair or revised copy.

Addressed from Garrard's Farm, Uffington, Berkshire (John's home in 1939), the letter begins:

Dear Mr Lewis,

Since I have just expunged from the proofs of the preface of a new book of poems of mine which Murray is publishing [*Old Lights for New Chancels*], a long and unprovoked attack on you, I wonder whether you will forgive my going into some detail with you personally over the reasons for my attitude? . . .

You were kind enough to say in a letter to me of about 1½ years ago that you had always regarded ours as a purely literary battle. I must say that it may have become that now, but it started on my side as a rather malicious personal battle. I think it only fair to explain why.

John reiterated his complaint that Lewis's damning testimonials had lost him three jobs 'in the inevitable prep-school mastering to which all unsuccessful undergraduates of my type are reduced' (when 'my father had quite rightly washed his hands of me').

Naturally [John continued] I was inflamed against you and thought, with the impulsiveness of a young man, that you had done it out of malice from the easy security of an Oxford Senior Common Room. The tragedy of it was heightened by the fact that I have always had a great love for English literature – and none for philology – and that it was my ambition to become a don and read English literature to the accompaniment of lovely surroundings. I thought of you as reading philology in surroundings which you did not appreciate. I visualized that white unlived-in room of yours in New Buildings, with the tobacco jars and fixture cards from Philosophy clubs and the green loose covers on the furniture which always depressed me. And when I was working in various far more repulsive surroundings in suburban and Industrial England, I often thought of those rooms and envied you . . .

He concluded by saying he could now put his letter into the post and sleep contented, 'for I still sometimes wake up angry in the night and think of the mess I made at Oxford'.

At Thorpe House, John was well liked by the boys. On 17 May 1928, he wrote to John Bowle:

I am surrounded by nineteen shrieking boys; I am settling quarrels and starting new ones. One blasted little brute is asking me a question now and I am ignoring him. Another is sulking because I have made him sit down. It is impossible to write coherently because I have continually to get up and go into the changing room to stop the bullying; wait a moment – oh God. The boys all got wet from cricket to-day & after we had changed their socks, I was left in charge of them while they were in the confined space within doors. How I loathe them all.

In 'Home Thoughts from Exile', the last poem he wrote for the *Cherwell* as an undergraduate, John chose 'St Ernest's Hall' as the name for an Oxford college. Relations with his father were becoming increasingly strained. Alan Pryce-Jones observed the tensions at 52 Church Street, where he was occasionally invited to dinner in the vacations. 'A lot of John's troubles', he said in 1976, 'arose from the great hostility he felt towards his parents when he was young.'

> His parents were always known to John as Ernie and Bess, never as Father and Mother, and he was extremely contemptuous of his father in those days . . . and very contemptuous of his mother, who he thought was a very stupid and tiresome woman; she was, as a matter of fact. They were a pretty con-straining couple, because old Mr Betjemann couldn't bear John's not going into the family business, and Mrs Betjemann was a nice cottage-loaf of a lady. They did not at all care for John's activities, and he did not care for theirs . . . Also, it has to be said, he is rather snobbish, and he didn't think they were very grand – and they weren't. They had pretty things and quite a lot of taste, the father especially. The house in Church Street was delight-ful – pretty eighteenth-century panelled house – but it wasn't somehow what John wanted. He felt that they were sort of 'people from Highgate' – rather as Evelyn Waugh felt about his parents in Golders Green.

John put all his resentful feelings about his parents into 'The Artsenkrafts', the short play he contributed to *Oxford Outlook* in 1927. The dramatic sketch is flimsily plotted. Mrs Artsenkraft (Bess Betjemann) chats querulously to the maid; Mr Jim (John) arrives and tells his mother about an 'awful business'; the dog, Sambo, which he was taking for a walk, has been run over by a bus. Then Mr Artsenkraft (Ernest) comes home from the works, and we are held in suspense: when will the news of the dog's death be broken? It never is; by the end of the play, Jim has still not summoned up the courage to confess. Whether the accident occurred in reality, or whether it is an example of John's wishful thinking, is not known; but much of the playlet's dialogue has the ring of authenticity.

Jim, described in the stage directions as 'anaemic-looking and repressed', is clearly a self-portrait. When Mr Artsenkraft – 'a fat person with sensual lips and a hard face' – comes in, he tells Jim to 'cut along and get me a whisky and soda'. When Jim returns, he is told to 'brace yer shoul-ders back!' and to 'cut up stairs and brush your hair properly. Don't come

down here looking like an inferior workman.' Jim shouts into his deaf
father's speaking-tube: 'I'm not going to be treated like a child of two.' And
the two men snarl insults at each other until the play ends with Jim's taking
'a feeble blow at Mr. A's bloated stomach'.

No doubt John exaggerated the friction with his father. If it had been
as extreme as 'The Artsenkrafts' suggests, it is unlikely that Ernest would
have written to him, as he did, in March 1928: 'I hope, old man, in the
coming vac, that you won't go away to study, you can work as well or better
in your own room at home. I have never been alone for a very long time,
and it is decidedly dull to have my small (but expensive) family continually
residing anywhere but under the parental roof provided for them, verily a
sign of the restless spirit of the age . . .'

In July 1928 John went to stay with Philip Harding in Dorset. One result
of this holiday was John's poem 'Dorset'. Another result was a fine for speeding. On 27 September Ernest wrote to him: 'Why on earth didn't you let
me know you had been fined £4 at Blandford on July the 28th and allowed
four days in which to pay? I've just had to settle with the police who were
on the point of issuing a warrant of arrest. It's too bad of you not to face facts
and humbug me so.' But this chicken had not come home to roost by 29 July
when Ernest wrote from St Enodoc View, Trebetherick, that he was very
pleased John had made a success of the schoolmastering. Ernest was in skit-
tish holiday mood: 'I find that small limpet shells with bright yellow tips
stuck over the face, give the most horrible effect of skin eruptions . . .'

In October 1928 John returned to Oxford for what was to be his last
term. As C. S. Lewis had suggested, he had written to the Secretary of the
Tutorial Board of Magdalen, stating his 'position'. The Secretary, G. C.
Lee, had replied that he would put his application to take a Pass degree
before the Board at its next meeting and reminded him that the Pass School
involved three subjects, one of which must be a language, 'presumably in
your case Latin or French'. It was always a mistake to presume anything in
John's case. When permission to read the Pass School came through, he
chose as his language, with maximum perversity, Welsh. Osbert Lancaster
suggests in his memoirs that John's failure in this subject was 'partially compensated for by the knowledge that in order to gratify this strange ambition Magdalen had been put to all the trouble and expense of importing a
don from Aberystwyth twice a week, first-class'. In view of the fact that
Jesus College was packed with Welsh-speaking dons, this seems a tall story;
but John did study Welsh for a short time.

Nonetheless, at the end of that Michaelmas Term of 1928, he was sent
down from Oxford for good. It was obvious to everybody by then that he

was not going to pass 'divvers'. But he was still of interest to Oxford under-graduates after he left. On 26 January 1929 his 'School Song' was reprinted in the *Cherwell*. 'A 'Varsity Student's Rag' was reprinted on 23 November – the poem's phrases were evidently part of normal conversational currency in Oxford by then – and it appeared for the third time almost a year later, for the benefit of a new set of freshmen. 'Sir John Matterhorn's Social Causerie' for 8 November 1930 reported: 'With Osbert Lancaster to the George. I saw that pretty Miss Harman* with my young friend Jack Betjeman . . .' The last reference to John in the *Cherwell* was in the issue of 31 January 1931: 'BETJEMAN: This past master was also in evidence last Saturday.' By then, John had been gone from Oxford for more than two years and had held four jobs.

---

* Elizabeth Harman, later Countess of Longford.

5

The Stately Homes of Ireland

JOHN MET PIERCE SYNNOTT (usually called 'Piers') in Maurice Bowra's rooms at Wadham College. Bowra was in love with Synnott and sent him love-letters and poems bad enough to suggest genuine emotion rather than a classical attitude. He and John were invited to Synnott's Irish home, Furness, Naas, County Kildare, in June 1926. Synnott owned the house, as his father had died in 1920. Furness had been built about 1740, probably to the design of Francis Bindon. The drawing-room ceiling was of delicate plasterwork, with a central medallion of Minerva attending a kneeling hero. In the grounds were a half-ruined monastic church, an eighteenth-century 'ice house', or primitive refrigerator, and yew trees from which rebels were said to have been hanged in the rising of 1798.

The three Oxford men drove to the restored sixth-century round tower and 'St Kevin's Kitchen' at Glendalough and on to Shelton Abbey, one of Billy Clonmore's homes. Clonmore himself was in London, but they were shown round the Abbey by the butler, Atride. John was entranced.

> Ireland seemed to me Charles Lever and aquatints come true [he recalled in 1976]. I thought it was the most perfect place on earth. Really what I liked was the Ireland of the Ascendancy, and I liked particularly people who'd gone rather to seed . . . The entrance to Shelton Abbey was the *dream* of the Gothic Revival, and all I could wish. It was by [Sir Richard] Morrison. You went in under a Gothick arch into a large hall, Gothick, lit with enamelled stained glass, purplish and amber-green, and that was called the Prayer Hall. Then there were rooms to left and right. I'd never seen such luxury and splendour – rolling parkland down to the river at Woodenbridge, the Meeting of the Waters. It was paradise.

Synnott wrote to Billy Clonmore in a 'vile temper', as he and John had walked half round Dublin looking for Mrs Synnott and her sister. Further, Ernest Betjemann had just telegraphed his arrival in Ireland, 'and is tearing the son to Galway to hold his [fishing] line while he jokes with Ranjitsinghi [the Indian cricketer, who had bought the 30,000 acre Ballynahinch estate]. Selfish and incongruous pursuits. He must be the vilest man ever lived, v. rich, gives his son nothing, forbids him to read poetry, kicks his wife, brings mistresses into the house, spends all on keeping shoots and fishing, makes his son go with him, makes scenes in public, and spends his spare time in persecuting people . . .' In retelling the tale of woe to Patrick Balfour, Synnott described how Ernest Betjemann had lost his temper in a Dublin hotel, throwing his cap across the lounge. 'Horrible scene: I was feeling sick, like sudden death.' Synnott's first-hand witness and shocked reaction corroborate John's allegations about Ernest, which might otherwise be taken for vindictive over-dramatization.

John left Naas to join his father. They went to the Ranjitsinghi estate at Ballynahinch, where John felt 'unwanted'. He fished in the heat, 'with my blood being drained by enormous flies and poison being put in its place by still larger ones . . .'. He claimed to have got sunstroke and to have arrived in Dublin, on his way back with his father, with a temperature of 101. Ernest Betjemann insisted on John's crossing with him that night. 'This I did suffering agony and vomiting the whole way.' But now John was better and was exploring Greek Revival churches in London.

John and Bowra again arrived in Ireland on 31 December, to spend the first two weeks of 1927 with Clonmore at Shelton Abbey. Bowra wrote to Patrick Balfour on 11 January: 'Betjeman is here in good form. He pretends to be in love with the Howard girl, Billy's cousin, a flaxen flapper with her bum swung very low and some large spots. There is also her brother here, but you probably know him.' John was indeed taken with Clonmore's cousin Katharine Howard. Recalling that second visit to Shelton, he said: 'Katie played the piano, and her brother Cecil was there; and we sang "The Meeting of the Waters" by Thomas Moore, Maurice very loudly and out of tune . . .'

Somebody who was not happy at the growing intimacy between John and Clonmore and his family, was Harold Newcombe, whom the Earl of Wicklow had appointed as a 'social tutor' to his son. Lady Wicklow (widow of Billy Clonmore, later Wicklow) recalled:

> Mr Newcombe was for upholding the social proprieties of life . . . He used to try to cure Billy of his friendship with John. He would say, 'That poor common little John Betjeman, he looks as if he'd been sent round with a brown paper parcel.' He didn't like John, but John seemed to like him – I suppose he never heard what Mr Newcombe said behind his back, spiteful old thing. John used to say, 'Oh, he's so *well connected*, Mr Newcombe.' He was a sort of introduction for John. It was from Mr Newcombe that he learnt all those 'U' and 'Non-U' phrases that he put into the poem in Nancy Mitford's *Noblesse Oblige* ['How to Get On in Society']. Billy said that John

had put in as many of Newcombe's 'don'ts' as possible. He said: 'Those are all the things that Newcombe used to correct *John* for saying.'

Clonmore invited John to Shelton again in August 1927, but Ernest Betjemann forbade him to go, claiming that he was ill and needed John to 'help around the house' in Chelsea, John wrote to Pierce Synnott from 53 Church Street on 7 August: 'It is hellish here. I lost my trunk – at least my suitcase was as good as taken from my hand – when travelling from Wilnecote to Bath, at New Street Birmingham station, the other day. Ernie proposed to make me a 21st birthday present of another suitcase back again; he was thwarted by the thing turning up from Bournemouth yesterday. I have to take the dog out at 8 o'clock for a ten minute walk EVERY BLOODY MORN-ING.' John was back at Shelton again in early November, Once more he flirted with Katharine Howard. On 14 November Clonmore wrote: 'Before you left I forgot to give you this Gothic Revival bookplate, which may please you. *Katie also* [Clonmore's emphasis] thought you might like it.'

Northern Ireland, with its harsh, Calvinistic Protestantism, never appealed to John as much as the south. But he enjoyed visiting Clandeboye, Basil Dufferin's home in County Down. He first stayed there in August 1928, when Edward James was also of the party. After the comforts of Church Street, Chelsea – cosiness incarnate – the big house must have seemed dark and forbidding, like the sinister Irish mansion depicted by Dufferin's kinsman, Sheridan Le Fanu, in *Uncle Silas*. Outwardly it was not a distinguished house. It had been superimposed by R. A. Woodgate in 1800 on a plain eighteenth-century block to which wings had been added. But the entrance-hall had an Imperial splendour. It had changed little since the days of Dufferin's grandfather, the Viceroy of India.

The rich Victoriana of Clandeboye delighted John, but living there was far from luxurious. Nobody has described that experience better than Basil Dufferin's daughter, Lady Caroline Blackwood, in her novel *Great Granny Webster*, a *roman à clef* in which Clandeboye appears as 'Dunmartin Hall'. The smells of damp-infested libraries mingled with those of cow dung, potato cakes and paraffin. There was something badly wrong with the plumbing; 'it was considered a luxury if anyone managed to get a peat-brown trickle of a bath'. Soggy strings hung from the ceiling to direct drips from the leaky roof into pots and pans and jam-jars. The food – often 'frizzled, unappetizing pheasants'– was usually stone-cold because it had to be carried by the butler from a dungeon-like kitchen in a different wing from the dining-room.

Frizzled pheasants and bad plumbing were not the only hazards at Clandeboye. There was also Basil's mother, Brenda, Marchioness of

Dufferin and Ava, who was regarded as more than half crazy by most of those who knew her. Edward James remembered her 'abject terror' of her servants – a trait confirmed by her portrayal as 'Lady Dunmartin' in *Great Granny Webster*. She claimed to receive messages from the fairies. Elated and jabbering, she would announce that they had chosen her as their queen. Her attitude to her son was unpredictable. She believed that he and his sister Veronica were demon substitutes for her real children, changelings left by evil fairies. John and the Marchioness quickly made friends, how-ever. John was used to humouring a mother who, though not mad, suffered from 'chronic nerves' and hypochondria. And he had a streak of zaniness to which the wilder eccentricity of Lady Dufferin could respond – he was quite equal to chatting with her about the Little Folk.

Back in Cornwall in early September 1928, John described the Clandeboye visit to Billy Clonmore: 'Oh how peaceful were those first few days with "the most intelligent conversationalist for his age" – laughing at Edward James's poetry and getting the enormous eyes of Bloody [Dufferin] to roll round in my direction.' John had been moved to compose some verse, which he sent Clonmore:

> Lord Ava had enormous eyes
> And head of a colossal size,
> He rarely laughed and only spoke
> To utter some stupendous joke
> Which if it were not understood
> Was anyhow considered good.

A letter from Patrick Balfour to his mother, Lady Kinross, suggests that it was Basil Dufferin's mother who obtained for John the job he began in February 1929 – as private secretary to the Irish politician Sir Horace Plunkett. John's own recollection was that the post was procured for him by Plunkett's principal secretary and adviser, Gerald Heard, and Plunkett's diaries confirm this. The diaries add that 'Betchmann [*sic*] . . . has just graduated at Magdalen, Oxford, in Modern Literature, is working in the City for his father, was offered a job by the *Daily Express* but doesn't like it and will take on my job.'

John seems to have been shooting a line to Plunkett. He had not gradu-ated in anything at Oxford, and it is unlikely he would have turned down a job on the *Daily Express* had it been offered. He was, in fact, desperate for a job. Since leaving Oxford, he had been 'knocking at editorial doors in Fleet Street in the hope of a journalistic opening', with no success. His father had obtained him a post with Sedgwick, Collins & Company, marine insurance brokers in Gracechurch Street, City of London, but John found the work dispiriting. So he jumped at the chance of working for Plunkett, who was the kind of aristocrat about whom he and Billy Clonmore enjoyed corresponding: son of the sixteenth Baron Dunsany, an admiral; uncle to the literary eighteenth Baron; cousin of Lord Fingall (and, some said, lover of Lady Fingall); cousin of the poet Emily Lawless, Lord Cloncurry's daughter; and formerly owner of the first motor-car brought to Ireland, a De Dion Bouton. Plunkett was seventy-five when John began working for him and had only three years to live. John Bowle, who succeeded John as his secretary, described him as 'tall and thin with a little goatee beard: he looked rather like a Van Dyck portrait'.

Plunkett had long pursued with monomaniac zeal his theory of Co-operative Creameries – the subject with which John was almost exclusively concerned during his service with him. Plunkett believed that Irish dairy farmers needed to combine, bringing their produce to big centres where new mechanical cream separators were available, and from which it could be efficiently marketed in bulk. Pessimists told Plunkett the plan was doomed. Irishmen, they said, could conspire but could not combine. By the time John became his secretary, the Co-operative Creameries scheme had been in existence for forty years, and Plunkett was still dissatisfied with its working.

He had early realized that he would only achieve wide currency and powerful backing for his ideas if he entered politics. He was elected for South Dublin in 1892. He called himself a Liberal-Unionist, but he lacked the taste and the guile for party politics. Except for a few extreme Republicans and extreme Unionists, most people who knew him agreed that Plunkett was sincere and disinterested, yet there was something unsympathetic about the man. 'Plunkett was a puzzle,' wrote G. B. Shaw. 'He devoted his life to the service of his fellow creatures collectively, and personally he disliked them all.' Plunkett was, as he admitted to Shaw's wife, 'a born bore', and probably wrote more letters to the editor of *The Times* than any other politician of his generation.

By the time John met Plunkett, the statesman's failings were aggravated by age, illness and drug addiction. Nightly morphine had been prescribed after an attack of pneumonia in 1918 and an operation for cancer of the bladder in 1919; Plunkett was unable to give up the drug. It caused wild fluctuations in his mood. 'We never knew whether we would find him manic or depressive,' said John Bowle.

In 1923, while Plunkett was on one of his 'dashes' to America, Irish republicans showed what they thought of him and his Co-operative Creameries by burning down his house, Kilteragh, at Foxrock, County

Dublin. After the fire, Plunkett did most of his writing at The Crest House, Weybridge, Surrey, and in a flat-cum-office at 105 Mount Street, London. John was in both the Weybridge house and the London flat a lot; Plunkett did not stay in either for long, but travelled restlessly about England, preaching the gospel of Co-operation.

John's opinion of his new employer is made clear in a letter he wrote Patrick Balfour from the Beresford Hotel, Birchington-on-Sea, Kent, on 10 February 1929:

> I am at the moment private secretary to Sir Horace Plunkett who in the early eighties was a big man in agricultural Co-operation. He is still more than keen on it and being slightly off his head has written the first chapter of a book of nine chapters no less than seventy-two times. He says the same thing over and over again and rarely completes one of his sentences which suits my style of thinking. The pay is fair and the food and travelling excellent. He is in bad health at the moment . . .

On the same day as John was writing this account of his master to Balfour, Plunkett was confiding his qualms about John to his diary:

> *10 February 1929*
> Tried to break in JB for my work. I think he will like it – only question is – can he stick to any definite work? His mind is most unsettled! This evening he went to Margate and worshipped at some strange sect – Countess of Huntingdon's Connection, I think.

Back in London, the daily routine was enlivened by visits from Plunkett's debonair principal secretary, Gerald Heard. Then aged forty, Heard was a brilliant conversationalist and a mystic who was later to become a guru in California and a great influence on Aldous Huxley, with whom he sampled mescalin and lysergic acid. John Bowle was less impressed by Heard:

> His idea was to get as much money from Plunkett as he could and to do as little work for it as possible. So he supplied Plunkett with a succession of bright young male secretaries, few of whom lasted for more than three months. Always at first Plunkett thought he had found the ideal man for his great enterprises; but he soon became disenchanted with them – and they with him. The only real attraction of the job was that Plunkett had two Chryslers, one a saloon, the other open. When high on morphine he used to drive the saloon round London at breakneck speed. The secretaries were usually allowed to drive the open Chrysler.

John found Heard's conversation too cerebral – 'Gerald Heard but not understood,' he quipped – but he was influenced by him. Heard was a man-about-town, with an entrée to the kind of society John enjoyed: literary parties in Bloomsbury, the high tables of Oxford and Cambridge colleges and fraudulent seances. It was probably Heard who persuaded him to become a Quaker. Heard was not a Quaker himself, but he considered the Society of Friends 'the most promising force for spiritual regeneration within the Christian Church'. John was already attending Quaker meetings in 1929; in 1931 he joined the Society of Friends in St Martin's Lane, London, and he did not formally resign until March 1937.

Unfortunately, John did not have the same kind of rapport with Plunkett as he had with Heard. Plunkett belonged to that minority of people who could not see the point of John because they were deficient in a sense of humour. Worse, he was never content with the drafts his secretaries made of routine circulars and other papers: several revisions were always insisted on. One of his assistants said: 'Lord! that man would amend the Lord's Prayer!' John, who prided himself on his prose, was prepared to have the odd split infinitive pecked out; but to have everything he wrote tampered with and revised was exasperating.

By 1 March, John had what the doctor considered influenza and was 'very depressed'. On 2 March, Plunkett recorded: 'JB more depressed than ever and made me doubt his being able to stand the strain of my rough [draft] which he has not yet faced. I am helpless.' On 3 March Dr Beare again had to be summoned for John 'who had diagnosed jaundice (rightly as it was found) and suspected cancer on the liver, the result of searching the Encyclopaedia on jaundice! He won't be fit, Beare says, for a fortnight for any serious work.'

John arranged with John Bowle that he should stand in for him as Plunkett's secretary until he himself was well again. Bowle arrived at Mount Street on 5 March and on the 10th John Betjeman went off to Sezincote for a week of convalescence. On 16 March Bowle agreed to stay with Plunkett for three months. John Betjeman was now summarily dismissed, and Plunkett even accused him of having deceitfully taken on the secretarial job, when ill, to obtain sick-pay. John, in turn, jumped to the conclusion that Bowle had ingratiated himself with Plunkett and had conspired to replace him permanently. Bowle indignantly denied this, and in a postscript to a letter which Plunkett sent John on 19 March 1929, Sir Horace wrote: 'I hope you will tell John Edward that you wronged him in suggesting that he had in any way been unfriendly to you. I never knew such scrupulous loyalty.'

The episode led to a breach between the two friends, which was not repaired for several months. Probably the truth was that Bowle, who had far more interest in politics and social theories than John, impressed the old man more. (When Bowle died, in 1985, Anthony Powell disclosed in his

– later published – journal that the quarrel between John and Bowle had inspired that between Mark Members and J. G. Quiggin over the secretaryship to St John Clarke in Powell's 1955 novel *The Acceptance World*.) At first Bowle, too, was Plunkett's blue-eyed boy, and he enjoyed charging about in the open Chrysler and reading, in Mount Street. But Plunkett was not sorry when Bowle left his service in May 1929. 'He is utterly incapable of any interest in life outside his own future,' he wrote.

Ernest Betjemann was concerned to hear of the new turn in his son's fortunes. It was beginning to seem that John was unable to hold down a job, and that he was going to be a wastrel like Ernest's elder brother Jack. John's relations with his father had in any case reached a new low point during his service with Plunkett. As usual, his financial mismanagement was the *casus belli*, though the underlying causes of estrangement were deeper and more complex. On 16 February 1929 Ernest wrote to John from the Pentonville Road works:

> My Dear Boy,
> I have your letter, my opinion of it is poor.
> You thank me, very properly, for paying the accounts, and express regrets for the worry these accounts cause me, as it is so often with you, you however grasp the wrong end.
> You are my son, the matter of the money is not the really most important point, and although I feel rather considerably your desertion, I would do a great deal more for you than pay out money.

He wrote to John again on 22 February:

> Dear John,
> Mother is very ill with pleurisy and bronchitis . . . She has not been well for some time, and I know how she has worried about you and your apparent carelessness. I ask you again to be very careful of her feelings in all things.
> Sorry you find your work a bore. I consider you fortunate in obtaining what with board and lodging is the equivalent of £450 to £500 a year, and my advice to you is to stick to the work all you can and hold the position.
> Why do you refer to Sir Horace as 'H.P.'? He has done much and such reference seems to me to be stupidly schoolboyish. I make the same comment on your addressing me as 'Ernie'. These, John, are *serious* times, serious for us, *very*, and a less flippant attitude more sensible . . .
> Your affectionate Father,
> Ernest Betjemann

This letter infuriated John. He sat down and wrote a passionately indignant reply. It was never sent, but remained among his private papers. Across the top he scrawled: 'What I ought to have said in reply.'

Dear Father,

I imagine it is your anxiety over mother that makes you write me a letter like the one you wrote on Saturday. It seems rather caddish to try to put the blame on me because mother is ill. As far as I remember you said to me some weeks ago that you were going to send her to the South of France. Since you do not have to pay for the extravagance of a son I think you might have afforded it. I do not think I can forgive your inferences. You can hardly think I am not dreadfully worried about mother. What I should have expected from you would have been a letter telling me details about her illness and offering something to cheer us both up, in the way of a hopeful sentence. Instead you seem to be an alarmist.

It is odd, too, that while you insist on the 'seriousness' of the times, half your letter consists of condemnations of the most trivial points in my remarks to you. I will answer them.

In point of fact I do not really find my work a bore at all. You and I at one time laughed about the abstruseness of agricultural co-operation.

A knickname [sic] is an expression of affection and I am very fond of the old thing and perfectly content. It will be quite simple to refrain from calling you 'Ernie'.

I do not think that what is said or written matters, but what is felt. Often most 'serious' feelings are expressed in a joke. I very rarely talk about what I really feel.

I have got flu and am in bed with it so I cannot be up today.

Yours

John B.

The news that John's illness had been diagnosed as jaundice brought a more sympathetic letter from Church Street, dated 8 March. Then came the disturbing news that John had been dismissed. Ernest decided to visit Plunkett to find out for himself what had gone wrong. Plunkett wrote in his diary for 17 March 1929:

Ernest Betjemann, father of JB, came to confer with me about his son who ought never to have taken on my job, in order to hold it while sick, got John Bowle (who can do it) and must now leave. The father is 10 years my junior. He is a manufacturer in the luxuries which adorn the Bond Street shop windows. Lives a double life, finds his staff no longer willing to carry on without an understanding as to their future interest (which E.B. wants JB to inherit but JB can't and won't) and practically asked me to help him in his perplexities. A bounder of the worst kind! I must try to help the boy to get away from the father – but how?

Plunkett seems to have convinced Ernest that John's dismissal was well merited. Ernest now refused to support John: he would have to 'learn to stand on his own two feet'. He may have hoped that economic necessity would eventually force John back into the family firm. As a temporary measure while looking for another job, John moved into a house at 28 Great Ormond Street, London, which Hugh Gaitskell was sharing with Lionel Perry. He wrote to Plunkett asking whether he could help get him into journalism. (Sir Horace had some experience of journalism: he had once owned the *Dublin Daily Express*.) Plunkett replied from Weybridge on 19 March, but – like so much that he had to say – his advice was kindly meant, sententious and useless. As crime reporters say of the police, he offered 'every assistance short of actual help'. John was hoping for a job on a Portsmouth newspaper, but it was not offered to him. So he once more joined the queue of Oxford and Cambridge down-and-outs at the door of Gabbitas-Thring, scholastic agents. They again found him employment as a preparatory school master, this time at Heddon Court, Cockfosters, at East Barnet on the northern outskirts of London.

6

Heddon Court

G ABBITAS-THRING'S RECORD card shows that John worked at Heddon Court from April 1929 to July 1930. His salary had risen from the £90 he earned at Thorpe House, to £180. To get the job, he had to pretend to be competent at cricket – as he recalled in his poem 'Cricket Master':

> 'The sort of man we want must be prepared
> To take our first eleven. Many boys
> From last year's team are with us. You will find
> Their bowling's pretty good and they are keen.'
> 'And so am I, Sir, very keen indeed.'
> Oh where's mid-on? And what is silly point?
> Do six balls make an over? Help me, God!
> 'Of course you'll get some first-class cricket too;
> The MCC send down an A team here.'
> My bluff had worked . . .

In a BBC television interview with Michael Parkinson in 1973, John again described this period of his life, recalling how in desperation he bought a Letts' Schoolboy's Diary 'to mug up the names of places on the field'. He added: 'I was soon found out and given the worst team to coach: the best one went to another master.'

Founded in the 1890s, Heddon Court was bought in 1927 by a rich Old Etonian called John Humphrey Hope, who had been an usher (assistant master) at Eton. Disconcertingly he was a Communist. David Soltau, a pupil of John's, remembered that 'After visits to Russia, Hope would come back and say how marvellous the Communists were, which of course did not go down well with most of the parents.' Under Hope's influence, John became a 'parlour pink'. 'Palme Dutt, Rust and Campbell were my new leaders. I bought *Das Kapital* by Marx in English translation, but could never get beyond the first two paragraphs. I subscribed to the *Worker's Weekly* and liked to be seen reading it in public transport.' But how were these left-wing attitudes (or poses) to be reconciled with his Anglo-Catholicism? John thought he had found the answer in the teaching of

Conrad Noel, the Red Vicar of Thaxted, 'with his lovely incense-laden, banner-hung, marigold-decorated church, with its folk-dancing and hand weaving, going hand-in-hand with joyous religion, in what was then unspoiled country'. John's weekend visits to Noel's Thaxted reawakened his interest in medieval churches. 'This time I visited them not just for their architecture, but also for their churchmanship.'

In spite of his radical politics, Hope did not change the regimen at Heddon Court much. He even continued the previous headmaster's practice of beating boys with a cricket bat. Also at variance with his professed Communism was the luxury in which he and his family lived. They occupied the fine Georgian house which was the core of the school buildings. 'The Hopes lived in great style,' David Soltau said, 'complete with a butler and full supporting staff.'

The Hopes had a daughter. Ann Hope (later Mrs Wolff) had no fond memories of John, on whom she based an unlikable character in her 1985 novel about a prep school, *The Grand Master Plan*. She recalled:

> I first knew him when I was four years old, and learning to read. I was being taught by a governess at home (i.e. Heddon Court), and she had an advanced technique of teaching the alphabet, not A ae, B bee, C see, but phonetically. So when I first met John Betjeman on the stairs, and he asked me what my name was, I, having just learnt to spell my name, said proudly, 'ă–n–n.' He screamed with laughter and shouted out, 'Hark to the trains they go ă–ner–ner.' I was much put out by this and went to my mother, and she said off-handedly that I should find something to say back to him. So when I next met him I shouted at him 'Hark to the bells they go Silly-Mr-Bee, Silly-Mr-Bee.' Thereafter we chanted these phrases at each other. And these were not fun exchanges, we were both in vicious earnest.
>
> . . . All the time I knew him he gave the impression of someone who has early looked closely at life and has profoundly despaired, and from then on he was filling in time until his death. He later mellowed, but at Heddon Court he seemed to be looking for a target on which to vent his unhappiness, e.g. me.

Mrs Wolff described her father as 'pompous and correct . . . not a dedicated headmaster, but an educated man turning his hand to a profession'. He does not sound a sympathetic character, but he and John were well disposed towards each other. Vera Spencer-Clarke (later Mrs Moule), the gym mistress mentioned in 'Cricket Master', declared: ' "Huffy" Hope loved John. They saw eye to eye.'

John made a less favourable impression on Walter Summers who, though a much older man than Hope, was his junior partner in the school.

Vera Moule thought that 'John was the bane of Summers's life, absolutely. When they were on duty on a Sunday, old Summers used to be in his sitting-room, which overlooked the courtyard. All the boys had to go through there. And suddenly, there would be a *tearing* crowd of boys going through, and he would go out and say: "Hrrrrumph! *Betjeman* on duty."'

Vera, John's main ally among the staff, was one of those dominant sports-girls to whom he was attracted. He was impressed when she threw to the ground the games master, Jack Malden, who had playfully gripped her wrist as she was about to take a cup of tea. She, in turn, thought John fascinating. 'There was such a depth there. And he was very, very funny.' She had become engaged to another master, Walter Moule, in 1927, but in that year he had gone out to Maseru, Basutoland (now Lesotho), as a school inspector ('because it was impossible to get married on a prep school master's salary') and had advised his fiancée, 'Take off your ring and have a fling!' Vera took the limited advantage of this invitation that was intended, and she and John engaged in a delightful and innocent flirtation. He wrote her several poems, which she preserved. In most of them he compares himself with the absent Walter Moule (whose surname is pronounced 'Mole', though John takes the poet's licence to rhyme it either with 'pole' or with 'pool'). Vera had a photograph of Walter in her bedroom. 'When I went back one day, one of John had been put in its place. And he found one of me and put it up in his room. It was all a lot of nonsense.' Even so, she was secretly pleased to hear that John had asked the headmaster's wife 'whether there was any . . . er . . . *hope*'.

One of the poems was written when John picked off Vera's desk a scrap of paper printed 'PLEASE SEND TO . . .' which somebody had cut off a bill to save paper. On the spot, John scrawled on the sheet eight lines of verse.

> PLEASE SEND TO Vera, by return of post,
> A portrait of the man she loves the most;
> Is he a fellow who, with pipe in hand,
> Teaches the natives in Basutoland?
> Is he a silent, strong-limbed sort of man,
> Whose sportsmanship is thorough as his tan?
> Was he at Lancing? No, I am appalled
> He's elegant, aesthetic too, and bald.

Another poem, said Vera Moule, 'he had the cheek to send to my future father-in-law, who was in a nursing-home in London having an operation on his eyes'. It ends:

When gloom is round your thinking,
  And gauze is round your eyes,
Then there will be no winking
  But when they loose the ties,
  Oh what a sad surprise!

Poor Walter as he ponders
  A few salt tears will shed,
Where lone Basuto wanders
  Along her chalky bed:
  Miss Vera will have fled,
  And married me instead.

What did her father-in-law think of that?

> He loved it! My father-in-law used to write poems, and he was very keen to meet John, but he didn't meet him till this occasion. His eyes were bandaged by that time, and I took John to visit him. We had to go on the Inner Circle, and of course he had to have Archie the teddy bear on his lap, with everybody staring. He used to bring him out of his little brief-case and sit him up on his lap and would talk to him: 'Now, Archie, you know where we are? We're in an Underground; some people call them "tubes". See that couple over there? They're looking at you. Behave!'

Vera made one journey with John which was still more embarrassing – the hair-raising ride in the bull-nosed Morris of another master, Huxtable, which ended in the desecration of the school's holy-of-holies, the cricket pitch, as described in 'Cricket Master'. The true events of that evening, recounted by Vera, were somewhat different from those described in the poem. The three teachers did not drive straight back to the school from the Cock Inn at Cockfosters. First they drove on to Haringey greyhound stadium, where they spent half an hour and each won a pound – 'which, in those days, was something'.

> So we got in the car, and chased up Piccadilly. And there we went into a pub, and John said, 'You'd better sit there,' and leaving me and Huxtable he went to the counter. He banged on the counter and decided what he wanted to drink, and didn't take any more notice of me or Huxtable. And then he listened to the conversation of some men at the side of him. I don't know what they were talking about, but he said in a rough voice, 'Well, my son's in a school, and they want 'im to learn Lat'n 'n' Greek. Now what's the use of Lat'n and Greek to a son of mine?' And they asked him, 'What do you do?' and he said 'I'm in *lino*.' So they carried on the conversation for quite a little while. Whether the men were taken in or not, I don't know. Screamingly funny.

On their return to Heddon Court, Huxtable zig-zagged across the cricket pitch. Unsurprisingly, he was sacked.

John burst on to the scene at Heddon Court as a new phenomenon. Sir Jasper Hollom – a Betjeman pupil who later 'signed the banknotes' as Chief Cashier of the Bank of England – remembered that 'his general approach to life came as something which was quite remarkably fresh, and extraordinary, and hence liberating'. Sir John Addis, a Heddon Court pupil who became British Ambassador to China, was not himself taught by John, but his brother Richard was. Sir John recalled: 'Dick was immensely exhilarated by this unusual master, and told us stories about his English lessons. Sometimes John wouldn't be standing at his desk, or sitting in his chair, but he'd teach lying on the floor. And on other occasions the class would be dutifully waiting for Mr Betjeman to arrive, and instead of walking in through the door, he'd come in through the window.'

Then there were the smart Oxford friends who visited John at weekends, such as Patrick Balfour, Edward James and the Marquess of Dufferin and Ava. Among them was Evelyn Waugh, who had also served his turn as a private schoolmaster, and told him, not entirely facetiously, 'You will remember these schooldays as the happiest time of your life.' In a BBC recording that John made for Waugh's biographer Christopher Sykes, he told how he and Waugh had lunch together at a Barnet hotel where they drank 'a lot of very strong beer, and I was so drunk when I came back that I wasn't able to take the game of football, and the boys kindly took me up to my room and never said anything about it. That was the effect Evelyn had on my schoolmastering, the only one I remember. But he felt that just being a schoolmaster was rockingly funny, and I remember him telling me, when I was offered a job on *The Architectural Review*: "Don't take it. You'll never laugh as much as you do now." And he was quite right, of course.'

The other staff were not just carping or being stuffy when they complained of John's subversive influence. He *was* subversive. One incident which got memorably out of hand is recalled by nearly all John's ex-pupils. He organized a riot, which centred on the 'bothie', a gardener's cottage in the angle between two walls, with one room upstairs and one down. With his 'court', Betjeman got into the upstairs room of the bothie and encouraged boys outside to throw acorns, conkers and apples, which Betjeman and his court threw back. The battle was fierce, and a few windows were broken. Eventually Summers appeared. John's good relations with Hope protected him from the fate of Huxtable. As Sir Jasper Hollom said, 'Disgrace came naturally to John Betjeman: there was a magnetic attraction between him and disgrace. But one always felt that he had a staunch ally in Hope, and so the risks weren't very great.'

John impressed the boys just as much inside the classroom as outside. Sir Jasper Hollom's elder brother Vincent (Hollom IV) wrote:

> Memories of John Betjeman tend to remain clear while others become hazy, which is an indication of the intense impression he made, mainly in his teaching of English literature. The hitherto familiar and laborious hours of 'parsing' and grammar were transformed into the sounds and usage and rhythms of words conveyed with such inspiration that sparks of under-standing seemed to be struck from every single and different boy in the classroom.

Paul Miller, a Betjeman pupil who became a Canon Residentiary and Precentor of Derby Cathedral, added:

> He cut at the foundations of the Establishment's regard for games, and this was obviously one of the things that Mr Summers hated. Our success at games simply plummeted. You see, John substituted one standard of snob-bery for another. The old snobbery was for games, and the people who were good at them. The new snobbery was for literature and architecture and those who could appreciate them.

John's classroom was at one end of a series of three classrooms which could be turned into one by folding-screen walls. Canon Miller recalled that John used to get his class to recite poetry together – 'what is now called "choral speaking"'. Miller remembered John's 'conducting' Vachel Lindsay's 'Congo':

> Fat black bucks in a wine-barrel room,
> Barrel-house kings, with feet unstable,
> Sagged and reeled and pounded on the table,
> Pounded on the table,
> Beat an empty barrel with the handle of a broom,
> Hard as they were able,
> Boom, boom, BOOM . . .
>
> 'BLOOD' screamed the skull-faced, lean witch-doctors,
> 'Whirl ye the deadly voo-doo rattle . . .
> Boomlay, boomlay, boomlay, BOOM.'

He would be waving his arms about in a frenzy at the front and bringing the boys to a crescendo – 'boomlay, BOOM!' – and at that moment Mr Summers would come in: 'Mr Betjeman, *do* you mind?' and John would look crest-fallen. In the end, he was given a classroom on its own, across a courtyard.

He even got the sporting boys to *write* poetry. Vera Moule was aston-ished that 'the most athletic boys who were really cricket and rugger mani-acs, boys who thought of nothing but games all day long, started writing poetry, which they got into the school magazine.' John always remembered the opening line of a poem by one such athlete, Robert Vernon Harcourt: 'The rain came down like a silver gown'. But Harcourt did not go on writ-ing verse. 'Modern poetry, like most modern art,' he wrote to John years later, 'has left me miles behind, dancing with the daffodils.'

John's considerable skill as a draughtsman also came into play. When he arrived in the classroom – before anything else happened and without saying a word – he would draw on the blackboard a series of pictograms of certain boys. Kenric Rice, whom John called 'the famine child', was given a skull-like head with deep-sunk eyes. Terence Glancy was depicted as a kind of Hallowe'en pumpkin lantern, with triangles for eyes and nose, a wavy line for a mouth, and a coconut tuft of hair. Murrant was a fish. Stevenson was always drawn in profile, as he had a head like a sausage-balloon. 'When John put up the lists of results at the end of each fortnight,' Kenric Rice remembered, 'there were no names at all, just these signs. I was a skull and crossbones. Vilvandré was a house-fly.'

Rice is the one Heddon Court boy who is mentioned in 'Cricket Master'. He was a particular protégé of John's, and there was more to his nickname than his slightly cadaverous appearance. The Rice family had moved to Tientsin in China. When it was time for Kenric to go to a preparatory school, he had to be found a home in England – he could not return to China every holiday – so his father advertised him in the personal column of *The Times*. He was taken by a family called Bruce in Sussex – 'and they charged my parents a whacking great fee for doing it'. Kenric Rice remembers 'the agony of the day that my mother – she went to China after my father – saw me into Heddon Court. It was pretty miserable, aged seven, suddenly to be dumped. I can see her now, walking down Cat Hill, I watched her till she disappeared. She said: "Cheer up, don't worry: the same moon shines over Cockfosters as shines over Peking." I mean, *that*, aged seven! And I didn't see her again for ten years.' Rice hid under his bed for a whole day and the staff could not find him. 'That is why John always called me "the poor little famine child" – he thought I was an orphan, you see.' At the end of term, John would see Rice safely across London from King's Cross to Victoria, telephone the Bruces to say 'Ken's on the 11.40 to Hailsham,' and make sure he got into the right train.

Paul Miller was another boy who had cause to be grateful for John's almost clairvoyant skill at finding out what was worrying people. Miller, whose parents were Plymouth Brethren, knew he was not one of his favourites. John did not draw a pictogram of him on the blackboard, as he did of Rice and Stevenson. But one half-holiday the new young master stopped to talk with him. Canon Miller recalled:

> The custom was, on certain half-holidays, that you took a rug out into the garden and read. I wasn't good at making friends – a very solemn, priggish little boy. So I took my rug out on my own and laid it out among the azalea bushes. And John Betjeman walked by, and out of an impulse of kindness, I suppose, sat down on my rug and started to talk to me. And that was when he discovered that I had a Plymouth Brethren background. And his way of making a discovery of this sort was highly characteristic. There was no reticence at all – I mean, he screamed with delight, and waited on your every word. Well, this was terribly flattering, especially coming from somebody who I had already decided was quite fascinating.

In both cases, the friendship was as lasting as the influence. Paul Miller went on to Haileybury, where he introduced John to Gerard Irvine, the beginning of another lifelong friendship. Miller's ordination in the church of England after the war brought him closer to John, who sent playful congratulations after Miller became Canon Residentiary of Derby Cathedral in 1966.

Paul Miller's father, a City of London clothing manufacturer who could afford to build a house on Hadley Common and send his son to an expensive private school (the fees were £52 a term), would have been considered comfortably off by most people in 1929; but many of the boys came from far richer families. Their parents arrived in Rolls-Royces and Bentleys. Alan Nightingale's family had the most coveted car, a 45hp Renault with a cocktail cabinet in the back. The masters' cars – Mr Godfrey's Clyno, even Mr Hunter Blair's Hupmobile – cut less of a dash. (A Hupmobile turns up in John's poem 'Indoor Games near Newbury'.)

John invited some of the boys to shows in London. He took Vincent Hollom to a film on the newly fashionable and shocking subject of lesbianism, *Mädchen in Uniform*, 'whose heroine victim', Hollom recalled, 'haunted me almost unbearably (as perhaps he intended)'. John gave John and Dick Addis lunch at the Café Royal and took them to see Nancy Price in Galsworthy's *The Silver Box*. Sir John Addis said: 'He made out that this was rather dashing for a schoolmaster taking out schoolboys – that it ought to have been Shakespeare, not Galsworthy.'

In August 1929 John was invited to the Addises' holiday home in Scotland. John and Dick Addis again had lunch with him in London when he was working as an assistant editor on *The Architectural Review* in 1931. 'I would probably be sixteen or seventeen by then,' Sir John Addis thought. But soon after that an incident occurred which severed relations between John and the Addis brothers for ever. The boys had once more been invited to lunch at the Café Royal. They went by Underground, and were going up the escalator at Piccadilly at the right time for their appointment with John, when suddenly they saw him haring down the 'down' escalator, two steps at a time. 'It was an agonizing moment, a nightmare vision,' Sir John Addis said. 'He did not recognize us and we were struck dumb and in a child-ish way didn't call out anything.' Whether John had forgotten their appoint-ment, or had remembered another, they never learned. 'What was really wounding was that he never followed it up with an explanation or apology. It was the end of the acquaintance. It was being dropped that hurt Dick.'

Against such occasional lapses into insensitivity must be set John's notable kindness to Rice and Miller and the exhilaration of his teaching and of his irresponsibility as an alternative to the code of self-control and team-spirit. As Vincent Hollom has suggested, John may have gained as much from his time at Heddon Court as his pupils:

> Heddon Court was a short chapter in J.B.'s long life and numberless acquain-tance. Even so, it was perhaps quite a formative experience for him also. Perhaps it was a surprise to him that his ideas could be so catching, so effective . . .
>
> Youthful adulation would not intoxicate such a man: but surely it did stimulate, might nourish. His eyes used to light up with . . . was it pleasure? was it just amusement?

7

'Archie Rev'

———————

J AMES LEES-MILNE, for thirty years architectural adviser to the National Trust, was a friend of John's from the early 1930s until John's death. (They went on holidays together when in their seventies.) They narrowly missed meeting at Magdalen, and met in 1931 through John's future wife Penelope Chetwode.

The traumatic event which turned Lees-Milne into a professional architectural conservationist happened during one of his summer terms at Oxford, when he was taken by friends to dine at Rousham, a Jacobean mansion on the Cherwell between Oxford and Banbury. The Cottrell-Dormers who owned Rousham had leased it to Maurice Hastings, described by Lees-Milne as 'a capricious alcoholic . . . rich, clever and slightly mad'. The young visitor was horrified when Hastings lashed at family portraits by Kneller and Reynolds with a hunting crop, and was even more outraged when he fired a rifle at the private parts of the garden statues. Lees-Milne looked back on the episode as his Damascus-road vision. That evening he made a vow to devote his energies and abilities to preserving the country houses of England.

So, in a negative way, Maurice Hastings was responsible for setting Lees-Milne on the course of his life's work. In a more positive way, he changed the direction of John's career, from prep-school master to architectural journalist. As both Maurice Bowra and Alan Pryce-Jones were friends of Hastings and frequently drove out to Rousham, it could be only a matter of time before John was taken there. In fact it was Bowra who made the introduction. The qualities which attracted John in Bowra he found reflected (if in a slightly distorting mirror) in the other Maurice; besides, a hedonistic eccentric, even one given to bouts of philistinism, would always have an appeal for him – far from diminished by wealth, good food and drink, and the setting of a historic house. For his part Hastings responded to John's charm, wit and bubbling enthusiasm for William Kent's decor at Rousham, and was impressed by his knowledge of architecture.

Maurice Hastings was a son of Sir Percy Hastings, head of the company which owned *The Architectural Review*, and since 1928 his brother Hubert de Cronin Hastings had effectively been in control of the magazine. Like most of John's friends, Maurice Hastings thought it absurd that John's unique talents should be wasted in teaching small boys and recommended him to his brother, who asked him for interview. John wrote some trial articles and on 1 October 1930 began work as assistant editor with a salary of £300 a year, in the handsome building which the company still occupies at 9 Queen Anne's Gate, London. This warren of eighteenth-century rooms was an improbable nerve-centre for the Modern Movement in Britain. As usual marking affection by a nickname, John and his friends called the magazine 'the Archie Rev' – an abbreviation used by the printers.

Hubert de Cronin Hastings became editor, aged twenty-five, early in 1928. Those who worked for him, whether on his staff like John, J. M. Richards and Hugh Casson, or as outside contributors, like John Piper and John Summerson, are agreed that he was a brilliant journalist but a difficult man. It was news sense, Richards thought, rather than any profound philosophical convictions about architecture, which caused Hastings to espouse the Modern Movement.

But against Hastings's originality and pioneering creativeness had to be set the problems which his personality caused those who worked for him. 'He had an obsessive dislike of seeing strangers,' Sir James Richards recalled. 'He never saw anyone at all. The rôle of the assistant editor was to deal with every person because Hastings never admitted anyone to his room when he was there except members of his staff and one or two old friends.' Although Hugh Casson worked at the *Review* every week after his initial interview with Hastings, he did not see him again for eighteen months, 'nor, for all I know, did many of my colleagues'. Hastings's appearances at editorial meetings were 'wildly irregular: once a month for two months, and then utter silence – not even a telephone call – for three months, followed perhaps by a draft for a special issue, a pile of magnificent photographs, a sudden bouquet, or a sharp reprimand'. The staff were left in no doubt of his wishes.

Hastings had the redeeming virtue which for John usually outweighed all faults: a highly developed sense of humour. It meant that he would put up with a lot of John's chaff, and he could not help laughing at his more outrageous pranks. 'He let John get away with murder,' said Piper. John jibbed at the petty rules imposed by the management. One was that bus tickets must be retained and stapled to expense sheets. John went to the bus station, obtained a sackful of used bus tickets, and tipped them over Hastings's desk. The only time one of John's escapades embarrassed

Hastings was retailed to Richard Holmes (who worked for Hastings some time after John) by the architect and Architectural Press journalist F. R. S. Yorke over a pub lunch. Holmes remembered:

> F. R. S. Yorke (referred to by H. de C. as Ferdinand Reginald Sebastian – which I naturally assumed were his names, but they weren't) told me: 'Betjeman comes into the office one hot mid-July day with a very small suitcase. "Ah! You don't know what I've got in here!" Whereupon he changes in the office and appears in the very briefest of brief swimming trunks. While he is in this garb, Hastings senior comes into the office with an eminent visitor. Betjeman advances across the room, utmost nonchalance, to greet them. Thumbs down for Betjeman, I heard.'

John was not intimidated by de Cronin Hastings. The friendship between the two is indicated by the nicknames they bandied, John called him 'Obscurity' (a reference to his shunning company) and Hastings called him 'Jaggers'. The warmth of feeling also comes through in Hastings's letters to John, full of easy badinage. In 1938, for example, three years after John had left the *Review*'s staff, Hastings wrote to him:

> My dear Jaggers,
> I quite forgot, when writing to you before, to tell you that Marx and I went together to Comper's church in Baker Street to make sure that you were mad. To our surprise – to our inexpressible surprise – we discovered it was absolutely lovely.

'Marx' was John's nickname for J. M. Richards. At first he had been called 'Gordon', after Gordon Richards the jockey, but John's nickname won the day. It was conferred, Richards remembers, after the two men had had a political argument, just before John left the *Review* in 1935. 'John was going through a rather extreme Anglo-Catholic right-wing phase; and I was going through a left-wing phase.' When Richards sent John an office memorandum later that day, he addressed it to 'Ignatius Loyola'. John promptly addressed a reply to 'Karl Marx'. 'He continued to refer to me as Karl Marx long after I had stopped calling him Ignatius Loyola,' Richards said.

Richards's office at Queen Anne's Gate was just across the landing from John's, which John had persuaded the company to decorate for him with a William Morris wallpaper. Richards recalls in his memoirs:

> The appearance and the contents of the *Review* were enlivened by Betjeman's personal enthusiasms: for the Gothic Revival, for Victorian typefaces, for the Arts and Crafts movement. Office life in Queen Anne's Gate was enlivened too by his mercurial personality and his pose of disrespect for authority. He practised at that time an undergraduate style of exhibitionism

which was tolerable because accompanied by wit and good humour. I remember, as an example of the kind of prank he took a pride in, his boasting to me one day that he had just come from the Geological Museum, then housed in a dusty, unvisited red-brick building in Piccadilly, by Pennethorne, and had contributed an exhibit of his own. 'Do go and look,' he said. So I went, and there indeed beneath the glass of one of the show-cases, which someone had I suppose carelessly left unlocked, was a small brown object with a neatly lettered card reading 'Horse Chestnut picked up in Bushey Park. Donated by J. Betjeman Esquire.' I believe it remained unnoticed and undisturbed until the building was demolished in 1935 to make way for Simpson's store [now Waterstone's bookshop].

Though Hastings ran the *Review* when John joined the staff, the nominal editor was Christian Barman ('Barmy'), who left the magazine just before John in 1935 to become publicity officer of the London Passenger Board. Richards described him as 'blond, bland, partly Swedish, really a conscientious editor but with very little impact outside.' The only other member of the *Review*'s staff, besides a couple of secretaries, was an older man, A. E. Doyle, who took part in the monthly laying-out of the magazine. Surviving letters from Doyle to John, signed 'A.E.D.' and accompanied by miniature self-caricatures with bowler hat, moustache and pipe, show the affectionate relationship between the two, mutual commiseration about their lot and an element of good-humoured conspiracy against de Cronin Hastings. John had less cordial relations with Mr Budd, the doorkeeper at Queen Anne's Gate. The elderly Mr Budd sat in the outer office with a list of members of the staff. His job was to write down the hour and the minute at which each arrived in the morning and left in the evening, and the times when they left for lunch and returned from it. 'He was a kind of human time-clock,' said Richards, 'so John had constant rows with him: why hadn't John been in the office longer that day, and so on. John never regarded himself as bound by office hours or disciplines or conforming to normal customs. He came and went as he liked. And I always had the feeling when I went into his room that the particular thing he was scribbling hard at had nothing to do with *The Architectural Review*.' Peter Quennell had a similar impression. Visiting John's office with some proofs, he found his chair unoccupied, though his desk was heaped with papers. 'Among them I saw a huge blotting-pad, evidently quite new, on which, using a sharp pencil and decorative Gothic script, he had inscribed the now familiar couplet:

> I sometimes think that I should like
> To be the saddle of a bike.'

Tom Driberg described this as 'the shortest erotic poem in our language', but in fact it was the opening of a long, indecent poem, now lost.

In spite of his sidelines, John contributed many articles, and some poems, to the *Review* during his four years on the staff. His first major article for the *Review* appeared before he joined the staff: '1830–1930 – Still Going Strong' (May 1930), subtitled 'A Guide to the Recent History of Interior Decoration'. It is a virtuoso performance for a man of twenty-three. His treatment of the subject is swashbuckling and erratic, but he has a confident grasp of the way cycles of taste succeed each other. He gives high praise to Charles Rennie Mackintosh, but also to Le Corbusier. Here is a child of the insouciant 1920s doing his best to adapt to the committed 1930s, and trying to reconcile what he likes with what he is required to like.

Doctrinaire adherents of the Modern Movement later denounced John as having been a kind of Trojan Horse within the Modernist citadel. The barebones architect Maxwell Fry, for example, thought that 'The key to John Betjeman's character is that he's a journalist and a Fleet Street man – and a popularist – and vain. He was the enemy to Modernism. I knew he would draw a facetious veil over our earnestness and that at the end he would find himself in some other camp . . . as far as I was concerned, he was a bloody nuisance.'

But the *Review*'s attitude to the Modern Movement was itself ambivalent. Hastings and Barman both professed to be for it. But, as John later pointed out, '*The Architectural Review* could not quite throw off classical town halls and civic centres partly because of the advertising revenue that came from makers of bronze doors, light fittings and from importers of marble and stone.' The old conflict which had plagued Percy Hastings in the early years of the century – architectural vision versus commercial profits – was still vexing to his son. John and his colleagues were expected at least to pay lip-service to the Modern Movement.

P. Morton Shand (grandfather of the Duchess of Cornwall, *née* Shand) was the most influential contributor to the *Review* during John's time there, and became a great friend of his. After an orthodox English education – Eton and King's College, Cambridge – he had gone on to the Sorbonne and Heidelberg and spoke both French and German fluently. Besides his keen and far-ranging interest in architecture, he was an expert on French wine and a student of pomology, cultivating varieties of apple that were no longer grown commercially and were in danger of becoming extinct. J. M. Richards, who thought him 'more responsible than anyone for the *Review*'s, and therefore for English architects', contact with modern Continental building', found him meticulously accurate, cynical, unhappy, always hard up (because of expensive divorces from several wives) and exceptionally good company.

Morton Shand was also an architectural historian. In a series of articles with the grandiloquent title 'Scenario for a Human Drama' (July 1934–March 1935), which John sub-edited, he pioneered the theory – also advanced with enthusiasm by Nikolaus Pevsner – that the Modern Movement was in clear descent from such Arts and Crafts men as C. R. Mackintosh and C. F. A. Voysey. This was a wonderful let-out for John, to whom Morton Shand expounded his theories some time before they appeared in print. The theory which ingeniously and improbably linked the folksy tiles and gables of Voysey with the 'architectural nudism' of Le Corbusier and Gropius gave John *carte blanche* to forget what Osbert Lancaster called 'the Bauhaus balls' and to devote much of his time to tracking down the Victorian and Edwardian architects who were now to be acclaimed as 'pioneers', and whose work was far more congenial to John than sheets of vita-glass and ferro-concrete.

Some of the Arts and Crafts men were still living. John visited Voysey in his St James's Street flat and found that he did not regard himself as a pioneer of the Modern Movement. The son of an Anglican clergyman and a descendant of John Wesley, Voysey disliked William Morris 'because he was an atheist'; had no time for the Glasgow architects Mackintosh and Walton, whom he called 'the spook school'; and thought the buildings appearing in the *Review* were hideous.

In October 1931 an exhibition of Voysey's drawings, designs for fabrics and furniture, was held under the auspices of *The Architectural Review* and B. T. Batsford Ltd, at the latter's galleries in North Audley Street, London. To mark the opening, John contributed an article on Voysey to the *Review* that month in which he gleefully suggested that 'Mr Voysey is as high a Tory as the old Duke of Wellington' (from whom, in addition to Wesley, Voysey was descended). But to justify the inclusion of such a benighted theorist in the *Review*, he was obliged to emphasize Voysey's alleged status as a 'pioneer': 'Although we see many of his decorative details reproduced *ad nauseam* in tea shop, waiting room and monster furnishing store, the simplicity to which he – as much if not more than William Morris – leads us back from the complex and futile revivalism in which many architects still remain, has made itself felt at least on the Continent.'

Sir Edwin Lutyens, John recalled in 1968, was the only classical architect he and his colleagues on the *Review* had been allowed to admire, though 'bankers' Georgian' was despised. An exception was made for Lutyens because in his youth he had been associated with the Arts and

Crafts Movement. Christian Barman sent John round to Lutyens's office to obtain drawings and photographs for reproduction. Lutyens was 'as welcoming as he was fascinating'. With the aid of a pencil and a penny he showed John 'how to turn a moulding from half a pipe into a living curve, by just stopping it being a quarter or a half and making it between the two'.

In 1931 John went to see M. H. Baillie Scott, another survivor of the older generation of architects, at his office in Bedford Row. He was not in, but John was cordially received by his partner Edgar Beresford, who had become Baillie Scott's assistant in 1905. Baillie Scott was in the country, but John must have made a favourable impression on Beresford, as he soon received an invitation from Baillie Scott to stay with him and his wife at their house, Ockhams, near Edenbridge, Kent. In his 'sleepy, laconic way with his melancholy expression, half-shut eyes and drooping moustache', Baillie Scott told John the events of his life with the kind of throwaway humour John enjoyed most. 'I went to the Isle of Man for a holiday,' he said. 'I was so seasick I couldn't face the journey back so I set up in practice there.' John especially relished the story of Baillie Scott's visit to Darmstadt to decorate the Grand Duke's palace. 'He was met at the station by the royal carriage. Behind it was a wagonette with four horses for his luggage. This consisted of a single grip.'

Charles Rennie Mackintosh, the *art nouveau* designer and architect whom John admired most, died in 1928, too early for John to meet him; but John was able to talk to Fra Newbery, who had taught Mackintosh at the Glasgow School of Art. And in 1933 he was just in time to meet Mackintosh's exact contemporary George Walton. In December 1933 John arrived without appointment at the Waltons' little flat in Greycoat Place, Chelsea. They had come to London as Walton wanted his young son Edward to go to Westminster School, and could not afford boarding fees. Edward Walton recalled: 'Betjeman was very enthusiastic about my father's work, called him "Architect" and wanted to write about him. My mother was pleased at the attention and after Betjeman left said how nice it was for [Walton] to be recognized still . . .'

On 7 December, George Walton became ill in the middle of the night. He was taken by ambulance to St John and St Elizabeth Hospital and died three days later. Unaware of this, John reappeared at the flat in a few days, bringing the text of an article on Walton for the architect to check and approve. 'On hearing the news of my father's death, he was stricken,' Edward Walton wrote. 'He left in great confusion.' During the next few weeks, John took the family's affairs in hand. On 10 January he waited on H. V. Vincent at 10 Downing Street to explain why Walton's Civil List pension should be transferred to his widow, and he persuaded the trustees of the Architects' Benevolent Fund to pay Edward's school fees. Walton's death was recorded in *The Architectural Review* of January 1934, in the caption to a large illustration of the Regency-like White House, Shiplake, which he had designed in 1908. A short obituary, presumably written by John, was published in the same issue.

Another of the older architects whom John was eager to meet was Ninian Comper, a hero to him since his childhood days in Cornwall when he had bicycled to Blisland, whose golden altars are among Comper's earliest work. He did meet Comper, and was a friend for the rest of the architect's long life (1864–1960) and an executor of his will.

The three architects whose friendship and influence were most important to John, both in his *Architectural Review* days and later, were Frederick Etchells and H. S. Goodhart-Rendel (both born in 1887) and John Summerson (born 1904). As a Vorticist Etchells had contributed, with Ezra Pound, to the first issue of Wyndham Lewis's magazine *Blast*. He had also worked in the Omega Workshops with Roger Fry. In 1927 he had given the Modern Movement in England the first of its gospels by translating Le Corbusier's *Vers une Architecture*. (Morton Shand provided the second in 1935 with his translation of Gropius.) John became a wide-eyed disciple of Etchells. It was Etchells whose 'inspired monologues on architecture' first made him realize the difference between 'modern' and '*moderne*'. *Moderne* (usually called Art Deco today) was virtually outlawed by the *Review*. After John's marriage in July 1933, he persuaded his father-in-law, Field Marshal Sir Philip Chetwode, to employ Etchells as the architect of his new house at 40 Avenue Road, St John's Wood, London. 'You can see the feller's never built a gentleman's house,' barked the Field Marshal. 'There's no brushin' room.'

H. S. Goodhart-Rendel's most celebrated building of the 1930s, Hay's Wharf, London (the *Review* devoted eight pages to it in February 1932) has been claimed for the Modern Movement but with its swaggering gilt letters, zig-zag window casements, marquetry lift doors and exterior reliefs by Frank Dobson it really has far more in common with the *moderne*. In his writings, Goodhart-Rendel made clear his distaste for the Modern Movement with a debonair facetiousness which outraged the more solemn ideologues. His detachment and wit seemed out of place in the committed 1930s, and Robert Furneaux Jordan has described him as 'an erudite flâneur'. But of course his humour recommended him to John, who particularly enjoyed Goodhart-Rendel's comment to Osbert Lancaster after inspecting the Parthenon: 'Well! Not what you'd call an unqualified success, is it?'

John Summerson was another subversive ostensibly within the Modern Movement. Like Betjeman, he was part of what Dr Gavin Stamp calls 'the

MARS gang': the Modern Architectural Research Group, founded in 1933 by Wells Coates and P. Morton Shand. But he had too subtle and dispassionate a mind to be altogether bowled over by what he later called 'the hurricane functionalists'. Even in 1938 he concluded that the only explanation of the wholesale loyalty of the Architectural Association school to Modernism was its 'poetic appeal; and the poet is the Ruskin of our age, Le Corbusier'. He later became assistant editor of the *Architect and Building News*, but moonlighted by writing articles commissioned by John for *The Architectural Review*, under the nom-de-plume 'Coolmore' – by which John addressed him ever afterwards.

Like Summerson, John's Oxford friend Michael Dugdale trained at the Architectural Association. Later he joined the avant-garde Russian architect Berthold Lubetkin in the Tecton partnership, whose best-known works were the gorilla house (1932) and penguin pool (1933) at London Zoo, and Highpoint Flats in Highgate (1935 and 1936–38). Apart from the expansive coverage given to Tecton buildings in the *Review*, John commissioned several articles by Dugdale and published three of his poems. But an unusually acid letter of 1931 from John to Dugdale suggests that Dugdale may have been talking out of turn and biting the hand which fed him:

> My dear Michael,
>
> I am told by various A.A. people that *The Architectural Review* is held in great contempt there. It therefore seems rather a waste of your time to send any articles up to it.
>
> – Seriously, though, I think it rather disloyal of you to run it down since it has to circulate among architects for its advertisement revenue – and they are bloody enough God knows – moreover by broadcasting the fact that no one on the staff knows about architecture – a fact which is quite untrue and seems a little jealous – you do it infinite harm in the future. Had I been given the chance that you have had to learn architecture, I would have taken it, tho' had I known that it would lead to my building in the style of ex A.A. students and developing a character like that heterosexual sycophant F. R. Yerbury [photographer and author of books on modern architecture], I should have desisted. You will probably do me a lot of harm. Please don't mention the paper at all, old boy, if you want 10/6
>
> for the sake of
> Your indignant and former friend,
> J.B.

Besides showing a certain jealousy of Dugdale on the part of the degreeless John, forced to earn his living by journalism, this letter prompts the question: how influential *was* the *Review* in the 1930s? John himself was in no doubt of the answer. 'If anyone asks me who invented modern architecture,' he wrote in 1974, 'I answer "Obscurity Hastings".' John Summerson has described the *Review* as 'the Diaghilev of the English architectural stage'. In the opinion of John Brandon-Jones, who was at the AA with Michael Dugdale, the influence of the *Review* was not only strong but pernicious:

> I never understood why so many of my contemporaries were taken in by the International Style, even though every generation tends to revolt against the one before. But the style was taken up and sold by people who were not architects but critics, like H. de C. Hastings and Pevsner. For years they published it and nothing else, and they managed to sell it to intellectuals . . . Architects took it up when it became clear that you could not get a building into the *Review* unless it was in the style. It was a propaganda exercise, unparalleled since Burlington brought in the Palladian style.

Brandon-Jones thought that much of the effectiveness of the *Review* as a propaganda instrument came not from the writing but from the artful photography. The buildings were always photographed when they were new and when the shadows and the background sky were right.

As third-in-command at the *Review*, then, John could have been a figure of some power on the British architectural scene of the early 1930s. De Cronin Hastings might be 'tyrannical' when he descended on the magazine to deliver his edicts and reprimands, but his long absences and his Tibetan inaccessibility even when he was on the premises, gave his lieutenants considerable discretion – and opportunities for indiscretion. John was more interested in contributing history, comedy and poetry to the *Review* than in trying to affect the course of the Modern Movement. In a prophetic article, 'Dictating to the Railways' (September 1933) he discussed the future of the Euston Arch.* 'For many years now there have been rumours about the reconstruction of Euston, the demolition of its great arch and its old booking hall, now known as the Great Hall.' John proposed that, if the arch had to go, it should at least be re-erected elsewhere.

His contributions on architectural history included an essay on Sezincote (May 1932). His reviews of such books as E. Jervoise's *The Ancient Bridges of the South of England* (1931), A. E. Richardson's *Georgian England* (1931), F. R. Yerbury's *Modern Dutch Buildings* (1932) and Noël Carrington's *Design in the Home* (1933) showed his learning, if not always the strictest impartiality: the despised Yerbury got short shrift. And John

*See Chapter 27, 'The Euston Arch and the Coal Exchange'.

could not keep his mischief and vivacity in check for long. They constantly showed through, like a brocade waistcoat under a sub-fusc jacket. Imaginary societies were advertised. Spoof letters were published and received spoof answers. An article by John on Wolf's Cove, Thirlwall Mere & District (January 1932), turned out to concern a miniature model village in the garden of Snowshill Manor, Gloucestershire, home of the architect Charles P. Wade, and John had named all the people in the village after his friends ('The Miller, George Kolkhorst, is old now, and young Toby, his son, is carrying on the business . . .'). Increasingly, the *Review* had a flavour of the *Cherwell* – cleverness and camp.

The *Review* published verses by John. In February 1930 it printed 'The Church's Restoration' (which had first appeared in the *Isis*) and in November 1930, 'Westgate on Sea'. (The first line of the last stanza read: 'For me in my Voisey [*sic*] arbour'; for subsequent publication in book form, John altered this to 'timber arbour', perhaps feeling that the general public could not be expected to understand the reference to an architect who was well known to readers of the *Review*.) 'A Railway Prospect of a Provincial Town' appeared in the issue of May 1935.

Working for *The Architectural Review*, John found, was not all fun – chatting with Edwardian architects or writing funny captions and verse. Much of the day's routine seemed drudgery. 'I write and I write and I write,' he complained in 1933, 'under different names and in different styles, yet no one has heard of either me or my pseudonyms. I must have written the word architecture more times than there are people in England who can pronounce it properly.' We get a glimpse of his more run-of-the-mill work at that time from a letter written to him in 1960 by Mr R. Morris. In about 1930, Morris told John, he had called at the *Review* with photographs of his own designs in stained glass and leaded lights.

> I was ushered into an impressive Editor or Assistant Editor's Office which was furnished in the very latest mode of chromium plated wonder that I had ever at that time seen. And at a super modern desk and in a super modern chair sat a gentleman whose name was Mr Betjeman. If this was you indeed, I must do you the justice to say that you interviewed me with every gesture of sympathetic interest and I presume controlled tolerance, tempered with kindness and not spoiled by any flavour of patronage. You struck me as being a real 'High Brow' but a pleasant one at that – although you deemed it wise, and I now know you to have been right, to have nothing to do with the wares I was offering at the time.

'Controlled tolerance' is probably a fair description of John's attitude to life on the *Review*. The tolerance could not last for ever; the control snapped. When growing rewards from the *Evening Standard* and from editing county guides for Shell-Mex offered him a measure of independence, he jumped at the chance and left the *Review* abruptly.

J. M. Richards happened to be in de Cronin Hastings's room discussing an article when John burst in to give his resignation.

> He flung into the room [Richards recalled]. John had a way that perhaps impressed Hastings more than my polite way of knocking at the door, of just storming in when he wanted to. Anyway, he flung into the room and shouted: 'Well, if you're not going to pay me another £300 a year I'm leaving tomorrow.' And he did leave shortly after that. But I don't think that was the reason he left. De Cronin wasn't ungenerous, financially. John obviously wanted to leave and his temperament was of that kind which made him want to create a scene in order to excuse him. He had decided he had other fish to fry and didn't want to spend his life being a magazine editor – still less an assistant editor.

In spite of his petulant flouncing-out, John remained on good terms with Hastings and continued to contribute to the *Review* for many years. But leaving the magazine released him from any further obligation to subscribe to the Modern Movement's philosophy of architecture. He no longer needed to claim that the Victorian and Edwardian architects and designers he admired were 'pioneers'. Neither did he have to pretend that steel pylons were an enhancement of the English landscape. In later years, pylons were to be among his favourite bugbears ('Encase your legs in nylons, / Bestride your hills with pylons / O age without a soul'). In a lecture at the Royal Society of Arts in 1956 he delivered a furious attack on pylons, but when the lecture was printed, George Mansell wrote to him: 'and if memory does not belie me, I remember in 1932 at Painters Hall in the City of London a certain young enthusiast for functional beauty showing a lovely slide of a PYLON in all its austere (and functional) beauty!! I was a fellow lecturer at that same event. TEMPORA MVTANTVR NOS ET MVTAMVR IN ILLIS.' John replied:

> I remember that slide of a pylon and I think I have still got it somewhere. Of course lecturing about it in that silly way does untold damage. A pylon in itself may be all right, but its setting is something in those days I did not regard. Pylons may look all right in large rolling landscape, but they look perfectly ghastly in quiet Cotswold country or among Essex elms. The same silly consideration of things caused the Royal Fine Art Commission, many years ago, to approve one kind of concrete lamp standard. Oh dear, one must be careful!

As his early imprudences reared up to haunt him, John's stance was somewhat like that of a 'good German', a Rommel who had worked for the Nazis without being tainted by their ideology. But when antagonism to the Modern Movement, led by Dr David Watkin and Dr Gavin Stamp, gained ground in the 1970s, he was sometimes made to seem more like an Albert Speer, denouncing the former masters whom he had served too well. Watkin and Stamp were both devoted to John, but they could not altogether exonerate him for suggesting, in *Ghastly Good Taste* (1933), that James Gibbs, who placed the classical Radcliffe Camera, Oxford, in the heart of a Gothic setting, 'would also have had the courage to build today as sincere an essay in modern materials in its place'. Even more damning, in Watkin's view, was a passage in John's pamphlet *Antiquarian Prejudice* (1939) in which he attacked 1930s buildings for exemplifying 'the timidity miscalled "tradition" but really antiquarianism, which enslaves beknighted architects' and urged architects to imitate the example of Soviet Russia in producing 'an honest plain structure of steel, glass and/or reinforced concrete'. John was also taken to task for having been a member of the MARS Group. John Summerson, another unlikely MARS recruit, had at least shown proper contrition in 1959 by describing the Group's New Burlington Galleries exhibition of 1937–38 as 'plastered with captions and exhortations of the most vacuous pomposity (I wrote them and I know)'.

A more surprising recantation than John's and Summerson's was that of P. Morton Shand. In 1958, two years before his death, he wrote John a letter from Saint-André-de-Sangonis, France, to which he had retreated because 'awful new buildings going up so rapidly drove me into a nervous frenzy':

> I have frightful nightmares, and no wonder, for I am haunted by a gnawing sense of guilt in having, in however minor and obscure degree, helped to bring about, anyhow encouraged and praised, the embryo searchings that have now materialized into a monster neither of us could have foreseen: Contemporary Architecture (= the piling up of gigantic children's toy bricks in utterly dehumanized and meaningless forms), 'Art' and all that. It is no longer funny; it is a frightening, all-invading menace.

John marked this passage and later reprinted it as evidence that Morton Shand had renounced what he had believed in the 1930s.

John's own recantation was as unequivocal as Mucius Scaevola's or Cranmer's. Expressions of it are to be found in many of his poems, articles and letters of protest in the press. But perhaps the most telling evidence of his volte-face is a letter which he wrote in 1943 to the man who had first led him up that shining path, Hubert de Cronin Hastings.

Why do we both live in farmhouses and not at High Point? Oh my dear Obscurity, we *must* make contemporary domestic architecture according to rules of proportion and with textures which will fit in with the buildings we have got. Is there no map of buildings which are built up to, let us say, 1850? And of the better ones after that date? And of skylines? and trees and prevalent materials and inbuilding? Is the flat roof essential in the pre-fabricated house? . . . If you can show one decent domestic unit – NOT A BLOCK OF FLATS – and not from Arizona or Sweden: if you can show it in *use* and in action in the photograph and if you can guarantee by imposing it on a photograph of a street of old houses, that it is the sort of house you wouldn't mind living in with a family or living opposite – then you will have . . . appealed to the heart as well as the head.

8

With the Bright Young People

SEVERAL OF JOHN'S contemporaries hated their fathers almost to the point of parricide. John Bowle, Clonmore and Lionel Perry are well-documented examples. The trouble usually began at Oxford over money. After Oxford, there was sometimes a tussle over the sons' choice of career – or over their failing to find a career. Their taste in girlfriends could also be a source of conflict. And if, as was the case with many of John's friends, the son was homosexual, that could cause further hostility. To these young men, Patrick Balfour's studio-flat at 26A Yeoman's Row – 'the Yeo', as they called it – became on a modest scale what the Prince of Wales's Carlton House had been during George III's reign: a place of refuge and a head-quarters of disaffection.

Balfour, a gossip columnist, for a while shared the flat with the writer Cyril Connolly, who later referred to this time when 'we didn't know where the next meal was coming from, nor whom to ask to it'. When John was dismissed by Sir Horace Plunkett in March 1929, Balfour offered him Connolly's old room, apparently rent-free.

The Yeo was John's London base during the whole time he taught at Heddon Court. His favourite pupils were invited there for tea or lunch at weekends or in the holidays, among them Marcus Sheldon (Sheldon IV) and his brother Stephen (Sheldon V). Marcus Sheldon wrote to Balfour in June 1930:

> In the dining hall there is a ghastly side-board, the sort all garnished with curtains and corners. While taking tea on Monday, Mr Betjeman looked in the mirror in it and said, 'Good looking fellow, eh?' to Miss Taylor. The maids were all standing by, so the direct effect was that they burst into a shriek of hysterical laughter . . .

Almost twenty years later, Balfour (by now Lord Kinross) sent John a photograph of Marcus Sheldon which he had been given in 1929 or 1930. John replied: 'Very nice to see that picture of Sheldon IV again. IV for love, but V for fun I suspect, don't you?'

John tended to exaggerate his homosexual leanings in his letters to Balfour, because he knew he was playing to a receptive gallery. Balfour was well known as a boy-fancier. But other friends noticed John's burgeoning interest in girls after he left Oxford. Elizabeth Longford, who as Elizabeth Harman was a fellow guest at Pakenham Hall, Ireland, in 1930, was surprised by the contrast with the aesthete she had known at university. In February 1929, when he was still with Plunkett at Birchington-on-Sea, he had written to Balfour: 'I am amazed at the beauty of Mary Erskine (Hamish's sister) and I love to contemplate the anger of Hamish if I were to elope with her.' In the winter of 1929–30 John did his best to turn this fantasy into reality.

Hamish St Clair-Erskine, younger son of the Earl and Countess of Rosslyn, was a friend of John's at Oxford. Mary Erskine was eighteen in 1929 and John was not the only young man paying court to her. Sir Michael Duff and Count John de Bendern were both admirers. Daphne Fielding met her in 1929 at Vaynol Park, Duff's home in north Wales. 'She . . . looked like a pretty and impertinent schoolgirl dressed up in her mother's clothes,' she wrote. 'She could get away with almost anything through her charm, and was always forgiven; and there was often plenty to forgive.' Lady Mary's escapades were already legend. She had been whirled around 'like an Indian club' by a roller-skating apache dancer in a London cabaret; only by biting him had she been able to stop his gyrations. At Vaynol she accidentally drove Richard Sykes's Rolls-Royce into Michael Duff's Rolls-Royce: the latter cannoned into the wrought-iron gates, 'which slowly toppled and crashed like the walls of Jericho'.

It was on this gossip columnist's delight that John had set his sights. But Mary Erskine was not just the socialite flibbertigibbet that Daphne Fielding's memories suggest. She was combatively intelligent and corresponded with John about poetry and religion. He was suffering from doubts about the after-life, and was wondering whether to become a Roman Catholic, perhaps even a Roman Catholic priest. The first of these alleged ambitions may have been intended to recommend him to Lady Rosslyn; the second, to pique Lady Mary into rescuing him from a life of holy chastity. He proposed to her in the winter of 1929–30 in his father's study in Church Street, Chelsea. 'It was lit entirely by stained glass,' Lady Mary recalled. 'John must have loved it. I was rather shocked – you know, there was a three-piece suite in violet brocade. And I was extremely flattered but said, "No thanks, I'd much rather have you as a friend." ' John remained her friend. In her copy of *Mount Zion* (1931), he wrote: 'Maria, good little thing, bought this. She is not only the only deep love of my life but she is the Angela Brazil of my dreams.' There follows a drawing of a hockey stick, a cricket bat, a tennis racquet, a skipping-rope, a lacrosse stick and cricket balls; and then: 'O hard – that husky voice – that simple school-girl. Don't get rid of your freckles.' Lady Mary married Sir Philip Dunn in 1933. 'I was rather cross when I found out there was a real Miss Hunter Dunn,' she said, 'because I thought John's poem was based on me.'

In July 1929 John again stayed with Billy Clonmore at Shelton Abbey. By late July he was in Cornwall. 'Ernie has built himself a most luxurious house here looking straight on to the villa of the local Baronet,' he told Balfour on 31 July. On 16 August, John travelled to Scotland to spend just over a week with his Heddon Court pupil Dick Addis and the boy's family at their rented house, Hartrigge, in the Border country near Jedburgh. Sir John Addis remembered that John had been 'the most enormous fun':

> He very quickly accommodated himself to this rather strange family, and I still remember the excitement of half a dozen or more of us sitting round, squatting on the floor, and him telling his anecdotes or talking in his amus-ing way – very much, then, taking off suburbia and all the standards that went with it.

One result of John's nine days at Hartrigge was a long friendship with the Addises' sister Margie, who married another of John's Heddon Court pupils, Alexander Geddes. She remembers that John's hair was so un-acceptably long that she offered to cut it for him with a pair of nail-scissors when they were about to visit some local grandees. 'I am afraid I was not a very expert hairdresser; and when we got to this family's house, the mother took me aside and said, "My dear, what is wrong with your friend Mr Betjeman? Has he got the *mange*?"' Though John's friendship with the Addis boys was cut short by the incident at Piccadilly Underground sta-tion, his friendship with Margie Addis lasted to the end of his life.

Early in 1929 Pierce Synnott and John joined Patrick Balfour and his family at their holiday home on the Isle of Skye. On 16 September, back at Heddon Court, John wrote Lady Kinross a thank-you letter decorated with caricatures. 'It was so depressing', he told her, 'to leave Skye & wait about two hours in Kyle of Lochalsh while men did nothing to the car, still in sight of the misty mountains, that my temper became very bad.' Although she had three marriageable daughters, Lady Kinross looked upon John with favour – a rarity among upper-class mothers. Knowing she was sympathetic, Balfour kept her well informed of John's plunges in fortune. On 29 October 1929 he reported:

> John Betjeman has finally broken with his father, who assaulted him – hit him on the head six times and went for his hunting-crop. John put up no

resistance, judging it the most dignified and humiliating course to take –
then got a letter from Ernie saying 'I am surprised I have received no
word of apology for your violent attack upon me. I only regret I had no
friend near me to give you the thrashing you deserved, and which you
have been badly wanting these last two years. However, you will one day
no doubt get laid out by someone whom you have insulted and derided;
until then you will probably tread the perfect cad's path.' It is magnificent,
isn't it?

On 3 January 1930 he wrote to her again: 'John's father has cut him out of
his will altogether. He gave him a long lecture on it, beginning, "My poor
boy, for poor indeed I must now call you." '

Balfour's accounts of Ernest's alleged behaviour provoke once again the
question: how true were John's stories of ill-treatment by his father?
Together, Balfour's two reports suggest Victorian melodrama garnished
with Wildean humour. Indeed, John might have been re-enacting Lord
Alfred Douglas's duels with the Marquess of Queensberry. Ernest's letters
to John, though often nagging in tone, are usually good-natured and for-
giving. Against this case for the defence, William Hammond's memory of
Ernest's flinging wood across the workshop and Synnott's report on the
tantrum in the Dublin hotel tell against John's father. John never failed to
exploit a good story for what it was worth, and sometimes for more, but
he may well have been predisposed to misinterpret, adversely, whatever
Ernest said or did. He seems to have been genuinely distressed by Ernest's
conduct; but that does not necessarily mean that Ernest's conduct was as
cruel as John thought it was, or said it was.

In late March 1930 John moved into a flat at 3 Middle Temple Lane
sublet to him by John Sparrow. He shared it with John Bowle, who was
teaching history at Westminster School. Angus Wilson, the novelist, then
a schoolboy at Westminster, was introduced to Lord Alfred Douglas at the
house. He also remembered John's coming to see a school play. 'John
Bowle got very drunk; and John Betjeman stood on a table and said: "I say,
you chaps aren't going to *peach* on John Edward, are you?" – in the manner
of a Victorian public-school novel.'

In April John travelled to Germany with Billy Clonmore and the ever-
vigilant Mr Newcombe. To some of John's friends, travel abroad was an
escape from unhappiness at home. Not so to John. 'Isn't abroad *awful!*' he
once said to Edward James; and Sir Osbert Lancaster said, 'When John is
abroad, he has to be surrounded by friends, like a rugby-football player
who has lost his shorts.' John wrote lugubriously to Patrick Balfour from
the Königshof Grand Hotel Royal, Bonn:

It is useless to pretend that I enjoy myself abroad. The continual difficulty of overcoming a foreign language which the meanest children in the public gardens opposite can speak with fluency, the constant frustration of natural impulse through inability to communicate with the object of one's desires overcomes the spirit as much as it mortifies the flesh. For instance I have drunk tea in my life, but never have I wanted to drink it so much as in this town. It is obtainable but I do not know how to ask for it; it is waiting steaming hot, but I have not the courage to depend on my Hugo's Simplified Course.

'Tea' was homosexual slang for boy trade.

Much more congenial for John was his first visit late that summer to Pakenham Hall in County Westmeath, the home of Frank Pakenham's elder brother Edward, sixth Earl of Longford. It was Frank who had invited John, but the Irish nationalist Edward and his wife Christine took to him at once. Edward Longford had come into his inheritance in December 1923: Pakenham and its demesne; the town of Longford; and half of Dun Laoghaire (Kingstown), a seaside suburb of Dublin. Outside the estate, his main interests were the theatre and folk-weaving. In 1930 he became chairman of the Gate Theatre, Dublin, two years after it was founded by Micheál MacLiammóir and Hilton Edwards – 'the Boys', as the Longfords called them. (According to Orson Welles, who arrived in Dublin in 1931, they were less delicately known in Dublin as 'Sodom and Begorrah'.)

The Longfords took John to the Gate Theatre. 'He was a very good critic,' Christine Longford said. 'I think his knowledge was wider than we knew, about *everything*. He would come to the Gate and made very sensible comments on the plays. We all would occasionally whisper; but I remember there was one performance of *She Stoops to Conquer* in which John whispered (and it pleased us very much) that our girl playing the principal part, and two boys, were as good as you could find anywhere; and while I was whispering in reply I was thumped on the back by a really well-behaved and devoted theatre-goer, who told me not to talk.' The actress was Cathleen Delaney, an attractive girl with 'dark, clustering curls'. John flirted with her and rowed her on Loch Derravaragh while she sang Moore's Melodies. When she married John O'Dea, an engineer, John Betjeman celebrated the event in a poem, 'The Colleen and the Eigenherr'.

When Evelyn Waugh arrived at Pakenham with his close friend Alastair Graham on 3 September, he recorded in his diary that the guests already there were John Betjeman and Elizabeth Harman – whom Frank Pakenham had invited to Ireland after dreaming about her in his Oxford lodgings in June. Waugh and Graham stayed for about ten days. Christine later recalled that Waugh, already famous as the author of *Decline and Fall* and *Vile Bodies*, was 'still the same little faun as at Oxford'. He would come down to breakfast with a determined face and demand, 'Who's got any funny letters this morning?' Christine wrote: 'That was the professional writer keen on the scent and we handed them over at once, as a solemn duty. He read rapidly and handed them back. The material was stored for the future.' The novelist was also diverted by his host's eccentricities. 'I have seen at Pakenham what I have seen nowhere else,' Waugh wrote, 'an entirely sober host literally rolling about the carpet with merriment. Edward soon became uncommonly stout, a condition which caused him no self-consciousness, and which, I think, he never took any steps to relieve. His butler and attendant footmen would gravely bestride the spherical form in its velvet smoking-suit as they carried their trays.'

'John B. became a bore rather with Irish peers and revivalist hymns and his enthusiasm for every sort of architecture,' Waugh noted in his diary. In spite of this grumpy comment, he seems to have enjoyed the singing as much as anyone. The house-party would stand round the piano or the wheezy organ, with Edward roughly playing the tune with his right hand 'and any old thing with the left hand'. In the evenings, in the great hall, John entertained the company with ghost stories by M. R. James and Sheridan Le Fanu, recitals of Vachel Lindsay's 'Congo', Gothic descriptions of 'basketings' at Marlborough, and parodies of Shakespeare. Elizabeth Longford recalled: 'Practically every evening John would be called on to do a Shakespearean dialogue, sort of "*Enter First Murderer.* 'Hast seen the light?' " and he'd go through the whole thing for about ten minutes. It was fantastic, you could not tell it wasn't some kind of Shakespearean discovery.' The Pakenhams made their own entertainments. These included charades, in which John excelled, and the 'marking game', with marks awarded for beauty, brains and other qualities.

Edward would drive his guests through the Westmeath countryside, stopping to look at some of the Protestant churches. 'They were usually locked,' Christine remembered, 'but John was extremely clever at finding out who had the key. There would be a notice on the door saying, key at a certain cottage, and the man would be out herding his cattle somewhere, but John would in the end get in.' John recalled how Edward would raise his wideawake hat when passing the Protestant churches, in emulation of the Irish who raised their hats or crossed themselves when going past a Roman Catholic church. Edward and Christine also drove John to the Celtic crosses of Clonmacnois and Monasterboice, 'scripture-lessons in stone', as the guidebook called them. They quoted to him T. W. Rolleston's poem about Clonmacnois, 'In a quiet watered land, a land of roses . . .' Rolleston was minor enough to attract John, who later paid him the tribute of pastiche in 'Variation on a Theme by T. W. Rolleston'.

'Dim peers' were what interested John most in Westmeath — obscure peers, not necessarily dim-witted ones. In 'An Impoverished Irish Peer' he mentions Lord Trimlestown. The quest for Lord Trimlestown took up so much of his time on that first Pakenham visit, that even Evelyn Waugh, whose tolerance of peers was high, felt the joke had been carried too far. Near the hamlet of Trim, on the way from Pakenham to Dublin, were the ruins of Trim Castle, where King John Lackland had lived for a time (John was photographed in the ruins), and Bloomsbury, the seat of Lord Trimlestown. John wrote to Patrick Balfour on 1 September:

> Lord Trimblestown's [sic] seat is called Bloomsbury near Kells and near this very remote place [Pakenham Hall], as you know. We devised a very clever scheme for calling on him. We made out a petition to prevent the demolition of Dublin Places of Worship — which, by the way, are of course, not going to be destroyed — and took it for him to sign. Bloomsbury is very difficult to find and when you do reach [it], it is very small. We asked about Lord Trimblestown in the district and no one had heard of him. Then we found Bloomsbury, an unpretentious William IVth structure in the Roman Manner and painted light mauve and brown. We learned at a lodge near the grass-grown drive and ruined gates that Lord Trimblestown had left it fourteen years ago — 'those were grand days' the old man said. His eldest daughter is a Mrs Ratcliffe who lives in an even smaller Georgian house near Kells. That is all. Four of his nine sisters are nuns and the rest have not married very well. I am so sorry.
>
> On the way back, heartbroken and stricken, we found an interesting sight on the roadside — An old man who lived in a wheel barrow with a mackintosh and umbrella over the top, all the year round. He was deaf and dumb but not dotty. I think he is the brother of Lord Trimblestown.

John referred to Lord Trimlestown ('whose peerage was created in 1462') in his article 'Peers without Tears' in the *Evening Standard* of 19 December 1933: 'Though over seventy, he is still, thanks to a hard early life before the mast, keen on dancing and racing.'

John and Waugh were taken to lunch with Lord Dunsany, the author, who was a nephew of John's recent employer, Sir Horace Plunkett, and was married to Edward's Aunt Beatrice, sister of the dowager Lady Longford. Waugh was not impressed by him. 'Lord Dunsany thinks his very nice eighteenth-century Gothic house is genuinely medieval. He was rude

to the servants and grossly boastful. He makes odious little faces of plaster.'
John, showing off his architectural knowledge, said quite the wrong thing.
'What I chiefly liked about Dunsany Castle', he remembered, 'was the
Strawberry Hill Gothic, because that's what it mainly was. I was a com-
plete failure with Lord Dunsany as I asked: "What date is this, sort of
1810?" "*Eleven hundred and six.*"'

John browsed happily in the library at Pakenham, the handsomest room
in the house. Its shelves were lined with leather-bound books and it also
contained first editions of Jane Austen, bought by the second Earl when
they were published. The book John enjoyed most was the bound record
of the probate trial in Dublin (1877) which followed the death of Adolphus
Cooke of Cookesborough, an estate bordering on the Pakenham demesne.
Cooke had believed that he would be turned into a screech-owl after his
death, or possibly into a fox which would be hunted down by the then Earl
of Longford and the Westmeath Hunt. Christine Longford turned the
Cooke saga into a comic novel, *Mr Jiggins of Jigginstown* (1934). By then she
had already published two well-received novels, *Making Conversation* (1931)
– 'the first novel that anybody can write, stories of my past life', as she
modestly put it – and *Country Places* (1932).

The success of Christine Longford and of Evelyn Waugh as novelists
may have revived John's ambition to write a novel; but the fragments of a
novella, written by him on Pakenham Hall writing paper in 1932, suggest
a parody of the Longford/Waugh society novel, rather than any serious
attempt to write one himself. Entitled 'Standish Mount Pleasant' (alterna-
tively, 'Standish O'Grady') and purportedly by 'Lord Belmont', it is an
even more 'camp' exercise than a Cornish novel he began two or three
years before, a *roman à clef* about Trebetherick. The hero, Standish, has
'yellow hair, blue eyes, yellow eyebrows and long tantalizing yellow lashes'
and sometimes paints his lips. When an official letter arrives for him, his
sister Emily ('who was always her brother's favourite since she was the most
boyish of his sisters yet a woman at the same time') asks him what it is.

> 'Well, I think I ought to tell you, Emily, that it is a warrant for my arrest for
> being detected in unnatural vice on the loop line between Westland Row
> and the Broadstone Station on the 21st of August 1932.'
>
> 'Then we had better send for a doctor at once, Standish: I will go and tell
> mother. Meanwhile, have some of Angela's prawns as I feel sure she will not
> want any more . . . '

The novella fragment ends with a scene which anticipates the end of
John's poem 'The Arrest of Oscar Wilde at the Cadogan Hotel' (first pub-

lished in the next year) – the arrival of two policemen to arrest Standish. ' "If only I could be sure that he was going away a Protestant," said Lady Guillamore between her tears.'

John continued to see much of the Longfords throughout the 1930s, both in Ireland and in London. The visits to Pakenham inspired some of his best poems and his most sustained piece of architectural research, into the life and work of Francis Johnston. And his weeks in the Irish heartland prepared him for his wartime service as press attaché to the British Representative in Dublin. They gave him an understanding of the Irish temper; some good names to drop; insights into the Irish theatre and Irish handicrafts; and a convenient bolt-hole in Westmeath when he needed respite from his duties. Christine Longford later wrote: 'If friends could be marked in arithmetic in a marking game, as we used to do in the evenings, I would mark John up as the greatest: he gave Edward the most and longest pleasure, either by his company or by letters and books for thirty years.'

Earlier in the summer of 1930, before the visit to Pakenham Hall, John had gone to Sezincote with Evelyn Waugh and Frank Pakenham for 'a delightful weekend'. It was there that he met Camilla Russell, daughter of Sir John Russell, known as Russell Pasha in Cairo, where he was head of the police. Her home was in Ghezireh, Cairo, but when in England she stayed with her great-aunt Gertrude Harris at Little Compton Manor, not far from Sezincote.

Camilla's friendship with John developed into a light-hearted romance. They wrote each other long letters, often using rebuses. ('I love you' was rendered as an eye, a dove with an 'l' substituted for the 'd', and a yew tree.) On 6 August 1930 John wrote to her from *The Architectural Review*: 'The more I see you the deeper my devotion to you becomes.' On 12 August he wrote, 'My hat I am cracked about you with those goo-goo eyes,' and added that he had written to Lady Harris that it was essential for Camilla to remain in England, 'not to go to Cairo there to lie on dromedaries & divans & be scolded [by her mother]'.

They became unofficially engaged. John wrote to Patrick Balfour on 18 August:

> I ought to tell you that I proposed marriage to a jolly girl last week and got accepted. It has left me rather dippy. It occurred at two in the morning. Suddenly two arms were raised from the floor and put round me, for I was sitting in a chair in an old world Tudor manor house [Little Compton Manor, by now restored] and then I was accepted and I kissed first the tip of the nose and then the neck and then the forehead and we took off our shoes in order to go upstairs quietly and we turned off the lights and stood

on the stone floor of the hall and suddenly the cool little hands were in mine and then a subtly unresisting body pressed against me and I kissed er [*sic*] full on the lips for the first time. Since then there have been other kisses. Patrick don't say anything about it because the parents are certain to object and with my reputation it would be very trying if it got about.

Balfour, whose profession was gossip, might just conceivably be relied upon to keep quiet, but others were already spreading the fascinating news. On 23 August John wrote to Camilla from Clandeboye: 'I find to my horror that John Sparrow knows I have fallen in love. But how? The Longfords & the Dugdales alone know the state of my affections & Maureen [Guinness, who had just married Basil Dufferin] guessed it to-day. They must be silenced. But if Sparrow knows the Dean knows & there's no silencing him . . .' And indeed Bowra already had the full story. 'Betjeman is said to be engaged to be married,' he wrote to Balfour on 23 August. 'She is called Camilla Russell, rather a crafty sort of tart, fond of practical jokes, water over the door, dogs in the bed, Eno's on the bacon. Very suitable for him so long as they don't marry.' Bowra also lost no time in telling Evelyn Waugh. Camilla, meanwhile, had confided in Mrs Dugdale, who was 'much amused at the marrying idea', Camilla reported to John.

When Camilla's mother, Lady Russell, got wind of the engagement, she did not find the prospect so entertaining. She took Camilla off to a house called Catball, not far from Little Compton, and forbade her to see John. 'This sudden blow', John wrote to Camilla, 'is no more than an incentive as far as I am concerned. Why the Ethel M. Dell are you not allowed to see who you like?' He suggested that Camilla should pick some deadly nightshade in the garden and put it in her mother's tea. In the couple's correspondence, the symbol for Lady Russell was a red nose – the nose which pried into their affairs.

It was not until the following August, of 1931, that John got round to sending his own mother the news that he was engaged to be married, without divulging Camilla Russell's name. Bess replied that she was not really surprised. 'I know the modern idea is that parents are the natural enemies of their progeny, but such is not the case with you and me, we are very closely allies.' She added an aggrieved postscript: 'My dear, I think you ought to tell *me* who the girl is, is it Mary Erskine or one of the Pakenham girls?' (Edward Longford and Frank Pakenham had four sisters, three of them unmarried.) John spent his summer holiday of 1931 in Ireland, staying first with Basil Dufferin at Clandeboye, then with the Longfords at Pakenham Hall.

Camilla, a talented artist, was planning to study at the Slade School of Art, London, with her cousin Karen Harris (the future Mrs Osbert Lancaster). John commissioned her to design a cover for his first poetry collection, *Mount Zion*, but her drawings were not used, probably at the insistence of Edward James. She had seen page-proofs, but not the finished book, by the time she left for Egypt in October. By then, it is clear, John's passion for her was waning. 'Try to see me if you can before you leave,' he wrote negligently on 2 October.

While Edward James was in America, John moved into 3 Culross Street, James's London house. He shared it with Randolph Churchill. 'You would certainly fall in love with him,' he wrote to Camilla, '– long hair, succulent lips & wide blue eyes – jungen style so popular in our more fashionable resorts.' He called Churchill 'the Mayfair Lady Killer'. Sir Osbert Lancaster said: 'You'd go round to 3 Culross Street and John would be shrieking with laughter while Randolph was on the telephone to some cabinet minister whose wife happened to be in bed with Randolph at the time.' When Camilla was about to return to Cairo for the winter of 1931–32, a *bon voyage* party was held for her in the house; the bill was footed by Peter Watson, a new friend of John's who had inherited millions from his father's dairy business. 'I went back to my parents in Cairo,' Camilla Sykes said, 'where I would be surrounded by very few girls and millions of young men. Betjeman wrote me a prayer, which was something like – "May God preserve me from cavalry officers and handsome Egyptians . . ."'

Back in August, when he was at Clandeboye, John had written to Camilla: 'I can't digest my food because in my plate I see your eyes & then when I look at a book I cannot concentrate because there they are again. You might blindfold yourself when I do see you or I shall go dippy.' And in early September, when she had several times kissed the margin of a letter, leaving red lipstick impressions, he had written: 'How I loved the red marks on your letter. They were a stroke of genius. It was almost as though you had come into the room & we had a passionate embrace.' But by late November there was a tepidity to his endearments which suggested that his heart was no longer in the affair. 'Darling, do pawn your blasted [?engagement] ring & come to Culross Street. I shall make no demands for I think you are more in love with love than with me, but I will do anything to help you because that woman [Lady Russell] is BLOODY AWFUL & will be your downfall. She has no right to have children.'

John had by now met Pamela Mitford and Penelope Chetwode, both of whom attracted him more than Camilla. And by early December, Camilla had met her future husband, in Cairo: 'A new man has arrived!!! Thrill!!

he is Christopher Sykes, friend of Robert Byron's, perhaps you know him? he seems quite nice though he had that same disconcerting stammer as Li [Lionel Perry] – *and* he rolled his eyes upwards at the same time just the same as Li!' But what really finished off the romance between John and Camilla was the discovery, by Russell Pasha, that John had sent her James Hanley's new novel *Boy*. Russell considered the picaresque life-at-sea book 'pornographic'. He forced Camilla to break off the engagement. It is unlikely that he would have reacted so strongly if a marquess or an earl had sent her the book. 'Later on,' Camilla Sykes recalled, 'when John was becoming well known, my mother said she would like to meet John again. But I refused to arrange it. I said, "You were poisonous to him when we were engaged. You can't just smile at him now and expect him to like you." ' The love affair fizzled out after the *Boy* episode. 'Partly because of opposition on all sides,' said Camilla, 'partly because I was very young and didn't know my own mind in those days, and I think John realized it. I was very frivolous – absolutely idiotic. I only thought about Paris clothes.'

On 10 January 1932, Edward James returned to London and John had to move out of Culross Street. There he had shared with Randolph Churchill the excitements of the 27 October General Election in which the National Government had beaten Labour, with a big Conservative majority; and there the copies of *Mount Zion* had been delivered in November and stacked in the hallway. As a temporary expedient, John now stayed in Peter Watson's house in South Street, London, while Watson was in Switzerland. Watson came back in March and in early April John moved to Jordans, the Quaker settlement near Beaconsfield, Buckinghamshire, where William Penn is buried.

At weekends he went away, as often as he could, to friends' houses in the country. One of his favourite retreats in 1931 and 1932 was Biddesden House, near Andover, the Queen Anne home of his Oxford friend Bryan Guinness, who had married Diana Mitford in 1929. At Biddesden, John met Pamela Mitford, Diana's sister, who was twenty-three in 1931. She lived in a flint-and-brick cottage on the estate. Guinness had asked her to manage the 350-acre farm with its fifty head of cattle. The farmhands called her 'Miss Pam', and it was not long before John was calling her 'Miss Pam' too. 'He was mad on kite-flying at the time,' Pamela (later Mrs Jackson) recalled. 'He used to bring his kite down for the weekend. I was in my cottage and on Sunday mornings he'd ring me up and say, "Is that you, Miss Pam?" "Oh, yes, it is." "Well, are you going to matins?" "Yes, I'm going to matins." So then we'd go off on bicycles to the little village church of Appleshaw, Hants.'

It was generally believed that John had become engaged to Pamela Mitford, though as Osbert Lancaster said, 'There is little doubt that her father, Lord Redesdale, would have regarded John as a "sewer".' Lady Chetwode, John's future mother-in-law, referred to the alleged engagement in a letter warning her daughter that John was fickle. But Pamela Jackson says that she never considered marrying John, though she now thinks he may have been in love with her for a while. 'He was essentially metropolitan, while I was rural,' she said. That is the word John used to describe her in a poem dated 1932:

SONG IN HONOUR OF
THE MITFORD GIRLS
BUT ESPECIALLY
IN HONOUR OF
MISS PAMELA

> The Mitford Girls! The Mitford Girls
> I love them for their sins
> The Young ones all like 'Cavalcade'
> The old like 'Maskelyns'.
>
> SOPHISTICATION Blessed dame
> Sure they have heard her call
> Yes even Gentle Pamela
> Most rural of them all.

John's romantic feelings for Pamela were at their height in February 1932, when he wrote to her sister Diana from the Salutation Hotel, Topsham, Devon: 'Alone in the cold Commercial Room, with a smelly & ancient dog looking at me & a child practicing [sic] scales next door, my thoughts are still with Miss Pam. I have been seeing whether a little absence makes the heart grow fonder and my God, it does.'

In 1932 John wrote to Nancy, whom he regarded as 'the warmest' of the sisters: 'If Pamela Mitford refuses me finally, *you* might marry me – I'm rich, handsome and aristocratic.' Nancy drew on John's character for the hero of her 1932 novel *Christmas Pudding*. Paul Fotheringay is an eccentric young man who flits from girl to girl. He has written a book which he intends to be serious but which all the reviewers and most of his friends think hilarious. He is a member of the Buchanite sect, founded by Mrs Elspeth Buchan, a Scottish prototype of Mrs Eddy and Mrs Besant. He earns £300 a year (exactly John's salary on *The Architectural Review*) as private tutor to an Etonian.

At the beginning of the story, Fotheringay is 'unofficially engaged' to

Marcella (Camilla), who dabbles in art and is going to the Slade. Later he proposes to Philadelphia (Pamela), but in the end he loses both women. Amabelle, a former call-girl who has been absorbed into the aristocracy, says of Paul and Philadelphia: 'He has far too weak a character to marry a girl of her sort. He needs something very hard-boiled.'

By the time she wrote those words, Nancy Mitford was well aware that John had fallen in love with Penelope Chetwode, a general's daughter, strong in body and in mind.

9

Steps to *Mount Zion*

⸻

B Y NOVEMBER 1928 Alan Pryce-Jones was working for *The London Mercury*. 'He and Mr Squire are great friends now,' the *Cherwell* reported on 3 November, 'and the London Mercury's getting ever so good.' This was John's entrée to 'the Squirearchy', the most powerful literary network of inter-war London. John Squire not only edited *The London Mercury* and until 1933 wrote regular reviews for *The Observer*; he knew everybody, and a word from him could set a young writer on the reviewing circuit or gain a publisher's sympathetic consideration of his first book. He was an adjudicator of the Hawthornden Prize. He persuaded Longman's to publish Thornton Wilder's *The Bridge of San Luis Rey* and Stella Gibbons's *Cold Comfort Farm*. He was a friend of the Prime Minister, Baldwin, who listened to his advice on Civil List pensions for writers. He even gave Paul Robeson advice on how to play Othello.

With an enthusiastic introduction from Alan Pryce-Jones, John received a warm welcome from Squire. In 1975 he wrote to John Jensen, who was writing a life of the Australian cartoonist Will Dyson, a friend of Squire's:

> Squire was a jewel of an editor to a literary adventurer like yours truly. He was always to be found during the week around noon at the bar of the Temple Bar Restaurant in the Strand below the office of the *London Mercury*. There he held his court . . . Squire liked people to read out their poems to him. He was generous, tolerant and without a trace of malice. The side of him which appealed to me was his passion for architecture, London architecture in particular.

John's first contribution to the *Mercury* (in December 1929) was a whimsical short story entitled 'Lord Mount Prospect'. A polished, if eccentric, performance, it owes much to the ghost stories of M. R. James and the novels of John Meade Falkner. It concerns a Society for the Discovery of Obscure Peers which attempts to track down the Irish peer Lord Mount Prospect. He is a member of the Ember Day Bryanites, 'that obscure sect founded by William Bryan, a tailor of Paternoster Row, and William

Reeve, a chandler in the city of Exeter . . . They believe in a bodily resurrection and the sleep of the soul. They declare that the sun is four miles
from the earth.' When the Society discovers Lord Mount Prospect, he is a
black-gowned skeleton lolling in the pulpit of his chapel. He has been
bodily resurrected with the Ember Day Bryanites.

'Death in Leamington' was published in the *Mercury* in May 1930;
'Dorset' (as 'Dorset Poem') in December 1932. John's next contribution was
a review in the issue of May 1933 which provoked an angry letter. The book
he reviewed was *A Pitman Looks at Oxford* by Roger Dataller, a miner from
the north who was a research fellow at Oxford from 1928 to 1931. John
criticized it with heavy irony. Commenting on a passage in which Dataller
records his failure to engage Dean Inge in conversation at a New College
luncheon party, John wrote: 'That is not the way to get on in Society, Mr
Dataller. Even the broadest-minded of us observe social conventions. The
Warden won't ask you again.' The point John was making here and throughout the review was that Oxford's failure to encourage Dataller was an indict-
ment of Oxford. Near the end of the review, he said so explicitly: 'his book
is the best condemnation of the University I have read.' But a New College
undergraduate, J. M. Bertram (a Rhodes Scholar from New Zealand), took
the review as literally as the authorities who put Daniel Defoe in the pillory
for *The Shortest Way with Dissenters* (1702) took that ironic pamphlet. He
wrote to John on 1 May 1933: 'Don't you think your review was quite as
class-conscious as Dataller's book? This, of course, won't worry you; but it
is pretty obvious. And I do think it was an unpleasant way to review a cour-
ageous book by a young man – a book with plenty of chinks where the
knowing could get a dig in; but would a generous critic have used them?'

A more serious article, simply headed 'Architecture', appeared in the
issue of November 1933. In it, John at his most punishing showed his
growing disenchantment with his work on *The Architectural Review*.

> I am fully aware that even the average reader of the LONDON MER-
> CURY will have passed over these boring looking pages on which I am
> about to spread myself. But I do not care, because years of unremunerative
> and heartbreaking work have brought me beyond caring . . . I remember
> recently a flannel bagged architect, wearing an arty tie, but possessing a
> shrewd business sense, saying to me between puffs at the foulest pipe I have
> ever been near, 'Well, it's through us that you get your living.' Apart from
> the fact that this truth is often the other way about, I felt obliged to burst
> out, 'Do you think it's any pleasure to me, to come round to offices and be
> patronized by art school students who crib Renaissance details and stuff
> them on to steel buildings? . . . Do you even realize that it is through people

like you that the word 'modern', connected with building, has become syn-
onymous with ugly . . . ?'

In May 1931 Edward James told John that he would like to finance the
publication of a book of his poems. John gave James a neatly written manuscript of each of the poems, in some cases adding written or sketched
suggestions for illustrations. James had already had a book of his own
poems published by the Curwen Press – *Twenty Sonnets to Mary* (1930). But
he decided to have John's book printed by the Westminster Press, then in
Henrietta Street, Covent Garden. He wrote to John on 11 May, before
taking the boat train *en route* for New York, to say that he had been round
to the Press and had discussed John's book with Mr Lowe, who was in
charge of the office. 'He is awfully slow on the uptake . . . but he is
infinitely well-meaning and obliging.'

The Westminster Press had undertaken to print the book in James's
absence, with the imprint 'The James Press' on the title-page. James had
explained to Lowe that for John's poems 'the type most suitable would be
a type in awfully bad taste – possibly an abortive Gothic'. But after
reflection he had realized that this would only be suitable for about 60 to
70 per cent of the poems. The remaining poems would be altogether
wrongly represented by such a type. 'For instance, "the bluish eyeballs of
my love" would look far better in graceful 18th or 19th century type.' He
had concluded that either the types must be varied from page to page,
'which would be extremely amusing if successfully carried out', or that
'one dull, sober, non-committal type' would have to be used throughout.
James had told Lowe to leave these matters to John's judgement, but not to
print the book without first sending James proofs in New York. James further suggested that the paper be fairly good and the cover nicely executed,
'so that while the book may present an epitome of everything that is the
worst taste in type and decoration, yet there be an underlying feeling that
the whole is well-produced. We must not allow the outside world one
moment to doubt the deep intensity of our sophistication.'

As we have seen, at the height of John's infatuation with Camilla Russell
he asked her to design a cover for the book. She sent it to him on 10
September, with a note: 'It somehow hasn't turned out quite what I meant
it to be like . . .' In the event, her design was not used. Instead, an old
engraving of a woman using a telephone was chosen – a joke on the book's
sub-title, 'In Touch with the Infinite'. Randolph Churchill corrected the
galley proofs. The book was published on 11 November 1931; copies were
stacked high in the hallway of 3 Culross Street. It was almost as eccentric a

production as James had proposed. While it was printed throughout in the same Victorian type, two different colours of paper were used inside ('God, how it smacks of Cecil Beaton!' John wrote to Camilla), and the cover was bound in paper obtained from Brock's, the firework manufacturers.

One of the first copies went to John's parents. Relations between John and his father had improved since 1930, partly because of John's steady job on *The Architectural Review*, but Ernest Betjemann could still be relied on for a candid opinion. In a letter of 15 November he took exception to a phrase in the book's dedication to Ethel Dugdale. Referring to Sezincote, John had written: 'Constantly under these minarets I have been raised from the deepest depression and spent the happiest days of my life.' Ernest thought the dedication 'would have lost nothing by the insertion of the two words "some of" before "happiest days" & would have been more complimentary to Mother & I'. Apart from that, he thought the book excellent: 'its chief charm is its obvious spontaneity'. But he added: 'Some of your verse reads a little hurried and loose & seems to want binding together a bit, & is not always sustained to the end . . . I feel all the time you can do much better. I expect that you feel the same.' He hoped John's royalties would soon equal those of Noël Coward (reported by the *Daily Mail* to be £40,000 a year) 'and then you can financially assist your parents . . .'.

Entranced with the novelty of being a published author, John sent out dozens of complimentary copies. Five years later, when he asked Edward James's permission to reprint some of the *Mount Zion* poems in the John Murray collection *Continual Dew*, James complained, from his suite in the Waldorf-Astoria, New York: 'Although the book is entirely sold out, I *lost* quite a lot of money on it – principally because you must have got a bit scared lest it wouldn't sell at first, and so, right at the beginning started by giving so many copies of it away free that there were *literally* only about 45 per cent of the copies left for me to sell. Now, ever since it has been out of print there have been so many demands for it that I could really have sold the whole of that first edition twice without giving any of the copies away.'

John wrote to Tom Driberg at the *Daily Express* on 10 November 1931: 'Here's the precious little work. I beg the favour of a notice. De Cronin Hastings did the drawings (many of them) . . .' *Mount Zion* was duly given a mention in Driberg's 'Talk of London' column on 12 November. Randolph Churchill did the book equally proud in the December issue of *The Architectural Review*: as John was assistant editor and Churchill was his friend and flat-mate, it was an outrageously partisan choice of reviewer.

Churchill wrote: 'If you like the genuine sublimation of the ridiculous you should read these poems. All the ugliness of the suburbs, all the vulgarity of human nature, are transmuted into golden beauty when touched upon by Mr Betjeman's pen.'

Alan Pryce-Jones's praise, in the December issue of *The London Mercury*, was more barbed.

'This precious, hyper-sophisticated book,' Mr Betjeman calls *Mount Zion* in his dedication, and thereby he disarms objection. For Mr Betjeman has invented a completely new attitude of mind, and therefore he cannot hope to escape objections . . .

The sophistication . . . is that the poems are deliberately not better. Whereas most poets, especially comic ones, polish their verses, Mr Betjeman unpolishes his so as to make them scratch more horribly on the reader. The ideal reader will be as tortured as the author, and as abruptly amused . . .

In 1932 John was too busy at *The Architectural Review* to contribute much to other periodicals. He was also writing his book *Ghastly Good Taste*. But through Gilbert Armitage, an Oxford contemporary, he submitted some poems 'grubbily written in pencil on torn bits of paper' to Geoffrey Grigson, who was preparing the first issue of the magazine *New Verse*, published in January 1933. One of the poems was 'The Arrest of Oscar Wilde at the Cadogan Hotel'. Grigson, whose taste was for bone-dry modernism, not for *fin de siècle* revival, rejected the poem as 'smart and frivolous'. This repulse, though it came in the form of a polite note, offended John so much, Grigson was told, that later, when John lived at Uffington, he stood on the backside of the White Horse above the Vale and 'gravely cursed' Grigson. The episode added Grigson ('Griggers') to John's demonology.

In May 1933 Randolph Churchill became assistant editor of the racy society magazine *Oxford and Cambridge*, which had been revived in that year after being founded in 1927 and going out of production in 1928. (This time it lasted until 1934.) On 18 May John sent Churchill two of his poems, with a story by Mary Erskine. Only one of the poems was published: the one Grigson had turned down. It appeared as 'The Arrest of Oscar Wilde' in the Summer Number (June 1933) with a full-page Art Deco illustration in colour by R. S. Sherriffs, showing the haggard Wilde being escorted from the Cadogan Hotel by two policemen.

A writer whose books are privately printed is usually one who cannot get his work published any other way. (Hence the term 'vanity publishing'.) This was not the case with John, and for his first prose work, *Ghastly Good Taste*, he was able to find a commercial publisher, Chapman & Hall, who had been Dickens's main publisher. John was a friend of one of the firm's editors, Eric Gillett, who had returned to the Squirearchy in 1932 after five years as an English literature professor in Singapore. It was Gillett who suggested the book's title.

Like *Mount Zion*, *Ghastly Good Taste* was given a presentation of Gothic eccentricity. When Anthony Blond said he would like to reprint the book, in the late 1960s, John re-read it, and was 'appalled by its sententiousness, arrogance and the sweeping generalizations in which it abounds'. The 'real point of the book', John thought in retrospect, was Peter Fleetwood-Hesketh's pull-out illustration of the 'Street of Taste, or the March of English Art down the Ages', with traffic to match each phase of the debasement of architecture. The pull-out 'was also an old-fashioned thing to do, and the style of architectural caricature was deliberately based on Pugin's caricatures in his book *Contrasts* (1836). This pull-out was what caused people to buy the book, and looking back at it, I regard it as far less modish and much more balanced than the rest.'

John had met Fleetwood-Hesketh through John Summerson. It was delightful for him to find somebody of his own age who not only shared his architectural interests but could speak of some of the great houses of England with an insider's knowledge. Peter Hesketh was equally charmed by John. 'He was very *simpatisch*; seemed to be amused by one's jokes and made some very good ones himself. And the interests we had in common weren't shared by many other people in those days. Architecture was then a very obscure subject.'

The reviews of *Ghastly Good Taste* were generally complimentary, though several of the reviewers, understandably, remained puzzled as to what John's own taste in architecture might be. 'Can it be', asked 'Ribax', 'that he dislikes anything and everything admired by other people?' As with *Mount Zion*, John managed to recruit a small claque of his friends to review the book in magazines where he had some influence. 'This is an important little book,' wrote Frederick Etchells in *The Listener* of 30 August, 'written with a disarming candour and a certain Puckishness which is attractive. But more than this, it deals in a fearless and simple way with questions which affect all of us and which are certain to do so still more as time goes on.' The prospective reader was not to be misled by the amusing title and cover into thinking the book an essay in playfulness, 'for behind Mr Betjeman's wit and fancy there lies a fund of common sense'.

Osbert Burdett, a fringe figure of both the Squirearchy and Bloomsbury who was on dining terms with John, reviewed the book not only for *The London Mercury* in September, but also for *The Architectural Review* in

October – a breach of critical ethics. Both reviews were eulogies. Perhaps for the sake of form, as John was still on the staff, the notice in *The Architectural Review* was toned down slightly with a few hints of adverse criticism. But the *Mercury* review was a straight 'rave', the kind any young writer would be happy to quote on the back jacket of a second edition.

> It is astonishing how mellow the mind of this young author seems to be . . .
> His pages appeal to tastes so various that I cannot conceive any type of discriminating reader who will not enjoy this book. It is a book to read, to master, to keep, to give to one's friends, and it shows so much talent that, remembering how disappointing precocity quickly rewarded has often proved, if this receives the success that it deserves I shall tremble for his literary future.

10

Marriage

J OHN BETJEMAN WAS fascinated by people's full Christian names and used them promiscuously. 'Nobody ever called me "John Edward" before he did; but then it caught on among all my friends,' John Edward Bowle complained. In the foreword to *Summoned by Bells* John wrote: 'The author . . . is particularly grateful to his friends John Hanbury Angus Sparrow and Thomas Edward Neil Driberg for going through the manuscript and proofs . . .'

Possibly the habit stemmed from early reading of William Brighty Rands ('Godfrey Gordon Gustavus Gore . . . / Was a boy who never would shut a door'). Or perhaps it was compensation for a resentment that his parents had given him only one Christian name, and that the commonest in England. Or it may have been a kind of 'sympathetic magic': knowing a person's full name – or his school – gave one an obscure power over him, like possessing a swatch of an enemy's hair.

When John was admitted to *Who's Who* in 1940 (giving as his hobby 'dirt track racing') he listed all three Christian names of his wife, the daughter of Field Marshal Sir Philip Chetwode. Her first name was Penelope, though she was the reverse of Ulysses' Penelope: it was John who stayed at home while Penelope travelled the world. Her second name was Valentine, because she was born on that saint's day, 14 February, in 1910. Her third name (her mother's second) was Hester: Penelope was to have much in common with Lady Hester Stanhope, whom A. W. Kinglake described, in *Eothen*, as 'cool, decisive in manner . . . full of audacious fun, and saying the downright things that the sheepish society around her is afraid to utter'.

Penelope Chetwode was not a serene *Tatler* beauty, like Camilla Russell. She was shortish and coltish. Later, John unkindly referred to her legs as 'Mr and Mrs Broadwood'; but she was proud of her full breasts; Lady Rachel Billington remembers her, in 1977, posing jut-chested in front of a voluptuous Indian statue of the goddess Durga in New Delhi and exclaiming: 'Look! *Just* like mine!' Penelope wore her hair in a Shetland pony fringe. Her eyes had the curious property of looking cold but conveying warmth. Her nose was '*retroussé*', 'button' or 'snub' according to the sympathy of the beholder. Her mouth had a natural droop which wrongly suggested sulkiness. Her voice was irresistibly imitable. At times of pitched emotion, it had an almost ventriloquial timbre, like that of a Punch-and-Judy man using his swazzle. Though she had picked up some cockneyisms ('Right you are' was her most frequent remark on the telephone) and in later years was prepared to muck along with drugged vagabonds on the hippie trail in India, she never forgot, or never escaped, her patrician caste. She could replicate, when it was needed, her mother's freezing stare, or quell a dissenting friend with the tally-ho tones of the hunting shires.

When John met her, in 1931, Penelope had a reputation as one of the more truculent debutantes of her year. Like her contemporary and friend Lady Mary Pakenham, who satirized 'the Season' in her 1938 book *Brought Up and Brought Out*, she rebelled against the vapid round of dances and parties where eligible young women were put on show, lightly chaperoned and heavily decked out in their mother's jewellery, in the hope that they would attract some eligible young men. Acceptably, she was interested in horses and loved riding; less acceptably, she was clever. She had already made herself as good a judge of Indian temple sculptures as of horseflesh. The writhings of Krishna and Kali were as intently studied and analysed as the Lippizaner curvetting of Moti, her Arab horse.

But though some might regard her as too brainy – a bluestocking in a riding boot, as it were – she was an attractive girl, and to the arbiters of 'society' she was 'eligible'. The Chetwode family had been established in Staffordshire from at least the fifteenth century, and had held a baronetcy since 1700. Penelope's father, who was gazetted field-marshal in 1933, the year she and John were married, was Commander-in-Chief of the Army in India. His service record was that of a *Boy's Own Paper* hero. By the outbreak of the First World War he was a brigadier-general, and he was the first British officer to be mentioned in dispatches in that war. The action which made him a national hero took place on John Betjeman's eighth birthday, 28 August 1914. Under his command the 5th British Cavalry Brigade engaged the German Cavalry in the Battle of Moy, in which the 12th Lancers and the Royal Scots Greys routed the enemy. 'We went through the Uhlans* like brown paper,' Chetwode told *The Times*.

Photographs of Chetwode's rather set, intense face now appeared frequently in the press. They were often accompanied by portraits of his

---

*The Preussisches Ulanen Regiment, a crack cavalry regiment.

elegantly dressed wife. In 1899 he had married Alice Hester Camilla, daughter of Colonel the Hon. Richard Stapleton-Cotton, a son of Lord Combermere. Their only son Roger was sent to Eton (where his great friend was Frank Pakenham) and to Oxford; and Penelope, their only daughter, went to Queen's College, London, and to St Margaret's, Bushey, Hertfordshire, a fashionable girls' school. Lord Vivian's daughter Daphne – later Marchioness of Bath – wrote: 'The shape of Penelope Chetwoode [*sic*], the shrill whine of her schoolgirl voice, highlights my short career at Queen's College. Whenever I see her now I feel she should still be in a gym-tunic . . .' At St Margaret's, Penelope's best friends were her cousin Audrey Talbot, daughter of Lord Ingestre, and Silvia Coke (afterwards Lady Silvia Combe), daughter of Lord Coke, later Earl of Leicester. Another early friend was the comedienne Joyce Grenfell, who was in the Brownies with Penelope – acutely observing the idiosyncrasies of Brown Owl for future skits – and joined the Girl Guides on the same day in 1921. To her, Penelope seemed at that time somewhat affected: 'She had a tremendous drawl and she was so lazy that when she saluted, instead of bringing her two fingers up to her head, she drooped her head down to her hand.'

Penelope was not affected. Affectation is the grafting on to one's natural character, appearance or accent assumed traits designed to impress. She never did that. She was brought up to talk in a certain way by her parents and her expensive schools: it would have been affectation in her to speak with a different accent. She moved in the grandest society: when her father had the Aldershot command (1923–7) the King sometimes came to luncheon or dinner and Penelope had to help entertain him. The Chetwodes often spent weekends with the royal family. After Sir Philip became Commander-in-Chief in India (1930), Penelope herself lived the life of a princess, with luxurious quarters, a Christian *ayah*, and a limousine always at her service.

Visits by friends from England made welcome breaks in the social routine. Basil Dufferin and his bride, Maureen Guinness, stayed with the Chetwodes for six weeks on their honeymoon in 1931. Another friend of John's who visited the Chetwodes in India was Robert Byron, who went out in 1929 to research the special issue of *The Architectural Review* devoted to New Delhi which was published in January 1931 to mark the Indian Round Table Conference in London. Byron was the first young man Penelope had met who understood and shared her passion for Indian architecture. There was vague talk of their getting married – which she flirtatiously passed on to him – though in many ways they could not have been more unlike, and in any case Byron was homosexual.

It was through Robert Byron that Penelope met John. In 1931 she had completed an article on the cave temples of Ellora in the Deccan. She showed it to Byron, who suggested she should take it to de Cronin Hastings at *The Architectural Review*. With his usual disinclination to see 'new people', Hastings refused to meet Penelope and she was shown into John's office instead. John was in the middle of a long telephone conversation with Pamela Mitford, but eventually Penelope was able to show him her article. 'We both got down on the floor on our hands and knees and I showed him all the photographs I had taken of Ellora,' she remembered. 'He wasn't the least bit interested in Indian art. Anyway, the long and short of it was that he did publish it, and that's how we met. And I was suddenly very attracted to him and started falling for him.' Penelope's article, 'The Paradise of Siva', appeared in the issue of October 1932.

By September 1932, Penelope and John were already writing to each other in the mock Irish brogue, interlarded with English passages in Greek characters, that they were to use for even the most serious correspondence for the rest of John's life. His nicknames for her were 'Ugly' (οογλι), 'Filth' (φιλθ) and 'Beastliness' (βεαστλινεοs), and she frequently signed letters or postcards with one of these sobriquets. She was just as playfully offensive about John, addressing him as 'Dung' (Δυγγ or Δοογγ) or 'Poofy' (ποοφy), short for 'Puffball', a fungus supposed to resemble his already balding head. (Unfortunately none of John's love-letters to Penelope has survived, because Lady Chetwode had advised her daughter always to destroy love-letters addressed to her – which advice she took.) Lady Longford, who had married Frank Pakenham in 1931, recalls that when Penelope visited their home, Stairways, near Aylesbury, Buckinghamshire, shortly after she had met John, and was asked what it was that she liked about him, she replied, 'He has green teeth.' When staying with her great-uncle, Lord Methuen, at Corsham Court early in 1933, Penelope wrote to John:

> You are a silly little boy to go on as you do about me not lovin you. You seem to have complexes about yourself and what-not. You certainly do smell very bad & are as yellow as a quattrocento Florentine, & you have earwigs in your nose which would revolt many people, but you must surely know by now that these defects only serve to enhance your charms in my sight, you στινχιν γελλοω τρεασυρε [stinkin yellow treasure].

James Richards, who joined *The Architectural Review* in 1933, remembered that 'Betjeman was at this time courting Penelope Chetwode, their courtship being conducted, or so it seemed to us, through exchanges of badinage between John, leaning out of his office window, and Penelope standing in the street below calling up in her penetrating upper-class cockney voice.' Penelope began asking John to her home in St John's Wood, London. The Chetwodes lived in the house in Grove End Road which had once belonged to Sir Lawrence Alma-Tadema, the painter of Grecian and Roman scenes. John called the house 'Tadema Towers'.

To the Field Marshal and Lady Chetwode, he was not a welcome suitor. He was a journalist and had neither land nor capital. He usually looked rather scruffy; though he possessed a few expensive suits, they were lacking in trouser creases. 'We ask people like that to our houses,' Lady Chetwode told Penelope, 'but we don't marry them.' The Chetwodes wanted for their only daughter a lord, an eldest son or at the very least 'somebody with a pheasant shoot', as Penelope later put it.

Parental opposition was not the only obstacle to a romance between John and Penelope. She was 'sort of unofficially engaged' to the artist John Spencer-Churchill, Winston Churchill's nephew. Johnnie Churchill had matinée-idol good looks and came from the kind of family Sir Philip and Lady Chetwode approved of; but the path of true love did not run smooth for him and Penelope. 'They quarrelled like Kilkenny cats,' said Osbert Lancaster.

Penelope's love-life was further complicated by an attachment she had formed in India. 'I was madly in love with Sir John Marshall, who was director-general of archaeology in India. He had been taken out by Lord Curzon in the early years of the century to organize the archaeology. He was a very distinguished scholar and he was, I'm afraid, rather one with the girls. Very good-looking.' Penelope had fallen in love with him in 1931 in the one summer she spent in Simla, and later he had come to England and asked her to go off with him and live on a Greek island. Marshall was fifty-five and Penelope was twenty-one.

Then she found herself falling in love with John Betjeman. 'So at that time I was really in love with three Johns, and didn't know which one I wanted to marry. Thank God I settled against Sir John Marshall, because I realized afterwards it is a terrible thing to break up a marriage with two children, I wouldn't have done it for the world.' Her ardour for Johnnie Churchill was cooling. 'He was very very fascinating and attractive, but I realized he wouldn't be an easy person to marry.'[*]

---

[*]See John Spencer Churchill, *Crowded Canvas*, London 1961, pp. 63–4, 80 and 82–5, for Churchill's own account of his romance with Penelope (whom he calls Sophie – 'to spare her blushes'). At one stage he pursued her across Europe wearing a false moustache to outwit her chaperone.

Penelope's feelings for John were intensified when he took her to Kew Gardens one day and they made daisy chains together. Her final choice between her three suitors was literally dramatic. She went with Johnnie Churchill to a performance of *The Merchant of Venice*. 'There are about twenty-two scenes in it. [In fact, there are twenty.] Each scene I decided on marrying a different John. And in the last scene of all I decided on John Betjeman. So then I stuck to that.' Penelope's choice mimicked that of Bassanio, who rejected the gold and silver caskets and chose the lead one. She declined the archaeological knight and the artistic scion of a ducal family, and chose the penniless poet.

John had already decided that Penelope was the girl for him. She was not quite the overpowering amazon of his poems, but she had the dominant quality that appealed to him:

> She stands in strong, athletic pose
> And wrinkles her *retroussé* nose.
> Is it distaste that makes her frown,
> So furious and freckled, down
> On an unhealthy worm like me?
> Or am I what she likes to see?
> I do not know, though much I care.
> εἴθε γενοίμην . . . would I were
> (Forgive me, shade of Rupert Brooke)
> An object fit to claim her look.

John had fantasies of submitting to masterful women. Once, when visiting the Tate Gallery with John Guest, he indicated a strapping woman on the other side of the room and sighed, 'Oh I say, wouldn't you like to be pushed in a pram by her round Hyde Park?' Penelope satisfied John's need to be dominated.

When Penelope told her parents that she wanted to marry John, they were predictably upset. However, they decided they must make an attempt to get to know John better, and invited him to a white-tie dinner at the Savoy. 'John went to amazing pains to get a made-up tie sewn on elastic,' said Osbert Lancaster. In those days, only waiters wore such ties. 'Throughout dinner he plucked the bow forward six or seven inches and let it snap back – purely to annoy his future mother-in-law.'

After this unpromising encounter, the Chetwodes insisted that Penelope should go back to India with them. When she complied, she was once again in the dangerous ambit of Sir John Marshall. But it was John who first proved fickle. He wrote and told her that he was engaged to one of her best friends, Wilhelmine Cresswell – 'Billa', who later married (Sir) Roy Harrod.

Penelope had known Billa since both were children. Billa's father was killed in the First World War, but her stepfather was a general at Aldershot when Chetwode was commanding there. 'I was absolutely furious and I wrote and told John where he got off,' Penelope recalled. 'Then he broke off the engagement with Billa and she said it would never have worked.'

In spite of this contretemps, the two were on good terms again by the time Penelope made the homeward journey in April 1933, stopping off to visit Greece with her mother. Penelope was not looking forward to this stop-over. 'H.L. [Her Ladyship = Lady Chetwode] is terribly difficult to sightsee with as you feel all the time that she's bored and wants to go to the cinema. As you know, I like sightseeing in a very pedantic and systematic way, especially places which I probably shan't see again, so it is all extremely trying and I wish to God we were cutting out Greece & coming straight home. But darlin you won't lose your temper & run off with another girl in those 10 days will you? Please please don't because I should go off my head. I love you so much . . .' Evidently the lesson of the Billa Cresswell episode had been taken to heart.

Penelope arrived home on 19 April to a rapturous welcome from John. Her father wrote from Simla on 14 May:

> Dearest Penelope,
>
> I have just got your letter of May 4th in which you say you have made up your mind to marry John Betjeman. I cannot pretend to be pleased, but you are a grown woman with more than the usual share of brains, and if after all this time you have had for reflection you are not certain of your feelings you never will be.
>
> I have told you the risks you are running and it is useless to repeat every-thing I have said or written – I love you more than I can say & hope & pray you may have chosen right, & that you will be happy.
>
> . . . Bless you darling.
>
> Your own daddy,
>
>   Philip W. Chetwode

But, when her father came home in June, Penelope changed her mind about marrying John. The reason she gave John was that she could not bear to sink herself in married domesticity before she had fully developed her mind. She wanted to become an Indologist and study with the archaeologist Giuseppe Tucci at the University of Rome. John and his friends thought that this was merely an excuse and that Penelope had given in to the objections of her strong-willed parents. On Sir Philip's return to England, John had written to him (6 June) formally asking for the hand of his daughter in marriage. On 8 June the Field Marshal replied that he could only reiterate that if the marriage to Penelope took place, it was against his desire and his advice to her – 'I cannot conceive that you can support her properly on the income you have or will have between you.'

Penelope was full of guilt and perplexity. So she went to the most worldly-wise man she knew, her mother's youngest brother Colonel Robert Stapleton-Cotton, 'Uncle Bertie'. He had been the black sheep of the family, but had made good: banished to South Africa at fifteen for getting a housemaid with child, he had made a fortune in gold-mining. Uncle Bertie saw that Penelope needed time to work things out, away from John and away from parental pressure. He paid for her to travel to France by train and stay with his sister Polly at Opio, near Grasse, Alpes Maritimes. Penelope had stayed there before with her parents and was fond of Polly. 'She was absolutely divine, a maiden aunt, and we all adored her.'

John was distraught. Penelope wrote to him on 14 June, admitting that it was 'useless' to say sorry: 'That I should make you suffer so terribly is unforgiveable [sic].' John saw that Ernest Betjemann had to be told of Penelope's action – if for no other reason, because of the financial arrangements he had been trying to negotiate with Sir Philip Chetwode. On 14 June Ernest wrote his son as sympathetic a letter as he ever sent him. He hoped John was not 'cut up'. He thought the break was all for the best – 'you know my opinion of military brass-hats and the family seemed to me to look upon their daughter's marriage too much from the cash point of view'.

John meanwhile had taken refuge with Pamela Mitford at Biddesden. All the Mitfords were full of sympathy for him and indignation over Penelope's behaviour. On 18 June, Bryan Guinness (who was still married to Diana Mitford, though the next year was to bring divorce) wrote Penelope a stern letter:

> John is a very great person. He is eccentric and needs looking after: but he has a genius of a very unusual kind . . . Such a person, endowed as he is for your service, with great emotional capacity, is not lightly to be cast on one side because your parents were not at the same public school as his. If you are ever to live a life of your own unhedged by the false barriers of snobbery you must stand fast . . . I can't bear to see John so unhappy – that is why I have been so impertinent as to write . . .

Penelope had probably not received this letter by the time she wrote to John on 22 June – the day *Ghastly Good Taste* was published. Over several pages she tried to explain her behaviour, stressing that 'when you used to say over & over again "I hate it abroad" & "you mustn't marry me if you can't do this or won't do that", I suddenly got terrified & thought that p'raps it was wrong, that p'raps your friends were right last winter when they told you we were both "positives" & could never fit in'. She concluded: 'My darlin darlin . . . I am so sorry, Oh God I am sorry – but can't we work it? Because we love, we love . . .'

This letter, with its mention of uncontrollable weeping, indigestion and insomnia, suggests that Penelope had suffered a minor nervous breakdown, caused far more by the conflict of loyalties between her parents and John than by that between married domesticity and the continuance of her studies. References to 'that Inn in Essex', of physical compatibility and of a subterfuge that was to be practised on her parents hint that John and Penelope had spent some nights together; and this is confirmed by her next letter from Opio:

> The actual facts of the case are as follows: we both love each other very very much, with a love that (should we part) will never come to either of us again, the φγσιχαλ στοοφ [physical stoof] is ideal & although it's of only secondary importance it is a thing which only comes once in a lifetime as perfectly as it has to us (I believe extremely few women get complete physical satisfaction from any man); we'll have enough money to live fairly comfortably, but, owing to capricious circumstances we each have very strong interests at opposite ends of the world. It's out of the question for you to give up yours (we'd have no money if you did!) & I'm too weak & SELFISH (that's what it comes to) to give up mine. *Can we effect a compromise?*

In the same letter, Penelope said that her plan was either to marry soon, secretly, or to live with John on and off for the next two or three years, at the end of which she would have the necessary knowledge to work on her own. If they were to marry soon, it would have to be secretly, or her allowance from her parents would be cut off and she would be unable to go to Rome. In his reply, John evidently insisted that they should marry rather than 'live in sin'. In her next letter, of 25 June, Penelope agreed, adding that John's suggestion of their living in Dorset did not appeal to her because she would get 'completely out of touch with all my Injun things'. She herself would prefer Ireland to anywhere, because it was so quiet and restful and ideal for work, '& also the people are so free & easy & independent . . .'. Much of the letter (even down to the living in Ireland) is an all too prescient forecast of their marriage, and of some of the reasons for its eventual breakdown:

> Our love has had wonderful moments, moments (minutes, hours sometimes) as you say, of complete understanding, but it's been terribly tempestuous & at times unhappy. Great love is of this nature I suppose. And our love has been great & passionate (& will continue to be so if we marry) but hardly calm & domestic. When you first saw me you said 'One shouldn't

John's father, Ernest Betjemann
(1872–1934)

John's mother, Mabel Bessie Betjeman(n),
née Dawson (1878–1952)

Even as a small child, John showed the
dramatic talent which was later so evident
in his television programmes

As an only child with few friends, John
made a confidant and companion of his
teddy bear Archibald, who survived into
patched old age

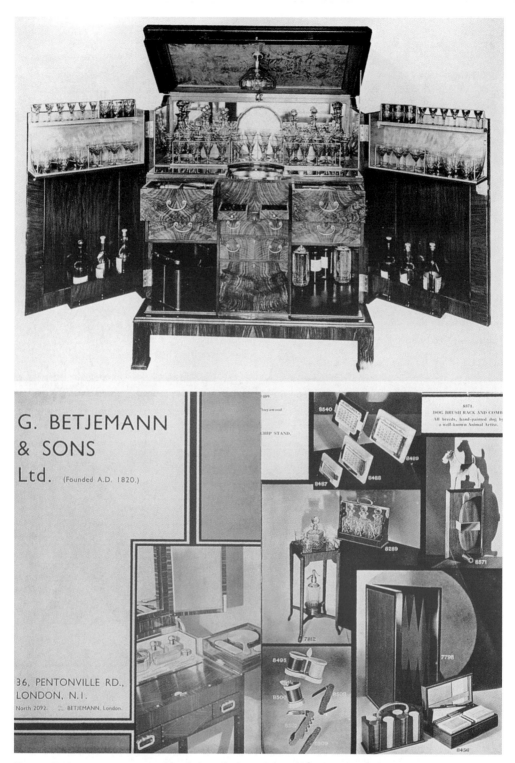

Ernest Betjemann was considered the Chippendale of his day. In the 1920s, G. Betjemann & Sons (founded 1820) became prosperous by making cocktail cabinets and dressing tables for Asprey's. Ernest hoped John would join the firm as 'the fourth generation', but John showed no interest in cabinetmaking

John and his mother: a studio photograph taken in
Kentish Town Road, London, about 1910

John about 1925, the year he went up to Magdalen

OXFORD FRIENDS

John Edward Bowle, historian

Lord Clonmore (later Earl of Wicklow)

Lionel Perry

Pierce Synnott

John, in a Magdalen College blazer, as an assistant master at Thorpe House School, Gerrard's Cross, in 1928

John at Little Compton, the home of Camilla Russell

John in 1931: a photograph by Camilla Russell

John at Dumbleton, Gloucestershire (the home of Sir Bolton Monsell), in 1933

Lady Mary St Clair-Erskine (later Lady Mary Dunn). John proposed to her unsuccessfully in the winter of 1929–30

Camilla Russell, 1931. Her engagement to John was broken off when he sent her an allegedly 'pornographic' book

Pamela Mitford and her motor car in Ludgershall. John, who was much attracted to her, called her 'Miss Pam', which was what the cowmen on Bryan Guinness's farm called her

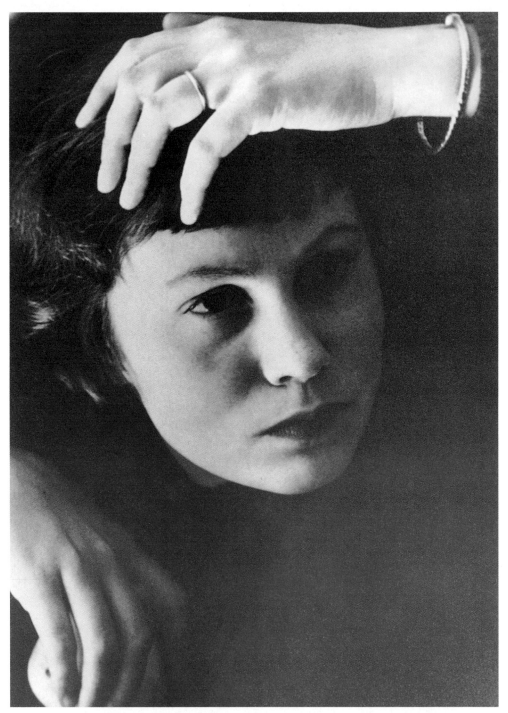

Penelope Chetwode: a photograph taken by the Hungarian designer L. Moholy-Nagy in 1933 after Penelope's clandestine marriage to John

marry for love as much as for friendship.' Well we are tremendous friends but do we fit in quite harmoniously enough for our love to turn domestic and calm?

Lady Chetwode was meanwhile writing long hectoring letters both to Penelope and to Polly, who left hers lying around for Penelope to read because she thought they were so funny. Penelope reported their contents to John, representing her mother's comments as a big joke. But inevitably some of the darts went at least halfway home. She commented on the extracts: 'I dare say you did say you meant to go out as much as possible & I know you were annoyed when I first wrote & suggested marrying in a few years, but when it comes to being engaged 5 *times* (actually it's only once besides me isn't it? & then only for 2 days to Billa!) & saying you take everything as a joke & have no depth of feeling it really makes one's blood boil.'

It was Nancy Mitford who goaded John into the action which won Penelope back. She said to him: 'Well, *go after her and get her*, don't just let it go like that. You must go out to the south of France and win her back.' And he did so, even though, as Penelope was so well aware, he hated 'abroad'. (He had received the same advice from P. Morton Shand, his *Architectural Review* friend.) Penelope recalled:

> He came out on the Blue Train and suddenly turned up at my aunt's house. My aunt didn't quite know what to do . . . I was in a way pleased that he'd come out and in a way upset. But then he was so insistent . . . And I said, 'All right, I will marry you, but I do want to get my qualifications first: then I'll be able to go on with a career after I'm married.' And he said, yes, I could do all that, it was perfectly all right.

John returned to England on 5 July, taking with him a piece of string which had been tied round Penelope's finger as measurement for a ring. Apparently the two had had a tiff just before he left, for she wrote to him the next day: 'You know I wasn't really angry with you or loved you less because of your tantrum. I just thought you a very silly little boy. Perhaps one day you will grow out of those tantrums.' Her two days in Opio with John, she wrote, had been 'bliss'. 'I know that it's inevitable we should marry, & I swear not to let you down.' She was sure that once they were married it would be easy for them to see each other, 'but we MUST keep it all secret for the next year or two' so that she would not lose her £250 a year allowance from her parents.

In her elation, Penelope wrote John another letter later in the day. Before she had gone to bed the previous night, she told him, she had walked into the garden and stood where she and John had stood. 'The moon was nearly full & the fireflies was fillin the olives with dancing lights.' And she had thought to herself: 'No I am too young to think of giving up love just yet' and had thanked God for bringing John back to her. She expected to be back in London on 19 July.

By 13 July the date of the marriage had been fixed: 29 July. The place was to be Edmonton Register Office – because Edmonton was sufficiently remote, and because it was near Heddon Court, where John was temporarily lodging with John Humphrey Hope. Penelope had her wisdom teeth out on 21 July. She recovered quickly, and the wedding took place on the 29th, with Isabel Hope and H. de C. Hastings (for once, not elusive) as witnesses. Under 'Rank or profession of father', John entered 'Art Manufacturer'. Penelope wrote: 'Baronet. Field Marshal. Army Commander in Chief'.

Ernest and Bess Betjemann attended the ceremony. Ernest's views on 'brass-hats' and his resentment about the slights to which his son might be exposed were no doubt counterbalanced by relief that he himself would not now be expected to haggle over a legal contract with the Field Marshal's solicitors; elopement has its own etiquette. Perhaps, too, the Betjemanns were pleased that at last, after all his romantic tergiversations, John was showing himself ready to 'settle down'.

John, with his love of Cowper, must have been put in mind of John Gilpin:

> Said John, it is my wedding-day,
> And all the world would stare,
> If wife should dine at Edmonton,
> And I should dine at Ware.

Instead of the grand reception John would have liked, there was roast beef and Yorkshire pudding with a few friends at the Great Eastern Hotel, by Liverpool Street Station. Not that the Great Eastern Hotel was a place lacking in romance for John. As Max Beerbohm said of Oxford, the very name was fraught for him with the most actual magic. The Great Eastern was and remained John's favourite London hotel, even though it was the Charing Cross Hotel which in 1978 honoured him by renaming its opulent Victorian dining-room after him.

As they had planned, the couple spent a few days in the Essex inn; their main honeymoon was to be a bicycle tour of East Anglian churches in September. Then Penelope went back to live with her parents – 'because, for all they knew, I wasn't married'. In the weeks that followed, John and Penelope played mouse and cat with the Chetwodes, arranging clandestine meetings when they could. A letter dated 24 August shows that Penelope was beginning to take John in hand:

> Mr Tennant (proprietor of Innes) has found a wonderful tailor in Bond St., a retired army officer who 'knows what a gentleman wants'. He is called Major Daniel Ltd. & makes suits of the best cloth for 8 guineas, his only stipulation being that you pay on the nail. That's an improvement on your £14 tailor, isn't it? . . . Is your light brown suit nice now it's been cleaned? And promise to ask Mrs Munn to take that *Revolting* blue one to Selfridge's please.

In a further letter, she returned to the subject of her studies abroad. She had decided that if, as was likely, Giuseppe Tucci – 'my Italian professor' – did not come back to Rome until Christmas, she would go to Germany for two months, 'as I have to learn German sometime & the only way to do it quickly is to go to the country'. Three-quarters of the books on Indian art and religion were in German and had not been translated, '& even if no more are written in future owing to the Nazis I've got to read some of the already existing ones.'

The newly wed pair stayed briefly with John Humphrey Hope, who had just sold Heddon Court as building land. He had joined the remnants of the school with Horton School at Ickwell Bury in Bedfordshire, and had settled with his wife and their daughter Ann in a cottage near by. Ann, who by now was eight, remembers the Betjemans' visit as by no means all billing and cooing:

> My mother told me that John Betjeman had eloped with Penelope and they were hiding with my parents to escape the wrath of her father. I have a vivid memory of JB pouring a full watering-can of water down the back of Penelope's neck, and she screamed and he screamed and they shouted at length and they threw things. So this, I noted, is how newly-married couples behave. The next village was Old Warden, about two miles from the cottage. JB had used letters from Old Warden in *Ghastly Good Taste* without knowing, or even bothering to check, whether the place really existed. I remember going to Old Warden church with JB and my parents. Screams of laughter – why, look, the place actually exists, and what a coincidence, with us living now so near.

When the couple returned to London, Penelope learned that her parents would be going back to India in late September. 'Then I thought, I must tell them about our marriage before they go back. I had the most terrible guilt about it. And I did tell them, and of course it was the most terrible shock. They were very upset. I had been going to Angkor Wat and all sorts of marvellous places that autumn, but of course I'd married so I couldn't.' A story went the rounds about how Penelope had broken the news to her parents. It suggested that she had waited until they were all three being ushered into a reception at Buckingham Palace. When the flunkey announced: 'Miss Penelope Chetwode', she squawked: 'No, I'm Mrs John Betjeman!' (Lady Betjeman said this was not true: 'I told my mother in her sitting-room at "Tadema Towers".')

On 27 September the news was at last made public, in the *Daily Telegraph*: 'SIR P. CHETWODE'S DAUGHTER. MARRIED AFTER BROKEN ENGAGEMENT'. Penelope's aunt, Lady Birch, had given the paper the story. 'My niece and Mr John Betjeman became engaged quite a long time ago, but the engagement was later broken off,' she told the reporter. 'This wedding was a complete surprise to all her relatives. Not even her parents knew anything about this marriage until after it was over. It took place very quietly indeed on July 29.' Lady Birch dismissively described John as 'the author of a volume of burlesque poems'. Nancy Mitford wrote to Mark Ogilvie-Grant on 3 October: 'Betjeman was married to Filth in July and announced it three days ago. They intend to live apart permanently – so wise.'

In fact, Penelope and John had set up house together – 'a really slummy sort of existence', as Penelope later described it. First they rented a small flat, one room and a kitchenette in Museum Street, London, by the British Museum. John was still on *The Architectural Review* earning £300 a year, and Penelope's marriage settlement had not yet been agreed. They then moved to what she considered a worse flat, near her parents' home in Grove End Road.

In October, Penelope went to Germany. She had intended to stay there for six months, 'but after three John was making a fuss and wanted me to come back'. He told her that Christian Barman, the nominal editor of *The Architectural Review*, who lived in Uffington, Berkshire, had found them a farmhouse there at £36 a year rent. By the time Penelope returned from Germany, the Chetwodes had decided to make the best of a bad job. Lady Chetwode, so implacable before the marriage, was the first to give in: she was more of an opportunist than Sir Philip, the rigid military disciplinarian. Within a few months of the wedding, Osbert Lancaster went round to the Chetwodes' house in St John's Wood. He had to wait a while for John to come downstairs. He looked for a clock, but all the clocks were wrong. 'Oh yes,' Lady Chetwode said, 'we've had to stop all the clocks in the house. The ticking keeps dear John awake.' Lancaster thought that she and John 'got on very well afterwards: she was an extremely intelligent woman, though utterly ruthless. John, also, finally got on quite well with the old Field Marshal. Chetwode was always saying, "Tell me, John, I don't drop me 'g's', do I?" '

But it was a long time before even that degree of rapprochement was achieved. To begin with, the Field Marshal found it difficult to remember John's surname. As Maurice Bowra commented, it was 'not the kind of name to be found in a cavalry regiment'. Not long after her marriage, Penelope said something to the Chetwodes' butler, who replied, 'Yes, Miss Penelope.' The Field Marshal snorted: 'She's not Miss Penelope. She's Mrs Bargeman.' Bowra recalled the difficulty Chetwode had in deciding how John should address him. ' "Sir" might be all right, but did not seem intimate enough. So he sought for a solution. "You can't call me Philip, that wouldn't do. You can't call me Father – I'm not your father. You'd better call me Field Marshal." So that was settled.'

The Chetwodes sailed for India in early October 1933. Chetwode wrote to Penelope *en route* on 6 October, from Marseilles: 'I *just hated* saying goodbye to my own darling. It would have been just the same whoever you had married. It is such a break when the young birds one has watched growing, leave the nest.' Penelope's brother Roger, who had sided with his parents in their opposition to the match, continued to stir up trouble, reporting that he had heard John had been doing comic imitations of them. On 20 November the Field Marshal wrote to Penelope (who was by then in Germany):

> Penelope darling, Your John must be a very stupid man. We have had quite a lot of letters from people who are cross with him because he mimics and mocks at me & mother – & imitates interviews with us. People all think it is in such bad taste. We have smothered our feelings & done all we can for both of you & it is so common & rude to mock at any older people let alone those who have done all they can for you. Several people have said they won't have you again because of it. Even Roger has heard of it in America. It is not only rude & common but it is surely very foolish if nothing else, & leaves a nasty taste in the mouth my dear, & makes us think we were right in our objection to the marriage. Try and stop him doing it.

John immediately wrote to the Field Marshal denying that he had imitated him. It is plain that Chetwode was not convinced (and Lady Chetwode wrote to Penelope: 'I believe it and always shall'), but he replied with stiff courtesy on 10 December: 'I naturally accept your denial at once, & can only suppose it must be enemies of yours who have sown these tares . . .' To Penelope he wrote (17 December): 'as he is your husband I have accepted his word at once. Someone must be maligning you as it is curious how many people have written about it.'

Chetwode became more cordial towards John when the Betjemans' first child, Paul, was born in 1937. But Frank Longford thought that John's kindness and sympathy after Roger Chetwode committed suicide in 1940 (when John called on the Field Marshal and wisely insisted he continue to go in to work to take his mind off the tragedy) finally ended the animosity.

Christopher Sykes, Evelyn Waugh's friend and biographer, was not so sure. He recalled meeting John in late 1945. John told him, half angry and half amused, that Lord Chetwode* had just given him a lift in his car. The Field Marshal had told his chauffeur: 'Drop me at the House of Lords – and then take Mr Thingummy wherever it is he wants to go.' If Chetwode indeed said these words (the story has a whiff of the apocryphal) John must have added them to his litany of slights – the snubs and rebuffs that he had hoarded, almost treasured, since childhood. They were his precious bane. Fermenting in him, they precipitated some of his best poetry. 'Why did I mind so much?' he asked of the 'common little boy' sneer. 'Heaven knows. But I still do . . .' Why did he sustain with such animus the vendettas against Jack Shakespeare, Kelly, Gidney and C. S. Lewis? Perhaps it was the response of injured innocence to a world where virtue was not rewarded, as it is in fairy tales. With rare exceptions, John was kind and well intentioned towards others. Why, then, must they be 'beastly' to him, victimize and insult him? His was the desolation of the Romantic whose vision of the world is eroded by the world's reality.

Rather as a Proustian invalid cosseting his ailments can outlive a fit man unprepared for sudden illness, John, by nursing the fleers and jeers, learned how to withstand them and how to hit back. Chetwode had gone through the Uhlans 'like brown paper' at the Battle of Moy, and John was the despair of the Marlborough OTC; but the Field Marshal met his match in his son-in-law. When Susan Barnes profiled John for the *Sunday Times* in 1972, a 'lifelong friend' of his told her: 'What the Chetwodes . . . didn't realize, toughies that they were, was that this shabby, shambling figure was tougher than they. John doesn't realize it himself.'

---

*Sir Philip was raised to the peerage as Baron Chetwode in July 1945.

11

Uffington

T HE YEAR 1934 brought three great changes in John's life. In January he
was appointed film critic of the London *Evening Standard* at a salary of
over £800 a year – at that time, a high income for a man of twenty-seven.[*]
The staff post marked the beginning of his public fame. His first book of
poems, *Mount Zion* (1931), and his light-hearted book about architecture,
Ghastly Good Taste (1933), had won him a small following; but now he was
writing for a leading London paper and his verdicts on films were placarded
outside the capital's cinemas.

In February, John and Penelope moved to the village of Uffington,
Berkshire. For the first time they had a house, not just a flat. Up to then,
apart from his Oxford years and his holidays in Cornwall and Ireland, John
had been essentially a 'townie'. His tastes were metropolitan; most of his
friends and interests were in London. Now he had suddenly to adapt to
country life – though, as his job took him to London, he was still to be
seen at the Café Royal and Boulestin's restaurant and in the cocktail bars
of the Dorchester and the Savoy.

In June John's father died. In 1927 when Ernest Betjemann's heart trouble had been diagnosed, John's anticipation of his death had been distasteful, almost vulturine. But now the sense of release he felt at the eclipse of
a figure who had seemed to him unsympathetic and domineering was
gradually overtaken by feelings of guilt – not only regret at having failed
to love or honour his father, but guilt at letting down the workers at G.
Betjemann & Sons. For this was the time when, if he had been the 'handy-
andy' son his father might have preferred, John would have taken over the
running of the family firm as 'the fourth generation'.

Christian Barman ('Barmy') of *The Architectural Review*, who lived in
Uffington, had found a house there for John and Penelope, a modest build-
ing in the high street called Garrards Farm. Late in 1933, John had gone to
Uffington to make the house ready, while Penelope was in Germany.

[*] See Chapter 12, 'Film Critic'.

Choosing between marriage to John and a career as an Indologist had been an acute dilemma for Penelope – one that their clandestine wedding in July 1933 had not resolved. She felt she could both be a wife to John and become a scholar. The Betjemans' daughter Candida Lycett Green goes so far as to suggest that 'my mother did indeed prefer her Indian studies to JB's affections', adding that Penelope's sojourn in Berlin left John feeling 'desperately insecure', even though it had the blessing of the couple's 'listening-post', P. Morton Shand.

If Penelope could desert the marriage for a spell, so could John. To help get the Uffington farmhouse straight, he employed a pretty girl with dark brown hair called Molly Higgins. He had an affair with her and at once admitted it to Penelope – perhaps in a spirit as much of tit-for-tat as of contrition. Penelope wrote to him from Germany: 'I did not realize until I got yours this mornin' that you were actually in love with Molly H. I thought you might be but did not let myself think that you really were.' She in turn confessed that she had been attracted by other people while in Berlin. She had resisted the temptations. By the time Penelope came back to England in January 1934, John's affair with Molly Higgins was over. Her attitude to the approaching reunion was curiously negligent. Considering that she was the wronged party, one of her letters to John from Berlin was oddly submissive and propitiatory. 'Darling, I'm so relieved you say I can come back. I think you will find it will work alright, anyway on my side now.' But she also wrote: 'I hope you'll be happy with me but if you aren't you can always go off with M.H. [Molly Higgins].' In spite of the bantering tone, there is a casualness about this, an air of 'Take me or leave me'. As it turned out, Penelope made friends with Molly Higgins, who sometimes stayed at the farmhouse and was no longer a threat. Somehow the assertion of independence by both John and Penelope seemed to have strengthened their marriage rather than exposed it as fragile – as it were, the aircraft could still fly on a single engine when the other failed, could glide when both engines were down.

The Betjemans went to Uffington early in February. The village, in the Vale of the White Horse, had changed little since Thomas Hughes described it in *Tom Brown's Schooldays* (1857). Although the railway had reached Uffington, it was a place of extreme rurality; it still is. Above, on the Berkshire Downs, was the White Horse carved through the turf into the chalk, the one genuinely ancient white horse in Britain, pre-dating by centuries the impostor of Westbury that John had known in his Marlborough schooldays.

The White Horse was an appropriate emblem for the terrain, since Uffington was in the heart of 'horsey' country, within easy reach of the trainers at Lambourn. The Betjemans' years together were all to be spent in Berkshire, first in Uffington, then in Farnborough and finally in Wantage, the largest town in the district. Their being uprooted from London and plunged into the centre of horse country did not benefit the marriage. Penelope was 'mad on' horses and was in her element in the world of hunts and gymkhanas. John was not only uninterested in horses, he actively disliked them. The couple's divergence of interests put strain on the marriage from the outset. Thirty years later, when a Wantage neighbour, Jessie Sharley, came to the Betjemans' house after church one Sunday and Penelope was nowhere to be seen, John remarked after a while, 'If we were horses, Jessie, we'd have had a cup of tea by now.' But the marriage's loss was poetry's gain. John's reluctant encounters with horseflesh led to such masterpieces of hippophobic satire as 'Hunter Trials' and 'Winthrop Mackworth Redivivus'.

Garrards Farm is a white clunch building with brick dressings round the casement windows. With it, in 1934, came a few acres of fields, some out-buildings and the stables where Penelope kept Moti, the Arab gelding her father had given her. The house was lit only by oil lamps. When Penelope's father, the Field Marshal, visited the couple, he insisted on staying at the Fox and Hounds across the road because he could not stand 'those stinkin' lamps'. There were other smells too. Penelope kept a goat in the yard, as somebody had told her that goats' milk was better for humans than cows'. Snowdrop the goat was allowed to come in and out of the house and it was not unusual to find chickens indoors too. 'Penelope invented "free range" long before anybody thought up the expression,' said Osbert Lancaster. 'The place was an animal sanctuary – and it stank.'

John asked Ernie Evans, the landlord of the Craven Arms, if he would let his bright teenage daughters, Gwen and Betty (later Mrs Packford), come and work at Garrards Farm. Gwen became the Betjemans' cook and Betty made the beds and waited at table. Later, after the girls left, the Betjemans took on a German maidservant, Paula Steinbrecher, who stayed for a year. When she arrived she spoke no English. For a long time she thought John's name was 'Shutup', as Penelope said that to him so often.

The couple attended Uffington Church, 'the Cathedral of the Vale' – a cruciform building which John considered 'the best and most complete' Early English church in the county. He became people's warden. The vicar was the Rev. George Bridle, an elderly bachelor – '*very* unmarried', as somebody described him. George Packford, who later married Betty Evans, introduced John to bell-ringing. What he learned from the Uffington ringers enabled him to set out, in his poem 'Bristol', the precise changes of 'the mathematic pattern of a plain course on the bells'. The book in which that poem appeared was called *New Bats in Old Belfries* and he gave his verse autobiography the title *Summoned by Bells*. His poem 'Uffington' begins:

> Tonight we feel the muffled peal
> Hang on the village like a pall;
> It overwhelms the towering elms –
> That death-reminding dying fall . . .

John and Penelope started an Uffington Parochial Youth Fellowship. John was listed as president on the printed events card, but Penelope did most of the organizing. 'I think the Betjemans did more good for Uffington than anybody else,' said Ken Freeman, who was eight years old when they arrived in the village. 'They brought the place alive. Pre-war, there was nothing going on. After the First World War there'd been a terrible agricultural depression. Even in 1939, a farm-worker's wage was thirty shillings. John and Penelope got things going, especially for us youngsters.' There were talks (Penelope later realized some of them may have been above the heads of the young audience), concerts, plays, tennis tournaments and garden fêtes. Every year a concert was held in the village hall in February or March. As well as making life in Uffington more entertaining, John took some of his protégés on jaunts, by river or road. Ken Freeman recalled: 'In the summer evenings the message would come round when I got back from school, "John Betjeman will pick you up at six o'clock tonight." And two or three of us with John, we'd go down to Radcot and he'd hire a punt with the old pole, and we'd go up the river.'

While making new friends locally, John and Penelope did not lose touch with their old friends. In April 1934 they started a visitors' book. Those who visited them before the end of the year, often staying for a weekend, included Lionel Perry, Billy Clonmore, Noel Blakiston and his wife Georgiana, Frank and Elizabeth Longford, Edward James and Evelyn Waugh. Waugh stayed from 5 to 7 November. Unfortunately there is a gap in his diaries from 18 July 1934 to 7 July 1936, no doubt depriving us of a more than objective description of the Betjeman ménage. Nancy Mitford wrote to her sister Diana Guinness on 25 April 1935:

> I saw the Betjemans a lot at Easter and dined twice with Gerald [Berners] who had Maimie [Lady Mary Lygon] and Hubert [Duggan] staying with him. The B's took me to see Ashdown and Coles Hill. They had the [Cyril] Connollys who made themselves very agreeable but looked strange in rural surroundings.

On one of the Connollys' visits John and Penelope had a violent row in which they rampaged over the house yelling at each other, passing straight through the bathroom where the Connollys were taking a bath together.

In November 1934 *The Sketch*, a *Tatler*-ish glossy magazine, ran a picture feature on the 'Uffington set'. One photograph was captioned 'MR JOHN BETJEMAN, who is definitely one of the Intelligentsia, is the author of "Ghastly Good Taste" and other books. He owns a Teddy bear, "Archie", which he is showing to LADY MARY PAKENHAM.' Another picture was of Penelope taking Peter Quennell and his future wife, Marcelle Rothe, for a drive in 'her old-world phaeton', drawn by Moti. In a third photograph, 'VISCOUNTESS HASTINGS is . . . posed with a charming little kitten.'

Along with all the Bright Young People from London, one local name appears in the Betjemans' visitors' book: Stuart Piggott the archaeologist, a learned and likeable man who became one of their best friends in Uffington. Piggott, who was twenty-four (the same age as Penelope) in 1934, came of Uffington stock. His parents moved to Hampshire but he spent many of his school holidays in Uffington with his grandparents and maiden aunts. He was a child prodigy of archaeology. At seventeen he made his first contribution to O. G. S. Crawford's magazine *Antiquity*. In 1931, still only twenty-one, he published an article on the White Horse of Uffington. In 1934, at a dig, Piggott told Reggie Ross Williamson, a friend, that he was going to visit his maiden aunts in Uffington.

> And Reggie, who knew John Betjeman from *The Architectural Review*, said, 'You must go and introduce yourself to the Betjemans.' And so I did. I went along to their house about tea time . . . and John came to the door and I introduced myself. But I said, 'Look, I'm sorry, you've obviously got some-body to tea, I'll go off and come back another day.' He said: 'No, for God's sake come in. We've got the prime minister of Nepal here. It's absolute hell. Come and help us out.' This was a wonderful beginning . . . And after that I used to see them fairly often. I'd see the maiden aunts as a duty, and the Betjemans for pleasure.

Piggott became Penelope's friend as much as John's. Like her, he was interested in Indian archaeology. They went together to the Royal Academy Indian Exhibition in 1935. At the show, various Indian Army colonels and proconsular figures came up to Penelope and greeted her.

'Congratulations on your marriage, Penelope,' one of them said. 'This your husband?'

'Yes, isn't he *sweet?*' Penelope replied. Afterwards she told Piggott, 'You'd better be John for the afternoon. It'll save a lot of trouble.'

John greatly took to Ronald and Rachel Bennett of Kingston Warren. 'Ronald Bennett was a racehorse trainer,' Penelope said, 'but he was one of the few people in the "horsey" world that John really liked.' The Betjemans often dined at the Bennetts' house. Sometimes John provided the entertainment at these dinners, by getting local girls to recite Berkshire dialect poems. One girl conscripted for this task was Marcella Ayres (later Mrs Seymour), the daughter of an Uffington farmer. John nicknamed her 'Caramella', perhaps from the sweets she received as a reward for reciting. He trained her to recite the poem 'The Berkshire Pig', which begins:

> Vathers' mothers, mothers' zuns,
> You as loves your little ones,
> Appy piegs among the stubble,
> Listen to a tale of trouble:
> Listen piegs in yard and sty
> How they Berkshire chaps zarde I [treated me].

When Marcella first recited the poem, she pronounced the word 'ones' in a BBC accent, not 'wons', the Berkshire way. 'Mr Betjeman stopped me dead. He made me recite the beginning until I got it right.' The routine was that, when dinner at the Bennetts' was over, John would pick up Marcella, she would recite a poem or two, then he would drive her home. 'One morning he came to book me for the evening performance, but I was ramping mad with toothache. He said to my mother, "Give her some Genasprins." My mother had never heard of Genasprins, but I was sent out to get some; and I did recite that evening, and received a small bar of chocolate from Mr Betjeman.' As Anthony Powell once wrote, John had 'a whim of iron'.

At Pusey House, near Faringdon, lived Michael Hornby, heir to the W. H. Smith newsagent and bookstall empire, and his wife Nicolette, a young couple who had married two years before the Betjemans. Penelope had been at school with Nicolette, whom John nicknamed 'Knee Coal'. 'Nicole could be very pompous,' a mutual friend recalled. 'And Penelope would prick any balloon. I remember once Nicole was being particularly pompous and Penelope said in her frightful cockney voice, "Oh, Ni-cole, do *shut up*! I remember when you put cream buns in your knickers."'

The grandest house in Faringdon, and that which the Betjemans visited most often, was Faringdon House, built about 1780 by one of Britain's more lamentable poets laureate, Benjamin Pye. It was now the home of Gerald Tyrwhitt-Wilson, fourteenth Baron Berners, who had been a diplomat in Constantinople and Rome before inheriting his uncle's title just after the First World War. Berners, an ill-favoured man in his early fifties, lived with a handsome young protégé, Robert Heber Percy, who was known in the Berners circle as 'The Mad Boy'. Heber Percy wore clothes of parakeet brilliance and was given to outbursts of rage. More than once he attempted suicide.

Lord Berners was something more than a dilettante of the arts. He had studied music with Stravinsky and is still well regarded as a Waltonesque composer. In 1934 his first volume of autobiography appeared, *First Childhood*: when John wrote the entry for Berners in the *Dictionary of National Biography*, he referred to the book's 'delightful and deceptively simple style'. Berners also painted, in a manner which those well disposed to him agreed was like Corot's; his limpid oil works included a sketch of Penelope galloping, adapted from a still from a Gaumont-British film. All of Berners's varied works had a tendency towards pastiche and parody. Nancy Mitford, who portrayed him as 'Lord Merlin' in *The Pursuit of Love*, wrote: 'As he was a famous practical joker, it was sometimes difficult to know where jokes ended and culture began. I think he was not always perfectly certain himself.'

In 1934–35 Berners built, in the best tradition of eccentric peers, a folly tower. It was designed by the architect Lord Gerald Wellesley (later Duke of Wellington). Berners liked the Gothic style but while he was away in Rome Wellesley built a tall classical tower. On his return, Berners was furious and insisted that a Gothic 'topknot' should be added. It was, and John and Penelope attended the grand opening in 1935. Edward James, John's first publisher, remembered:

> My mother knew Penelope's mother, 'Star' Chetwode [Lady Chetwode], very well. She would say, 'I must ask Star Chetwode's advice about that' – just as she would write in the margin of a poem of mine, 'Very morbid. Must ask Florrie Bridges' – the niece by marriage of Robert Bridges. Lord Berners held a party to celebrate the new folly, and Star arrived, still thinking it deplorable that her daughter had married this 'little Dutchman', John Betjeman. And at the party John got on tremendously with Gerald Wellesley. So Lady Chetwode went round saying, grudgingly, 'Well, I must say, Gerry Wellesley quite likes him.' It was an eye-opener to her, that John was so accepted in that *galère*.

Berners was delighted to have the Betjemans as neighbours. They were often invited to dinner. Heber Percy noticed that 'Penelope seemed overpowering when John was there, because she really didn't let him get a word in edgeways. John would be telling you about something very interesting when in would come Penelope and tell you a very funny story about what

was happening among the chickens or cows; and then John used to sub-
side. Equally, Penelope was tremendous company when *John* wasn't there.'

Heber Percy remembered that, at one dinner-party, John claimed that
Sir Walter Scott was a most erotic novelist:

> Gerald said he didn't believe it. So after dinner a volume of Scott was pro-
> duced and John began reading. After he had been reading for quite a while –
> innocuous passages about knights and turrets and so on – something per-
> fectly disgusting came out. And then John went on reading again, more tame
> stuff, when another passage of pure pornography was read out – all of course
> invented on the spot by John. John completely straight-faced and reading in
> a soporific voice.

Berners invited the Betjemans to lunches with Aldous Huxley, H. G.
Wells and Wells's mistress Baroness Moura Budberg ('Baroness Bedbug', as
John called her) and Penelope was deputed to take these celebrities for
jaunts in her phaeton. One day Berners invited Penelope to bring Moti
into the great hall at Faringdon, with its neo-classical chimneypieces at
either end, so that he could paint the horse's portrait with her standing
beside it. This diversion was repeated to amuse or shock visitors: a photograph shows Evelyn Waugh sitting beside Moti on the drawing-room
carpet, while Penelope and Heber Percy look on.

Sometimes Berners took his guests to visit the Betjemans at Garrards
Farm. This happened when Gertrude Stein and her friend Alice B. Toklas
stayed at Faringdon to discuss the chorus that Stein was to write for
Berners's ballet *A Wedding Bouquet*. Stuart Piggott was roped in to help
entertain the daunting pair when they were brought to the Betjemans' for
a drink. John asked if he had ever met Stein.

> I said, 'No, I never have.'
>
> 'Nor have I,' he said, 'and I've never read a word of hers; that's the
> trouble.' He said, 'I've found a quotation and it doesn't say what it's from,
> but it is Gertrude Stein.' . . . He said, 'I think it would be a good idea if I
> produced that, don't you?' . . .
>
> So then the party arrived. 'Oh, Miss Stein, it's wonderful to see you. You
> know, knowing that you were coming, the whole day a line of yours has
> been running through my head, and I can't think where it's from. I wonder
> if you can tell me?' And he produced it. And Gertrude Stein sat there firmly
> and squarely – as she was – and said, 'Well, no, Mr Betjeman, I can't quite
> think where that is from. Alice, do you know?' And Alice paused for a
> moment, then said, 'No, I don't know either.'
>
> So Gertrude Stein said, 'Well, you may rest assured, Mr Betjeman, it's not
> from one of my *major* works.'

And after that, of course, it became a phrase with John and myself – 'It's not from one of my *major* works.'

What Oxford was to John, Rome – to which he had been sent in a junior diplomatic post in 1912 – had been to Berners. In 1928 he bought a house there, 3 Foro Romano. Its balcony commanded a fine view of the Forum. The artist Rex Whistler, who stayed there in 1929, wrote to his mother that he could see the wonderful view while lying in his bath. A postcard of his bedroom notes: 'Isn't it delightful? The walls are dirty parchment colour and the bed, curtains etc. are crimson damask. The head of the bed is carved and gilt.' Berners took on a cook–housekeeper, Tito Mannini, who came to regard the house as his own. Edward James, who was meant to be staying indefinitely, found Mannini so rude and unbearable that he left after a month and alleged that he was using the front part of the house as an antique shop. In 1936 John, never one for foreign travel, was lured out to stay there with Penelope. Tito was, Penelope thought, 'rather out of sorts'; but John wrote to Berners: 'This is the first night in your house and I must write at once to thank you for lending it to us. It really is a bit of all right with that view of all those ruins and the charming Tito to whom I speak French, Italian, Deutsch or English very clumsily.'

Though John could take a tease in good part and had a gift for getting on with people whom others found 'difficult' (Tito Mannini is an example), he was never content to be surrounded only by friends and figures well disposed towards him. As a good story needs a villain, so his variegated nature demanded the ennui-dispelling stimulus of a bugbear. In Farmer John Wheeler, his landlord in Uffington (Wheeler himself rented Garrards Farm from its owner, the Earl of Craven), he found a satisfying new hate-figure to succeed A. R. Gidney of Marlborough and C. S. Lewis of Oxford. Like them, Wheeler was to be pilloried in a Betjeman poem. John's dislike for Wheeler went beyond his usual rebellion against authority. 'If John saw Farmer Wheeler coming, he would hide behind a wall or start walking fast the other way,' a friend remembered. 'It was absurd, really, because although Wheeler was a bit rough, he wasn't an unpleasant man.' A stout figure, Wheeler suffered from diabetes and was a teetotaller. When he went to a neighbouring house after a shoot, and others were asking for 'a drop of whisky' or 'a drop of gin', he would ask for 'a drop of your water, moi boi', in the high-pitched voice which earned him the nickname 'Squeaky'. (In his poem, John called him 'Farmer Whistle'.)

Money was the root of the ill-feeling between John and Wheeler. John was nearly always late with his rent, though when he brought it round

Wheeler sometimes tried to sweeten the pill by offering him a 'Berkshire Special' – gin and ginger wine. Wheeler's daughter Peggy (later Mrs Phillips) took her father's view of John. 'Father was down to earth,' she said. 'He'd got no time for airy-fairy nitwits. We all thought he was that. Mrs wasn't, but he was.' She had not forgotten the 'dreadful state' of Garrards Farm when the Betjemans left it. 'All the animals had been inside. Father said they had to put it back in the same order as they'd found it, and of course they didn't want to.'

John found three ways of taking revenge on Farmer Wheeler. First, at the invitation of a farm-worker known as 'Little Titch', who had formerly worked for Wheeler, he became secretary of the Uffington branch of the Farm Workers' Union. John got to know Little Titch, whose real name was Oziah Johnson, because the farmhand often did jobbing work for Penelope. John presided over the Union's meetings and sent out entertaining memoranda. It greatly amused him to be the Wat Tyler of Uffington, encouraging the workers to ask Farmer Wheeler for higher wages and more days off. John joked that when the socialist 'slave state' arrived, he would be spared from immediate execution because of his good work in Uffington.

Another way in which he was able to get at Wheeler was in his rôle as people's warden of Uffington Church. The Vicar wrote to John:

Dear Mr Betjeman,

I am writing to you as People's Warden to request you to take steps, in conjunction with Captain Piggott, to prevent another incident such as occurred on Sunday morning last at the eleven a.m. service.

When Mr Wheeler brought the collection to the chancel steps he deliberately jostled me with his shoulder and if I had not been fairly firm on my feet I should have been knocked over. His manner in church is never very reverent and has been commented on many times, but it must be made clear to him that his action of last Sunday must not be repeated.

To make amends for his irreverence, Wheeler gave some land to the church so that the graveyard might be extended. (By a nice irony, he was the first to be buried in it.)

John also took revenge on Wheeler in verse. In his poem 'The Dear Old Village' he wrote:

> See that square house, late Georgian, and smart,
> Two fields away it proudly stands apart,
> Dutch barn and concrete cow-sheds have replaced
> The old thatched roofs which once the yard disgraced.

Here wallows Farmer WHISTLE in his riches,
His ample stomach heaved above his breeches.
You'd never think that in such honest beef
Lurk'd an adulterous braggart, liar and thief.

There is no evidence that Farmer Wheeler was 'adulterous' (or indeed a liar or thief): here John may have been visiting on him the sin of which he accused his own father.

12

Film Critic

‾‾‾‾‾‾‾‾‾‾‾‾‾

SIR ROBERT BRUCE LOCKHART, the diplomat, British agent and writer, had enjoyed a career of high drama. In 1911 he had taken first place in the Consular Service examination – largely, he claimed, because a chat with two French prostitutes in Green Park just before his French oral test had given him unusual fluency in it. At twenty-seven, newly married, he was acting British Consul in Moscow. He was sent home shortly before the revolution of 1917, ostensibly on sick leave, in fact to extricate him from the scandal of an adulterous affair. After the revolution the War Office sent him back to Russia to try to persuade the Bolsheviks to come into the Great War on the allies' side against Germany.

When the Bolsheviks and the allies fell out, he was imprisoned in the Kremlin. It seemed more than likely that he would be shot. The Bolsheviks also jailed Lockhart's most recent lover, Baroness Budberg. He managed to obtain her release and the two remained friends long after she became H. G. Wells's mistress. Lockhart himself was freed in exchange for Maxim Litvinov, whom the British had imprisoned in retaliation for Lockhart's arrest. 'Over my body,' Lockhart wrote, 'two world systems had wrangled.'

In 1928 Lockhart joined the *Standard* as joint editor, with Harold Nicolson, of the 'Londoner's Diary'. In 1933 Nicolson, who had little taste or aptitude for gossip journalism, resigned. ('I have won fame and lost reputation,' he wrote to his wife.) Lockhart was left as sole editor of the 'Diary'. It is likely that he obtained John the post of film critic. Lockhart was, with the columnist Lord Castlerosse, one of the inner court of the newspaper's owner, Lord Beaverbrook – Malcolm Muggeridge described them as 'the two wild ones, *avec peur et avec reproche*'. Lockhart was by now the lover of the Countess of Rosslyn, mother of Lady Mary St Clair-Erskine to whom John had unsuccessfully proposed marriage. Both Bruce Lockhart and Castlerosse were often at the Rosslyns' house, Hunger Hill, Coolham. John is first mentioned in Lockhart's private diary in 1931, as one of a gathering of socialites who included John de Forest, William Astor, Lord Hinchingbrooke and a friend of Lady Castlerosse known as 'the belching baronet'.

Osbert Lancaster said that what commended John to Beaverbrook was an article, 'Peers without Tears', which John contributed to the *Standard* in December 1933 – an essay on 'dim peers' such as Lord Trimlestown, whom he had hunted down in Ireland. It was probably Lockhart who helped place the piece; he was also in a position to draw it to Beaverbrook's notice. The *Standard*'s editor, Percy Cudlipp, wrote to John on 15 January 1934 offering him a job on the editorial staff from 29 January at 16 guineas a week.

Malcolm Muggeridge, who joined the newspaper while John was film critic, recalled that the *Standard* was produced in a single large room, 'the idea being that thereby the whole operation of bringing it out would be integrated and cooperative'. In the 'Londoner's Diary' corner, Bruce Lockhart reigned as 'a quasi-independent satrap'. He had a direct line to Beaverbrook, and could treat Cudlipp, the editor, as more or less an equal. Even when not on the premises, Beaverbrook kept close control of how the *Standard* was run and what went into it. The peer had no principled views, Muggeridge thought, 'only prejudices, moods, sudden likes and dislikes'. Overnight, he might reverse a previously held position as a result of a conversation. John may have found it easier to accommodate Beaverbrook's whims than did the newsmen and leader-writers. He did not come to film-reviewing as a learned *cinéaste*, or with any deep feelings or preconceptions about film as an art form.

He arrived in late January 1934, and was given a desk near Bruce Lockhart's. He had other friends at the *Standard*. On the 'Londoner's Diary' were Randolph Churchill (who may have owed the job to his father's friendship with Beaverbrook) and Patrick Balfour, who had been trained as a gossip columnist and in 1933 had enjoyed some success with his book *Society Racket* – John had been caricatured in one of the illustrations. Muggeridge joined the team slightly later, as did Lady Mary Pakenham (later Lady Mary Clive), whom John had first met four years earlier in Ireland.

Muggeridge recalled that it was part of John's duties to contribute occasional paragraphs to the 'Londoner's Diary', helping out with 'architectural and ecclesiastical news, especially clerical appointments'. He liked John, yet felt 'a sense of mystery' about him.

Never did I meet any of his relations, nor do I recall anyone who did. There was in him too a certain coolness or standing-offness in personal relationships which can even be read into the famous poem about Miss J. Hunter Dunn. He also had a predisposition to melancholy, which led him often into practical joking. One of the more serious instances of this occurred when he met the Liberal Foreign Secretary, Sir John Simon, a severe, stuffed-shirt sort of character, on a London street. John Betjeman fell down in front of him, feigning an epileptic fit, which left the politician helpless and at sea, wondering what to do. Who would have thought then that Betjeman would become Poet Laureate?

Sir John Simon was Foreign Secretary from 1931 to 1935, so this incident must have taken place while John was on the *Standard*.

The first film John had to review for the paper was *Catherine the Great*, starring the German actress Elisabeth Bergner, one of the foreign-accented stars who had successfully made the transition from silent films to 'talkies'. Because John was not a film-fan, he did not know that for the past few months the British trade press had been abuzz with speculation as to which would be bigger box-office, Bergner in United Artists' *Catherine the Great*, or Marlene Dietrich in Paramount's rival film on the same subject, *The Scarlet Empress*. By some impulse of the *Zeitgeist*, two movie moguls had had the same idea at the same time.

John's review of *Catherine the Great* appeared on 10 February 1934 under the headline 'LITTLE CATHERINE *IS* GREAT'.

> The best film of the week is 'Catherine the Great', at the Leicester Square Theatre.
>
> After all, most pictures that you go to see you regard as temporary relief from the misery of being alive. You visit them in the same spirit in which you get 'a novel' from the circulating library.
>
> You don't demand more than a joke or two, a love interest and a sustained plot, and the book goes back to be read and forgotten by someone else, in the same way that you have read and forgotten it yourself.
>
> But there are some books which you will want to buy and keep in your memory. So there are some scenes in films which one can never forget. I remember as I write, 'Poil de Carotte' hanging in the barn; Manuela being called on that bleak school staircase in 'Mädchen in Uniform'; I also remember a chandelier twinkling with glass and hanging from a dark painted ceiling. This last is from 'Catherine the Great'.

In this first review, John sets the tone of the articles that were to follow in the year and a half he remained film critic. He is quickly establishing himself as a 'character', entertaining and quirkish. He treats his readers as intimates, allowing them to see the depressed state of his mind. Films are 'temporary relief from the misery of being alive'; *Catherine the Great* is 'an event in my gloomy existence'. These asides suggest something more than a comical glumness *à la* Buster Keaton. Perhaps the strains of marriage were beginning to tell. Perhaps he felt that in accepting a well-paid job as a journalist he was betraying his vocation as a poet. Or Muggeridge may have been right when he wrote of 'a predisposition to melancholy'.

Gradually John settled into the routine of the job. He would get up about seven in the morning. After breakfast Penelope would drive him to Uffington or Challow station and at about 7.30 he would catch a slow train to Didcot; after that, a fast one to London. He saw the films in the morning, wrote about them in the afternoon, then caught the train home. 'It was always a bit of a rush,' he told his granddaughter Endellion in 1977, adding, 'The slowest part of the journey was the underground railway from Paddington to Farringdon Street, the nearest underground station to the *Evening Standard* office [in Shoe Lane].' It was while travelling to work on the Underground, on 26 June 1934, that John had an uncanny experience. In recalling it, for Endellion, in 1977, he described it as 'the only ghostly experience I had which can be witnessed'.

> One morning I was travelling down on the Inner Circle underground from Paddington to Farringdon Street when the train did a very unusual thing. It waited for a long time at King's Cross station. My father, your great-grandfather, had a factory, founded in 1820, on the Pentonville Road (it is still there and now owned by the Medici Society). King's Cross underground was the nearest station. I remember thinking as the train waited at King's Cross, 'Shall I go out and see my father?' A voice inside me seemed to say, 'Yes, do go and see him. It won't take you long and you won't be too late for the film.' The train went on waiting but I felt too lazy at that time of the morning to bother to get out and take a tram up the hill. Then we went on and with other film writers I saw an American musical film called *George White's Scandals*.
>
> When I got back to Uffington that evening the telephone rang. It was my father's managing clerk, Mr H. V. Andrew, and he told me that my father had died that morning while talking to him. He was recalling a date. Do you think my father was trying to get through to me? Do you think he knew he was going to die so swiftly? I don't know. All I can tell you is that it happened and Gramelope [Penelope] will remember it.
>
> She offered me a strawberry that we had grown in our garden at Uffington when I heard the news and I remember being too upset to want to eat it.

There was a further shock at Ernest's funeral, which took place in Chelsea Old Church. John's Oxford friend Alan Pryce-Jones recorded in his memoirs:

> John was an only child, and while he and his mother were waiting for the ceremony to begin a scene occurred like that in the second act of *Der*

Rosenkavalier. A second, unknown, Mrs Betjeman suddenly irrupted with a second family, and it turned out that for many years Mr Betjeman [*sic* for Betjemann] had lived a second and hitherto secret life.

Ernest was buried in Highgate Cemetery, where an obelisk marks his grave; and a slate tablet to his memory, designed by Frederick Etchells, was set in the wall of St Enodoc's Church in Cornwall.

Ernest had not cut John out of his will, as he had allegedly threatened to do in 1930. His properties were to be sold to form a trust fund which would benefit Bess in her lifetime and, after her death, would be held 'in Trust for my Son John Betjemann absolutely'. Within ten years the business Ernest and his forebears had built up was liquidated. During those years, John did his best to help when asked – for example, writing, at Horace Andrew's request, some advertising copy to promote the company's 'Datoclock'. But there was never any question of his taking over. Some of the men who lost their jobs when the business failed were bitterly resentful. 'John Betjeman let a great business go to rack and ruin,' said William Hammond, one of Ernest's most skilled workmen.

John seems to have displayed a conventional grief at his father's death. Later, Lord Clonmore wrote to Lionel Perry: 'You will remember the crocodile tears which were shed over Ernie, after all the abuse the poor man had to suffer when alive.' John's writings suggest that only over many years did he come to feel he had misjudged his father and had failed to obey the Fifth Commandment, 'Honour thy father and thy mother . . .' If there were tears, crocodile or genuine, they did not last long. Nerina Shute, film critic of the *Sunday Referee* in 1934–35, remembered John as anything but melancholic – always sunny, full of vivacity and mischief.

> He and I used to meet at every film show; and we had a feeling of rapport, because I couldn't take it seriously and neither could he. To us it seemed mad that we should be doing this, and that all this money should be spent on film shows. We had two or three film shows a day. We drank enormous amounts of gin and whisky provided by the publicity people. We had parties, we had huge meals at the Berkeley and the Ritz and the Savoy, with directors and stars. I couldn't believe this was happening to me and I don't think he could believe it was happening to him. Anyway, we used to giggle together.

In 1934, at twenty-three, Shute was the youngest film critic in Fleet Street. Four years younger than John, she appealed to his snobbery and to his taste for boyish girls. Her grandfather, Sir Cameron Shute, had been a major in the cavalry charge at Balaclava; the family property, Woldhurstlea, near Crawley, Sussex, a Victorian mansion surrounded by 200 acres of field and forest, was turned into a housing estate whose roads included – to the satirical glee of John and Nerina – Humpty Dumpty Lane. Nerina was strikingly good-looking: her dark, ambiguous beauty later caught the eye of Lord Beaverbrook, who paid her a backhanded compliment: 'You know, you're a beautiful woman. But very few men will realize it.' (She later married the radio commentator Howard Marshall; but she spent her later years with women lovers and in 1992 'came out' as a bisexual in her memoir *Passionate Friendships*.)

John and Nerina were something of a 'twosome'. They sat next to each other in the cinemas and sometimes went on jaunts together to the British studios. The young film director Dallas Bower encountered them when making his first film, *The Path of Glory*, in 1934. He recalled their arrival on set:

> The man was wearing a hat he'd obviously bought in Whipple's [the ecclesiastical outfitters], a flat hat of the kind you only see now in television adaptations of *Barchester Towers*; and the lady looked an odd companion for him. I thought: what are they doing here? And I became slightly irritated. Most directors don't like visitors unless they're told who they are. And in due course I discovered that the man in the hat was Mr John Betjeman and that the lady was Miss Nerina Shute.

Bower welcomed them and gave them lunch.

> And then a very odd thing indeed happened . . . I wanted to re-run my rushes, so I opened the door to the box – and there was Mr Betjeman standing in the box with the projectionist.
> He said: 'Oh, I'm awfully sorry, old top.'
> So I said, 'Well, *really*! May I ask what you're doing here?'
> He said, 'Oh, I feel very embarrassed indeed.'
> I said, 'Well, not a bit.' I *was* slightly irritated. But I said, 'Not a bit. But you know if you'd wanted to see the rushes, there's no reason whatever why you shouldn't have asked and I would have been delighted for you to have sat in with me.' . . . What I really wanted to do on this occasion was to choose takes; so I had old John come back – by this time looking very humble indeed, hat in his lap, I might say. Now, whether he had slipped a coin to the projectionist, I have no idea; more probably he said: 'I wonder if . . .' – you know, he had the most enormous charm which he could turn on at the biggest possible wavelength. He said to me: 'Well, I've enjoyed my day enormously.' I took to him but I was rather frightened of him – what he might write about us. He said: 'I want to do a piece.'
> I said: 'Delighted. What do you intend to say?'
> 'Oh, the usual sort of stuff, you know.'
> To the best of my knowledge, nothing ever appeared.

The next time the two men saw each other was in 1940, when Dallas Bower was 'fished out of the army' to join the Films Division of the Ministry of Information, and found himself sharing an office with John.*

John knew few people who could give him a direct entrée into the film world or feed him its secrets. Two of the British stars – Heather Angel and Evelyn Laye – happened to come from Faringdon, so he heard something of them on the village grapevine. Emlyn Williams, whom he had known in the Oxford University Dramatic Society, acted in *My Song for You* and *Roadhouse* in 1934, as King Christian VII of Denmark in *The Affair of the Dictator*, and in *City of Beautiful Nonsense* in 1935, among other films. John's Magdalen friend Gyles Isham went out to Hollywood to appear with Garbo in *Anna Karenina* and sent him useful gossip about her – for example, her ability to gobble up the entire top tray of a trolley of canapés in two minutes flat. Anthony Bushell, a friend of John and of Evelyn Waugh, acted in British films and was good for a story or two. Robert Donat (pronounced 'dough-nut', John told his readers) was a nephew of the architect C. F. A. Voysey, whom John had met when on *The Architectural Review*. But John had one contact who was in the vanguard of the British film industry – his old school-friend Arthur Elton. After experience in Gainsborough's script department and cutting-room and on the studio floor in England and Berlin, Elton had become a leading figure in the documentary-film movement.

The word 'documentary' was first used by John Grierson in a review written for the *New York Sun* in 1926. It was derived from *documentaire*, a term which the French applied to their travel films. Grierson used it to characterize Robert Flaherty's *Moana*, an account of the daily life of South Sea islanders. Later, Grierson defined this film genre as 'the creative treatment of actuality'. Flaherty, fifty in 1934, was the oldest of the documentarians. When John began reviewing for the *Standard*, Flaherty was on a barnstorming tour of England to promote *Man of Aran* (1933–34), about life on one of the Aran islands off the coast of Ireland. He appeared at cinemas with Aran islanders in homespun and tam-o'-shanters. His life story was published in a Sunday newspaper and copies of it were handed out by usherettes dressed in fishermen's jerseys. In the Edgware Road, London, an excited crowd tried to cut locks of hair from Tiger King, the film's hero. On 30 July 1934 John wrote: 'The most important general release this week is Bob Flaherty's "Man of Aran". Do not let it be said that I didn't warn you. If you are going to this film expecting to see a tale of smuggling off the Irish coast with a lot of colleens keening and calling out "Acushla,

---

* See Chapter 15, '"Minnie"'.

Machree" you will be disappointed.' Flaherty became a drinking companion of John's. Over the drinks, he heard about Flaherty's latest projects, and brought his readers news of them.

The Hollywood film-makers are just names in John's column; but through the introductions he gained from Arthur Elton he was able to present the documentary-makers as flesh and blood. Elton himself he had known too long to take quite seriously.

> Talking of films without sex in them, let me introduce you to Arthur Elton, a director of sexless films. He is a peculiar figure in Wardour-street.
>
> He has a yellow beard, dresses in rustic style, and lives in Bloomsbury. I remember that at school he always used to carry a peculiar umbrella in which he kept his books. It must have been made of some extra strong material.
>
> Now he carries films in huge tins slung across his back in some string contrivance. He always was an ingenious man.

Lord Beaverbrook, with his jingoist British Empire campaign, encouraged his journalists to favour British products, and the British studios were near at hand. Among the directors John met besides the documentarians were the 'nervous and aesthetic' Anthony Asquith, Basil Dean, Alexander Korda, Michael Powell, Sidney Bernstein and Alfred Hitchcock. But American movies dominated the British cinemas. The public wanted to see them, and John had to cover them; but he was determined not to be taken in by Hollywood hyperbole. At first he decided not to write about stars more than was necessary. 'I considered them as "pandering to the box office and to the lowest elements in a cinema audience",' he wrote in his farewell article of 1935. 'But now if I were to meet Greta Garbo in the street I would faint right away with excitement.'

John overcame his distaste for the star system. His favourite film star was Myrna Loy – 'my beloved freckled Myrna Loy, with auburn hair and blue-green eyes'. She visited London and he interviewed her for the *Standard*. When the conversation became slightly sticky, he asked, 'Do you mind if I say you like English Perpendicular?' Miss Loy said it was fine by her, honey; and the interesting insight into her taste in architecture was duly relayed to the British public. Reviewing *Evelyn Prentice* in 1935 he wrote: 'I am still in love with Myrna Loy, despite the hats she wears in her new film.' He was less enthusiastic about Joan Crawford. 'I think she is a splendid actress,' he wrote, 'but I am always a little repulsed by her shining lips, like balloon tyres in wet weather.' In January 1935 he advised his readers: 'If you want to see Joan Crawford soundly beaten with a hair-brush by Clark Gable . . . go and see *Forsaking All Others* at the Empire.'

Next to Walt Disney's 'silly symphonies' with Mickey Mouse and the rest, which he considered the best things on the screen, John liked comedies. W. C. Fields was by far his favourite male star. 'A creative genius' he called him in December 1934. 'I have only to see his face to laugh.' John did not think Bing Crosby mixed well with Fields on screen. He disliked all musicals, quoting in support of his view 'a Neasden correspondent'. He missed no opportunity of savaging Bing Crosby. He wrote of *We're Not Dressing* (1934):

> The interminably crooning sailor is Bing Crosby: he croons when he is on board the yacht; he croons when he is nearly drowning in the vasty deep; he croons when the sun sets on the desert island; he croons when the moon rises, and of course he falls in love with Carole Lombard, the little rich girl who gets prettier and less useless as she settles down to desert island life. But why must we see so many close-ups of Bing Crosby? He has a nice innocuous face, but he is not a great actor.

Eight months later, reviewing *Here Is My Heart*, John speculated, 'I suppose this is the swan-croon of Bing Crosby': wishful thinking.

The 'purity campaign' was an issue that all film critics had to address in 1934–35. In 1934 the Hays production code, governing movie morality, was imposed on the Hollywood studios, with severe sanctions against transgressors. A phrase much bandied about in the ensuing censorship controversy was 'good taste'. The production code imposed in 1934, for example, stipulated that 'The treatment of bedrooms must be governed by good taste and delicacy.' The subject, and of course its antithesis, 'bad taste', were in the air. Here John, after the publication of *Ghastly Good Taste* (1933), could be considered an authority. In the spring of 1935 Montagu Montagu-Nathan, a British expert on Russian music, and Arnold Haskell, the ballet historian, organized 'An Evening of Bad Taste' at the Garden Club in Curzon Street, London. John may have had a hand in the design of the printed programme. The front was decorated by irregular type and a drawing of a garden gnome; on the back cover was a badly designed advertisement for Shell; and an inside page promised 'CROONING', that pet hate of John's, and 'BUFFIT'. It also promised that 'Mr John Betjeman, author of "GHASTLY GOOD TASTE", will hold forth.'

Despite this star billing, John was unable to attend the party: he had to write his *Standard* column. Instead, he sent along a 78rpm gramophone record of his voice, to be played to the guests. The record survives. On it can be heard the voice of the twenty-eight-year-old Betjeman, sounding slightly more affected than it was later in his days as a television celebrity.

Mr Chairman, art lovers and art haters –

I can think of nothing in poorer taste than accepting an invitation and coming like this. When you know why I am here in such record form you will find me in poorer taste still. I am at the present moment, while you are sitting here, writing rubbish about what sort of throat pastilles Bing Crosby uses, what sort of lingerie Garbo wears, why Clark Gable always has a bath in melted butter . . . And yet, when I come to think of what I am writing, it seems to me to be in better taste than what I used to write. For what is bad taste? If you will forgive my saying so, it is what is usually called good taste. It is self-consciousness. It is refeenment. If someone says to me, 'Do you know Mrs So-and-So? She's such an artistic woman. Her house is in fearfully good taste,' I know what she must be like. I can see the good taste of that house. Mentally, I bark my shins against the unstained oak table and trip over the expensive steel furniture of that artistic woman's drawing-room. Good taste nowadays is an aping of mass-production, which sends up the price of what should be cheap. Good taste nowadays has come to be identified with the expensive; and so I thank God that I am poor.

'Montie' Montagu-Nathan wrote to John on 11 March 1935 to thank him for his contribution to the evening. 'The thing "got over" with complete success. And your proxy received such a greeting that instead of wishing you were present on the platform I should like you to have been in the audience.'

Though John was playing for laughs, the pettishness in his recorded voice as he describes his work for the *Standard* suggests how irksome he was finding the job. As he became increasingly bored by reporting on films and stars, he hit on an ingenious way of writing instead about the London suburbs, which interested him far more – Wood Green, Acton, Ealing, Stepney, Maida Vale, Kilburn, Hammersmith and Streatham. He pretended to be doing 'field work', analysing what kinds of film were most popular in each suburb. In reality he was portraying the character of the suburbs – as he was to do in his 'Metroland' film on television almost forty years on.

Ninety-nine years ago Wood Green became a place of retirement for Aged Fishmongers and Poulterers, who still have an institution there.

Now it is hardly a place for the noisiest fishmonger to retire to. It is busy making sweets, stockings and batteries. It resounds with trams, roars with buses, blazes with lights and squelches with shops. Long streets struggle up the hill to where, like a broody flamingo, the 'Ally Pally' reigns over all. She even broods over the Gaumont Palace, which is big enough, heaven knows.

Another diversion John allowed himself as a change from the drudgery of workaday film-reviewing, was to make up verses about the films and stars. Sometimes indulgent sub-editors let these through. He broke into verse – which anticipates his 1940s poem 'How to Get On in Society' – to comment on an American report that Hollywood (because of the attack on it by the purity movement) 'has its back to the wall and is breathing hard . . . It is fighting for its very life.' He imagined Mae West, Marlene Dietrich and Jean Harlow singing a dirge:

> I can offer you tea and a biscuit,
>   Will you please go and shout at the door,
> Over there at the end of the ballroom,
>   As the bell doesn't work any more?
>
> It's terrible, all this privation,
>   I can't understand what they mean,
> If we give up our platinum bathrooms
>   Well, how can we ever be clean?

Occasionally the *Standard* would let John off the leash to write feature articles on subjects other than films: 'How to Look at the Map'; 'Museums Should Be More Attractive'; 'How Do the Clergy Live?' and 'Why I Am Glad that We Are Negotiating with Ireland'. Stuart Piggott gave him help with a debunking piece headed 'The Druids Were Over-rated'. The most vivid of the general articles were on afternoon teas and preparatory schools. In the teas article, he mocked the names of country tearooms – 'Dame Nature's Pantry', 'Primula's Kitchen', 'At Ye Signe of Ye Olde Spynnynge Wheele' – and warned of what awaited people who braved teatime in country hotels.

> The afternoon is sleepy. The porter is having his nap. No one is about. 'Ring bell for waitress.' You ring. A long pause.
>   'May I have tea, please?'
>   'Will you have it in the lounge, or in the coffee room?'
>   If you choose the coffee room, you will sit among the tables laid for dinner, looking at someone's special bottle of sauce and someone else's bottle of spa water, not quite finished, waiting for the next meal.
>   If you choose the lounge, be it wicker chair and palm variety, or mahogany and stained glass, there will be out-of-date numbers of weekly periodicals to look at. Tea will be brought eventually, and you will be glad to step out into the open air.

As with Harold Nicolson, the *Standard* job was bringing John fame, if not reputation, and he received many requests to write articles, collaborate on 'projects' and make public appearances. One commission he accepted was to write for *Kinematograph Weekly* an article criticizing the architecture of London movie theatres. The piece appeared in the issue of 17 January 1935 under the headline 'Has England Any Artistic Kinemas?'. Because this subject engaged John's interest, the article is more spirited – more Betjemanesque – than the general run of his *Standard* film critiques.

> When I write about kinemas as buildings, I cannot help thinking, without any disrespect, of churches. Kinemas are often the churches of to-day. In the provinces and in the suburbs whole families attend the kinema with the weekly regularity that their grandparents attended church or chapel. They have their special seats, just as their forebears had their special pews.
>
> But there is this difference. Churches, until a hundred years ago, led the way in architecture. Kinemas lag behind.
>
> The new Gaumont Palace at Chelsea . . . is in a pseudo-Swedish style that is already out of date. In ten years that interior will be a curiosity like the echoing vaults of the St Pancras Hotel or the terra-cotta fastnesses of the Hotel Grand Central. It will cost a mint of money to bring it 'up to date'.

When leaving the *Standard* job in 1935, John wrote that he had been more a 'film informer' than a film critic. As well as reviewing, he was expected to tell his readers facts and news about the stars. But he was not a success as a newsman. One story of his hopelessness as a reporter became Fleet Street legend. As told to Simon Jenkins, who was a journalist on the *Evening Standard* in the 1970s and became its editor in 1976, the story runs like this. John knocks at Percy Cudlipp's door. 'Come in. Oh, hello, Betjeman. What's the matter?'

'Please, sir, I think I've got one of those "scoop" things.'

'Oh, really? How do you know it's a scoop?'

'Well, I've rung the *Evening News*, and they haven't got it.'

A genuine scoop of John's – one of only two pieces by him that made the front page of the *Standard* – was about Merle Oberon's breaking off her engagement to the movie mogul Joseph Schenck. According to Osbert Lancaster, Schenck 'made such a stink' about the story that Beaverbrook ordered Cudlipp to fire John; but (Lancaster said) the British film industry advertisers protested strongly about the sacking – threatening to withdraw their advertising – and John was reinstated.

John's other front-page scoop was that Lady Caroline Paget, eldest daughter of the Marquess of Anglesey, was to star in a film. John had good reason to know the inside story on that, since he himself took a small part in the film, as a clergyman. The film was made at Ashcombe, Cecil Beaton's Georgian house in Wiltshire. Beaton's and John's friend John Sutro, who was a director of London Film Productions, had often wondered why even the smallest movie should cost such a lot of money. Would it not be possible to produce something worthwhile for only a few hundred pounds? Sutro and Beaton decided to attempt at Ashcombe an amateur film of David Garnett's story *The Sailor's Return*, about a Victorian sailor who brings back to his village from overseas a black wife named Tulip, a small dark daughter and a parrot. The cast was to consist of friends, neighbours, farmhands and the family of Betteridge, the Ashcombe game-keeper. From Denham Studios came make-up men, electricians and photographers with their arc-lights. The studio became a dormitory and the dining-room a canteen. The costumes were run up in a day.

The Sailor's Return was never completed. 'As with many amateur enterprises,' Beaton wrote, 'there was no enthusiasm left to supply the dreary but essential finishing touches, and the film was never finally cut or the sound-track added.' If John had intended to remain a professional film critic, the experience of helping to make a film – however amateurish – might have been of value to him. But a month after taking part in the Ashcombe film, he was writing an acerbic farewell article in the *Standard*, 'Good-bye to Films'. Nerina Shute's recollection was that he was fired, this time without reprieve. 'Someone had arrived from Hollywood, I can't remember who, but some very well-known star; and it was a *news* story – you had to go and meet this person and interview them and it was very important. And he just didn't go. He couldn't bear to go to Southampton or wherever it was to meet a film star. And the editor said, "Why didn't you go?" and he said "Well, I didn't feel like it." That was the end of John Betjeman on the *Standard*. I remember his telling me about it and laughing. He thought it was terribly funny, and so did I; because anybody in Fleet Street, as I'm sure you know, thinks that the most important thing in the world is a news story – it's the Holy Grail.'

As when leaving *The Architectural Review*, it seems likely that he precipitated his own downfall at the *Standard* when sick of the job. In the farewell article he spared no one's feelings.

> Yesterday I wrote my last article as film critic in this paper. When I started off, a pale green bogus-intellectual, a year and a half ago, what a different man was I.
>
> A visit or two to some Continental films, a sarcastic sneer to any people who told me they were in love with Greta Garbo, and that was the sum of my cinematic experience. The word 'montage' was on my lips, 'art' was written in poker work across my heart, 'prose style' was embroidered with raffia on the reverse side of it.
>
> I was as typical a middlebrow as ever thought he was highbrow and tried to write poetry in Hampstead.

And now what would you see, were these lines of type to fly about and form themselves into a portrait of the author, as in some French surréaliste short film? You would see a bald elderly man, still pale green, but with a tough expression, grim business-like lips and a pair of unscrupulous eyes gleaming behind recently acquired horn-rimmed spectacles. In fact, you would see a typical member of the film business.

The farewell article appeared in the *Standard* eight days before John's twenty-ninth birthday. He still had the resilience of youth. Even when venting his exasperation with film-reviewing, he kept his sense of humour. 'Films were gradually turning me dotty. I used to come out of a Press showing and caress the bricks in the street, grateful that they were three-dimensional. If I saw a thuggish-looking man with his hat pulled down over his face, I expected to be shot in the back.' John considered he had done well to stick at such a mind-numbing job for a year and a half. 'The old old story seven times a week is . . . more than enough for the most willing ears after a year.' And brief as his reviewing stint was, it made him – in 1930s Britain with its cult of the gentleman amateur – a 'films expert'. When, in 1938, Charles Davy edited a book entitled *Footnotes to the Film*, John was one of the contributors, alongside Alfred Hitchcock, Robert Donat, Graham Greene, Alberto Cavalcanti, John Grierson, Alexander Korda and Sidney Bernstein. And during the Second World War, when a medical board pronounced John unfit for any war service, his reputation as a films expert enabled Kenneth Clark to find him a job in the films division of the Ministry of Information.*

---

* See Chapter 15, ' "Minnie" '.

13

'That's Shell – That Was!'

After resigning from the *Standard*, John had time on his hands. He used some of it to keep a diary, intermittently, during the second half of 1935 and the first few months of 1936. As far as we know, it was the only journal he ever kept. Parts of it are gossip, and there are jottings on architecture, but the diary also gives a view of him in his late twenties more intimate than any of his printed writings, where his frankness about his appearance and his melancholia conceal as much as they reveal. In the diary his preoccupations and fears are naked, not dressed up for public consumption. There is no sense that he is writing with an eye on posterity.

It was a meeting with George Bernard Shaw and his wife Charlotte, at Lord Berners's house, that inspired him to begin it, in August 1935, but he stopped a few days later. After a long gap John resumed the diary on 5 October, at which time Penelope was in Rome, attending a Conference of Orientalists. John dined with Berners, Diana Guinness (later Lady Mosley) and W. H. Auden.

> We all went to W[ystan Auden]'s play 'Dance of Death' well produced & impressive satire, wish there had not been the clumsy attempt at realism at the end. D[iana] thought Mosley bits excellent & pro-fascist, clapped. Hissed when red flag appeared . . . Diana took us back to Eaton Square & played the leader's speech & Hitler's on gramophone. W[ystan] unimpressed. As Gerald says 'I feel I may have a row with Diana any minute.' W finds Gerald a v sympathetic character.

On 6 October John lunched with Auden at Curtain's restaurant. 'No talk about literature thank God,' he wrote. 'Find him refreshingly unchanged. Said I wished he'd kept D[ance] of D[eath] satire all through. "You forget my views, my dear." Saw his piece [a boy Auden admired at the Downs School, where he had been teaching until recently] accompanied by master arrive at Waterloo. W dashed back to say, "What do you think?" "Not bad." Big ears.'

After another hiatus in the diary, John wrote up a visit to E. E. Bradford, the 'Uranian' poet whose verse made him scream with laughter. However comic John found the verse, he was sympathetic to the poet.

> Funny bald head flat on top & pearshaped. Blue eyes. Poor old man obviously cataract coming on. Won't admit he is failing. Knocked over firescreen & broke it. Quiet hurried little movements. Frail sweet little person. Walks 16 miles on some days. No car, walks everywhere. Thrilled at sight of motor. Ran 3 miles 2 years ago when late for a funeral. Found he was not tired afterwards. Believes in helping young.
>
> . . . Cold supper in vicarage . . . Felt the better for seeing such a sweet & saintly little man . . . Surely never did a bad thing in his life.

Meeting W. H. Auden again had made John want to see more of him. On 16 December he wrote:

> Wystan Auden stayed. P[enelope] in London to see her father Sat night so W & I got tight or at least mellow & went through the whole of Evensong (broad to high). More fun later. Sunday went to hear [the Rev. S. E.] Cottam preach [another paedophile vicar]. Ch v empty. Terrific attack on the people of Wootton he knew of no parish which helped its clergyman so little. As W says he is obviously going mad. His eyes roll & he never looks at one but out of the corners of them – persecution mania. W thinks he will have to be taken away soon.

The diary then jumps to 7 February 1936, for an entry about Uffington villagers.

> To-day poor old Mrs Townsend died getting out of bed. 'I heard the death rattle last night,' said T[ownsend] '& then this morning she said the bottle was cold & I thought, "that's funny" for it was warm enough to wash up the tea things. So I brought her another & then found her all in a heap on the floor.' He changed into his Sunday clothes at once & went off on his old bicycle. Old Mrs Norton died in the Radcliffe at 2 a.m.

The diary of 1935–36 is fragmented and truncated; but it gives us a direct conduit into John's thinking at the age of twenty-nine. One strand in it is the peculiarly eager interest in literary homosexuals, not to say paedophiles. The visits – almost pilgrimages – to S. E. Cottam and E. E. Bradford have later analogies in his seeking out the Uranian novelist and art historian Forrest Reid, in Belfast, and in his suggestion to Siegfried Sassoon, in the 1950s, that they should call on Sidney Mavor, the last surviving boyfriend of Oscar Wilde. (It turned out that he had just died.) Too much should not be read into John's renewed friendship with Auden and his light-hearted appraisal of Auden's 'piece'. Much more significant are the entries which show that John was anti-fascist, convinced that a war was coming and determined not to fight in it. At that time he was still formally a Quaker: that fact, as well as his admitted fear of death, may have been a motive for wishing to avoid the battlefield – fighting shy of it, one might say. Most of the Oxford undergraduates who in 1933 caused national outrage, when they voted that they would not fight for King and Country in a future war, served in the armed forces when war broke out. John's outlook was also to change completely by 1939. Then, it was the armed forces that rejected him, not he them.

Another literary activity at this time, and one which brought in a little money, was John's rôle as editor of the Shell Guides to English counties. He had been introduced to Jack Beddington, the dynamic publicity manager of Shell-Mex BP, in his (John's) days on *The Architectural Review*. Operating from Shell-Mex House, the monolithic, much reviled new building by Francis Cashmore which replaced the old Hotel Cecil on the Victoria Embankment of the Thames, Beddington was an inspired patron of artists, many of them young and untried. Among them were John Piper, Graham Sutherland, Ben Nicholson, Duncan Grant, Rex Whistler (who caricatured him), E. McKnight Kauffer, Edward Bawden, Edward Ardizzone and Mary Kessell, who became Kenneth Clark's lover. Beddington commissioned several of them to contribute to a great poster campaign. Instead of getting safe academic poster artists to paint landscapes of local beauty spots, as the railway companies were doing, Beddington relied on the humorous approach. The poster that caught on best was the 'double-headed man' designed by John Reynolds, son of a *Punch* art editor: the idea was that the man's head was swivelling violently from one side to the other as a car full of Shell petrol roared past in a blur of dust. The slogan was 'CRIKEY! THAT'S SHELL – THAT WAS!'

Beddington gave work to writers as well as artists. Evelyn Waugh and Peter Quennell both contributed. Early in 1933 John suggested to Beddington the idea of the Shell Guides – a series of guidebooks to British counties that would display the individuality of the writer as well as of the county. John was to be general editor. At first he did the work at weekends and on holidays but after he stormed out of *The Architectural Review* in 1935, he was able to devote much more time to the project. This was perhaps the first paid work he had undertaken – apart from writing poetry – which promised to be really congenial.

No sooner had he embarked on this enterprise – which was to occupy him on and off for over thirty years – than he wrote Beddington a panicky letter attacking Maurice Regan, part-owner of the Architectural Press. 'I do not wish to be unpleasant about the Regans, but they are not our sort. They all live in Wimbledon, have closed saloons, see no one but each other and are not interested in anything but getting money which they do not know how to spend.' Regan's offence was to have told Percy Hastings all about the Shell Guides without mentioning that the idea was John's.

The morose, somewhat paranoid letter reveals John's depressed state of mind at that time. But it also shows the political skill with which he could always urge his case when he wanted something. First, there is the background summary of the situation at the Architectural Press, with just enough malice and piquant detail to hold Beddington's interest as the long moan continues. The sub-text of the letter is: 'I would like to leave *The Architectural Review* and come and work for you at Shell.' This plea is implicit throughout and John comes close to making it explicit.

Jack Beddington picked up every nuance of the letter and knew what he could promise and what, at this stage, he should not promise. On 19 August he wrote John a soothing letter, beginning, 'My dear John, You do want a holiday — what a cri de coeur!' He could and would insist that John was to be responsible for the whole make-up and was to get the credit for the entire job. He could also promise the same for future guides, though he did not think he would be able to issue them without the aid of the Architectural Press. On John's ambition to join Shell he put a damper: he could see little chance of that happening and was convinced that 'it would be a great mistake for you at the moment to try to do such a thing'. Beddington added: '*Private*. Secretly between you and me personally for my part I rather liked Regan (as I believe that privately for your part personally you do too) . . .'

In fact, John continued to feel resentment towards Maurice Regan and his family. His satirical poem 'Kegans', first published in *Uncollected Poems* (1982) but written years before — probably in the 1930s — was originally entitled 'Regans'. The last two stanzas run:

> And bridge and golf and golf and bridge
> > And travels in the car,
> A large saloon with all aswoon
> > From Reginald's [Maurice's] cigar;
> From three to four an A.A. tour
> > And then the cinema.
>
> We've left our hearts in Wimbledon
> > Our feet are in the waves,
> And when the rain comes down again
> > We'll shelter in the caves,
> And if we see impurity,
> > Remember 'Jesus saves'.

John wrote the first Shell Guide, on Cornwall. Published in 1934 at 2s 6d, it had a title-page of fantastical typography, reminiscent of the covers of *Mount Zion* and *Ghastly Good Taste*; but the new cover was a simple photograph with the title in austere sans-serif lettering. The endpapers were photographs of shells and the book had a spiral wire binding – very Modern Movement. Besides topographical and architectural details and photographs, *Cornwall* contained a recipe for Cornish pasties and an article on fishing in Cornwall, contributed by Ernest Betjemann. In the acknowledgements John thanked his father for the article and added: 'If an Editor is allowed to dedicate a book, he would like to dedicate this one to him. His father first taught him to love Cornwall.' This, in the last year of Ernest's life, was as near as John came to a gesture of reconciliation.

The Cornwall guide was very successful and Beddington asked John to plan guides for other counties. In January 1935 John sent him a progress report. The Northumberland guide was under way, but he wanted Beddington's permission to offer W. H. Auden money to contribute a general article on the county. Paul Nash's *Dorset* was in final page form at the printer's and Peter Quennell's *Somerset* was 'on the way'. John was often described – in his later years especially – as 'bumbling'; but this letter to Beddington again shows how businesslike he could be when he chose. He is aware that Beddington wants to know what has been done, what is being done, what difficulties may arise, when he can expect results – and what it is all costing. ('The setting up of the type [of the Northumberland guide] has cost £12, we have spent another £88 in blocks & maps . . .')

John's second guide, *Devon*, appeared in 1936. Other guides followed in quick, efficient succession. 'John farmed out the Shell Guide commissions to all his cronies,' said Sir James Richards. '*Kent*, I remember, was edited by a slightly dissolute peer.' The dissolute peer was Lord Clonmore, whose account of Canterbury Cathedral began: 'To travel in Kent without visiting Canterbury is rather like eating plum pudding without brandy butter.' Robert Byron edited *Wiltshire* (1935), for which Lord Berners designed an extraordinary collage cover. Edith Olivier, with her intimate knowledge of the county, wrote the gazetteer section of the Wiltshire book. It has been plausibly suggested that the elegantly compressed style of her entries influenced John's later topographical writing.

The success of the Shell Guides and the fun of working with John finally persuaded Jack Beddington to take him on to the staff at Shell as a copy-writer. John was given a desk in a large office at Shell-Mex House, near the company's Church of England chapel which he called 'St Mary Mex'. He shared the office with Beddington's other aide-de-camp William Scudamore

Mitchell, a gentle, good-humoured man whom John and his friends called 'Scudamore' to tease him about his kinship with the Lords Scudamore whose baroque tombs were illustrated in the Shell Guide to *Wiltshire*. Like Philip Harding at Marlborough, Mitchell was a quiet, sympathetic figure who played stooge to John's fizzing vivacity. John tried out new poems on him. Mitchell was given a manuscript of 'Holy Trinity, Sloane Street', headed in John's best Arts and Crafts lettering embellished with Voysey hearts.

Part of John's job was to think up slogans for the poster campaign. He was especially adept at the punning topographical slogan — 'Ashby-de-la-Zouch but SHELL sur la route'; 'Stow-on-the-Wold but SHELL on the Road'. The cartoonist Nicolas Bentley rendered 'Wormwood Scrubs but . . .', 'Gerrards Cross but . . .' and 'Mother Shipton's Well but . . .'. Edward Bawden designed the Freudian nightmare of 'Stonehenge Wilts but SHELL goes on for ever' — the giant stones actually drooping.

E. McKnight Kauffer (1890–1954) was the finest poster artist employed by Shell. He made typography an integral part of his designs, not just an added label. Like John — and often with him — 'Ted' Kauffer and his girl-friend Marion Dorn enjoyed the *bon vivant* entertainment that Beddington offered his friends at the Café Royal and the Gargoyle Club in London. Kauffer and Dorn became John's friends. He visited them in their successive ultra-modern flats, furnished in beige, dove-grey and aluminium, with modernist rugs by both of the couple. Kauffer designed a surreal jacket for John's collection of poems *Continual Dew* (1937). At the time the artist was strongly influenced by the work of the French posterist A. M. Cassandre; it was perhaps the resulting European look that caused the volume to be reviewed, by one English paper, as *Continental Dew*.

Anthony Powell, whom John had known slightly at Oxford, but now knew much better through Powell's marriage into the Pakenham family, was encouraged to try his hand at slogans for the old-and-new 'Times Change . . .' advertising campaign. Powell commented in a letter of 1988:

> Shell did indeed use at least two of my suggestions for Old & New; so far as I can remember, an Old Time Sergeant saying 'Fall in, defaulters', New Type, 'Fall in, Trigonometry candidates' and Old Time actor, 'I trod the boards with Irving', New Type, 'Noël's practically offered me a part', but Shell never sent me a halfpenny for using them which I thought pretty shabby as a couple of guineas would have been most acceptable at that moment.

In recounting this episode — in almost identical words — in his journal (31 October 1988), Powell added: 'I always thought that rather discreditable on Betjeman's part.' Since John was Powell's contact at Shell, it was perhaps natural for Powell to bear him a grudge over the non-payment; but as Beddington held the purse-strings at Shell he was probably more to blame than John. The publicity manager was not universally popular. The film director Dallas Bower, who in the early 1940s shared a room with John in the films division of the Ministry of Information – a division headed by Beddington – left the Ministry because he 'could not bear him'. But, to John, Beddington was one of his guardian angels, one of the people who could do no wrong for him, while Gidney, C. S. Lewis, the Regans and Pevsner could do no right.

It was through the Shell Guides that John was to meet his dearest friend, John Piper. In 1936, when Piper was thirty-three – three years older than John – J. M. Richards suggested that he might write the guide to Oxfordshire. Piper went along to the Shell offices to meet John and be introduced to Jack Beddington. He was shown into an office where William Scudamore Mitchell and John were amusing themselves by writing limericks about the Shell secretaries. 'Some of them were fairly indecent,' Piper said. 'And I thought the atmosphere in the office was more amusing than anything I'd seen, because I had never been in an office before.' John and Piper soon found that they had given themselves the same kind of training, bicycling round the countryside looking at church architecture. Neither man yet knew it, but there was another link between Piper and the Betjemans: Myfanwy Evans, then his girlfriend and soon to be his second wife, had been at school with Penelope at Queen's College, London, during the First World War. And Myfanwy independently knew Jack Beddington, because she was involved in the Group Theatre's meetings in Great Newport Street, London, which he chaired.

John Piper and Myfanwy had been together since they were introduced by the painter Ivon Hitchens in 1934; Piper's first wife, Eileen Holding, had gone off to France. Piper was still an almost exclusively abstract artist. But he was also a photographer. It was through his photography that he had built up a reputation as a topographer and architectural historian. He and Myfanwy had been driving round England in a 1920 Lancia which he had bought for £15, photographing Romanesque font-carvings.

At the Shell-Mex House meeting, Piper was given the commission. John Betjeman suggested that the guide should be called simply *Oxon* – and so it was. 'John just let us get on with Oxford,' Piper said. 'He didn't exercise editorial control. He was amazed by the production that he got; he thought that everything was absolutely super. He got funny pictures of signposts at Salford and articles by Myfanwy about Deserted Places. He was shattered by the manuscript he got, and he didn't alter one sausage of it.

The only intervention he made was to write the most frightfully funny captions — including the celebrated "tree of knowledge" one [John's description of a multi-flanged signpost].'

In 1937 Myfanwy became pregnant and she and John Piper decided that they ought to get married; he was by then divorced. In the same year Piper's mother bought them a farmhouse at Fawley Bottom, Henley-on-Thames ('Fawley Bum', as the Pipers and Betjemans called it in their correspondence) and the Pipers had water put in, though, like Garrards Farm, the house was still without electricity. It was their home for the rest of their lives.

Piper was to be not only John's dearest but also his most compatible friend. His modesty was a foil to John's exhibitionism. His gifts as an artist and photographer complemented, and did not challenge, John's as a writer. As Richard Ingrams has pointed out, the two had a great deal in common. They were both children of the middle class. Both had rebelled against fathers who wanted them to take over the family business: after Epsom College, Piper had become an articled clerk in his father's firm of solicitors, but on his father's death in 1928 had at once given up the law to become an artist, studying first at the Richmond School of Art, then at the Royal College of Art. Above all, the two men shared a sense of humour. Late in life, Piper said on a television programme: 'If a Mephistopheles were to say to me, "You can have your life over again; but you must make a choice. You can either give up creating all your works of art, or you can give up all the jokes you have enjoyed with John Betjeman" – unhesitatingly, I would give up the works of art.'

And then there was Myfanwy. She was to be one of John's muses, the inspiration of two poems. The 'golden Myfanwy' of Arthur Machen's *The Secret Glory* was an almost mystical harbinger of his meeting her. He loved her. She had the 'schoolgirl' look that always appealed to him; but also there was something austerely mystical about her, something of the Celtic enchantress, of witchcraft, medievalism, Pre-Raphaelitism and the young Edith Sitwell. He called her 'Goldilocks' – sometimes 'Goldilegs'. In the poems 'Myfanwy' and 'Myfanwy at Oxford' (both written in the late 1930s and published in *Old Lights for New Chancels*, 1940) he fantasized about her schooldays and her life as an Oxford undergraduate, teasingly implying in both poems that she might be the object of lesbian longings.

John and Myfanwy Piper were introduced to the Betjemans' circle of friends. Piper credited John with having converted himself and Myfanwy to Christianity. John modestly denied this: 'It was probably looking at all those Norman fonts,' he said. The Pipers were baptized, though Piper thought the officiating priest 'a pompous old trout'. The introduction to Osbert Lancaster was the most successful. 'Osbert was sent to Fawley Bottom by John,' Piper said. 'He arrived on his bicycle one day and said, "I'm Osbert Lancaster" and I said, "Well, anybody could see you were." And we got on like a house on fire. He was then living in a cottage with Derek Verschoyle, the literary editor of *The Spectator*, who was married to Osbert's future wife Anne Scott-James.' Lancaster and his first wife Karen became such great friends of the Pipers that they moved to Leicester House, Henley, to be near them; and in 1951 Piper and Lancaster together designed the Grand Vista for the Festival of Britain's Pleasure Gardens at Battersea.

One of the introductions John made to Piper was, in Piper's view, the making of his own career as an artist. The introduction was to Lord Alfred Douglas. John had interested Piper in eighteenth-century guidebooks illustrated with aquatints, and Piper began making a series of sensitive aquatints of Brighton. John suggested that they should be published as a book, and that Lord Alfred Douglas should be asked to contribute a preface. 'John got Bosie to come up from Brighton,' Piper remembered. 'We all had lunch – Myfanwy, John, Bosie and I – at Overton's outside Victoria station, so that Bosie could get back to Brighton where he could see up the little girls' skirts from his basement flat as they went over the iron railings – his tastes had changed.'

Brighton Aquatints was published in 1939 in two editions, one of them limited to fifty copies in which the prints were coloured by hand. One of these, 'Brighton from the Station Yard', was hand-painted in all fifty copies by John Betjeman. Piper always claimed that it was *Brighton Aquatints*, and in particular Douglas's foreword, that 'put him on the map'. He thought it was probably the Douglas foreword that had attracted Osbert Sitwell to write a full-page review of the book (with an illustration) in *The Listener*. Sitwell wrote that Piper's drawings manifested 'all the quality, the ease and speed, of beautiful handwriting'. Piper said: 'After that I became one of the boys.' The article was immediately followed by an exhibition at the Leicester Galleries, which sold out.

The two Johns agreed to write the Shell Guide to Shropshire together. (Although written in 1939, the book was not published until after the war.) It was a county neither knew well, though John had read the book on Shrewsbury by W. H. Auden's father and had been to Apley Park, a Berners property. They drove up to Shrewsbury in Piper's car – by now the 1920 Lancia had been replaced by a Citroën Light 15 – and made their headquarters at the Prince Rupert Hotel, conveniently near St Mary's Church where John Betjeman attended Communion each day. 'It was marvellous going with Mr Piper for the first time,' John told Richard Ingrams. 'It was like going to Brazil or somewhere.' In all, the two men made about five separate journeys to Shropshire, sometimes accompanied by Myfanwy. Piper took photographs and made sketches.

In a biography of Piper (1979), Anthony West, the son of Rebecca West by H. G. Wells, persuasively suggested that there was a cross-pollination of talent on the journeys John and Piper made together for the Shell Guides. Piper 'gained a great deal from this intimate working association with a poet who, whatever his carefully maintained public persona and his lighter verse may suggest to the contrary, combines a profound seriousness with a refined sensibility'; while 'The poet's eye fed on what was valued by the painter's . . .'

However, light-heartedness was in the ascendant on the topographical jaunts. Piper told Richard Ingrams that it was at Much Wenlock, on the Shropshire trip, that he got his Betjeman nickname of 'Mr Piper' (or, as John usually wrote it, 'Mr Pahper'). They called at a hotel for tea and were told to sit in a waiting-room. Finally a waitress came in and said in a strong North Country accent, 'Will you two men come forward, please?' When they sat down, John started talking in a similar accent, pretending to be a businessman and addressing his colleague as 'Mr Pahper'. Stuart Piggott recalled that when he first met John Piper, 'he and John Betjeman were just back from a tour in connexion with the Shell Guides . . . and kept up conversations in a comic Shropshire accent, full of flat vowels and hard "g's" – "swimmingg" and "singgingg" . . .'

Myfanwy loved John too; but it was not an uncritical love. Five months after his death in 1984, when the exhibition 'John Betjeman – A Celebration' opened at the National Theatre, London, she wrote in *The Times* that it was 'hard . . . not to feel a little jealous of an old friendship with someone whose store of acute perceptions and eccentricities has, as it were, gone public'. John, she suggested, had approached all human relationships by way of an idea of character or an invented situation. '"Approached" is perhaps the wrong expression: "staved off" is more like it. When I first met him, nearly fifty years ago, the game had to be played; the invented character and ambience discovered, then accepted with a good grace and then exploited to mutual satisfaction and many jokes. All the people accepted and loved by him had to put up with it, even and especially his own family.' Myfanwy added:

It was when he carried the game beyond affectation and into social comment and alien territory that 'long-suffering' was an appropriate term. There was an occasion in an apparently empty bar at the Mytton and Mermaid near Shrewsbury when the Shropshire guide was being written. He suddenly spied, in a corner, a commercial traveller writing up his notes. We were then treated to a long imaginary sales talk about a whistling kettle in a persistent, boring Midland undertone. It was very funny and we were appalled: hopeless tears of laughter were mixed with tears of embarrassment – could what was going on be heard, or guessed at?

14

Decoration

A T FIRST THE VILLAGERS of Uffington viewed the Betjemans as strangers and Bohemians, exempt from the rules by which they themselves
lived. Gradually this attitude changed. The newcomers' warmth and sincerity established a rapport with all but a few of the local people. Even so,
there were limits to the pleasure John and Penelope could derive from
conversations about the price of bran or about the macabre agricultural
accidents which are part of folklore.

Three men who took houses in the Uffington area in the 1930s became
friends of the Betjemans: Adrian Bishop, Christopher Blunt and Arthur
MacKenzie. Bishop was a friend of Maurice Bowra. He had come to
Uffington to recover from a bout of *encephalitis lethargica* (sleepy sickness)
from which he had almost died. Bowra had first met him in 1921 when he
visited Oxford, and was not sure that he liked him. 'He was tall and heavy
and dark, with slightly curly hair, a receding forehead and noticeably bad
teeth. He was used to dominating any group in which he mixed, and in
this, as in other ways, he resembled Oscar Wilde, who came from the same
layer of Dublin society.' This was Bowra's way of indicating that Bishop
was homosexual; as Penelope put it, 'I'm afraid he liked the gentlemen.'
Bowra respected Bishop as a classical scholar. He relished his 'overpowering vitality, his gift for juggling with words, and his quick, satirical wit'. In
1936, when Bowra was lecturing at Harvard, he received a letter from
Bishop saying that, no doubt as a result of his brush with death, he had
been brought to God. 'His hostility to religion and his derisive jokes about
it', Bowra wrote, 'indicated that it played a larger part in his mind than if
he had been merely indifferent.' To John Betjeman, the combination in
Bishop of wit, homosexuality, religious conversion and a recommendation
from Maurice Bowra made the Irishman an interesting neighbour. Bishop
was invited to dinners, introduced to the Berners circus and dragooned
into Penelope's village entertainments. He was eventually to become an
Anglican novice at Nashdom Abbey.

Christopher Blunt, the brother of John's schoolfriend Anthony (there was a third brother, Wilfrid, who taught art at Eton), lived with his wife Anne at Woolstone, the village next to Uffington. Two years younger than John, he had been at Marlborough with him. A merchant banker by profession, he was also the leading expert on Anglo-Saxon coinage. Wilfrid considered Christopher 'by far the best of the Blunts', though he added that 'both Anthony and I thought him a shade pompous . . .'. John too thought Christopher 'a bit of an old stuffy', but went over to Woolstone when Anthony visited his brother. Anthony was still on good terms with John, though according to Wilfrid 'his close friendship in early days with John Betjeman later fell apart because he felt that John, who had the makings of a scholar, elected – as Anthony saw it – to prostitute his talents by popularizing what he could have directed into serious study'.

Arthur and Eileen MacKenzie lived just down the road from John and Penelope. The archaeologist Seton Lloyd recalled in 1989, at the age of eighty-seven, 'They lived in a rather disorganized house in Uffington, the wife bringing up five sons on practically no money at all while he worked assiduously and continuously in the hothouses producing innumerable incomprehensible sculptures, which nobody, at that time, bought.' John procured MacKenzie a job as art master at Oundle, where he created many more sculptures. (Eventually he was given a one-man show in London under the pseudonym George Kennethson, and sold about half a dozen.) Arthur's parents lived in Beaulieu and in 1945, recovering from an operation, John would go to stay with them, and write 'Youth and Age on Beaulieu River, Hants'.

In August 1936 a chance encounter on a train brought the Betjemans two new friends: the Rev. Francis Harton, Vicar of Baulking, four miles from Uffington, and his wife Sibyl. In her nineties, Mrs Harton recalled her first meeting with John and Penelope. She was in a train on the little line that ran under White Horse Hill. Her husband had become vicar three weeks before. In the railway carriage, besides herself, were a young couple and an elderly woman – 'very much a countrywoman, and in those days they were very poorly clad'. The young couple attracted Sibyl Harton's attention at once because they were bickering. 'They were glaring at each other. I hadn't met that kind of thing before. They were quite oblivious of being in public.' Sibyl Harton did her best to concentrate on a book.

> But about the second station the old lady was preparing to get out. And, this is what was so noticeable and so typical of John. At once he was up opening the door, handing her out her old country parcels, without any

self-consciousness and without a great deal of attention to her personally –
but just doing it. It struck me very much. He would do just the same, in the
same sort of way, for anybody. That's what I always noticed about John: he
had this innate kindness which was more than ordinary, and it would be the
same whether you were in rags or in a crown.

The next Sunday, the young man (she had not yet found out who he was)
was in Baulking church, with another man. After the service, the two
introduced themselves as John Betjeman and Adrian Bishop.

Both became devoted disciples of Father Harton, as he liked to be known.
John read his book *Elements of the Spiritual Life*, on a holiday in Rome with
Penelope and Joan Eyres Monsell in 1937, and felt his faith renewed by it.
Maurice Bowra, who also became a great friend of the Hartons, commented
that it must be the first time anybody had been converted to Protestantism
by a journey to Rome. John often attended church at Baulking, rather than
Uffington, and Harton became his confessor.

Father Harton was one of the few people capable of putting Penelope
in her place. She was renowned for her dislike of cocktail parties. She drank
only ginger beer and did not enjoy trivial chat. At a party given by her
cousin Lord Methuen at Corsham Court near Bath, she spent some time
ostentatiously darning two pairs of John's socks. Sibyl Harton remembered
a party at Baulking Vicarage. 'We had four or five people in. She came in,
wasn't interested in them or didn't like them, and promptly – I can see her
– went up to the bookshelves and turned her back on us all and browsed.
When our guests had left, my husband said to her, "Penelope, you're *the
rudest woman in Berkshire*."'

The Betjemans loved and respected the Hartons, but that did not stop
them making fun of them behind their backs. Harton they dubbed 'Father
Folky', while Sibyl was 'the Abbess'. The folky-ness really belonged to
Sibyl, who was apt to offer her guests Blue Vinney cheese and raspberry
cordial. She was the author of several books with somewhat twee titles,
such as *Once Upon a Bedtime, Being 52 Delectable Stories from the Bible for the
Want-to-Be-Read-tos* (SPCK, 1937). A later book, *Stars Appearing: Lives of
68 Saints of the Anglican Calendar* (1954), she dedicated 'To John Betjeman,
a good friend'. She radiated goodness; one's own character seemed shoddy
by comparison. A neighbour described her as 'scraped pure'. But there was
an edge of intolerance and censoriousness to her saintliness.

Four years into their marriage, John and Penelope had still had no children. The Field Marshal began to think that another of his suspicions about
John might be well founded. Maurice Bowra wrote a long humorous poem

in which the philoprogenitive Frank and Elizabeth Pakenham (later Earl and Countess of Longford) point out to the Betjemans a stallion serving a mare in a field and suggest they should take heed of this practical sex education. Penelope stood on the White Horse's eye and prayed to the pagan gods for fertility. In 1937 she became pregnant. 'I wish it could be a little horse,' she said to Sibyl Harton. Paul Betjeman was born on 26 November 1937, with wispy blond hair. Penelope had had an agonizing time, with three days of labour followed by a Caesarean.

When it was known that Penelope was expecting a baby, the Betjemans paid for Betty Evans to take a six weeks' training course at the Truby King School for nannies in London. A very experienced nanny from the School came to Uffington for the first fortnight after Paul's birth; then Betty took over. When she was asked in 1989 what Paul had been like as a baby, her husband George chipped in: 'A little ruffian!' She corrected him: 'No, he was quite sweet. Yes, he was a little bit on the wild side as he got older, rather strong-willed; he was nearly five when I left him. But he was a very good baby. His dad used to call him "Egghead" because he had a very oval head and very little hair, to start with. They always used to say, "Oh, come on, Egghead!"'

Betty Packford recalled some of the hazards of life with the Betjemans at Garrards Farm:

> The getting-up routine, with John Betjeman, was pretty awful, because he nearly always went off with either odd socks or odd shoes and he walked around with his Bible while he was dressing – reading a chapter of the Bible. You all had to keep well out of the way, because he never looked where he was going. The Bible-reading took him an awful long time. He was very slow in getting down to breakfast.

Betty remembered frequent quarrels. 'Oh dear, yes. There was always arguments. They used to shout at one another. He'd be upstairs and she'd be shouting downstairs, or the other way round. And also the bathroom was never vacant when she wanted it because he took such a long time. And he could never find his hat; he could never find the right shoes. There were lots of arguments, but they were nice ones – they didn't come to fighting.'

At eight weeks old, Betty remembered, Paul was put 'straight on the back of a horse'. The moment was photographed for the album Penelope had given her with 'Betty' in gold paint on the front. Later Penelope bought a goat cart, like that in which Queen Victoria's children were tugged about the grounds of Balmoral. Paul was sat in the cart and Betty had to walk in front of Snowdrop with a carrot. Betty also had to milk the goat twice a day, as Paul was brought up on goat's milk.

Betty Packford's opinion was that 'John Betjeman was not what you'd call a good father. He very rarely came up to the nursery. John Sparrow, who used to come for weekends, liked to come up to the nursery. We used to call him "Tweet tweet", he was ever so nice. And John Piper used to come up, he was interested in Paul. Osbert Lancaster came sometimes, and Graham Sutherland quite often. But we didn't see much of Mr Betjeman in the nursery.' It was not, Betty thought, just a matter of John's being too involved in his work: 'I don't think he was fond of children anyway.' This lack of sympathy for children is suggested in such poems as 'Sun and Fun' and 'Original Sin on the Sussex Coast'. One might have expected John, after his unhappy relations with his own father, to have lavished special affection on his son. Rather, his behaviour towards him seemed to recreate his own miseries.

Most of John's friends were agreed that he was a failure as a father. Alan Pryce-Jones said: 'Of all the fathers I have known, not excepting myself, he was the worst. I think he liked the *idea* of being a father – the notion of the Victorian *paterfamilias* presiding over the roast beef at Sunday luncheon. But he found that being a father was no fun at all. He was actually cruel to Paul. I have been there when he said, "Look at the Egg. If we sit here long enough, it may say something." A child doesn't like being exposed to that, in mixed company.' In later years John and Penelope more commonly referred to Paul as 'The Powlie', a corruption of his name that fitted into the semi-Irish, semi-Cockney dialect they used in private. The teasing and taunting continued well after infancy. Sibyl Harton remembered travelling to London in the train 'with John teasing Paul until he said, very quietly, "If you don't stop it, I'll get out."'

One of Paul's main playmates, Roy Weaver, lived next door to Garrards Farm. He was the son of Queenie Weaver, Ken Freeman's 'Auntie Queen'. Mrs Weaver said:

> Paul and my boy got into a lot of mischief. I remember once Mrs Betjeman came round and she said, 'You're not to let Roy come down to play with Paul for a week, because they're getting in so much mischief.' Well, partly it was her fault; because she used to take up the carpet in the hall of their house and let them go racing up and down. One day they got a saw and sawed a leg off a little chair. So I said, 'All right, I'll keep Roy home. He shan't come up to play with Paul.' I kept him home two days and she was down and said, 'Let Paul come and play with Roy. He gets into more mischief without him.'

Both Paul's waywardness and Penelope's sublime tactlessness are illustrated by a story told by Robert Heber Percy. When Paul was a small boy, Penelope brought him to tea with Lord Berners at Faringdon House. Paul was throwing a golf ball about in the grand salon, and to Penelope's horror smashed a fine rococo looking-glass. With great courtesy, Berners made light of the accident, assuring Penelope that he could easily find a replacement for the mirror in the Portobello Road market. After tea he saw them into their car. Penelope told Paul to wave goodbye and began to drive off. Suddenly there was a screeching of brakes and a grinding of gears as she reversed up the drive. Arriving outside the house again, she stuck her head out of the window and shouted to Berners:

'I'm awfully sorry, but we've forgotten our golf ball!'

Three weeks before Paul was born, a second collection of John's poems was published. His first collection, *Mount Zion*, published by his rich Oxford friend Edward James in 1931, had been something of a private joke – as it were, an amusing literary party held for friends. Five years later, he began looking around for a 'proper' publisher to present his poetry to the world. The book would contain the best poems from *Mount Zion*, with others written since. T. S. Eliot, John's old prep-school master, courted him in 1936 as a possible Faber author; but he was too late. By then, John had agreed to be published by his friend John ('Jock') Murray. The book, *Continual Dew*, appeared in November 1937.

After Eton, Jock Murray had been at Magdalen, Oxford, from 1927 to 1930, and had thus overlapped with John for one year. The two men kept up their friendship after Oxford, and the care with which Jock Murray preserved John's early letters suggests that he had some inkling of his future fame. Jock was in the know about John's engagement to Penelope in 1933. On 5 May of that year, three months before the marriage, John wrote to him, 'I am so sorry I could not come to your pretty little party last night but Philth [Penelope] was coming to see me, & although I should have had no qualms in bringing her, she came too late to make it polite for me to come . . .' In October of the same year, John wrote:

> Dear Jock,
>   Thanks, old boy, for the congratters. They were topping. Penelope goes to Germany for three months on Sunday while I have to look for a house in the country but within easy reach of London. This will not be bad fun provided P comes back faithful and not a Nazi. I have a lot of funny things to tell you.
>   Would you care to reprint Mount Zion with considerable additions?
>   I will be in London Monday for the rest of my life . . .

This was John's first tentative overture to Murray, but no further move was made until 1936. It was uncertain whether Edward James held the copyright in the *Mount Zion* poems and, if he did, whether he would allow them to be reprinted. John knew how difficult and cantankerous James could be; but luckily there was something James wanted from him, and in return he was prepared to let the *Mount Zion* poems be reissued. James wanted poems and essays by John for *Minotaure*, a new review in which he had a financial interest; he also wanted John to use his influence with his literary friends to get them to contribute.

In a letter to Jock Murray of 28 September 1936, John listed the poems from *Mount Zion* which he thought could be omitted from the new collection '& any others you like to remove'. In February 1937 he sent Murray a new poem for the collection, the famous 'Slough' ('Come, friendly bombs, and fall on Slough / It isn't fit for humans now . . .'). He asked that Murray should include in the contract, or in a letter, the author's veto on copies being sent to the *London Mercury*, *New Verse*, *Contemporary Poetry and Prose*, the *Morning Post*, the *New Statesman* and if possible the *Times Literary Supplement*. The request shows how morbidly sensitive he was to adverse criticism.

The new book was to be almost as striking and eccentric in appearance as *Mount Zion*. Osbert Lancaster designed arborescent lettering and mock hinges to be stamped in gold on the cover. For the title-page and the jacket, John had more avant-garde plans. The book's title was of course taken from *The Book of Common Prayer*; to absolve himself of maudlin religious sentiment, or perhaps just to shock, he proposed a diagram of a dripping tap for the title-page. He wrote to Murray on 20 July 1937: 'Here is the tap and tracing with the way to draw the drops of water. You might make a test and see whether they fall from the outside rim of the tap. Certainly not the middle . . . I think it ought to look very nice indeed. Perhaps you will let Ted Kauffer know of this. He might incorporate it in his dust jacket.'

Edward McKnight Kauffer, with whom John had worked on Shell posters, did not use the tap on the jacket. He drew a surreal design of a severed hand, the wrist sprouting into fleshy leaves, with heavy dew falling from fluffy white clouds. John received an early copy of the book in October. He wrote to Jock Murray expressing his delight, adding: 'My dear Jock, I feel it unlikely that you will sell more than a dozen copies and I do appreciate the charity, for I can only call it that, which has made you publish the verse in so exquisite a style. You and Lord Gorell [editor of the *Cornhill Magazine*] will get your reward in heaven . . .'

Jock Murray indeed deserves credit for persuading his traditional-minded firm to publish the book with such lavishness and eccentricity. He may have thought it as well to humour John, to keep him as an author. He may also have recognized the publicity advantages of the flamboyant production. Or he may just have enjoyed entering the spirit of the enterprise. There were disadvantages too, however. Had T. S. Eliot not been pipped at the post by Murray, John's poems would probably have appeared in the normal chaste Faber format with elegant letterpress but with no decorations, dripping taps, dendriform lettering, leaf-sprouting hands or prayer-book paper. The reviewers might then have taken John more seriously, as one of the 'Thirties Poets', along with W. H. Auden, a Faber author – though, as John wrote to Edward James, 'It would not have been fun to come out uniform with Stephen Spender.' Eliot might not have allowed John his facetious sub-title, 'A Little Book of Bourgeois Verse'. John may have hoped that the sub-title would disarm criticism by forestalling it, but it did not work. His aggressive flippancy was a red rag to some critics. An English master, reviewing the book for the Dragon School magazine, *The Draconian* (in which Betjeman verse had first appeared in print), accused him of preciosity, unkindness, snobbishness and affectation, and advised him to confine his humorous writing to subjects in better taste. (Pillorying this critic in the preface to his next book, John noted, 'He has translated Homer into Esperanto.')

Evelyn Waugh, however, writing in *Night and Day*, gave bantering praise to the book's originality and modernity. 'Mr Betjeman's poetry is not meant to be read, but recited – and recited with almost epileptic animation; only thus can the apostrophic syntax, the black-bottom rhythms, the Delphic climaxes, the panting ineptitude of the transitions be seen in their true values.' Maurice Bowra's review in *The Spectator* was kindly but pedestrian (it was said of him that 'His talk was brilliant, but it died on the page').

In spite of John's injunction that no copy should be sent to the *New Statesman* (he had sour memories of what its critic had said about *Mount Zion*, and a left-wing magazine was hardly likely to welcome a book of confessedly 'bourgeois' verse), Peter Quennell reviewed it for that magazine. The heading under which the review appeared, 'Flowers of Mediocrity', must have prepared John for the worst; but it referred to the subject-matter, not the poetry. On the poetry, Quennell (a friend of the Betjemans) was complimentary: 'He is a writer of very remarkable wit and facility; but he is something more – a passionate observer of the second-rate who (just as a physician might become positively enamoured of the various morbid phenomena he has selected for clinical examination) is now almost attached to the life he condemns . . .'

Continual Dew, dedicated to Gerald Berners, was published on 2 November 1937. On 5 November, John wrote to tell Jock Murray that Auden (it was he who had suggested to Eliot that Faber should publish a Betjeman collection) had asked if he might include two of the poems in his *Oxford Book of Light Verse*. 'Very flattering, I'm sure,' John wrote. 'I don't want a copyright fee. Are you entitled to one?' Auden's anthology was published in 1938. In the same year appeared John's book *An Oxford University Chest*, a companion volume to Mary Benedetta's *Street Markets of London* (1936) and *Eton Portrait* (1937) by a young Black Watch subaltern, Bernard Fergusson (later Lord Ballantrae). The publisher, John Miles of Amen Corner, London EC4, was a newly established subsidiary of Simpkin Marshall, a large firm of wholesale booksellers. It was intended that Miles should launch out initially in a small way, with a short list of high-quality books. Those by Benedetta, Fergusson and John were all to be illustrated with photographs by the Hungarian-born László Moholy-Nagy, a member of the Bauhaus.

The pictures were to be on shiny art paper, the text on rough paper. There could be wide margins and in the headings 'black letter type such as might have pleased Caxton' was allowed. Osbert Lancaster drew some caricatures of Oxford characters – lady dons on bicycles, swells in the Bullingdon Club and scarfed rowing men. Line drawings from *The Adventures of Mr Verdant Green* (1853) by the Rev. Edward Bradley mixed in well with Lancaster's. But the main illustrations were the magnificent photographs by Moholy-Nagy.

Writing in 1977, John insisted that his text was designed to be 'entertaining reading only, and useless in the examination industry'. It was an odd mish-mash, combining a furious polemic on the way the colleges had allowed their estates round Oxford to be developed; an architectural tour; observations on undergraduates, dons and scouts; and deeper thoughts about 'the three Oxfords' – the old city, or 'Christminster', the university and what he called 'Motopolis', the hateful creation of 'William Morris the Second' (Lord Nuffield). The reviewers took the book more seriously than he did. *The Listener* judged: 'Mr Betjeman's book is funny but not frivolous; he is not facetious or whimsical and does not patronize his subject . . . He is not behind the times, yet he seems to wish he could be.' *The Spectator* sent the book to Graham Greene, who wrote a page full of praise ('Nobody can catch atmosphere better than Mr Betjeman').

The only hostile notice appeared in *The Architectural Review*. It was by the editor's brother, Maurice Hastings, a man John and his friends regarded as a philistine of philistines – it was his shooting the genitalia off the statues at Rousham that had outraged James Lees-Milne. Hastings began approvingly enough, writing of 'Mr Betjeman's great powers of heart', but then he became severe. 'Alas, much though we may admire the brilliance of the prosecution, we are bound to admit the weakness of Mr Betjeman's case.' He took issue with John's maledictions on specialist dons. John had, Hastings thought, no idea of the proper function of a university.

> He implies continually [Hastings complained] that Oxford offers her children a stone for bread, that for Culture is substituted pedantry. He remarks that the English School is really Anglo-Saxon, Northumbrian, and tedious medieval poems. He draws a sad picture of Miss Angle extending her few wits over Gutnish in the Bodleian . . .
>
> Scholarship is only dry as dust to the non-scholar, and the University must cater for the highest, not the lowest, standard of scholarship. There is no law to compel people to take academic courses, and if you don't like Gutnish, or think it a waste of time, don't do it.

Fair comment; but when John criticized the Oxford English School he was not concerned to be fair. He was sustaining his relentless vendetta against C. S. Lewis (that enthusiast for Nordic languages).

The last two years of the 1930s were not a happy time for John. In the surviving letters of his friends we find variations on 'I am sorry you are so depressed'. His *Angst* went beyond the gloom that most Englishmen felt as the 'low, dishonest decade' drew to its close and war with Germany began to seem inevitable. It is hard to account for the degree of his misery. Ostensibly he was a success. But by 1939 his state of mind was such that Penelope insisted he see a psychoanalyst 'to get rid of his persecution mania'.

Much of his anxiety could be traced to money troubles. He had flounced out of *The Architectural Review* and had lost his job as film critic of the *Evening Standard*. His work at Shell was only part-time and ended in 1939 when it became clear that the Shell Guides would have to be 'held over' until after the war. Like most freelances, he missed the assurance of a regular pay-packet. Farmer Wheeler pursued him for his rent. The baby was a new expense. John ate humble pie and begged to be restored to his job on the 'Archie Rev'. Much as de Cronin Hastings liked and admired him, he was not able to oblige him in this. 'The board is damned,' he wrote, 'if it is going to switch everything round again to please you. It admits that you leave a gap. Already you have fulfilled the prophecies of those who shall be nameless, who in their wisdom laughed and said, "In six weeks he'll be wanting to come back." I said: "Nonsense. You've lost a genius. In six months you will be wondering why you were so mad as to let him go . . ."'

John flailed around, trying to find ways of making extra money. His best journalistic contacts were with the *Daily Express*. His Oxford friend Tom Driberg was writing the 'William Hickey' gossip column. Osbert Lancaster began drawing his 'pocket cartoons' for the paper in 1939. The features editor, John Rayner, married another of John's friends, Joan Eyres Monsell, who had earlier been engaged, briefly, to Alan Pryce-Jones and was later to marry Patrick Leigh Fermor. Rayner liked to set writers challenges at odds with their characters. A dog-hater would be invited to write up a poodle parlour, a butterfingers to extol the joys of village cricket. The resulting friction, he thought, would strike sparks. For John he found the most perfectly unsuitable of commissions: to write a regular column of household handyman hints entitled 'Man about the House'. John, who hardly knew how to change a fuse, was expected to tell his readers How to Unblock That Sink or What to Do with That Cupboard Under the Stairs. 'All he used to do', Penelope remembered, 'was to go straight along to Bill Packer, the Uffington blacksmith, with each problem. Bill would tell him what he needed to say; John would put it in his own words and send off an article to John Rayner.' For a sub-series on 'Furnishing the Perfect House', John received further tips, with scale drawings, from his Oxford friend the architect Michael Dugdale. If anything could be less congenial to John than writing the household hints articles, it was answering readers' letters about their domestic problems. At least he got paid for writing the articles. In compensation, one reader's letter was a source of unending hilarity to John and his friends. (He recalled it yet again in conversation with Jonathan Stedall in the 1982 television series 'Time with Betjeman'.) It was from a desperate man who wrote: 'Dear Sir, The man in the flat next to mine has an enormous frig that makes a terrible noise all night long. What can I do about it?'

Lucy Milner, the women's page editor of the *Express,* further bolstered the Betjeman family exchequer by commissioning a long-running cookery series from Penelope, who wrote the articles under her two middle names, Hester Valentine. John praised her culinary and journalistic skills to others, though once or twice he reflected wryly on the disparity between the mouth-watering dishes she described in the *Express* and the more humdrum fare she commonly served at home. When John unexpectedly brought Cyril Connolly home to dinner, Penelope squawked from the kitchen: 'I'm going out in ten minutes. I'm sorry, you can only have hard-boiled eggs.' John took Connolly to the well-stocked wine cellar and said, with an air of solemn rumination and fastidious connoisseurship, 'Now, Cyril, I wonder what goes best with *hard-boiled eggs.*'

Connolly asked John for poems for the early numbers of *Horizon,* the

arts-and-letters magazine launched in 1939. Another editor who commissioned work from John was T. S. Eliot of *The Criterion*, of which the last
issue appeared in January 1939. The two men had met again, after a gap of
over twenty years, in 1937. As we have seen, Eliot courted John as a possible Faber author. John Murray beat him to the poems, but Faber's did end
up publishing the Shell Guides for a time.

Eliot and John became friends, drawn together by old acquaintance and
by their allegiance to the Church of England, their interest in English
topography and their similar senses of humour. They lunched and dined
together. Eliot came to stay at Uffington. John persuaded him to open an
exhibition of original Shell advertising drawings at Shell-Mex House.

Early in 1938 John was discussing with James Shand of the Shenval
Press and the designer Robert Harling the possibility of starting a weekly
magazine called *The Christian*. The scheme fell through, but later that year
Shand approached John with a new idea: would he like to take over from
a man called Smitthels the editorship of the quarterly magazine *Decoration*,
which was in the Shenval Press stable? John accepted the offer. Again
Harling was to be the art editor – 'a dapper, urbane figure with a stake
in a number of diverse projects', among them an advertising agency in
Park Street, London, which promoted the furniture shop Heal's and
Boot's the Chemist. John's deputy editor was Hugh Casson, the future
president of the Royal Academy. Later on, when Casson's practice as a
very 'modern' architect expanded, he and John did not always see eye to
eye; but, looking back, he saw a likeness between John and himself in the
Thirties.

> He was very amusing, which shows, as a rule, that you're not confident, I
> think. You're hiding your shyness or unease under a constant lightning of
> sparklers and hoping people won't notice you aren't as interesting as you
> think you are. I think John was unconfident and not entirely happy all the
> time, until his last years when he enjoyed being a telly star. Rather like me.

Antagonism soon developed between John and Robert Harling. It came
into the open in March 1939, when Harling wrote to James Shand about
'the problems involved in the editorial direction and details of production
of DECORATION'. He wrote: 'Obviously Betjeman is in disagreement
with the way I have gone ahead with certain things on the editorial side of
the magazine. I think it would be a good idea, therefore, if at this stage
(which allows a reasonable time for the production of the next issue) we
were to decide exactly what the respective jobs of Betjeman and myself are
to be.' Harling sent a copy of this letter to John.

A few months later Harling had become exasperated by John's lacka-daisical attitude to his job. He wrote to him very directly on 12 July 1939, in reply to an apparently contrite letter.

> As far as I can see you have taken your editorial duties very lightly indeed, and somebody had to write captions and the rest of the gubbins. Calling (and breaking up) occasional meetings to fit in with the GWR [Great Western Railway] time-table seems to me an odd way of editing a maga-zine; and that an editor should need gentle reminders concerning the necessity for a leader is, of course, almost incredible, but it happened.

Five days later, Harling sent an irritable chaser to Pakenham Hall, County Westmeath, where John was staying with the Longfords.

John spent most of his holidays of the late 1930s at Pakenham Hall, seldom accompanied by Penelope. He was there early in 1938 when he designed the sets for a play Christine Longford was producing at the Gate Theatre, Dublin, her own adaptation of Maria Edgeworth's *The Absentee*. She was thrilled with the 'gorgeous designs . . . The Gothic library is pecu-liarly lovely.' Cathleen Delaney, the 'Colleen', played the heroine, Clare Nugent. It is clear from a letter she wrote John in February 1938 that she had developed a *tendresse* for him.

> I'm afraid I sound full of self pity which is not true. I am very happy really, and you mustn't think I'm not. It's only your leaving was such a wrench. It made me feel so dreadfully alone . . . If your name comes up when I'm in the room I've got to put on a fairly detached air, and look appropriately dis-interested. I can't tell anyone in the world how I really feel about it, or ask anyone all the things I long to know about you, things I shall never have time to learn, because we'll never be alone together – and yet, I love you, John, though I have no right to do that either . . .
>
> John, nothing in this world could please me more than to think I've in any way helped you to write poetry. If I can help you at all darling, I'll understand why all this happened.

Cathleen Delaney's mention of having helped John to write poems – perhaps meaning that she had inspired some of them – leads one to look at John's verse of 1938 for a poem referring to a 'colleen'. Just such a poem is found in *Sir John Piers*, the verse sequence published as a pamphlet by a newspaper at Mullingar, near Pakenham Hall, late in 1938. The second poem in the sequence, 'The Attempt', begins:

> I love your brown curls, | black in rain, my colleen,
> I love your grey eyes, | by this verdant shore

Two Derravaraghs | to plunge into and drown me,
Hold not those lakes of | light so near me more.

Some of the romantic afflatus may have gone from this relationship by
January 1939, when Cathleen Delaney wrote to John: 'I think you flatter
yourself a great deal when you make up your mind that the village suspects
you of fathering your maid's child. A Don Juan is the last thing I would
credit you with being. Odd, if you like, but not amorous.' Or perhaps the
taunt was intended to kindle or revive his ardour.

Cathleen Delaney's presence in Ireland is unlikely to have been the
reason John began looking for a house there in 1938. He may have had
some idea of saving his family from bombs if war broke out. What weighed
with him more was his feeling that Ireland had not been 'ruined', as in his
opinion England was being ruined. In July 1938, when Robert Harling
berated him about some missing proofs, John wrote to T. S. Eliot from
Pakenham Hall:

> In the silence here – a silence so deep one hardly dares speak in it and where
> there is no sound over the hills except at evening when you can hear the turf
> carts rumbling over the bog two miles away – I will be able to get it all in
> the right perspective. London seems like some mad dream in all this green,
> wet civilization.
>
> In the city dusty
> Is the old lock rusty
> That opens rasping
> On the place of graves.

> Do you know Oireland? It is what England was like in the time of
> Rowlandson with Roman Catholicism thrown in. I can't think why we
> don't live here. If I had any competence of my own I would.
> There aren't any aeroplanes.
> The roads are too small for many motors.
> The Church of Ireland is 1835 Gothic and 1835 Protestant . . .

John corresponded with estate agents in Waterford and Clonmel. He
was tempted by Belline House, Piltdown, Co. Kilkenny, 'about eleven
miles from Waterford and close to the late Lord Bessborough's estate', but
money seems to have been the sticking point. He may also have paid some
heed to the wise advice of Constantia Maxwell, a distinguished historian
at Trinity College, Dublin, who had first written to him for help with her
book *Country and Town in Ireland under the Georges*, eventually published in
1940. When, in his reply, he mentioned that he was looking for a house in
Ireland, she wrote: 'You would enjoy Ireland for 6 months, then you would

begin to get melancholy, & long for English intellectual society & the comforts of your own country.' For somebody who had never met John, this was a remarkably accurate prophecy of what actually happened when he became a diplomat in Dublin during the Second World War.

Robert Harling was outraged to discover that not only was John staying at Pakenham Hall, blithely uninterested in the fate of proofs, but that he was also going straight on to Swanwick, Derbyshire, to lecture at a Student Christian Movement summer camp. It was T. S. Eliot who had let John in for this experience. Eliot was friendly with Mary Trevelyan, the warden of Student Movement House in London, and with Brother George Every of the Society of the Sacred Mission, Kelham, Nottinghamshire, who was also a leading organizer of the summer camps. Eliot first asked John to lecture at the camp in 1938:

> Respected Betje,
>   Soft you, a word or two before you go: I have done the Shell some service, and I know't. Now is the chance for your good deed . . . So listen. By none but me may the tale be told, the butcher of Rouen, Big Berold.
>
> > Betjeman must betake himself to Swanwick
> > To prattle about Art and Architectonic.
>
> The good Bro. George Every, S.S.M. of Kelham, a charming and saintly young man whom you ought to know, has arranged a set of informal lectures for the summer course of the S.C.M. at Swanwick . . . He only wants the best . . .

John replied that he could not accept, because he was due to stay at Pakenham Hall on those dates. He was approached again in 1939, this time agreeing to lecture just after his visit to Pakenham. He gave a comic account of the ordeal – with illustrations – in his thank-you letter of 31 July to Edward and Christine Longford.

> The food was very, very plain and in the camp, one had bits of last meal's butter on our knife and some cabbage on the spoon for tinned apricots. Then all the spoons would be beaten on the table and the students would shout, 'We want a story from JIM DOWSER.' Up would stand old Jim and tell us a funny anecdote about the Archbishop of York or a verse from the *Bab Ballads*.
>
> 'Art and Values in the Conservatory' were a complete failure. I was too doped to notice many of the questions. But I remember one, 'Will Mr. Betjeman explain his theory systematically?' I could not remember what my theory had been. On the spur of the moment I had decided to judge architecture by the criterion of the Seven Deadly Sins. It seemed as good as anything else, though Lust was a bit difficult.

On John's return to London and Uffington from Pakenham and Swanwick in July 1939, he wrote to James Shand, frothing with anger at the hectoring tone of Harling's letters. 'Am I not editor, and is Harling not my subordinate?' was the burden of his *cri de coeur*. Shand knew how to soothe John. He wrote: 'Dear Betjeman. O.K. Toots! Let us meet and discuss these large issues. I will come to Shell Mex House at 3 o'clock on Wednesday, unless you command to the contrary.' But, as it turned out, the outcome of the Betjeman–Harling spat was of academic interest. A greater conflict supervened. On 26 September 1939, James Shand wrote to John, after Britain's declaration of war on Germany, to tell him that a lack of advertising obliged him to shut down *Decoration* until peace returned. With the end of *Decoration* and the temporary end of the Shell Guides, John was once again badly in need of a source of income.

One apparently promising source was the BBC. By the late 1930s John was already well known as a radio broadcaster. His BBC programmes were reaching far more people than his poems. He had become a minor celebrity; and this had not happened by accident. He was ambitious, avid for fame. Without appearing to be scheming or pushy, he had used his contacts to get work in this relatively new medium, in spite of some early rebuffs which would have discouraged anyone less determined.

John's first radio broadcast was produced in 1932 by Lance Sieveking. Lionel Fielden, who had shared an office with Sieveking on Savoy Hill before the BBC moved into Broadcasting House in 1931, wrote: 'Lance lived somewhere among the rolling clouds of his vivid and sometimes erratic imagination, and occasionally from these clouds there fell a shower of brilliant ideas. His impact on broadcasting . . . was considerable. He was in the forefront of all experiments and afraid of nothing.'

Here was somebody who could appreciate the wilder flights of John's jokiness. In a pamphlet entitled *John Betjeman and Dorset* (1963), Sieveking recalled what he claimed was John's first broadcast: 'I put a sort of variety show into the microphone in which was a turn billed as "Betjeman major, the Highbrow of the Upper Fifth".' Sieveking remembered 'the spontaneous enthusiasm with which the young Betjeman threw himself into the job of preparing to appear in public disguised as a sort of mockery of himself . . . a sort of gentle satire on one side of himself, yet with the other side, the romantic, showing through'. When Sieveking asked John to take part in the programme, 'he immediately saw what fun it could be, and, by Jove, what fun it *was*!' Sieveking quoted chunks of the script John had given him: 'I'm going to recite poetry with action (*bicycle bell*). You won't be able to see the action, but, my hat, you'll hear it all right (*Rifle report and thunder*).'

In his 1963 pamphlet Sieveking noted that the second verse of 'Westgate-on-Sea' which John read in the broadcast was not included in the poem as published in his *Collected Poems* of 1958. Other verses in the programme which were not reprinted in 1958 were those of 'The Most Popular Girl in the School', which John said were by his sister, Miss Jessie Betjeman. Sieveking quoted two stanzas.

> It isn't the same at St Winifred's now Monica's left the school –
> She was so calm and collected, cultivated and cool;
> I shall never forget the example she set to a girl like me
> By the way she carried her rifle in St Winifred's OTC.
>
> Gosh, I was fond of Monica! She was a regular sport,
> It was rotten for her her complexion seemed to fall rather short
> Of what is expected of schoolgirls, but I think it's a filthy disgrace
> To say that a girl looks ugly just 'cos she's spots on her face.

Though John was always prepared to have fun on the radio, he also realized, early on, its potential as an instrument of propaganda. The first script of a Betjeman talk which survives in the BBC archives is 'Waterloo Bridge Is Falling Down', broadcast on 17 February 1932. In its original, unedited form it began:

> I have in my hand today's paper. The headings read 'Old Waterloo Bridge Doomed – To be pulled down this summer – LCC [London County Council] Decision'. Eight years ago the cracks in Waterloo Bridge were noticed by the *Architects' Journal*, and the agitation started. Mr Herbert Morrison, a late Minister of Transport, said that before the agitation started ninety-nine people out of every hundred had not noticed the beauty of the bridge, which is a 'debatable' point. (Meaning the beauty of the bridge is a debatable point.) I will not contradict him, although it was Canova, the great sculptor, who said that it was the finest bridge in Europe. I shall leave Mr Herbert Morrison to quarrel with Canova.

John was twenty-five when, with this mixture of humour and anger, he told Government ministers and the rest of the population why Old Waterloo Bridge should not be replaced.

In March 1934, only two months after he became film critic of the *Evening Standard*, John tried to persuade Fielden to appoint him film critic of the BBC. Fielden sent a sniffy reply: '. . . I doubt very much whether you are "a master of the microphone". I think your writing is admirable, but that's quite a different thing, and particularly in the case of film criticism, where we want someone who will ring the bell every time.' In any case, Fielden wrote, the pay – only ten guineas a fortnight – was unlikely to tempt John away from the *Standard*. Nevertheless, John was increasingly in demand as a broadcaster. He was a natural choice for any programme that required some erudition and wit.

Guy Burgess, at this time a BBC talks producer, who already knew John through Anthony Blunt, wrote to him in July 1937: 'Dear John, We are having a series of talks called "Eccentrics", and I said to myself who more suitable than you to talk about one of the others?' He added: 'When are we going to meet again? The last meeting was a great success at least from my point of view, as you will remember.' It might be carrying speculation too far to discern a sexual undercurrent in this, though Burgess's promiscuity and indiscretion were notorious. (John's reply ended: 'I hope your evening meeting continued as successfully as it started'; and Burgess wrote in his next letter, 'I had a very nice evening yesterday.') Burgess suggested that John might choose the troglodyte Duke of Portland as his eccentric; but in the end he spoke on Adolphus Cooke, the nineteenth-century neighbour of the Pakenham family in Ireland who feared that he might be turned into a screech-owl after his death, or into a fox that would be hunted down by the then Lord Longford. 'He beats anything I have heard of,' John wrote to Burgess in August 1937.

Although in 1934 Lionel Fielden doubted that John was 'a master of the microphone', in 1946 the BBC accounts official Ronald Boswell wrote to the Talks Booking Manager, 'As Mr Betjeman is a speaker of great reputation and experience, I am wondering whether we could not consider putting his standard fee for a fifteen minute talk up from 10 guineas to 12 guineas.' The increase was agreed. In the intervening twelve years, John had gradually improved his broadcasting technique. In the early days, he was amusing, but mannered and a little toilsome. Later on he developed a more conversational style, less laboured and less patronizing.

In his two talks entitled 'Seaview' (April 1938) the pontifical aesthete had given place to someone familiar with the practicalities of ordinary people's lives. There is still a garnish of humour.

'Come away, Henry, from those common little children: they're only visitors.'

'Don't have anything to do with those people, Bertie – they think they own the place.'

Who of us does not know that eternal struggle between Residents and Visitors which goes on from year to year round our wave-washed shores? I have arranged the first two of these talks like a boxing match. Round one, which I propose to describe now, is going to be a victory for the visitors. I'm going to show you that the poor visitors have a good deal to complain of.

At times John's levity and insouciance worried the BBC mandarins, who as the leaders of a comparatively new institution were concerned about 'standards'. He gave in gracefully when challenged, but in January 1940 he got into a scrape from which it was hard to extricate him. In a talk on the poet Sir Henry Newbolt, whom he much admired, he said that Newbolt's only son had been killed in the Great War. Unfortunately, Captain Newbolt was very much alive, and 'hopping mad'. John said he had been misled by a phrase in Major R. Furse's preface to Sir Henry Newbolt's *A Perpetual Memory* (1937), which even Sir Henry's widow later agreed was ambiguous. But Captain Newbolt was not to be easily appeased. Through his literary agent, A. P. Watt, he demanded to be sent a copy of the talk, so that he could correct it before it was published in *The Listener.*

A stiff letter shortly arrived from Captain Newbolt himself. 'Let me say at once', he wrote, 'that I recognize that [the talk] was written in a spirit of appreciation, not to say admiration.' But John had referred to Sir Henry's cigars ('He was a non-smoker all his life,' Captain Newbolt expostulated), to his motor cars ('He never possessed one') and to the loss of his only son ('who now has the unpleasant task of writing this letter'). Captain Newbolt next demanded that the BBC should commission a second, more accurate, talk about his father by Sir Henry's friend Walter de la Mare. Eventually a compromise was reached: a reading of Newbolt's poetry was to be broadcast on 23 March 1940, with a short introduction by de la Mare. George Barnes, head of the Third Programme, wrote to Pennethorne Hughes: 'The (dead) son and the son-in-law and the widow are all in on it. You will be glad to hear that my patience is almost exhausted.' The new programme was not exactly scheduled for a peak listening time: it ended at midnight.

But these difficulties did not conceal John's talent. With admiring allies at the BBC and compliments coming in from listeners, he seemed set for a more prominent broadcasting rôle. In the early 1940s he might have become a radio star to rival J. B. Priestley; but war service supervened.

15

'Minnie'

———◦◦◦———

JOHN HAD NOT waited until the outbreak of war to do his bit to oppose Nazism. In 1938 he had joined the Observer Corps (later styled the Royal Observer Corps), the volunteer force responsible for tracking and recording the movements of aircraft over Britain. The Corps had its origins in the First World War, and in the Twenties. Networks covering first Kent and Sussex, then Hampshire and the eastern counties, were established, with Observer centres linked to air defence headquarters. All personnel were unpaid special constables. On a gridded operations room table, aircraft positions were plotted with coloured counters. On 26 September 1938 the Corps was called out for the first time as a fully fledged organization, and on 24 August 1939, while holidaymakers sunned themselves and one newspaper proclaimed there would be no war, it manned its posts and centres and began a watch on the skies which was to continue for six years.

Post X2, which John helped to man, was in Parrot's Field, Uffington, and was connected to Oxford, Wantage and Sutton Courtenay. Among those who served with him were Bill Packer (the head of the post), Ron Liddiard, an old tailor called Lovegrove and Harold Long, head gardener at Kingston Lisle. They wore Air Force-blue battledress blouses, armbands with the Observer Corps badge and berets with the badge. The men had a hut to protect them from bad weather. A plotting instrument, familiarly known as 'Heath Robinson', about twenty yards from the hut, was surrounded by a makeshift shelter of corrugated iron which John called 'the urinal'.

'If there was a 'plane coming in fast', Liddiard recalled, 'someone would shout, "Look out, chaps!" and John, who was usually reading a book or writing something, would yell, "Out to the urinal!"' The corrugated iron was to protect the operators from blast, if there was a bomb. 'One day John got halfway to the urinal and got entangled in the wire – fell arse over tip before he got there, shouting, "We're going to lose the war!" He spoke to Oxford on the walkie-talkie set while rolling about on the ground trying to free himself.'

Although in later years John had warm memories of the Observer Corps, back in 1939 he was less enthusiastic. He wrote to the architect Ninian Comper on 12 October: 'I am here in a silly thing called the Observer Corps, and hope to get into the RAF. But only if I can persuade myself it is right to fight at all. At present fighting in a war seems to me to be committing a new sin in defence of an old one.' The letter to Comper illustrates John's ambivalence about the war. He had written in his short-lived diary in 1935: 'Imminence of war. Damned if I will fight. Rescue work, yes, but not killing. Dread death.' Those words were written in low spirits and may have been partly inspired by the pacific Quakerism which he still formally professed until 1937. At any rate, despite his views in 1935, in 1939 John pulled all the strings he could to try to get into the armed forces. He applied for an Intelligence post with the RAF.

In January 1940, however, he was turned down by the RAF on medical grounds. In later years, his encounter with the medical board became the subject of one of his set-piece anecdotes: he claimed he had been rejected because the interview exposed his terror of spiders. A more plausible explanation was offered by H. Beauchamp, a Roman Catholic staff chaplain who was an acquaintance of John's. Beauchamp wrote: 'I am afraid it is impossible to make an appeal or find out why you were disqualified. From my knowledge of medical examinations, it was probably caused by your casual remark that you had once been treated therapeutically.' John next applied to join the Royal Marines, which had commissioned his Marlborough and Oxford friend Philip Harding. Again he was turned down. He had one last, powerful string to pull. He persuaded his father-in-law, the Field Marshal, to write on his behalf to contacts in Government and the forces. But privately Chetwode – who must have had many reservations about John's suitability for a commission – was urging him to take a job offered by Sir Kenneth Clark. 'Get a written offer of the film job [in the Ministry of Information] and *accept it at once.*'

Since John had first met Clark in Maurice Bowra's salon at Oxford, the young art historian's rise had been meteoric. At twenty-nine, in 1933, he had become the youngest ever director of the National Gallery. A popular legend about his appointment as head of the Films Division of the MoI was that Churchill had growled, '*He* knows about pictures, doesn't he?' On paper, John had a strong qualification to be Clark's assistant in the Division: he had been film critic of the *Evening Standard*. But that was not why Clark chose him. 'I wanted his flexibility and originality of mind,' he said, 'and also his charm – because, essentially, ours was a public relations rôle.' So John moved into a third-floor office in the University of London's Senate House, an Art Deco ziggurat of Portland stone by Charles Holden which had been completed in 1938. By 1940 the Ministry of Information ('Minnie' to John and his friends) needed all the charm and flexibility of mind it could get. The war was going badly for Britain; the Ministry was in chaos; the press were antagonistic, the film-makers disgruntled.

In September 1939 the Labour MP Ellen Wilkinson wrote to the film impresario Sidney Bernstein, who was wondering whether to apply for a post in the Ministry: 'The Ministry of Information is in chaos . . . The place is stuffed (rather than staffed) by Everyone's relations . . .' The Ministry's prime duty on the home front was to sustain civilian morale and produce long, detailed weekly reports on public opinion and public spirits. To begin with, it had four other broad functions: the release of official news; security censorship of the press, films and the BBC; the conduct of publicity campaigns for other departments; and the dissemination of propaganda to enemy, neutral, allied and Empire countries. By April 1940 the Ministry's responsibility for censorship and news had been lost to the newly created Press and Censorship Bureau. It was quickly clear that the MoI was going to be a Cinderella among wartime Government departments. It did not help that Lord Reith, the Minister, was not a member of the war cabinet.

John's main work was to commission films and to read the scripts as they came in. Many of the films were 'five-minuters' on such subjects as 'Careless Talk Costs Lives' (the slogan of a famous series of posters by Fougasse), the uses of dried egg, economizing on bath water, the need for blackout at night, and 'Dig for Victory'. Sidney Gilliat, whose career in films had begun with British International Pictures at Elstree in 1928, was asked to call on John at the Ministry. 'All I knew about him', Gilliat recalls, 'was that he had been film critic of the *Standard*, that he was a poet and that he had some interest in architecture.' Gilliat had imagined that John would be 'rather a quiet, withdrawn person'. Instead he found 'this extraordinarily extrovert man – or maybe he was *acting* the extrovert, I don't know'.

> He didn't start by saying what he wanted. He said, 'My dear fellow, come into this refined gentlemen's lavatory. Take no notice of the carpet. As a temporary civil servant, largely unpaid, I'm not entitled to a carpet, so this is my own carpet. The lamp and lampshade, the same. I'm not entitled to a lamp or lampshade of this description.'
>
> And then, before we could get on to anything, the 'phone would ring and he'd say, 'No, no; this is not Mr Findlay, or in fact Mr Findlay's office. Mr Findlay has for six weeks been occupied for the Ministry in – I forget whether it's Rio or Buenos Aires, but he's not been here. I have told them on the exchange. Please try somewhere else or get back to the exchange.'

Then he put the 'phone down and said, '*The fucking lot of cunts.*' And of course in those days you didn't use language as freely as we do today; I certainly didn't expect it from the Films Officer of the Ministry of Information. And this went on all the time. Each time it was a call for Findlay – whom I happened to know, he was a Hugh Findlay, had been a PRO at Gaumont. And this went on all the afternoon. Each time Betjeman would get more icily polite on the telephone and more foul-mouthed when he put the 'phone down.

Then there was a tap on the door and a man came in with a paint-pot and a piece of rag and overalls and a cloth cap.

'Oh,' he said, 'I'm sorry, sir.'

Betjeman said: 'I don't blame you for mistaking this for a gentlemen's urinal; but what can I do for you?'

So he said: 'Oh, it's all right, sir. I only wanted to wet my rag, sir.'

He said: 'My dear fellow, if you must wet your rag, there is the tap, there is your rag, pray go across and wet it. Pay no attention to us; we're merely supernumeraries in this tiled palace.'

And the poor wretched man, trembling, wet his rag under the tap – 'Thank you, sir' – and went out. And of course Betjeman then exploded again.

One day in 1940, John arrived in his office to find that a second desk had been moved in. The man sitting at it, with sleek black hair and spectacles, looked slightly familiar.

'Hello! How extraordinary we should be together!' said the newcomer.

'I'm sorry,' John said, '– I feel I know you, but I can't quite put two and two together.'

'*The Path of Glory* – remember?'

John did not.

'You came down with Nerina Shute and hid in the projection booth.'

It was Dallas Bower, whom he had last met in 1934. Since then, Bower had moved out of films into television. Kenneth Clark took him into the Films Division, as he was recommended to him by their mutual friend, the composer William Walton. Bower's brief was to bring some professionalism into the Division; and, having invaded John's office, he lost no time in letting him know how things were going to be from now on – even though the two had the same rank of Films Officer, and John had seniority of tenure.

Even with Bower added to the team, the Films Division was still badly understaffed. Bower found his workload gruelling. 'John said, "You're getting very overwrought, old top, very overwrought indeed. It won't do. Come along, now, we're going across to the Bedford. We'll have a nice sandwich and a lager, then I'll take you up to Islington and show you a beautiful altar screen." And that's exactly what we did. We came back about three o'clock and I must say I was jolly pleased to have seen the altar screen. It completely relaxed me – I was fussed, something had gone wrong, we had to re-make.'

Just occasionally, John was less sympathetic and added to Bower's burden, turning the tables on him perhaps in mild retaliation for his over-bearing 'This is my production office' line. Bower wanted to commission a 'five-minuter' for the Ministry of Food, starring Alastair Sim.

> . . . John and I were both present when there came up on screen – thank God in rush, not in any kind of cut – a staircase that went nowhere. John made the most tremendous fuss about this, although it didn't really matter a damn. He said, 'I think it's quite dreadful. Somebody like you should know better.'
>> I said, 'All right, John, all *right!*'
>> 'Well, how much is it going to cost to redo that long shot?'
>> I said, 'Well, it's going to cost whatever it costs.'
>> He was so insistent – and he wasn't my boss, we were neck-and-neck.

The 'production office' became still more crowded when a desk was brought in for Graham Greene, who was working on some scripts. He was not with the Division for long, but while he was there Penelope came up to fetch John for lunch. 'Apparently Graham Greene had never met Penelope,' Bower said. 'Poor Penelope, there she was, and John – "Oh!" he said, "well now, you don't know old Graham, do you? This is my wife Propeller. She's *hipposexual*."'

John usually had a beer-and-sandwiches lunch at the Rising Sun public house in Tottenham Court Road, often with his old schoolfriend Arthur Elton. But sometimes he went to the Ministry's canteen. There he chatted to MoI personnel outside the Films Division, including Henry Maxwell, who was a Regional Information Officer – one of the people who, if the Germans landed, were to be the core of the Resistance and set up a com-munications system. Maxwell remembered the time when Kenneth Clark's loyalty to John was put to its severest test.

> As well as a Minister, we had these directors-general, and their deputies. We were always having people brought in from outside, often senior civil ser-vants who were supposed to pull us together, because most of these little departments were staffed by amateurs who were a perpetual pain in the neck to the established civil servants, so despairing efforts were made to impose some sort of discipline. And they brought in, as deputy director-general, this man called Colonel Scorgie. He was sent to us from the Stationery Office;

although he was moving from one civilian ministry to another, he insisted on calling himself 'Colonel'. He had a reputation as an efficient, no-nonsense man. With a flourish of trumpets he was to bring order out of chaos. We were told that this fire-eater was coming, who would see to it that we conformed and behaved. And he hadn't been in the Ministry a week before he issued a letter to all staff, very much the sort of naïve pi-jaw the headmaster of a prep school would give to the school if he thought they were being 'slack' – to 'pull up our socks' and 'put our backs into it' and 'all pull together'. It was rather resented, I must say, by people many of whom were eminent in various walks of life, and were not accustomed at their age to be addressed in that way – but there it was. Anyway, two days later, John found himself in the same lift as Scorgie, whom he recognized. And turning to the lift-man, an old catch-'em-aliveo from the '14-'18 war with one arm and practically stone deaf, John said, 'I say, have you seen anything of this fellow *Scroggie*? They tell me he's not really *pulling his weight*.' It was all round the Ministry by lunch-time. It was the beginning of the end for Scorgie.

Clark remembered the Scorgie episode. 'Colonel Scorgie said to me, "That fellow Betjeman will have to go. He's half-baked." I replied: "John Betjeman has one idea a month that is better than all the other ideas of my Division put together. You must, with respect, keep him."' But even Clark found John's prankishness tiresome at times. Nicolas Bentley, the cartoonist, remembered Clark's pausing in the middle of an address to his staff to say, 'Betjeman, I shall be obliged if you will remove those bicycle clips from your ears.'

On 10 May 1940, Chamberlain resigned and Churchill became Prime Minister. In June, Reith was replaced by Duff Cooper, who lost no time in offering Sidney Bernstein the job of Films Adviser. Not long afterwards Kenneth Clark had moved upstairs at the Ministry, and Jack Beddington – another old friend of John's – had succeeded him as head of the Films Division. Opinions about Beddington at the MoI were mixed. Michael Balcon thought him 'the ideal man for the job', a 'real expert salesman', and found him easy to deal with. But Sidney Bernstein did not like him and Dallas Bower could not stand him. 'He was aggressive in a way John Betjeman could never be aggressive,' Bower said. 'And there was something rather flash about him.' Sidney Gilliat gave Beddington credit for setting up, on his suggestion, an 'ideas committee', but thought he had an ulterior motive. 'He saw his job as a shop window for himself; and if he could bring important people together in an ideas committee, that was a bigger and better shop window.' John served on the committee, but was disdainful, calling it 'Beddi's Brain Box'.

After Beddington's arrival at the MoI, the four main executives of the Films Division all had surnames beginning with 'B'. John wrote a poem about 'The Four B's' which, as Bernstein's biographer Caroline Moorehead writes, 'conjured up the spirit of the place, with its camaraderie, its touch of whimsy and its absolute exclusion of all things bureaucratic':

I wish I were – I often think –
Another Maurice Maeterlinck
So I could write a play with ease
About four little busy B's
Who fly about and buzz and buzz
And stay exactly as they wuzz
And buzz about and fly and fly
About the spacious MoI
Then settle in the glittering sun
Content with having nothing done.
Sing,
Beddington, Bernstein, Betjeman, Bower
Sing,
Winken, Blinken and Nod
Sing,
Shell, Granada, sing Norman Tower
Make a five minute treatment of God.

Almost fifty years later, in 1989, Sidney Gilliat took part in *Filming for Victory*, a television programme about wartime films, presented by Professor Christopher Frayling. Later he said: 'I noticed that in the film there was a tendency to write Betjeman off as an eccentric who had a brief, hilarious and unproductive spell at the Ministry; but I think that in many ways, given the difference in their areas of operation, he was a lot more effective than Jack Beddington, because Beddington used the Films Division to promote himself, whereas Betjeman didn't appear to give a damn about what happened to him so long as he got something going . . . Also, John was very approachable. You could say to him, "I think that's a bloody silly idea," and he'd listen; you wouldn't dream of saying that to Kenneth Clark or Beddington.'

Gilliat did have one complaint about John. He thought that because of John's schooldays with Arthur Elton (whose services were much used by the Ministry, and whom Beddington eventually appointed to the Films Division) and his friendship with Bob Flaherty when film critic of the *Evening Standard*, John was prejudiced in favour of the documentary film-makers and against makers of commercial feature films of the kind made by himself and his business partner Frank Launder. Gilliat may, however, have been overestimating John's reliance on the documentarians. As he himself conceded, 'The documentarians felt they were a lowlier species with higher ideas; and we were a higher species with lower ideas. Something roughly like that. Each side had a chip of a different kind on their shoulder.' Michael Balcon, of Ealing and not a documentarian, had however no complaint about the volume of work he got from the Ministry.

The Boulting twins, still in their twenties, also got work from the Films Division. John Boulting was in the RAF, Roy in the Royal Artillery. John Betjeman first met Roy, who was in his army captain's uniform, in the brasserie of the Café Royal in 1940. They drank some bottles of 1924 Cheval Blanc, a fine claret which the restaurant served as a table wine until supplies ran out. They had a conversation about films. The next time John Betjeman saw what he took to be Roy, he continued the conversation; the thread was picked up very quickly. He wondered why Roy was now wearing RAF uniform, and assumed he must be in some high-up Intelligence unit which required him to dress up in different uniforms. After a while the young man said, 'You think I'm Roy Boulting, don't you? Well, I'm not. I'm his twin brother.' The Boultings had reason to be grateful to John when he defended them at a preview of their MoI film *Dawn Guard*. Clive Coultass writes in *Images for Battle: British Film and the Second World War, 1939–1945* (1989):

> *Dawn Guard*, which was finally released in January 1941, is an unusual film for that period because it was not content only to emphasize the need to stand up to Hitler, but also took a reformist view of the social outlook for postwar Britain . . . According to Roy Boulting's account, the MoI's Films Division knew nothing of the content of the film until it was previewed. He also recalled that its official reception was cool, the only MoI officer to make brief favourable comment being John Betjeman, although the left-wing aspirations of the script surely sound too mild for serious objection.

At the end of December 1940, after apologizing to Sidney Gilliat in the wake of a clash about favouring the documentarians, John wrote to him: 'Are you feeling OK about it all? If in any way offended, sore, angry, hurt, diddled, please write to me & quote reference number above [F/149/66].' Changing the subject, he added: 'I have fallen in love with a girl in the catering department here who is a doctor's daughter from Aldershot. She was lacrosse captain & tennis champion at Queen Anne's Caversham.'

The girl in the catering department was Miss Joan Hunter Dunn, the subject of John's best-known poem, 'A Subaltern's Love-song' –

Miss J. Hunter Dunn, Miss J. Hunter Dunn,
Furnish'd and burnish'd by Aldershot sun,
What strenuous singles we played after tea,
We in the tournament – you against me!

Love–thirty, love–forty, oh! weakness of joy,
The speed of a swallow, the grace of a boy,
With carefullest carelessness, gaily you won,
I am weak from your loveliness, Joan Hunter Dunn . . .

In a radio programme of 1976, John remembered how he had first
encountered Joan Hunter Dunn. 'I was walking down a corridor at the
Ministry of Information with my friend Reggie Ross Williamson when
we saw a beautiful girl with red hair. "Gosh, look!" I said, "I bet she's a
doctor's daughter from Aldershot." And she was.' Joan Hunter Dunn had
been appointed to the catering staff of the University of London before
the war. When war came, and the University moved out of the Senate
House, she stayed on. With the arrival of the MoI and the constant stream
of visiting journalists, writers, officers, film-makers and artists, life became
much more hectic for her.

In their memoirs, Lord Clark and the fashion writer Ernestine Carter
(whose husband, the bibliophile John Carter, worked at the MoI) both
claimed that they had introduced John to Joan Hunter Dunn and that they
had been the first to read the celebrated poem. In 1995 Joan described what
really happened.

Michael Bonavia summoned me into his room. 'I've got someone here who
would like to meet you,' he said. Inside was John Betjeman, who went down
on his knees. I just burst out laughing. My first impression was one of
extreme humour. I thought anybody who got down on his knees to say
'How d'ye do' to me must be mad. He asked Mr Bonavia if he could take
me out to lunch. 'Certainly,' he said.

In a *Sunday Times* interview of 1965 she told what happened next.

In the taxi on the way to the restaurant he put a copy of *Horizon* magazine
into my hand and said, 'I hope you don't mind, but I've written a poem
about you.' I must say I was absolutely overwhelmed. It was such a marvellous break from the monotony of the war. It really was remarkable the way
he imagined it all. Actually, all that about the subaltern, and the engagement
is sheer fantasy, but my life was very like the poem.

John told the same interviewer: 'When I showed her the poem she told
me she lived in Farnborough, Hampshire, but I considered that near
enough Aldershot to count.'

Joan married a MoI civil servant, H. Wycliffe Jackson, in January 1945. John was invited but sent a telegram to say he was unable to attend. 'I never got to know John well at the Ministry,' Joan said, 'but when I did get to know him was in 1963, when my husband suddenly died, of a coronary, in Rhodesia. Our three sons were at school in England, one of them at Winchester, the two youngest at prep school. John wrote to me and was so, so kind. He took each of the boys out to lunch, separately, and helped to make arrangements for the rest of their education.' In the *Sunday Times* article two years later, John recalled Joan in the war. 'When the bombs fell she bound up our wounds unperturbed. She was so marvellous at first-aid – I used to wish desperately for a small wound from a bomb so that she would minister to me.'

A new collection of his poems had been published a few weeks after he began work at the Ministry. In October 1939 John had written to tell Jock Murray that John Miles, the publisher of *An Oxford University Chest*, wanted to publish twenty-two new poems of his. 'As you took the risk of publishing *Continual Dew*, I don't want to do anything without first getting your permission.' Murray sent the no doubt hoped-for reply that he would like to publish the collection himself. On 20 October John wrote to him: 'The poems are being typed & when they are ready I will send them. A cheap, unillustrated edition like a Victorian hymn book would be nice.' Most of the new poems had never appeared in print.

Murray, who once he had made a decision did not let the grass grow under his feet, on 1 November sent John a specimen page set in Plantin type. John replied on 2 November that, though he was delighted Murray would publish the book, he hated Plantin. 'Do you remember how they printed Robert Bridges's *New Poems*? The type there seemed absolutely right for poetry. Plantin is too heavy & looks like the Shropshire Lad.' He enclosed a book of Henry Lyte's poems, which struck him as 'the ideal way of printing poetry'. As before, Jock Murray showed himself ready to indulge John in almost all his whims. On 7 November John came up with a new notion: 'What would you say to a silhouette of me for a frontispiece?' Murray gave enthusiastic approval to this, too; on 20 November he wrote, 'I look forward to the silhouette with enormous curiosity!' With the silhouette frontispiece, John was reinforcing the 'personality cult' that always meshed with his literary reputation. It was arranged that John Piper would draw the silhouette by projecting John's profile on a wall at Garrards Farm like a children's entertainer bunching his fist into a bunny-rabbit head for a shadow-pictures show. John wanted the words 'Frontispiece by John Piper' to go on the title-page (a further plume for his own reputation), but Piper refused as it was 'only a tracing'. He continued to refuse even when Murray telephoned to try to cajole him, on John's insistence. But John did find a way of bringing Piper's name into the book, by dedicating it to him and Myfanwy in amusing dog-Latin, corrected by John Sparrow:

AD

M. ET J. PIPER

FELICES ET DULCES

APUD

VILLAM FAWLIENSEM PROFUNDAM

HENLEY

HIC LIBER

CUM

GRATIIS ET FIDELITATE*

The title was still giving trouble. John was fecund with suggestions.

An Old Clergyman & Other Poems? There is no poem called An Old Clergyman, which would make it interesting. Or The Negligent Incumbent?* Or Sir John Piers or Topographical & Amatory Verses? or Nave & Chancel*? Or The Baptistery? Stained Glass Windows? Or Squint & Squinch? Decay? Damp Rot? Or Death Watch Beetles? Or Cemetery Gates? Or From Holloway to Mullingar? Or Holloway to Multifarnham?* Or Upper Holloway*? The Tortoise Stove*? Heating Apparatus? Oil & Gas? or New Lights for Old Chancels? or Old Lights for New Chancels?** Or By Southern Electric & Great Southern? The Parish Room**?

I favour those marked with a star. Perhaps you can think of others. Second title should be Topographical & Amatory Verses . . .

John added a preface. This was a bid to throw off the irksome label of 'satirist' and to be recognized by the critics, if not as a serious poet, at least as a sincere one. After sketching in his literary ancestry – Crabbe, Clare, Hardy, Tennyson – he mounted a pugnacious self-defence.

I see no harm in trying to describe overbuilt Surrey in verse. But when I do so I am not being satirical but topographical. No doubt many of the lines of Tennyson I have quoted have been quoted by those who have other ideas about poetry, as examples of bathos. The suburbs, thanks to *Punch* which caters for them, are now considered 'funny'. Some people still think Victorian industrial scenery is only fit for invective. Churches are always 'funny' unless they are written about by a devotional writer. Gaslight is funny, Pont Street is funny, all sorts of places and things are funny if only the

---

* To M. and J. Piper, happy and sweet, of Fawley Bottom House, Henley, this book with gratitude and fidelity.

funny writers are funny about them. I love suburbs and gaslights and Pont Street and Gothic Revival churches and mineral railways, provincial towns and Garden cities. They are, many of them, part of my background. From them I try to create an atmosphere which will be remembered by those who have had a similar background, when England is all council houses and trunk roads and steel and glass factory blocks in the New Europe of after the War.

This was disingenuous: clearly John intended to poke fun at, for example, Pont Street (also satirized by Osbert Lancaster as 'Pont Street Dutch'). But in the closing words of the preface, John begged:

> my old Esperanto friend whose disgust I aroused with my last volume [the schoolmaster who had reviewed *Continual Dew* in *The Draconian*] to accept that though this may be 'minor' poetry, its author is
>   his *sincerely*,
>   JOHN BETJEMAN

Jock Murray told John that he found the preface 'most moving'. But though Murray was still humouring John – he had even agreed that one of the poems could appear in Welsh translation opposite the English original – he could not resist adding: 'I am just wondering how far the joke under your silhouette is quite in keeping with your introduction. However, we can think that out in a quiet hour.' What the joke was is not clear, but it must have been pretty extreme, considering the toned-down version John proposed in a letter of 26 November 1939: 'I feel that if we just put "Apollo" under the silhouette & excise "Betjeman" from the signature, the difficulty will then be met. Those who know me will understand, those who don't may think it is Apollo.' That was how the silhouette eventually appeared.

John had left it up to Murray what to call the book. The publisher chose *Old Lights for New Chancels*. In early December John was still uneasy about this title, which he thought 'a bit of a mouthful'. He was pressing again for 'The Negligent Incumbent'. He added: 'Perhaps "Old Lights for New Chancels" is rather nice, but "Old Lights for Restored Chancels" would be more true.' He returned to the subject a month later: 'The title page is a great improvement but I honestly do not like the title. I would much prefer "Cheltenham & Clifton" or merely the sub-title. I feel the present title is too humorous and cancels out my preface. I hope that it is not too late to alter it . . . "First Edition" is a bit like counting your chickens before they are hatched . . .'

Jock Murray replied that there was a great deal to be said for counting chickens before they were hatched. 'The title is a very different matter. Your suggestion of "Cheltenham and Clifton" is horrible, and to call the book by its sub-title is to put a weight against success. I do not really feel that "Old Lights for New Chancels" is any more contrary to your preface than is the frontispiece. One of the points of the book seems to me to be that humour and a serious purpose are not incompatible.' John, who usually had such a feel for the popular pulse, was curiously uncertain of touch in his choices of titles. Here his genuine eccentricity skewed the composition. Murray's strong objection to 'Cheltenham and Clifton' was all the more forceful because of his normal compliance with John's wishes – it was as if a vicar swore. John eventually deferred to his judgement.

The book was published on 14 March 1940 – an ordinary edition at 5s and a special edition of only twenty-nine copies on blue-laid paper, 'outrageously bound and signed by the author' (Murray wrote to a friend) at 10s 6d. William Plomer's review in *The Listener* said about John exactly what John wanted to hear: 'He still produces more or less violent reactions and gets called precious, snobbish, reactionary, bourgeois, anti-Christian, and so on and so forth. He naturally causes alarm by being clever, observant, and sometimes satirical, and it seems that to be good-humoured is to be mistaken by solemn persons for a fribble.' Plomer, three years older than John, was perhaps the contemporary poet who had most in common with him, sharing his taste for Victoriana, sinister Gothicism ('The Dorking Thigh') and jokes.

John can have been scarcely less happy with the review by 'Senex' of the *New Statesman*.

> Is it a clue to his temperament to say that he is in love with the past, and that the suburban landscape which is for many of us the background of childhood – the bright smelly shops, oozing railway arches and dusty privet hedges – has a romantic quality that he has never quite outgrown? Childhood associations abound in his verse, either conveyed directly, as in *Trebetherick* – one of his most successful metrical experiments – or imaginatively, as in the first of the three *Amatory Poems*, with its memorable evocation of the black-stockinged bicyclist tinkling her way home towards school-room tea . . . *Myfanwy* – Beatrice to Mr Betjeman's Dante – supplies the starting point of yet another journey in pursuit of the past – this time to the dim paradise of Oxford women's colleges, cocoa parties, reading circles and girlish enthusiasms . . .

Andrew Wordsworth, who reviewed *Old Lights* for *Time and Tide*, had been at Marlborough with John – a son of the Bishop of Salisbury and a younger brother of Matthew Wordsworth with whom John ran *The Heretick* magazine. (He had gone on to teach at Westminster School with John Edward Bowle.) He made use of his inside knowledge in the review.

When I was fourteen I thought school slang silly. Then I went to tea with John Betjeman and heard him use as much as possible but in inverted commas. It was the revealing light. Keats left Leigh Hunt 'Brimfull of the happiness Which in a little cottage he had found'. I left Betjeman's *bin* converted. The world of school could never again be dismissed as something you tried to avoid because its values were not of the aesthete and the intellectual. You were in it. *Barnes, tolly, oiler, bolly* – these were no longer the words of Marlburians with false values; they were your own words, words by which the extraordinary business of being at a public school could be made fun of, yes, but also understood and controlled.

Betjeman has always chosen to live in the background in which he was brought up. Not for him the Waste Land, the Proletariat or the Tower, but the actual geographical world of his own life, the actual world sweating only in sports and in bed, of that slice of the middle-class he has lived through. He loves it and hates it all and knows all its slang, using it to control it, and, because he is a genius, to preserve it for ever in poetry of obsessional power.

In March 1940 the *Times Literary Supplement* added its carefully measured encomium to the other tributes.

Because he has a definite aim and definite interests, and has limited himself to these, his verse, if minor, is not so through failing to be major. It is perfected achievement in its kind.

16

Dublin

————

O N 24 JANUARY 1941 John's mother wrote to Ernest's old friend and patron Philip Asprey: 'John and family go to Dublin next week, he has been transferred from the MoI to the Embassy there, a very lucrative post. I do hope the Huns don't invade Ireland.' The British did not in fact have an embassy in Dublin; because of the ambiguous relationship between southern Ireland and Great Britain, the senior British diplomat in Dublin, Sir John Maffey (later Lord Rugby), had the title 'United Kingdom Representative in Eire'. John was to be his press attaché. Writing to Gerard Irvine on 27 January to give him his office address in Dublin, John added: 'I am very sad to be going.' He signed the letter 'Seán O'Betjemán'.

Penelope was no better pleased. Having witnessed her mother's wearisome routine of entertaining at Aldershot and in India, she had sworn she would not marry anybody in the services. In marrying John she 'little thought that he would become a sort of bogus diplomat'. Uprooting themselves from Uffington and finding a suitable home in Dublin was an ordeal. Penelope recalled: 'We were given the names and address of two old maids, the Misses Hamilton, who had a house on the outskirts of Dublin – *just* country – and took PGs [paying guests]: we could PG there until we owned a house.' The Betjemans and Betty Evans, the nanny, stayed with the Hamiltons for three months. All that time, Penelope was looking for a house in Dun Laoghaire, Blackrock and Killiney – seaside suburbs of Dublin – but found nothing she liked. Then at a party she and John met Billy Kirkwood and his wife Peta, who was of the Jameson Whiskey family. 'They knew I was mad on horses,' Penelope recalled, 'so they said, "Why don't you have Collinstown? We're going to live in our other house outside Dublin, and we want to have Collinstown aired. You can have it on a caretakers' arrangement at £10 a month." There was no polo in the war so all the eleven polo ponies were turned out there and I was allowed to ride any I wanted. The house was beautiful, but in terrible condition and very damp.' Collinstown was at Clondalkin, near Dublin, and next to an aerodrome – one of the first places the Germans would have overrun if they had invaded.

The post of British press attaché in neutral Ireland was one of great sensitivity. Henry Maxwell, John's Ministry of Information colleague, heard that he was sent out on the suggestion of Brendan Bracken, whom Churchill had made Minister of Information. 'It was felt', Maxwell said, 'that the German Minister in Dublin, Eduard Hempel, was making much too good an impression on Eamon de Valera, the Irish leader; and that it would be a good idea to send out somebody of charm and wit to keep de Valera sweet, and the Irish press and public opinion sweet. And it worked: once John was out there, reports came in of improved Anglo-Irish relations.'

Bracken may have had a hand in John's appointment; but the person most directly concerned with it was the head of the MoI's Empire Division, Harry Hodson, a fellow of All Souls and a future editor of the *Sunday Times*. Hodson thought John was 'the sort of chap who could get on with the Irish'. It was not only his charm that qualified him; there were also his varied experience of Ireland over more than ten years, and the good contacts he had made while staying with Billy Clonmore, Pierce Synnott and the Longfords. He had even had a taste of Northern Ireland while at Clandeboye. And he was a poet, coming to a land where poets were more honoured than in his own.

John was made welcome at the Representative's office in Upper Mount Street, Dublin. He painted his third-floor room 'boudoir pink' and hung it with Piper paintings of bombed London churches – a political, as well as aesthetic, statement. Maffey briefed John on the other diplomats in Dublin; and gradually he got to know them. John was amused that his own opposite number, the German Press Attaché Karl Petersen, had the same name (though differently spelt) as the arch-villain of the Bulldog Drummond stories by 'Sapper'. Petersen was causing difficulties for Hempel by his drunken indiscretions. There was some fraternizing between the British and Germans – 'The German diplomats used to come to Maffey's parties and vice-versa,' said Ruth-Ellen Moller, a granddaughter of the novelist Erskine Childers. But John was asked not to fraternize with Petersen, 'because then Sir John wouldn't be able to cut him dead in the street'. The Japanese Press Attaché, Mr Ishihashi (John called him 'Mr Itchy-Scratchy'), went riding with Penelope until the attack on Pearl Harbor in December 1941, after which she was asked not to see him again.

It was not the Germans and Japanese who gave Maffey and John most trouble. A delicate aspect of the two men's position was the poisoned relations between de Valera and Churchill. The two statesmen had disliked each other as young men; age had not mellowed them. Churchill remembered de Valera as a terrorist. De Valera was also the man who had done his best to scupper the 1922 treaty which Churchill, as Colonial Secretary, had signed with Michael Collins – the treaty which gave Ireland, not the home rule that de Valera wanted, but the status of a dominion. In Churchill's view, de Valera had 'broken the word of Ireland'.

What above all rankled with Churchill was that the three Irish ports which, under the 1922 treaty, were to be kept available for Britain's use in time of crisis, had been meekly ceded to de Valera by Neville Chamberlain's Government in 1938. Churchill regarded these ports – Queenstown (now Cobh), Berehaven and Lough Swilly – as 'sentinel towers'. He protested in 1938 and warned that the ports might become 'nesting places for our enemies'. Throughout John's three years with Maffey, Churchill kept up a constant growl about the cession of the ports, with occasional threats that it might be necessary to seize them by force. These were the times when Maffey's calm diplomacy and John's wooing of the Irish press were most needed.

When Britain declared war on Germany in 1939, de Valera insisted that Ireland would be neutral. Many British people – Churchill among them – thought that Ireland's neutrality was craven. And as Maffey put it to de Valera in May 1940: 'Here is a maniacal force let loose in the world. It is not a time to talk of Anglo-Irish disputes . . .' How long did de Valera imagine Ireland would remain free if Hitler conquered Britain? There were several other reasons for the Taoiseach's policy. Anti-British feeling was widespread in Eire. De Valera himself had been condemned to death by the British, and the Black and Tans' atrocities were not forgotten. The propagandist commentary of a British Pathé film might suggest, with sublime euphemism, that 'Britain and Eire may not always have seen eye to eye in the past' and that 'today all that is forgotten in the common danger', but in fact old hatreds were not so easily obliterated. The novelist Elizabeth Bowen, in a secret report for the British Government in 1940, relayed a 'typical' Dublin comment: 'What right have the British to keep denouncing the Nazis? Haven't they been Nazis to us for centuries?' Hempel reported back to Berlin a nationalist commonplace, 'England's difficulty is Ireland's opportunity.'

John's duties in Dublin were not confined to 'keeping sweet' de Valera and the Irish press. He had also to send regular reports to London. The reports went to the Dominions Office and to the Ministry of Information. Dr Nicholas Mansergh, a young historian who was later to be Master of St John's College, Cambridge, was appointed by the MoI to be John's opposite number in London. He was an Ascendancy Irishman.

The circle in which John moved in Dublin consisted mainly of Irish Government ministers and civil servants, diplomats, Irish and visiting

British journalists and literary people. Sometimes he accompanied Maffey to see de Valera; occasionally he was sent on his own as a 'messenger boy'. John was virtually apolitical, the Irish leader steeped in politics; yet perhaps the two men had more in common than either would have acknowledged. Both had foreign names and forebears. (De Valera, born in New York of a Spanish father, was once called 'the Spanish onion in the Irish stew'.) Each immersed himself in the culture of the land in which he grew up, and became a voice and a personification of that land's character.

Maffey told John which of the Irish Government ministers he thought more or less friendly. He considered Seán MacEntee, Minister for Industry and Commerce and later Minister for Local Government and Health, 'a strong Anglophobe'; in spite of that, John sat with MacEntee in the front row of a concert and went on to drinks with the MacEntees at their home. Diplomacy is not the art of courting one's friends. In fact, John and Penelope became very friendly with the whole family. MacEntee's daughter Máire (later Mrs Conor Cruise O'Brien) recalled:

> Mr de Valera was his own foreign minister, but was not over-fond of entertaining diplomats and making small-talk, so he often delegated that task to my father. Both my parents absolutely loved the Betjemans. And – I was only a teenager – I think the Betjemans loved them, too. John wrote a very nice poem about my father's holiday house in Brittas Bay . . .
>
> My father had been condemned to death by the British for his part in the Easter Rising of 1916 (he was released under the amnesty of 1917) – but I think he felt he had settled scores with them. He was emphatically *not* anti-British. He loved Shakespeare and Browning and wrote poetry in English himself.

Ruth-Ellen Moller has less happy memories of Penelope and horses. When John was in Dublin, her father, Erskine Childers (a son of the novelist of the same name shot by Michael Collins's faction in 1922), was secretary of the Federation of Irish Manufacturers, though he was soon to be one of de Valera's ministers and was another future President of Ireland. He and his American wife Ruth became friends of the Betjemans. One day, Penelope telephoned Childers and asked, 'Do your children ride?' Childers said they did. 'Well, send them over. I'd love to have an afternoon with them and they can do some riding with me.'

> I was twelve and my brother Erskine was ten [Ruth-Ellen Moller remembers]. We were at boarding school and we'd ride at school but we never hunted. We arrived at Collinstown – a Government car had picked us up – and John opened the door. He said, 'Wait a minute.' Then he called up

the stairs, 'Penelope, your slaves for the ponies have arrived.' No answer; so he said, 'Propeller! Your slaves for the ponies are here.' Still no answer. He said, 'Dammit, I can't *stand* it,' and shouted, '*Filth!* The children are here to exercise your beastly ponies.' So Erskine and I just stood there in wonderment – wondering what was going to come down the stairs. Anyway, down she came and she took us by the hand and brought us out to the stables and put us on two ponies. John came out too and looked on rather bleakly, as if to say to Penelope, 'I hope you're going with them.' But she didn't come with us, we were on our own.

We were not well up in various kinds of horses, so we had no idea we were on polo ponies – very dangerous to ride. She gave their rumps a good slap and off we went into the middle of yonder. And Erskine must either have put his knee into the pony's side or pulled on the rein – anyway, complete circle; he came down heavily, his head protected by his arm which broke in two places, the bones sticking out. I didn't know what to do. I thought he was going to die, he was absolutely unconscious and I thought, 'If I run to the house he'll be dead; I've got to stay here.' Eventually, some farm worker came across and carried Erskine back to the house. Penelope paid little attention. She said, 'What a silly boy! I suppose the two of them will have to go to hospital.' But John was incredibly upset. And furious. Livid with Penelope for not going with us; furious with himself for not realizing what she was capable of. He drove us to the hospital – the nearest was near the main station – and stayed with us until my parents arrived. Erskine had a double compound fracture. He was never able to straighten his arm after that.

Ruth-Ellen's parents often held parties at their house in Highfield Road, Dublin. She remembers one party at which John's diplomatic *savoir-faire* was urgently called upon.

The party was in honour of Udo Udoma, the son of a Nigerian chief. He was very talented and had become president of the Philosophical Society of Trinity College, Dublin. I was allowed to stay up that night. After a while there was a hammering at the front door. My father said to John, 'I've got a horrible feeling this is going to be bad news' – because somebody had told him that Francis Macnamara, Dylan Thomas's father-in-law, was going to gatecrash the party.

So John and my father – I was watching from the stairs – went to the door. My father was very tall and John wasn't; they couldn't stop Macnamara, he just burst in. My father said, 'Francis, you just have to behave yourself.' Macnamara was a *wild* man, much given to drink. So they went on back to the party. I crept back into the drawing-room. I had a feeling that something exciting was going to happen. When I went in, there wasn't a sign of Macnamara – I couldn't think where he had got to.

Udo Udoma was on the sofa beside my mother. Suddenly a huge hand came up from behind the sofa and grabbed his shoulder. Then a big head popped up and said, 'Hiya, nigger!' Deathly, horrified silence. My father tried to get hold of Macnamara but he couldn't. He dodged behind an arm-chair and said it again, even louder – 'HIYA, NIGGER!' Then he went back behind the sofa. John told my mother he would try to get him to leave but he came back and said he thought Macnamara had reached the 'incapable' stage. So my father, John and a well-known American war journalist, Raymond Gram Swing, a very strong man, got hold of Macnamara, threw him out into the garden and locked the door. We were relieved and a little surprised that there was no further sound. The party progressed.

Because John's house was quite distant, he stayed the night with us. In the morning I heard him calling out to my father, 'Erskine! Erskine! You must get down here at once!' So my father rushed down in his dressing-gown – I was close behind, to see what the excitement was. I heard my father give an awful groan; and John was in hysterics. I went out on to the lawn. Cut into the turf was a huge swastika. In neutral Ireland! It was a ter-rible embarrassment. And Macnamara had just thrown the turf he removed over the fence into the next-door garden. So John and my father set to – scrambled over into the neighbours' garden to retrieve the turf and put it all back before breakfast.

Censorship was a subject that could cause friction between the Irish Government and the British Representative's office. Normally, the censor was less concerned to prevent information coming into Eire from outside than to suppress any propagandist material from within Eire that might compromise neutrality. British newspapers and magazines were on sale in Dublin throughout the war. Neither BBC nor German broadcasts were jammed. However, the Dublin cinemas were not allowed to show Charlie Chaplin's satire on Hitler, *The Great Dictator*. Where the Irish censor departed from strict neutrality, it was usually to avoid giving offence to the Germans rather than the British. The vast, Chestertonian editor of the *Irish Times*, R. M. Smyllie, was strongly Anglophile. As he never tired of reminding his readers, he had been in a German prisoner-of-war camp in the First World War. He was adept at sliding pro-British stories past the censor, and protested fiercely if he thought the censor was failing to be impartial. His biographer, Tony Gray, writes:

A typical example of his artfulness occurred when I was editing the Book Page and we ran a short review of a schoolgirl's romance entitled *Worrals of the WAAFS*. When the proofs reached Dublin Castle, the review was imme-diately banned. Smyllie then re-wrote it carefully, giving the girls names like Gretchen, Eva and Lilli, and retitling the book *Lotte of the Luftwaffe*. The resultant review was passed by the censor without comment, and of course Smyllie then raised all hell on the grounds that this incident proved that the Irish censorship was biased in favour of the Germans. It didn't, of course; all it proved was that at this particular stage of the war the Irish Government ministers were far more afraid of the Germans than they were of the British.

A spirited joker like this was likely to get on with John; and obviously it was in the interests of the British Press Attaché to cultivate the editor of the leading Irish newspaper. The two met often in the inner-sanctum 'snug' of the Palace Bar in Fleet Street, Dublin. At the back of the main bar, a door led through a screen, 'rather like the iconostasis in a Byzantine church', into an area where journalists and other writers were served drinks by barmen in long white aprons. Cyril Connolly, who was brought to Dublin by John in 1941, thought it 'as warm and friendly as an alligator tank; its inhabitants, from a long process of mutual mastication, have a leathery look, and are as witty, hospitable and kindly a group as can be found anywhere'. Among the regulars were the poet Patrick Kavanagh, the novelist and *Irish Times* columnist Brian Nolan (alias Flann O'Brien and Myles na gCopaleen), the poet Austin Clarke, who lived mainly on what he earned from Radio Éireann for a weekly poetry programme; the literary editor M. J. MacManus; the journalist and former trade unionist Cathal O'Shannon; the one-legged wit and raconteur G. J. C. Tynan 'Pussy' O'Mahony (father of the comedian Dave Allen); and the poet Seumas O'Sullivan. John came to know all these men.

He enjoyed the company of the Rabelaisian Kavanagh, who was usually in debt. John introduced him to John Lehmann, who published poems by him in *New Writing*, and to Cyril Connolly, who found space for him in *Horizon*. 'He used [my father] mercilessly to help him promote his work,' writes Candida Lycett Green. John helped many other writers and artists to 'place' their work, too. He obtained the painter Jack Yeats an exhibition at the National Gallery, London. Nolan's novel *At Swim-Two-Birds* (1939) was 'experimental' in the Joycean manner. That might not have recommended him to John; but, as Myles na gCopaleen, he was also the *Irish Times*'s star humorous columnist, and John found his 'Cruiskeen Lawn' column hilarious. They often met for a drink or lunch, and Nolan made a friendly reference to John in the 'Cruiskeen Lawn' column.

Occasionally John came to London to report in person to Mansergh and to Professor Hugh Pugh in the Dominions Office in Downing Street. Mansergh was in the London University building where John had previously worked. 'Betjeman regarded my office as "dim",' he said. 'He asked the porter at the entrance where I was to be found, and he didn't know.

Betjeman was rather shaken by this.' Mansergh noted that John was usually able to get access to people in high positions. At the MoI John would call on Brendan Bracken himself, or one of the directors-general, Sir Walter Monckton or Sir Cyril Radcliffe. (He had first met Radcliffe and his antique-dealer brother at Camilla Russell's house in the 1930s.) John was known at the MoI and his eccentricities were tolerated, even enjoyed. He was less cordially received at the Dominions Office, where the permanent under secretary was Sir Eric Machtig and the deputy under secretary was (Sir) John Stephenson.

Mansergh thought that John 'either consciously or subconsciously knew how to exploit the advantages of the curious triangular situation between the MoI, the Dominions Office and himself'. Mansergh was mildly irritated at attempts to play him off against Pugh, though he was amused when (Sir) Norman Costar, Machtig's private secretary, remarked, after John had crossed him in some matter, 'It says much for the British Civil Service that, in an hour of grave peril for the nation, it has actually been able to find something for John Betjeman to do.' John was in still less favour with the Dominions Office after the episode of the sticky diplomatic bag. One summer morning, Lord Cranborne, who had succeeded Anthony Eden as Dominions Secretary, found that the pile of letters on his desk was sticky. Enquiries were made, and it was found that the diplomatic bag in which the letters had arrived had been used by John to send a pound of butter over to a friend in London.

John's visits to the MoI were never less than exhilarating for Mansergh.

> Once, when Betjeman was in London on a week's visit, the Germans showed signs of attacking Bermuda. There were headlines in the papers. Betjeman came to a meeting of the Dominions Section and I remember well his coming into the Senate House room for the meeting, a little late, in marvellous Irish tweeds and looking sunburned and happy.
>
> 'Doctor, dear doctor, how nice of you to ask me round,' he said. 'Bermuda! I could *die* for Bermuda. Where is it?' This disrupted the morning's meeting. Then I had another meeting with him, and in the course of some great discussion about something, he heard that Joan Hunter Dunn was in the building. He had lost track of her. He was wildly excited – only stayed with me a minute or so longer – raced off to see her. Actually, I knew quite a lot about Joan Hunter Dunn, because my wife had been at school with her. They had played lacrosse together.

According to Mansergh, John was 'dedicated to being as co-operative as possible to the Irish while preserving the priorities of Britain's wartime interests', and he felt that he was the ideal person to put across the idea that 'what the Embassy [*sic*] was really interested in was fostering cultural links – literature, the arts, and so on.' Certainly John made himself popular on the Irish literary scene. He became a lasting friend of the writer Sean O'Faolain – novelist, short-story author, travel writer and editor of *The Bell* – and of Frank O'Connor, another master of the short story.

John also spent time with O'Faolain's sometime lover Elizabeth Bowen at her flat on St Stephen's Green. John Lehmann has described her at that time as 'in high spirits, radiating charm and vitality, the slight impediment in her speech giving an attractive touch of diffidence to the eager flow of her wide-ranging conversation'. Bowen was both a British Intelligence agent and a contributor to the *New Statesman*. She and John saw each other both professionally and socially; though O'Faolain, in the tell-all revision of his autobiography, *Vive Moi!*, which was published in 1993 after Bowen and others of his lovers had died, writes that she 'scornfully dismissed' John, after having lunch with him in 1946, as 'that silly ass'.

One of the powerful Dublin figures whom John was most eager to court was the formidable Archbishop of Dublin, John Charles McQuaid. John knew that he was close to de Valera and that he had been as responsible as anyone for drafting the Irish Constitution of 1937; also, that through the priesthood he exercised an immense influence over the thinking of Irish people. John's great interest in religion was one of his many assets in a country where religion was all-pervasive. He distributed copies of the Roman Catholic journals *The Universe* and *The Tablet* (the latter edited, since 1936, by his friend Douglas Woodruff); organized broadcasts on St Patrick's Day; publicized the exploits of Irish Catholics fighting in British forces; urged London to get *Picture Post* and *The Universe* to publish straightforward illustrated accounts of Nazi persecution of Polish Catholics; and made friends with Peter O'Curry, editor of the influential Catholic *Standard*, setting out 'to persuade him of Nazi anti-Christianity and to steer him away from the anti-British slant taken in his paper'. And to some extent he gained the interest of Archbishop McQuaid.

In a letter of 1942, he gave the prelate his views on ecclesiastical architecture and, in effect, told him what he wanted to hear – that if English parish churches 'become simply & traditionally Catholic (the Communion Service, the Central Service & the Catholic teaching of the meaning of that service), so, I believe, we will enlarge the nucleus which is to bring England back to Catholicism'. Unfortunately, there were several ways in which, directly or indirectly, John managed to annoy McQuaid. In January 1941, when he brought over Count Jan Balinski from the Polish Research Centre in London, a branch of the exiled Polish Government, Balinski antagonized McQuaid by complaining about the Irish censor. In June 1941 McQuaid wrote to Archbishop William Godfrey, the Apostolic Delegate to Britain, to tell him how angry he was at 'the Balinski incident' and of 'the caution that I feel obliged to show in the future'.

In September 1942 Patrick Kavanagh wrote a poem to celebrate the birth of the Betjemans' second child, Candida Rose. She was born in the Rotunda Hospital, Dublin: Elizabeth Pakenham (later Lady Longford) told Penelope that it was 'like being born in the Parthenon'. On 22 September, John's mother, who was recovering from illness at her sister's house in Wimbledon, London, wrote to Penelope to congratulate her and to ask what 'woollies' the baby needed – 'I will at once start knitting.' Paul, sturdy and flaxen-haired, was five that year. He took lessons a few miles away at Johnstown with a family named Warham who had a governess. John wrote a nonsense rhyme about him:

> There is a Paulie with no head,
> he runs about at the bottom of the bed
> There is a Paulie with no feet,
> he runs about at the bottom of the street
> There is a Paulie with no arms,
> he runs about and plays with the Warhams.

Ruth-Ellen Childers (now Mrs Moller) and her brother Erskine thought the rhyme was 'a bit off. Perhaps it was innocuous, but we thought it odd that a father would write that about his son. We certainly wouldn't have liked to have a rhyme like that written about *us*.'

Family life took second place to John's diplomatic duties. Even he, a natural socialite, found the pace gruelling.

> I am in hell [he wrote to John Piper]. A hell of my own choosing. I begin to hate Ireland and feel it is all playing at being a country . . . This eternal lunching out is getting me down and dining out and drinking and high tea . . . It feels like St John's Wood in Leicester.
>
> Thank goodness Propeller and the Egg and 'Bet' [Betty Evans] are happy enough. They like the country and Moti has arrived to cheer Propeller.

Penelope was not in fact particularly happy, though she dutifully played her part as a diplomat's wife. In another letter to the Pipers, John wrote: 'Propeller presided at a luncheon I gave to sixteen fifth columnists the other day. It was funny but sad. We all went in taxis to look at a church afterwards – double bluff.' Penelope wrote to Myfanwy Piper:

> As John has probably told you, we are both madly homesick and loathe all the social life here. We have to go to large cocktail parties, dinners and lunch

parties and, worst of all, a special brand of Dublin party when you arrive after dinner: about nine pm and are expected to stay till at least two am . . .

An important part of John's work was to look after visiting celebrities. The popular journalist Beverley Nichols was invited to stay at Collinstown, but found mushrooms growing on his bedroom walls in the damp mansion, and moved into the Shelbourne Hotel. In May 1943 Laurence Olivier came to Ireland to film the Battle of Agincourt for *Henry V*. Ireland was chosen because the skies above England were scored with the vapour trails of marauding Luftwaffe aircraft and defending Spitfires and because the able-bodied men of England were fighting a real war, while in Ireland extras could be easily and cheaply recruited. Olivier first came over on a reconnaissance trip accompanied by Dallas Bower, who seemed to appear at intervals in John's life like a recurring figure in an Anthony Powell novel.

Olivier and Bower arrived at Dun Laoghaire in the mail-boat and were met by John who took them to their Dublin hotel in a taxi. During the taxi-ride, John said, 'You do like Palestrina, don't you? I'm sure old Larry does, because he was a chorister; but I'm not certain whether you do, Dallas.'

Bower said, 'Well, yes, John, I do like Palestrina, of course I do, yes.'

'Ah, good,' John said. 'I'm afraid you'll both have to come with me to High Mass at Maynooth tomorrow morning.' (The next day was a Sunday.)

Olivier looked very dubious at this and said to Bower, when John had left them, 'What do you think of this?'

'My dear chap,' Bower said, 'we are absolutely in John Betjeman's hands and we must do whatever he says.' Later, he recalled, 'we realized that John knew exactly what he was doing – because on the Monday morning, all the Dublin newspapers had banner headlines, "LAURENCE OLIVIER ATTENDS HIGH MASS AT MAYNOOTH", or words to that effect. And after that we had no trouble at all with the Irish Government.'

John gave Olivier and Bower lunch with Edward Longford, who said, 'The man for you is Mervyn Powerscourt.' Longford pointed out that Lord Powerscourt's demesne at Enniskerry, Co. Wicklow – one of the scenic marvels of Ireland – had the advantage of a permanent Boy Scout camp in the grounds, in which Olivier's armies could be billeted. John drove Olivier and Bower to see him. 'Without John Betjeman, we could not have made that sequence there,' Bower believed. 'And, as it was wartime, we might not only have been unable to make the Agincourt sequence – we might not have been able to make the film at all.'

The centre of pro-British society in Dublin was the Shelbourne Hotel. In this luxurious, cushioned environment, the world of the pre-war

Ascendancy, a Molly Keane world of affectations, brittleness and Bright Young People, seemed to survive. As a superannuated Bright Young Thing himself, John knew how to make himself interesting in this society. It was at a literary party in the Shelbourne in 1941 that he met the young British writer Sylvia Stevenson. She introduced him to her friend Eleanor Butler, whom he, in turn, was to introduce to her future husband, Billy Clonmore (later Earl of Wicklow).

Eleanor Butler and John soon discovered a common interest in architecture. Her father, Professor R. M. Butler, had been Professor of Architecture at Trinity College and was 'one of the few people in Dublin at that time who knew anything about Georgian buildings'. Eleanor brought John to see her father, who was recovering from a heart attack. John had learned to do some research into people before he met them. One thing he had found out about Butler was that his mother, by birth a German from Schleswig-Holstein, had become interested in the Irvingites, whose small sect, the Catholic Apostolic Church, had flourished in Germany. They had one little church in Dublin, one in Belfast and a number in England which had been designed in the late nineteenth century by some of the Gothic architects whom John most admired. So, instead of talking about Georgian Dublin, John plunged into the history of the Catholic Apostolic Church. By this date the Church was in decline, and Professor Butler, as the only descendant of anybody connected with it, had been appointed a trustee to wind up its affairs. When John began to say how fascinated he was by the Irvingites, Butler was not really interested. John was full of the correct terminology – the Catholic Apostolic Church called their pastors 'angels', and above them was a number of 'archangels'. Lady Wicklow recalled:

> John went on with his usual thing: 'Oooh, how marvellous! Are you visited by the *angels*? How often do you meet an *archangel*?' Well, up to a point my father went along with this and joked about it; but then John said, 'Really what I would like, Professor Butler, if you could arrange it, is to join the Catholic Apostolic Church in Ireland.' . . . About a week afterwards a friend, Senator Douglas, who was a leading Quaker, came to see my father and said, 'Have you met this fellow Betjeman?' My father said yes. And Douglas said, 'Well, it's an extraordinary thing, he's come to me and says he wants to become a Quaker.' So from that point on, my father always said of John, 'That *mountebank*!'

Though John was fond of Eleanor Butler, she did not inspire one of his extravagant crushes. 'I think the person he really fell for in Ireland', she said in 1976, 'was Lady Hemphill, now Emily Villiers-Stuart. He wrote one of his best poems about her, "Ireland with Emily".' Emily was a New England American, daughter of a rich shoe manufacturer – the kind of heiress who marries English lords in P. G. Wodehouse novels. She had married Lord Hemphill, a Dublin lawyer, but by now the marriage was under severe strain because of his chronic alcoholism. The Hemphills lived at Tulira in Co. Galway, an accretion of 1880s Victorian Gothic around a much earlier building. Soon after meeting the Betjemans in Co. Cavan, Emily Hemphill invited them to stay at Tulira. She recalled:

> John had a motor-car – *no* one had a motor-car then, the only people allowed to run one were priests, doctors, vets and race officials. But he was on the fringe of the diplomatic world, so he had one. Well, Penelope went off in the car straight away to look for a Connemara pony. So John and I had nothing but bicycles, and we went on the ride John describes in 'Ireland with Emily'. I said the nicest place we could go was where the St George family lived. John was thrilled with them, because they were rather aristocratic and very profligate gamblers. The lovely Georgian house had been burned down. 'Let's go there,' I said, 'and let's go to the sea and swim.' So off we went, and picked up beer at a pub. Then he saw the ruins – very attractive ruins, a shell with lovely festoons of plasterwork hanging down like stalactites. And across the road was the mausoleum which he describes in the poem. The door of that was hanging open, the sarcophagi had been robbed, the lead had been taken, naturally, and sheep used it as a refuge. After that, we did swim, halfway up Galway Harbour, about twenty miles from the Clare border. Then we bicycled back down the 'bohreens' (that means lanes) described in the poem.

> Penelope was miserable on that first visit to Tulira.

> John absolutely fell for Emily, and I'll never forget the agony of jealousy, the only time I've ever felt jealousy, I think, when he stayed up talking to her till about 1.00 a.m. and I went up to bed and he never came in. In point of fact I needn't have worried a bit; she was already secretly engaged to someone called Ion Villiers-Stuart who lived in a very beautiful and famous house called Dromana which has now been pulled down. I mean, she wasn't in the least in love with John, but he was mad about her. She subsequently married Ion Villiers-Stuart, then he died beside her in bed after two years. She had to get a Reno divorce from Lord Hemphill, because you couldn't get a divorce in Ireland. Ion Villiers-Stuart's wife, too, was an alcoholic, oddly enough; she died, and he married Emily.

The idea voiced by both Eleanor Wicklow and Emily Villiers-Stuart, that John may have been a spy – for Britain, of course – has been treated with some derision; but it deserves open-minded consideration. The degree to which it has simply been taken for granted, in Ireland, that he was a spy in 1940s Dublin is remarkable, and in 1941 the IRA took the notion seriously enough to plan to assassinate him. In 1967 he received a letter from Diarmuid Brennan, of Stevenage, Hertfordshire:

> I was in Dublin in 1940–41. I was responsible for all matters relating to civilian Intelligence for the Army Council of the Irish Republican Army . . . Oddly . . . you became a source of much anxiety to the Army Council of the IRA. I got communications describing you as 'dangerous' and a *person of menace* to all of us.

In mid-1941 elements within the IRA decided to embark on terrorist activities, and John was watched. Brennan continued: '. . . I sent word to these two fellows and told them that one of our contacts in Dublin Castle – a Special Branch man – had passed on word that they had been spotted around the area of the British Embassy. I emphasized that as they were now under police surveillance they hadn't a chance of "taking care" of you. This, I should stress, was pure invention; but they called off the job.'

The letter has to be read with the caution that any IRA document merits, but the main burden of Brennan's story, taken with the circumstantial trimmings – such as his use of the correct surname of John's assistant Joan Lynam, newly appointed in 1941 – is convincing. John was luckier than Cinna the poet, in *Julius Caesar*, who is first confused with a conspirator, then murdered for his bad verses.

There is some evidence that John went beyond the alertness expected of a diplomat and ventured into the 'grey area' between diplomacy and espionage, not least that he was privy to Elizabeth Bowen's secret reports to the British government. Stronger evidence is presented by Robert Cole. He writes of the IRA plot to assassinate John:

> It came to nothing, and . . . responsible IRA leaders apparently never thought that Betjeman was other than what he appeared. But then, in January 1942, an Irish acquaintance on the West Coast begged Betjeman to come down because 'something very important has turned up about the fishing. It is urgent that you should come here and see me *now* . . .' Betjeman contacted Brigadier Woodhouse immediately, saying: 'This may be important.' Did 'fish' refer to German submarines? Was Betjeman acting as liaison with naval intelligence?

The message John received was almost a parody of a spy message. As he was no keen fisherman, he would not have regarded any aspect of fishing as 'important'. And Cole's tentative hypothesis about naval Intelligence reminds us that, in the year after John left Dublin, he had a 'hush-hush' post with the Admiralty in England.*

David O'Donoghue's scholarly book *Hitler's Irish Voices: The Story of German Radio's Irish Service* (1998) offers even more convincing evidence. Part of the book is about Mrs Susan Hilton, who, although born in India of British parents, had Irish connections. Using her maiden name, she began broadcasting to Ireland from Berlin in January 1942, and 'warned listeners against allowing Ireland to be turned into a battlefield following America's entry into the war'.

> On 26 March 1942 she used official German Radio notepaper to write a letter to her brother Edward, then living at the Moat House in Oldcastle, County Meath . . . As well as being read by the Gestapo, the letter was intercepted by British Intelligence who tipped off their Irish counterparts in G2 . . . The official sent to the Moat House was John Betjeman, then attached to the British diplomatic representation in Dublin, officially as a 'press and cultural attaché', but actually involved in intelligence work. Sweney remembers that Betjeman 'called at my place in the 1940s in a car when no one had cars, and asked whether the local church had pews in it or not. I told him I didn't know but suggested he could get a chair to stand on and look through the church windows to see for himself.' Betjeman's question was a pretext to engage Sweney in conversation but the wily farmer did not take the bait.

The message about the 'fish' and the Edward Sweney affair suggest that, on at least two occasions, John trespassed into the grey area. But if indeed he had some kind of Intelligence rôle – and the evidence suggests he had – it is likely to have been only a minor and fitful aspect of his work, not – as implied by David O'Donoghue – a major task for which his formal title of press attaché was only a cover.

One piece of evidence which weights the balance against major Intelligence duties for John is the mock timetable he wrote of his typical day's work, 'A Representative Day in the Press Attaché's Office'. It was presumably written to amuse his secretary, Miss Whitehorn, and others of the staff at Upper Mount Street; perhaps it was also a sidelong way of making Maffey aware of some of his grievances. There is a clear element of spoofery, and in the sustained *jeu d'esprit* of this Pooterish timetable, John may well have belittled his importance to add to the comedy: he depicts himself as put-upon dogsbody. But some observers thought him just such an insignificant figure. Hector Legge said in 1976: 'John Betjeman was small

---

* See Chapter 17, 'Admiralty'.

boys' stuff – Maffey's little boy. Nobody took him very seriously, and there wasn't much for him to do. The papers were all down to a minimum – the *Sunday Independent*, which I edited, was only four pages. So there wasn't much point in Betjeman's churning out press releases.' Professor R. F. Foster has formed a similar impression of John's wartime rôle from the surviving documents in the Public Record Office, London. He writes that in Dublin John 'indulged in a camp Hibernian High Church fantasy'.

John Lehmann, editor of *New Writing*, gave in his memoirs a more sympathetic and probably fairer assessment.

> John Betjeman had taken on a cultural liaison job in neutral Dublin in the UK Representative's office, and fulfilled his duties with immense aplomb and zest, charming the most suspicious among the local intelligentsia into at least keen interest if not wholehearted engagement with what writers and artists were thinking and doing in war-shattered Britain, and keeping an easy lead over his Axis opposite numbers all through the course; thus proving, not for the first or last time, that in such a job a dram of personality is worth a hogshead of bureaucracy.

Why did John and Penelope leave Ireland, late in 1943? Given their growing disenchantment with the pattern of their life there, John may well have been pulling strings. On 14 June, 'Mr John Betjeman Leaving' was front-page news in the *Irish Times*. The MacEntees gave an informal leaving party for John and Penelope. 'Towards the end of it,' Ruth-Ellen Moller recalls, 'my mother said to John, "Why don't you sing?" So he sang, in fluent Irish, "Dark Rosaleen" – sixteen verses – with the tears pouring down his face. My mother accompanied him on the piano. The tears were terrible, because others started to cry, too. The tears were genuine; but the letters which have been published show he was glad to leave.'

De Valera's friend Frank Gallagher organized the formal leaving party in Dublin Castle. Terence de Vere White, another friend the Betjemans had made in Dublin, remembered: 'The *gardaí* controlled the traffic as it piled up in the Lower Castle Yard, and there must have been a sinking in the hearts of many who had seen themselves as choice spirits.' Gallagher made the farewell speech. 'One thing', he said, 'they will carry with them as proof of Irish hospitality. Came three. Went four . . .'

On 25 August 1943 John and Penelope went together to say goodbye to de Valera, who signed and dated a photograph of himself. Some four months later, John, over lunch at Brooks's with James Lees-Milne:

> Said he loved Ireland but not the Irish middle class. Only liked the country eccentrics like Penelope's distant relations, the Chetwode [*sic*]-Aikens.

When they claimed to be cousins Penelope retorted, 'No, you can't be. Your branch was extinct fifty years ago.' When the Betjemans left Ireland, de Valera sent for them. Penelope said to him, 'My husband knows nothing of politics; or of journalism. He knows nothing at all.' She offered to plan an equestrian tour for de Valera, and her last words to him were, 'I hope you won't let the Irish roads deteriorate. I mean I hope you won't have them metalled and tarmacked.'

17

Admiralty

I N 1940 PERCY CUDLIPP, John's old boss at the *Evening Standard*, became editor of the *Daily Herald*. In 1943 he needed a new book reviewer – a single writer who would select and pronounce on the books of the week. He chose John. Evidently he did not hold against him his naughtinesses as *Standard* film critic – in that post John had proved his ability to write entertainingly and had been a draw to advertisers. Cudlipp, himself a doggerel versifier, also admired John's poetry.

John began reviewing for the *Herald* in November 1943. His then agent, Edmund Cork, negotiated a fee of fourteen guineas a week, which was to increase to eighteen in July 1945. John used his first 'About Books' column to set out his stall. 'If you see a book at a booksellers which you like the look of, buy it while it is still there. Books are not rationed, but good books are scarce.' Only two of the thirty words of this 'intro' are of more than one syllable: like George Orwell, in his journalism of this same period, John understood the power of plain writing – in this trait, both men were perhaps influenced by the Authorized Version of the Bible. In the rest of the article, John hammered the 'mad situation of English literature' in the war, by which publishers had become arbiters of public taste, because the public appetite for books was such that they would buy anything publishers chose to print.

John had only one serious disqualification as a writer for the *Herald*: his political views, or rather his lack of them. It was a Labour paper. Started as a strike journal in 1912, for several years it was edited by the Labour politician George Lansbury. It was the *Daily Express* of the left. But, luckily for John, neither the proprietor nor the editor of the *Herald* was zealous in adherence to Socialist dogma. 'Lord Southwood was really an absurd figure to be in charge of a Labour paper,' said Michael Foot, who contributed a political column. 'He was a small-minded man interested only in profits.' Foot had a much higher regard for Percy Cudlipp, 'although maybe he was not a tremendously enthusiastic Socialist'.

He was an extremely efficient editor in every way [Foot said in 1990]. He could do anything on a newspaper. He could take anybody's copy and make it better; he could make up the paper; he could write the political leader; but he could also write poetry of his own peculiar debased kind – it didn't claim to be anything of any great moment . . .

Percy was the brightest and best of all the Cudlipp family . . . and certainly the most interested in light verse. His relationship with John Betjeman was a very close one; I often heard Percy talk about Betjeman.

One committed Socialist on the staff was Marjorie Proops, later the queen of agony aunts on the *Daily Mirror*. She was on the *Herald* throughout the war, first as a fashion artist, then as fashion editor, later as women's editor. Her overriding memory of the *Herald*'s offices in Long Acre (the building was demolished in 1984) was 'a persistent smell of rotting cabbages'. Covent Garden market was still below. Marje Proops said that she did not meet John often, because he had no desk at the *Herald*, but hand-delivered his copy to the cabbage-smelling office every Tuesday. This chore was often combined with an architectural exploration. On 15 December 1946 he wrote:

To each his private pleasure. Mine is looking at buildings old, new and middle-aged. So soon as I have delivered these reviews to the 'Daily Herald' I go off for the afternoon on a tram.

Away in the suburbs I watch the sun redden behind high Victorian churches, children scamper over municipal asphalte [*sic*], cats dash into speckled laurel bushes, and I think myself back into my childhood.

I am perfectly happy. Mr **J. M. Richards** clearly has the same pleasure. His book, THE CASTLES ON THE GROUND (*Architectural Press*, 8s. 6d.) is the first study of the modern suburb which looks at it from my own point of view that I have read . . .

This passage shows how winningly John could write when his interest was engaged. Often it was not. His mother 'gutted' many of the books for him and he frequently used her brief reports verbatim. Colonel Kolkhorst, by contrast, sent John long and minutely detailed reports, which had to be drastically boiled down in the *Herald*. John's critiques were marred by a disinclination to write anything but good of the writers under review. One reason for this was that he was so acutely sensitive to adverse criticism himself that he shrank from visiting it on others. On 7 March 1945 he wrote: 'When a man lays bare his soul he should be treated kindly, whether he does it in prose or verse. Reviewers killed Keats . . . I feel qualms of conscience towards an author's feelings and would prefer not to review a book at all rather than review it unkindly.' A. L. Rowse had a more

cynical explanation of John's benevolence: 'He didn't want to make enemies in the literary world.'

When Holbrook Jackson's edition of *The Complete Nonsense of Edward Lear* was published by Faber's in 1947, John drew a significant contrast. 'Lewis Carroll, by comparison, is a pedantic don in his nonsense poetry, but Lear was a true Victorian poet and a true artist. Most of us can bear poetry only if it has a story or sounds marvellous when it is read out and makes us want to shout and dance. Lear knew this. First he wrote his famous illustrated Limericks. Then he wrote whole poems which sounded like those of his friend Tennyson, and which were, in their mad way, as poetical.'

In June 1945 John complained: 'Now we have a system of paper control which rigorously keeps down the printing of good literature, the slow-selling classic, in favour of what will sell off rapidly in a month.' But, during the time he was reviewing for the *Herald*, several books were published which are now regarded as classics – among them Evelyn Waugh's *Brideshead Revisited*, Albert Camus' *The Outsider*, John Steinbeck's *Cannery Row*, L. P. Hartley's *Eustace and Hilda*, Joyce Cary's *The Horse's Mouth*, Malcolm Lowry's *Under the Volcano*, Elizabeth Bowen's *The Demon Lover* and Mervyn Peake's *Titus Groan*.

John's almost unerring recognition of exceptional quality is the most impressive aspect of his reviewing. Of course a critic who praises virtually everything he reviews is not going to miss many winners, but the purr of his approval rose to a noticeably higher frequency – like a Geiger counter in the presence of uranium – when he encountered a masterpiece.

He found Camus' *The Outsider* 'so well written and profoundly disturbing that it is in a class by itself'.

> What makes so short a book so moving, so true to its Paganism, is that although, by our own standards, this highly intelligent and physically attractive young man has no morals, no conscience, no motive in life, we still sympathize with him.
>
> Throughout the trial we see that the French are imposing the alien moral and Christian code of Europe on a sun-soaked Pagan.
>
> Seldom have I read a work which says so much in so short a space.

In May 1945 John wrote to Evelyn Waugh:

> You are very much in my thoughts, for I am reading for a second time *Brideshead Revisited* since it has come in to me for review in the bloody old *Daily Herald*. It will get a spanking good notice. To me it is a great treat to read a book with a standard of values behind it. Christian values what is more. I shall have somehow to hint this fact to readers without letting it be apparent to the

Editors, since recently I had a letter from them to say that I was using the paper for *Roman Catholic propaganda* and that 'The *Daily Herald* finds itself in conflict with the Catholic Church on several points.' I was also accused of 'Jesuitry'. This made me rather proud. Of course, I have not altered my tactics.

John reviewed the book in June. 'Evelyn Waugh is about the only living writer whose novels I can read a second time with pleasure. This is because he hates writing and does not suffer from verbal diarrhoea, as do many lengthier novelists . . . His new novel is, I think, his best yet, and that is saying a lot.'

John was one of the most insular of English poets; yet he was not insular in his literary taste. In 1946 he gave high praise to Vladimir Nabokov's *The Real Life of Sebastian Knight*, acclaiming him as 'a novelist in the forefront'. He admired Nabokov's use of adjectives.

> See how he describes a European express train at night: 'The long sad sigh of brakes at dimly surmised stations, the upward slide of an embossed leather blind disclosing a platform . . . the clank of an invisible hammer testing wheels; the gliding move into darkness; the passing glimpse of a lone woman touching silver-bright things in her travelling case on the blue plush of a lighted compartment.'

On the same day John reviewed Mervyn Peake's book *Titus Groan*, about the Earl of Groan and his mad sisters, Cora and Clarice. 'If you can tuck yourself into the dream world Mr Peake creates – and I was able to do so – this book is a cobwebby, candle-lit escape from life.' (Only later editions of the book were enhanced by Peake's illustrations of Gothic 'gloomth'.)

John was less enthusiastic about the modern movement in poetry. Two of the movement's leaders, Eliot and Auden, were friends of his, and he wrote carefully about them; but he could not conceal his distaste, which was more for their influence than for their own works. 'Please don't try to imitate Mr Eliot' was the headline above John's column on 18 October 1944.

> There is little doubt that the greatest established poet writing in Britain today is T. S. Eliot.
>
> There may be other potential great poets lurking among the pages of that excellent periodical 'Poetry', edited by Tambimuttu, in 'Horizon', and other periodicals like a new one called 'Prospect' (*Claremont Press*, Little Chalfont, Bucks, 9d.).
>
> But Eliot is established, and anyone who is interested in literature has heard of him.
>
> But not everyone likes him. They say he is obscure, that he doesn't scan or rhyme properly.

Certainly his influence has been disastrous, for his mannerisms are easy to imitate. Eliot writes lines which are each their own rhythm and poem, and yet together they form a poem which is a sort of outer-covering to the numerous little poems which are each line.

Imitators have hit on this manner of writing as an excuse for composing 'poems' which are really just prose sentences chopped up to look like Eliot on the printed page. Read the description of the sea . . . from Eliot's poem 'The Dry Salvages' in his new collection FOUR QUARTETS (*Faber*, 6s.) which are his four newest poems in one volume.

If you were to string these lines together like prose, they would be very odd prose and you would soon want to separate them again into Eliot's arrangement.

In 1945 John wrote of his friend:

Wystan Auden, the poet, has reverted to religion. His new book, FOR THE TIME BEING (*Faber*, 8s. 6d.) contains one long poem on the birth of Our Lord and it is clear that its author has been influenced by the thinking of three other British writers from these islands who are in the United States – Aldous Huxley, Gerald Heard and Christopher Isherwood.

Though I cannot get the general drift of the whole poem, being too near to it in time, I find it flowering with mature and beautiful lyrics.

By contrast with these restrained plaudits, there was heartfelt praise for Dylan Thomas in 1946: 'The Welsh poet, Dylan Thomas, is not only the best living Welsh poet, but is a great poet. His DEATHS AND ENTRANCES (*Dent*, 2s. 6d.) proves this. He is sometimes difficult, but always rewarding, rich and arresting . . .' Quoting 'A springful of larks on a rolling Cloud', John wrote: 'I wish there was space to quote more; for Dylan Thomas deserves a whole page of this paper and it is unfair to him to quote part of a stanza as I have done – it is too like cutting a bit out of a painting and asking you to judge the whole picture from it.'

This was the highest praise John gave to any contemporary poet. That said much for his objectivity, because Thomas's floodtide lyricism is far removed from John's own poetic style. When John discovered a poet of his own metal, such as William Plomer, D. B. Wyndham Lewis or 'Sagittarius', he praised freely but less ardently. He knew how the trick was done. In Plomer (who became a friend) he at once recognized a kindred creator. Plomer's *The Dorking Thigh* (1945) contained 'splendid poems for reciting to a not too squeamish audience'.

Many of the writers John reviewed were people he knew, often friends. He seldom revealed that he knew them. It was not primarily a case of his giving friends special treatment; it was simply that he had come to know many of the leading and minor figures on the British and Irish literary scenes – at his schools and at Oxford, and in his later jobs. Then there was the happy chance of having Mary Renault as his nurse in the Acland Nursing Home, Oxford, in 1945 before she moved to South Africa. Reviewing her novel *Return Tonight* in 1947, he wrote, 'The authoress is so good and knowledgeable about doctors and hospitals and has a touch, terrible and tender, when she describes suffering.' He had copious compliments for society friends of the pre-war years, such as Nancy Mitford and Cecil Beaton. In December 1945 he wrote to Nancy Mitford: 'Cold from the G[reat] W[estern] R[ailway], in which I have just been finishing *The Pursuit of Love*, I write to tell you on this lovely *writing* paper how v. greatly I enjoyed it . . . Oh you clever old girl. How I am going to break this lovely book to the drearies of the *Daily Herald*, I don't know. I shall enjoy trying. Clever, clever Nancy. I am proud to know you.'

In spite of his antipathy to 'kiddiz', John did not neglect to review children's books. 'The toyshops may have let the children down, but the bookshops have not,' he wrote just before Christmas 1944. His own children gave him insight into young children's tastes. 'I have been trying to get *Grimm's Fairy Tales* for my son,' John wrote in 1944. 'He has reached the age when he enjoys miraculous stories, especially those involving the mystic numbers of three or seven – seven wishes and three giants or three visitors and seven adventures for each.' But Grimm and Hans Andersen were 'unobtainable'. In 1947 he recommended, for children of eight and younger, Enid Blyton's twenty-one new stories in *The Little White Duck*.

John's review of 30 December 1947, headed 'Handy Guide to Modern Novels', began:

> Mind you, I don't say it always works. But, as a general rule, you can tell what a novel is going to be like from its first sentence. Supposing you read this one:
>
> > His demob suit pinched him behind the shoulders, and the wet, rain-soaked streets of a typical London November day seemed singularly uninviting.
>
> Well, I can tell the book is unlikely to be any good. There are several obvious errors. His demob suit would have pinched him under the arms or drawn his shoulder-blades together, but it would not have pinched him *behind* the shoulders. If the streets were rain-soaked they were presumably wet. A 'typical London November day' means nothing definite. Foggy or dry or fair, or windy or cold?
>
> 'Singularly uninviting'. If it were a 'typical' day, it would not be *singularly* uninviting; it would be as uninviting as usual. In fact, this author is a bore

who does not think before he writes, but just jabbers away, putting in need-
less dead words which add nothing to the picture.

John's columns would have been of value to a reader who wanted to be
a writer. His most effective critical technique was comparison, either with
another book in the week's batch, or with inventions of his own. His
column of 31 July 1946 was headed 'How NOT to write'.

If you want an example of bad writing, take this: 'Frank, aware that he
looked guilty, made *frantic efforts* to *banish the maiden blush* which was *suffus-
ing his face.*'

I have italicized the outworn clichés which this writer brings into the
sentence. What he means is 'Frank, aware that he looked guilty, tried not to
blush.'

Because he is writing a 'funny book' he thinks funniness consists in spinning out a sentence.

I will not bother you with the name or author of this book. The publishers should not have wasted paper on it. They are to blame. Every page
has dozens of such dead sentences.

'It was not, therefore, until the next morning that the *full tragedy of the
previous night* was *laid bare to his horrified gaze.* The four rabbits were still *repos-
ing* on the lawn and *with some distaste* he collected them up, *depositing* them
in the tool shed.'

This is a 'funny' way of saying 'He found the dead rabbits on the lawn
next morning and put them in the tool shed.' Funny my foot! And no funnier tricked out in fourth-form frills.

If you want an example of better writing, take this, which describes a
wife saying good-bye to her husband at a station:

'John has gone. The last brass carriage handle has disappeared, and the
empty track yawns greasily in front of me.'

That is felt and observed and simply described. Of course she could have
said:

'John has departed. The iron monster has steamed forth on its
appointed journey, leaving to my distracted gaze a dreary expanse of
shining rails.'

But because she is an artist, she does not. I do not know her real name,
this **Elizabeth Evelyn**, who writes NO PROMISE IN SUMMER (*Cape*,
8s. 6d.) . . .

By 1947, John was losing interest in book-reviewing. His notices were
becoming ever shorter and more perfunctory. He made no attempt to dis-
guise the fact that reviewing had become a grinding chore. Sometimes he
frankly washed his hands of a book. In June 1947 he wrote: 'If you ask me

what TREADMILL, by **Michael Harrison**, is about, I don't know. All the same, I enjoyed it.' It was clear that he was suffering from reviewer's fatigue. He hated the work and despised his readers. In 1951, by mutual consent with Percy Cudlipp, and with no hard feelings, John ceased to be the *Herald*'s book critic.

When he began his stint on the *Herald*, John had been back in England for two and a half months, and had resumed work, after his adventures in Dublin, at the Ministry of Information's Senate House. By March 1944, however, he had managed to get himself moved to a section of 'P' Branch of the Admiralty, which was stationed in Bath. Though some of his former colleagues thought him disorganized and flippant, he had won the approval of senior figures – such as Sir John Maffey and Sir Kenneth Clark – whose opinions counted when appointments were being made. Their glowing commendations helped to gain him his new, responsible and 'hush-hush' post. A month after his arrival in Bath he had a letter from Honor Tracy, the future novelist and humorous journalist. He had known her at the Ministry of Information, where she served in the Japanese department. Clearly she felt for him something more than friendship; and it is possible that their affectionate relationship was later the inspiration for a Betjeman poem.* In the 1944 letter Tracy wrote:

> Please send me your Bath address because I am writing a farewell poem for you. At present I am drunk, I was picked out of the canal last night by PC Smith at two am. Case coming up on Tuesday . . . How I love you. I am very drunk. There is no need to read this letter to everyone who comes into your office. Don't tell Arthur [Calder-Marshall] about the canal.

John's immediate superior in Bath was the novelist Richard Hughes, author of *A High Wind in Jamaica* (1929), an adventure story about a family of children captured by pirates. 'Diccon' Hughes and John had at least known *of* each other since John was a schoolboy at Marlborough, when Hughes was one of three literary judges who chose a poem of his for the anthology *Public School Verse*. When war broke out in 1939 Hughes was considered too old for active duty in the Royal Navy (he was six years older than John). But through his friend Jack James, who was a godfather of his daughter Llecky and one of the 4,000 Admiralty staff whose departments had been evacuated to Bath soon after war was declared, he was offered a post as a temporary assistant in the Administrative Service. He arrived in Bath in June 1940.

---

* See Chapter 18, 'Farnborough'.

Hughes had expected to be 'licking envelopes'; but in fact he was made personal assistant to the head of one of the departments. That head in turn answered to Jack James, who, with the rank of assistant secretary, was in charge of the Bath section of 'P' Branch. (The 'P' stood for Priority.) This was an independent secretariat within the Admiralty. Its task had originally been 'the rigid administration of production priorities'; but it had gradually become 'the administrative pivot of a very much wider field of work, wherever the Admiralty supply machinery came into contact with the ever more complex central machinery of Government and with the other supply departments'. In September 1940 'P' Branch officially became the '*Production and* Priority Branch' and Hughes was promoted to be 'Head of the General Section of the "P" Branch'.

John was billeted on Mrs Helen Holmes of 16 Macaulay Buildings, Widcombe Hill, Bath. He got on very well with Mrs Holmes, who remained a friend and correspondent for many years after he left the city. A warm, kindly woman with a lively mind, she enjoyed having intellectual arguments in the evenings with John and her other lodgers. In 1949 she wrote to him: 'I have often thought of you and longed for some of the old exhilarating conversations that made you tear your hair at my rash statements . . .'

On 1 May 1944 John reported for duty. The Admiralty offices were in the Empire Hotel, a grotesque, cavernous building overlooking the Avon and its shop-lined Adam bridge. Some of John's colleagues in 'P' Branch felt slightly resentful that he was literally a 'Johnny-come-lately', who had missed the really hard work and the pressures that they had endured. The Battle of the Atlantic had been won, and the preparations for the Normandy landings had all been made by the time John joined the Admiralty a month before D-Day. He had also missed the heavy bomb raids on Bath.

John found the Admiralty's bureaucratic procedures, as he wrote to Nancy Mitford after less than a fortnight in 'P' Branch, 'wonderfully boring'. After a while Hughes found some limited use for his literary talents. He was put in charge of two publications which were circulated to Admiralty branches around the country: the 'Green 'un', as it was called, supplied up-to-date bulletins on the best places to find supplies of labour, steel, wood and so on; and the more 'hush-hush' 'Pink 'un' (originally the title of a famous Victorian sporting paper) gave reports on recent damage – for example, 'Don't try to find labour in Acton because it has been bombed.' John had three people working for him in his office. One of them was Arnold Weinstock (later Lord Weinstock), who remembered him as 'frightfully scruffy' and chain-smoking, with a cigarette always hanging from his top lip. Weinstock noticed that John swore a lot – a habit, it seemed to him, oddly at variance with his professed Christianity. He also remembered John's using the staff as 'slave labour' for his book-reviewing.

Dawn Macleod, a young woman who was made John's personal assistant, has left two vivid accounts of 'P' Branch in 1944 and the impression he made there. In 1958 she asked John's permission to write about her wartime encounter with him in her autobiographical *Oasis of the North*. He replied: 'Say what you like.' But in fact, only too well aware of the thinness of John's skin, she wrote about him with a polite wariness. '*Dear* Mr Betjeman, don't think me rude! Anyone who could make a Civil Service office amusing and lively, as you did, has genius enough to stoke the warmest fires of gratitude and praise. Our essential part in the war effort had been virtually completed before D-Day, and until you came we found the ensuing boredom much harder to bear than bombing.'

In 1984, however, just six months after John's death, Dawn Macleod felt free to write, in a *Spectator* article headed 'Betjeman at War', a much more candid account, contrasting John with the bearded, imposing Hughes.

Betjeman proved to be a completely different fish: plain John Dory to a lordly salmon. He sought no technical details and did not even feign interest in my talk of welded hulls, Oerlikon guns and the latest radar equipment. What, then, could a well-meaning personal assistant do for him? His chief need, a shoulder to moan upon, had never been listed in Fleet Orders. But this was autumn 1944, with the war all but won, the air-raids on Bristol and Bath at an end, and a surfeit of tinned spam to fill our shrunken stomachs. It seemed opportune to relax my official attitude a little. While most of us felt cautiously cheerful, poor JB so hated being confined to an office that he drooped and wilted day by day, appearing to be on the brink of suicide or at best an early Victorian decline.

His curious complexion reminded me of some chameleons with whom I once cohabited in the East. It kept changing its hue, not to match the background but apparently influenced by some inner alchemy of thought and emotion. At times he was a flat Egyptian yellow, which would turn by stages to a lurid gypsy bronze with gold trimmings. In his most miserable moods he displayed a countenance of ghastly peasoup green, truly alarming until you got used to it. After all, he never quite passed out: yet none of us would have risked a sixpenny bet on his chances of living to be seventy-eight.

Dawn Macleod thought that Hughes, although he made no comment, guessed that John's need for constant sympathy was a drain on her. Hughes's remedy was to take her and John on lunch-hour strolls around Bath's crescents and squares. She noticed how the architectural merits of any building were 'instantly reflected by the poet's countenance'.

His sagging cheeks puffed out, pink and soft. His wet-spaniel eyes developed glamorous sparkle. Without delay he launched us on a sea of inspired documentary, so that we lost our bearings and all track of time. On one occasion the punctilious Hughes disgraced himself by forgetting an appointment with a VIP.

We must have made an odd assortment of characters even for an ancient city accustomed to freaks, from Bladud to Beau Nash and Beckford. Richard Hughes, in harmony with his erect posture and stately, unmodern pace, was invariably well barbered and tailored, while roly-poly John Betjeman looked as if he slept in his clothes – and someone else's garments grabbed after a shipwreck at that . . .

One event in Dawn Macleod's life as John's assistant stood out in her memory. She mentioned it briefly in *Oasis of the North*, but twenty-six years later, in the *Spectator* article, pulled out all the stops to describe it in its full absurdity.

We had compiled a long and boring paper about some plant extension at a shipyard. In it, reference to 'a bed of retorts' was seized upon by my superior with infantile glee. Opening the docket out flat, he used the inside of its smooth cover to draw a picture of the great bed of Ware, at the Victoria & Albert Museum in London. The illustration, perfect in every detail, showed the entire Retort family tucked up beneath a quilt, heads of all sizes in a row on the bolster. Having put his signature to the report and dropped it into the messenger's bag for Whitehall, the artist leaned back with a happy smile.

This euphoria did not last. He was utterly downcast next day, when the docket came back with a curt note attached: 'Please instruct your staff to refrain from scribbling on dockets.' It was that cruel word 'scribbling' which caused such pain. *Scribbling.* He read the insult aloud in a hoarse voice. His face, already green, turned eerily blue, the sort of leached colour seen during an eclipse of the sun.

For the first and only time in my life I tried a homeopathic remedy, using like to cure like. Outside in my car, some fine purple plums, picked from our orchard, waited for delivery to an aged aunt. She had to go without, for Betjeman's need was paramount. I fed him the luscious fruit, the blue bloom on the fat plum cheeks matching exactly his facial hue. Quickly he recovered, flushing crimson with pleasure. I still have the book of poems which he pressed upon me in gratitude. It is inscribed:

from J. Betjeman
  Hell,
  Bath,
  1944

John had a few other solaces in Bath, besides Georgian architecture and homeopathic plums. Hughes took him to dinner with the writer Horace Annesley Vachell, on whom Hughes was billeted. (The old man died in 1955, aged ninety-three.) And John's and Penelope's friend and mentor P. Morton Shand lived in Bath with his family. John and he were always on the same wavelength. The Shands lived in Darlington Place on Bathwick Hill, with a view right over the city. John visited them often and was captivated by Morton Shand's schoolgirl daughters, Elspeth and Mary, who were to marry, respectively, the politician Geoffrey Howe (later Lord Howe) and the architect James (later Sir James) Stirling. He had a special crush – romantic and platonic – on Mary, whom he saw as some idealized figure from a medieval legend illustrated by William Morris or Edward Burne-Jones. He jotted down some rough notes for a poem about her, which included the lines:

> Pale Pre-Raphaelite Mary Shand
> Swung her satchel and waved her hand;
> Her every step on the wet Bath pavement
> Bound me more in a ~~deep~~ sweet enslavement . . .

John kept in touch with the Stirlings, visiting them at their house in north London. The last time Mary saw him was at a 10 Downing Street reception in the early 1980s. 'He was in a wheelchair.'

For John, the proximity of Bristol was one of the great compensations for being at 'P' Branch. He found that city even more interesting than Bath. Bristol had been far worse hit in the Blitz. A historian of Bristol later wrote: 'For the first time a city which had always played safe with history, secretly disliking the political wars that interrupted trade with France, Spain and the American colonies, found violent history on its doorstep.' To John, who had known Bristol before the war and lavished praise on it in a radio broadcast of 1937, the damage inflicted by the Luftwaffe was agonizing.

His greatest friend in Bristol was Mervyn Stockwood, the future Bishop of Southwark, who since 1941 had been Vicar of St Matthew, Moorfields, Bristol. (The roof had been severely charred in a German air raid on Good Friday 1941.) John had first met him in 1939 at the table of Father Cyril Tomkinson, the ebullient and high-living Vicar of All Saints, Clifton. Stockwood, whose childhood was spent in Clifton, was an intense young cleric who had been converted to Socialism in 1937 by a Bristol speech of Sir Stafford Cripps, the future Labour Chancellor. Stockwood had a deep, resonant voice that seemed designed to echo round cathedrals. He was a man in whom piety and sensuality seemed constantly at war: he was described as having 'the eyes of an angel, the mouth of a devil'. Like Tomkinson, he was a *bon vivant* and a spirited talker. Some of John's friends could not understand his liking for Stockwood, whom they found vain, overbearing and bombastic. But the two men just 'clicked'; and they remained lifelong friends. Penelope Betjeman once said, 'John likes all his friends to be homosexual,' and Stockwood's biographer, Michael De-la-Noy, writes of his subject: 'His heart he only ever gave to men . . .' The last line of John's poem 'Bristol and Clifton' was an in-joke intended specially to amuse Stockwood –

> 'I know the Inskips very well indeed.'

The poem is a monologue by the pompous churchwarden of Emmanuel parish church, Clifton. There were three eminent brothers called Inskip in the Bristol and Clifton area. Stockwood had had a spat with Sir John Hampden Inskip, a right-wing Conservative who deplored the priest's leftward leanings.

John's 1944 poem 'Bristol', published in *New Bats in Old Belfries* the following year, was written in a mood of exalted melancholy. It begins:

> Green upon the flooded Avon shone the after-storm-wet sky
> Quick the struggling withy branches let the leaves of autumn fly
> And a star shone over Bristol, wonderfully far and high

and ends with 'the mathematic pattern of a plain course on the bells'. Showing off the knowledge of campanology gained in Uffington, John added, in a footnote, the actual sequence of changes.

He had absolutely no wish to stay at the Admiralty; he could not get out of it quickly enough. Three months after describing his work to Nancy Mitford as 'wonderfully boring', he was calling it 'hellish'. He left at the end of October 1944. On 31 October his colleague Pamela Barlow wrote to thank him for some flowers, adding, 'I do hope you will be happy in your new work.' Morton Shand wrote on 4 December: 'The family are bitterly disappointed you've turned your back on Bath. Mary is already renouncing Anglicanism in consequence.'

In December 1954, Helen Holmes wrote to him:

> I was looking through some old letters just now to find a lost document and came across a letter of yours dated 14.i.XLV and a poem, 'Bristol', which you composed on Widcombe Hill and sent to me. I have read and re-read it this afternoon instead of going on with my hunt for lost papers. It is just lovely, and again from our windows we see the flooded Avon and the after-storm-wet sky . . .

18

Farnborough

ARLY IN 1945, Farmer Wheeler told the Betjemans that he needed
Garrards Farm: his son Peter was going to live there. It was a bad blow
for John, who never welcomed sudden changes in the pattern of his life.
It intensified his dislike of Wheeler, which was to surface in his poem 'The
Dear Old Village'. John and Penelope began house-hunting. They looked
at a farmhouse at Stanford in the Vale, and another house at Avebury. Then
Sir Ralph Glyn, the local MP, told them that the Old Rectory,
Farnborough, was on the market, a squarson's house of 1749 in grey vit-
rified brick with red-brick dressings, a panelled parapet and a columned
porch. Penelope bought it at auction for £5,100.

Because John and Penelope had married clandestinely, her parents,
Lord and Lady Chetwode, had never given them a wedding present.
Now, reconciled to John, Chetwode paid for the Farnborough house and
gave it to the couple. For the first time John, who had spent his life in
little houses in north and south London, in London flats and then the
Uffington farmhouse, was moving to a 'gentleman's house', rather as
Evelyn Waugh, another north Londoner, had done when he bought Piers
Court, Gloucestershire, in 1937. For the first time, too, John would have
a library for his hundreds of antiquarian books. It was a topic of amused
comment in the neighbourhood, that the Betjemans, on coming to the
Old Rectory, *removed a bathroom*. John was not renowned for cleanliness;
in 1943 he contributed an article to the racy magazine *Lilliput* in praise
of dirt.

The Betjemans found themselves having to explain to many of their
friends that they were moving not to Farnborough in Hampshire, where
in 1887 the Empress Eugénie had built a mausoleum for her husband (and
where Joan Hunter Dunn had grown up), but to the Berkshire
Farnborough, near Wantage. With a population of just over a hundred, it
was the highest village in Berkshire, situated idyllically amid ancient tracks,
notably The Ridgeway. Penelope had hopes of running a smallholding
there, the profits from which would enable John to give up his book-

reviewing for the *Daily Herald* and devote himself to the work he enjoyed, writing poems and books on architecture and topography.

On 27 May 1945 John wrote to Evelyn Waugh:

Propeller's father has just bought Farnborough Rectory, Nr. Wantage for us: 1730-ish. Red brick seven hundred feet up on the downs. No water, no light, no heat. Beech trees all round. We shall be at Uffers till September at least.

In the meantime, there was a medical problem that needed attention. 'I am feeling so ill and tired . . .' John wrote to Geoffrey Taylor on 8 June. Later that month he went into the Acland Nursing Home, Oxford, to have a sebaceous cyst removed from his stomach. He was nursed there by the historical novelist Mary Renault, who was nearing the end of her nursing career and was soon to emigrate to South Africa. She remembered that John's window overlooked a girls' school and that he told her, 'The girls are just like St Trinian's' – the incorrigible schoolgirls of Ronald Searle's cartoons. He was invited to convalesce at Friar's Oak, Beaulieu, Hampshire, the home of Jack and Vera MacKenzie, the father and step-mother of his Uffington friend Arthur MacKenzie. Their house was beside Beaulieu River. There he met Brigadier Buckland and his daughter Clemency, whom he introduced into one of his most poignant poems, 'Youth and Age on Beaulieu River, Hants' (see below).

On Sunday 22 July John wrote to Penelope from Friar's Oak to say that he was planning to remain with the MacKenzies until the Wednesday, when he would stay with Penelope, moving on to Colonel Kolkhorst's at Yarnton on the Thursday, with a morning visit to his doctor 'as he alone can determine my convalescence' – a euphemism for 'decide how many weeks he will sign me off work'. John spent much of the summer of 1945 at Yarnton. It was handier for Oxford than either Uffington or Farnborough; in a time of petrol shortages, he could bicycle to work. Yarnton also took John out of the milieu of screaming children, horsiness, animals and rows with Penelope, into the relaxed bachelor ménage in the Tudor manor house. Osbert Lancaster joked that 'John liked large girls and the Colonel liked small boys'; but John was able to enter amusedly into the campery of Kolkhorst's circle, which included the dons John Bryson and Toby Strutt, the aesthetes Hedley Hope-Nicholson and Stuart Hill, two servants, Fred and Souch, and Soda the dog. Stuart Hill spent an hour and a half each morning putting on his make-up. Hope-Nicholson, though married and the father of Marie-Jaqueline Lancaster who was to edit a book on John's friend Brian Howard, also applied a bit of 'slap'. In a libellous rhyme, John alluded to this habit and to his owning More Place in Chelsea, the former home of Sir Thomas More –

> H is for Hedley,
> Who lives in a Place;
> What he makes on his bottom
> He spends on his face.

Another frequent visitor to Yarnton was Gerard Irvine, who used to bicycle over at weekends from St Stephen's House in Oxford, where he was training to be a clergyman. John had met Irvine through his former pupil at Heddon Court, Paul Miller. Miller had gone on to Haileybury, where Irvine was one of his best friends. He had introduced Irvine to John, who in turn – tempting Providence – had taken the two schoolboys to lunch with Tom Driberg in Fleet Street. Irvine became a great family friend of the Betjemans and John's long correspondence with him – because the two men wrote to each other with utter candour on all sub-jects and with no posing or posturing – is one of the most reliable sources as to what John was thinking or feeling at any given time between the late 1930s and the early 1980s.

One was as likely to find village boys as Oxford dons enjoying the Colonel's hospitality. John brought his son Paul to Yarnton several times. Kolkhorst at least affected to be in love with the 'golden lad'. (In 1937 he had declined to be his godfather, on the grounds that it would mean renouncing 'the Devil and all his works'. Tom Driberg was chosen instead.)

One other visitor to Yarnton was the future MP and notorious hetero-sexual Alan Clark. In 1949 John wrote to his father, Kenneth Clark: 'I remember how marvellous Alan was in the Boys' Club at Yarnton which he visited for about two minutes, joining in *boxing* – the greatest asset for a "social worker" – with terrific success.' In 1999 Alan Clark recalled the occasion.

> One evening Betj. did take me out to Yarnton. In those days I was extremely innocent and didn't realize that the 'Colonel' hosted the Boys' Club and laid on an *ex tempore* gymnasium for them from motives that were voyeuristic if not actually predatory. I had been runner-up middleweight champion at Eton the year before and so it was no problem for me when invited to 'spar' with one of the boys. Actually I have had guilt about it ever since because he was a pleasant self-effacing youth and I was much too rough with him.

In January 1946, John began a long campaign to obtain a public honour for Ninian Comper, which eventually led to the architect's knighthood. John thought he should be appointed to the Order of Merit, but wrote to

Kenneth Clark on 28 January: 'Tom Boase does not think Comper "enough guns" for an OM. I doubt if he knows Comper's work.' Boase, a historian of both medieval and Victorian art and architecture, became President of Magdalen College, Oxford, in 1947; the letter shows John's low opinion of the man with whom, seven years later, he was to have an ill-tempered battle over Magdalen's plan to create a rose garden opposite the college, in the High. In March, John asked Comper if he would design the lettering for a Memorial to his beloved friend Basil Dufferin, killed in the last days of the war. John and Maureen Dufferin had decided on these words for the memorial at Clandeboye:

IN MEMORY OF
BASIL SHERIDAN,
4TH MARQUESS OF DUFFERIN AND AVA
CAPTAIN, ROYAL HORSE GUARDS

A MAN OF BRILLIANCE
AND OF MANY FRIENDS

HE WAS KILLED IN ACTION AT LETZE ON MARCH
25TH 1945 AT THE AGE OF THIRTY-FIVE,
RECAPTURING BURMA THE COUNTRY WHICH
HIS GRANDFATHER ANNEXED TO THE BRITISH
CROWN

On 18 April John attended Dufferin's memorial service at which, Evelyn Waugh wrote, 'White's turned up in good numbers.' Waugh made his first visit to Farnborough in October. He told Nancy Mitford that the house 'smelled like a village shop – oil, cheese, bacon, washing . . .' and that 'The Betjemans both put on Jaeger combinations on the 1st of September & keep them on for all purposes until the 2nd week of May. A horse sleeps in the kitchen.' In his diary he wrote:

Wantage, Thursday 31 October 1946

In the late afternoon to stay with the Betjemans in a lightless, stuffy, cold, poky rectory among beech woods overlooking Wantage. Harness every-where. A fine collection of nineteenth-century illustrated books. Delicious food cooked by Penelope. I brought sherry, burgundy, port. A daughter of grossly proletarian appearance and manner.

John's comment on this, when the Waugh diaries were published in 1976, was: 'How very Evelyn, to write so readably and so inaccurately.' Candida Lycett Green agrees the Rectory was cold, but denies that it was lightless or poky and that one could see Wantage from it. As for her seeming 'proletarian', Waugh may have got that impression because, at that time, Candida's playmates in Farnborough spoke broad Berkshire and she picked up the accent – that pleasant yokel murmur in which, characteristically, a cactus is described as having 'noice little spoikes'.

An exception to Berkshire accents in the village was Mr and Mrs Dowkes who ran the village shop. They came from the Midlands and John taught Paul and Candida to recite a rhyme about them –

> Hickory Dickory Dowkes,
> I'll tell you some Birmingham jokes.

The children never realized that the nursery rhymes they learned were different from those chanted by other children. John's favourite was:

> Ba Ba centipede,
> Have you any jelly?
> No sir, no sir, it's all gone smelly.

Candida was only three, and Paul seven, when the family moved to Farnborough. Both of them attended the small village school until Paul left for the Dragon School. Candida, a pretty, fair-haired child, was her father's pet. She was allowed great freedom and was seldom reprimanded. John often kissed the top of her head. He first called her 'Waba' or 'Wuba', then 'Wabz' or 'Wubz', then 'Wibbly' or 'Woebley', and finally 'Wibz'. That was the nickname that stuck; so she called him 'Dadz'.

In later life Candida realized that John had avoided household chores and the discipline side of bringing up children; these were left to Penelope. Paul and Candida connected John with treats and presents; Penelope with disagreeable work and crossness. The only physical work John undertook was preparing the paraffin lamps, trimming the wicks and lighting the fires – all quite good fun for the children to join in. To Penelope fell all the cooking, the vegetable gardening, milking the cows, Buttercup and Daisy, morning and evening, feeding the horses, goats, rabbits and chickens, and making the bright yellow butter which Paul and Candida hated. John was seldom found at the kitchen sink, where Candida spent a lot of time complaining to her mother about having to wash up. Penelope did all the ticking off over table manners and all the bossing about. Paul and Candida soon learned that being near their mother usually meant being given a job and being near their father usually didn't.

The Betjemans' marriage could not exactly be described as unhappy; but it was turbulent. The friends from Uffington days observed that John and Penelope had not given up their habit of having rows in public. The rows had become a sort of ritual: point, counterpoint. The great crisis of the marriage came in 1947. A religious schism opened between the two. John had resigned from the Society of Friends in 1937, and now, ten years on, was a fully committed Anglican. The first strong hint of a religious rift with Penelope appeared in a letter from John to Gerard Irvine on 20 March. 'Your prayers are asked for a quandary I am in. Propeller is toying, nay more than toying, with Rome (keep to yourself) and I do not feel any urge to go over. Indeed I think it would be *wrong* for me to go over, mainly betraying the Church of God.'

It has been claimed that Evelyn Waugh and Frank Pakenham (later Lord Longford) converted Penelope to Roman Catholicism; but in fact she made the decision quite independently, after experiencing 'a vision of the heavenly host' while on holiday in Assisi. Nevertheless, Waugh was a close friend of hers; and as she moved Romewards he tried to bully John into joining her, in a series of hectoring letters. The bullying began in 1946. Although the two men were on friendly terms, the respect John felt for Waugh was tinged with terror. In this year, too, Waugh was busy satirizing John in his novella *Scott-King's Modern Europe*. When it was published in 1947 he wrote to Penelope: 'I hope John did not resent the parody of his erotic rhapsodies in *Scott-King*.' In the book John is unmistakably travestied as Mr Whitemaid, who, with the schoolmaster Scott-King, is attending a conference about the poet Bellorius in the republic of Neutralia (a thinly disguised Yugoslavia). Also apparently at the conference – though in fact she is with another group of physical training experts – is Miss Sveningen, a 'giant carnivore'. Whitemaid thinks she looks superb in shorts: 'I can imagine a whole life lived riding tandem behind her, through endless forests of conifers, and at midday sitting down among the pine needles to eat hard-boiled eggs.'

Waugh had also appropriated John's love of Victorian architecture in *A Handful of Dust* (1934), in which he had teasingly given him a walk-on part as 'a very civil young man' from 'an architectural review'; and in *Brideshead Revisited* (1945) he had brazenly pirated John's teddy bear, and his treatment of it, for Lord Sebastian Flyte. Beyond these minor sources of tension was Waugh's manifest affection for Penelope: there were persistent rumours of an affair. John already knew in 1945 that Waugh was making Penelope the heroine of his novel *Helena* – which, when it appeared in 1950, was dedicated to her.

On 22 December 1946, Waugh wrote John his first long letter about religion. He had been reading his contribution to *Five Sermons by Laymen*, and was 'painfully shocked' by it. 'Last time I met you you told me you did not believe in the Resurrection. Now I find you expounding Protestant devotional practices from the pulpit. This WILL NOT DO.' On 9 January 1947 he wrote again: 'You cannot rely on a death bed conversion. Every hour you spend outside the Church is an hour lost. I well know the vast handicap of having started my Catholic life 27 years too late. Think what it must have been like for poor Charles II who only had a few minutes' Catholic life!' Waugh's belief, expressed in the same letter, that John was 'being allowed to see a glimpse of the truth broad enough to damn you if you reject it now' was well calculated to revive the fear of hellfire instilled in him by his Calvinist nurse in early childhood, as he described in his poem 'N.W.5 & N.6'. John wrote back politely: 'I deeply appreciate your zeal on my soul's behalf. Indeed I have never been more exercised by a correspondence in my life.'

By April, Waugh's letters had become a torment to John. Penelope, who unlike Waugh had to live with John, intervened to ask the novelist to lay off.

Dearest Evelyn,

I am very grateful to you for writing those letters to John tho' it is very disloyal of me to write to you and say that still I hope you will pray very hard indeed during the next few weeks for him because he is in a dreadful state he thinks you are the devil and wakes up in the middle of the night and raves and says he will leave me at once if I go over . . .

Waugh did not take the hint. He shot another salvo at John in May, which drew a heated reply. John was particularly upset by Waugh's suggestion that he stayed in the Church of England for purely aesthetic reasons. 'Really you are wrong in thinking that I regard religion as "the source of pleasurable emotions and sensations". I used to, as an undergraduate, but it has been a stern struggle for the last fourteen years.' He said he felt obliged to support his local church: 'In villages people still follow a lead and we are the only people here who will give a lead. I know that to desert this wounded and neglected church would be to betray Our Lord.' Waugh riposted: 'Blind worm, who are you to lead? You should humbly follow.' Penelope was by now so concerned at John's state of mind that she postponed her instruction. In a letter to her on 4 June 1947 Waugh at last promised to lay off John. 'I am by nature a bully and a scold and John's pertinacity in error brings out all that is worst in me. I am sorry . . . But really when he says that the truth of the Petrine claims is dependent on his place of residence, the mind boggles. I think there is very clearly a devil at work in him . . .'

The tension began to ease. In July, John wrote to Waugh affably, with no mention of religion, telling him he wanted his opinion of a stained-glass window which he was sure was by the Pre-Raphaelite Ford Madox Brown. In August Waugh, rarely a bearer of olive branches, made a special effort to heal relations with John. He wrote in his diary: 'To Farnborough to make my peace with the Betjemans. Successful in this. A drive with John looking at 1860 churches. Penelope seems resolved to enter the Church in the autumn.' But somehow the friendship was never the same again after the epistolary battering and Penelope's conversion. Waugh had proposed John for membership of the Beefsteak Club and he was elected in December 1947; but on 9 January 1948 Waugh wrote in his diary: 'To the Beefsteak to induct Betjeman, but he had taken ill or frighted and would not come.' Two years later, Waugh was writing to Penelope: 'It is nice of you to ask me to visit you but (a) I don't think John likes me (b) I don't think I like your children (c) I know I detest all talk about the varying fads of heretics.'

Penelope was received into the Roman Catholic Church on 9 March 1948 at St Aloysius, Oxford. It was an agonizing time for John. As so often through history, religion, intended as a beneficent force, had brought discord and misery. He could not follow Penelope. As she had told Waugh, he regarded Roman Catholicism as 'foreign'; and he 'hated "abroad"'. He had no taste for ecstasiated Bernini virgins, *baldacchini* and Salomonic columns. He preferred the more temperate beauties of English parish churches. If he 'went over to Rome', in defiance of all the indoctrination of his youth, he would be giving up not only those churches but most of the hymns he loved, and relinquishing the Authorized Version for intoned or gabbled Latin – a language which, from his days under Mr Gidney at Marlborough, had never been his forte. Rome would also mean submission to authority, which did not come easily to him. Rome stood for absolutism and infallibility, as against the easy latitudinarian ways of the Church of England.

Three days before Penelope's 'reception', John wrote to his friend Geoffrey Taylor that he was making himself scarce, in Cornwall, for the event, 'and for the recovery I am going to Denmark (paid for by the Danes) for a week the week after'. He enclosed a poignant sonnet he had written on Penelope's apostasy.

> In the perspective of Eternity
> The pain is nothing, now you go away
> Above the steaming thatch how silver-grey

Our chiming church tower, calling 'Come to me

My Sunday-sleeping villagers!' And she,
    Still half my life, kneels now with those who say
    'Take courage, daughter. Never cease to pray
God's grace will break him of his heresy.'

I, present with our Church of England few
    At the dear words of Consecration see
    The chalice lifted, hear the sanctus chime
And glance across to that familiar pew.
    In the Perspective of Eternity
    The pain is nothing – but, ah God, in Time.

This poem, which became known as 'The Empty Pew', had been through several earlier versions. When it reached the page proofs of *A Few Late Chrysanthemums*, the third line from last read, 'And glance across to that deserted pew'. Jock Murray thought the poem might cause Penelope distress and it was pulled out at the last moment. For the same reason I did not include it in the *Uncollected Poems* published in 1982, when both John and Penelope were still alive. It was first published in Volume One of John's *Letters*, edited by Candida Lycett Green in 1994.

John told Susan Barnes in 1972: 'I had thought that however much Penelope and I quarrelled, at any rate the Church stayed the same – rather like old Archie, something you can always turn to. And Penelope was really very Anglican by temperament – the sort of person who always quarrels with the vicar.' Now Penelope quarrelled with Father Wixted, priest of the 'hideous Roman Catholic church' in Wantage which she attended each Sunday, picking up on the way Irish farm labourers' children and the Italian servants of the local gentry. Paul and Candida noticed little difference in life, except that a 'Hail Mary' was added to 'Our Father' at their nightly prayers. Candida remembers John's making fun of the 'Hail Marys' and reciting them in a broad Irish accent, 'which I assumed, not unnaturally, was how we were meant to say them – "Hooley Merry, methyr of Guard . . ."'

In May 1949 John went into the Acland nursing home in Oxford for the removal of another cyst. This enforced distance from Farnborough and his marriage gave both him and Penelope a chance to reflect on their changed situation. Penelope wrote to him:

> You must be really honest and admit we were never religiously at one in the Anglican Church. I wanted to become RC when Fr Burdett tried to convert us both and you said, 'You ought to try your own Church first.' Then

I was completely converted to Catholicism by Fr Folky [Harton]'s book . . . When we went to Eire I became more and more convinced of the truth of the Roman claims and hoped that you were feeling the same way . . . Life simply is NOT long enough to go on like this and personally I think it would be idiotic to separate, we would neither of us be any happier and the children would be very *un*happy. Let us forgive and forget and both admit that we have colossal faults and different temperaments and different approaches to religion and have been very bad husbands and wives though I think we are BOTH good parents, and let us each lead our own lives as far as friends are concerned and not try to conceal things any more but let us LOVE AND BE HAPPY. Yours very truly, Morwenna Plym Woad. [Morwenna was the Cornish saint's name which Penelope had added to her own Christian names on being received into the Roman Catholic Church.]

John replied from the nursing home on 2 June. He had been suffering intense physical pain which, he thought, had 'an excellent purifying and clarifying property'. It had enabled him to realize that he must for a long time have been going through 'some sort of breakdown', marked by excessive bad temper. 'The peace of this place now I am out of pain makes me see how tiresome I have been and cruel and bullying. *Oi am very sorry.*' In response to a renewed suggestion by Penelope that she should pay for him to give up his uncongenial work for the *Daily Herald* and let her minister to him, he replied:

I don't really mind doing degrading work like book-reviewing (I doubt if I am now fit for anything better) provided I have your love. And having your love doesn't mean being told I have got it 'underneath all our quarrelling'. It doesn't ever entail on your part mending my clothes. It means seeing you and being with you *alone* much more than I am.

Whatever the circumstances of our marriage in its beginnings, I had grown to love you so much by the time Powlie was born, that you were more important to me than anything else. And you still are. I have always prayed in my heart that I will die before you because I feel that I could not live without you.

Analysing the course of their marriage, John thought that his main trouble had been jealousy. It had not been too acute at Uffington, where they saw a lot of each other and could always get together and make up after a row. But 'Ireland was just hell.' John's war work had taken him away from Penelope just when she needed him most. 'Farnborough gets me down because the farm and the children between them have taken you away from me so much that I only see you alone late in the evening when you and I are both tired and touchy. Or rather I am touchy and you are tired.' And now something had happened to take her further away still: her defection to Rome. 'That is really why I have an "obsession" about Rome, because I love you so much.' He asked for more time alone with her – ideally one full afternoon a week, including lunch and tea.

Gerard Irvine thinks that Penelope's conversion was 'the beginning of the end of John and Penelope's marriage'. And Candida, although her childhood was not disrupted by the event, realized in retrospect that 'It was a watershed, for it saw the beginning of JB's being able to love other women whilst continuing to love my mother.' He was smitten by a lady glider he met at a John Murray party, but nothing came of the encounter. In June 1949 he fell in love with Margaret Wintringham, the blonde, buxom wife of Edmund Penning-Rowsell, the wine expert. The couple lived in Hinton Parva, a village at the foot of the Berkshire Downs. They were both Communists: John called them 'the Party Members'. He first met Margaret at a Swindon Poetry Society meeting. In early autumn he went to supper with Margaret and her husband and left behind his handkerchief, which seemed almost to take on the significance of the handkerchief in *Othello* when Margaret returned it, washed and ironed, with a note saying how much she had enjoyed doing it. He tried unsuccessfully to get her work at the BBC but gave her children's books to review for *Time and Tide* when he became the magazine's literary editor.* They met for coffee – this was the decade of *Brief Encounter* – when John was on his way to Bristol or London. He encouraged her in her poetry-writing. She tried to convert him to Communism: he called her 'my Stakhanovite'. Margaret often brought her family to Sunday lunch at Farnborough. Penelope, who referred to her as 'John's Poitry Girl', would take the children off in the pony cart, Candida recalls, 'so that Margaret and JB could be left alone to talk about poetry'.

Was there more to it than that? John's main confidante in these years was Anne Barnes, the wife of George Barnes, his friend and patron at the BBC.* In July 1949 he wrote to her from Farnborough:

> Like a fool I went there. With priggishness and self-righteousness, with fear and love, I insisted on doing nothing. She – oh God I can't put it down in ink or pencil or charcoal or anything – she put up with my priggishness. And now what have I? Remorse, internal writhings, detestation of everything here, inability to concentrate, fear of her revenge on me and the prospect of several more deliciously wonderful visits each with its sad ending. Sad for her, self-righteous for me, misery for us both. Yet if one 'went the whole hog' as we used to say at Marlborough, the guilt would be worse still and I wouldn't see her again.

* See Chapter 21, 'Wantage'.

It is the very voice of *Brief Encounter*. Three days later he wrote to Anne Barnes again.

> I received a beautiful slap-in-the-eye from my Stakhanovite yesterday in the form of this quatrain:
>
> For J.B.
> Remember when in your philosophy
> Human relationships take second place
> Your chastity is founded on my charity
> And through my grief you reach your State of Grace.

Of course, she's quite right. If I'm not prepared to risk mortal sin, then I shouldn't go on with it. Anyhow she leaves today for three weeks in France and I shall begin to breathe again. She is very funny. But oh that Party line, that runs through her! It is shiveringly attractive and horrifying at once. There is always that delicious sense . . . that one has gone just a little too far.

Margaret disappeared from John's letters to Anne Barnes after 1950 and was gradually relegated to the status of old flame. In 1950 another love-interest came into John's life: his new secretary Jill Menzies, whom he called 'Freckly Jill'. She was twenty-two, an Oxford graduate who had taken a course at St Godric's Secretarial College. John interviewed her in the offices of *Time and Tide* and appointed her even though she admitted she was not good at doing up parcels – a skill useful when sending back review books. Providing John with a secretary was part of Penelope's plan to relieve him of some of the chores that made him fractious; this new luxury could be afforded because the Betjemans no longer had to pay rent to Farmer Wheeler. Jill Menzies arrived in Farnborough in May 1951 and lived as one of the family. For her, Candida writes, 'he developed a grand, long-lasting, platonic passion'. On 3 June John wrote to George Barnes: 'On Tuesday I will be accompanied by my new Scottish-Canadian C of E Secretary with freckles, grey eyes, tip-tilted nose and grey flannel skirts and cream shirts and furry skin.' In later letters to others he rhapsodized about her 'sultry lips and darkish hair', her 'tall hiking figure and high Scottish cheekbones'.

John's secretaries helped to bring some order into the haphazardness of his work – his book-reviewing for the *Daily Herald* and the *Daily Telegraph*; radio scripts; poems for the *New Statesman* and *The Listener* – and wrote kind letters of encouragement to the often hopeless would-be poets who wrote to him enclosing their verses. Though John had found reviewing for the *Daily Herald* an intolerable chore, he still needed the extra

259

income that this kind of part-time job brought him. As a result he began writing for the *Daily Telegraph*, and his association with that paper lasted from 1951 until 1969. John had two links with the Berry family which owned the *Daily Telegraph*. His brother-in-law, Roger Chetwode, who committed suicide in 1940, had married Patricia Berry, Lord Camrose's daughter. And Michael Berry, Patricia's brother, had married Lady Pamela Smith, sister of John's friend Freddy Birkenhead. Through these connections, John became a book reviewer for the paper a few months after giving up his *Daily Herald* column. He was hired as a fiction critic, though occasionally he was also sent poetry, 'funny' books or works on architecture and the railways. From 1949 he also put in an afternoon a week at the London offices of *Time and Tide*.

Having a secretary and becoming more 'organized' also allowed him some free time to drive off to Oxford and give talks to undergraduates. He enjoyed these jaunts, in which he could exercise his histrionic side. He learned what the young were thinking and became well known to those who were to become political and cultural leaders in Britain. Denis Healey, a future Chancellor of the Exchequer, invited him to talk about Victorian architecture. In 1946 the future drama critic Kenneth Tynan – like John, a Magdalen man, but unlike him a favoured pupil of C. S. Lewis – wrote to his friend Julian Holland:

> John Betjeman spoke on Thursday about Tennyson. He completely succeeded in rehabilitating him as a man: he was apparently a great wit and a humorist of boundless, spasmodic energy. In fact, Betjeman suggests that the last lines of 'Enoch Arden' 'The villagers had never seen a costlier funeral' may be intentionally amusing.

Penelope did not worry too much about John's undisguised 'pashes' for Margaret Wintringham and 'Freckly Jill'. They became her friends too, and that seemed to neutralize them as threats to her marriage. Apart from the couple's religious schism, life at Farnborough continued much as before. Penelope still ran the local Women's Institute and organized fêtes and gymkhanas. She and John kept up with all their old friends: the Pipers, the Lancasters, John Sparrow and Maurice Bowra. One friendship was maintained in the face of some controversy: that with Sir Oswald Mosley and his wife Diana, both of whom had been imprisoned in the war because of their pro-Nazi views.

Most of the people Paul and Candida met at Farnborough were of their parents' generation, or older. An exciting exception was Patrick Cullinan, who came to stay in April 1950. Today a well-known South African poet, he was then a seventeen-year-old schoolboy at Charterhouse – Osbert Lancaster's old school. He and John had met in January 1950 when John came to address the school's Poetry Society in the drawing-room of Cullinan's housemaster, Vincent 'Sniffy' Russell. John invited anyone who wrote poetry to send him their work. Cullinan sent him a poem entitled 'England 1950' and a short story. John wrote back enthusiastically. 'If you knew what a treat it is to have something worth considering sent to one after the heaps of mediocre verse [sent to *Time and Tide*], you would know how grateful I am to you.' Cullinan sent more poems. John wrote back, on Valentine's Day:

> Your Joyce–Auden–Eliot MS hot from the soul . . . pleased me a lot.
>
> What I like in it is not the thought (if there is any) nor the emotions (turbulent) nor the transitions (inexplicable), but that same delight in words and ability to use them that I mentioned before.
>
> You may not agree with me, but I think
>
> 1) Poetry should not be private but easy for all to understand.
> 2) It should have tones of meaning beyond the surface one.
> 3) It should read out loud well.
> 4) It should be memorable.
> 5) It should very clearly not be prose.
>
> I would like to see what you did using rhyme (which often provides more inspiration than the human fancy can devise without it) & an accepted metre & writing quite clearly & obviously but out of anger, love or sadness, exaltation or self-pity whichever inspires you most.
>
> Your poems bring back to me my own delight when literature first opened to me & I wish I had your vigour & hope now.

Cullinan first went to stay at Farnborough on 6 April 1950. His memory of the Rectory is of 'a dark but friendly kitchen where we had our meals and I remember John opening and decanting the most delicious bottles of claret'. Cullinan's mother had died of a brain tumour the year before and his grief had made him introspective. John helped him get over the tragedy. The youth had a blond lock of hair which constantly fell over his blue eyes. Candida, now eight, 'became completely transfixed by him and watched with fascination as he cleaned his teeth each morning with an almost supernatural vigour'. His extravagant good looks, charm and vitality were not lost on John, either. In a letter to Candida in 1993, Cullinan tackled head-on the (not directly asked) question whether there was anything more to it than that.

> I don't think for a moment that JB worshipped me. I just think he needed to have some sort of acolyte at that period in his life – fortunately for me.

We had so much fun together . . . Obviously, you would want to know if there was anything beyond our friendship, i.e. a physical relationship. There was nothing. Never at any stage was there any move from him or from me to get involved sexually. I was crazy about girls and, quite frankly, so was he.

On Cullinan's second visit to Farnborough, in April 1950, Penelope's father was staying. He told the young South African stories of his experiences in the Boer War – in particular, how he had allowed Kruger's train to escape capture by his troop because his horses were tired and needed a rest.

CULLINAN: But, Good Lord, sir, if you had captured Kruger then it would
    have shortened the war by at least a year!
CHETWODE: Yes, I know.
CULLINAN: But didn't anyone find out?
CHETWODE: No. I never told anyone! (*Looking very pleased with himself.*)

Lord Chetwode died three months later. 'Very sad it will be for Penelope,' John wrote to Cullinan on 15 July. 'Losing one parent is bad enough. When you lose both, you suddenly know you have stepped out in loneliness, there's no one to back you up or even to quarrel with except other lonely people like yourself.'

Cullinan's visits were cheering; but John had become depressed by life at Farnborough. That it was the scene of the first great rift in his marriage had soured the place for him. In any case, essentially metropolitan in temperament, he was ill suited to village life. Living in a comparatively grand house brought unpalatable financial demands – for roof repairs and fencing, for example. An estimate for putting electricity down the drive showed it was beyond the Betjemans' means. John was upset when Fritz the cat, who had been with them since Uffington days, died behind the boiler in the kitchen on the day after Boxing Day 1950. And he 'minded intensely' when the elm trees by Farnborough Church were felled and the ancient barn next to their garden was demolished by Mr Laurence, one of the local farmers. In 1951 John and Penelope decided to sell the Rectory and move to the less isolated town of Wantage.

In the last months at Farnborough, John took time off to attend an unmissable social event, the marriage of Tom Driberg in London on 30 June. Driberg's engagement to Ena Binfield, a Labour Party worker, had been announced in *The Times* in February. That this most confirmed of bachelors should choose to marry was a surprise to everyone, and a joke to many. (A House of Commons policeman muttered, 'Poor lady, she won't know which way to turn.') Osbert Lancaster and John went together to the service in St Mary's Church near Sloane Square. Driberg wrote in his diary on the day of the wedding: 'As we went out at the end, I remember seeing my old cronies John Betjeman and Osbert Lancaster standing together regarding me quizzically.'

In the same month, the Old Rectory, Farnborough, was auctioned at the Bear Hotel, Wantage. 'We have put a reserve of eight and a half thousand on it,' John wrote to Patrick Cullinan, 'and I don't think it'll reach the reserve. But the woodlice still walk on the landing here unperturbed. And what am I more than a woodlouse?' The house was sold for £11,000.

During their first year at Farnborough John had been preparing *New Bats in Old Belfries* for publication. As far back as December 1941, Jock Murray had been encouraging him to marshal enough poems for a further Betjeman collection. On 12 December John sent him, from Dublin, the manuscript 'of what little I have done of my Epic' – the long autobiographical poem of which the greater part was published in *Summoned by Bells* (1960). In April 1943 Murray again pressed him to let him know what poems he had amassed, but plans for the book hung fire from mid-1943 to mid-1945. Not only was John busy with secret war work for the Admiralty at Bath:* Jock Murray was serving as a lance-bombardier. But on 11 July 1945 John sent Jock 'what, with two other poems which I must ask you to get, should be enough to make a book'. Murray wrote on 19 July: 'It was very good to get the poems . . . If we get them all into proof we can then best decide if any should be taken out.'

This proof survives: Murray later had it bound in leather. A blank had been left for the title, which John filled in, with his usual maladroitness in the matter of titles, 'ROPES & RINGERS'. The poems 'Cheshire Lines' and 'Monody' were printed but crossed out, as was 'To Uffington Ringers'. A poem printed with the heading 'Fragment of a Poem for Emily Hemphill' was changed to 'A Fragment for Emily', then to its final title, 'Ireland with Emily'. Some comic misprints were put right – as in 'Invasion Exercise on the Poultry Farm', in which the printers had rendered 'I've trussed your missing paratroop' as 'I trust your missing paratroop'. Other lines were altered to improve them. Basil Dufferin, of whose death in the Burma campaign John had heard on VE Day (8 May), was described in the original threnody as 'Curious, reckless, loyal – / The last of civilized Oxford'; in the revised version as 'Humorous, reckless, loyal – / My kind, heavy-lidded companion'. The same poem was given a far more poignant and effective ending.

* See Chapter 17, 'Admiralty'.

Thirty-five years later, John told James Lees-Milne that he had been 'more in love with Ava than with any human being he had ever met in the world. His Oxford career was ruined by this unrequited love for "Little Bloody". He loved his gutter-snipe looks, his big, brown, sensual eyes, sensual lips, dirtiness generally. Never received so much as a touch of a hand on the shoulder.' That day, Lees-Milne had just met, for the first time, Basil Dufferin's daughter, the novelist Lady Caroline Blackwood. When he mentioned this to John, 'He told me he once saw her twenty years ago and was so moved by her resemblance to Ava, and so attracted to her, that he decided he could never meet her again.'

On 20 July 1945 John, recovering in Beaulieu from his operation, sent these suggestions for possible titles to Jock Murray: ' "Grandsire" "Triples" "Bob Major" "Bats in the Belfry" "Triple Bob" "A Ring of Twenty" "Call Changes" "A Touch of Twenty" "Belfry Jottings" "Louvred Steeples" "Spires & Towers" "Ropes & Ringers" "Mr Murray's Surprise Method" "Homage to Newbolt". I don't know JB.' Eventually *New Bats in Old Belfries* was agreed on, as a neat counterpoise to *Old Lights for New Chancels*. The volume included what was to be perhaps John's most famous, most quoted poem, 'A Subaltern's Love-song'. It also contained the cryptic poem whose title mystified Philip Larkin, 'The Irish Unionist's Farewell to Greta Hellstrom in 1922', apparently a *poème à clef*. It is about a man saying a regretful farewell to a woman – allegedly 'my Swedish beauty' – in the small town of Dungarvan, Co. Waterford, Ireland; and it involves a car driving away from Dungarvan. The final stanza runs:

> Had I kissed and drawn you to me,
>   Had you yielded warm for cold,
> What a power had pounded through me
>   As I stroked your streaming gold!
> You were right to keep us parted:
>   Bound and parted we remain,
> Aching, if unbroken hearted –
>   Oh! Dungarvan in the rain.

No celebrated Greta Hellstrom (or Hellström, as she would need to be) is known to Swedish history; so it is natural to wonder whether the poem is a coded account of a meeting between John and a woman. Who is the strongest candidate? In the Betjeman archive at the University of Victoria, British Columbia, is a letter written to John on 21 September 1946 by Emily Villiers-Stuart (formerly Lady Hemphill), in which she thanks him for having been kind to her son Peter Patrick (now Lord Hemphill) on his visit to Oxford. The stationery on which the letter is written has the printed letterhead 'DROMANA, CAPPOQUIN, Co. WATERFORD', but Emily Villiers-Stuart has crossed this out and superscribed it 'Helvick Lodge, Tring, Dungarvan'. Dromana was the home of Ion Villiers-Stuart. Years later, John was reported as having said that the woman he met in Dungarvan was 'staying in Helvick'. Does that mean that the friend to whom he was saying farewell was Emily Hemphill (as she still was)? We know from Penelope that he found her very attractive. She was certainly the central figure of one poem in *New Bats*, 'Ireland with Emily'; was she the heroine of this one, too?

There is possibly a rival candidate, Honor Tracy. We have already seen that she wrote to John as early as April 1944, 'How I love you.'* They had been friends at the Ministry of Information, where Tracy worked in the Japanese section and for a time as secretary to the Sinologist Arthur Waley, also in John's circle. In a handwritten postscript to a typewritten letter of 11 September 1946 from the offices of Sean O'Faolain's magazine *The Bell* in Dublin she wrote, 'Dear, dear John'. And a letter from her to John dated simply 'April 23' begins 'Dearest Johnny' and ends, 'It would be lovely to see you again, you forcibly illustrate my favourite maxim, namely, the ones we don't sleep with are the dearest and the best.' That would fit with what he wrote in the poem.

The matter is likely to remain a tantalizing mystery – unless, some day, a cache of hitherto unknown letters should come to light, with indisputable revelations. For the time being, the most plausible hypothesis is that Emily was the object of a tactfully deflected pass by John, whose later letters to her suggest that he was still greatly smitten by her.

By September 1945 last-minute corrections were being made to *New Bats in Old Belfries*. At the eleventh hour, John sent a further poem for inclusion, 'Youth and Age on Beaulieu River, Hants'. At the twelfth hour, he realized that he had not asked permission of three women mentioned in three different poems: Emily Hemphill, of 'Ireland with Emily', Joan Hunter Dunn of 'A Subaltern's Love-song', and Clemency Buckland of the Beaulieu River poem. Emily cabled from Reno, Nevada, where she was getting a divorce from the drunken Lord Hemphill, 'OF COURSE DON'T OBJECT'. The reference to Joan Hunter Dunn had the most terrifying legal implications, since at the end of the poem John claimed 'And now I'm engaged to Miss Joan Hunter Dunn', whereas in fact she had married H. Wycliffe Jackson on 20 January. Fortunately she made no objection either.

* See Chapter 17, 'Admiralty'.

As with Joan Hunter Dunn, John had used Clemency Buckland's name *en clair*. In reply to his request to print the poem, she wrote:

Dear Mr Betjeman,

Thank you for your letter and the poem. It is alright, neither my father nor I mind your publishing it. It certainly came as a surprise though, we little thought this would come of just asking the time!

I am glad you did write it, as it will commemorate for me some very happy evenings spent on the river. You see the MacKenzies got it wrong, it was a friend of mine with me, and not my brother. We had just borrowed his sharpie [the flat-bottomed, two-masted vessel mentioned in the poem]. Unfortunately our time was all too short, and he has now got sent to America for some months. So I remember very well the times we met you. Would you mind keeping it private, though, please, as you doubtless know what gossip in small villages is like, and I do happen to like him very much.

I'm sorry if I have bored you with all that, but I thought I should explain things to you, after writing such a nice poem. I like it. And as you do ask my opinion, I think 'limbs' goes better than 'form', giving a clearer picture.

My father thought it might interest you to know that my grandmother had a poem written to her, by Robert Louis Stevenson, who was her first cousin. It was called 'To Minnie with a Looking Glass' . . .

Yours sincerely,

Clemency Buckland

Murray did not quite manage to meet his self-imposed deadline of 12 December. *New Bats* was published on 19 December in two editions, one at 6s, the other (on better paper and signed) at 10s 6d. On 23 December Tom Driberg reviewed the book in *Reynolds News* ('Betjeman specializes in nostalgic, exact, topographical, metrically archaic, only half satirical descriptions of middle-class life . . . The thing about Betjeman that probably annoys some fools is that they don't know if they are meant to laugh or not'). But, because of the delayed publication, the main reviews did not appear until January and February 1946. Like *Old Lights*, the book was very well received by the *New Statesman*, *The Listener*, *The Spectator* and *Time and Tide*.

The anonymous *Listener* reviewer found it exciting 'to read poems which are so sentimental, and also self-conscious, self-mocking, and often very funny'. It was, he thought, 'like listening to an exile making fun of his homesickness'.

Betjeman is exiled in time not in space. He looks for the spirit of the English past which is his home, and he finds it lingering in odd places pathetically; he conveys not only the pathos but also the absurdity of the odd places, and of the people who live in them. It is not comic verse (the horrible hearty tradition) or sentimental verse, but comic-sentimental, usually something more than the mock-Victorian valentine, because of the extraordinary sensitiveness to the mood and life of places. Within a single idiom and attitude there is great variety in this book, certainly great differences of depth and interest. There are the easy running magazine poems which are always funny and have jingling metres. But there are also the lyrical and more metrically elaborate poems, which are sad and sentimental, with beautifully contrived mournful echoes and a depressing nostalgia for dying ways of life; the best and most original poems are the meeting-places of the two styles.

If one had to choose any passage of criticism to sum up the strengths of John's poetry, this might be it; and John must have basked in the praise.

In July 1946 *The Architectural Review* published a rather late notice of the book, by Hugh Casson. John and Casson knew each other well from working together on the *Review* and *Decoration*, and were outwardly friendly; but they had never really clicked. Casson was aware that John only paid lip-service – if that – to the Modern Movement, to which he himself was committed. Already plans were in train for a 1951 Festival of Britain, of which Casson was to be the architectural director. As an architect of the brave new Britain, he could take only so much of what he clearly regarded as an increasingly tiresome pose; though, by the same standards, he was generous about John's more serious poems.

> . . . Mr Betjeman's belfry is no ivory tower. Sturdily built – to the design perhaps of Butterfield? – it stands firmly on English soil, buttressed with affection, ivy'd with nostalgia . . . And the bats, are they really new? Well, we've met some of them before – the toothbrush airing on the N. Oxford window-sill, Miss Hunter Dunn, 'Furnished and burnished by Aldershot sun', the poultry farm girls, the barking athlete, the village organist – but how nice to see again their familiar furry little faces and hear the effortless beating of their wings. And those of you who still think Mr Betjeman is just a funny man read the last verse of 'Parliament Hill Fields', or 'Before the Anaesthetic' or 'Sunday Afternoon Service in St Enodoc Church, Cornwall'. Send not to enquire, then, *Review* readers, for whom Mr Betjeman's bell tolls – it tolls for all of you – and each note is a summons.

Did the conflation of 'bell' and 'summons', in that last sentence, plant in John's mind the phrase which became the title of his verse autobiography, fourteen years later?

19

British Council

IF JOHN HAD lived in the eighteenth century, he would probably have found himself a rich patron. At the *Daily Herald*, it was one of his *cris de coeur* that the only reason he took employment – the war effort apart – was to buy time to write poetry. By September 1944 he was as discontented at the Admiralty as he had become with all his previous jobs. He was flirting with the BBC, which was holding out the possibility of a staff post based in the Devon and Cornwall area. More attractive to him was the prospect of a senior appointment with the British Council, which he was discussing with Brian Kennedy-Cooke, director of the Council's production division. Kennedy-Cooke was one of a number of Council officials who had served in the Sudan – they were known as 'the Camel Corps' – and it is possible that Sir John Maffey, who had been Governor-General of the Sudan, recommended John to him. Kennedy-Cooke obtained John an interview with the Council's well-loved Secretary-General, A. J. S. White, who had served with the Indian Civil Service before the war. White was ten years – to the day – older than John. In 1984 he recalled the interview.

> We had been to the same school and as he sat down I said, 'You were at Marlborough, weren't you?' To which he replied – 'That stinking place. Yes I was.' Hardly an ingratiating remark from a candidate for a job, as I and my four sons were very enthusiastic Old Marlburians and I was ten years his senior! But of course he was the last person one could expect (or want) an ingratiating remark from. I was glad I brought him into the Council though I think I may have had to invent that job for him!

John was to be assistant director, under Kennedy-Cooke, in charge of the books division. The British Council had been created as a voluntary body in 1934, and was essentially a trade propaganda organization, though its aims were expressed in high-flown language – 'To make the life and thought of the British peoples more widely known abroad; and to promote a mutual interchange of knowledge and ideas with other peoples'. A prime aim of the campaign was to encourage the study and use of English.

A single department with a staff of two dealt with Books and Periodicals in 1939. By the end of 1943 work and staff had grown so much that there were three departments – Books, Periodicals, Publications – each under its own director. In Kennedy-Cooke's view, these directors had become warring 'primadonnas'. He thought that putting John in charge of them would make for harmony.

The Admiralty gave John his release, and by January 1945 he was an officer of the British Council. He first worked at St James's House, South Leigh, Oxfordshire, where the books departments had temporary quarters. It had been a school for 'backward boys'; above the entrance was a carving of the hare and the tortoise, with the legend 'FESTINA LENTE'. Shortly after John joined the Council, the books departments moved into Oriel College, Oxford – exchanging the carved tortoise of St James's House for a live college tortoise which had the Oriel coat of arms painted on its shell. John found that he knew three of the staff already. Renée Tickell he had known at Oxford, where, like himself, she contributed to *Oxford Outlook*. He always called her Renée Haynes, her maiden name, though in reference to her married name he made the Biblical pun, 'Renée, Renée Tickell, Upharsin'. Molly Fernald he had known as Molly Kidd. They used to drive out to the Spread Eagle inn at Thame together. She had married John's Marlborough and Oxford friend John Fernald, but by now they were divorced. 'There were those who called her Mrs *In*fernald,' Renée Tickell recalled. 'They had reason.' A third Oxford friend was Jack Yates (who as an undergraduate had called himself Theodore). Between Oxford and the Council appointment he had been a prep-school master. Always an aesthete, he had developed into a richly camp figure.

In theory John was answerable to Brian Kennedy-Cooke for the efficiency of the book departments. In fact, however, almost all his dealings, by memorandum and by telephone, were with Kennedy-Cooke's assistant, Joanna Collihole. 'John Betjeman was not remotely suitable for the job,' she considered.

Mrs Ormrod [later Lady Ormrod] was in charge of the books department. Its business was, during the war, to supply libraries in those countries where you could send books. Joan Barton was in charge of the periodicals department. John Hampden was publications department . . . Mrs Fernald was in charge of the book exports scheme. Renée Tickell was in charge of reviews.

So there was this group of primadonnas, largely isolated down at Oriel College, getting awfully sick of being down in the country when they would much prefer to be up in London – and *he kept them sweet*. That, in my opinion, was John's greatest contribution.

He was an appalling administrator. This is my view – rather pompous, I suppose. I was a good administrator. My business was to see that John provided Mr Kennedy-Cooke with what he needed in the way of confidential reports and returns and all the things that didn't matter to John one iota. So he was always late; and he must have hated my guts . . .

Knowing what Miss Collihole thought of him, John went out of his way to make his messages to her sound as maddeningly scatty as possible. One of his memos to her that has survived (because he eventually crossed it through and used the rest of the sheet to write to one of his assistants about poetry) begins: 'Miss Collihole from Mr Betjeman III II XLV: I have bicycle oil on my hands which has got on to the minutes. Miss Craig [John's secretary] is on leave – hence longhand . . .'

In view of her own difficulties with John, Joanna Collihole found it slightly galling that he got on so well with her boss, Brian Kennedy-Cooke. 'They liked each other very much,' she said. 'Mr Kennedy-Cooke found John enormously amusing – as *everybody* did!' John did not in fact manage to keep everybody happy; even in his limited mission of keeping the 'prima donnas' sweet he was not invariably successful. Mrs Ormrod, who had done more than anyone to create an effective books department, was not best pleased to have him put above her.

> . . . We were at Oriel [Lady Ormrod recalled], and the Council had been offered the possibility of a very fine house on the river. None of my people wanted to go, and it wouldn't have been suitable for me at all . . . And he accused me of influencing my staff not to go and I denied this, which was absolutely true . . . And he said, 'That's an absolute lie.' And I said, 'That is no way to speak to me; and it's not so.' . . . And he said, 'But you don't want to go.' And I said, 'No, I don't.' He said, 'Well, there you are, you've influenced your staff.' And he went on bullying me. So I got up and walked out and the meeting broke up.
>
> At lunchtime, I was just going out when somebody tapped me on the shoulder, and it was Betjeman, smiling and saying, 'I was a swine to you this morning.' And I said, '*Why* were you a swine to me?' He said, 'I felt like it.' So I said, 'Well, that was very unkind, because you upset my whole morning, making me feel beastly.' . . . Then he said, 'Oh, let's stop this and go and have a look at Oxford.' So he put his arm in mine and out we went; and, you know, to be with him . . . I knew Oxford pretty well, but he'd say, 'Stand in this doorway and look at that corner . . .' and see this or that. He was wonderful to be with. We had a very happy lunchtime together.

Late in 1945, the books division was moved from Oriel College to Blenheim Palace – the Duke of Marlborough's house, where Winston

Right: Farmer Wheeler, the Betjemans' landlord and a bugbear of John, who put him in his poem 'The Dear Old Village' as 'Farmer Whistle'

Below: In John Sutro's *The Sailor's Return*, Cecil Beaton played the sailor and John a clergyman. *The Bystander* called it 'The film with a Mayfair cast'

Father Harton, John's confessor, whom he both liked and mocked

Adrian Bishop, a raffish figure who later became a monk

Evelyn Waugh, who after Penelope's conversion in 1948, tried to bully John into becoming a Roman Catholic too

Osbert Lancaster, a friend from Oxford days

John in 1934 with Marcelle Rothe, who later married Peter Quennell

John holding his bear Archibald Ormsby-Gore

Stuart Piggott, the young archaeologist who helped John out when the Prime Minister of Nepal came to tea

John expressing with a scowl his dislike of horses

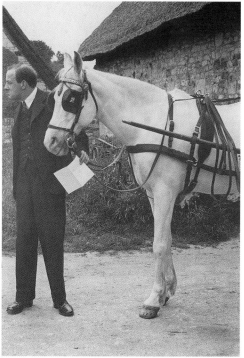

Tea at Faringdon. *Left to right*: Diana Heber Percy ('Bubbles'), sister-in-law of Robert Heber Percy, Moti, Penelope, Robert Heber Percy and Lord Berners

The opening of the Faringdon Picture Theatre in 1935: John sits in the back row with Penelope to his right; in the front row Lord Berners 'exchanges a joke' with Mrs MacDougal; to his left is the film star Stewart Rome

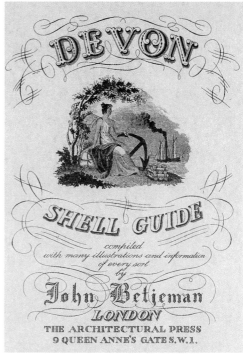

Jack Beddington, by Rex Whistler. He was Shell's publicity manager at the time of the Shell Guides to English counties, edited (and in some cases written) by John

The title page of John's *Shell Guide to Devon* (1936)

Field Marshal Sir Philip (later Lord) Chetwode with his grandson Paul Betjeman

The film director Dallas Bower, whom John met when on the *Evening Standard*, and later at the Ministry of Information and in Ireland

John Piper by Osbert Lancaster

Myfanwy Piper. She was a muse of John's; he put her in two of his poems and nicknamed her 'Goldlilegs'

E. McKnight Kauffer's surreal design for the jacket of *Continual Dew*

Miss Joan Hunter Dunn

John in Ireland in 1941, with Paul

Candida with her Christmas presents, Dublin 1942

R. M. Smyllie, editor of the *Irish Times*, with Penelope in Dublin's Fleet Street. John is at right, in the flat cap

Penelope, John, Candida and Paul in the garden at Farnborough

Churchill had been born. Most of the staff were to be housed in offices which were converted railway carriages in the Palace grounds; but a few rooms in the Palace, just vacated by MI5, the security service, were available, and for these there was ill-tempered competition. The practical Anne Ormrod quickly decided that she would much prefer to be in the trains. 'Everybody was fighting for rooms in the Palace, and bargaining. They were great, draughty rooms, and the tapestries were all covered with white dust-sheets, which had to be removed by men on ladders whenever the Duke wanted to show the tapestries to visitors. I wanted the trains, they were perfect for me. I had the end carriage and it had a telephone to the Continent. It had been the headquarters of the British staff until the Germans got to know where it was and threatened to bomb it – which was pretty nice for us, but we were expendable.' Molly Fernald bagged a room in the Palace. John Hampden was also in the Palace; and John, as head of the division, took the best room. Ralph Glasser, who worked for Molly Fernald, has written a brilliantly observed portrait of him *in situ*.

> Talking to John Betjeman in his room at Blenheim Palace, I happened to mention that I had come up to Oxford from the Gorbals. Part of the palace was in use by departments of the British Council, still in wartime evacuation quarters. He was standing before one of the huge panels of biscuit-coloured plywood covering the walls of the little salon which, like most of the rooms put to office use, still carried this protection for delicate surfaces beneath. He had been chalking on it a complicated notation of change-ringing . . . His present duties could not have been burdensome; to judge from the vast arrangement of chalk marks he had drawn on the board, he had spent most of the morning at it. He turned, the loose lower lip, drawn to the left as always, sagging further, and searched my face, plainly wondering what to say, which was unusual for him. Then, resuming the habitual mandarin drawl, half-eager, half-blasé, said, 'You *must* tell me how the place struck you – I suppose "struck" is the word! Dear boy, did the architecture transform you?'

John made himself an expert on the architecture of Blenheim. He produced a typewritten guidebook and set a competition for the office juniors to draw or paint anything they chose in the Palace and grounds. John was on hand to show visitors around. A. J. P. Taylor recalled that on VE Day in May 1945, his son Giles had a holiday from the Dragon School. 'He and I bicycled out to Blenheim where we picnicked in the park. We also called on John Betjeman who conducted us over Housemaids' Heights, the extremely uncomfortable servants' quarters, not usually shown.' The Duke of Marlborough was incensed when he learned that

John was making so free with his house. He was particularly annoyed to hear that John had taken some visitors out on to the roof – 'treadin' on me leads', as the Duke put it. John was forbidden to go roof-climbing again.

The Duke was not popular with the Council staff, nor they with him.

He was an old beast [Lady Ormrod said]. He would stamp about in a Norfolk jacket. If he could find a complaint he made it. He used to come and say to me, 'Would you please stop your staff doing something-or-other?' – whatever he could think of. And I used to say, 'In what way is it inconveniencing you?' And he didn't like that.

One of the troubles was, you had to go to the loo in the Palace. You had really almost to be introduced to the loo – it was in a room twice the size of this [a fair-sized drawing-room], and on the door was somebody-or-other's name. When you opened it, in the far distance you could see a loo, then you swept up the steps.

The Duke complained to John Betjeman that people were jumping out of my train and walking to the Palace to relieve themselves and were wearing the grass out. And Betjeman replied, 'But, surely, Your Grace, you are aware that it is not permitted to use the train lavatory when the carriages are stationary.'

John's secretary was Diana Craig. One of his first acts at South Leigh had been to prowl around looking at the secretaries. 'He stole Diana from me,' Rosemary Pearce complained. Barbara Watson, another British Council officer, thought Diana Craig 'a luscious-looking girl, rather plump, lovely fair hair'. John used often to disappear with Diana Craig for the afternoon. 'He took her off to lunch, and sometimes took her to Magdalen Chapel. I shouldn't think Diana Craig had been in a church since she was baptized – *if* she was baptized.'

Diana Craig figures with another Council secretary, Daphne Dunlop, in the one Betjeman poem directly inspired by his spell at the British Council. Entitled 'A Romance', it was not published until *Uncollected Poems* (1982), but it was a comic fantasy about the twenty-first birthday ball of a girl called Carol on the Council staff. It ends:

> 'Two thousand pounds it cost me,'
>   Said the Captain to his mate,
> 'And there's our daughter Carol
>   And she hasn't made a date.
> I fear we made our guest-list
>   Far too wide and vague
> When we asked that cold Miss Dunlop
>   And that fast Diana Craig.'

Happily for John, the Marlborough Arms in Woodstock had been taken over by Max Ehrsam, the Swiss restaurateur who in John's undergraduate days had presided over the George in Oxford. 'John and Jack [Yates] welcomed Max with open arms,' recalled Michael Hooker, who worked in book exports.

> Some of the lunches tended to go on . . . and I remember John coming back to Blenheim Palace and lying on his back on the floor of a corridor and waggling his arms and legs in the air like the man turned into a beetle in Kafka's *Metamorphosis*. We tried our best to get him to behave. He wasn't at all drunk, he was playing a part. As the registry clerks went by carrying files from one department to another, he would call out, 'Miss Smith, I'm as tight as an owl!' And she would say, 'Yes, Mr Betjeman,' and walk on . . .
>
> I remember coming back from the Marlborough Arms on one occasion – *more* than one occasion, we always tried to egg him on to repeat this, because once John got into his stride, nothing would stop him. Good company rather than good food or drink, I think, probably had this stimulating effect. He would give a one-man performance of the OUDS [Oxford University Dramatic Society]. He would stand behind some curtains in one of the state rooms of Blenheim Palace where we had our offices, and would produce pseudo-Shakespeare by the yard. Somebody had 'engendered ten thousand horse' or something, and he would play the part of the prompter getting it wrong and he would come on to the stage and somehow, with another hand, drag himself back off. There were mutterings behind the curtain, between two or three imaginary people. I've never laughed so much before or since. I remember lying on the floor there, thinking my ribs were going to crack.

By 1946, the Duke of Marlborough was agitating for the British Council to be cleared out of his palace and grounds, bag and baggage. He had taken to going round with a spiked stick, ostentatiously stabbing at litter. Later that year his wish was granted and the books division moved back to London. But by that time John had found himself another job, as secretary of the Oxford Preservation Trust (see below). He left little mark on the Council; but, as usual, he had made more friends than enemies. He kept in touch with some of the friends, especially with Jack Yates.

After the war Yates found the British Council uncongenial. A native of Lincolnshire, he decided to return to Louth to live with his elderly mother Emily and to buy Goulding's, a musty eighteenth-century bookshop in the middle of the town, unheated and lit by flickering gas. Goulding's Bookshop did not have much competition. Yates liked to recount how he had gone into the town's only other bookshop and asked if they had Pepys's Diary. 'No, only Letts's,' was the reply. When Yates moved back to Louth,

John became a regular guest. 'He stayed about twice a year,' remembered Yates's niece, the artist Gill Foot. John was predisposed towards Lincolnshire. His mother's family, the Dawsons, were Lincolnshire folk. 'My grandfather', he told the Lincolnshire Association in 1963, 'was a Spalding builder who went bankrupt.' John admired the Lincolnshire poet Jean Ingelow, to whom Tennyson exclaimed, 'Miss Ingelow, I do declare you do the trick better than I do.' And Lincolnshire was the county where Tennyson himself had lived. John loved Lincolnshire because, he said in 1963, 'it is so beautiful, so unobtrusively beautiful, and from the landsman's point of view it is saved from much hideous destruction by the Humber stopping things going straight through'.

In the late 1920s John stayed in Kirkby-on-Bain with Canon Felix Blakiston, the father of his friend Noel Blakiston, and was 'first excited by the county'. With comic variation, the place-name was absorbed into his poem of 1945, 'A Lincolnshire Tale' –

> Kirkby with Muckby-cum-Sparrowby-cum-Spinx
> Is down a long lane in the county of Lincs.

John liked the place-names of Lincolnshire – Clixby, Claxby, Claxby Pluckacre, Ashby Puerorum, Bag Enderby. Gill Foot remembered his glee on encountering a signpost on the Spilsby–Boston road which read 'TO MAVIS ENDERBY AND OLD BOLINGBROKE'. Somebody had scrawled underneath '– the gift of a son'.

John did not care to join Yates for his early-morning run, in pyjamas, along the sea-front at Humberstone. After breakfast, the two men would set out for a day of exploration, often accompanied by Emily Yates. Sometimes they went by car, sometimes by bus. The places associated with Tennyson were visited, from Parker's in Mercer Row, Louth, where his *Poems of Two Brothers* was first printed, to Somersby Rectory where he grew up, and Harringdon Hall, whose garden was the one into which 'Maud' was invited to come. Another favourite trip was to Woodhall Spa, described by John as 'that unexpected Bournemouth-like settlement in the middle of Lincolnshire'. The place is also mentioned in his poem 'House of Rest'.

Whether or not she was to be of the party, Emily Yates prepared a picnic hamper for each expedition, with bottles of wine as well as food. Jack Yates usually found a brook in which to cool the white wines, tying strings round the bottle necks. A Yates picnic was not a casual affair. A linen tablecloth was spread out, with napkins in ivory rings. The wine was drunk from stemmed glasses, not plastic beakers or paper cups.

One of the many churches John and Jack visited was St Margaret's, Huttoft. In his poem 'A Lincolnshire Church', John wrote:

> There in the lighted East
> He stood in that lowering sunlight,
> An Indian Christian priest . . .
> I thought of the heaving waters
> That bore him from sun glare harsh
> Of some Indian Anglican Mission
> To this green enormous marsh.

The Vicar of Huttoft from 1943 to 1959 was the Rev. Theophilus Caleb, who was indeed an Indian. He died in a tractor accident in November 1959 and is buried in Huttoft graveyard.

John and Yates remained friends well beyond the 1940s. When, in 1960, Jack Yates had the first of three heart attacks and gave up his bookshop, John, who always moved swiftly to help friends in distress, said to Henry Thorold, the squire of Marston, Lincolnshire, and the two men's companion on many church crawls, 'Dear boy, our friend Jack is a bit bored, I'm afraid, now that he hasn't got the bookshop. I was thinking, we really do need a Shell Guide to dear old Lincolnshire and I was wondering if you'd like to do it together.' He added: 'Of course, Jack'll do all the work, and . . . you can have some jollies round together.' John then went to Yates and said, 'I say, old man, I've just been talking to Henry and I think that you and he ought to do a Shell Guide to Lincolnshire together, because after all we do need one. He'll do all the work, of course, because you don't want to be overdoing things now with your heart. But you could have some expeditions together, and I thought you might enjoy it.' Yates died in 1971, the year John became Poet Laureate.

Years later, John wrote to Thorold: 'My dear Henry, last week I took up your Lincolnshire Guide, thinking of you and our late friend Jack and read it as though it were a thriller. Such it proved to be. It is funnier and succincter than any Shell guide. Norton Disney is the funniest entry I know.' (The entry stated that 'the creator of Mickey Mouse' was 'a descendant of a junior branch' of the Disney family.)

John continued to work in Oxford after he had left the British Council: between 1946 and 1948 he was secretary of the Oxford Preservation Trust. But on this episode in his history there is a puzzling lacuna in the printed records of his life. He omitted any mention of it from his *Who's Who* entry. No allusion to it appeared in any of the obituaries, even that in the *Oxford Times*. He seems not to have spoken of it to either of his early biographers,

Derek Stanford or Patrick Taylor-Martin. He was happy enough to be offered the job. The pay seemed good: £300 a year for a minimum of one day's work a week; he was allowed to continue reviewing for the *Daily Herald*. His office was in one of the most historic rooms in the city, the Painted Room in the Cornmarket, part of the old Crown Tavern where Shakespeare was alleged to have slept. John was allowed to recruit Diana Craig, his British Council secretary, as assistant secretary of the Trust. It was a job for which he was well cast. He had known Oxford since his prep-school days in the Great War, and was nothing if not a preservationist.

The Oxford Preservation Trust had been founded in 1926 by Sir Michael Sadler, Master of University College, and others who wanted to preserve the old Oxford and to ensure that any new building was in keeping with the old. In particular, they were alarmed at industrial encroachment on the outskirts of Oxford by the Cowley motor works of Lord Nuffield – 'William Morris the Second', as John ironically called him in *An Oxford University Chest*. Industrialization was leading to a rapid increase in the population which had to be housed.

Sadler had died in 1943, and others of the original Trustees, including the sub-Stracheyesque historian Philip Guedalla, had resigned. Among the most influential of the Trustees in 1946 were Lionel Curtis, the Rev. J. M. Thompson and H. S. Goodhart-Rendel. John was on good terms with all three. Curtis, who had fought in the Boer War, had become acting town clerk of Johannesburg and was now a fellow of All Souls. John knew him through his Magdalen friend Lionel Perry. A further link between Curtis and John was John Sparrow of All Souls. It was he who suggested to Curtis that John would make a good secretary for the OPT. John was already a friend of J. M. Thompson, his favourite don at Magdalen. Thompson was a key figure in the Trust, with the title 'Convener'. The architect Goodhart-Rendel John had known and praised in his days on *The Architectural Review*.

John was duly interviewed and at a meeting of the Trustees in Lionel Curtis's All Souls rooms on 28 April 1946 it was agreed unanimously that he be appointed, the Trust to bear as well the cost of an assistant secretary, who would also act as caretaker of the Painted Room. It was open to the public most days. Combined admission receipts and postcard sales for the previous year amounted to £400. The position would be reviewed at the end of the first year, when it was hoped that an increase in the Trust's revenue would enable it to raise John's salary: payment by results.

Diana Craig and John moved into the Painted Room and the adjoining office in September and were given £100 to spend on essential office furniture. Even at Blenheim, John had not had an office so splendidly appointed. The Painted Room was on the second floor of No. 3 Cornmarket Street, above a J. Lyons restaurant. The ground floor had formerly been occupied by Hookham's, a gentleman's outfitters. The building behind the shop front had been part of the Crown Tavern kept between 1564 and 1581 by John Davenant, the father of the dramatist and Poet Laureate Sir William Davenant to whom Shakespeare 'stood god-father' in Oxford. In 1934 E. W. Attwood, who owned Hookham's, stripped away seventeenth-century panelling in the upper rooms and revealed remarkable Tudor wall-paintings. Against a rich orange-scarlet background, probably of red ochre mined on Shotover Hill, were painted stylized flowers and fruit – white Canterbury bells, windflowers, roses, passion flowers and grapes. The materials used for colouring were lime, charcoal and ochre; the fixative, beer. Over the fireplace was painted the Christian monogram IHS and around the room ran a set of pious verse exhortations known as 'the Girdle of Holiness'.

John Aubrey tells how Shakespeare 'was wont to go into Oxfordshire once a year and did in his journey lye at this house in Oxon, where he was exceedingly respected'. It became settled belief that the Painted Room was the poet's bedroom. By the time of John's appointment, a panelled screen mounted on rollers had been set in front of the floral wall. He would draw it back with a flourish to surprise visitors. Osbert Lancaster liked the paint-ings but said he thought the rooms were rather dark. 'What was good enough for Shakespeare is good enough for me,' John said.

The Trust was, however, an impotent body. It had no statutory powers. Too often it was reduced to asking plaintively, 'Can something be done . . . ?' Much depended, as those who appointed John understood, on diplomatic relations between the secretary and the Town Clerk and other officials. John knew how to charm; but there was another aspect to his character which sometimes militated against his power to do so. If he was involved, as often happened with the OPT, in a business dispute over land or buildings, he was inclined to interpret the opposing point of view – even when it was expressed with no animosity – as hostile criticism directed at himself. Then he bridled and spat back. This trait was aggravated as John's work-load became heavier.

In the first months there was little sign of bile, though there was a touch of it in the minute he wrote on 'Cherwell Dredging' on 29 October 1946: 'The Secretary was instructed to write to Sir Ralph Glyn [an acquaintance of John's from Uffington days] asking him, as a Thames conservator . . . whether dredging operations necessitated the felling of trees on river banks, as had been done on the New Cut above Gosford, and whether it was beyond the wit of man to devise a dredging plant which did not cause the destruction of trees.' The minute immediately after the 'Cherwell Dredging' item reads:

BINSEY POPLARS. The Secretary to arrange with the Town Clerk for Mr Emden, Mr Sanzen-Baker and himself to visit these sites with the Parks Superintendent.

Though John was never an enthusiastic Hopkinsian, he knew Hopkins's poem 'Binsey Poplars'; and the Town Clerk's name was Harry Plowman – phonetically, at least, the title of another Hopkins poem.

In every job he held, John needed a *bête noire*, somebody on whom he could vent the frustration he felt at not being free to write poetry. Harry Plowman was the official with whom he had most dealings while with the OPT. The Town Clerk was, by all accounts, a likeable and intelligent man, but John seems to have taken against him and his tough, no-nonsense memos. Perhaps as John's duties increased, Plowman made it too obvious that he thought he was getting out of his depth, and teased him a little about his inefficiency. There can be small doubt that John had Plowman in his sights when he wrote his poem 'The Town Clerk's Views', published in *Selected Poems* in 1948, a few months after he left the Trust. The poem begins:

> 'Yes, the Town Clerk will see you.' In I went.
> He was, like all Town Clerks, from north of Trent;
> A man with bye-laws busy in his head
> Whose Mayor and Council followed where he led.
> His most capacious brain will make us cower,
> His only weakness is a lust for power –
> And that is not a weakness, people think,
> When unaccompanied by bribes or drink.
> So let us hear this cool careerist tell
> His plans to turn our country into hell.

Later in the poem are the pointed lines

> Oxford is growing up to date at last.
> Cambridge, I fear, is living in the past.

John Edwards, who was Plowman's deputy at the town hall, remembers the Town Clerk as 'a consummate advocate and diplomat, coupling this with great charm, imperturbability, and a sense of humour'. Loyal to Plowman's memory, Edwards does not think he would have been capable of formulating the philistine opinions with which he is credited throughout the poem. 'Moreover, on no occasion would there be any question of HP sending for the Secretary of the OPT to hold forth about general national planning.' But Edwards admits that when John arrived at the Town Clerk's department, he might well have been invited in with some such formula as the first line. 'In view of line 2, it should be mentioned that HP was a Londoner, but as he had been Town Clerk of Burnley, Lancs, before coming to Oxford, JB might be pardoned for thinking he was a northerner. As to line 4, I can quite imagine that anyone not familiar with Council procedure might be given this impression at a meeting of the City Council, whereas all HP would be trying to do from time to time would be to see that the Council did not stray too far from its own standing orders.' John is unlikely to have had regular dealings with any other town clerks. It is probably safe to conclude that Plowman is being 'got at' in what was largely a work of John's imagination, a generalized onslaught on the town planners.

John's job was no sinecure; he put effort into it and he got results. His two years at the OPT were a critical period in the history of British town planning. The Council was required to prepare a development plan under the Town and Planning Act 1947, and to that end commissioned Dr Thomas Sharp to advise it. Five years older than John, Sharp had been educated at Council schools and had worked for twenty years in local government before becoming a town and country planning lecturer at Durham University. While preparing his report for the Oxford Council, he rented from them the floor below the Painted Room. Against all the prognostics, the pugnacious Sharp got on well with John, often joining him and Diana Craig for tea. John was to describe him as 'our most sensitive and controversial town planner'. Most of those who had dealings with Sharp found him considerably more controversial than sensitive.

Sharp's report on the city, *Oxford Replanned*, was published as a book in 1948, before John left the Trust. The lavish avant-garde production showed that post-war paper shortages and austerities were coming to an end. It was part of John's job to canvass opinions about the report from the Trustees, college heads and others who had, or thought they had, a right to be consulted. On 21 January 1948 he wrote to J. M. Richards at the Architectural Press:

Dear Boy
For goodness sake help me, and I repeat, for goodness sake help me.
Here am I Secretary of the Oxford Preservation Trust & asked to obtain 27 copies of Thomas Sharp's Plan for Oxford on the day of publication, for distribution to each of my Trustees. Oh for God's sake get them for me. I will send you a cheque so soon as you tell me you can get them. Ask old

AED, ask the Regans, ask Tatters, ask Mr Pierson, ask Obscurity himself, but get them for me.

Thomas Sharp has moved into this old-world building with me, and very happy we are together . . .

Sharp's proposals quickly attracted strong criticism. L. Bellinger, vice-president of the Oxford Trades and Labour Council, declared: 'The future prosperity of this country depends on industry, and it is no good trying to re-establish Oxford University with a monastic atmosphere. It seems to me that the report, which shows so much concern for the University, might have been issued by the Oxford Preservation Trust.' Perhaps John's teatime conversations with Sharp had had some effect.

But as time went on there were further signs that John was chafing against the restrictions the job put on his freedom. As so often before, novelty degenerated into routine, routine into drudgery. In June 1948 John resigned from the Trust; Diana Craig resigned at the same time. Recording the annual general meeting in Brasenose College on Saturday 26 June, John wrote in the minutes:

> *Resignation of Secretariat* ~~was accepted with regret~~, Mr Betjeman as Secretary and Miss Craig as Assistant Secretary was accepted with much regret. The appointment of Alderman Sam Smith as Secretary, with effect from the date of transfer of change, is approved . . .

The Trust forgave John for deserting it; but did he forgive himself? The absence of any later mention of his secretaryship suggests a deliberate or subconscious attempt to wipe the episode from his record. Did he perhaps feel that his credibility as a passionate preservationist would be impaired if people learned how he had not made more of the biggest chance he ever had to preserve? In Oxford his authority as a preservationist was never taken quite seriously again. In 1962, when he expostulated to President Boase of Magdalen that his college's new Waynflete Building, on the other side of Magdalen Bridge, was 'a hideous monstrosity that will ruin Oxford for ever', Boase felt able to treat the criticism dismissively, patting it away with a droll Irish bull – 'Oh, I don't know, John; it's not as ugly as it looks, you know.'

20

A Preservationist in the Making

IN THE SIX years before his abrupt exit from the Oxford Preservation Trust, John had steadily built up his reputation as a 'natural' on the radio. Earlier, his wartime service in the Ministry of Information and in Ireland had caused a big gap in his broadcasting career, though on one visit to London, in 1943, he had taken part in *The Brains Trust*, the weekly discussion of current affairs and other topics, with Professors C. E. M. Joad and Julian Huxley. In February of that year he had also given a heartfelt talk on 'Coming Home – or England Revisited'.

> It is something really terrible, this longing for England we get when we are away. The other month I found my eyes getting wet (fortunately there was no one about) at the sight of moonlight on a willow stump covered with ivy. It reminded me of a willowy brook in the Berkshire village where we used to live before the war . . .
>
> I do not believe we are fighting for the privilege of living in a highly developed community of ants. That is what the Nazis want. For me, at any rate, England stands for the Church of England, eccentric incumbents, oil-lit churches, Women's Institutes, modest village inns, arguments about cow-parsley on the altar, the noise of mowing machines on Sunday afternoons, local newspapers, local auctions, the poetry of Tennyson, Crabbe, Hardy and Matthew Arnold, local talent, local concerts, a visit to the cinema, branch line trains, light railways, leaning on gates and looking across fields.

On 18 September 1943, John wrote to Ronald Boswell from the Films Division, Ministry of Information, 'Here I am back, grinding at the mill.' Shortly afterwards, Geoffrey Grigson, who worked at the BBC's Bristol studios, told Winifred Salmon, the assistant director of talks, London, that John wanted to talk on 'war weariness'. Grigson commented:

> That would be too bald a title, and would, perhaps, put you off, but he means the state of mind after several years of war, the necessity for thought and silence and some point of meditation in one's life . . .
>
> I believe he would do a talk of this kind really well. Last Thursday was

the first time I'd produced him myself and he seemed to me to have control over his speaking, and a marvellous ability to be on the listeners' side.

Winifred Salmon sent a lukewarm reply.

By all means encourage Betjeman to talk about war-weariness, but I see certain snags in this.
(a) that having lived in Dublin for so large a part of the war he has less excuse than most people to be war-weary;
(b) that his particular voice and manner (no offence intended) might make a good many people think that he was weary before the war began. He must contrive to sound entirely sincere . . .

Grigson replied:

You rather suggest that Betjeman might not sound sincere or that, as a broadcaster, he sounds tired. That isn't my impression of him on the air. Whatever one may know about him oneself, I find that he sounds sincere, convinced and vigorous. The fact remains that we get a bigger correspondence after his talks down here than we get after talks by any other speaker, and that correspondence is always 99% appreciative.

John might have been surprised if he could have seen this inter-office correspondence. He had been ill-disposed towards 'Griggers' ever since, in their Oxford days, Grigson had rejected his poem 'The Arrest of Oscar Wilde at the Cadogan Hotel' for an undergraduate magazine. In John's view, Grigson was a sucker for avant-gardism in verse; and Grigson made no secret that he thought John's poetry indefensibly anachronistic. It was magnanimous of Grigson to praise John to Winifred Salmon in 1943; only four years earlier, John had had to write him a grovelling apology for using something very close to his name for a character in a published short story about commercial travellers.

Ingredients of future poems are found in two of John's radio talks. In 1937, in a talk on Exeter, he said: 'Another part of Exeter that still survives almost intact, is the Georgian district . . . Walk in the miniature dell of beech and ilex-shaded lawns called Rougemont Gardens . . .' Later in the talk he again referred to the Exeter trees – 'copper beech, beech, oak, and best of all the ilex whose olive leaves look grand against the yellow, red or cheerful plaster'. The ilex reappeared in his poem 'Exeter', published in *Continual Dew* that year –

> The doctor's intellectual wife
> Sat under the ilex tree
> The Cathedral bells pealed over the wall
> But never a bell heard she

> And the sun played shadowgraphs on her book
> Which was writ by A. Huxléy.

A much more developed blueprint for a poem formed part of his talk 'Christmas Nostalgia', transmitted on 25 December 1947.

> Last week I was in the most beautiful building in Britain – King's College, Cambridge. You know it. It is a forest glade of old coloured glass, and between the great windows columns of shafted stone shoot up and up to fountain out into a shower of exquisite fan-vaulting. It is the swan-song of Perpendicular architecture, so immense, so vast, so superbly proportioned, so mysterious, that no one can enter it without gasping. All the school children of Cambridge had filed into a Carol service and there they were in the candle light of the dark oak stalls. We stood waiting for the choir to come in and as we stood there the first verse of the opening carol was sung beyond us, behind the screen, away in the mighty splendour of the nave. A treble solo floated up to the distant vaulting

> *Once in Royal David's City . . .*

> It was clear, pure, distinct. And as I heard it, I knew once more – knew despite myself – that this story was the Truth.

There – even down to certain phrases – is the inspiration for John's poem 'Sunday Morning, King's Cambridge', published in *A Few Late Chrysanthemums* (1954). But in a 1949 recital of his poems on the radio, with his own commentary, his listeners were not only given an early version of the poem, but were made party to the very workings of the poet's mind.

> Well, there's one other [poem] I might as well give you on a more serious topographical note, before we come to the suburbs, which is 'King's at Cambridge'.
> Do you know King's at Cambridge? I always think Cambridge really beats Oxford . . . Its architecture. And I'm trying to do a poem on King's Chapel. Haven't finished it yet. Keep writing the last verse and it doesn't work. Sounds too grand. Sounds like a sort of state poem in *The Sunday Times* when I get the – when I put the last verse on, so I'm just going to read you the first two. I've crossed out the last one. I don't know whether they are much good, but King's Chapel really is such a blaze of glory and beauty, especially inside, that I've always wanted to get it into verse. If you can compose the last verse in this metre I should be very grateful and would give anybody who writes it full acknowledgement . . .

> File you out from yellow candle light
> Fair choristers of King's,

And leave to shadowy silence
These canopied Renaissance stalls.
In blazing glass above the dark
Go skies and thrones and wings,
Blue, ruby, gold and green
Between the whiteness of the walls.
And with what rich precision
The stonework soars and springs
To fountain out, to spreading vault
A shower that never falls.*

Then, I've tried to give the impression of all the colours that you see in
Cambridge, and Cambridge is full of them in its stonework and in its mead-
ows, and in all its scenery, its flint, and everything outside and in its sky.
They're all – they become transmuted through this stained glass, just into
pearl on the stone shafts that go sprouting up the walls and bursting into the
fountains I've described of fan-vaulting.

The white of windy Cambridge courts,
The cobbles brown and dry,
The gold of plaster Gothic
With ivy overgrown.
The apple red, the silver fronts
The deep green flats and high
The yellowing elm trees circled out
On islands of their own.
Oh! Here beyond all colours change
That catch the flying sky,
To waves of pearly light that heave
Along the shafted stone.†

And now I don't know how to complete it, you see. One wants to get the
impression, really, that brings King's Chapel finally to life when one's inside
it, which is when the organ is going, and that choir is singing, so brilliantly

---

* In the published version the first stanza reads:

File into yellow candle light, fair choristers of King's
Lost in the shadowy silence of canopied Renaissance stalls
In blazing glass above the dark glow skies and thrones and wings
Blue, ruby, gold and green between the whiteness of the walls
And with what rich precision the stonework soars and springs
To fountain out a spreading vault – a shower that never falls.

† In the published version the second stanza is almost the same; except that the twelve lines
are regrouped into six lines; 'the deep green flats' become 'the wide green flats'; and
'beyond' (presumably a typist's error in the BBC script) is corrected to 'behold'.

conducted by – run by, Boris Ord, you know. Then you get such a sort of fourth dimension in the place. It's absolutely the one experience, I think, that England has got above any country in the world, in the way of architecture and music welded together. That last verse, I don't think I shall ever be able to write it. But I hope somebody will one day write a poem about King's Chapel. Wordsworth's sonnet, to me, though very wonderful, doesn't quite bring it off as I should like to see it done, to hear it done, by some great man. It can never be done.*

Against John's wishes, 'Sunday Morning, King's Cambridge' was excluded from his next book, *Selected Poems*. In June 1946 he and Jock Murray began discussing a new book which would bring together poems from the three earlier Murray volumes. Though it was early decided that a selection would be made, both men referred to the book as *Collected Poems* until just before publication. 'I would prefer to leave the selection to you or to who you like to get,' John wrote to Murray on 22 June. Murray asked whether there were any poems John would like to omit. 'As far as possible,' Murray thought, 'they should all be included.' On 10 July the publisher wrote again to ask for any new poems that had appeared in magazines since *New Bats in Old Belfries*. He had asked John Sparrow and Peter Quennell to read through the earlier volumes and give their views.

Quennell marked with an 'X' 'the poems I like least. Naturally this doesn't mean that I don't like them.' He blacklisted five poems from *Continual Dew* (including 'Slough'), three from *Old Lights* and two from *New Bats*. Sparrow's advice was to select only the best – 'the best *poetry*, light or serious – not the most typical . . .' He wanted to include twelve poems of the thirty-three in *Continual Dew*, eleven of the twenty-one in *Old Lights* and fourteen of the twenty-four in *New Bats*. So Quennell's and Sparrow's estimates of the three books, in terms of quality, were strikingly similar: both men thought Betjeman the poet had improved over the years. Murray agreed with Sparrow that 'The ideal is certainly only to include the very best.'

Sparrow wanted to discuss with John not only the selection, but also the arrangement of the poems under thematic headings. And indeed it was

---

* As published, the third stanza John wrote was as follows:

> In far East Anglian churches, the clasped hands lying long
>   Recumbent on sepulchral slabs or effigied in brass
> Buttress with prayer this vaulted roof so white and light and strong
>   And countless congregations as the generations pass
> Join choir and great crowned organ case, in centuries of song
>   To praise Eternity contained in Time and coloured glass.

soon accepted – though exactly when, how or why is unclear from the Murray archives – that he would be a sort of ringmaster for the selection. It was also agreed that he would write a preface to it. Sparrow had been one of John's closest friends since they were undergraduates together. To have him, with his double First and All Souls fellowship, introduce the poems might not confer gravitas on them; but it would set on them a seal of Establishment recognition which John, for all his pot-shots at society's grandees, craved. Sparrow's attitude to him was unengagingly *de haut en bas*. For his friend, he would deign to dip a fastidious toe into the popular market; but in return he expected absolute control over the contents of the book. His strictures on the poems he wanted excluded were severe. There was perhaps an element of jealousy in this. Though he held the blue riband of academe, he published little more than a few collections of essays. His poems never caught on. His name was unknown to the man in the street – except, possibly, in 1962 when he suggested that D. H. Lawrence had introduced buggery into *Lady Chatterley's Lover*. It was satisfying to subject John to his authority.

W. H. Auden, who was living in Long Island, New York, selected and wrote the introduction to an American collection of John's poems – a book quite distinct from Sparrow's selection. It was issued in 1947 as *Slick but not Streamlined*. John's daughter, Candida Lycett Green, recalls that her father detested this title. Auden wrote to John on 9 August: 'I was furious about the title they gave your book but the sales department insisted . . .' He said he had wanted to call the book *Betjeman's Bust*. This was probably disingenuous. In his 'Verse-letter to C. Day-Lewis' (1929), Auden had described the poetaster Humbert Wolfe, whom he despised, in these contemptuous lines:

> While Wolfe, the typists' poet, made us sick
> Whose thoughts are dapper and whose lines are slick.

It seems rather too much of a coincidence that the epithet 'slick' should occur in the American title too; and was it really likely that an American publisher's sales department would have thought of such an untempting title and insisted on it in defiance of the anthologist's wishes? It is more probable that Auden, like Sparrow, slightly resented his old Oxford friend's growing fame, and intended to put him in his place. He was also, perhaps, not amused by the suggestion in *The Listener* by 'Beachcomber', reviewing *Continual Dew*, that he, Auden, had 'begun to imitate' John. With the honesty that belongs to great poets, Auden candidly admitted his jealousy of John in the first sentence of his introduction; and while the tone of this piece was friendly, its effect was to depreciate John by treating him as a very English joke.

> It is difficult to write seriously about a man one has sung hymns with or judiciously about a poet whose work makes one violently jealous. Normally when I read good poetry, for example Mr Eliot's line
>
> > The place of solitude where three dreams cross
>
> my reaction is one of delighted admiration; a standard of excellence has been set in one way which I must try to live up to in mine: but when I read such lines of Mr Betjeman as
>
> > And that mauve hat three cherries decorate
> > Next week shall topple from its trembling perch
> > While wet fields reek like some long empty church
>
> I am, frankly, rather annoyed because they are not by me. My feeling is similar to that one has when, on arriving at some long-favorite picnic spot in the woods, one finds that another trespasser has discovered it too.

In October 1947, Sparrow at last produced the preface for his own selection. Murray was delighted with it, an urbane, thoughtful and entertaining piece. Sparrow had two main themes. He wanted to show that John was pre-eminently a poet of place (Harold Acton was to call him 'the genius of the *genius loci*'). And he tried to distance him from his early 'amusing' phase, and to illustrate his new maturity.

Sparrow was having second thoughts about some of the poems he had turned down. 'I have been haunted for days', he wrote to Murray on 25 November, 'by the feeling that we ought to have included *Invasion Exercise on the Poultry Farm* in the Selection . . .' There was still time, and it was reprieved. However, Sparrow was adamant in refusing to admit 'Myfanwy at Oxford'. He also had reservations about 'Sunday Morning, King's Cambridge'. After Jock Murray had passed these and other criticisms on to John, the poet replied, on Christmas Day 1947:

> I am delighted with Spansbury's comments, on which I find myself in complete agreement with the dear old thing. With others I am not.
>
> But before I deal with these I will tell you one thing I must write to him about (and I have not yet had time to do so) and that is the Preface. I said I would like to be as dead about it, but there is an inaccuracy in the beginning which, since I am alive, I MUST correct. I am not a pure poet of place. I bear no resemblance to Bloomfield or Clare and very little to Crabbe and only a little to Cowper but much more to him than the other three. This means to say that I write (and I know this) primarily with *people* in mind

and relate the people to the background. When I am describing Nature, it is *always* with a view to the social background or the sense of Man's impotence before the vastness of the Creator. That is what makes my satirical poetry and the earlier stuff different (and I think feebler) than the later. You will also find this in my prose work. For instance, the only merit of Ghastly Good Taste was that it treated architecture sociologically.

John was upset that Sparrow wanted to omit 'Sunday Morning, King's Cambridge'. After dealing with Sparrow's textual criticisms of the poem ('I always pronounce Renaissance Rĕnăĭssănce'), he burst out: 'But this poem is a corker! and Spansbury is mad not to include it, though I admit it gives the lie to his theory about my being a poet of place; back your own judgment, Jock; you know it is the best poem I've ever written; so do I.' In sending Sparrow's comments to John, Murray had written, 'If you think his suggestions are improvements and decide to adopt them, I personally very much hope that he will, in the end, include it.' But in the upshot the King's, Cambridge poem was left out of *Selected Poems*; it appeared in *A Few Late Chrysanthemums* (1954).

On 4 March Murray wrote to the printer, William Clowes, 'We shall be sending you shortly a printing order for 4000 copies of Betjeman's *Collected Poems*.' There was also to be a limited edition of 100 copies on handmade paper, with marbled endpapers from Douglas Cockerell of Letchworth, Herts. John returned to Murray what he called 'the Spansburied proofs' on 3 March, making a last vain plea that 'Myfanwy at Oxford' should be used instead of 'Invasion Exercise on the Poultry Farm' ('but it is not a vital matter'). On 3 May Murray wrote to him that 'The Collected, Selected Opus will be the advance guard of the autumn season – that is to say a September book.' The title *Selected Poems* was finally decided on. In letters to Sparrow about last-minute corrections, Murray referred to the book as 'the Betje-bus'.

Murray sent John the first completed copy on 16 September and asked him to lunch on 4 October (Sparrow was invited too) to 'drink a health'. John replied two days later: 'I am DELIGHTED with the book of Selected Poems and with the preface by Spansbury. I cannot bring myself to read the verses.' The book was published on 5 October 1948. The next day, it was reviewed in the *Evening News* by the short-story writer Frank O'Connor – John's friend from Dublin days – under the heading 'A POET FOR ALL'.

Mr John Betjeman is, for me, the most interesting figure in English poetry today. He approaches you with the most disarming air of being really a disappointed contributor to *Punch* who has been barred from its pages owing to his eccentric passion for Victorian bric-à-brac . . .

Mr Sparrow seems to be writing something perilously like nonsense when he says that 'the gift of poetry was not bestowed on Mr Betjeman to enable him to unlock his heart.' Betjeman is, I think, a religious poet in the line of Donne and Hopkins, with the same crude, unqualified tension between his love of God and his natural sensuality, though in him the sensuality is mostly expressed in adolescent terms. He is developing on seven-league boots . . .

The Spectator bracketed Auden and Betjeman, in a review by H. A. L. Craig. Craig thought John deserved the dedication of Auden's *The Age of Anxiety*. 'Indeed, John Betjeman deserves much, for he is that rarity, a poet who chooses his own limitations and is completely successful within them. Auden sets himself a big test, and fails; Betjeman a lesser test, and passes it, taking again the prize of the senior freshman year. This is not to belittle Betjeman, but to place him . . . John Betjeman is a minor poet, but an original one. The exactness of his expression, the lightness with which he lays down serious moods, the disarming way he codifies the unwritten and terrifying laws of middle-class behaviour, are the works of a master.' The anonymous reviewer in *The Listener* also praised John. 'This descendant of Crabbe, Calverley and Praed, this poet of the local gazette, of parish, school or regimental magazine, writes with assurance, wit and style.' The reviewer thought that the tender last lines of 'Parliament Hill Fields' were 'almost Blake-like' –

> And my childish wave of pity, seeing children carrying down
> Sheaves of drooping dandelions to the courts of Kentish Town.

This Blake-like view of the world invigorated John's other great passion. He had the same belief about architectural appreciation as Freud had about the human psyche: that experiences in early childhood are crucially formative. 'What makes you like architecture', he wrote in 1971, 'are the things you have seen and reacted to as a child.' The first buildings he could remember were on Highgate West Hill. 'I did not realize that some of them were charming Georgian.' He thought that tall buildings near his parents' house, in a Pimlico style, were very ugly. So as early as that – before the First World War – he was exercising his own taste, deciding for himself what he liked and disliked. The spiky skyline of Holly Village, Highgate, built by Alfred Darbyshire in 1864 to house Baroness Burdett-Coutts's servants, gave him a frisson of horror. Also, he thought that anything in grey or stock brick was ugly and that red brick was beautiful. 'I remember my father telling me that this was not so.'

What made John realize that there was 'more than surface' to architecture was *The Ghost Stories of an Antiquary* by M. R. James, which Skipper Lynam used to read the boys at the Dragon School. 'Those stories', John said, 'bring out the Norfolk landscape, Perpendicular churches, Georgian squires' houses in red brick, Strawberry Hill Gothick, mezzotints and the eighteenth century as well as the Middle Ages – and with that touch of horror which is essential to keep one's attention.' On sketching expeditions at Marlborough, in the 1920s, he became infatuated with Ramsbury Manor, a classical building of the late seventeenth century. During the school holidays, he explored the City of London churches, which he had already discovered in holidays from the Dragon School. He also began buying second-hand books, among them Thomas H. Shepherd's *Metropolitan Improvements* – 'steel-engravings of London in the 1820s, the sort of things that are now tinted in by watercolour and put on to dinner mats.'

> And then my eyes were opened by looking at a book called *Monumental Classic Architecture in Great Britain and Ireland* by A. E. Richardson. That was folio with whacking great sepia photographs by Bedford Lemere. Those pictures opened up a world to me that I did not know existed – that you could go beyond Sir Christopher Wren and even admire Somerset House, and still more the Greek Revival, and notice things like Waterloo Bridge, and the British Museum, and branches of the Bank of England, in the Romano-Greek style, in Bristol and Birmingham.

At Marlborough, too, John waged his first conservation campaign on behalf of the eighteenth-century grotto of Lady Hertford.* Letters sent in his Oxford days show John's continuing interest in eighteenth-century architecture. Writing to Pierce Synnott in 1927, he praised 'a beautiful baroque church at Edgware built by an eighteenth-century Duke of Chandos' and a church of 1760 at West Wycombe, where the politician Bubb Dodington, Lord Melcombe, was buried. A taste for the Georgian, let alone the Victorian, was revolutionary enough at that time. Looking back, as president of the Georgian Group, in 1969, John's friend Lord Rosse said, 'It must be remembered that the period between the wars was that of Jacobean cocktail bars and spurious Knole sofas, when Georgian buildings were dismissed as dull square boxes.' John Rennie's Waterloo Bridge was destroyed in 1934; and the destruction of Adelphi Terrace, London, an Adam building, in 1937, provoked the formation of the Georgian Group, in which John took part with Douglas Goldring, the older poet viewed by some as a proto-Betjeman.

---

* See Chapter 3, 'Marlborough'.

More than anybody else, John is credited – and rightly – with having established the taste for the Victorian; but he was not the first in the field, and his own appreciation of Victorian work was slow to develop. Harold Acton, Robert Byron and Henry Green (Henry Yorke) had all collected Victoriana before they came to Oxford; and Osbert Sitwell had indulged a similar taste before them, not only in his collections, but also, like John, in poems. In 1923 John's lifelong friend Philip Harding recorded in the minutes of the Marlborough literary society how he had read a paper on early-Victorian art and literature 'which he very aptly illustrated by passing round examples to prove to what artistic depths the Victorians had debased themselves'.

In 1932 John mounted the first of his campaigns to try to save a historic piece of architecture – Rennie's Waterloo Bridge (1810–17). He was in favour of reconditioning the bridge, and in *The Times* put forward precise, practical suggestions as to how that operation could be financed. He failed: the bridge was destroyed and a new one was designed by Sir Giles Gilbert Scott. John's defence of a pre-Victorian bridge – 'industrial architecture' – would not have jarred on de Cronin Hastings. But four months later, in an address at Painters' Hall to the Incorporated Institute of British Decorators, John made some remarks about the International Style that were distinctly 'off message'. He was only twenty-five; but his speech was reported at length in the home news pages of *The Times*. Part of the talk was wholly in line with *Architectural Review* dogma, but in a later passage John suddenly veered away from such orthodoxy and revealed what he really felt about the Modern Movement.

> After referring to the architecture of today as 'chaos', Mr Betjeman spoke pessimistically of the future. Architecture, he said, would not consist of the varying indigenous styles of a county or a country, but of one style for a continent. The increase of transport, the spread of knowledge, the universality of many materials would cause most of Europe to have the same style. We were being levelled down . . . The motor-car had become more important than the house, the petrol than a picture. In the house the sitting-room was less important than the kitchen, and artists would be required to dispense with mere ornament and create things severely of use.

John's somewhat pontifical *Times* letters of the late 1920s suggest a man implacably hostile to all things Victorian; but even then in talk with his close friends he revealed a more catholic taste. Kenneth Clark, whose pioneering book *The Gothic Revival* was published in 1928, later acknowledged that John was one of the people who had opened his eyes to Victorian architecture:

The most important name of all [in writings on Victorian architecture] will
not appear in my footnotes because his influence has not been exerted
through learned articles, but through poetry and conversation. It is that of
Mr John Betjeman, one of the few original minds of our generation. His
first interest in Gothic Revival architecture may have been part of his over-
flowing love of the neglected; but his sensitive response to architecture, as
to everything which expresses human needs and affections, allowed him to
see through the distorting fog of fashion, and to recognize the living force
of the Gothic Revival in Voysey and in Mr J. N. Comper. The changed
point of view which underlies all recent articles on nineteenth-century
architecture . . . is due directly to the stimulus of his talk; which proves once
again that history is not to be found solely in files and learned publications,
but in human contacts and in the radiation of a single personality.

In 1930, Evelyn Waugh, in his travel book *Labels*, called John 'the chief
living authority' on the *art nouveau* architecture of Antoni Gaudí. In 1933,
reprinting the 'Church's restoration' poem in *Ghastly Good Taste*, John
added: 'But it is tiresome to laugh at Victorian solecisms. It has been done
too often. For those who wish to read a far from laughable study of the
earlier part of the Gothic Revival, I can recommend Mr Kenneth Clark's
book on that subject.' Here was a distinct thawing. In 1934 John wrote to
Bryan Guinness that he was going to stay in the (Victorian Gothic)
Charing Cross Hotel, London, 'as I am very fond of it there . . .' In that
year, too, Evelyn Waugh, in *A Handful of Dust*, teasingly associated John
with the appreciation of Victorian architecture.* An appreciation of
Victorian art and architecture was among the many bonds between Waugh
and John, before differences over religion caused their rift.

On 8 February 1936, at twenty-nine, John was for the second time the
subject of a news report in *The Times*: 'OXFORD ARCHITECTURE
CRITICIZED'. In a lecture on 'Modern Oxford Architecture' he had said
that the factors which had made such a muddle of the city were antiquarianism and a desire to preserve. There was, he said, no point in preserving
'an early English arch or a squalid little block of medieval buildings' if
undergraduates were to be forced to live miles down the Iffley, Banbury
and Botley roads. Better build 'new and higher blocks of college buildings
as they did in the eighteenth century'. The buildings need not be of steel
and glass, but they could be convenient and up to date. 'Modesty and the
desire to leave everything to the specialists, without knowing who the
good specialists were, had resulted in the present architectural disasters of

* See Chapter 18, 'Farnborough'.

Oxford.' De Cronin Hastings would have had nothing to complain of in that speech.

Though John was always at his most passionate in defending the City of London, especially its churches, he had homes in the country for much of his life, and often intervened in disputes on rural issues. In July 1937 he wrote to *The Times* to support the Dowager Duchess of Norfolk, who had written to the paper about rural housing and who had asserted that 'There is a class in this country simply at the mercy of the local authority.' John agreed: council houses were too big for old-age pensioners, even if they could afford them, and old people were not strong enough to start a new garden on virgin soil. Beyond the tender concern for pensioners that the letter might suggest was probably the desire to score a point against the balefully regarded 'local authority' (the very word 'authority' was a red rag to John) and to release bile at the council houses springing up in Uffington.

By 1937, John's conversion to Victorian architecture was well advanced. In that year he warned John Summerson that the 'magnificent' Mary Ward Settlement in Tavistock Place, London, an early 1900s building by Dunbar Smith and Cecil Brewer, was to be demolished, and suggested it should be photographed. A month later he wrote to Bryan Guinness, after the Crystal Palace had burned down: 'I haven't recovered yet.'

John wrote no letters to *The Times* during the war period; he was pre-occupied, and as a civil servant could not express private views in the press without permission. Towards the end of 1948, he took a leading part in a significant controversy. On 30 October, F. T. Barrett, chairman of the parish meeting of the Berkshire village of Letcombe Bassett, wrote to *The Times* to say that a threat of such serious import hung over the village 'that it must concern all who dwell in small villages'. Letcombe Bassett, with its thatched cottages and barns, an old church, elms and beeches above water-cress beds in a gorge of the downs, was 'a singularly beautiful place'. The village appears as Cresscombe in Hardy's *Jude the Obscure*. 'Indeed [Barrett wrote], Arabella's cottage of that novel is likely to be one of the casualties in what may happen.'

Rather than build twelve new cottages and recondition the existing ones (involving main sewerage at a cost of £4,500), Wantage Rural District Council seemed disposed to take the advice of a Reading planning officer and 'disrupt the whole village community'. Its plan was to shift most of the population, against its will, to a larger neighbouring village. Letcombe Bassett would then be left as 'a few farms and associated dwellings, and a sprinkling of cottages which may, or may not, be taken by retired people, and with the church in decay'. Barrett added: 'If, instead of being one of the loveliest villages in Berkshire, Bassett were a nest of bungalows, the plan would still be sinister, for it strikes at the root of an Englishman's love of his home surroundings . . . Are all our small villages to be allowed to decay, while their luckless inhabitants are shifted to "larger units"?'

In November, Dr C. S. Orwin of The Malt House, Blewbury, Didcot, wrote to *The Times*, ridiculing the village's houses and asserting that 'there are no buildings of historical or architectural importance in Letcombe Bassett . . .' This was more than John could bear. On 3 December he wrote to *The Times*:

> I must join issue with Dr Orwin on a number of matters which arise from his letter . . . First, no purpose is served by his listing, as he does, the few modern and unattractive buildings in Letcombe Bassett and omitting the many old and humbly beautiful ones which preponderate. On the same principle, I could produce a proportionately greater list of ugly buildings in the village of Blewbury from which he writes. His final paragraph comes as a shock. He implies that because there is now no school or resident priest or 'social institution' (there *is* an excellent inn) or athletic club, therefore 150 people should be moved elsewhere. This is rather like saying that because a person who can be cured is ill, it is wiser, if it is cheaper, to kill him . . .

John applauded the Minister Lewis Silkin's statement that he was opposed to the destruction of small villages, and his assurance that the people of Letcombe would be allowed to speak for themselves at a public inquiry. On 15 December 1948 H. J. C. Neobard, Clerk of the Council at Shire Hall, Reading, wrote to *The Times*: 'In view of the publicity given to the development of this village, the planning committee of the Berkshire County Council wishes it to be known that no decision has been reached by the council as to the future planning of Letcombe Bassett.' The white flag was being shown, and Letcombe was saved.

Writing from Denchworth Manor, by Wantage, John's friend Compton Mackenzie, never one to pull his punches, started another conservation row with a letter to *The Times* on 17 September 1949.

> Is it too late for sane, decent and civilized public opinion to shame Mr Silkin into withdrawing the permission he has accorded a private company to quarry along the whole length of Dulcote Hill and thereby ruin the natural frame of the lovely city of Wells? . . . 'Progress must come before sentiment,' the Minister . . . warned . . . But why stop at the frame? Why not sell the stones of Wells Cathedral and indeed the stones of every old edifice in England which has survived the Reformation and the German blitz?

On 24 September, in response to questions in the House, Silkin said he would take legal advice to see whether he had the power to reopen the inquiry. On 1 October, J. Foster Yeoman, a director of the quarrying company in question, wrote what he no doubt intended to be a reassuring letter. This provoked one of John's most stinging attacks. He excoriated the company which intended 'to slice the top off Dulcote Hill'. Yeoman, he wrote, was 'hardly fair to those who object to such a drastic operation to a panorama so beautiful that it is of national and even dollar-earning interest'. No one had minded quarrying on Dulcote Hill for the last seventy years, because it had all been done on the side of the hill that did not face Wells. The stone was certainly very fine, but there was more elsewhere, 'all the way from Frome to the sea'. It was not true to say the shareholders had no redress. Under the Town and Country Planning Act, if quarrying were stopped, they would be compensated.

> Finally, I do not see how there can be a 'reasonable' or any other kind of 'balance between the claims of amenity and the requirements of productive industry'. As well try to balance the claims of Wells Cathedral against those of dried eggs. There can be plenty of dried eggs so long as we have hens and chemicals and factories. But there is only one Wells. So there is plenty of limestone, but only one Dulcote Hill and one Wells of which it is a part.

By 12 October 1949 the story had escalated into *The Times*'s main home news item. 'THE THREAT TO WELLS: CATHEDRAL SETTING ENDANGERED', though a *Times* reporter who visited Wells found to his surprise that 'of the 5,000 citizens of Wells, not more than a score or so really care'. The MP for Wells, Dennis Boles, who was on John's side, wrote to *The Times* on 20 December: 'It seems that in being able to mobilize public opinion early, to inform the public in time of any future threat, lies our best hope of protection.' Boles announced that a Somerset (or Wells) Protection Society was to be formed. Here was another lesson for John: prevention was better than cure. Such thinking was behind the foundation of the Victorian Society eight years later, though its founders were to learn that public opinion had to be educated before it could be mobilized.*

---

* See Chapter 24, '"Vic. Soc." and "The Dok"'.

21

Wantage

A FTER LEAVING THE Oxford Preservation Trust in 1948, John made his living for a while as a freelance journalist, contributing promiscuously to *The Strand* (magazine), *The Listener* (spin-offs from his broadcasts), the *Church Observer*, the *Evening Standard*, *The Architectural Review*, *The Countrygoer*, the *Cornhill Magazine*, *The Harrovian* (the magazine of Harrow School), *Horizon*, *The Observer*, *Leader Magazine* and *The Author*. This kind of work continued for years but became more of a sideline than a lifeline in 1949, when John wrote to T. S. Eliot, 'I have become "Literary Advazer" to *Tame and Tade* which means going in on Mondays from two-thirty till five and distributing the books.' John sometimes called himself 'literary adviser', sometimes 'literary editor' of the magazine. He succeeded the historian C. V. Wedgwood, who had been literary editor since 1943. How he got the job is not known. Under Veronica Wedgwood he was already a contributor of poems and reviews, and she may have recommended him to the magazine's formidable founder-proprietor-editor, Lady Rhondda.

Lady Rhondda founded *Time and Tide* in 1920 as an independent political and literary magazine. She was born Margaret Haig Thomas in 1883, daughter of David Alfred Thomas, a coal owner and politician. A militant suffragette, she jumped on to the running-board of Asquith's car and was roughly handled by the crowd; burned the contents of a pillar box with a chemical bomb; was sent to Usk Jail and went on hunger strike. She was returning from America with her father in the *Lusitania* in 1915 when the ship was torpedoed; both were saved, though she floated in a lifebelt three hours before being picked up unconscious. In 1918 David Thomas was created Viscount Rhondda with special remainder to his daughter 'in default of heirs male of his body'. A month later he died and Margaret inherited the title and a fortune. In a long legal dispute she claimed the right to sit in the House of Lords, an attempt which was finally defeated largely by the opposition of Lord Birkenhead.

Though she married in 1908 (Sir) Humphrey Mackworth, later the seventh baronet, of Caerleon-on-Usk, the two were amicably divorced in

1923. Lady Rhondda was widely regarded as a lesbian. She surrounded herself with others of like tastes, such as the novelist Winifred Holtby (who died young in 1935) and Theodora Bosanquet, with whom she lived. *Time and Tide*, it was said, wait for no *man*. Confusingly known as 'Bosie', Theodora Bosanquet had once been secretary to Henry James and had preceded Veronica Wedgwood as literary editor (1935–43). She was still coming into the office in John's time, arriving each morning on her motorbike dressed from head to foot in black leather. Veronica Wedgwood lived with the high-ranking civil servant Jacqueline Hope-Wallace, sister of Philip Hope-Wallace, the magazine's flamboyantly camp drama critic.

John found Lady Rhondda a difficult taskmistress, and he was not alone in that. Vera Brittain wrote glowingly of her in *Testament of Friendship*, the book in which she recalled her own intense relationship with Winifred Holtby; but when Brittain's diaries were published in 1986, almost thirty years after Lady Rhondda's death, a less flattering portrait appeared. Lady Rhondda would never allow her staff any initiative; she did not work hard enough herself, was just 'a rich leisured woman who runs the paper as a hobby'; and she had been Winifred Holtby's evil genius – 'used her time, health & energy, & gave little worth having in return for all that she took'. Holtby's letters revealed, Brittain thought, Lady Rhondda's 'selfishness and possessiveness' when, 'even in the appalling days of work & correspondence after [Holtby's] father's death she was apparently still expected to do Notes for T. & T.' John may not have been the ideal employee, but Lady Rhondda was far from being the ideal boss.

In 1949, when John arrived at the offices of *Time and Tide* in Bloomsbury Street, where the ill-starred *Decoration* had also been based, Margaret Rhondda was sixty-six. Asked what she had looked like, John described her in Seven Dwarfs terms, 'stumpy, dumpy and grumpy'. Her control over the magazine was absolute. In 1949 she seems to have allowed John little discretion, as his influence on the magazine is scarcely discernible. But from 1950 he made his presence felt in three ways: by importing his friends as reviewers, by contributing articles and poems himself, and by setting and judging imaginative literary competitions. Among the reviewers he inherited from Veronica Wedgwood was C. S. Lewis. One can only guess at the embarrassment he suffered in dealing with his hated former tutor. John did commission one review from Lewis in 1950. After that his name disappeared from the roll of contributors, which now included Gerard Irvine, Roy and Billa Harrod, Stuart Piggott, Jack Yates, Renée Haynes (Tickell), Robert Bruce Lockhart, Randolph Churchill and other friends. John was happy enough to inherit Wolf Mankowitz, who had met Veronica Wedgwood when doing research for his book on her ancestor, the potter. And John soon made friends with Rose Macaulay, whose Anglicanism was of the same dye as his own, and who also became a friend of Gerard Irvine at this time. The acute and incisive Rose Macaulay found John a somewhat woolly thinker ('one can never bring him down to exact facts', she wrote), but the two remained affectionate friends long after he left *Time and Tide*.

The years John was at *Time and Tide* were those of the Festival of Britain, the King's death and the accession and coronation of Queen Elizabeth II. There were expectations of a new English renaissance, a second Elizabethan age. The Festival of 1951 was ostensibly a commemoration of the anniversary of the Great Exhibition of 1851, but symbolically it was more: a defiant statement of Britain's recovery from war and austerity. As revealed in a long article in *Time and Tide* (5 May 1951), John's feelings about the Festival were ambivalent. The 'Crystal Palace' aspect attracted him, and he was all for having some fun. On the other hand, the Festival had been a Labour Government ('Slave State') initiative; Evelyn Waugh attacked it in prose, Noël Coward in a song. Significantly, John took only a negligible part in the Festival, though eleven years later, when asked to help with a Festival of London, he wrote amusing lyrics and performed alongside Sir John Gielgud and Tommy Steele.

On 16 June 1951, John contributed to *Time and Tide* an article unrelated to books, one of the most vitriolic things he ever wrote in prose or verse. Headed 'A Martyr to Income Tax', it was provoked by a paragraph he had read in the *News of the World*. James Morrison, a forty-nine-year-old boot-repairer, who had boasted in a public house that he was successfully 'diddling' the Inland Revenue by claiming allowances for two children he did not have and a 'dependent' mother-in-law who was dead, was reported to the authorities by one of his listeners and was jailed for four months for fraud. John wrote that this was 'a picture of such horror that I have been thinking about it ever since'.

> Let us examine the queue of stinkers lined up before us . . .
>
> Of course we do not quarrel with the law. There is obviously an Act of Parliament which enables one man to sentence another to four months' imprisonment for defrauding the State. No one questions that, just as no one questions the State's right to pay out our money for atomic research, community centres and the destruction of small village schools.
>
> Similarly we dare not challenge the Minister of Transport's right to ruin old towns with concrete lamp-standards. If we did, his PRO would be hot on our tracks. But one of the surprising things about this case is that Mr James Morrison is a boot-repairer. I have seen many men glide by me in long new

motor-cars with a wireless set in the dashboard. They were obviously not boot-repairers . . . And there are those restaurants where the waiter will buy your bill from you if you have paid in cash, and sell it to an executive who can show it in for expenses. I doubt if Mr James Morrison did that kind of thing. He was a boot-repairer. But it will not do if we have mere manual workers defrauding the State. We will have authors trying to do it next.

Though John is often accused of having been snobbish and apolitical, the emotions of this article were genuine. But his rant is not from the far left; rather it is the polemic of a Tory inveighing against the intrusive state and siding with the individual and his right to privacy, even in a public house. Still more, it is the rhetoric of a Christian denouncing the Pharisees: 'He that is without sin among you, let him first cast a stone . . .' (John 8: 7).

John was much exercised at this time by unsympathetic additions to church architecture. On 5 December 1953 he and John Piper contributed to *Time and Tide* a feature headed 'Glories of English Craftsmanship – Electricity and the Old Churches'. The illustrations, specially drawn by Piper from 'authentic examples in Buckinghamshire', showed how electrical fittings were ruining church architecture. John supplied trenchant captions.

During the years he was literary editor, several of his own poems were printed in the magazine: among them 'Original Sin on the Sussex Coast' (8 December 1951), 'Hunter Trials' (5 January 1952), the elaborate spoof of Longfellow in 'A Literary Discovery', with all its footnotes (6 December 1952) and 'Devonshire Street W.1' (8 August 1953). Young poets were encouraged, including Edward Lucie-Smith and James Kirkup, an 'out' homosexual who later won notoriety when his poem about Christ provoked Mrs Mary Whitehouse to instigate the last trial for blasphemy held in Britain.

John printed a number of Kirkup's louche verses. He failed, though, to get a poem by Tom Driberg into the magazine. Entitled 'Cycle with Masks', it was an almost parodic exercise in free verse, not unlike his 'Spring Carol' of 1927 which had been guyed (probably by John) in the *Cherwell*. In his diary of 1952, published in 1953, Driberg wrote of 'Cycle with Masks': 'I showed it to one or two friends: John Freeman was non-committal; Nye Bevan approved of it; Tony Crosland roared with laughter and said it was the greatest nonsense he had ever read.' Driberg recorded those reactions in May. Five months later, he wrote in his diary:

That unfortunate (and, no doubt, unworthy) poem, *Cycle with Masks*, having been rejected by three literary editors in quick succession, I was naturally delighted when John Betjeman said he liked it very much and asked me to let him have it for *Time and Tide* (whose literary side he helps to look after).

They kept it for some time. Then it came back, with the following remarkable letter from the editor of *Time and Tide*, Lady Rhondda:

> Dear Mr Driberg,
>
> John Betjeman has given me your poem of which he thinks highly, as does Theodora Bosanquet, to whom I showed it.
>
> But I am, I am afraid, a little worried. Our views – yours and *Time and Tide*'s – are so extremely widely divergent that I cannot feel it to be suitable that you should appear in its columns. It would seem to me really almost as unsuitable as if the Archbishop of Canterbury were to be printed in the *New Statesman*!
>
> So I am very regretfully returning it.
>
> Yours sincerely,
>
> Margaret Rhondda

To which I have replied:

> Dear Lady Rhondda,
>
> Thank you for taking the trouble to write to me personally about my poem, and for writing so candidly.
>
> I am surprised to learn your reason for rejecting the poem, for I had thought that political tests were applied to non-political writings only in Soviet Russia and possibly in some quarters in the USA. However, I suppose that such literary applications of the doctrine of infection by association are but a small part of the *Gleichschaltung* to which we are being subjected in the course of the Cold War; and, in any case, your editorial discretion is absolute.
>
> Yours sincerely
>
> Tom Driberg

This episode may well have raised, in Lady Rhondda's mind, doubts about John's judgement.

The long illness of his mother contributed to John's lowness of spirits in the *Time and Tide* years. She was the one person who had always had faith in him – 'The Only John', as she wrote on a baby-photograph of her son for Penelope. Her love was unconditional. In the autumn of 1952 she lay dying in a Bath nursing-home. John's daughter recalls: 'JB and I used to visit her together. She sat swathed in shawls, forlorn and tiny on a window seat. After our last visit she wrote to JB, "I was so glad to see you and Candida yesterday. It was very kind of you to come. Give Candida my love and tell her the eau de cologne she gave me is sprinkled on my hand-

kerchief and the scent of it wafts across the room. All love, Bess."' In the
final stages of his mother's illness, John visited her alone, staying in Bath
with John Walsham, his childhood friend from Trebetherick who worked
in the Admiralty, and his wife Sheila. He was with Bess when she died on
the evening of 13 December. He returned exhausted to the Walshams'
house. 'He sat down with a glass of whisky,' Candida writes, 'and the telephone immediately rang. (Granny Bess had been an inveterate telephoner.)
He said to Sheila, "Oh, my *God*, she's come alive again."'

Colonel Kolkhorst wrote to John on 23 December: 'I think you saw a
lot more of her latterly. That is a good thing. It will be a real consolation
to you now that you pleased her and were dutiful. Duty, I found, came a
lot into the picture on these occasions . . . As a son one is given the initiative; one has a special power to do right. Your Victorians – like the Romans
– knew this; and it fortified them . . .' But John knew he had not always
been so dutiful. After Bess's death he wrote the moving poem 'Remorse',
which ends:

> Protestant claims and Catholic, the wrong and the right of them,
>   Unimportant they seem in the face of death –
> But my neglect and unkindness – to lose the sight of them
>   I would listen even again to that labouring breath.

In his depressed mood, John felt out of tune with the magazine's earnest
political campaigning. In December 1950 he contributed a poem entitled
'The Weary Journalist', satirizing the stock of clichés on which the
magazine drew so heavily. The poem may not have been intended as
autobiographical in every detail but it is unlikely to have endeared him to
Lady Rhondda.

> Here, on this far North London height
> I sit and write and write and write.
> I pull the nothings from my head
> And weigh[t] them round with lumps of lead
> Then plonk them down upon the page
> In finely simulated rage.
> Whither Democracy? I ask
> And what the Nature of her Task?
> Whither Bulgaria and Peru?
> What Crisis are they passing through?
> Before my readers can reply
> Essential Factors flutter by
> Parlous, indeed, is their condition
> Until they find a Key Position.

A part of his job that John really enjoyed was setting some of the weekly literary competitions. One of these (29 December 1951) brought him lasting and not altogether welcome renown. Competitors were asked to add a final verse to his poem 'How to Get On in Society'. The poem, beginning 'Phone for the fish-knives, Norman', was a collection of the words and phrases that upper-class people were not supposed to use. It was already in existence in 1949, when Randolph Churchill, who had heard the first line from somebody, asked him for a copy. In his report on the *Time and Tide* competition, on 19 January 1952, John wrote that he had been 'dazzled by yards of splendid verses from over a hundred entrants'. He awarded the first prize to 'HMB' for this verse:

> Your pochette's on the pouffe by the cake-stand
> > Beneath your fur-fabric coatee.
> Now, before we remove to the study
> > Let me pass you these chocs from Paris.

John liked the way this entrant used rhyme to get in one more *faux pas*.

John's friend Nancy Mitford had started the hunt for 'social errors' in her novel *The Pursuit of Love* (1945), in which 'Uncle Matthew' (the character based on her father, Lord Redesdale) attacked the vulgarizing effects of education on Fanny's vocabulary, in particular her use of the word 'notepaper'. When John, who had once light-heartedly proposed marriage to Nancy Mitford, wrote her a fan letter about the novel in December 1945, he showed that he had read the 'notepaper' passage by joking, 'I write to tell you on this lovely *writing* paper how v. greatly I enjoyed it,' and added that Uncle Matthew was his favourite character in the book. It may well have been the 'social errors' passage in *The Pursuit of Love* that inspired him to write 'How to Get On in Society'.

In 1954 Nancy Mitford met Professor Alan Ross, a philologist from Birmingham University, who told her he was writing an article on sociological linguistics for a learned Finnish journal, to be entitled 'U and Non-U', denoting upper-class and non-upper-class usage. In 1955 she wrote an article for *Encounter* entitled 'The English Aristocracy', based on his material. 'Of course it was all a tremendous joke,' writes Mitford's biographer Selina Hastings; 'but a joke which Nancy herself more than half took seriously.'

The issue of *Encounter* sold out almost immediately. It provoked a flood of letters, newspaper articles and cartoons, and a *New Yorker* poem by Ogden Nash, 'MS Found Under a Serviette in a Lovely Home'. In 1956 Hamish Hamilton reprinted the essay in book form under the title *Noblesse*

Oblige, together with Ross's original article, John's poem, a piece by Peter Fleming ('Strix' of *The Spectator*) on 'Posh Lingo' and an open letter by Evelyn Waugh, 'To the Honble Mrs Peter Rodd [Nancy Mitford] On a Very Serious Subject'. The book was illustrated by Osbert Lancaster: John's poem faced a drawing of a 'cosy lounge' with Art Deco clock, brick 'mantelpiece', pouffe, neo-classical table-cigarette-lighter and the inevitable flying ducks on the wall. By the end of the year nearly 14,000 copies of *Noblesse Oblige* had been sold in Britain; in America 10,000 went in the first week. Nancy Mitford's sister, the Duchess of Devonshire, dismissively said: 'If it's me, it's "U"' – a quip quickly appropriated by Osbert Lancaster for a pocket cartoon of Maudie Littlehampton. The book made John's poem famous, rather to his embarrassment, as it seemed likely to link his name for ever with petty snobberies. 'JB never thought of his verses as anything but a journalistic joke,' his daughter writes. As Gertrude Stein said to Stuart Piggott and John, 'not one of my *major* works'.

Towards the end of 1953, Lady Rhondda invited him to lunch (U: 'luncheon') at the Caprice restaurant in Arlington Street, St James's, where a table was permanently reserved for her. Over the coffee, she told him he was fired. In her forthright way, she probably thought she was doing the right thing in breaking the news to him herself, rather than delegating the task to some underling; but John felt ambushed and humiliated. Relations between them had been deteriorating for some time. John had enlivened the magazine, but circulation had not risen. When asked later why she had dismissed John, she said that the reviews he commissioned never came in on time or to length or about the right books. A woman sub-editor who worked on the magazine with John and liked him thought that the last straw may have been an exchange which she overheard between the proprietress and the literary editor.

'Mr Betjeman!'
'Yes, Lady Rhondda?'
'I want to give the magazine a more European flavour.'
'Oh, so do I, Lady Rhondda, and you will be glad to hear that I have just ordered a review of a book on the architecture of fourteenth-century Spanish monasteries.'

That was not what Lady Rhondda had in mind at all.

In 1956 John wrote a poem entitled 'Caprice' about being fired from *Time and Tide*. In 1957, as a visiting professor in Cincinnati, Ohio, he recited it to a party of academics under the seal of silence. When the poem was first published, the last six lines were omitted as, in John's words, 'too strong meat'; they have since been restored to the version in the *Collected Poems*.

Caprice *

I sat only two tables off from the one I was sacked at,
      Just three years ago,
And here was another meringue like the one which I hacked at
      When pride was brought low
And the coffee arrived – the place which she had to use tact at
      For striking the blow.

'I'm making some changes next week in the organization
      And though I admire
Your work for me, John, yet the need to increase circulation
      Means you must retire:
An outlook more global than yours is the qualification
      I really require.'

O sickness of sudden betrayal! O purblind Creator!
      Oh friendship denied!
I stood on the pavement and wondered which loss was the greater—
      The cash or the pride.
Explanations to make to subordinates, bills to pay later
      Churned up my inside.

I fell on my feet. But what of those others, worse treated,
      Your memory's ghosts,
In gloomy bed-sitters in Fulham, ill-fed and unheated,
      Applying for posts?
Do they haunt their successors and you as you sit here repleted
      With entrées and roasts?

After Lady Rhondda's death, *Time and Tide* limped along under different proprietors. In 1965 Anthony Lejeune said in a BBC talk on weekly magazines that it was 'weirdly changed'. In February 1977 the once feminist publication was relaunched as 'The Business Man's Weekly Newspaper'. It survived only until July 1979.

In the summer of 1951 the Betjemans had completed their move from Farnborough to The Mead, their new house in Wantage. Their friend Douglas Woodruff, who lived not far off at Abingdon, believed that The Mead stood on the site of the palace of King Alfred the Great, whose axe-brandishing statue by Queen Victoria's nephew, Count Gleichen, dominates the town's market square. But there was nothing ancient about the

---

* A restaurant in Arlington House [John Betjeman's footnote].

house. In moving to it, John was certainly practising what he preached. With its Gothic gables and bargeboarded porch, it was almost a caricature of the kind of Victorian building he was famous for admiring.

The house came with seven acres of land, later increased to nine before Penelope began selling off fields to pay for the upkeep of her ponies. There were nineteenth-century stables. At the entrance to the drive was a Victorian lodge where Mr Gardner lived, the Betjemans' part-time chauffeur. Dick Squires, the son of their neighbour Dr Vaughan Squires, noticed that the usually genial John was sometimes 'horrid' to Gardner.

> There was a very naughty side to John. When he got annoyed, he could be very unkind to what you might call 'the humble folk' – and I was very much surprised at this. Once he and I were going to lunch somewhere in Smithfield Market, and an innocent little chap in the car park told him where to park his car. John suddenly went almost white with rage.
>
> It was partly to do with cars, I think – letting off his resentment of having to rely on motor cars and his intense dislike of anything mechanical. And Gardner, who was very loyal to the Betjemans, drove one of those old shooting-brakes . . . 'half-timbered cars', as John's friend Barry Humphries once said. Gardner was a lovely chap . . . but if things weren't going well and John got rattled, he used to be very unkind and . . . [call him] 'that fool Gardner!' and so on.

Also on the estate was a cottage known as The Gogs, where Mr O'Brien, the Betjemans' gardener, lived with his family. As well as looking after the grounds, O'Brien did odd jobs about the house. Unlike Gardner, he did not suffer in silence when John became autocratic.

> I used to clean his shoes [he recalled] . . . When [he] came home, if he was in a little bit of a hurry, he never undone the shoelaces . . . So I cleaned the shoes and sent them back with the shoelaces still done up. He said to me one day, 'O'Brien, you never undone me shoelaces.' I turned round and said, 'Mr Betjeman, if you'm too bloody lazy to do it, *I'm* not going to do it.'

The Squires were already friends of the Betjemans. The Letcombe Brook, mentioned by John in two of his poems about Wantage, separated The Mead's ground from the Squires' garden. Dr Vaughan Squires was fifty-six in 1951, his wife Ottilie twelve years younger. He had become the Betjemans' doctor when they lived at Farnborough. 'My husband went up to Farnborough to see Candida once,' Ottilie remembered, 'when Candida was still riding quite a small pony, and he had to examine her throat while she was sitting on the pony, because Penelope said she didn't want to lift her off and on again.' Dr Squires shared Penelope's love of horses. Their two children, Dick and Judy, were, respectively, about the same age as Paul and Candida.

It has been said of the second Earl of Ashburnham, an ancestor of Swinburne, that 'he gravitated naturally to the rich'. The same could fairly be said of John and Penelope. Their greatest friends, among the local land-owners, were the Loyds of Lockinge and the Barings of Ardington. The Loyds' fortune came from the Victorian S. J. Loyd, later Lord Overstone, a self-made banker from Northampton. His daughter developed an exist-ing Georgian house into a vast mansion of geometric brickwork, and was, with over 20,000 acres, the largest landowner in Berkshire. The Betjemans became friends with Christopher ('Larch') Loyd of Betterton House – in 1944, the largely Victorian house had been demolished – and his sisters Hester ('Heck') and Catherine ('Ag').

Hester remembered her first encounter with Penelope. She 'brought Paul over when he was a baby; and she suddenly decided to breast-feed him. I had never seen that done, in a drawing-room. Then she proceeded to give my mother a tremendous lecture on that aspect of life, and I remember sitting there with my jaw gaping.' John struck her as equally out of the ordinary when she met him at dinner-parties. 'If he was really amused by something, he'd pick up the table-napkin and throw it over his face, shrieking away underneath it.'

Mollie and Desmond Baring, who were of much the same age as the Betjemans, lived at Ardington House, an assured baroque building of 1719–20 by Thomas Strong. Mollie Baring had been at RADA with Vivien Leigh and could do an imitation of Penelope almost as life-like as Joyce Grenfell's. Her father was the successful racehorse-owner Ben Warner, who also founded the Queen's Hotels Group (later taken over by Moat Houses). Desmond Baring, related to the banking Barings, ran the hotels group for his father-in-law.

The Betjemans were still at Farnborough when the Barings first encountered them. During the move to Wantage, Candida stayed at Ardington House and became great friends with the Barings' daughter Anne, whom John always called 'Arne', after Dr Arne who wrote 'Rule Britannia'. Paul was a friend of the Barings' sons, Peter and Nigel. As for their parents, Mollie felt it was 'a friendship that absolutely "went" – sur-prisingly, because we were not in John's world at all'.

> We were at that time very much in the racing world; and even Penelope, though she loved horses, was not interested in racing. But we all got on so well . . . We saw each other almost every day . . . I don't think [John] ever

got off the train at Didcot without calling in at Ardington. We spent about twenty Christmases together.

By the mid-1950s, Anne (later Dalgety) recalled, the two families had become 'so intertwined that no important decision could be made in either household, without consultation with the other'.

Through his catering contacts, Desmond was able to obtain exceptional wines. 'Oh, a Margaux! It never lets one down,' John wrote to him after a gift of a magnum. He created a comic persona for Desmond. Mollie Baring recalled: 'John had the theory that the more drink he and Desmond had, the gayer he himself would become, but Dezzie would get quieter and quieter. And once John got hold of something like that, he never let go. He would look across the table at me and say, "It's going marvellously, darling – Dezzie hasn't said a word." It was a running joke . . .' Penelope, who stuck to ginger beer, was very disapproving about the drinking. After one dinner she said John smelt of 'dead codskins', opened all his whisky bottles and poured the contents down the sink.

On 6 December 1951, John wrote to his BBC friend George Barnes: 'My new friend Elizabeth Cavendish is just our kind of girl. She is as bracing and witty and kind and keen on drink as Anne [Barnes's wife]. I long for you to meet her.' Lady Elizabeth Cavendish, then twenty-five, was a daughter of the tenth Duke of Devonshire. She and John had first met on 29 May, at a London dinner party held by Lady Pamela Berry. John had known Lady Pamela for over twenty years as she was the sister of his Oxford friend Freddy Birkenhead. She often invited him to dinner, *sans* Penelope, and usually asked him to sing for his supper by reciting some of his poems. John thought it as well to keep in with her, as her husband Michael (later Lord Hartwell) had great power at the *Daily Telegraph*, for which John began reviewing books that year. Neither John nor Elizabeth thought that the dinner-party in Lord North Street was going to be anything more than the usual agreeable mix of the Berrys' artistic, literary and political friends; but to historians of espionage that evening is counted as a critical moment in the dénouement of a great scandal. Among the other guests were Anthony Blunt, who by now was Director of the Courtauld Institute of Art; Sydney Butler, wife of the politician R. A. Butler; and Isaiah Berlin. Also expected for dinner was another friend of John's, the diplomat Guy Burgess. These people were loosely linked in an Establishment mesh: R. A. Butler, John and Blunt had all been at Marlborough; the Courtauld Institute was named after Sydney Butler's father, Sir Samuel Courtauld; Blunt and Burgess had been together at

Trinity College, Cambridge, where a kinsman of R. A. Butler had earlier been Master; and Michael Berry and Burgess had been friends at Eton, where Berry had tried to get him elected to the exclusive Eton Society – 'Pop' – but had failed because 'The majority simply "preferred not to have him".' Now, twenty years on, Burgess had asked Berry to give him a dinner-party and a job on the *Telegraph*. In his book *The Climate of Treason* (1979), Andrew Boyle wrote in all innocence:

> The press lord had intended to tell Guy over dinner . . . that there would be no immediate opening for him on the staff of the *Daily Telegraph*. When Blunt . . . had arrived, alone and rather downcast, having waited in vain for Burgess to join him at the Reform Club as arranged, Hartwell said lightly that their friend was not noted for his punctuality. They lingered, and there was an empty place at table when they sat down thoughtfully to dine. Blunt evidently did not enjoy the meal. He appeared sickly, pale and increasingly distraught. Suddenly he got up and said apologetically: 'I feel I must go now and look for him.'
>
> Only the day before, Blunt had dismissed with disdainful logic the theorizing of Goronwy Rees about the likely destination of Burgess. Hartwell learnt later that the eminent art critic and connoisseur, prostrated by his unavailing efforts to solve the mystery of Guy's disappearance, had taken to his bed, sick with anxiety.

On 25 May, four days before the dinner-party, Burgess had left England with Donald Maclean, another diplomat spying for the Russians, who was due to be interrogated by MI6 on the 28th. We now know that, by the day of the dinner, Blunt was not only fully aware of Burgess's defection, but had managed to scoop up two incriminating letters from his flat. Blunt's distress at dinner – Hartwell recalled that he 'went noticeably white' – may be ascribed to his fear that MI6 would now turn the heat on him. As Burgess's close friend, he was bound to fall under suspicion, perhaps be exposed as a spy.

Somewhat off-target as it now seems, Boyle's account at least shows how things appeared to the Berrys and their guests on 29 May. Oblivious of any historical undercurrents, John and Elizabeth gazed at each other. 'They did not speak to each other that night,' writes Candida Lycett Green, 'nor did they need to. It only took seconds . . . for JB and Elizabeth to know that they had fallen in love.' Here, love was not blind, but dumb.

In that year, Lady Elizabeth had become a lady-in-waiting to Princess Margaret. She was just three days younger than the Queen; her mother had been a childhood friend of the Queen Mother, and Elizabeth had known the two princesses since children's parties at 145 Piccadilly. ('It can't have been easy for Princess Elizabeth,' she commented in a television programme about the Queen in 2001, 'always being curtseyed to, and with everybody falling silent when she entered the room.') Princess Margaret's biographer writes of Elizabeth Cavendish: 'Like Princess Margaret, she had also been brought up in palaces with chilly State rooms beneath painted Verrio ceilings . . . and, like Margaret, she set little store by such trappings.'

We catch a flamelit glimpse of Elizabeth in adolescence, in a letter of 1943 from Kathleen 'Kick' Kennedy, sister of the future American President, to her father, Joseph P. Kennedy, describing a London party attended by Irving Berlin:

> The party ended at 1.00 . . . However we had an incident before it was all over. Lord Edward Fitzmaurice, a young Guardsman of 21, had rather too much to drink and set a match to Elizabeth Cavendish's new evening dress. She is Billy [Lord Hartington]'s younger sister and it was the first party she had ever been to so we were all afraid it might have scared her away from other parties. She stayed on and told her mother, 'before I was set on fire the boys didn't pay much attention to me, but afterwards I was very popular. An American boy put the flames out' . . . Angie Laycock said that she said to her brave husband Gen Laycock 'why didn't you do something about putting those flames out?' He replied, 'I thought it was a firework display.'

Kick Kennedy married Lord Hartington; Elizabeth tried to console her when he was shot and killed by a sniper in Belgium in 1944. She later recalled:

> I never met anyone so desperately unhappy in my life. I had to sleep in her room night after night. Her mother had tried to convince her that she had committed a sin in this marriage, so that in addition to losing her husband, she worried about losing her soul.

Elizabeth became a friend of John F. Kennedy too; in 1948 Kennedy met Kick at Lismore, the Duke of Devonshire's estate in Co. Waterford; shortly afterwards, Kennedy fell ill with Addison's Disease in London, and Elizabeth visited him. The three vignettes from Elizabeth's youth reveal something of her character: her sang-froid and ability to deal with an emergency; her sense of humour; her enjoyment of attention from young men; and her compassion. All were brought into play in her long relationship with John.

The day after the dinner-party in Lord North Street, Pamela Berry rang Elizabeth to tell her the sensational news of Burgess's disappearance. She also mentioned that she was trying to get John to take a trip to Copenhagen on the Camroses' yacht *Virginia*. She added that he was unhappy, that 'his marriage was going wrong' and that he would come on the yacht only if she came too. Elizabeth agreed to join the party. Alan Pryce-Jones, by now editor of the *Times Literary Supplement*, was also on board with his wife Poppy. 'It is often said that John hates "abroad",' Pryce-Jones said in 1976, 'but I can tell you he certainly didn't hate "abroad" on that voyage!' After that, John's friends had to get used to the idea that, although he and Penelope were still together, he had 'found someone else'. How serious the affair was became clear in 1952 when he took Elizabeth, not Penelope, on holiday with the Barneses in France.

In *Summoned by Bells* (1960), John wrote of his childhood love for a little girl in Highgate, adding:

> . . . all my loves since then
> Have had a look of Peggy Purey-Cust.

Comparing photographs of Peggy as a child and Elizabeth as she was when John met her, one can see that both had the same kind of patrician good looks, with fair hair and a slight natural frown in the set of the eyes. John nicknamed Elizabeth 'Feeble' (or 'Phoeble') because she wasn't – rather as short men get called 'Lofty'. He liked dominant women, but it amused him to keep up a teasing pretence that Elizabeth was shy, nervous and ineffectual. 'Come and meet the palest, wispiest, least-known lady-in-waiting in the world,' he wrote to a friend. Because Elizabeth was tall and willowy, and Princess Margaret was not, John referred to the Princess as 'Little Friend'. Elizabeth could be very winning and had a varied set of friends, including the Bohemian, slightly raffish group known as 'the Princess Margaret set'. But a word sometimes used to describe her was 'reserved', and her reserve could be misconstrued as coolness or hauteur. The American critic Edmund Wilson, who admired John's poetry, was told by him at a London party in 1954 that he had invited 'a jolly girl' to join them. 'This turned out to be some titled lady,' Wilson wrote in his diary. 'She did not seem particularly jolly.'

Not all John's friends welcomed his new romance. 'Is it not about time you gave your heart a rest, for a little while, anyway?' Colonel Kolkhorst asked in 1951. 'You have been at it non-stop now for I don't know how many donkeys' years. It is not good for you.' Some friends, who loved and were loyal to Penelope, were frosty towards Elizabeth. At first, Penelope herself was not too concerned. 'John had had crushes before,' she said in 1976. 'But always, I met those girls, they became my friends too and somehow that sort of "defanged" the thing and John lost interest after a while. But with Elizabeth it was different. She just wouldn't agree to see me.'

Penelope's friends were not the only people who looked with disfavour on John's relationship with Elizabeth. Some of her own friends and relations saw her as 'throwing away her life' on a married man twenty years her senior. She had not been without admirers – among them Evelyn Waugh's brother-in-law Auberon Herbert. Iris Murdoch and John Bayley recalled how, when they had stayed with Elizabeth's uncle Lord David Cecil, at Cranborne, Dorset, in the early 1950s, he had expressed disapproval of the liaison. It is likely that her nearer relations, too, were less than happy with the situation. But, as with John's relations with the Chetwodes in the 1930s, he was able to disarm criticism and to win over his detractors. Dick Squires remembered David Cecil rolling up to The Mead in a Bentley, about 1953. 'Penelope was weeding in the drive, pulling up dandelions in her jodhpurs, when he arrived. "My God, David! I'd completely forgotten you were coming to lunch. I must finish this weeding. Can you possibly scramble some eggs?" And there was poor Lord David, who had probably never cooked an egg in his life, having to go into the kitchen. Luckily, John was there and helped him.' The Devonshires were soon placated, too. John had known the Duchess, the former Deborah Mitford, since the days when he had proposed marriage to two of her sisters. He also made a hit with the Dowager Duchess, Elizabeth's mother, whose house at Edensor, Derbyshire, 'was like another home' for him. She enjoyed talking to him about the pomps of the 'old days'. In October 1951 Evelyn Waugh wrote to Nancy Mitford: 'Betjeman has the flu and has retired to the house of the Dowager Duchess of Devonshire where he is waited on & washed by Lady Elizabeth while the high-church butler reads *The Unlucky Family* aloud to him. Meanwhile he has sold Penelope's house & purchased a villa in the centre of Wantage – "Oh the joy of being back in real suburbia old boy" – and has left Penelope quite unaided to make the move.'

When John was with Elizabeth, she ministered to his comfort in a way that Penelope rarely did. Penelope could cook superbly, but most visitors to The Mead had to take pot luck. The episode of Lord David and the scrambled eggs was not unusual. Life at The Mead was often chaotic. In August 1953 Lady Silvia Combe, Penelope's old schoolfriend whom she called 'Cackle', visited her there. Shortly afterward she wrote an account. Although John was away at the time, this vignette is an unrivalled evocation of everyday life in the Betjeman ménage. As Lady Silvia arrived at the house, a man was turning into the drive with a yapping pekinese in his car. 'The Warden' (John Sparrow), who was staying and hated dogs, told her he wished she had run over Marco Polo and added: 'I was asked to lunch by Penelope before being given a jumping lesson, but she only appeared at *three*, there was no horse, and the entire afternoon has been spent transporting to and from the timber yard enormous planks of wood to make wings for her gymkhana jumps.' Sparrow took Lady Silvia's case up to what he guessed would be her room, but warned, 'For goodness sake don't leave your hairbrush lying about on the dressing table. Last time I was here the daughter of the house cut all the bristles off mine, and with my own nail scissors, what's more!'

The sound of a car stopping and a piercing shriek from the drive, 'Gina, fare mangiare alle anitre!', announced the return of Penelope, who, on seeing Lady Silvia, said, 'God, I quite forgot you were coming today, but it's nice to see you, Cackle.' (Gina was a new maid. The garbled Italian was intended to mean 'Go and feed the ducks!') They went into the dining-room.

> The table was devoid of cups and the usual paraphernalia associated with afternoon tea. Instead a charming young lady was already seated there, with Bible and prayer books laid out before her. 'Oh God!' said Penelope. 'I quite forgot you were coming for your Catechism lesson. However, as you're here, you can help get the tea and also milk Clara. Gina won't give us any tea today, as she's always cross on wash day, and John's had his four Frog cousins to stay for the weekend so she'll be crosser than ever.'
>
> A loaf of bread was suddenly hurled through the hatch, the catechist miraculously produced some cups and a tiny pot of tea. Half a Swiss roll and two partially nibbled biscuits were pulled by Penelope out of the pocket of her milking smock (which I felt would not exactly match the standards set by the Milk Marketing Board for their country-fresh dairy maids). 'I saved these from the W.I. [Women's Institute] tea,' she said. 'In these days one simply can't afford to waste anything.'

They had hardly begun eating when Mr Levy arrived, a 'grey-faced, grey-suited' musician who had been examining the girls of St Mary's School, Wantage, on their piano-playing. 'Mr Levy sat down, and after eyeing the two half nibbled biscuits, the *passé* Swiss roll and the khaki-coloured tea, said that he'd already had tea, thank you.'

> Not another remark did he make except when asked whether he didn't miss the Stones very much who'd left his neighbourhood. 'No, why should I?' he replied. 'I left Newbury two years ago. Why does *everyone* think I live there still?' he plaintively added. This temporarily silenced the conversation until Penelope looked at me and burst into uncontrollable giggles. 'Do have some cake, Cackle, it's delicious,' she said, and on seeing my hesitation, the Warden put in, 'You'd better, you won't get any dinner tonight, judging by my lunch.' Penelope shrieked, 'What do you mean? Cackle will have a delicious dinner, we've got a riding mistress coming who's so mean, she only

eats when she's asked out, and I've ordered *Uove in Purgatorio.*' 'John's got a book about Purgatory by his bed,' said the Warden musingly.

Suddenly Penelope remembered that Clara had yet to be milked and the religious instruction still to be administered, so she said, 'Now you'd better all go home, the Warden must give Mr Levy a lift in that precious car of his, and Cackle must help with the cows, although she's too incompetent to milk them.' 'My car doesn't happen to be going in Mr Levy's direction,' said the Warden firmly and, as we all thought, quite finally. 'Then,' said Mr Levy with a sudden startling display of spirit, 'if your car does not intend to travel in my direction, *it must be coaxed to do so!*'

Visiting the Betjemans for a day or so could be stimulating, but being their neighbour could be more testing. 'We were all very fond of Penelope,' said Ottilie Squires, 'but I don't think I've ever known anybody who could use other people so much.'

She was so bright, she found just running the house was boring. So she gave lectures or went out in a pony-trap. Somehow she always needed your help more than you needed hers. She used to palm off Candida on us. Candida, who was older than my youngest, could be delightful; but she could also do everything she could to upset – like when nanny went to get the pudding course from the kitchen downstairs Candida would put stew on the chair, that sort of thing.

Dick Squires also remembered Candida's naughtiness. 'One day my sister came in with wet knickers and my old man said, "Why have you wet your knickers?" "Well, Candida told me to."' He also remembered Candida's bloodcurdling threat to Georgie Sale.

The Sales were our other next-door neighbours – on the opposite side of us from the Betjemans [he explained] . . . There were two elder boys and then Georgie, who drove us all mad, always knew the answer to everything. But he was terrorized by Candida. At a children's party we held, he came up looking very frightened and said, 'Ottilie (he always copied his parents in calling my parents by their Christian names), please help me, Candida and her friends say they are going to hang me.'

Mollie Baring recalled: 'Anne had had a bad go of 'flu and Vaughan Squires came over to see her. I said to him, "I think Candida's coming over," and he said, "Well, if she can stand Candida she must be well, she can take any-body." Candida used to do *such* naughty things. Perhaps it was because she did not get enough attention from either of her parents.'

'I'm sure it came as a shock to John, sometimes, to realize he'd *got* chil-dren,' said Ottilie Squires. 'That was the impression I got. The children rather did what they liked and then suddenly Penelope would realize that things were getting out of hand and she'd say, "Breakfast at eight o'clock; you've got to be down and you've got to make your beds and tidy your bedrooms." But it never lasted for more than about two weeks, and then they'd slip back into the old ways.'

Now that the children were growing up, John became more interested in them. Though he was satirical about the horse world, he was proud when Candida won prizes on her pony Dirk and amused when asked by a Post Office assistant whether he was related to the little girl who was carrying off all the trophies. He took her sketching and was pleased when Miss Wimpress, the art teacher at St Mary's, Wantage, complimented her on her drawing. He went to the cinema with the children; Candida remembers his explaining the plot of *The Third Man* (1949). Every Christmas holiday he took them to see the Crazy Gang. Every summer he drove them down to Trebetherick for two weeks. On the way down, he fumed behind long-distance lorries and stopped at nearly every church. One year he tried surfing but realized on emerging from the sea that he had lost his trunks. He walked up the beach with the surfboard held in front of him and Candida walking behind him, both helpless with laughter.

Paul was at Eton much of the time. He was embarrassed when his father turned up at the school in his usual harum-scarum clothes, sometimes to give poetry readings. John was mortified when told about this and tried to look smarter. Paul's housemaster, Oliver Van Oss, had been at Magdalen with John and had acted with him in college plays. 'Paul's reports are good, he is an entertaining and independent boy with a clear mind, rather too clear at times,' Van Oss wrote to John in 1952. 'He likes things to be definite. He proved a hopeless library fag and was dethroned for casualness, etc. He has also become rather a good footballer. Very much of a character is Betjie and I value his presence a lot.' In the school holidays Paul saw a lot of Dick Squires, who was about the same age.

> Paul was keen on jazz at that time, and so was I [Squires recalled]. He was always one stage ahead of me in liking a different form of jazz . . . It was the Brubeck Storyville concert that first got me hooked, but Paul was one stage more advanced in liking Coltrane, Miles Davis and so on . . . We used to play music for hours. We had a huge old-fashioned gramophone with a horn up in the hay-loft. One was able to put hawthorn spikes into it as needles.

London, always a lure to John, was made yet more tempting by the chance to be with Elizabeth Cavendish; and in 1954 he rented a London flat.* But he did his best to fit into Wantage life. He became a church-warden at the Church of St Peter and St Paul, 'the Cathedral of the Vale', and a governor of Candida's school. He opened church bazaars. In 1953 he took part in a Coronation Pageant organized by Penelope and filmed by Tommy Clyde, father of the actor Jeremy Clyde. And he appeared in local Brains Trusts held in St Mary's School and the Corn Exchange, both as a question-master and as a panellist. One question was, 'Would the panel prefer to look clever and be stupid, or look stupid and be clever?' John replied that he would rather look stupid and be clever. A voice from the audience: 'Your wish is granted!'

The Betjemans were usually short of money. John and Penelope were both extravagant in their own ways: he in travelling first-class to London and back, and paying for expensive lunches; she in keeping her ponies and buying carts. Penelope decided she must think of ways to make extra money. First she set up as a duck-farmer, but 'It was never really a paying concern.' The Betjemans' next venture was John's idea.

> John gets manias for people [Penelope said in 1978]. He got a mania for a very sad married couple in Wantage, Peter and Dorothy Martin. Mr Martin was a failed actor who dealt in a small way in antiques and she was rather lit-erary and had a lending library, 6d a book. And she wasn't making much money because the county library had started and people were getting their books free, so naturally they weren't going to pay poor Dorothy her six-pences for the lending library. So John suggested that he and they should start a sort of cafeteria in conjunction with the books, which was what the Newman Bookshop in Oxford was doing very successfully. John rented an upstairs room from the chemist who lived on the opposite side of the road. It was in a funny little long building on a sort of island site. Dorothy had the ground floor and the chemist had most of the upstairs floor and John man-aged to rent just one end, where the cooking would be done. They called the café 'King Alfred's Kitchen', and John was a director of it.

Penelope, who was still running the duck farm, did not want to get involved with the café.

> However, the trouble was that neither John nor the Martins knew the first thing about cooking – but, I mean, not the first *thing* . . . They only had a tiny electric stove meant for a family of two; it was just hopeless. One day I went in to have lunch and I said, 'Dorothy, what's for lunch today?' And she said, 'Oh, I couldn't care less; ask Mary' – the cook upstairs. In point of

---

* See Chapter 22, 'Cloth Fair and Rotherhithe'.

fact there was nothing but Spam salad with a lot of rather dirty lettuce. I was getting very worried about it. It was bad for our reputation in Wantage.

After the restaurant had been open for almost a year, Penelope offered – 'Dorothy was looking very drawn and worried' – to run it for a fortnight while she took a holiday. It was agreed that Dorothy would go away on her own.

> I found to my great surprise and horror that they were buying nut-and-date loaves on the opposite side of Wantage market square, a cake shop, and removing the trade labels and selling them in King Alfred's Kitchen as home-made. And I said to John, 'This is going to be a scandal – you are one of the leading Anglicans in England' . . . And he got in an absolute panic.

The Martins resigned. 'But then I realized the full horror of the situation: which was, that John had got a "repairing lease" of twenty-one years, of which only seven years had elapsed while the Martins had their library. It was a most appalling prospect.' The Betjemans bought a commercial gas stove and new tables and chairs. There was a grand reopening in 1956 by Father Trevor Huddleston, who had recently become the most famous Church of England priest (the sacerdotal equivalent of C. S. Lewis in the laity) with the publication of his book *Naught for your Comfort*, exposing the malevolence of apartheid in South Africa. With Penelope in charge of the kitchen, the restaurant became a meeting-place for Wantage folk and a popular rendezvous for undergraduates motoring out from Oxford. 'Everything was beautifully done,' recalled Kathleen Philip, a local historian who helped out in the café. 'You used to get a "King Alfred Special" – ice cream, nuts and burnt sugar, with chocolate sauce in little pots.'

There was the odd mistake; two scones were burned black. Penelope put them into the window with a label: 'Original cakes burnt by King Alfred the Great'. Dick Squires recalled a day when Penelope had been cooking sausages for late breakfasts. 'And you know what a frying-pan looks like when you've done a lot of frying and haven't changed the fat. Well, a vicar ordered an omelette and he sent it back to the kitchen with a note on the plate that said: "Please will you do me another omelette. This one looks as if it has been cooked in a coal-scuttle."'

At its best, the cooking was exceptionally good; but Penelope periodically went on foreign tours, leaving the catering to others. In any case, she wearied of the 'caff'. 'She was always too busy,' Mollie Baring said. 'The worst period for all her friends was the café. She got very tired, very irritable, and she and John lost a lot of money on it.' Candida remembers that her father 'complained about the funds he had to keep pouring into the "caff"'. For a long time the repairing lease deterred people from taking it off the Betjemans' hands. 'I felt it was going to be a millstone round our necks for ever,' Penelope said.

Both John and Penelope still allowed themselves some extravagances. He bought a new Peugeot 203 estate car – 'the first and last smart car we ever owned', Candida writes. Penelope acquired first a Vespa motor-scooter, then a 500cc Norton motor-bike. Even she came to realize that the motor-bike was too powerful for her; but Paul enjoyed riding it. Dick Squires recalled:

> Paul was riding the bike one day when he saw a car come out of a drive. It drove straight into the road in front of him. He went into the side of it, doing some body damage to the bike but not hurting himself. The car belonged to Father Wixted, the Irish Roman Catholic priest in Wantage with whom Penelope had quarrelled – she went to services in Hendred instead.
>
> At the court hearing the judge said, 'Did you not see Father Wixted in the entrance of his drive, and why did you not slow down?'
>
> Paul replied: 'I certainly saw a car, but did not know it was Father Wixted. Knowing what a reputation he has in a motor car, if I had known it was him I would not only have slowed down but I would have got off my motor-cycle and walked.'

Paul was coming to the end of his time at Eton. Unlike his father, he excelled in gymnastics. Van Oss wrote to John in the Lent term of 1955: 'Paul has an alert and critical mind . . . I mean that he gets the answers right, but seems desperately anxious to leave next half [that is, term]. He is vividly aware that his parents are unusual and gifted people, with strongly individual personalities. This makes him watchful and wary even in religious matters. He very much wants to be himself and not JB's son. It may be an argument against Oxford, I don't know . . .' This was a wise and prophetic assessment; but in discussing Paul's future another factor had to be taken into account. In the mid-1950s, every fit young male had to do two years' National Service in the armed forces. On John's fiftieth birthday (28 August 1956) he wrote a long letter to Penelope, heading it 'The 50th birthday of a failure'. Penelope had written to him about Paul and about The Mead. John addressed them 'in order of importance', putting 'The Powlie' first. He thought there was no harm in Paul's sitting an entrance examination to an Oxford college while waiting to be called up.

> Trinity might be able to take him now. But if you think, & I'm inclined to think with you if you do, that National Service in a good regiment w^d be the making of him, then even if the P[owlie] passes the exam to Trinity, he

should do national service first. I don't think this is a decision we should leave to him. We should make it ourselves.

It is curious to find John, never gung-ho or instinct with *esprit de corps*, suggesting that army service could be the 'making' of his son; odder still to find one who rebelled against an authoritarian father, intent on deciding for his nineteen-year-old son what was best for him. But the birthday letter shows that John had gone to some trouble on Paul's behalf. He had written to Michael Hornby, Michael Balcon and Sylvester Gates, as 'three representative business men', to ask whether they thought an Oxford degree was a help in getting a job in business, 'as the Powlie, though not an academic type, will have to earn its own living'. In the event, Paul did his National Service, then went to Oxford.

On 31 August 1956 John published a *cri de coeur* in the *Spectator* column he was by then writing:

> This week I had my fiftieth birthday. I had felt it coming on for some time. Standing nude in the bathroom two months ago, I suddenly realized I could not see my toes any more because my stomach was in the way. I started reviewing my past life first through a magnifying mist of self-pity – never quite made the grade, not taken seriously by the *Times Literary Supplement*, Penguin Books, the Courtauld, the Warburg, the *Listener*, the University Appointments Board, the Museums Association, the Library Association, the Institute of Sanitary Engineers. I thought of the many people at school with me who were now knights and politicians. I wanted to cry. Then I thought of my many friends who are now dead, and terror of eternity made me want to scream.

It is the mark of a poet that he can express what he feels more powerfully in a few lines of verse than in several of prose. In a poem about Archibald, John wrote:

> The bear who sits above my bed
>   More agèd now he is to see,
> His woollen eyes have thinner thread,
>   But still he seems to say to me,
> In double-doom notes, like a knell:
>   'You're half a century nearer Hell.'

22

Cloth Fair and Rotherhithe

IN 1945 THE Oxford historian A. L. Rowse suggested to John the idea for what was to be his best prose book. John wrote to Jock Murray from Oxford on 6 February 1945: 'I have made the acquaintance of A. L. Rowse since I have been here and I find that he thinks a lot of my work. He says I ought to publish the broadcasts, articles &c I have written on topography and architecture in a single illustrated volume. He says it would sell like hot cakes. What do you think?' Murray replied that he thought the plan was a good one. Surprisingly, however, considering the eagerness of both these letters, nothing further was heard or done about the 'collected prose' project for three years. It became clear to Murray that, for John, gathering together his broadcasts and articles was a chore with little appeal. It would not get done unless somebody else did it. So he volunteered the services of his secretary, who wrote off to the *Daily Express*, the *New Statesman*, *The Architectural Review* and other magazines to which John had contributed, asking for their help in listing his pieces. But there seems still to have been no hurry on anyone's part.

In November 1951 Myfanwy Piper was brought in to make the final selection of articles and broadcasts, to save John from the anguish of 'murdering his own babies'. She also thought of a title for the book – *First and Last Loves*. John Piper made drawings of Nonconformist chapels and designed the dust-jacket. In April 1952 John wrote an introduction to the book. Headed 'Love is Dead', it reflected his depressed state of mind at the time.

Publication was finally achieved on 10 September 1952. Jock Murray sent 'birthday greetings' for that day: 'I know you are a little nervous and off-hand about your paternity of *First and Last Loves*, but at any rate I have enough pride for both of us. I am delighted that we should be publishing it and I know that it will make a lot of people happy.'

The reviews were generally excellent. John had the happy knack of being reviewed by friends. They gathered, like a theatre claque, to applaud his work. Osbert Lancaster, in a flagrant infringement of reviewing etiquette, wrote notices of the book in both the *Daily Telegraph* and *The Listener*. In the *Listener* review he remarked that 'No task is more difficult for a writer on art than to persuade people to see merit in the unfashionable, and nothing is ever as unfashionable as the immediate past.' Betjeman, as Sir Kenneth Clark had 'generously pointed out in his preface to his own work on the Gothic Revival', had done more than anyone to rehabilitate the Victorians. 'The secret of his success is that for Mr Betjeman all works of art exist in their human context.' Lancaster had a special word of praise for the introduction which had worried Jock Murray a little. 'Some may think that the preface "Love is Dead" bears little relevance to the essays which follow; few lovers of good, minatory hell-fire prose will wish that it had been omitted. Since Ruskin we have become unaccustomed to passion in writing of this sort and our responses are the poorer.' In the *Telegraph* review he again compared John with Ruskin – both masters of *saeva indignatio*.

The review in the *New Statesman* was less fulsome. There, too, the reviewer was a friend; but that friend was John Summerson, by nature a supercilious carper – somebody said he kept his lip in curlers. He began with a prolonged sneer at the very convention of anthologizing a living author. There was no real sting for John in this ironic preamble, and Summerson conceded that 'Mr John Betjeman is a writer worth collecting.' He thought John's essays should be bound up with pretentious papers by other people – 'just so that they have companions to embarrass'.

> That is part of Mr Betjeman's function and his art. What an embarrassing, what an out-of-step, singular author he is! There is nobody like him, nobody with that particular intuition for knowing when a thing has been forgotten but is not yet decently out of date, for recognizing the vanishing point of some word – 'electrolier', 'metro-land' – and bringing it back to use with a shock of pathos so striking that these resurrected words become Betjeman-words. He has created an attitude, a myth perhaps, almost a dialect.

Even this acute analysis of John's gifts had a light frosting of disdain; and there was more to come. The review ends: 'There is one thing I forgot to say about his book, which is that it is prefaced by one of the most savage Jeremiads on English life today that I have ever read. It is a little embarrassing.' It was just this irresistible tendency to deprecate, even when he felt much admiration, that lured Summerson, nine years later, into writing the article on the Euston Arch which led Sir William Haley to write the dismissive *Times* leader which in turn encouraged Harold Macmillan and his Transport Minister Ernest Marples to ignore John and the other protesters who wanted to save the arch.

Evelyn Waugh, writing in *The Month*, also laced praise with severities – warning John off his own territory of prose, satirizing his narrative methods and reprobating his, to Waugh, illogical allegiance to the Church of England. The piece began with high commendation.

> In the small, shrinking, perhaps vanishing society which honours beauty and humour, Mr Betjeman is literally a household word. His name has passed into the vernacular as surely as Spooner and Banting. 'A Betjeman character', 'a Betjeman house', have plain meanings. His poems are the best remembered, the most quoted, of any writer's save Mr Belloc. Are there circles where after-dinner revellers leap to their feet uninvited and declaim Mr Stephen Spender's verses for the sheer delight of hearing them again? . . . 'Betjemanism' is a mood of the moment like Existentialism. His following is among the gayest element of his contemporaries . . .

However, the review soon lapses into a series of complaints. 'The collection', Waugh thinks, 'does not show Mr Betjeman at the top of his form. He is, first and last, a poet – one of high technical ability – and prose does not become him.' Not only that, too many of the pieces in the collection were broadcasts and still bore 'the awful stains of their birth – the jauntiness, the intrusive, false intimacy, the sentimentality – which seem inseparable from the medium'.

Waugh pokes fun at the set pattern of the typical Betjeman essay.

> The normal process of Betjemanizing is first the undesired stop in a provincial English town, then the 'discovery' there of a rather peculiar police station, *circa* 1880; the enquiry and identification of its architect. Further research reveals that a Methodist Chapel in another town is by the same hand. Then the hunt is up. More buildings are identified. The obscure name is uttered with a reverence befitting Bernini. The senile master is found to be alive, in distressed circumstances in a northern suburb of London. He is a 'character'; he has vague, personal memories of other long dead, equally revered contemporaries. In his last years he is either rejuvenated or else driven mad to find himself the object of pilgrimage. It is all very beguiling and beside it there flourishes a genuine, sound love of the simpler sorts of craftsmanship.

Other reviewers were less ambiguously critical. The bookman Daniel George, speaking on the BBC's General Overseas Service on 13 October 1952, found the book 'rather frivolous' – 'I often felt a little irritated by his lighthearted assumption of superiority and by his humorous touches of what intolerant readers might regard as intellectual snobbery. I think he's just a big tease.' When he read 'Love is Dead', George felt, 'O Lord, here it all is again, the old familiar diatribe.' He was suspicious of a writer 'whose Utopia is in the past'. Under the heading 'Betjeman's Bogey', the young art philosopher John Berger mounted a more forceful attack on John's alleged snobbery in the socialist paper *Tribune*, and concluded by asking 'why bother to consider the book at all? Because it shows, I think, how silly an imaginative and knowledgeable writer can become, if he loses touch with the real issues of the time.'

A number of reviewers agreed with John Summerson that the introductory essay was too extreme. Edmund Penning-Rowsell, writing in *World Review*, found in it 'a dispirited note, a tone of defeat, which is at variance with the zest for life and people which is Mr Betjeman's most engaging quality'. Hugh Casson also took exception to 'Love is Dead'. By contrast, Cyril Connolly, reviewing the book in the *Sunday Times*, admired the preface more than anything else in the book. 'It is a cry of despair from the heart,' he wrote, 'and I would like to see it plop through every letter-box in the country for the despair is under control and the simple artless sentences state facts with but an undercurrent of contempt . . .' Connolly concluded: 'In another age or another country, Mr Betjeman would not be a "failed literary gent", by which I suppose him to mean a scholar and a poet who makes his living as a journalist, but a national celebrity and arbiter of taste. Lovers of good writing would hang on his words. Lovers of good building would submit him their plans. He would not be relegated to the limbo of the professional humorist or the clever fellow . . .'

In mid-1952 Jock Murray and John were already making plans to publish a volume of *Collected Poems* to follow the 'selected prose' of *First and Last Loves*. John wrote to Murray on 6 June: 'I would like to see my Collected Verse published cheaply, in paper, with a cover by Walter Crane of daffodills [*sic*] and bluebells. I would call it *Jocund and Blythe*.' On 18 July Murray wrote John a more businesslike letter, asking him to list the poems that had not been included in *Selected Poems* but which he would like to see in the *Collected* volume. As with *First and Last Loves*, there was a hiatus between thought and deed. The *Collected Poems* were not published until 1958. In the meantime, another slim volume of new poems was issued by Murray in 1954, entitled – perfectly in character with John's new-found pose of premature Grand-Old-Mannishness – *A Few Late Chrysanthemums*.

John prophetically wrote to Murray on 17 May: 'I think that if we put in "Phone for the Fishknives" ["How to Get On in Society"] I will be dogged by the blasted thing as I am even now dogged by Westminster Abbey, so let's leave it out.' However, Murray persuaded him to leave it in. On 28 May Murray sent John a complete set of the poems to be considered for the slim volume. He knew that John had doubts about publishing 'Easter 1948' ('The Empty Pew') and 'Dr Ramsden', an elegy for a don at John's favourite – because 'dimmest' – Oxford college, Pembroke. The Easter poem was 'too personal' and might upset Penelope; the Dr Ramsden poem might give offence to the don's surviving colleagues at Pembroke College. 'I am sure that Dr Ramsden must go in, he is so good,' Murray wrote; but added, 'I would not mind leaving *Deux Poésies françaises* out.' Murray had also read through a separate batch that both men had agreed were 'doubt-fuls'. Of 'The Dear Old Village' he wrote, 'You are rather fond of this and inclined to inclusion and so am I, but I am quite sure that it should either be cut or changed where you deal with the beastly farmer, because now some of that part reads as an excrescence on a beautiful poem. The farmer goes on too long.' John had let his hatred for Farmer Wheeler of Uffington run away with him. 'Easter 1948' was omitted. The French poems were also axed, but 'Dr Ramsden' went in, as 'I. M. Walter Ramsden, ob. March 26, 1947, Pembroke College, Oxford'.

The two men agreed that McKnight Kauffer, who had designed the wrapper for *Continual Dew*, would not be the ideal jacket-designer for this book. John thought he 'would not grasp it enough' and suggested instead a jacket 'like some of those home hobby books you publish'. Murray agreed that the poems should be divided into three sections headed 'Light', 'Medium' and 'Gloomy', the last, in John's words, 'concerned with death and self-pity'.

As usual, John had a lot of suggestions for titles. Myfanwy Piper had thought of *A Few Late Chrysanthemums* and he liked that; but 'The most honest title would be *Gloom, Lust & Self Pity*', and Murray might also like to consider *Baker Street and Other Poems*, *Neither Jocund nor Blythe*, *Grandsire Doubles*, *Cemetery Verses* or *Necropolis*. 'This last', John added, 'has a good "twenties" ring about it.' (Was he thinking of Fritz Lang's 1926 film *Metropolis*?) A postcard followed on 21 October: 'Elizabeth and I thought also of these titles: *Skin in the Coffee*, *Jam on the Handle*, *Marmalade on the Wrists*, *The Struggle for Freedom*, *Whither Democracy?*, *Dying Dahlias*, *Painful Extractions*.' Jock Murray blandly thanked him for the suggestions and made no further comment on them. On 27 October he wrote to John: 'O[sbert] L[ancaster] suggested *A Justification by Works* but it looks to me as though up to the present *A Few Late Chrysanthemums* has it.'

Page proofs were ready by mid-February. One set was sent to John Sparrow, who wrote to Murray: 'Betjeman's new poems are $\alpha+++$, to use our old-fashioned academic ratings. I expected a scanty bunch of draggled old flowers – and instead I find that it is perhaps the best of the collections you have yet published for him. Some of the new ones, e.g. "Remorse", are as good as, if not better than, anything he has yet written. "Congratulations" to you both!' Murray wrote back, on 16 February, that he might later ask permission to quote Sparrow's opinion. 'I am going through the proofs now and it will take a lot of chasing to get them out of JB . . .' John returned his set on 24 February. 'I think it unlikely', he wrote, 'that the book will have any success and I should not print more than a few hundred copies.'

A Few Late Chrysanthemums was published on 2 July 1954: the main run was of 6,000 copies, and fifty special copies were printed on hand-made paper with full buckram binding. John was sent his first copy on 9 June. He thanked Murray and said, 'it looks very nice'. The most significant reviews, in terms of reaching large numbers of potential readers, were in *The Observer* and the *Sunday Times*. Both appeared on 11 July. The *Observer* review, by the paper's resident critic John Raymond (it was a sign of John's growing celebrity that it was headed simply 'Mr Betjeman'), was damning: 'In far too many of the poems contained in this new slim volume Mr Betjeman has traded his unique sense of place for the all too fashionable sense of Guilt. The exchange is entirely to his disadvantage . . . The old magic has fled. There is nothing in this book comparable to "Youth and Age on Beaulieu River, Hants."' Evelyn Waugh reviewed the book in the *Sunday Times*: the notice was headed 'Mr Betjeman's Bouquet'. Now that John had moved off Waugh's turf and back into verse, the novelist was prepared to praise his friend once more, and his review must have given John some salve for Raymond's: 'He has named it *A Few Late Chrysanthemums*. At first glance those mid-Victorian exotics, heavy and haunting in scent, rich in autumnal colours, might seem a happy epithet. But those ragged mops of petals? – no, in form Mr Betjeman's poems have the crisp precision of the iris.'

For the most part, the other critics were polarized into the Raymond camp or the Waugh camp: those who thought the new book an unfortunate departure and those who thought the poetry as good as ever. (A third group maintained that the poetry had never been any good.) The critics who saw the book as a falling-away disliked two aspects in particular: its melancholy, and the acerbity of its satire, especially in 'The Dear Old Village' – the poem about which Jock Murray had worried. Geoffrey Taylor in *Time and Tide*: 'It is rather as though something friendly, familiar and furry and easily frightened had turned at bay and bitten one in the bathroom.' There were the usual complaints about John's right-wingism and snobbery.

The most punishing onslaught on the book, apart from Raymond's, came in *The Critics* programme on BBC radio on 1 August. The session was chaired by John's friend John Summerson, but he held the stance of a strictly impartial chairman and did nothing to restrain the participants – all three of whom agreed that the book contained nothing as good as his best work – from savaging him. By grouping some of the poems under the heading 'Gloom', John no doubt invited the complaints that he was 'mournful', 'mopish', 'sentimental' and 'sour' – the *New Statesman* reviewer wrote of 'a prevailing slightly liverish note'. But a few of the critics welcomed the new, less comedic Betjeman. In a radio broadcast, the Cornish poet Charles Causley said: 'I think his new book is his best. Some of the poems touch depths of feeling, and reach heights of imaginative invention, that I don't think Betjeman himself knew he possessed.'

From Betjeman loyalists came a chorus of praise, and on 14 July 1954 *The Times* sympathetically assessed John's current standing.

> In an age which positively enjoys wrestling with words, and far more readily spends its time upon the sibylline than the enjoyable, he has built up a steady following, both in England and America, by employing for the most part the easy grace which in the past has been associated with names like Tom Moore, Thomas Haines Bayly, and Jean Ingelow . . .
>
> He is often in love – but with the gym tunic quite as much as with its wearer . . . He suffers agonizing twinges of guilt, but bravely incurs the reproaches of a delicate conscience by going on exactly as before. And all this is set down in strains of deceptive innocence . . . while the reader, ever prepared to be amused, suddenly finds his heart touched as well by an entirely original skill.

In October *The Spectator* gave John a page and a quarter to reply to his critics. He resisted the temptation to slang them back, allowing himself one jab: 'I was not addressing myself to the *vieux jeu avant garde* – if I may string four French words together – which still lingers on in the "Critics" programme of the BBC.' The article contained the most cogent description he ever gave of his method of writing poetry.

> Verse-writers will know the lengthy and painful business of giving birth to a poem. First there is the thrilling or terrifying recollection of a place, a person or a mood which hammers inside the head saying, 'Go on! Go on! It is your duty to make a poem out of it.' Then a line or a phrase suggests itself. Next comes the selection of a metre. I am a traditionalist in metres and have made few experiments. The rhythms of Tennyson, Crabbe, Hawker, Dowson, Hardy, James Elroy Flecker, Moore and Hymns A & M are generally buzzing about in my brain and I choose one from these which seems to me to suit the theme. On the backs of cigarette packets and old letters, I write down my lines, crossing out and changing. When I reach home

I transfer the whole to foolscap and cross out and change again. Then I start reciting the lines aloud, either driving a car or on solitary walks, until the sound of the words satisfies me. Then I try reading the poem out to a patient friend whose criticisms I gladly accept, provided they are of detail only. After that I may have the courage to send it all to a magazine.

At the suggestion of Eric Walter White of the Arts Council, Jock Murray had delayed publication of *A Few Late Chrysanthemums* to allow it to be submitted to the Poetry Book Club for their summer selection of books. It was not selected; but, as consolation, in 1955 William Foyle, the bookseller, awarded John the £250 Foyle Poetry Prize. The cheque was presented to him at one of Miss Christina Foyle's literary lunches, at the Dorchester Hotel on 11 March – William Foyle's seventieth birthday, as it happened.

The sensational event of the luncheon became a big news story in most of the papers, including the *Telegraph*. John's cheque was presented by the eighty-four-year-old Lord Samuel, whom he had known at the Oxford Preservation Trust. Praising John as a rare contemporary poet who was comprehensible, Samuel made an intemperate attack on modern poetry. Having examined some anthologies of modern verse, he said he had been 'appalled to find the degree to which the vice of obscurity was afflicting English verse'. It was, he thought, 'self-conscious posturing'. To illustrate what he meant, Samuel quoted, in a 'stumbling' voice for comic effect, from Dylan Thomas's 'A Grief Ago' –

> A grief ago,
> She who was who I hold, the fate and flower,
> Or, water-lammed, from the scythe-sided thorn,
> Hell, wind, and sea . . .

The *Daily Sketch* recorded what happened next. 'Up sprang 46-year-old [Stephen] Spender. He bristled with indignation, glared at Lord Samuel and stalked out of the door.' 'Afterwards,' the *Daily Mail* reported, 'he said he was "furious" and "disgusted" and went on: "I was a great admirer of Dylan Thomas, and was the first person to write to him about his poetry. It seems that if you are going to give £250 to a modern poet you have to denounce modern poetry. It is the price you have to pay."' The drama of Spender's exit turned into farce when he bumbled by mistake into the Dorchester's kitchens, from which he emerged sweating, blinking and 'poppy-faced'.

Although Spender had been seated at the top table, he was some way from the speakers, and John did not see him leave.

Mr Betjeman stopped staring intently at the ceiling [the *Manchester Guardian* reported] and rose hesitantly to his feet. He said that he hoped Mr Foyle's prize will encourage all poets because 'poets don't hate each other like some other people do who are in a less creative capacity, shall we say.' Turning to Lord Samuel, he said that some very great poetry seemed difficult when it first appeared – Mr Eliot's for example – but that after ten years it became a commonplace. Poets are prophets.

The Bookseller printed one of John's sallies: 'He himself had struck lucky, he was fashionable, he said; "but, my goodness, I'm in for it in ten years' time!"'

For some years John's friend Patrick Kinross had been providing him with a London *pied-à-terre*. In the 1920s he had given him shelter in The Yeo, his house in Yeoman's Row, South Kensington. By now, Kinross lived in Warwick Avenue in London's Little Venice near the Grand Union Canal. He was making a name for himself as a travel writer, particularly on Turkey; and while he was away John was given the run of the Warwick Avenue house.

In May 1953, much to John's dismay, his secretary Jill Menzies resigned. 'I think I was getting too fond of him,' she said. 'I thought it would upset Penelope if I stayed.' This may have been a polite way of saying, 'I think he was getting too fond of me.' In her place John appointed a new part-time secretary, Anita Dent, the daughter of Major Leonard Dent, a friend of his and John Piper's who lived near Reading and collected Rowlandson paintings. She agreed to accept the same salary as Freckly Jill, £3 10s for three days a week, with her keep.

John's cuckoo-nesting in Kinross's house was inexpensive, and he liked Little Venice; but he felt the need of a London flat of his own – no doubt as much as anything because he wanted Elizabeth Cavendish to be able to visit him without the threat of a sudden incursion by the gossipy Kinross, or in view of Kinross's neighbours who might tattle to him and others. He soon found 'a very cheap flat in the City in Cloth Fair' owned by a homosexual couple, Paul Paget and Jack Seely. (Seely had succeeded his father as Lord Mottistone in 1947.)

John moved into 43 Cloth Fair in August 1954. It was the brief Fifties lull between Hitler's bombs in the 1940s and the 'new brutalist' architecture of the 1960s – the 'eggbox' buildings which in John's view 'nearly killed' the City's character. He was returning to his roots – to the land of his fathers, the 'cavernous streets' where his ancestors had lived and worked from the eighteenth century to the twentieth. Aldersgate Street, where his immigrant great-great-grandfather, George Betjeman, had lived, was just a step away, and Pentonville Road, where his father had made dressing-tables for maharajahs, was not far off. John had explored the City since childhood, had known it intimately before much of it was lost in the Blitz. He expressed his affection for it in several poems.

In 1977, five years after leaving Cloth Fair, he described in the *Observer Magazine* what it had been like to live in the City.

> This was the nicest place in London to live in, because everything could be reached on foot, down alleys and passages. Like all county towns it had a bit of every trade. I was lucky enough to live in Cloth Fair where there was still a shop which sold cloth. On some weekly nights there was bell-ringing from the tower of St Bartholomew the Great, just such bells as the walled city must have heard when there were 106 churches in its square mile. Behind me was Smithfield meat market with its cheerful, Chaucerian characters and medieval-looking handbarrows . . . Just over the boundary were the rag trade and the print and down in Clerkenwell the clocks. Southward, the City became a river port with wharves and cobbled quays and a smell of fish from Billingsgate where alleys plunged steeply to the river.

Candida often visited and sometimes stayed at Cloth Fair. She would be treated to lunch at Coltman's restaurant in Aldersgate, where there were bentwood chairs on a sawdust floor and John would be served champagne in a pewter mug. She noticed that on Thursday mornings John disappeared. 'I never thought to ask why, but years later I discovered it was something he never talked about to anyone.' Through the hospital chaplain, Mr Bush, whom he met at church on Sundays, he began visiting patients in St Bart's. He made friends with two of the hospital's Sisters, Winifred Hector and Mary Bland, and came to drink coffee in Mary Bland's room every Thursday morning before visiting the patients in her ward. 'He was able to make all the patients laugh,' she remembered, '– he was a wonderful mimic.' She thought that it was his horror of death which 'helped him to see dying patients'. Hugh Dunn was a cancer patient in Percivall Pott ward. His widow wrote to Candida in 1994: 'Your father certainly cheered up his days by his visits when they discussed London before and after the war. Mr Betjeman was at the time a very busy man but he still found time to visit us, and attend Hugh's funeral at Mortlake Crematorium.'

In May 1958, when John's secretary Anita Dent announced that she was leaving to get married, John took on in her place Tory Dennistoun (later Lady Oaksey), the daughter of the racehorse trainer Ginger Dennistoun who trained at Letcombe Regis and was a friend of the Betjemans. She worked for John four days a week for seven pounds.

John was a lovely employer and I was *hopeless* [she told Candida in 1994]. Sometimes he would sigh and gaze wistfully at a photograph on the mantelpiece of a pretty girl, saying, 'Oh, for Freckly Jill!' – his perfect secretary . . . Archie, propped up on the top of a bookcase, looked over us all the time and probably saw me forget to turn off the Stenorette tape machine one night. I always suspected it was the cause of the fire which nearly destroyed the house, but John never blamed me.

The fire damage was severe and John had to move out while the flat was restored. He wrote to Candida on 26 November 1958:

> Through the kindness of Tony Armstrong-Jones, the photographer, who has just gone to the USA for a month, I have been lent a room in Rotherhithe while 43 is being repaired . . . It is so nice I never want to leave it and I long to take you to see it. I sleep there at nights and am writing this now in it with the sound of a spring tide lapping against the walls under my window.

Antony Armstrong-Jones was the son of Lady Rosse, with whom John had founded the Victorian Society in 1957.* Rotherhithe Street SE16 is the longest street in London. Pier-like, it stretched between Cherry Garden Street and Cow Lane, with the Thames on one side and the Surrey Commercial Docks on the other. It was from this waterfront that the *Mayflower* sailed to Plymouth to take on board the Pilgrim Fathers. Among the warehouses and blitzed sites opposite the Victorian headquarters of the river police was a row of eighteenth-century houses which ships' masters had built right on the river bank, so they could keep an eye on their vessels at their moorings. No. 59 was the shabbiest of these. It looked across moored barges and tugs to a tangled skyline of cranes and the portal of Tower Bridge, with the dome of St Paul's beyond; at the back of the Georgian street façades was a Dickensian jumble of wooden platforms and wharves. In 1954 William Glenton, a London shipping reporter, had bought the house as a combined home and office. Paint on the panelled interiors was flaking and some of the wooden floors sloped so badly that 'it was like being on the deck of a listing ship'. An upstairs room overhung the Thames, with a view of a mile and a half of the river from London Bridge to Limehouse.

Glenton was a tough character who thought he had been lucky not to be hanged during the war when he and other ratings of the Royal Navy ship HMS *Lothian* had mutinied at Balboa against living conditions on the lower deck. They had refused to take the ship to sea on the way to the

* See Chapter 24, ' "Vic. Soc." and "The Dok" '.

Pacific campaign and were court-martialled. Glenton was confined to ship for six months. Now he divided his time between the waterfront and Fleet Street and used a bare ground-floor room of the Rotherhithe house to hold high-spirited parties with journalist friends. He also frequented the local pubs. At one of them he met some 'Chelsea-ites' in search of excitement in the East End. One of them asked if he would help him find a *pied-à-terre* along the river for a friend. The friend turned out to be Armstrong-Jones, who said he could get no peace at his Pimlico studio now he had become a well-known 'society' photographer. Glenton and Armstrong-Jones cruised dockland in the latter's Morris 1000 saloon, with no success. Then Armstrong-Jones asked if he might lodge in Glenton's house, 'in the empty room overlooking the river on the ground floor'. Glenton agreed to this.

Armstrong-Jones was in the 'arty' circle of Elizabeth Cavendish and it was at a dinner-party given by her at her mother's house in Cheyne Walk, Chelsea, in February 1957, that he had first met Princess Margaret. The Princess's biographer, Helen Cathcart, writes: 'Tony, who loved investing himself with an air of mystery, had occasionally spoken to Elizabeth Cavendish of a Room (which had seemed even then to be invested with capital letters) where he could escape at times from the bustle of his studio to work in peace and quiet.' In March 1958, just back from inspecting, in Germany, two regiments of which she was Colonel-in-Chief, Margaret crossed the Thames by the Deptford ferry, 'incognito, muffled up and unrecognizable', to have drinks with Armstrong-Jones in the Rotherhithe flat, after an official visit with Lady Elizabeth to the Dockland Settlement in the Isle of Dogs. As the romance between Margaret and Armstrong-Jones intensified, the Princess often visited the Room.

In November 1958 William Glenton received a telephone call from Pimlico.

> Speaking more excitedly than usual [he recalled], Tony asked if I could do him a great favour. Would I mind if a friend of his were to use The Room for several weeks? I imagined it would be someone of around Tony's age and of his usual circle. When he told me who it was I hardly knew what to think.
>
> My house, with its broken-down, half-starved look, certainly did seem more appropriate for a poet than a fashionable photographer – but the beaming, well-fed, almost Pickwickian figure of John Betjeman, who appeared a few hours later on my doorstep, looked in no way like the conventional idea of the threadbare, starving poet. When Tony had told me who it was that wanted somewhere temporary to live, I knew of John Betjeman sufficiently well to be surprised, but I had never even seen a photograph of him. Now that I was getting my first look at him I was even

more startled. But it was pleasant astonishment, for he radiated a warm friendliness that made me respond enthusiastically. He captured my attention so well that I hardly paid any notice to the tall, obviously well-bred woman in her thirties who had arrived with him by car. Indeed, she seemed to prefer to remain in the background while John explained how he had the night before been made homeless by a fire at his own ancient house in Cloth Fair . . . He became as excited as a small boy when he saw The Room and then the view from it. 'Oh, how jolly! This is going to be fun! I shan't want to go back to my own place.'

John insisted on seeing the rest of the house; but, an hour later, the woman with him reminded him that he was late for an appointment.

With his coat flapping and with wisps of grey hair poking out from beneath the wide-brimmed, well-dented trilby clutched to his balding head like the feathers escaping from a cushion, John rushed out of the house shouting promises not to be in late that evening. They had both gone before I realized that I had not been introduced to his female companion. Perhaps she was his secretary, I thought . . .

As a friendly gesture, Glenton took a cup of coffee down to John the next morning. The guest came to the door in his striped pyjamas, sleepy but cheerful. 'I've never slept so well for years,' he said. 'I'm almost glad there was a fire.' He explained about the lorries that rattled past Cloth Fair on their way to Smithfield meat market. The two men talked for a long time, as they were often to do in the weeks John spent in the house; but John found the view distracting.

While still in his pyjamas he stood at the open windows, watching the river craft bustling by with all the deep satisfaction of a boy studying a demonstration of model trains. He seemed unable to tear himself away, and then, suddenly, he began throwing off his pyjamas and putting on his suit, in a frantic hurry to be on time for his first appointment of the day. He was still buttoning up his clothes as he rushed from the house.

It seemed to Glenton that John always had 'some desperate business to perform, making it additionally difficult for me to realize that he was a poet and not some slightly eccentric businessman'. Glenton could not understand 'the need for his constant rushing here and there' until, later, he learned that John had been involved in preparations for the imminent publication of his *Collected Poems.*[*] Glenton never saw him at work on a poem. John was constantly looking out of the windows.

[*] See Chapter 25, '"A Really Thrilling Moment of Triumph"'.

He wanted to know the reason for everything he could see, and to find out more about the people who worked on the river he went with me to several of the waterfront pubs. The watermen, bargehands and dockers he met knew little of, and cared even less about, poetry – but John's genuine and enthusiastic interest in them won them over, and they spent hours yarning about their work to him.

When John left the Rotherhithe house – leaving an electric toaster as a thank-you present – Glenton was sorry to see him go. John was regretful too, and promised to visit him again as soon as he could. Knowing of John's busier public life ahead, Glenton did not expect to see him again; but two weeks later he reappeared at the house. 'As on the first visit he arrived with the tall, unknown woman, but this time Tony was with them. He, too, appeared to be a close friend of the woman's, and some of the mystery was cleared up when he introduced her to me. "Do meet Lady Elizabeth Cavendish," he said.'

> The visit of this oddly assorted trio [Glenton adds] signified a definite change in Tony's use of The Room. He never again used it to bring down any of his usual Chelsea friends or for any large parties. The people who did come down with him were older, and just two or three in number at the most. Lady Elizabeth was usually one of them, and proved to my surprise that she could be much jollier and less dignified than I thought. The three, including Betjeman, acted like happy playmates, as though they shared some secret joke.

One evening Armstrong-Jones decided to test his friends' athletic prowess by seeing which of them could get into the fishnet hammock he had installed in the Room, the easiest and quickest way.

> He, of course, leaped in and out of it in a matter of seconds [Glenton recalled], while John, carrying a far greater weight disadvantage, had to be almost levered in. I wondered if Lady Elizabeth, who is somewhere around six feet tall and has very lanky legs, would even bother to try. But she was as keen as both the others, and with great glee threw herself up into the hammock. Instead of landing inside it, however, she went right over the top – and crashed to the hard floor on the other side. We rushed to pick her up, thinking she must have broken a few bones or cracked her head, but she brushed us off and once again tried to get in the hammock. This time she succeeded, and she lay sprawled along its full length like a highly bred saluki dog.

Glenton remembered that evening not only for its fun but because it was the last time, for several months, that Armstrong-Jones invited him to join his guests. Glenton had the feeling that his tenant was becoming 'exceptionally secretive'. One day, about teatime, Glenton entered the house and met Lady Elizabeth coming down the stairs. They discussed the weather with strained casualness, 'and then Lady Elizabeth, who must have felt that some explanation of her presence alone was necessary, told me that she had just dropped by to tidy Tony's Room. With no further explanation she excused herself and hurried out to her car . . .' Later that evening, Glenton discovered that a roll of violet-tinted toilet paper had been hung in the lavatory. 'It did not need my reporting intuition to make me realize that there had to be some very special reason for a duke's daughter to act as a home help.' A fortnight later, he was glancing through a glossy magazine at his barber's and came across a photograph of Lady Elizabeth with a caption identifying her as a lady-in-waiting to Princess Margaret. An 'almost unbelievable thought' entered his head. Then, returning from a newspaper assignment, he was about to go up the stairs when the door of Armstrong-Jones's room opened and silhouetted against candle-light was 'the unmistakable figure' of the Princess. Helen Cathcart writes, 'Here was a working journalist with the greatest romantic scoop story of the century within a floor's depth of his typewriter. Yet to his lasting honour Mr Glenton kept the secret through all its developments, until the demolition men razed 59 Rotherhithe Street . . .' Princess Margaret and Armstrong-Jones (by now Lord Snowdon) continued to use the Room as a hideaway after their marriage in 1960, until the house was pulled down.

23

'City and Suburban'

A T A TIME when the BBC was still standing on its dignity (radio announcers were required to wear evening dress at the microphone), John was lucky to gain the trust and admiration of a number of senior officials, who were not deterred by his irreverence and occasional facetiousness. Chief among these was George Barnes, the first head of the Third Programme. His acquaintance with John began inauspiciously with the contretemps over Captain Newbolt* but developed into one of the great friendships of both their lives. In March 1944 Barnes invited John to lunch at the Oriental Club in London. On 6 April, writing to tell Barnes that he was going to the Admiralty, John addressed him for the first time as 'Dear George'. Barnes reciprocated with 'Dear John', but grumbled that he deplored 'this modern habit of using Christian names'. Later that month he invited John down to his home, Prawls, near Tenterden, Kent, giving him the advice – 'hardly necessary in your case' – to wear his oldest clothes. John met Barnes's wife Anne and the couple's thirteen-year-old son Anthony, whom he called 'Little Prawls'. Barnes himself was soon given a Betjeman nickname, too.

> John always called my father 'The Commander' [Anthony Barnes recalls]. My father had been at Dartmouth Naval College; he desperately wanted to be in the Navy, but because of the cuts after the First World War and his poor health he had to give up that career. He always regretted it. When Independent Television started, there was a Commander Brownrigg at Associated Rediffusion, so John's nickname was particularly embarrassing to my father. John would go round saying, 'Do you know my friend Commander George Barnes, who has made a little niche for himself in television?'

Anne Barnes was bilingual; her second language was French. She had become John's confidante, and by slow degrees she managed to overcome his antipathy to 'abroad' and he went with the family on holidays to France. In 1949 they travelled to Auxerre, Chartres and Vézelay – 'and then he

---

* See Chapter 14, 'Decoration'.

went racing back to stay with Diana Cooper in Paris and got 'flu on the way', Anthony Barnes recalls. In 1950 they went to Albi and Armentières. 'But he was desperate to get back to Vincent's Garage in Reading, where his car was,' Barnes says. 'He was genuinely terribly homesick.' After the 1951 holiday, John wrote to George Barnes: 'Oh, *wasn't* it fun! The best ever, ole man. And Bourges. I shall remember that all my life. Oh ta ever so. My breath is still bad from all that overeating.' The 1952 holiday was cut short by Bess Betjeman's illness. Anthony Barnes took a photograph of John 'lying on the ground at Le Touquet in a sulk because the 'plane was delayed. I think my father delivered us to Prawls and then took John straight to his mother.'

When Anthony was at Eton, he wrote to John about his problems. In October 1949 he told John about an affair he had started at Eton with another boy. John wrote to him: 'I had better not write too openly on the subject you mention for fear that letters are read by your comrades in arms. But of course the affair is a splendid thing and probably will prove the deepest, purest and most remembered emotional incident of your life . . . Don't bother yourself about the rights and wrongs of that sort of love in relation to the Faith. The whole question, so long as it is love, is Academic. When it turns into lust (and there often is a certain amount of lust can drive out love or an affair can be wholly lust) then whether it is hetero or homo makes little difference . . .' When Candida Lycett Green published her father's letters, she asked Anthony Barnes if he would prefer her to exclude that letter. But Barnes, by then twice married, asked her to leave it in 'because it showed a side of John which wasn't always visible. It showed, too, in the letter he wrote me when my father was dying – and in his hospital visiting of which there is no detailed record.' John also turned Anthony Barnes into a confirmed church-crawler; in later life he became director of the Redundant Churches Trust.

Besides Barnes, John had two other great allies at the BBC: Harman Grisewood and Douglas Cleverdon. Both had known him at Oxford. It had been Grisewood who had insisted on John's expulsion from the Oxford University Dramatic Society for publishing a spoof photograph of the OUDS rehearsing; but the friendship had been soon patched up. Grisewood had joined the BBC as an announcer in 1933 and succeeded Barnes as Controller of the Third Programme in 1948. Cleverdon had been an antiquarian bookseller in Bristol before joining the BBC in 1939. He was to be midwife to Dylan Thomas at the difficult birth of *Under Milk Wood*. Cleverdon wrote to John in December 1945 commissioning a talk on 'How to Look at a Town'. He was also in charge in 1947 when Osbert

Lancaster and John read extracts from *The Adventures of Mr Verdant Green*, the first Oxford novel. (John and Lancaster got the giggles so badly that Cleverdon was almost sacked.)

In 1952 John presented a series called 'Landscape with Houses', each centring on a famous building. After the first, on William Morris's house Kelmscott Manor, Sir Sydney Cockerell, the private press printer, wrote: 'I have just been listening to your enchanting talk on Kelmscott Manor which brought tears to my eyes again and again, so dear has it been to me since I first stayed there with Morris sixty years ago.' Next, John turned to William Burges's Cardiff Castle. At that date it was still thought most eccentric to praise a Victorian building; but John did not pussyfoot. 'A great brain has made this place,' he declared. 'I don't see how anyone could fail to be impressed by its weird beauty . . . You see people coming out blinking their eyes, awed into silence, punch-drunk as it were, from the force of this Victorian dream of the Middle Ages.'

In 1956 there was a gap in John's broadcasting career. His then agents, Pearn, Pollinger, were pressing for an inclusive contract for both radio and television broadcasts: could something be worked out like the arrangement with Malcolm Muggeridge, who received £1,500 a year for a maximum of twenty-six television programmes? Consulted on this, the Head of Talks (Television) reported that John was 'not such tremendously good value as a Television performer as we first thought, largely because he will not take sufficient trouble'. For their part, the radio producers felt that John's hesitations, which seemed engaging on television, just came out as awkward pauses on the radio. So on 30 April 1956 a polite refusal was sent to Pearn, Pollinger. Mortified, John immediately brought down an iron curtain.

However, financial need soon forced him to end his strike and accept freelance work. In February 1958 Pat Dixon persuaded him to be a panellist in *These Foolish Things*. Different sounds would be played to the panel to provoke 'a series of interesting, amusing or dramatic stories'. The sounds would be: the Angelus, a sneeze, a poetry reading by Edith Evans, the music of a Russian dance, and bolts being drawn on a heavy door.

Despite the misgivings voiced by the Head of Talks (Television) in 1956, it was in that year that John's value as a television performer was properly recognized. His career in the new medium had been launched nearly twenty years before by the BBC's first woman producer. Mary Adams, according to her *Times* obituary in 1984, 'was a typical pioneer. Ever eager to press on to new ground, she would not stay to tidy up that on which she was at any moment standing. She had little use for formal procedures . . . She was the despair of administrators.'

Luckily it was this rule-breaker, humorous and open to new ideas, who first invited John to appear on television, and arranged his programmes. On 31 May 1937 she wrote to him:

I don't know whether you have seen the television screen, or whether its problems interest you, but I should very much like you to come up to Alexandra Palace [then the headquarters of BBC Television] and discuss with us the possibilities of this new medium.

We have in front of us a period of experimentation, and we should like to think that you were interested in how it can best be used.

Unfortunately, John turned up at Alexandra Palace on a day she was away. 'I was greatly disappointed to have missed you,' she wrote on 13 July, 'but I hear you provided those who remained with a certain amount of fun . . . It occurred to me that it might be possible to give a television programme showing how Guide Books are made.' On the same day she sent him a second note: 'If you don't like the Guide Book idea, what about having a shot at a *Museum*?' In reply, John wrote, with a visionary prescience:

I was interested by television. But I feel . . . that these initial stages are a little boring. The value of television seems to me to be its possibility of outside work. I mean, when television cameras can show to millions of people actual scenes of shooting and dying in Spain, then it will become the most valuable propaganda medium in the world. When it can actually drive down the Great Worst Road picking up the noises, and then catch the silence of a cathedral close, it will awaken people to the repulsiveness of their surroundings. Beside this, 'How to Make a Guide Book' seems an unimportant thing, but more important to me than Museums which I simply loathe – except the Soane, Saffron Walden, Dulwich Art Gallery and minor provincial collections.

John's reservations were overcome and it was decided to proceed with *How to Make a Guide-Book*. On 14 September 1937 – just a week before the programme went out – John sent Mary Adams his ideas for it. The setting, he suggested, should resemble a village hall. There should be a blackboard. He also asked her to procure these objects:

a good-sized Cornish pastie
a waste paper basket
a hanging oil lamp.

He enclosed a sketch, with self-portrait, to show what he meant.

John received eight guineas for this first television appearance. Two years later, when asked to summarize John's performance of 1937, Mary Adams's assistant Andrew Miller Jones wrote:

John Betjeman drew us several types of tourists, and suggested the appropriate guide book for them. The bulk of the talk, however, dealt with a
guide book for ordinary folk. He showed a milking stool, a piece of
Cotswold stone, some wild flowers, a weather cock made from the hub of
a cart wheel, and several other objects of interest which are not referred to
in the average guide book containing a preponderance of information on
ecclesiastical architecture.

Mary Adams sent John a 'still' of his performance, as a souvenir. He wrote
back: 'Thank you so much for the excruciatingly funny photograph. I shall
certainly have it framed. It is the maddest thing I ever saw.'

John took part in a few more television programmes before the service
closed down for the duration of the war. A photograph shows him blind-
folded as a participant in a 'Tactile Bee' at Alexandra Palace, with
Christopher Stone as master of ceremonies and Andrew Miller Jones as
scorer. (The object of the game was to identify things, such as a lady's elas-
ticated swimming costume, from their feel.) But his television career did
not really take off again until the early 1950s, when George Barnes was
promoted to be Head of Television. Mary Adams was still involved in television. In June 1951 she wrote to John: 'Does the medium interest you any
more now that you have had practical experience of it? I enjoyed your programme [a debate on guidebooks with Geoffrey Grigson] and as we discussed it afterwards we all agreed that you had a Television personality
capable of development.' She suggested he might like to appear fortnightly
over three months, adding: 'I thought that John Betjeman talking about
something that had excited him during the week might make quite a dent
on viewers. You could choose something you hated or something you
liked.' John replied that he did not want to commit himself to a fortnightly
series. 'Strain, lack of experience and finance are some of the consider-
ations.' What would interest him, he wrote, would be to make a film about
a church. But at this stage nothing came of the idea.

In 1954 John made the earliest programme of his that is preserved in the
BBC's recorded archives – *Conversation Piece*, a televised chat with Lord
David Cecil and A. L. Rowse. In the same year he agreed to take part in a
programme called *Where on Earth*. Inviting him to join Peter Fleming and
Merlin Minshall, David Attenborough, then a talks producer, told him that
the idea was to show 'much-travelled people' pictures of places and buildings to identify. John was ill-travelled, except in England, but knew he
would be able to give value by jokes, aesthetic verdicts and ridiculous
guesses. Sir David Attenborough recalls that one photograph was of
burning-ghats in Benares, 'all temples, turrets, burning pyres and naked

people washing themselves in the Ganges'. After the rest of the team had rather surprisingly failed to identify this scene, John, 'after a moment of bafflement, responded triumphantly, "Got it – the Thames just above Maidenhead!"'

John liked this kind of panel programme which required him to do no gruelling research, but just live by his wits. In November 1955 Nancy Thomas, a production assistant on Television Talks, asked him to take part in an 'art' version of the popular quiz *Animal, Vegetable, Mineral?* The show, which ran from 1952 to 1958, was a brainchild of Mary Adams, who had adapted it from an American programme called *What in the World?* Museums and galleries submitted objects from their collections, challenging the panel of the night to identify them. Dr Glyn Daniel chaired the series, but its star was his fellow archaeologist Sir Mortimer Wheeler, craggily handsome, moustachioed and bombastic. When John was on the panel with Wheeler, the two showmen egged each other on in a kind of contest of Edwardian courtliness.

Though in demand for off-the-cuff contributions, John was still not being offered by the BBC the kind of television programmes he wanted to make. What sharply changed the BBC's mind was the growing threat from commercial television from the mid-1950s on. John's old friend Kenneth Clark was head of the Independent Television Authority; another old friend, Sidney Bernstein, founded Granada Television. And Jack Beddington of Shell was still around to help until his death in 1959.

It was Beddington who introduced John to Peter Mills, the director and producer of motor-racing films. Together they made, under Shell's auspices, twenty two-and-a-half-minute films on British scenery and buildings which were shown on commercial television under the running title *Discovering Britain*. John wrote to John Piper in July 1955, 'I don't think I've enjoyed anything so much since our Shell and Murray Guide days. Of course the secret is keeping the camera on the move, whether looking at a flower, or a box pew or a painted ceiling.' He described Peter Mills as 'a fast motor maniac', but thought him 'just the chap for these films and as funny as you and I are in the same way . . .'. Paul and Candida went on location for some of the filming.

George Barnes saw the Shell films. Annoyed that the competition had been allowed to steal a march on him, he gave orders that every reasonable inducement was to be offered John to persuade him to make television films. A programme on parish churches was commissioned. For the first time, BBC viewers were to see John's arts as a cicerone: the way he took off his shapeless hat and gazed reverently upwards before entering a church;

the conspiratorial gesture with which he beckoned them into the gloom to peer at a carved bench-end.

A new series was planned on 'The Englishman's Home'—meaning stately homes. 'The building', John told Barnes, 'should be more important than the commentator who should let the building speak for itself as much as possible and draw people's attention to what they might not notice, not emphasize the obvious . . .' John was to receive 50 guineas a programme; but after filming at Syon House and Uppark, he wrote to Miss Knight of Programme Bookings to argue that this was not enough. He pointed out that for a 'light entertainment' programme he received a minimum of 25 guineas, usually with a lunch and drink thrown in and only half an hour's work, with perhaps a quarter of an hour's rehearsal. 'All is smooth and merry and well paid.' But for an 'Englishman's Home' programme, he had to visit the house with the producer to work out which rooms should be filmed ('a day and very often a long journey by train'); then spend two hours at the studio dubbing the preliminary film ('a whole morning'); then on the day of the transmission he had to be at the house in question for most of the day, with two half-hour rehearsals. As a result of this remonstrance, his fee was raised to £60 a programme. Three further houses were filmed: Berkeley Castle, Castle Ashby and Tower House, Kensington, with its eccentric Victorian décor by William Burges – the house that was to be bequeathed to him in 1962.

The casual television work that he found so untaxing and congenial continued to be offered. In 1956 the BBC asked John's old school friend Anthony Blunt, director of the Courtauld Institute, whether he would take part in an 'architectural' *Animal, Vegetable, Mineral?* at the Soane Museum with John and Sir John Summerson. He replied: 'I hate *Animal, Vegetable, Mineral?* more than anything in the world and have always refused to do it, but the constitution of the panel is tempting, and so is the idea of doing architecture.' He agreed to appear. In December 1956 Glyn Daniel retired as chairman of the programme, and Nancy Thomas asked John if he would take over, at thirty guineas a programme. He replied: 'My dear thing, I should love it. It is money for jam and it is a pleasure.'

John was now writing a column that was at first sight just as congenial. From 1954 to 1958 he appeared every week in *The Spectator* under the heading 'City and Suburban'. In a decade that relished whimsy and nostalgia, his rôle was that of the resident eccentric. He was encouraged to be as quirkishly Betjemanesque as he liked. His main topic was architectural conservation, with frequent 'casualty lists' of buildings demolished or threatened;[*]

* See Chapter 24, '"Vic. Soc." and "The Dok"'.

but he also wrote about the railways, class distinctions, schools, horror comics, etiquette and accents, and relayed some good jokes, well told if not always pristine. There were intermittent flashes of autobiography.

The Spectator was setting a new course after a year of editorial turmoil. The magazine had been sold to a rich young barrister, Ian Gilmour (later Secretary of Defence and Lord Privy Seal in a Conservative Government, and afterwards Lord Gilmour of Craigmillar). After a power struggle among the senior staff, Gilmour decided he had picked up enough journalistic technique to edit the paper himself. He was editor for the whole of John's stint as columnist, leaving one year after him to become Conservative MP for Isleworth. *The Spectator* was known as a Conservative magazine, but Brian Inglis, Gilmour's assistant editor, thought he 'appeared more in sympathy with Labour'. Gilmour took on 'the Establishment' – a term first brought into popular usage by *The Spectator*'s political columnist, Henry Fairlie. Gilmour wrote exposés of the conduct of the police and the prosecution in the case which led to the conviction of Lord Montagu of Beaulieu for homosexual offences; he vigorously backed the campaign for the abolition of capital punishment, denouncing the Home Secretary in 1955 for his decision not to reprieve Ruth Ellis, the last woman to be hanged in England; and he opposed the Government over the Suez invasion of 1956. As Inglis later wrote, 'People in libraries and clubs who had regarded *The Spectator* as a soporific were woken up to the fact that it was now beginning to mount a challenge to the *New Statesman* as the journal to be picked up first.'

John's first 'City and Suburban' column appeared in October 1954, but he made his début in the paper on 12 March. At the start, he seems to have been typecast as a specialist on religion. Only later does his column give us a view of the range of his preoccupations in his fifties. On 27 August he was allowed to try his hand at 'A Spectator's Notebook' and used most of the space to protest about the Bishop of Ripon's 'determination to pull down the beautiful eighteenth-century church of Holy Trinity, Leeds, which stands in the heart of that city and is, as it were, the St Martin's-in-the-Fields of those crowded industrial streets'.

The Archdeacon of Leeds, C. O. Ellison, replied in a letter more than a column long. As the Bishop of Ripon was in America, the Archdeacon took it on himself to say that 'Mr John Betjeman unfortunately misrepresented the facts.' The Pastoral Committee, he wrote, was bound to question the existence of three or four churches near the centre of the city. 'Holy Trinity is one of these churches, and it stands on an extremely valuable site in the midst of shops.' He added, 'The wish to preserve

Holy Trinity church for its undoubted architectural interest and merit is a natural one, but to wish to keep it for this reason alone is to shirk reality and to ignore the spiritual and pastoral needs of the population as a whole.' This was too much for John. On 1 October a derisive poem by him appeared in the magazine, entitled 'Not Necessarily Leeds'.

I wish you could meet our delightful Archdeacon
There is not a thing he's unable to speak on.
And if what he says does not seem to you clear,
You will have to admit he's extremely sincere.

Yes, he is a man with his feet on the ground,
His financial arrangements are clever and sound.
I find as his Bishop I'm daily delighted
To think of the livings his skill has united.

Let me take for example St Peter the Least
Which was staffed by a most irresponsible priest;
There are fewer less prejudiced persons than I
But the services there were impossibly High.

Its strange congregation was culled from afar,
And you know how eclectic such worshippers are.
The stipend was small but the site was worth more
Than any old church I have sold here before.

John's views prevailed, and the church was saved.

One thing that the columns reveal is how peripatetic he was in these years. He was constantly on the move across Britain. Why did he travel so much? Partly, perhaps, to check up on the buildings which his readers warned him were falling into decay or otherwise threatened. Partly because he enjoyed journeys by train in that last age of steam. Possibly, too, the column began to write him – a common fate of diarists who may begin to do interesting things just to have something worth putting in the diary. In February 1955, motoring near Hull, he spied the Italianate towers of Tranby Croft, a Victorian house which had been the scene of the baccarat scandal involving Edward VII when he was Prince of Wales. 'It is now a girl's school, and the headmistress told a friend of mine that the girls know one of the rooms as the Baccarat Room. "And what is it used for now?" "Prayers."' Eight years later, John's daughter married Rupert Lycett Green, a kinsman of one of the baccarat players of Tranby Croft.

Trains, like buildings, were a staple ingredient of John's column. Like most of the largely Conservative readers of *The Spectator*, he thought the

British railway system should not have been nationalized by the post-war Labour Government, and he was full of complaints. In December 1955 he wrote:

> In order not to offend countries on the Continent, British Railways have decided to abolish third class and call it second. I wonder what is going to happen to the second-class carriages on the continental boat trains? I think this absurd slavery to formalism is just the same as that futile erasure of the old company lettering that went on when British Railways were started. It descended even to the tea-cups.

He waged a running vendetta against Sir Brian Robertson, the retired general who was chairman of British Railways. After visiting Cheshire in April 1956, John wrote:

> Oh sad Sir Brian Robertson, England's most unpopular general, how heavily hung your spirit over my train journey from Congleton to Oxford! I remember Mr Chuter Ede telling me that the idea behind the nationalization of the railways was that they should be a public service and not run from the profit motive. All the way along I saw sad little, weedgrown branch lines curving away to forgotten termini in midland towns. This devastation the general leaves in his trail is due to his determination to make the railways show a profit rather than perform a public service.

Religion, from High Church observances to Muggletonian survivals, continued to be a dominant interest. On 30 August 1957, John began his column:

> I would like to record something about Monsignor Ronald Knox* which may otherwise go unnoticed. At a time when there is a strain in the relations between the Church of England and Roman Catholics in some quarters, it ought to be mentioned. The chimes in the beautiful Parish Church of Mells were in need of repair, and Ronnie Knox wrote to me to ask me to come and open a fête in aid of them. This was held in the gardens of the Manor House where Mrs Asquith† lives and where Ronnie spent the last years of his life. Many prominent Roman Catholics had helped the vicar to organize the fête. Of course, it rained, like it always does at village fêtes, but Ronnie, though he was then very ill, came out into the rain to the little opening ceremony. I think he had much affection for the Church of his birth, and he certainly greatly appreciated its variety and added to its humour.

---

* Knox (1888–1957), a prolific author, had been received into the Catholic Church in 1917. He was Catholic Chaplain at Oxford, 1926–39.
† Katherine Asquith was the widow of Raymond Asquith, son of the Prime Minister.

John's rosy view of Knox on this occasion can be offset by Knox's less kindly memory of John, which Anthony Powell recorded in his journal over thirty years later:

> V [Powell's wife, Lady Violet] recalled that when Betjeman was staying with the Clives at Whitfield, the house was not yet 'on the grid' for electricity, so Betjeman could not use his electric razor. Someone therefore had to drive him to the nearest house in the neighbourhood (in fact on the outskirts of Hereford), which had electricity laid on. (Betjeman was then not Poet Laureate, tho' widely known from TV, other public appearances.)
>
> V told this story to Ronnie Knox (Katherine Asquith's chaplain at Mells), who burst out: 'What a hypocrite that man is!' It turned out that an electric carillon had recently been installed at Mells Church and Betjeman had been invited down to speak in celebration of its arrival. His speech fiercely inveighed against modern, especially electrical, technology, regretting the old days of bell-ringing by hand. A slightly piquant trimming to this story is that the Mells chimes played hymns, which Ronnie had more than once mentioned greatly disturbed him, possibly hymns reminding him too vividly of his own apostasy from the Church of England.

Most of John's columns were brightened by jokes, some supplied by friends. A 'new train of deliciously futile thought' was set up by a story about surnames and place names. 'The late Lord Salisbury is said to have sent the following telegram to his son: CRANBORNE, CRANBORNE. ARRIVING SEVEN SEVEN SALISBURY – SALISBURY.' John was tickled to hear from the County Surveyor of Northamptonshire that he had received a letter addressed to 'The Countess of Ayr'. And a friend in the City of London told him he had 'lately seen a man working a pneumatic drill there and wearing a deaf-aid'.

In private, John enjoyed scatology; but in judging whether a risqué joke might be passed as fit for *Spectator* readers he was more circumspect than the editor, twenty years his junior. A friend whose son was at Winchester College showed him a circular the school had sent to all parents, advising them that fees were to be increased by a certain amount *per annum*. The typist had missed out one of the 'n's in the Latin phrase; and John's friend had written to the school to say that, if it was all the same to them, he would prefer to continue paying through the nose. 'I urged him to put the story in his column,' Lord Gilmour recalls, 'but he never did.'

In some of the columns the germ of a Betjeman poem is found. On 29 October 1954 John laments that 'Aldersgate Street Station as our fathers and grandfathers, and, for younger readers, great-grandfathers knew it, is to be destroyed . . . No longer will we be able to ascend those dizzy heights of branching iron staircases to where the bombed refreshment room reminds us of how once there used to be written, in white china letters, on its plate-glass windows "Afternoon Teas a Speciality".' In an extra article on 'The City Churches' he wrote of the models of old London which used to be in the London Museum and which enabled one to imagine oneself back in the medieval City. 'With this picture of a walled city, with red roofs and white stone and many turrets and a wide, slow-flowing Thames, held up from the sea by the sluice of waters under London Bridge, leave Kensington and go to Aldersgate Street.' This sentence anticipates the fourth stanza of his poem 'Monody on the Death of Aldersgate Street Station' –

> Then would the years fall off and Thames run slowly;
> Out into marshy meadow-land flowed the Fleet:
> And the walled-in City of London, smelly and holy,
> Had a tinkling mass house in every cavernous street.

John wrote about schools in September 1956.

I remember Canon Demant saying to me that as soon as a nation started discussing education it was a sign of decadence. Let me discuss it here. Is it still true that there are two roundabouts which never touch each other? The one, State school and red-brick university or 'student' at Oxford or Cambridge and a career in the Civil Service or local government with a pension at the end, the other private school, public school and an undergraduate at Oxford or Cambridge and luck or influence afterwards?

A reader wrote in to charge John with snobbery – Graham Hough, a future Professor of English at Cambridge, educated at Prescot Grammar School.

Sir, – The point of Mr Betjeman's suburban drooling frequently escapes me: I am particularly baffled by his antithesis between a 'student' at Oxford or Cambridge and an undergraduate at Oxford or Cambridge. This distinction is unknown at Cambridge [Hough was then a fellow of Christ's College], and I should be glad to know what Mr Betjeman supposes it to be.

Later, in his valedictory column of 1958, John wrote, 'I am even grateful to those many correspondents I have infuriated . . . I was particularly glad at one time to have stirred so placid a writer as Mr Graham Hough into a positively interesting fury.'

John would probably have pleaded guilty to the charge of 'mischievous silliness' levelled at him by Hough. He ended one column: 'Is this all a bit arch and E. V. Lucas-y and 4th-Leaderish? Yes, it is, and all the better for

that. This column is the home of lost causes.' In 1956, at the height of the
Suez crisis, he complained of people who cornered him and made him discuss politics.

> Because I write in this paper, people assume that I share its Editor's views
> about Suez, and I expect if I had read them I would have shared them for a
> time, for I am always persuaded by the last argument I have heard. But I
> don't know what the views of this paper about Suez are, because I never
> read the political stuff in front. I take the *Spectator* to see whether there are
> any misprints in this column and for the book reviews and for dear old Strix
> [a column by Peter Fleming] and the angry letters.

This airy assertion brought a sharp rebuke from Ian K. McDougall of
San Francisco.

> Sir, – I have just read, in your Christmas number, 'City and Suburban' by
> Betjeman.
> I have lost all respect for this dodo as of this moment. I would remind him
> that 'that political stuff in front' is more than people's opinions. It is the very
> essence of our survival in these modern times . . . BAD LAWS ARE
> ALWAYS MADE BY GOOD PEOPLE WHO DON'T VOTE. How can
> Betjeman expect to get support from all those from whom he seeks it, to
> preserve old buildings and streets, if they share his views in relation to, shall
> we say, election of borough councilmen, and if they feel that such 'political
> stuff' is not for them? Such blindness is folly of a supreme nature . . . To the
> block with this hermit.

Francis Schwarzenberger of New York sprang to John's defence: 'I just
cannot let the insults to Mr Betjeman . . . pass without comment . . .
Actually, Mr Betjeman pointed out that the world's difficulties, "the political stuff" included, in all their vital significance, must not excuse disregard
or lack of care for the precious heritage of the nation which will survive,
God willing, the great international and political crises . . . Let us hope and
pray that Mr Betjeman continues his panoramic perusal of our times from
his peculiar point of vantage . . .'

John was no doubt right in thinking that most of his readers found of
absorbing interest nice points of etiquette, snobbery and accent. It was the
decade of Nancy Mitford's *Noblesse Oblige*, the guide to 'U' and 'Non-U'
usage to which he contributed. In November 1954 he wished someone
would publish a little book on the correct etiquette for typed letters.

> Rich and influential people who write to me by typewriter leave, I notice,
> a blank at the top and bottom and write in 'My dear Betjeman' or 'My dear
> John' at the top in long hand, and also sign 'Yours sincerely' or 'With much

love' in long hand above their signatures. Those who are frightened by their secretaries correct the typewritten part in ink. Those who frighten their secretaries either have the mistake rubbed out or the letter done again. But there are further subtleties, and I notice that employees of the BBC delight to put 'Dictated by . . . and signed in his absence by . . .' To them I always reply with a letter signed 'Written by his secretary and signed in her absence by J. BETJEMAN'.

Etiquette was not just a matter of academic interest to John. Bad manners could goad him into a choleric outburst, as in October 1957.

'Excuse me,' said a lady to me when I was crossing Hammersmith Broadway. She elbowed me off the traffic island and asserted her rights on the zebra crossing in front of a bus. When people say 'Excuse me' I always reply 'No', and they look round, as this lady did, risking her life in doing so, in pained amazement. 'Excuse me' is only one of the phrases current today which has lost its original meaning. Today it means 'Get out of the way.' 'Can I help you, sir?' means 'What the hell are you doing here?' 'With due respect' . . . means 'I have no respect for your opinions at all.' For years now 'To be frank' has meant 'To be unpardonably rude'.

John enjoyed talking to readers who talked back. He complained to Brian Inglis (so Inglis recalled) that 'he got no feed-back (not a term, I suspect, he would ever have used) from the *Telegraph* column'.* But, always morbidly sensitive to criticism of any kind, John did not appreciate the brickbats that arrived with the bouquets. Candida remembers that 'He had become tired of the constant complaints about his articles that they printed in the *Spectator* . . .' In October 1957 John wrote to Michael Berry asking whether he would commission a regular feature on architecture for the *Daily Telegraph*, with an illustration, 'which unfortunately I cannot put in the *Spectator*'. Berry agreed to this and John resigned from *The Spectator* in January 1958 – although the first of his 'Men and Buildings' columns did not appear in the *Telegraph* until April, and the column did not become a regular commitment until May 1959.

'This is the last paragraph I shall be writing in "City and Suburban",' John wrote in *The Spectator* of 10 January 1958. 'I have not been sacked, but the effort, week after week, of compiling this column is proving too much for me . . .' On the same day, 'A Spectator's Notebook' paid tribute to him in an affectionate farewell.

---

* It is not clear whether Inglis was referring to John's book reviews in the *Telegraph*, or to his later 'Men and Buildings' column.

'I should like to see John Betjeman added to his own casualty list,' a truculent correspondent informed the *Spectator* recently, but I wonder whether – now that 'City and Suburban' is to be with us no more – he will not come to regret his words . . . For myself (if a colleague may be permitted to write the *valete*) I have not always seen eye to eye with him about many of his enthusiasms . . . But I entirely agree with another correspondent who, in answer to a recent *Spectator* questionnaire, called him 'always constructive in his destructive criticism of official vandalism' . . . I suppose there could be no higher praise than to say that . . . unlike in the case of most columnists . . . the appointment of a successor has never even been considered. 'City and Suburban' *is* John Betjeman; that is all.

24

'Vic. Soc.' and 'The Dok'

I N AUGUST 1950 John launched what was to become one of his most
tenacious crusades, in a *Times* letter headed 'UGLY LAMP POSTS'. He
was sure he was not the only one to object to 'the present craze for erect-
ing lamp posts like concrete gibbets with corpse lights dangling off them
in old country towns'. He had seen a catalogue of some of these standards
which advertised on its cover that the contents had been 'passed by the
Royal Fine Art Commission'. Could it really be true that the Commission
approved their being set up in old and beautiful towns?

In 1951, he took the lead in a campaign to save Carlton House Terrace.
The Ministry of Works had asked the architect Louis de Soissons to incor-
porate part of the Terrace in a new Foreign Office building. John wrote to
The Times on 8 February: 'The new design looks top-heavy on Nash's
Doric plinth. It overpowers Benjamin Wyatt's beautifully related Duke of
York's column, sentinel between the terraces. It is ridiculous to say that
"the essential character of Nash's work has been preserved".' Others wrote
in support, including the architect Sir Alfred Bossom, who had lived at
Carlton House Terrace for the past twenty-five years. The pressure building up had its effect. On 20 April 1951 the Town Planning Committee told
the Minister of Works that the appearance of the existing Carlton House
Terrace building should be retained 'substantially intact'. Later, de Soissons
was asked to modify his plans.

There was another side to the medallic image of John Betjeman, gallant
preserver of Britain's heritage. Sometimes his mission was not so much to
save the old as to prevent the new. In this rôle he could seem just a benighted
reactionary. In February 1953 he and Osbert Lancaster appeared together in
a *Times* news story, as objectors to the proposal of the LCC to acquire a site
of eight and a quarter acres at Campden Hill, Kensington, London, for the
construction of a secondary school for 2,200 children. At a public inquiry,
Lancaster, supported by John, protested against the provision of 'huge permanent schools that would be but partially occupied after a few years'. This
was an argument they did not win. Holland Park Comprehensive was built

and became the most famous school of its kind in the country. Forty-five years later, in his half-historical, half-autobiographical book *Comp*, John-Paul Flintoff gave a bilious account of the early opposition to the school, at which he was a pupil from 1979 to 1986. He quoted some of the letters from rich residents of Campden Hill to local papers. One described the school as 'a ghastly, gargantuan gasometer'; another as 'an educational abortion, a vast factory, mass-producing units for the prefabrication of the classless dictatorship of the proletariat'. Flintoff singled out John for special ridicule.

> In the best traditions of middle-class protest, the school's opponents founded a pressure group, the Campden Hill Preservation Society. Members included the South African High Commissioner, the widow of a former governor of the Bank of England and the future Poet Laureate, John Betjeman. All of them opposed the idea of grubby teenaged rowdies, and angular, 'modern' municipal buildings, popping up in their midst – but each of them had other arguments, too . . . Lady Norman opposed the plan because it involved a compulsory purchase order on her own home, Thorpe Lodge. Here, after a hard day in Threadneedle Street, Her Ladyship's late husband Baron (Montagu) Norman of St Clere had tried to take his mind off the complexity of the gold standard, and the sheer effort involved in keeping sterling a hard currency; he'd sit with Her Ladyship, beside the grand Medici fireplace, cheerily admiring the works of art they had collected, or the rare species of tree and flower they'd assembled in the garden.
>
> And that's where the conservationist poet stepped in: John Betjeman was anxious about the effect of boisterous schoolchildren on certain pleached limes, a wall-trained fig, a wistaria and a tulip tree. He allowed his anxiety to be published, but after a public inquiry the purchase order was pushed through.

In April 1955 the Inland Waterways Association appealed for £25,000 for a campaign against the closure of canals. The next day, C. Dexter Watts of Stroud, Gloucestershire, wrote to *The Times* to point out that nearly all the National Coal Board's output was rail-borne. A rail strike was threatened and, Watts wrote, canals would be the obvious alternative transport – 'except that many canals are rapidly falling into disrepair from sheer neglect'. In May, Lionel Curtis, John's old champion at the Oxford Preservation Trust, wrote to *The Times* without consulting John first, 'Mr John Betjeman should receive support from everyone who enjoys the best form of holiday, i.e., camping out by waterway . . . We should all join in Mr Betjeman's movement to prevent Parliament from taking from us one of our best amenities.' John, surprised to find himself suddenly hailed as the head of a movement, wrote on 18 May to point out that he was not its instigator.

Lionel Curtis's elevating John into leader of the canals campaign is the first example of a trait that was to become endemic, and later chronic, in British preservation – the idea that no respectable campaign could afford to be without John's name. The enemies of conservation were thus able to depict him as a sort of 'Rentaprotest'; even his friends at *Private Eye* satirized him as bleating, 'It's those awful *developers*, old thing . . .' His main contribution to the canals campaign was made in 1974 when, in the presence of Queen Elizabeth the Queen Mother and Robert Aickman, he declaimed a specially composed poem at the opening of the Upper Avon at Stratford.

As his fiftieth birthday approached, John needed all his new-found kudos in the bruising campaign to save the Imperial Institute, London, a building of 1887–93 by Thomas Edward Collcutt. There was a Cold War drive to match the Soviet Union's technology; the Government had decided to demolish the Imperial Institute to make way for a more spacious block. John wrote to *The Times* on 13 February 1956: 'If this masterpiece is to be taken down by the Government it will surely be the first time a British Government has committed such a crime for many years.' But R. Long of the Imperial Institute strongly supported the Government's decision to demolish 'this anachronism', and suggested that the 'Victorian sentimentalists' should be left 'to contemplate the splendours of the Albert Memorial'. Nikolaus Pevsner wrote in February 1956 pleading for 'a new start on the site'. But, although the tower was spared, the rest of Collcutt's building was torn down. In an outburst of contrition for having promoted the Modern Movement, P. Morton Shand, writing to John two years later, singled out the new Institute building, with its offensive 'cladding', as a prime example of the horrors to which the Movement had led. 'Thank heavens you were able to save the tower of the Imperial Institute, but just look at the accepted model of the sort of penitentiary cantonment which is going to surround it!'

Albert Bridge, spanning the Thames between Cheyne Walk and the western boundary of Battersea Park, was threatened in May 1957. The LCC wanted to demolish it and build a larger bridge. 'The structure has its modest degree of loveliness,' an LCC spokesman said, 'but is regarded as having ceased to be a useful bridge for purposes of carrying modern traffic.' Built in 1873, Albert Bridge was the second-oldest of the ten bridges maintained by the LCC between Hammersmith and Waterloo Bridge. Only Westminster Bridge, opened in 1862, was older. The LCC appointed the engineers Rendel, Palmer and Tritton to report on the matter.

John's friend Richard Church, the poet and novelist, wrote to *The Times* that he had known the bridge since his childhood. 'This fairy-tale structure is part of the aesthetic character of the approach to that unique marshland where William Blake and subsequent writers lived . . . Without the Albert Bridge, Battersea will lose much of its distinction. This graceful signature in suspended iron gives an authority to the Park, and an introduction to Chelsea. A concrete bridge can never work with such grace . . .' On 7 June I. D. Hill of the Royal College of Science wrote: 'It seems to me that the retention of the Albert Bridge because your correspondent enjoyed swinging on it when he was young is carrying democracy too far.' The letter contained less amusingly disobliging remarks. John swung in to Church's – and the bridge's – defence.

> I question the statement of your correspondent of June 7, Mr Hill, that it is a sign of progress when a nation destroys the buildings of the days of greatness. I cannot believe he wants this country to be all airports, glass towers and sodium lights . . .
>
> He ends his letter by bringing democracy into the argument. It will be a sign of a return to democracy when the aesthetic opinions of scientists are not always preferred to those of people who have been educated in the liberal arts.

J. E. Rupp of Chelmsford commented on this: 'Why drag in the Imperial Institute, glass towers and sodium lights when a clear analogy is at hand? I thought the Battle of Albert Bridge was fought – and lost – at Waterloo.' (He was referring to the demolition of the old Waterloo Bridge in 1934.)* But the Battle of Albert Bridge was not lost. Perhaps less through Church's and John's eloquence than through the disinclination of the influential residents of Cheyne Walk to have increased traffic thundering over a big new concrete bridge near their front doors, the LCC scheme was abandoned. Today the bridge remains, festooned with fairy lights at night – a Whistlerian vision.

As the 1950s advanced, John found that more and more often he was resisting threats to such Victorian structures as the Imperial Institute and Albert Bridge. By now, the merits of good eighteenth-century architecture were generally acknowledged. Thanks largely to his proselytizing in verse and broadcasts, there had even been a slight shift in public opinion on the Victorians. We get some idea of what the general public thought about Victorian architecture in the Fifties from Agatha Christie's murder novel of 1952, *They Do It with Mirrors*.

> 'Have you been to Stonygates before?'
> 'No, never. I've heard a great deal about it, of course.'

---

* See Chapter 20, 'A Preservationist in the Making'.

'It's pretty ghastly, really,' said Gina cheerfully. 'A sort of Gothic monstrosity. What Steve calls Best Victorian Lavatory period. But it's fun, too, in a way.'

In 1952, then, an intelligent lay person probably found Victorian architecture ugly. But at the same time the character in Christie's novel allows the possibility that a Victorian building can be 'fun', can even be regarded with affection. ('"Hideous, isn't it?" said Gina affectionately.') Even this small concession suggested that the public's mind was not absolutely closed to the appreciation of Victoriana. However, the enthusiasts for Victorian buildings were still a small group and the words 'Albert Memorial' were still good for a laugh. John and his pro-Victorian friends came to realize that architecture of the later nineteenth century needed its own pressure group to fight for it. In 1957 they founded the Victorian Society.

In October 1957 John was once again called on to defend John Nash stucco – not, this time, Carlton House Terrace, but the terraces of Regent's Park. On 19 October he ambushed the Crown Commissioners, in a *Times* letter signed by a formidable list of *eminenti* – William Holford, Ralph Vaughan Williams, Lord Mottistone, Arthur Bryant, Kenneth Clark, Richard Costain, Philip Hendy (director of the National Gallery), Basil Burton, Henry Moore, Basil Spence and Woodrow Wyatt. They understood that the Commissioners were on the brink of announcing a decision on the future of the terraces. The signatories felt that the Nash façades were designed to be seen as a whole, and 'would lose much of their attraction and merit if they [were] even partially mutilated'. Not all art-lovers shared this view. On 22 October, R. Gainsborough, editor of *Art News and Review*, wrote, 'These gloomy terraces have overshadowed the park for long enough; built in imitation stone for an upper class . . . they have outlived their utility. Not only are the buildings worn out, but the aesthetic on which they are founded has outlived its day.' He wanted London to be rid of 'this pastiche of the Acropolis'.

In the top *Times* letter of 24 October, John replied with scathing irony.

How shocking it is, to carry the arguments of your correspondent of today, Mr Gainsborough, a stage further, that so many outmoded memorials of our decadence survive in London alone: St Paul's Cathedral, for instance, with its wasteful dome, and those of Wren's City churches built in imitation of Italian architects who in their turn imitated Greece.

If he finds the Nash Terraces gloomy, I dread to think of what he has to say about the Temple, Somerset House, Queen Anne's Gate, and other buildings of an age earlier than Nash which we have foolishly allowed to survive. As for Eaton and Belgrave Squares and towns like Cheltenham and

Brighton, built in the stucco which your correspondent and the late Sir Reginald Blomfield and John Ruskin so deeply disapprove, such offensive memorials of class distinction should obviously be destroyed.

T. Bedford suggested that the buildings in Regent's Park should be gutted but the outer shells kept – and this was precisely the compromise later reached.

John's campaign to save the Regent's Park Terraces showed that he had learned from his failure, four years earlier, to prevent Magdalen College creating a 'suburban' rose garden in the High Street, Oxford.* Now he mobilized all the media. The young presenter Woodrow Wyatt, himself a kinsman of Regency architects, made a plea for the terraces on the television programme *Panorama* and elsewhere. In 2002 Anthony Hobson, the former head of Sotheby's books department, recalled that Wyatt and John also took more direct action over the terraces: 'Woodrow Wyatt and Betj went to the Prime Minister, Macmillan, and got it stopped.'

John had also remembered the lesson that prevention is better than cure. The idea of a pressure group to protect Victorian art and architecture was hatched between him and the Countess of Rosse in 1957. Michael Rosse, the sixth Earl, was exactly a month younger than John and had known him at Oxford. In 1935 he had married Anne Armstrong-Jones, sister of the designer Oliver Messel and mother of the future Lord Snowdon. The first informal meeting was held in the Rosses' London house, 18 Stafford Terrace, an appropriate venue since the Victorian interior had remained – as it still remains – almost undisturbed from the days when it had been owned by the Countess's grandfather, the *Punch* cartoonist Linley Sambourne.

Two of the people the forceful Anne Rosse wanted to attend this first meeting on 5 November 1957 were brave enough to decline. Nikolaus Pevsner, showing the sense of humour that John always denied existed, wrote to her on 30 October, 'I deeply regret that a long-standing engagement with Guy Fawkes makes it impossible for me to be present at the meeting next Tuesday.' However, he wanted her to know how much in sympathy he was with the forming of such a group. He suggested that the society should set itself four main tasks, the first of which was 'To draw up a list of Victorian buildings which must be preserved'. Reasons for preserving buildings, he suggested, might be:

1) Pure architectural value.
2) Historical value.

---

* See B. Hillier, 'The Boase Garden', *The Betjemanian*, Vol. 9, 1997–8, pp. 10–38.

3) A special and exceptional importance in the history of Western architecture.

Pevsner confined his comments to architecture; but Sir Kenneth Clark, who also had to decline Lady Rosse's invitation, mentioned the decorative arts as well, and gave shrewd advice on the politics of such a group.

> As to buildings, your list will have to be severely critical, otherwise you will find yourself called in to try to save two-thirds of the town halls in the Midlands, practically all the Insurance Offices in the country, and many other buildings, which, although they have something to commend them, must take their chance in the general course of architectural development.
>
> With regard to decorative objects, the problem is almost of the opposite kind because so many of these have been destroyed already . . .

Both these responses correspond with their authors' comic stereotypes – Pevsner's for categorization and 'admin', Clark's for love of 'agreeable' objects.

Most of the other art-world grandees Lady Rosse had invited were present among the aspidistras and antimacassars in the first-floor drawing-room of Stafford Terrace on Guy Fawkes' Night, 1957. Besides Lord and Lady Rosse, John, and James Lees-Milne, they included Lord Esher (who became the first chairman), Oliver Messel, John Pope-Hennessy of the Victoria and Albert Museum and his brother James, the architect H. S. Goodhart-Rendel, John Piper, Osbert Lancaster, Sir Hugh and Lady Casson, Belinda Norman-Butler (a great-granddaughter of Thackeray), J. M. Richards of *The Architectural Review*, the art critic Nigel Gosling, Christopher Hussey of *Country Life* and the novelist Rosamond Lehmann. Among the younger people present were Peter Clarke and his friend from Cambridge days, Thomas Greeves, who had both met John in 1938 when he gave a lecture at Cambridge on 'Antiquarian Prejudice'.

Until the Victorian Society could attract enough members and subscriptions to afford its own premises, it was allowed to hold its meetings in the rooms of the Society for the Protection of Ancient Buildings at No. 55 Great Ormond Street, London. On 16 December 1957 the organization committee met representatives of the SPAB there. J. M. Richards chaired the meeting. John was among the Victorians' delegates, with the Rosses and Lord Esher. It was decided that the Victorian Society should be a sub-committee of the SPAB but with its own chairman and secretary. That was just how the Georgian Group had started in 1936.

Ian Grant, an architect, who was thirty-two in 1957, was the first young blood to come into the society, though by 1958 Mark Girouard, the architectural historian, and his friend Thomas Pakenham, the journalist and historian – both eight years younger than Grant – had joined the committee. The following year Grant agreed to be the society's secretary. A few weeks later, at a meeting on 16 December, the committee decided, with an irony that would only afterwards become apparent, that 'the Boardroom at Euston station would be a suitable place to hold the Annual General Meeting', but British Railways cannily refused permission. At the same meeting, a proposal for a Victorian fashion show was discussed. It was eventually held in 1960. Ian Grant described what happened:

> It was the first really important activity the Victorian Society ever had. A woman called Charmian Lacey undertook to arrange [it]. She managed to borrow an enormous collection of genuine Victorian clothes and found a collection of girls to model them. At first we were terrified there weren't going to be enough people, so the other amenity societies were circularized, the Georgian Group and the SPAB. We did actually turn people away in the end.
>
> It was a marvellous occasion . . . brilliantly organized by this girl. I was upstairs, faffing around trying to make myself useful. And one of the uniformed porters came up to me and said, 'Mr Grant, there's a man downstairs making an awful fuss. He's trying to get in without a ticket. He's called Mr Bet-something-or-other.'
>
> I said, 'Oh my God, he's on our committee; and I'm sure he hasn't got a ticket.'
>
> I went downstairs and John, wearing his grotesque old hat, all out of drawing, and carrying his fish-bass, had managed to make his way from the entrance right to the bottom of the staircase, but they wouldn't let him in. He was absolutely furious. He said, 'Oh, I see that you've got to be properly dressed to get into places like this.' And fortunately I just burst into fits of laughter, in which, in a moment, he joined. It must just have been instinct. But it was a difficult moment. I mean, he was meant to be on the receiving line – receiving guests with Anne Rosse.

At the meeting of 19 January 1960 (by now the society had 289 members) John was congratulated on his CBE, announced in the New Year's honours list. At this meeting, too, the threat to Euston station appeared for the first time, a faint storm-cloud on the horizon.*

Ian Grant's architectural practice was growing. In February he had announced that he would like to resign, and the committee agreed to employ a new secretary at a salary of £500 a year. The post went to John's

---

* See Chapter 27, 'The Euston Arch and the Coal Exchange'.

old friend with the stage-aristocrat drawl Peter Fleetwood-Hesketh, who had illustrated *Ghastly Good Taste* with many a Victorian fane. From his ornate flat below the SPAB'S committee-room in Great Ormond Street, Fleetwood-Hesketh ran the society and fought the Battles of Euston and the Coal Exchange.

The National Provincial Bank building at Bishopsgate was one structure in which John took the keenest interest. It was 'a marvellous Victorian, slightly curved building in Bishopsgate, ostensibly a single-storey building of the 1860s by Parnell.' Its case was raised at the meeting of 6 March 1962. Fleetwood-Hesketh reported that he had consulted a friend who was a director of the bank and who thought 'that rebuilding might eventually be necessary but not for several years'. John was not going to be fobbed off with that kind of evasiveness. 'Mr Betjeman suggested that the Secretary try to have a preservation order made on this building, which the City Architect is said to be fond of. It was decided to press for up-grading and that a letter be sent to the chairman of the bank and the City Architect asking what proposals were envisaged, and saying that this Society would object to demolition; also referring to Professor Pevsner's published opinion in *Buildings of England*.' A public inquiry later found in favour of its preservation. 'And this really set the City developers absolutely on their elbow,' Ian Grant recalled, 'because they suddenly realized that just because it was "Victoriana", it didn't necessarily mean that they were going to be allowed to pull it down. It was a real turning-point.'

John's attendance at the Victorian Society's meetings had become gradually more intermittent. Monica Dance, secretary of the Society for the Protection of Ancient Buildings, warned Ian Grant: 'John is a great one for lost causes and new societies, but when they begin to gather momentum he loses interest.' John was far too easily bored to be a good committee man. Canon Eric James gave an example of his fragile attention-span.

> I first met John Betjeman when the future of St Peter's Vauxhall was under discussion in the Sixties. We were both appointed to a Commission which the Bishop of Southwark, Mervyn Stockwood, had set up. John Betjeman represented the Victorian Society. I was then Canon Precentor of Southwark Cathedral.
>
> The meetings . . . began at 5.00 p.m. and the members of the Commission sat round a large rectangular table which virtually filled the room and allowed little or no space for movement in the room once people were sat at the table.
>
> At the first meeting . . . we were just about to begin when John Betjeman arrived, looking very flustered and embarrassed. There was only one vacant

seat, next to me, and I tried to look welcoming. He came and sat down and huffed and puffed and unfolded his papers which seemed to be in complete disarray.

The meeting had not been in session for more than half an hour when I noticed he was scribbling furiously. Suddenly, he pushed what he had written in front of me. It said: 'Do you know the Two Chairmen?'

I thought he must be going gaga, and simply wrote below what he had written: 'It is not two chairmen but the chairman and his male secretary,' and pushed the note back to JB.

Immediately he started scribbling furiously again, and then back came the piece of paper on which he had now written capitals:

'WRONG! 1 out of 10. "The Two Chairmen" is a pub near here. If you had the courage to say to *the* Chairman soon that you had a train to catch you would give me the courage to join you, and we could repair to "The Two Chairmen."'

It was just after opening time when we arrived and just before closing time when we left, having laughed our way through most of the evening.

When in 1963 Lord Esher died and Nikolaus Pevsner succeeded him as chairman, John virtually ceased to attend meetings. He detested Pevsner, who became a hate-figure in his later years to rival those demons of his youth, A. R. Gidney, C. S. Lewis and Farmer Wheeler. Immediately Pevsner was elected chairman, John suggested that a new post of deputy chairman should be created, and proposed for it his old friend John Brandon-Jones, who was elected. It is possible that this was his way of ensuring that there would be a counterbalance to Pevsner at the top, somebody he himself could 'nobble' if Pevsner tried to push through unpalatable measures.

Nikolaus Pevsner was four years older than John. He had seen the way things were going in Germany and had come to England in 1930 in the German intellectual diaspora. At first he taught Italian to History of Art students at the Courtauld Institute. His *Pioneers of the Modern Movement from William Morris to Walter Gropius* was published in 1936. In 1939 he was interned for two months as an enemy alien, then released. Offered a choice of several jobs, he said yes to a staff post under J. M. Richards at *The Architectural Review*; to editing King Penguin books (when the original editor was killed in an air raid in 1941); and to teaching art history at Birkbeck College, London. He was Slade Professor of Fine Art at Cambridge from 1949 to 1955. His great series the Penguin *Buildings of England* began in 1951, the year in which his *High Victorian Design* was also published.

Dr Timothy Mowl, who has written a book on the rivalry between the two men, thinks it likely that John was first antagonized when Pevsner, in the foreword to his 1936 book, made the implausible claim that he had not known of articles by P. Morton Shand on which the book's theme – that Morris was forefather to Gropius – was evidently based. Even if that did not upset him, what happened in the 1940s must have done. In 1941, when the architect and designer C. F. A. Voysey died, John sent an obituary appreciation of his old friend to *The Architectural Review*. It was not used; instead, a tribute by Pevsner appeared. Because of his *Pioneers* book, *he* was now seen as the expert on Voysey and all that school.

Richard Ingrams and others have suggested that there was 'nothing personal' in John's low view of Pevsner. It was (they contend) simply a matter of colliding tastes: John, whose response to buildings was largely instinctual and related to the people who lived or had lived in them, deplored the 'Teutonic thoroughness' with which Pevsner categorized architecture, with hardly any mention of human associations, his 'graceless' prose and lack of humour. John did indeed hold those opinions; but the bitterness of his animus against Pevsner suggests a more personal vendetta. Pevsner, after all, pulled academic rank on John. The only book of his which he ever deigned to notice publicly was *Ghastly Good Taste* (1933). This he described as 'memorable', but only for the eccentric typography of its title-page. He understood that Betjeman had been 'an undergraduate at Oxford' – a dry way of sneering at the poet's degreelessness.

In the post-war period, there was competition between the county guides John edited for Shell and for John Murray, and Pevsner's Penguin series of *The Buildings of England*,* with their very different approaches. The Murray guides got off to the quicker start, with *Buckinghamshire* and *Berkshire* in 1948 and *Lancashire* in 1950. Mowl judges that by the time the first *Buildings of England* volume was published, 'the race was running level'.

Open warfare between the two men broke out in 1952. In January, reviewing L. T. C. Rolt's *The Thames from Mouth to Source* in *Time and Tide*, John delivered a sideswipe at Pevsner: '[Rolt] writes with an eye for landscape unimpaired by antiquarianism. He sees a building and he knows its history, but he does not isolate it from its setting and function and classify it as though for a museum, as do our Herr-Professor-Doktors of today.' In March, John complained in a letter to James Lees-Milne: 'I travel third and am cut by people who count and looked down upon by the new refugee "scholars" who have killed all we like by their "research" – i.e. Nikolaus Pevsner that dull pedant from Prussia.'

---

* Now published by Yale University Press.

Whatever the reason for John's attack on him, Pevsner did not take it lying down. He fired back what Mowl considers 'a raking, provocative and deliberately hurtful broadside'. In his *London: Volume 2* of 1952, he disparaged John's favourite living architect, Sir Ninian Comper – and his admirers. Of Comper's St Cyprian, Marylebone, he wrote: 'If there must be medieval imitations in the C20 it is here unquestionably done with joy and care. Beyond that appreciation can hardly go. There is no reason for the excesses of praise lavished on Comper's church furnishings by those who confound aesthetic with religious emotions.'

The Betjeman–Pevsner feud continued in 1953. In June, sending on to Osbert Lancaster a note from Lord Chetwode in which the field-marshal expressed admiration for one of Lancaster's cartoons, John added: 'See me on Pevs in next TLS . . . INTEGRITY & TRUTH must be safeguarded against official closed shop of ART HISTORIANS.' The anonymous review appeared in the *Times Literary Supplement* of 3 July. In it, John tore to pieces the latest Pevsner on County Durham, pointing out many inaccuracies. Pevsner's letter to the *TLS*, replying to the criticisms, is described as 'an incoherent, apologetic disaster' by Mowl, who adds: 'He had deliberately hurt Betjeman in that vulnerable area where religious enthusiasms and aesthetic judgments interact. Now he himself had been ridiculed as an outsider whose scholarship was inadequate in an English context.'

Bruising as such encounters could be, Pevsner's ruthless insistence on efficiency was what the Victorian Society needed at that stage of its development. Under the Esher–Rosse–Betjeman régime, it had shambled, in a gentlemanly, shabby-genteel way, from crisis to crisis. On 16 October 1963, Thomas Pakenham presented a report, as clear-eyed and unsentimental as even Pevsner could wish, on the working and future expansion of the society. 'For virtually all its life,' he said, 'the society has been living beyond its means and now the reckoning approaches. Four fifths of our accumulated funds have been dissipated . . . We have continued to spend nearly double our income.'

It was largely thanks to the efficiency of Pevsner, aided by a crusading woman, Jane Fawcett, that the society achieved so much in the years that followed the destruction of the Euston Arch and the Coal Exchange. St Pancras station and the Foreign Office were saved. The appointment of Lord Kennet as the minister responsible for preservation and his introduction of the 1967 Town and Country Planning Act and the 1968 Civic Amenities Act gave the society essential powers; official recognition and compulsory notification of threatened listed buildings came with the first, while the 1968 Act, by establishing 'conservation areas', helped stop the systematic destruction of Victorian cities. With the arrival of 'spot listings' in 1974 the society was able to short-circuit the inadequacies of the post-1830s lists by ensuring that full statutory protection was given to threatened buildings, under emergency regulations, within twenty-four hours. St Pancras and Liverpool's Albert Dock were spot-listed as Grade I. In important campaigns, such as that to save St Pancras, John continued to play his flamboyant rôle in public; but after 1963 he was seldom seen at the committee meetings, where Pevsner hustled the members through the agenda.

By the time John died in 1984, Victorian architecture was being studied seriously, with university lectures on such as Pugin and Baillie Scott. Pevsner's disciples gave their master nearly all the credit for the Victorian reprieve; 'he saved a century', it was said, a tag which adhered to him. To John, too, however, must go much of the kudos for de-stigmatizing Victorianism – as co-founder of the society with Lady Rosse, as affectionate champion of Victorian architecture in poetry and prose, and above all in his television broadcasts, which won over the public to Victoriana more effectively than a hundred well-researched works by Pevsner could have done. Only with the public on its side could the society persuade MPs and other powerful figures that they would not become laughing-stocks by supporting its campaigns. Neither man's achievement is diminished or eclipsed by that of the other. One might see them as the 'tough cop' and the 'gentle cop' going to work on an obstinate customer – the firm smack of *Kunstgeschichte* followed by the soothing caress of poetic nostalgia. But even this contrast is unfair: Pevsner had his moments of geniality, and John was not all smiles.

Pevsner won the battle of the guidebooks. In the long run the tortoise beat the hare – Pevsner's dogged application outdistancing John's inspired dilettantism. But it was John who triumphed in the battle of the styles. After the war, Pevsner's views seemed temporarily to prevail. With a Labour Government, a shortage of materials, and an urgent need to rehouse bombed-out people, his pro-Bauhaus theories and taste for austere buildings had more appeal than John's and Piper's arguments in favour of individuality and decoration and against doctrinaire aesthetics. But history eventually settled for John's more catholic taste, comprehending Victoriana, suburbia and decorative eclecticism, not for Pevsner's fealty to the International Style. Mowl attributes John's win to his 'sheer omnipresence' in the 1970s, but some credit, too, must be given to human nature, which rebelled against 'a machine to live in' and craved some 'chintzy, chintzy cheeriness'. It has been claimed that John came to 'like and recognize' Pevsner; but the hatchet was never quite buried. In 1982 John said to me: 'Why is it that when you've read what Pevsner has to say about a building, *you never want to look at that building, ever again?*'

25

'A Really Thrilling Moment of Triumph'

O N 6 OCTOBER 1946 Miss George Elliston died in Madisonville, Ohio, at the age of sixty-three. From 1901 until 1942 she had been on the editorial staff of the *Cincinnati Times-Star*. As a young woman, she was a tough reporter: she had obtained an 'exclusive' from a murderer on his way to the electric chair and was proud of having climbed into a fifth-storey window to steal a photograph to accompany another scoop. Later she became the paper's social editor, a powerful arbiter of who was who in Cincinnati society. She also had a reputation as the dewiest of poetesses. Her 'Every Day Poems' in the *Times-Star* mixed sentimentality and moral uplift in the manner of Ella Wheeler Wilcox and Patience Strong.

During her lifetime, it was generally believed that, with all her fame as a Cincinnati 'character', George Elliston was poor as a church mouse. She wore cast-off clothes given to her by the society ladies whose parties she wrote up; even on her deathbed she borrowed $10 from a friend. Yet her will revealed that she had left $250,000 to found a chair of poetry at the University of Cincinnati. (She had inherited money from her father and invested it well in property.) The will stipulated that the Elliston Chair was always to be held by a poet, not by an academic. The person responsible for making the choice was William S. Clark II, chairman of the English department at UC. Some of the Elliston Poets were strikingly unsatisfactory. John Berryman, who held the chair in 1952, was an alcoholic. Stephen Spender (1953) was at first refused a visa by the American Embassy in London, because he had been a self-confessed Communist for a few weeks in 1937. The biggest disaster was the tenure of Robert Lowell in 1954. He went to the Gaiety strip club twice a day. Returning to his lodgings on one occasion, having run out of money, he jumped from a moving taxi to avoid paying.

After these and other débâcles, William Clark decided that in future he was going to be far more stringent in vetting candidates. Stephen Spender, who had charmed Clark, was asked whom he would recommend for 1957. He suggested John Betjeman. 'You won't have any trouble with him,' he said. But this time Clark was taking no chances. In June 1955 he and his

wife Gladys went to England to see for themselves whether John Betjeman
would be suitable. Spender had already told John about the chair, in particular about the $3,000 he could expect for giving five lectures and some
'workshops'. At about three dollars to the pound, this was a tempting prospect for the hard-up Betjemans, and Penelope made sure that the Clarks'
visit to Wantage would be both enjoyable and impressive.

As soon as the Clarks arrived back in Cincinnati, Clark wrote to offer
John the post. Quite apart from the Betjemans' charm, erudition and
fluency as conversationalists, Gladys (regarded as a bit of a snob by some of
the academic establishment in Cincinnati) had been impressed by their
grand friends and by Penelope's 'Honourable'. John asked Penelope
whether she would accompany him. She was dubious as to whether she
would enjoy '*Chinchin-náti*' – as she insisted on pronouncing the city, in the
Italian manner – but it was a good pretext to get John away from Elizabeth
Cavendish. So she agreed; but she made it part of the bargain that, if she
'did her time' in Cincinnati, she should be allowed to take Candida on holiday to Italy afterwards.

After sailing to New York, John and Penelope spent one night at the
Algonquin Hotel as guests of the *New Yorker*. The magazine wanted to
publish a profile of John, and sent Brendan Gill to interview him. Gill
wrote:

> He sat sipping a bourbon on the rocks and bubbling over with delight at the
> American scene: 'My first visit you know,' he said. 'I ordered a bourbon
> because I understand it's the authentic American drink. I mean to be thor-
> oughly American during my stay at Cinci – I hope it isn't disrespectful of
> me to call Cinci Cinci so soon.

(John had got it wrong. The accepted abbreviation of Cincinnati is not
'Cinci', but 'Cinti'.) John also told Gill that he thought the Woolworth
Building – an early skyscraper – 'enchanting . . . all that Gothic work so
high in the air, so close to eternity!'

On 4 March, the Clarks held a party for the Betjemans at their home in
Hyde Park, Cincinnati. Two days later, John was to give the first of his
Elliston lectures, on 'The Visual and Sensual Approach to Poetry'. Van
Meter Ames, the University's professor of philosophy and himself a pub-
lished poet, recorded both events in his journal:

> *7 March 1957.* Monday evening was the Clark party for this year's Elliston poet,
> John Betjeman and his wife Penelope, who runs his farm near Oxford and is
> a famous cook . . . Much interested in Indian thought, and from it discovered
> western mysticism, Von Hügel and then St Theresa and was converted to

Catholicism, after being 'damn glad I wasn't a Christian'. . . Didn't get much impression of her husband, and Betty [Ames, Van Meter's wife] and Liz Bettman were afraid he would not be interesting, and all he drank was grapefruit juice. But I caught a glimpse of the red lining in his coat and thought he might surprise us.

Sure enough he did, in his first lecture yesterday. Simply captivated the full house in 127 McMicken [Hall]. When the photographer thought he had finished snapping him, Betjeman opened his coat to cause a universal gasp over the flaming lining and equally red broad suspenders [braces]. Then he took the coat off and proceeded in his shirtsleeves which he rolled up.

Asked his first impression of the University of Cincinnati, John said: 'It is impossible for me to understand how anyone could possibly get any work done in a co-educational university. If I had been here as an undergraduate I would have been in love all the time because your American co-eds are so beautiful.'

Very few undergraduates were admitted to John's lectures, which were for select members of the community. But John did meet some undergraduates and recent graduates in the poetry 'workshops' which were among his duties as Elliston Poet. Completely at home on the public platform, he was daunted by the idea of a workshop: the very word, jarringly modern in an academic context, had, for him, unhappy associations with his father's cabinet-making firm. The workshop consisted of eight to twelve people, about evenly divided between the sexes. One member was Alvin Greenberg, later a novelist and poet and professor of English literature at Macallister University. In 1957 he was twenty-five. He had graduated from UC in English in 1954, had been briefly in the Army, had married and was working in Cincinnati in the family wine business.

So now I was delighted to be back . . . Workshops were always a real high point in the year for me. Betjeman was just a delightful person to be with – a wonderful spirit, and he always had that smile. I think it was also fairly evident, early on, that he didn't have the slightest idea what to do with us.

That was the time when the teaching of creative writing was just beginning to make inroads into the American universities . . . I'm sure it wasn't being done at the British universities.

Aside from the workshops, John's timetable was arranged by William and Gladys Clark, and the Betjemans saw a lot of them. Clark was a tall, handsome New Englander of fifty-six. He was considered autocratic. 'Some people thought him a benevolent despot,' said Alvin Greenberg. 'I wasn't sure about the "benevolent".' Gladys Clark was also a New Englander, Vassar-educated. A faculty wife spoke of her 'frozen smile'.

John seemed to enjoy being lionized. Elizabeth Bettman said: 'He put himself out enormously. He made a conscious effort, it seemed to me, every time I saw him, to entertain and to give pleasure.'

Liz Bettman was the woman who overcame Clark's resistance to having women in the English department. 'I *broke* him,' she joked. 'After me, he let women in.' Clark had a crush on her 'but he was, for him, very shy about it'. She was the young, attractive wife of Gilbert Bettman, who was forty in 1957 and had been elected a municipal judge in Cincinnati two years before. 'Liz is a bit wild,' was a general, if affectionate, view. She was a red-hot radical on almost every political and social issue. An unlikely person, perhaps, for the conservative Clarks to entrust with any aspect of entertaining the Betjemans – but she was shiningly sincere, sympathetic and learned in English literature, and had become a friend of visiting poets as disparate as Spender, Berryman and Lowell. The Clarks gave Liz Bettman the job of chauffeuring John around Cincinnati. He was captivated by her: she seemed an American Joan Hunter Dunn. At first, she 'found it hard to get past his bonhomie'; but later, when she was driving him to his appointments or on sightseeing jaunts, their relationship grew a little closer. He would give her sidelong looks from the passenger seat and would 'gently interrogate' her about her private life. 'I knew he was trying to get me to talk about my marriage, which he realized was already a little rocky. What I didn't realize was that his marriage was rocky too.'

John threw himself manfully into party-going. After being sighted with the misleading grapefruit juice at the first Clark soirée, he took to strong martinis. Penelope, as ever, was much less keen on parties. In a letter to Lady Silvia Combe she wrote: 'The Americans are, as one has always heard, the most friendly and hospitable people in the world, and we are asked out to every meal and meet new people every day, so that we are nearly mad and shall need a long rest-cure on our return.' Every member of the English department held a dinner-party for the Betjemans.

Among the leading families of Cincinnati were the great Jewish dynasties, the Fleishmanns, the Bettmans and the Ransohoffs. The Fleishmanns, arriving in Cincinnati in the 1860s, had made a fortune from a Hungarian process of manufacturing yeast. Julius ('Junkie') Fleishmann was often host to the Betjemans in his 1927 Lutyens-like house in Indian Hill. The Camargo Hunt, with which Penelope often rode, met in the courtyard of the house and the hounds were from the Fleishmann kennels. Penelope had not come to Cincinnati prepared to ride – 'so I just wore ratcatcher', she wrote. This shocked the huntsmen of Indian Hill.

Danny Ransohoff and Gil Bettman sometimes had a friendly argument over whose family had been longer established in Cincinnati. Ransohoff was a fifth-generation Cincinnatian. His grandfather, Dr Joseph Ransohoff, had been a well-known medical doctor and scientist in the city. Ransohoff liked to act as a guide to eminent visitors to the city. He had shown Berryman, Spender and Lowell the sights; he found John Betjeman more receptive than any of them.

If the guest was staying for any length of time, Ransohoff would give him two tours of the city: one of its architectural showpieces, the other of its slums. John was taken on both. We know which buildings he liked best, from an article he contributed to the *Cincinnati Enquirer* after he returned to England in April. He liked the Taft Museum, the beer barons' mansions, the City Hall, of 'streaky bacon' Gothic brick, and the German domestic architecture of the downtown area known as 'Over the Rhine'. His 'favourite skyscraper' was 'your Union Central Building by Cass Gilbert, architect of the Woolworth Building, which is still New York's handsomest bit of skyline'. John paid tribute to a house designed by Frank Lloyd Wright in 1953 for Cedric Boulter, the Professor of Classics, and his wife Pat. The luxurious suburbia of Walnut Hills and Avondale also appealed to him. But he added that he could not end with a good conscience without mentioning the slums between Third Street and Seventh Street – which he had seen on his second tour.

> I know the London slums, but they are not as bad as these, partly because of bylaws which make windowless rooms illegal and which insist on fire precautions.
>
> I went up black evil-smelling stairs from a front hall studded with mailboxes in houses where there was only one sink and an outside toilet which had to be emptied by a vaultman after use by 40 people. I was amazed at how well kept these waterless, brittle, insanitary rooms proved to be once one was inside them. There was garbage in the streets piled feet high. What these places must be like in hot weather I dread to think . . . The many kind friends I have made in Cincinnati will not, I hope, feel I am unaware of their generosity to me, their hospitality and their welcome if, remembering the slums so near the padded luxury of the Terrace Hilton, I end with these Victorian lines:
>
> > '*Oh loved Cincinnati, I bid thee farewell,*
> > *Thy heights are perfection. Thy basin is hell.*'

On 11 March the *Cincinnati Times-Star* took the Betjemans through the riverside towns of the Ohio Valley. 'Cincinnati has the most beautiful gas-

lights in the world,' John told the gratified reporter. The Royal Fine Art
Commission, of which he was a member, had been 'looking for something
like that for a long time. I must have a picture of it to show the others . . .
We just don't have any lights in England as pretty as that.' In the same park,
John was photographed, in one of his most punished felt hats, sketching the
neo-classical Temple of Love, which he called 'a perfect crown to the hill'.

On 14 March he delivered his second Elliston lecture, on 'Tennyson:
Master of Landscape and Sardonic Wit'. It was as well received as the first.
Two days later, the *New Yorker* published Brendan Gill's profile of John. As
a fillip to his reputation in Cincinnati, it could not have been better timed.
Cincinnatians had had two weeks to decide what they thought of him;
now they realized that he was not just a British celebrity, he was an international celebrity. John's third lecture, 'Local Poetry and Love of Place',
was on 20 March. 'There's an immense field of inspiration for poetry to
come from this district,' he told his large audience. He suggested that
Cincinnati poets should investigate the possibilities in 'the extraordinary
landscape of used car marts'. 'The flashing lights, the brightly coloured
cars! They're hideous but surely they could be turned into poetry. It could
be either satirical or inspirational.'

John's last lecture in Cincinnati, on 28 March, was a triumph. His subject was 'The Nineties'. He spoke of Oscar Wilde and Ernest Dowson, and
told the audience, 'I was the last gasp of the Nineties.' The *UC News Record*
reporter wrote that the lecture closed 'amid a storm of applause mingled
with a feeling of sadness'.

> This middle-aged man with the pixy smile had completely won the hearts
> of all who attended his lectures and as he left the lecture room there were
> audible comments from every side which served as sufficient proof that Mr
> Betjeman will be long remembered.
>
> Dr Clark, head of the Department of English, said afterwards that the
> attendance at this year's lectures averaged higher than at any time in the past.
> Mr Betjeman spoke to standing-room-only audiences . . .
>
> Dr Clark compared Mr Betjeman's interest in cities to that of Charles
> Lamb. 'He wanted to see and know everything about Cincinnati. His curi-
> osity reminded one of a charming small boy who is seeing the world for the
> first time.'

The Clarks held a small party for John to say goodbye to the members
of his workshop. Alvin Greenberg recalled:

> Betjeman presented each of us with an inscribed copy of one of his books,
> which had to have cost him a good bit of money because he surely didn't

bring them with him; but, most amazing of all, he gave each of us . . . probably each of us in the class had bought one of his books; he managed to give each of us the *other* book, the one we didn't have. I guess that at one time or another we'd each asked him to sign a copy – and he had paid attention. That was such a generous, thoughtful, kind thing for him to do. In the long run, it would be hard for me to detect Betjeman's influence on the ways I write. But I think what he did show me – which I haven't seen a lot of in other writers that I've known – is that you can be an artist and be a decent human being at the same time.

Penelope left for New York, before John, on 27 March; she was back in England on 1 April. John left on 31 March. Before he went, he recorded an interview which the Ames' daughter, Damaris, heard on the local radio station that evening. In it, he said again that he had never had such a responsive and appreciative audience. He had been afraid they wouldn't understand his 'Limey' accent, but he had enjoyed his audience so much that 'it was a form of self-indulgence'. The less pleasurable aspects of his month in Cincinnati were trenchantly described by Penelope in a letter to Mollie Baring: 'John's lectures are being a great success, but he is so exhausted from the entertaining that he can hardly wait to get home, and the central heating nearly *kills* us.'

John kept up with some of his Cincinnati friends. William and Gladys Clark made a second visit to Wantage in 1962. Penelope had become a vegetarian, Gladys noted; and Candida, just married, was 'off round the world in a van'. Later in 1962 Elizabeth Bettman also came to Wantage and was photographed by John Lehmann at an evening picnic on the downs with the Betjemans and Jock Murray. (Beside the camp-fire, John gave a bombastic performance of Vachel Lindsay's 'Congo', with saucepan *obbligato*.) Penelope, well aware of the *tendresse* that had developed between John and Liz, wrote on the back of Lehmann's photograph of the two of them: '"LUST"'.

Despite the impression he gave, did John in fact 'loathe' Cincinnati, as he later told Stephen Spender? A letter of 12 March 1957 to Candida suggests that he did.

> Darling Wibz,
>
>   Mummy has bought you a very pretty pink dress here and the other day I saw in a delicatessen store the following things for sale – broiled octopus, English liquorice allsorts, rattlesnake meat, fried Japanese grasshoppers, fried Mexican worms. I get very tired here, nobody stops talking, the wireless is on everywhere even in the hotel elevators, and sometimes two different programmes in the same room. I can make little contact with the students I have

to teach as I have so little in common with them. We are foreigners here. The English are either much liked or not liked at all. The city is a collection of different frictions – Jewish v Christian, Negro v White, RC v Protestant, North v South (for Cincinnati is on the Mason–Dixon line which divides the old southern states who practised slavery from the ascetic, hard-working, rather egalitarian and self-righteous North). And oh my goodness it *is* ugly though the Arts Museum is good. The nearest main road to this hotel is appropriately called 'Reading Road'. Most roads and towns look like the approach to Didcot from Wallingford and big towns are like the Great West Road. The suburbs in Treeclad Hill alone are pretty.

I long to see you and Wantage again – my goodness, I do. Don't forget Mummy and me. We think of you a lot and envy you *even* at school. It could not be worse than here.

Tons and tons of love from MD [Mad Dadz]

Setting down this very English poet in this very American city had almost the character of a chemistry experiment – it was like dropping a piece of sodium into a dish of water and watching it fizz about. The entertainment certainly exhausted John. He was parted from Elizabeth Cavendish and exposed for weeks on end (not just at weekends) to Penelope at her most horse-mad and cantankerous. Clearly he enjoyed the adulation of the crowds. But he never returned to Cincinnati, or indeed to America.

John was relieved to be back with Elizabeth. Although their liaison did not get into the gossip columns until the 1970s, the couple were not particularly circumspect about it. As early as 1954 Violet Trefusis – the daughter of Edward VII's mistress, Alice Keppel – put their names side by side on a list of people to be invited to a party she and Patrick Kinross were organizing together. The invitations were printed *Please bring your comb*: combined with lavatory paper, the combs were to become primitive kazoos for a concert in which the guests would be the musicians. In 1957 Ann Fleming, perhaps the most malignant gossip in England (she was married to Ian Fleming, the creator of James Bond), sighted the lovers at a much more public gathering. She wrote to Evelyn Waugh on 5 July:

You made a mistake in missing Lady Pamela Berry and Mr Mike Todd's party at the Festival Gardens to aid the Newspaper Benevolent Fund and publicize the film of *Round the World in Eighty Days*. Those of us who wished the maximum pleasure embarked at midnight from Charing Cross pier in a flotilla of river steamers, rain was falling and the cabins and bars were filled with Jewish film producers, publishers and interior decorators. On each deck was a brass band playing 'Rule Britannia' and other appropriate tunes and the remaining available space was occupied by us foolish goys . . . Present Paddy

Leigh Fermor, Vivien Leigh, Stephen Spender looked handsome in a black sou'wester, the Warden of All Souls [John Sparrow] was in transparent white plastic, John Betjeman and Elizabeth Cavendish wore identical pale transparent blue . . .

In August, Penelope went to Italy – her reward for having endured the cocktail parties and central heating of Cincinnati. She returned to Wantage, at the end of September, with an idea for revitalizing King Alfred's Kitchen. In Rome she had seen the up-to-the-minute Gaggia machines for making espresso coffee. She now ordered one and installed it in the 'caff'. The silvery Gaggia machine, with its one-armed-bandit handle, was a piece of impulse buying which Penelope later regretted. It was true that undergraduates, in their tweed sports jackets and cavalry twills, still drove out to the Kitchen, particularly when there was a chance to see the Betjemans' beautiful daughter. But this was also the time of the Teddy boys – teenagers who dressed in an ersatz 'Edwardian' style, with 'DA' (duck's arse) haircuts, bootlace ties, long 'drape' jackets with velvet collars, drainpipe trousers and 'winklepicker' or 'brothel-creeper' shoes, sometimes with flick-knives as accessories. They tended to buy one 'Expresso' and lounge around all morning or afternoon drinking it, frightening off the genteel ladies who used to come in for tea and toasted teacakes. John was increasingly worried about the café's drain on the family finances.

Early in February 1958 he and Elizabeth stayed with the Devonshires at Lismore Castle, their house in Ireland. Then John, Elizabeth and Princess Margaret attended a concert at the University College of North Staffordshire, Keele, where John's friend George Barnes was now Principal. The Princess had recently become the University's Chancellor. Thanking the Duchess of Devonshire for her hospitality, on 15 April, John wrote: 'The visit to Keele was uproariously funny and we all had the giggles on our return just as though we were kiddiz. Little Friend [Princess Margaret] was on her best form.' Late in April John took Candida on a tour of the Scottish islands. He and Penelope knew the Earl and Countess of Wemyss, whose daughter Elizabeth ('Buffy') Charteris was a schoolfriend of Candida and had stayed at The Mead in 1954. In 1957 John had been the guest of David and Mavis Wemyss at Gosford House, East Lothian, when giving a lecture at Edinburgh University. Wemyss was chairman of the National Trust for Scotland and in 1958 invited John and Candida on an 'experimental tour' of the islands, including Fair Isle and St Kilda, two of the Trust's properties. John wrote an article about their experiences ('Guano and Golden Eagles') in *The Spectator* of 16 May.

In the same month Candida went to stay with a family in France, an experience she hated. John wrote to her:

> . . . I miss you very much. I went into your room and it looked just as though you were there. It was harvest festival this morning and it went on for hours and hours . . . I had to sit beside that pair of little old women who cough gently every other minute. Glory to God in the highest! I had to concentrate a lot to keep charity and God in my heart.

Just as John had prescribed, Paul had done his National Service before going up to Trinity College, Oxford. He served in Lord Chetwode's old regiment, the 19th Hussars (now the 15th/19th). Dick Squires remembered: 'He arrived in Northern Ireland on a motor-bike with a saddle and a saxophone. Penelope said, "No one will have his own car; there's a marvellous saddle club, nobody will have his own horse." Paul wrote back and said, "Everybody's got his own car, or two, and everybody has a hunter and polo ponies. There's no such thing as a saddle club and they're all enormously rich."' While he was in the Army, National Service was abolished for anyone born in 1938 or later; so when he arrived at Oxford many of the undergraduates were at least two years younger than he.

Tall, fair-haired and good-looking, he cut a dash at the University. Both Penelope's father and John's mother had left him some money. He used it to buy a vintage Rolls-Royce – to Penelope's disgust. 'Paul rather fancied himself,' said Squires. 'He went through a stage when he was very dandyish. His tie had to be just right. He had terribly smart luncheon parties. The *Isis* gossip columnist wrote: "The other day I went down Beaumont Street and passed Paul Betjeman, hand-in-hand with Paul Betjeman." Paul had two saxophones. He was on a gig somewhere, I think at Henley, and he ran over the saxophones in the Rolls in a pub car park.' Paul took a Fourth in geography. The idleness required to obtain a Fourth had to be nicely gauged.

In September, Colonel Kolkhorst died. John contributed an obituary notice to *The Times*, which ended: 'He was kind and gentle to the humble and unknown, and, which is harder, to the famous . . . Though a don, he valued Oxford as a place and way of life rather than an exam. factory and had no tolerance for pedantic research.' He attended the funeral and described it in a letter to Billy Wicklow, who was in hospital in Dublin. 'I very much enjoyed your account of the Colonel's funeral,' Wicklow replied on 3 October, 'and of Hedley [Hope-Nicholson] saying, "that horrid Mr Bryson, I meant to cut him and I smiled at him."'

In February 1959 John wrote to an old friend, the author Cecil Roberts: 'I dare not drop journalism until my son (now at Oxford and with two years and a bit to go) and daughter (in France and aged sixteen and pretty and clever) are off my hands. Then, by Jove, I will. I'm now fifty-two. Can I last the course? I must. Penelope has a small income and so have I, enough to live on, just – but only just.' Because of the great success of his *Collected Poems*, published in December 1958, his financial situation improved. He was even prepared to be indulgent about King Alfred's Kitchen. Writing to Penelope in May 1959, after she had had to pay for the café's roof to be repaired, he complimented her on the way she was running the business, adding, 'I daresay I had better cough up for the roof out of shares . . . NIL DESPERANDUM things might be much worse.'

In the same month, John wrote to thank the Duchess of Devonshire for another week he and Elizabeth had enjoyed at Lismore Castle in April.

> I find it hard to believe that this time last week Feeble and I were sitting in a bar in Mallow eating our sandwiches and drinking Guinness after testing the mineral water in Mallow Spa, an 1840s building near the gasworks. Those glorious days of Lismore were some of the best and most fruitful I have ever spent in my life as I was able to write verse, talk rubbish to Feeble and you and the kiddiz, play with Andrew [the Duke] and admire the castle and cathedral. The phrase 'play with Andrew' is Feeble's. She said one morning I was to go upstairs and write poetry and 'not go playing about with Andrew' until after I had written it.

He was writing *Summoned by Bells*.

Had the Betjemans been living together at The Mead full-time, a 'devoted couple', we should know far less about their preoccupations at this time than we do. As it was, letters flew back and forth between Wantage and Cloth Fair or Edensor. John's were full of protestations of his love for Penelope, in Irish-accented babytalk. Now that Paul's immediate future was settled, Candida's became the principal topic of the correspondence. In November 1959 – she was seventeen – the Betjemans were debating whether she should go to Italy, be sent to a crammer's for the spring and summer and forgo the London Season, or start in a job, perhaps as a trainee window-dresser, in January. 'It is not easy to talk to her,' John wrote to Penelope, 'and she is too old to be ordered about & accept what is planned for her. Girls develop earlier than boys.'

While, to some extent, John had played the heavy father with Paul, his instinct with Candida was to allow her considerable freedom. Penelope was less sure that this was a good idea. On 12 November 1959 John wrote to her from Edensor:

> I will promise not to let Wibz be rude to you these hols if I can help it.
>   I think it much better that she should find a place of her own as she has

done. It is to be allowed to stand on her own feet more & more & not have things planned for her.

I wish I were with you to help & comfort you in your arguments about Wibz. I see you in my mind's eye lying in bed & thinking of Wibz in desperate situations, no Tewpie [himself] by you.

But let me tell you this. Wibz is healthily 'reacting' against both of us. She hates Art History in the Courtauld sense because you like it & she probably is bored by Mrs Lestrange (who is now 30 years older than when you knew her) partly because Mrs L. did *not* bore you. She hates looking at churches because I like them. She is not in the least interested in what interests us just because these things interest us.

This was a singularly enlightened attitude for a father to take in the 1950s; though, once again – as he sheepishly admitted – John was leaving Penelope in the front line.

The *Collected Poems* had been a long time coming. On 24 March 1955 Jock Murray had written to John:

I hope you will approve of a plan of doing a complete edition of your poems in the autumn of 1957. By complete I mean that it should include those poems that you can be persuaded not to feel embarrassed to see in print. It would include the Selected and Chrysanths, about four additional early poems which were left out of Selected and poems written after Chrysanths and it is for consideration whether we try to make arrangements for Poems in the Porch to be included also.

Poems in the Porch – a set of Betjeman poems about churches, with illustrations by John Piper, published by SPCK in 1954 – were eventually excluded from the 'collected' volume. John thought them not up to standard; but some of his admirers regretted that the hilarious 'The Friends of the Cathedral' was not admitted. (It was admitted to the 2001 edition.)

Murray's hopes of publishing the *Collected Poems* in the autumn of 1957 proved too optimistic. On 19 November 1957 he wrote a memorandum for his staff which mentioned that Lord Birkenhead would be shown the collection and should suggest which poems might be deleted and which included. Why Lord Birkenhead? He had been a friend of John's at Oxford and had written an able biography of his father, the great F. E. Smith. But he was not among John's closest friends; and in the past John had relied on Tom Driberg and John Sparrow for advice on his poems. It was probably the influence of Birkenhead's sister, the forceful Lady Pamela Berry, rather than his own merits, that prompted the choice of Birkenhead, who eventually both garnered the poems for inclusion in the volume and introduced them. Lady Pamela was not only a significant figure in the social life of

Lady Elizabeth Cavendish and John; she liked, as Osbert Lancaster put it, 'to have a finger in every cultural pie'. She had introduced John to Elizabeth; now her brother would introduce him to the world.

On 27 January 1958 John went to tea with Lord Birkenhead to discuss which poems should go into the *Collected* volume. Most had been published in Murray books but some had never appeared in volume form. Birkenhead telephoned Murray on 12 March. He agreed to send the poems in three weeks and his introduction in a month: that would mean an early start could be made on printing the poems. John had proposed that the poems should be illustrated by Michael Tree of Mereworth Castle, Kent, who was Elizabeth Cavendish's brother-in-law, having married her sister, Lady Anne.

John needed the money that the poems would bring. On 17 April he sent Jock Murray a *cri de coeur*.

> Will you put in any money that is owing to me to my bank, Brown, Shipley & Company . . . ? I have been faced with an overwhelming demand for income tax for past years. It seems that Percy Popkin [his then accountant] whose health broke down about six months ago, had not been declaring my income right. I have no redress and will have to give up a secretary, clubs and sell some books. If you ever hear of a weekly job for me which will bring in a weekly sum, I shall feel most relieved. This free-lance existence at my age and with my family at its most expensive is becoming unendurable.
>
> I enclose Freddy's selection of my poems.

Murray obliged with a transfer of funds to Brown, Shipley.

The book was published on 1 December 1958 – rather late for the Christmas market. Besides 10,000 ordinary copies, a special edition of one hundred copies was printed, with marbled endpapers and a leather binding on a thin board in the same style as George Borrow's *Bible in Spain*. John had made a great deal of fuss about the cover, with designs being shuttled back and forth between London and Elizabeth Cavendish's house in Derbyshire, but the ordinary copies were finally issued with the plainest of covers, stamped only with a rule set about half an inch from the book's edges all round. The jacket had simple typography against a pink background. Jock Murray sent Lord Birkenhead an advance copy on 19 November. 'I hope you will approve of its modest elegance,' he wrote. 'As you know, the temptation to make it Art Nouveau in appearance was very great.' A launch party was held on 3 December.

The runaway sales of *Collected Poems* were the publishing phenomenon of 1958. One week after the initial order of 10,000 copies, a further 8,000 copies were ordered for the second printing. The book was selling at the rate of just under 1,000 copies a day. The printers worked through the night. Hatchard's bookshop received fifty copies one morning and were sold out by lunch-time. The reviews were predominantly good. Raymond Mortimer, in the *Sunday Times*, described himself as 'one of his earliest and still most fervent admirers'. John's book criticisms seemed to him 'sometimes too idiosyncratic, always too insular', but 'in his verse and poetic prose, his peculiarities become bewitching'.

Anthony Powell reviewed the book in *Punch*, under the heading 'The Swan of Wantage'. He had particular empathy with John, who could be seen as achieving in verse what Powell was doing in prose – using traditional forms to write about contemporary Britain. Powell wrote:

> Impressions shower down on the reader of this volume, among them – perhaps the most overwhelming – that of the personality of the poet. We feel ourselves in the presence of a man of strong will; indeed, a man of iron. Nowadays the term 'Betjemanesque' may be found even in letters to the daily papers (usually employed to deprecate those who delight in good architectural design in contrast with an urge for concrete lamp posts) . . . The interesting thing is that all those kestrels and pylons of the early 'thirties have, in their way, dated more distinctly than Betjeman's pitch-pine and stucco. Crashing his way through the *zeitgeist* to the swelling notes of the church harmonium, John Betjeman has become, perhaps, the poet through whom the vagaries of our age will in the last resort be remembered.

Powell ended his review with words that were to appear on countless future editions and printings of John's poems: 'It would be difficult – in my opinion impossible – to point to a contemporary poet of greater originality or more genuine depth of feeling.'

Frank Kermode praised John in *The Spectator*, Anthony Lejeune in *Time and Tide*. In *The Listener*, W. G. Hoskins, who is credited with inventing the subject of landscape history, claimed the *Collected Poems* was 'beyond question the best book to be published in 1958 about the landscapes and towns of England'. One review that gave John special pleasure was Philip Hobsbaum's in *Gemini*, which compared him with his old Marlborough rival Louis MacNeice, to the latter's detriment.

In the *New Statesman*, the book was reviewed by the magazine's literary editor, Janet Adam Smith, widow of the poet Michael Roberts who had edited *The Faber Book of Modern Verse* in 1936. John was not her sort of poet, but she did her best to be fair.

> Three cheers for Betjeman the celebrator of oil-lit chancels and bargeboarded country stations; two for the recorder of nostalgia in Brentford, lost

innocence in Norfolk; not much of a cheer for the Betjeman who looks at the social scene today; and no cheers at all for Lord Birkenhead, who does no service to this excellent writer of light verse by claiming too much for him [in his preface]. I can't think that he is likely to win Mr Betjeman new admirers by remarks like 'one who has always stood aloof and alien among the modern poets upon many of whom the autumnal blight of obscurity seems finally to have settled.' Who is he talking about? Empson or Auden? Larkin or Enright?

The name of John Betjeman was becoming known abroad. Houghton Mifflin in New York ordered 250 unbound copies and bumped up the order to 500 when the book 'took off' in London. John fitted the American stereotype of the Englishman as cultured eccentric. *Time* magazine published a full-page profile by Michael Demarest. ('John Betjeman, 52, is a gentle, witty, rumpled Englishman who has been called "the greatest bad poet now living". It would be in character if he agreed with that estimate, although he can be called "bad" only in the sense that his rhymes sometimes jingle like a song writer's . . .') The *Collected Poems* received long, favourable notices from Orville Prescott in the *New York Times* and Walker Gibson in the *New York Review of Books*. 'He is a very attractive poet,' Gibson wrote, 'and the reader never knows when the most frivolous passages may dissolve into deep and finely controlled feeling.'

In December 1958 there was a new boost to John's fame and sales when Princess Margaret presented him with the Duff Cooper Prize. The judges were Maurice Bowra, Lord David Cecil and Harold Nicolson, all old friends of John. The ceremony took place on 18 December at the home of Lady Jones (the writer Enid Bagnold) near Churchill's house at Hyde Park Gate. The *Evening Standard* reported that day: 'Poet John Betjeman, 52, whose London home in Cloth Fair was recently swept by fire, was at work today in the house of his neighbour and landlord Lord Mottistone, the architect. Betjeman is sleeping in a room in Rotherhithe lent to him by photographer Tony Armstrong-Jones.'

Among the guests at Hyde Park Gate were the Duke of Devonshire, Joan Aly Khan, Lord Sheffield and Rupert Hart-Davis. The Princess looked like a 'jewelled, silky bower-bird, with a close-fitting, wild duck's preened feather hat, no hair, skin like a tea rose, wonderfully pretty – and she made her funny, faultless speech with art and sophistication,' Lady Diana Cooper wrote. Presenting John with a cheque for £150 and a leather-bound copy of Duff Cooper's memoirs, *Old Men Forget*, the Princess said it was a particular pleasure to her that that year's recipient of the prize should be 'a friend of mine'. ('John London' of the *News Chronicle* explained: 'The poet first met the Princess five or six years ago. He has taken her to look at some of the old churches about which he is so enthusiastic.') The Princess continued: 'Anyone who has studied John Betjeman's poems closely will have learned not only all about England's lovely old churches but also how to move in society with confidence.' This drew laughter by its obvious reference to the poem beginning, ''Phone for the fish-knives, Norman . . .' Diana Cooper recorded that 'Poor Betch was crying and too moved to find an apology for words,' though next day the *Daily Telegraph* reported him as saying, 'I am overwhelmed by getting the prize. Duff Cooper was a friend of mine, and of many of my friends. I served under him for a short while at the Ministry of Information. We exchanged some very funny notes.' The *News Chronicle* man observed that 'The poet clean forgot at the appropriate moment to present the Princess with a copy of the poems bound in red velvet. He slipped it to her later under the table – but then it had to be given back to him again for an inscription.'

Sir Roderick Jones, the head of Reuters news agency and 'the only living man shorter than the Princess', insisted on winding up with an interminable speech about the Empire, 'punctuated by whispers from his wife – half proud, half explanatory – of "You know, he's eighty one!"' He gave some offence to the chairman of the judges by referring to him as 'Sir Horace Bowra'. Whether from this slight or from jealousy at John's success, Maurice Bowra later composed a malicious poem about the occasion. The first of the seven stanzas ran:

> Green with lust and sick with shyness,
> Let me lick your lacquered toes,
> Gosh, O gosh, your Royal Highness,
> Put your finger up my nose,
> Pin my teeth upon your dress,
> Plant my head with watercress.

John received one of the three velvet-bound copies of the *Collected Poems* from Jock Murray for Christmas, with a case of wine. He wrote a thank-you letter on Christmas Day:

I've never seen anything quite so swish as that red velvet edition in its morocco box except that which was in the long, royal fingers on that horrifying occasion. No man ever had a kinder or more considerate publisher than you. All I've had from Collins is a bill for £21 against some extra copies I ordered of Parish Churches. How different is Mr Murray, who sends delicious wine as well as the books, in which we drunk [*sic*] your health at lunch today.

Of course next year there will be the reaction and I shall suffer contempt, neglect & frustration, but I can now always look back to a really thrilling moment of triumph . . .

26

Summoned by Bells

CANDIDA NEVER QUITE forgave her parents for moving, in 1951, from the Georgian Old Rectory in Farnborough, downhill to their almost parodically Victorian new house, The Mead, in red-brick Wantage. But there was one compensation for the move: it brought the family much nearer to Desmond and Mollie Baring and their children at Ardington House. The Barings became the Betjemans' best friends in the district.

Desmond and Mollie did everything they could to help the Betjeman family. 'Candida was virtually brought up at Ardington,' Mollie said. In 1960 John was able to make some return for the Barings' kindness in what seemed, at the time, an episode of high drama. On 20 April 1960, the *Wantage Herald* reported that an outrage had been perpetrated in the Berkshire town. Under the headline 'KING ALFRED IN THE RED', the newspaper stated: 'Workmen were busy on the statue of King Alfred the Great in Wantage Market Place today removing paint from it. Dark red paint was found today daubed on the face and on the battle-axe. Police are making enquiries.' The granite effigy of Alfred had been sculpted by Queen Victoria's nephew, Count Gleichen, in 1886, and the craggy face was said to have been modelled on that of Lord Wantage, a kinsman of the Betjemans' friends the Loyds.

The police investigation exposed the culprits – fifteen girls at St Mary's School, among them Anne Baring. Mollie, on her way to Goodwood, was summoned back to be interviewed by the police. 'I was a magistrate at the time and so were most of my friends. Someone said to Anne, "You'll probably end up in court." And she said, "Well, what will that matter? It will only be in front of Mummy, Mrs Lonsdale and Mrs Knight!" '

Of the fifteen graffiti artists, twelve had just left St Mary's; but three were staying on, including Anne. Sister Brigitta, the school's formidable headmistress, decided that they must be expelled. Though Candida (who was not involved in the incident) had left the school some time back, John was still a governor. He went to work on Sister Brigitta. He had already had one brush with her, in 1958. Candida was in trouble then. She had copied

378

out some lines from Andrew Marvell's 'To His Coy Mistress' which she had found in the school library –

> My vegetable love should grow
> Vaster than empires, and more slow.

She had substituted the words 'D-cup bras' for 'empires' and passed the lines to a friend. 'Her explosion of laughter caused the piece of paper they were written on to be confiscated and shown to Sister B. who, not knowing her Marvell, took the lines to be an invitation to lesbian frolics. She was at the time cross-questioning the whole school on the question of masturbation.' John and Penelope were called in to see the headmistress, after which meeting John wrote to Sister Brigitta with some asperity:

> One thing on reflection greatly disturbed me in that shattering interview I had with you (and may I say that Mrs Betjeman was even more shattered than me), and that was that you told me the chaplain had said to you he was greatly disturbed by the sex in the school, because of what he had heard in the girls' confessions. I do not think that even in the most general terms a priest should make such a breach of confidence.

When necessary, John could be very tough. He told Sister Brigitta that if the statue-painters were expelled, he would resign as a governor. Given his fame, this would ensure that the vandal-scandal reached national newspapers, not just local ones. 'And I grovelled,' Mollie Baring said. 'The girls were going to be in the sixth form, which carried tremendous privileges. I said, "Why don't you let them stay but take away all their privileges?" – Anne was very upset about that. And Sister Brigitta accepted that compromise and let them stay on.'

In the middle of the crisis over King Alfred, his descendant Princess Margaret married Antony Armstrong-Jones (Lord Snowdon), on 5 May 1960, in Westminster Abbey. John and Penelope were invited. So was William Glenton, Armstrong-Jones's landlord in Rotherhithe. He and the Betjemans agreed that 'for moral support' they would go to the Abbey together.

> As part of the arrangement [Glenton recalled] I was to collect them in my car – but when I arrived at the Kensington house where they were spending the night there was, at first, no reply to my knocking. Only after I had hammered hard for several minutes did the door open, and the plump figure of John, still in pyjamas, appeared. Both he and his wife had overslept, and when I announced that we had only half an hour to get to the Abbey, there was pandemonium. As I helped John to find his clothes, half of which he had mislaid, I kept catching glimpses of a half-dressed female figure dashing up and down stairs – his wife was hunting for her belongings. It was more like

a quick change at the Windmill, and how John managed to get ready in time without putting his ancient morning suit on over his pyjamas I do not know.

Three days after the wedding, Noël Coward wrote in his diary: 'I forgot to mention that during the week I met, at long last, John Betjeman and, of course, loved him immediately.' (The friendship developed. John read the address at Coward's memorial service in 1973 and the playwright left him one of his own oil-paintings in his will.)

After the first two public events that affected John in 1960 – Alfred red, Margaret wed – came a third: the arrival in Wantage of a new vicar. John had always found the previous vicar, the Rev. Arthur Chetwynd-Talbot, a 'dull old stick', and disliked his wife, who had annoyed him by uprooting all the box hedges in the vicarage garden. So he was delighted when a new priest, John Schaufelberger, came to the town. In September 1960 John wrote to Harry Jarvis: 'He is full of jokes, calls everyone "my dear", likes embroidering and I think cats or maybe dogs, lives with his old mother, is dark-haired and forty-four and thank God is *very High*. I hope that Our Lady will come back into prominence and life and a little vulgarity.' A ribald nickname for the new incumbent was soon in circulation: 'Shufflebugger'. The curate, the Rev. Harry Bloomfield, was his boyfriend.

'John came to church very faithfully,' Schaufelberger recalled in 1976. It was at church that John met Bart and Jessie Sharley, who lived in a small terraced house in the road called Portway, in Wantage. John invited the Sharleys back to The Mead for a drink with Penelope, and the two couples became friends. The Berkshire society in which John and Penelope normally moved was of people whose sons were sent to public schools and whose daughters became debutantes. Some of these friends could not understand why the Betjemans spent so much time with the Sharleys. Bart and Jessie were not at all grand. He was a primary-school teacher at King Alfred's School in Wantage; she had been secretary to a director of the Rootes company in London. They had two daughters, slightly younger than Candida – Veronica (Ron) and Diana. 'Penelope called us The Bug Family,' Ron recalled. 'She always said that John should have married Mummy and she should have married Daddy – and all the children would have been prime ministers.'

The Betjemans' and Sharleys' children were less close to each other than their parents were. 'Paul I adored,' Ron said. 'I had a wonderful schoolgirl crush on him. He was always very kind, just like his father, but I don't think he specially noticed me. At that time he had this terrific thing with serpents, he loved snakes. He kept a snake in a glass tank in the library at The

Mead, with a volume of the *Encyclopaedia Britannica* balanced on top to stop it escaping.' Ron saw little of Candida. 'Candida was very much with the yuppies – my sister and I didn't fit into that group. We were sort of glorified village kids, I suppose. She mixed with the Old Etonians and so on – people like Herki [Hercules] Bellville. He was quite sweet – just like a streak of lightning, very tall, very slim.'

Many of Candida's friends were the children of her parents' friends – the Barings, Clives, Harrods, Lancasters, Pipers and Powells. But in Oxford she met a new group of friends, the pioneers of the 1960s satire movement, including Richard Ingrams, Willie Rushton, John Wells and Paul Foot. She fell in love with Ingrams, who had film-star looks to match her own. Ingrams and Rushton were both involved in producing the undergraduate satire magazine *Mesopotamia* (*Mespot* for short – it was named after a spit of land in the River Cherwell). Candida – then taking a sculpture course at the Oxford 'Tech' – went round college rooms selling the magazine. *Mespot* was a prototype for *Private Eye,* which she helped to launch in 1961. By then she had a job sub-editing copy about fur coats for Jocelyn Stevens on *Queen* magazine.

She later wrote of her friends of that time: 'If they seemed like eager university students, they often alarmed my father. He felt vulnerable among them.' At first, he took against the lymphatic and noisy Rushton, and wrote a rude rhyme about him. Rushton retaliated with amusing caricatures of John. But in time John came round to Rushton. Ingrams, too, became a friend and in 1971 John began contributing a 'Nooks and Corners' column to *Private Eye,* pillorying bad architecture and the assaults on good buildings. He always called Ingrams 'old Pressdram' – the latter word was the magazine's telegraphic address.

After Candida was fired from *Queen* magazine, and before she became secretary to John's former Admiralty boss Richard Hughes, she was invited to a house party in Venice. Penelope remembered in 1976: '. . . John said, "On no account must Candida go." He was not going to pay for her to go . . . We had an awful row about it. He was so self-contradictory: I mean, he loves grand people himself. Finally, I paid her return fare; and there she met Rupert Lycett Green – one of the most successful marriages of all time!'

John and Penelope were delighted and relieved when Candida and Rupert became engaged. Twenty-five in 1963, Rupert Lycett Green was Byronically handsome. In that year he founded Blades, the tailors, in Mayfair, London, naming it after the elegant fictional club where James Bond had his greatest gambling triumph in *Moonraker.* The wedding took place on 25 May. At the lunch, which was at Faringdon, Robert

Heber Percy released a flight of Lord Berners's coloured doves. John Schaufelberger, who might have been expected to enjoy such campery, felt that 'it was a falsity'. All the *Private Eye* crowd were at the ball that evening. Candida recalls: 'Nicole [Hornby], who was very tall and quite alarming, waltzed JB, who was smaller, around the dance floor at great speed. My mother . . . bravely intercepted and put an end to it, insisting that JB would be sick.'

In September 1963 Diana Sharley made a tape-recording of an evening that John and Penelope spent with the Sharleys at their home in Portway. The Betjemans knew the recorder was on, and there was some playing to the gallery; but gradually they forgot about it. This unique 'oral document' takes us, as closely as it is possible to get, into the Betjemans' company when John and Penelope were in their fifties. Bart and Jessie Sharley, Diana and Ron were all present.

DIANA SHARLEY (*to Penelope*): You're looking very tired.

PB: Terribly tired. I awoke at four o'clock.

JB: It's very good that she should look tired. Because she's been over-excited and wrought up for so long, it's very much better she should go to bed tired.

PB (*indignantly*): Not over-excited! My God, I haven't been excited. I'm absolutely bored stiff with that house and our possessions.

RON SHARLEY: Where are you going for Christmas, Mr Betjeman?

JB: I don't know, haven't thought about . . .

PB (*interrupting*): Cornwall, you always go to Cornwall.

JB: Generally. I expect I shall go and stay with Joc Lynam and Peggy Lynam Thomas down at Trebetherick. Or I shall be with Mr Piper.

Inconsequential as it is, the 1963 tape gives a fly-on-the-wall view of the Betjemans' strained relationship at that time. There is still affectionate fun between them, but she flares up at his suggestion that she is 'over-excited': on the contrary, she is fed up with having to take responsibility for The Mead and their chattels. Her snappish interruption to insist that John will be spending Christmas in Cornwall illustrates her displeasure over his separate life with Elizabeth Cavendish. (John is dissimulating when he suggests that he may stay with Joc Lynam and Peggy Lynam Thomas in Trebetherick, or that he will 'be with Mr Piper' – when in fact he will be at Treen, his own house in Trebetherick, with Elizabeth.)

Though John's relationship with Elizabeth was now generally accepted in and some way beyond his circle it was still causing awkwardnesses. Ron Sharley remembered that 'Penelope used to have to say to his London secretary, "Can I make an appointment to see John?" ' For a while, Ron had a job in a golf club in Cornwall. 'I used to visit him in Trebetherick,' she said. 'He would say to Elizabeth, "You go and do the shopping, then Ron and I will go for a walk." We used to walk for miles along the beach. Everyone down there called Lady Elizabeth "Mrs Betjeman", but I'm afraid I blurted out: "*That's* not Mrs Betjeman."' Some people who had been friends with John and Penelope for years still kept their distance from Elizabeth.

> It was always slightly embarrassing [Mollie Baring said] because I didn't ever ask Lady Elizabeth to stay at Ardington. I was Penelope's friend. He would have stayed with us more often if I had said, 'Will you and Elizabeth come?' Also, there was a celebrated party held by the d'Avigdor-Goldsmids, at Somerhill. My daughter Anne was Chloë d'Avigdor-Goldsmid's best friend, and Chloë asked Anne to the party. But she also asked John and Elizabeth. Anne rang me and said, 'But I can't go, Mum, can I?' And I said, 'No, I don't think you can.' She said: 'They don't understand. Loving Penelope as I do, I just don't feel I can go.'

Candida, on the other hand, accepted Elizabeth; naturally, she did not want to be alienated from her father. 'I certainly never thought twice about the situation,' she writes. 'Like JB, Elizabeth was a listener and easy to get on with.' In 1964 John and Elizabeth had supper with the Lycett Greens at their new house in Chepstow Villas, Notting Hill Gate, London – 'and from then onwards [Elizabeth] was part of the Lycett Green family'.

In that year, John Osborne exposed to public view John's guilt over his double life, in his play *Inadmissible Evidence*. Improbably, he and John had become friends and, possibly as early as 1958, John had stayed with him at his mill house in Sussex. It is hard to think of anyone less likely to get on with John than the bileful playwright, angriest of the Angry Young Men. The pioneer of 'kitchen sink' drama might have been expected to lump John with Noël Coward as a reactionary fribble, and the title of one of Osborne's later books, *Damn You, England*, could stand as the exact antithesis of John's outlook. But Osborne's sharp, often scatological humour amused John. Still more winningly, it was clear that Osborne was a genuine fan of his. In May 1963 the dramatist wrote in his diary: 'Max Miller, the great priapic God of Flashness, dies. "There'll never be another." As old John Betjeman says, an English genius as pure gold as Dickens or Shakespeare – or Betjeman, come to that.' And again, on receiving a 'spiffing note' from John on his birthday in December 1965: 'What did Trollope say – muddle-headed Johnny? It's deep honesty that distinguishes a gentleman. *He's* got it. He knows how to *revel* in life and have no expectations – and fear death at all times.' A wit and a fan of John's Osborne might be; but, as his wives and most of his friends found out sooner or later, he could suddenly turn on them and spit venom. He might have echoed one of the speeches in *Inadmissible Evidence*: 'I myself am more packed with spite and twitching with revenge than anyone I know of.'

John attended the first performance of the play at the Royal Court Theatre in Chelsea on 9 September 1964. He wrote next day to congratulate Osborne on 'a tremendous play', adding: 'It is the most heart-rending and tender study of every man who is not atrophied. We want to avoid giving pain and we want to be left in peace. Love makes us restless and we resist it. I felt increasingly that the play was about *me* . . . Oh, my dear boy, I can't exactly thank you for such an agonizing self-analysis. I can only reverence the power and generosity in you which makes you write such a shattering and releasing piece.' John was almost certainly dismayed by the play, but realized there was no point in protesting about a *fait accompli*. Osborne was in any case a dangerous man to offend.

Of John's two children, Candida was now 'off his hands', but Paul continued to give some concern. In 1963 Penelope had come to see John Schaufelberger, 'dressed as usual in a pair of old jodhpurs'. She burst out: 'The Powlie has embraced the Mormon faith. At his age, of course, anything like that is permissible. I, in my youth, embraced Zen Buddhism. But at least that has some authenticity – but he has wedded himself to *a bloody fairy story!*' Paul had come back for the wedding from America, where he had enrolled at the Berklee School of Music. Dick Squires, the Betjemans' next-door neighbour in Wantage, saw him on that visit. 'We had tea in our garden,' Squires recalled. 'Paul said, "This is a very nice cake, delicious," and I said, "Oh yes, it's coffee cake" – and he immediately, without thinking, spat it out on the lawn, because coffee's a stimulant forbidden to Mormons.' Osbert Lancaster commented, 'If the Field Marshal knows that his grandson is playing the jazz saxophone and has become a Mormon, he must be rolling about in his grave.' Paul's conversion was less of a joke to John. He wrote to his friend Father Harry Williams, at that time Dean of Chapel at Trinity College, Cambridge, for his advice and was much consoled by it. Williams wrote:

> You must inevitably be very worried about your son Paul. But what occurs to me is that if he wanted, as most sons do, to be different from his parents and didn't want to be an agnostic, you and his mother haven't left him a great deal to choose from. He could have become a Methodist or Baptist, but that would have been frightfully dull. Mormonism is different, calculated to surprise and shock, and a positive religion.

Sending this on to Penelope, in the hope it would help her as it had helped him, John said that when he wrote to Paul he would merely say,

'Love to the Mormons', or 'God moves in a mysterious way His wonders to perform', and make no fuss about it. But he asked her not to tell people about it too much. 'It will probably pass off & if it doesn't it's better than Marxism I suppose or nothing at all & may be full of charity & make the P[owlie] less selfish.' One perennial difficulty for Paul was that, with his distinctive surname, wherever he went in Britain people said to him, 'Oh, are you related to that marvellous . . .?' In America, hardly anyone had heard of John Betjeman. There, Paul could be – as his Eton housemaster had discerned he wanted to be – himself. Eventually he became an American citizen and taught music in New York.

With Paul in America, with Candida married and John, for the most part, in London, The Mead was even less a centre of family life. In November 1963 the Betjemans let it, for eight months, to an interior decorator called Tom Parr. From the early 1960s onwards, Penelope did a lot of travelling. King Alfred's Kitchen was at last sold in 1961, as 'more trouble than it was worth'. In 1965 Penelope decided to write a book about the Kulu Valley in northern India. Published in 1972, it showed how impressive an Indologist she could have been if, instead of marrying John, she had dedicated herself to scholarship. In the later Sixties and the Seventies she spent several months at a time in India, sending him regular letters about her adventures. Her attitude to Elizabeth Cavendish softened a little. When she heard that Mollie Baring was going to Cornwall and would be seeing John and Elizabeth, she asked her to tell Elizabeth how much she appreciated the devoted way she was caring for John. 'How else could I go gallivanting off to India?' she asked. Mollie recalled: 'I told Elizabeth, who said, "How very kind of you." She invited me to visit her when I was in London. But I never went.'

In June 1964 John reported to Penelope, who was in India, that The Mead had been well cared for by Tom Parr and, according to Candida, had become 'a fashionable rendezvous'. He was relieved to find that he did not feel chained to his library there; and he suggested they look for a smaller place. This might have been a moment for the Betjemans, while remaining on affectionate terms, to go their separate ways, to sell The Mead and make good use of the proceeds. Neither John nor Penelope seems to have contemplated this course. Why not? John's letter implied that his whole concern was for Penelope: 'Like you, I have shed much of the need for possessions but know you will want your pony and field for it to graze – and a smaller house.' In other words, he was not going to shrug off his share of financial responsibility for her. This probably was in the forefront of his thinking; but a sub-motive may have been that it suited him, as the very public figure he now was, to continue to seem conventionally and happily married. For her part, Penelope still loved him, had found no other partner and hoped he might one day come back to her; also, her religion was particularly hostile to any backsliding from the marriage vows. And John, in his way, still cared greatly for her, telling friends, 'I love nobody in the world more; but we just can't live together.'

In 1965 the Betjemans divided the house in half, letting the front part to a middle-aged lady with a terrier, and occasionally spending time together in the other part. Candida noted sadly that The Mead was now 'altogether different from how we had found it when we first came in 1951': new houses had been built on the fields which had been sold on either side of the drive, and the houses were soon surrounded by 'municipal shrubs'.

John's prominence as a public figure had been boosted by the publication in 1960 of his verse autobiography *Summoned by Bells*. As long ago as 1941 he had sent John and Myfanwy Piper the typescript of a lengthy autobiographical poem in blank verse to which he referred in letters as 'The Epic'. At that stage, most of the poem was about the Betjemanns' Cornish holidays. Large parts of it were siphoned off and published, with some emendations and changes of names, as 'North Coast Recollections' (first in the *West Country Magazine*, Spring 1947, then in *Selected Poems*, 1948). Other extensive passages were used, again with some changes, in *Summoned by Bells*. A few passages in the early version of the 'Epic' were never published – less because John thought them of inferior quality than because he felt they were too harsh about his parents and might give offence to surviving relatives.

The bulk of *Summoned by Bells* was written between the early months of 1958 and the early months of 1960. When the poem was broadly completed, a typescript was sent first to Tom Driberg, then to John Sparrow, for them to make comments and to suggest possible changes. Preserved in Murray's archives, the typescript bears copious marginalia by Driberg, Sparrow and John, with the odd addition by Jock Murray. Driberg and Sparrow expressed themselves with great freedom and often with a jocose *de haut en bas* tone, as when the word 'proffering', in John's line 'My father, proffering me half a crown, said . . .', draws from Sparrow the comment, 'How many times must I tell you that you must not drag out such words into three syllables. TD is right.' (Driberg had written: 'Awkward scansion – As he proffered half a crown?' In the published version, John opted for 'My father, handing to me half-a-crown'.) Driberg is severe on mixed tenses. Sparrow is forever replacing 'which' with 'that' – 'John Sparrow is a great which-hunter,' Jock Murray quipped.

John agonized most about the lines that described the love he had felt for Donovan Chance at Marlborough. Partly at Sparrow's urging, partly on his own initiative, he deleted large passages from this section of the poem – which, however, survive in the typescript at Murray's.

> O dreadful sin against the Holy Ghost!
>   Sin for which ~~Blanksome~~ Major was expelled   Branksome
> The only sin which could not be forgiven
>   Even by God in chapel.
> 'Break temptation's fatal power,
>   Shielding all with guardian care;
> Safe in every careless hour
>   Safe from sloth and sensual snare
>   Thou our Saviour
> Still our failing strength repair.'

> This nameless evil sapped one's strength for games,
> It made the mind too weak to pass exams,
> Rotted the will, for ever stained the soul
> And drove its victims on to suicide.
> There were unmentionable forms of sin
> For which one went to prison. Oscar Wilde
> Had practised them. Thus life was only safe
> Exchanging scandal with contemporaries:
> And love, of course, was poles apart from sex.

In the original, these lines were followed immediately by the lines which introduce Donovan Chance in the published poem, beginning, ' "Coming down town?" I had not thought of him . . .'

Other early drafts of the Marlborough poem which, in the published version, begins 'The smell of trodden leaves beside the Kennet . . .' contain these stanzas:

> ~~I could not analyse the new emotion~~ Intense and inexplicable emotion
>   Here by the fives-courts, by myself at last
> ~~I revelled in the warm enclosing ocean~~ I longed to meet the
>   warm enclosing ocean
>   Of love to come and persecution past
> Here 'twixt the church tower and the chapel spire
> Rang sad and deep the bells of my desire.

> Sad, deep and vast, bells through the branches pealing
>   Under the clouds which raced from Granham Hill
> Gave me that guilty, dread religious feeling
>   Those lovers know whom only dreams fulfil.

Lit windows rose impersonal and grim
But lights in one house class-room shone on him.

Though Mr Gidney's hours were now no brighter,
   Nor could I concentrate on verbs ~~in Greek~~   in μί
Yet dark school passages were made the lighter
   By the mere whirlwind of his rushing by.
The labs might show him meddling with retorts
Or goalposts frame him in his muddy shorts.

'Vainly we offer each ample oblation.'
   The hymns in chapel had a meaning new
'Richer by far is the heart's adoration'
   Lucky, by Jove, were his hymn book and pew
He read the one and rested on the other
'Oh brother man, fold to thy heart a brother.'

(Then followed the stanza beginning 'The smell of trodden leaves . . .',
later transferred to the beginning of the poem.)

   How could I have withstood those five years flowing
      From boredom on to boredom; how endure
   Without romantic love to keep them going –
      Romantic love so rarefied and pure
   That the sole reason why it never died
   Was just because it was unsatisfied.

   Hot summers of discovering liberation
      Moving from Oscar Wilde to *Antic Hay*
   Commanding Officers' exasperation
      On Corps parades: The tedious Molière play:
   Escaping cricket by the skilful ruse
   Of biking off to sketch with Mr Hughes.

   'Castle and Ball' when stopping in my motor
      To drink within your warming-pann'd recess
   I still recall my mother's fearful floater
      ~~By coming down in far two young a dress~~ When she came
                   down in far too young a dress
   For Prize Day and I recollect my dread
   As the lounge listened to the things she said.

(Sparrow wrote of this: 'Irrelevant stanza. It's not good. It doesn't reproduce the anguish or the [romantic?] ecstasy.')

   Fresh and refreshed I motor past the College
      Whose prison walls look still the same and close

> Round those grim classrooms of pedantic knowledge
>> Where the years showed me who were friends and foes
> Two things your stern conventions taught me well:
> What joy it was to love and to rebel.

(Sparrow wrote: 'This lyric is not up to standard. Try to remember what being in love at school was *really* like.')

In the original version of the Marlborough poem, John wrote:

> Was God what I was waiting for, or love?

Sparrow commented: ' "Was God what I was waiting for?" is a false note. God was not what you were waiting for, nor did you think it was Him. Don't mention Him.' For the published version, John changed the line to

> Perhaps what I was waiting for was love!

In the early draft, John's description of his love as 'a delightful illness That put me off my food and off my stroke' is followed by the couplet:

> Electric currents racing through my frame –
> Was this the love that dare not speak its name?

These lines were cut from the printed version and replaced by a less explicit couplet; however, John recycled the 'electric current' notion in the next chapter, in recounting his love for Biddy Walsham in Cornwall –

>> If my hand
> By accident should touch her hand, perhaps
> The love in me would race along to her
> On the electron principle, perhaps . . . ?

In the typescript, the Marlborough poem, in its six-line stanzas, was followed by the continuation of the main narrative of *Summoned by Bells*, beginning:

> Desire for what? I think I can explain
> The boys I worshipped did not worship me
> The boys who worshipped me I did not like . . .
> And life was easier in terms of jokes
> And gossip, chattered with contemporaries –
> Till one there was – yes one there was whose light
> Irradiated all the summer term
> Neither through what he did nor what he thought –
> His interests were chiefly motor-cars,
> His friends not my friends – did we come together
> The usual greetings in the gravel court,

The shouted joke, flying along with books
He to the Science, I to the History Sixth,
The wink across the parted chapel pews.
Occasional visits after lunch down town.
To Stratton, Sons & Mead for groceries,
Agreement upon masters we disliked
And priggish boys and prefects in the house –
These were of each of us the outward sum
And sex, the sin against the Holy Ghost,
Was quite unthinkable. It would pollute
The freckled innocence of one who seemed
So perfect that I now believed in God
So handsome his existence was enough . . .

Very little of this passage survived in the published poem, perhaps as a result of Sparrow's remonstrance in the typescript's margin:

'The boys I worshipped . . .' These lines just won't do. Who are these 'boys' (plural)? *What is this 'worship'?* You introduce this whole poignant theme with two flat lines and it turns out to be only *one*, after all. And you don't give the feel of it. He might be anybody. Try to *remember* Donovan C! Give personal details of *him*! Recreate your feelings for him – if you ever had any, and I am beginning to suspect you of not having done so. Don't insist too much on the innocence of the passion (which I readily accept), but convey its intensity (as you do so well for 'John Lambourn' in 'North Coast Recollections'). In short this is NOT up to snuff. You must try again. Sorry, but so it is.

Sparrow, supremely uninterested in girls, also wanted John to cut the lines about his childhood feeling for Biddy Walsham, in the 'Cornwall in Adolescence' chapter. Opposite the last line of the penultimate 'paragraph' of that section, ('She would explain that I was still a boy') Sparrow wrote: 'PLEASE end this canto here. It is such a good end and leads on so well to the next, "The Opening World". And the lines about Biddy Walsham are not in keeping or in context and are NOT good in themselves – second-grade Betjeman. What goes before is first-grade. Don't spoil it.' John took Sparrow's criticism seriously, and right up to a late proof stage was un-decided whether to cut the Biddy Walsham passage. Eventually he followed Elizabeth Cavendish's and Jock Murray's advice and left it in.

John for the most part left people's real names in the typescript, chang-ing them to pseudonyms in the published version. The boy who was covered with ink and treacle and hoisted in the giant waste-paper basket was Ingle – L. D. C Ingle, who had entered the school with John in 1920 and, according to the *Marlborough College Register*, did indeed leave early, as recorded in the poem ('Never to wear an old Marlburian tie'), and became a horticulturalist. In the poem, John called him 'Angus'. Though this retained the 'ng' sound and had the right number of syllables, it caused diffi-culties with the original line –

> Though Ingle's body called 'Unclean! Unclean!'

'Though Angus's body . . .' disrupted the scansion; so John had to change the line to –

> Though the boy's body called 'Unclean! Unclean!'

As early as 29 April 1959 Jock Murray could write to Leonard Russell, the literary editor of the *Sunday Times,* 'The vicissitudes of the present work have already been considerable.' There were many more vicissitudes to come, chiefly relating to John's heavy revision, to negotiations for the print-ing of an extract in the *New Yorker,* and to the book's design, including its brown-paper jacket and the bell changes illustrated on its endpapers. (Philip Larkin, in his review of the book, described the endpapers as 'awful'.)

At last, in August 1960, page proofs were ready. A set was sent to Stephen Spender, who wrote to Jock Murray, 'It is his best work and certainly a classic of our times because it is so beautifully founded on experiences intensely lived and accurately remembered.' Murray asked permission to use this comment in pre-publication publicity. Spender wrote back: 'Yes. I meant it!' The *New Yorker* extract had appeared on 27 August. Philip Larkin wrote to Murray on 14 September, 'I am greatly looking forward to *Summoned by Bells,* something of which I have already seen in the *New Yorker.* I wish there were more of it, but there it is. One cannot be lengthy without being tedious (see Coleridge) and Betjeman is incapable of that.'

Not since the Festival of Britain nine years earlier had there been a pub-licity campaign so clamorously and successfully orchestrated as that for the launch of *Summoned by Bells.* It began as early as 24 July with a note by Leonard Russell, in his 'Mainly about Books' column in the *Sunday Times.* 'John Betjeman has just completed his finest work, a long autobiograph-ical poem in blank verse called *Summoned by Bells* (Murray, November). Fresh from reading it in manuscript, I abandon all the usual literary equivo-cations, and call it a masterpiece.' By this stage the *Sunday Times* had secured the serial rights.

On 4 November the *Daily Telegraph* trumpeted: 'more than a literary sensation – an experience all must share. The life poem of John Betjeman . . . John Betjeman recites a passage from his autobiography to Leonard

Russell, literary editor of the *Sunday Times*.' Two days later, the *Sunday Times* published the first of three serial extracts under a Gothic canopy ornamented with gargoyles of mischievous schoolboy heads. The artist Charles Mozley also drew an impression of the schoolboy John, based on early photographs.

John's Oxford friend Michael Dugdale – mentioned in the poem – wrote up the publication-day party on 28 November in his diary.

> Back to finish the Betjeman poem so as to be able to say, this evening, that I had done so. It is successful, I think, but not his masterpiece. Would I have read it had I known neither the author nor some of the events and people it describes? I doubt if I should have got to the end.
>
> Then to the party, and a very good evening it proved to be. We met at Jock Murray's beautiful office in Albemarle Street. We were the following: Jock, Betjeman, John Bryson, Ben Bonas, John Dugdale, Tom Driberg, Philip Harding and myself. In fact the entire available cast of 'Summoned by Bells'. Some talk and drink and laughter – for none of us have been in the habit of meeting a great deal of late. We then moved off to a near-by restaurant, and dined off oysters and sole bonne femme, and a bottle of white wine which Tom ruthlessly sent back as being corked. I sat between Betj. and Bryson with Driberg opposite, and got, therefore, the pick of the conversation . . .
>
> 'Will John Wain spoil my sales?' asked JB in the voice of one who did not think that anyone could do that.
>
> A very perfect evening.

John was in need of some affection and comforting at the party. The day before, *The Observer* – whose cantankerous literary editor, Terence Kilmartin, thought he had been promised the rights and was furious at being scooped by the *Sunday Times* – published the brutal John Wain review mentioned by Dugdale. Deriding 'timid reviewers', with their 'squeals of adulation' for John's work, Wain scorned his 'complete lack of the skills of the true poet, his wooden technique, his watercolours slapped at the canvas, his incuriosity about literary art', and added:

> Most of his poems are written either in hymn-metres or in metres usually associated with 'light' and comic verse. These forms, themselves loaded with the kind of suggestion he means to convey, are the literary counterpart of Betjemanian *bric-à-brac* in the world of objects – yellow-brick steeples and the rest. To manipulate them needs no more skill than is shown by the men who write the jingles on Christmas cards. And that so many people find Mr Betjeman the most (or only) attractive contemporary poet is merely one more sign that the mass middle-brow public distrusts and fears poetry.

The Bookman quoted these dismissive lines under the crosshead 'Summoned by Jingle Bells'.

Punch, which had also been eager to secure the serial rights, now published a similarly disobliging review, by Julian Symons, under the heading 'Private Giggles'. A whiff of sour grapeshot?

> The Betjeman, like the South Sea Bubble, grows and grows . . . here indeed is a poet for the Plain Man. But Mr Betjeman's critical reputation at least must surely be badly damaged by this long stretch of autobiography, written for the most part in singularly blank verse which contains so many object-lessons in the art of sinking. ' "Haven't you heard," said D. C. Wilkinson, "Angus is to be basketed tonight." ' 'Ah-hah,' say the Betjemanites, 'but Betjeman himself knows that such lines are funny. Yes, and a little bit sad, too. He anticipates all your criticisms.' Perhaps he does: but still the product of this tear-in-the-eye whimsicality is not poetry.

In the *Sunday Times* on the same day as Wain's *Observer* diatribe, Raymond Mortimer, a friend of John's, could muster only a qualified enthusiasm for the book.

While Wain and Mortimer criticized the poetic technique, Robert Pitman, the *Sunday Express* columnist, attacked what he took to be the 'kinkiness' of its subject-matter, in a parody of John's more familiar style.

> But before the bit on Oxford
> There is something rather *odd*
> In the way he notes each belting,
> Each debagging, every rod,
> Every nurse's spanking fingers,
> Every bully's boot unkind
> Which made imprint almost daily
> On the Betjeman behind.
> He gives each humiliation
> In such detail that you'd say
> There'd be not much book left over
> If you took the pain away . . .

December brought a kinder press. On the 1st, the *Times* reviewer had some patronizing things to say, but conceded: 'The more one reads through it all, the more plain does it become that what Mr Betjeman has brought off is not the *Prelude* of today but a lightweight version of *Sinister Street*. The young John and Michael Fane in Sir Compton Mackenzie's once best-selling novel have much in common.' P. N. Furbank in *The Listener* tried to fathom why John's poetry was so popular.

Betjeman's present vogue is part of contemporary English chauvinism. The English cannot hear too much about themselves at present. In the decline of their imperial greatness they are studying and inventorying themselves with passion and the richness of their preposterous socio-architectural inheritance dazzles them. An eye trained simultaneously upon class and architecture, and a tone which parodies both, have thus made Betjeman peculiarly topical . . .

On 2 December William Plomer, perhaps the poet of that time who had most affinity with John, gave him a straight 'rave' in the *Daily Telegraph*. ('In this poem his humanity, his precision in detail, his powers of enjoyment, and the playful wit that never quite hides his seriousness are all to be found in plenty. It will increase the admiration and affection he has won by being himself . . . But it may annoy literary prigs who find popularity unforgivable.') John wrote to him: 'The last sentence of your kind review . . . has saved me from a nervous breakdown brought on by persecution mania. I really thought the verse not bad and complete in itself and it was much worked on. Fuck Wain and the prig in *The Times* who was probably Griggers [Geoffrey Grigson]. I've gone away to escape further blows.'

Philip Larkin's review in *The Spectator* was all that poet and publisher could have hoped for. 'He is an accepter, not a rejecter, of our time, registering "dear old, bloody old England" with robustness, precision and a vivacious affection that shimmers continually between laughter and rage . . . Although it remains a mystery how Mr Betjeman can avoid the traps of self-importance, exhibitionism, silliness, sentimentality and boredom, he continues to do so. Why should we accept his teddy bear when we want to stuff Sebastian Flyte's down his throat? . . . No doubt sincerity is the answer, a sincerity as unselfconscious as it is absolute . . .'

In compensation for the many reviews which failed to take John seriously, V. S. Pritchett's *New Statesman* review, on 3 December, observed that 'Mr Betjeman's real subject is not nostalgia, but the sense of insecurity, the terror of time and pain. The laughs come at the point of agony. If it sounds like the chuckle of *The Diary of a Nobody*, it has far more of the delighted scream of the fiend.' Pritchett thought that John's genre was very English: 'it is perpetuated only by very clever, frightened, defensive people who are given sedulously to ritual . . .'. At a second or third reading, the verse disclosed its essence: 'he is a true excavator of drama'.

On 9 December, sending John a favourable but uninspired review by Peter Quennell in the *Weekly Post*, Jock Murray wrote:

A survey of all reviews makes most fascinating reading. Though the envious sharks got the lead at the start, they have been well and truly routed now, so

394

you have no excuse for indulging in symptoms of persecution mania.

News of progress: the approximate figure of sales before publication was 35,000. Sales today are passing the 50,000 mark.

I have just seen – for approval – the first copy of the limited edition which in modern parlance looks smashing. The edition should be ready for signing just before Christmas. I am afraid you will have to keep the major portion of an afternoon for this.

The full 75,000 first printing of the book was soon sold, and Murray reprinted. By the end of 1960 John was to many Britons not just one of the most famous Englishmen, but one of the best-known people in the world. In a 'round-up of the year' cartoon for New Year's Eve, Cummings of the *Daily Express* showed him with (among others) Prince Philip, President Kennedy and Chancellor Adenauer.

In February John received a warmly appreciative letter about the work from his old Magdalen friend Martyn Skinner, writing as one poet to another. The two men had kept in touch. John had admired Skinner's *Letters to Malaya*, a wartime poem in heroic couplets which had won the Hawthornden Prize; and from time to time he gave his opinion on the majestic epic 'The Return of Arthur' that Skinner was writing, for which John would eventually write a foreword. He replied to Skinner on 23 February 1961:

What pleases me most is that you (& John Sparrow) alone know – or at any rate have expressed – the laborious technique that went to make it seem effortless & readable & concise at the same time. I knew that I had done that, but until you wrote I did not realize anyone had consciously seen that I had made that particular effort. It involved cutting out a lot of dead stuff. Now that you have written I feel immensely cheered up for this awful publicity (much of it well-meaning) has been getting me down.

Another spirit of the Oxford past summoned up by the book was Edward James, who wrote several rambling letters to say how much he had enjoyed the poem, especially the parts about himself. A friend had sent him John's *Punch* poem 'Edward James' of 1958, which was incorporated in *Summoned by Bells* ('They tell me he's in Mexico, / They will not give me his address . . .'). James had given strict orders to his agent at West Dean, Sussex, that he was not to divulge his Mexican address to anybody; but on the illogical whim of the petulant, spoilt rich man he was, he fired him for not having given John his address. In return for a complimentary copy of *Summoned by Bells*, James prepared a magnificently bound copy of his own recent poems written under the pseudonym

'Edward Silence', and hand-painted an elaborate dedicatory title-page for John; but when he had finished the decoration, he was so pleased with his artistry that he kept the book and never sent it – at least living up to his pseudonym.

In March 1961 a biography of John by Derek Stanford was published. Philip Toynbee, who roasted it in *The Observer*, took the chance to summarize what he took to be John's achievement.

> It had to happen soon, but it does seem a pity that it had to happen through the dull and obfuscating medium of Mr Stanford. (He was first on the ball with Dylan Thomas too; and this ordeal is not the least of the dubious fates which seem to attend the achievement of popularity in verse. Think of Mr Stanford, all you young poets, when you set foot on the primrose path!) This is a bad book indeed and my only excuse for reviewing it is that I find the subject of it deeply interesting.
>
> Mr Betjeman has three more or less distinct claims on our attention. There is the simple claim of his verse itself – its uniqueness of tone and method. There is the fact that the 'Collected Poems' have sold over 80,000 copies and 'Summoned by Bells' 60,000 copies. There is finally the fact that Mr Betjeman has changed our vision to the extent that certain English scenes or buildings immediately evoke his name.
>
> It is fashionable – which does not mean that it is wrong – to decry the verse; but my own view is that the point is usually missed in the more savage attacks. Betjeman is a pasticheur – which means that the claims made by the verse (they are not the same as the claims made for them by its more ardent admirers) are obstinately modest . . . I must add, with a real regret, that I cannot apply this approbation to Mr Betjeman's last poem. 'Summoned by Bells' seems to me to be an almost unmitigated disaster – a gross case of a writer miscalculating not only his capabilities but the whole nature of his talent . . .

'An almost unmitigated disaster' was the most crushing of the verdicts on John's most ambitious poem. But in his otherwise ambivalent *Sunday Times* review, Raymond Mortimer put the case for it: 'We say to ourselves, not "This is poetry" but "This is the truth."'

27

The Euston Arch and the Coal Exchange

IN 1959 JOHN came back to a Cloth Fair restored and titivated by 'the Partners', Lord Mottistone and Paul Paget. Tory Dennistoun had left to marry John Oaksey – then a successful point-to-point rider and later a popular racing commentator. John now decided to employ male instead of female secretaries. Through his friend Canon Freddy Hood, who tried to find jobs for clergymen who were in 'a spot of trouble', he employed several in the early Sixties. 'Perhaps he thought they would not be constantly leaving to get married,' Candida speculates; but there was another reason, too, for his taking on Hood's protégés. 'There, but for the grace of God . . .' he would say. Asked by Osbert Lancaster what an ex-priest had been 'done' for, he replied, 'Bare ruined choirs, where late the sweet birds sang.'

Harry Jarvis, who had been chaplain at Summer Fields prep school, Oxford, was one of the priest–secretaries. His rôle was not only secretarial. It also resembled that of a batman to an officer ('Make the bed, make the tea, open the champagne at midday') and private chaplain to a lord. Sometimes he took John's confession formally, in church; more often John used him as 'a confessor out of the confessional, so to speak'. The two men became great friends.

Jarvis was a sympathetic confidant on John's private life. In August 1960 John wrote to him from Wantage:

> As the calm mentor of my life and the only person who knows its twisted strands, please remember in your prayers Phoeble [Elizabeth Cavendish] and me and Penelope and Paul and Candida. I must not make Phoeble unhappy as I do with my ties here. How can I hurt least? It is all very fraught, I know that.

John's relationship with Lady Elizabeth, so settled in later years, was still in the balance. Elizabeth did not want to break up the Betjemans' marriage and had tried to give him up. In 1954 John had written to Jack Beddington: 'I am ill from a broken heart at present and the pleasures of life seem very far away.' Elizabeth's distancing herself from him at that time provoked a poem for and about her, 'The Cockney Amorist', which, because of its sensitive personal context, John witheld from publication for twelve years –

> Oh when my love, my darling,
> You've left me here alone,
> I'll walk the streets of London
> Which once seemed all our own.
>
> . . .
>
> I love you, oh my darling,
> And what I can't make out
> Is why since you have left me
> I'm somehow still about.

Was there a veiled threat of suicide in that last stanza? Or just the romantic implication, 'I shall die of a broken heart'?

In March 1960 John wrote to Father Harry Williams:

Feeble is getting v[ery] pale and washed out again. Partly it is insecurity about me. I love her. But I also love – and very deeply – Penelope and the kiddiz. If Feeble falls in love elsewhere, I will be able just to get along. Of course, without her, I would probably write nothing more except the dreariest hackwork and would get still more into debt. But I don't really mind about that. I do mind about not hurting Feeble. I'm so glad we are in your prayers.

At his most tormented, John put his feelings about the situation into his poem 'Guilt' –

> I haven't hope. I haven't faith.
> I live two lives and sometimes three.
> The lives I live make life a death
> For those who have to live with me . . .

In contrast with the tribulations of his private life, John basked in public fame after the publication of *Summoned by Bells*. Journalists beat a path to his door. One of the best writers among them was Kenneth Allsop, who wrote a profile of John for the *Daily Mail* in December 1960. Allsop, who had lost a leg in a road accident, limped up the narrow staircase of No. 43.

The Poet of 1960 [he wrote], the only English mass-circulation bard since Kipling . . . is flat out in his flat spin through his London morning.

John Betjeman, the minstrel of middle-class suburbia as well as Top People's unofficial laureate, is floundering bemusedly about his tiny house in Cloth Fair, behind Smithfield meat market, looking like a flood victim in search of somewhere to be cast up.

His ash-powdered suit apparently clove to him some time ago down-stream. He has two cigarettes going at once. He has just been gulping a cup of tea and is now sloshing out some whisky.

His secretary is vainly trying to get his pen to connect with the bottom of some typed letters. Christopher Hollis drops in, so does a young woman wanting the Betjeman autograph on her copy of his new smash best-seller . . . *Summoned by Bells*. The telephone bell shrills continually, relentlessly summoning him.

In a brief interlude between calls from an importuning TV producer and an editor Mr Betjeman relates a conversation a friend has just had with Earl Attlee: 'Attlee's a dear old thing. He said "Betjeman's such a relief." "A relief from what?" my friend asked. "From other poets," Attlee said.'

Mr Betjeman screeches with laughter, revolving once or twice inside his motionless suit, and, forgetting the whisky, snatches at the teacup.

Then the laughter dies as if a fuse has blown and his face crumples back into its more customary sag of apprehensive dolour.

John's new worry, he tells Allsop, is of not being able to pay his taxes. His old apprehension about death is always there. 'I dread the idea of extinction, and I think about death every day.' As the whisky takes effect, John lets some of his resentment at the criticism for *Summoned by Bells* glint through.

'Well,' Mr Betjeman reflects kindly, 'I could hardly expect the approval of these poor accentless, rootless, joyless brain-boxes.

'It is understandable that, not being very good poets themselves, they are envious if one is lucky enough to be more widely read. However, to keep this in proportion I keep reminding myself that Ella Wheeler Wilcox sold like this.'

John's nearest neighbour in the City, except for the Partners, was Andrew Graham, the wine correspondent of *The Times*, who lived in the Charterhouse and needed help to empty the many cases of wine he received. The Garrick Club was another temptation. Fleet Street, today no more than a metaphor, was then still a thrumming reality. (It can be seen as it was then, in the 1963 comedy film *Brothers in Law*, based on Henry Cecil's novel.) John's freelance journalism took him to Fleet Street; and the Garrick was a convenient haven near the City and the newspaper offices. Too often for the health of his bank balance, he entertained there. His publisher, Jock Murray, recalled:

He was a marvellous host. And unfortunately he was fond of oysters, smoked salmon and champagne. And I remember his accountant, a Mr Masterson, who was also a poet (which is perhaps why he stayed with that accountant) coming into the office and saying, 'Oh, Mr Murray, is there any royalty?

Because John is rather in the red.' And he said, 'You know, there are times when I find myself going down on my knees and praying, "O Lord God, prevent John Betjeman from going to the Garrick Club."'

Among the friends John most enjoyed seeing were Ian and Ann Fleming. Ian Fleming was becoming famous through the James Bond books and films. John had first known Ann through her brother Hugo Charteris, novelist and playwright. Her celebrated bitchiness was entertaining so long as it was not turned on oneself; John, who had taken against Evelyn Waugh when the novelist tried to bully him into becoming a Roman Catholic, especially enjoyed the story of how, when Waugh affectedly proffered her his Victorian ear-trumpet, she had banged it smartly with a spoon. In December 1963, a few months before Ian Fleming died, John wrote him a fan letter to cheer him up. Fleming replied: 'A thousand thanks, my dear John, for, I think, the most unexpected and charming letter I have ever had. But as Annie said when she delightedly read me the letter, "Tell him that *he's* the person that created a world."'

For John to create his world, it had become important for him to battle against the destructive urges of others. In 1960 the Euston Arch became the latest target of developers, exactly as he had anticipated. As he had declared when accepting the Foyle's Poetry Prize in 1955, 'Poets are prophets.' There would seem to be a mysterious link between poesie and prophecy; William Blake is only the most obvious example. John, too, had this gift. In 1933, still in his twenties, he wrote in *The Architectural Review*: 'Hardwick's Doric Arch at Euston is the supreme justification of the Greek Revival in England . . . If vandals ever pulled down this lovely piece of architecture, it would seem as though the British Constitution had collapsed . . .' He lived to see the arch demolished. Its destruction became a *cause célèbre*, an oriflamme for every future conservation battle. As Dr Dan Cruikshank has said, 'The arch had symbolized the might of the railways. Now it was to symbolize institutionalized vandalism and the triumph of stupidity and greed over beauty.'

Euston station was built by the London and Birmingham Railway, a company formed in 1830. The directors of the company wanted the new station to express the importance of the first trunk railway to link the capital and the provinces. It was planned by their engineer, Robert Stephenson, son of George Stephenson of *Rocket* fame. The design was entrusted to Philip Hardwick. The Doric arch was the central feature, a gateway linked to flanking lodges by ornamental gates.

The Euston Arch stood seventy feet high and was supported on four fluted columns each eight feet six inches in diameter. The total length of the façade was 300 feet and it cost the company £35,000. It was built by W. and L. Cubitt using some 80,000 cubic feet of stone from the Bramley Hall quarries in Yorkshire. Behind this entrance were the arrival and departure platforms, offices and waiting-rooms. Although at the time the line to Birmingham was far from complete, Euston station was opened on 20 July 1837, with a service between London and Boxmoor in Hertfordshire. As Victoria had become queen exactly a month before on the death of her uncle William IV, the station just came within the purview of the Victorian Society.

The first reference in the press to the possibility that the arch might be threatened was on 22 January 1960. In a paragraph headed 'PROPOSALS FOR EUSTON STATION ARCH', *The Times* reported that the London County Council town planning committee would have no objection to the removal of the Doric arch at Euston Station – so that the site might be used in the London–Manchester electrification scheme – provided it were re-erected in another 'appropriately dignified and open setting'. The LCC was deferring a decision on the station's Great Hall, which the British Transport Commission (the body charged with overseeing the nationalized British Railways) wanted to remove for the same purpose, to obtain professional advice.

The British Transport Commission had long wanted to see the station redeveloped. Since the building was put up in the 1830s the needs of passenger, freight and parcels traffic had, like the population, vastly increased. The main-line and Underground stations were unequal to the demands made on them. These demands would become greater still when the Commission electrified the main line from London to Birmingham, Manchester and Liverpool. Euston station occupied a large area of land, set back from the Euston Road. The Commission wanted to bring it forward, with longer platforms – which would also be more suitable for trains which were longer and faster than those of the nineteenth century. In addition, London Transport wanted to resite the entrance to Euston Underground station. Beyond these practical issues was the question of 'image', to use a term that became popular in the 1960s. Bernard Kaukas, then deputy to the chief architect of the London Midland Region of British Railways, and – perhaps surprisingly – later a good friend of John's, recalls that the attitude of the Region's general manager was: 'We are coming to the end of the electrification. What an embarrassment if at Euston there is what everyone but the conservationists considers a wretched mish-mash of buildings and platforms, in which it is hellish to try to get a train.' Kaukas concluded: 'No way were they going to have this archaism at the end of the electrified line.'

The British Transport Commission's architects, led by Frederick Curtis, decided that the Doric arch could not be retained in its then position on Drummond Street, facing the present Platform 9. The Commission therefore notified the LCC, as planning authority for the area, of their intention to demolish it. They had to give such notification because the arch was listed by the Ministry of Housing and Local Government as a building of special historic or architectural interest. In the list prepared in 1951 the arch had been registered as Grade II* – meaning that it was outstanding in the second class. Although copies of the list had been issued to the Society for the Protection of Ancient Buildings and the Georgian Group in 1951, no suggestion that the building was incorrectly listed was made until 1960.

The first public figure to campaign against the proposed demolitions at Euston was not John, but Woodrow Wyatt, a maverick politician who was then in the Labour Party but who, twenty-five years later, would be among Margaret Thatcher's and Rupert Murdoch's closest friends. John wrote to Wyatt on 28 January 1960 to congratulate him on raising the matter of the arch and to tell him about a piece he was writing for the *Daily Telegraph*. John's article duly appeared on 8 February. He could not conceal his anger:

> There is very little written about railway buildings. The names of the architects of some of our grandest stations such as Temple Meads are forgotten.
>
> Partly because of this and partly because of an incredible insensitivity to architecture on the part of the British Transport Commission in the past, a great many splendid buildings have been mutilated or allowed to decay.

Meanwhile, Woodrow Wyatt was getting his campaign under way. Sir Keith Joseph, then Parliamentary Secretary at the Ministry of Housing and Local Government (but twenty-five years later the 'Mad Monk of Monetarism' and 'a Thatcherite before Mrs Thatcher'), reported to the House of Commons that the British Transport Commission had given notice that it intended to remove both the Great Hall and the Doric arch at Euston. The Ministry was 'considering the matter'. Wyatt intervened: 'It would be an act of vandalism to destroy the Great Hall and Shareholders' Room at Euston, which was the first railway station to be built in any capital city in the world, and has been designated as an historic monument.' A speech by Julian Snow, Labour Member for Lichfield and Tamworth, showed that the conservationists were not going to have things all their own way. 'There are mixed views about the Doric arch,' he said. 'While it has an historic quality, not everybody is convinced that it has artistic merit.'

On 19 April *The Times* published a strong letter from Nikolaus Pevsner. 'If the Euston Arch were destroyed,' he wrote, 'that would be the worst loss to the Georgian style in London architecture since most of Soane's Bank of England fell shortly before the war.' No doubt Pevsner calculated that there would be more sympathy for 'Georgian' than for 'Victorian'. On 11 June John's friend Sir John Summerson contributed a long signed article to *The Times*, 1,600 words of damning faint praise. John always called Summerson 'Coolmore', not just because it was his mother's maiden name, but because it seemed to fit him: there was something of frigid neo-classicism in his character. His article on Euston was severe to the point of disparagement. Its first sentence was defeatist and deprecating. 'Euston station as it stands at this moment (but will not stand for very much longer) is, perhaps, the greatest railway curiosity in the world.' A *curiosity*: something that had no place in the brave post-austerity Britain of the 1960s. He added: 'Today the Euston portico or "arch" (as it is wrongly but perhaps irrevocably called) stands in grossly embarrassed relationship to everything around it.'

John had in the meantime been stirring things up behind the scenes. Although in 1953 he had lost a battle to prevent Magdalen College, Oxford, from creating a rose-garden in the High Street, it had taught him the value of a decision by the Royal Fine Art Commission. No public body could wholly ignore such a recommendation, even if the intention was to defy it eventually; so the Commission could at least defer catastrophe. John used his influence with the RFAC, and his vote; the Commission recommended that the Euston Arch should be preserved. In the Commons on 21 July 1960, Woodrow Wyatt asked the Prime Minister, Harold Macmillan, whether he would appoint a minister with the responsibility of implementing the RFAC's recommendation. 'No,' Macmillan replied. 'Such action would be entirely inconsistent with the Commission's status as an advisory body.' Wyatt was not to be put down.

> Will the Prime Minister look into this, and check the careless vandalism that is going on under his Government? The RFAC have recommended to the Ministry of Housing and Local Government that Euston Station should not be pulled down and the Doric arch not destroyed. It has been totally ignored. These are wonderful monuments to the railway age which should not disappear entirely. (*Some Ministerial laughter.*)

That was the trouble with having Wyatt on one's side: no one took him very seriously.

Representing the Victorian Society, John made a television appeal. By now the arch was covered in scaffolding, bearing the signboards of the general contractors, Fairclough, and of the demolition firm, Valori. Standing in front of the arch, John's bespectacled interviewer said:

> The Victorians built to last. They built this gateway to Birmingham in granite. Now, 125 years later, it is to come down. But who is this, pushing his way to the foot of the gallows with a last message of hope? Who but Mr John Betjeman of the Victorian Society?

Turning to John, he asked, 'Why should we bother with this arch?' John replied:

> It was the first bit of railway architecture in the world of any size – it's very grand-scale. Fine stone – granite. And if it were moved forward in front of the new Euston Station, it would be the most magnificent public monument in London.

On 17 October 1961 *The Times* reported that the possibility of moving the arch had been put forward by a Canadian firm, Nicholas Brothers, which had offered to move it on rollers at an estimated cost of £90,000. The Victorian Society had raised a forlorn £1,000 towards this.

On the same day, *The Times* published an editorial headed 'NOT WORTH SAVING'. It was the arch's death-warrant. John's old colleague from 'Archie Rev' days, J. M. ('Karl Marx') Richards, had been *The Times*'s architectural correspondent since 1947. He had got on well with the editors Robin Barrington-Ward and William Casey, but found their successor, Sir William Haley, far less easy to work with. Unfortunately, Richards's rather prickly personality was of exactly the kind to cause friction with Haley.

One suspects that Haley was out to teach Richards a lesson: you don't argue with the editor, whose decision is final. But Haley was not without subtlety. He wrapped his criticism of the arch in a more general attack on conservationists who were indiscriminate in their crusades and thus weakened their case when something worth saving was threatened. Many would have seen these remarks as aimed directly at John, the most persistent campaigner, and the best known. Haley seized on Summerson's too cool appraisal of 1960, which was now flung back in his face – 'stands in embarrassed relationship to everything around'. Haley concluded: 'Whether we dismiss [the arch] as some of our ancestors did as "Glyn's Folly" (in reference to SIR STEPHEN GLYN, the first chairman of the London and Birmingham Railway) or hail it as a Hardwick masterpiece, we should think twice before devoting to its preservation funds that could be so much better spent elsewhere.'

As a desperate last measure, the Victorian Society and other groups had approached Macmillan and he had agreed to receive a deputation. The meeting took place on 24 October. The deputation, led by Sir Charles Wheeler, president of the Royal Academy, included John, Richards, Summerson, Pevsner, the then Earl of Euston, Hugh Casson and Peter Fleetwood-Hesketh. Richards later wrote: 'Macmillan listened – or I suppose he listened; he sat without moving with his eyes apparently closed. He asked no questions; in fact he said nothing except that he would consider the matter . . .' Fleetwood-Hesketh recalled the Prime Minister as slightly less taciturn:

> We'd provided Macmillan's people for months with all the information. We all sat down at this table. Macmillan was there; on his right was Ernest Marples; on Marples's right was myself and then the rest of the deputation. And within a minute or two of the beginning of the meeting it transpired that in spite of our having supplied them with all the relevant information, Macmillan knew absolutely nothing about it. You would have thought he'd never heard of the Euston Arch. He said: 'I understand you want to pull it down stone by stone and build it up again.' Well, *months* before we had said that was out of the question. What we proposed to do was to move it on rollers, which had been done in every other country for years – Canada, America, France, Germany. But whatever information we had fed into that Prime Ministerial office, evidently hadn't percolated. And that beautiful thing could have been left where it was, or moved forward on rollers for £90,000. Why didn't they agree to that?

Ten days after Macmillan saw the deputation, Sir Charles Wheeler, as its leader, received his reply. *The Times* gave the gist of it in a main home-news story headed 'EUSTON PORTICO FATE INEVITABLE, SAYS MR MACMILLAN: LITTLE OR NO PROSPECT OF FINDING AN ALTERNATIVE SITE'. The Doric arch could not be saved, Macmillan wrote. There was the question of time: 'It is urgently necessary to get ahead with this work [of rebuilding the station].'

A movement needs a martyr. A religion needs a human sacrifice; a conservation movement needs an architectural sacrifice. Though the loss of the arch was grievous – 'Eustonasia', it was called at the time – the conservationists learned new cunning. They realized they had left everything too late, they had not mobilized their forces in time, they had failed to raise enough money, their generals were too far from the front line. Developers learned something too. The row brought odium on the Railways and the Government. In future, developers perhaps thought twice before planning the casual demolition of a listed building. 'Remember the Euston Arch' was the word in boardrooms.

Frank Valori, managing director of the company responsible for demolishing the arch, was so upset at having to do it ('he cried all the way to the bank', as a cynical later commentator said) that he presented the Victorian Society with a silver model of the arch, 'to perpetuate the building's memory'. On 6 March 1962 Lord Esher, as the society's president, accepted the gift. *The Times* reported:

> Lord Esher frankly admitted that this generous gesture made him feel as if some man had murdered his wife and then presented him with her bust by Epstein. But, he added, Mr Valori was a benevolent executioner who, as a man of taste with a respect for the architecture, had undertaken the demolition without pleasure . . . The guilt lay in the low mental capacity of what were called top people. [This was a snarling reference to the then familiar advertisement, 'Top People Read *The Times*' and hence to Haley's editorial.]
>
> It was to the retarded mentality of those who set out to govern us that this artistic outrage was to be attributed. It would happen again and he foresaw dozens of silver replicas passing into the society's headquarters in Great Ormond Street.

After this speech of graciousness, ungraciousness, good taste, bad taste, wit and bile, drinks were served. John was at the party. In this less formal setting, and not for the notebook of the man from *The Times*, Esher was heard to remark, in his booming, bassoon-like voice: 'I am often accused of preferring buildings to people. Well, the Euston Arch is *irreplaceable*. People? They can be replaced quite easily. And with a certain amount of pleasure.' Later, as if in mimicry of the granite original, the miniature silver arch 'went missing'. It has never been recovered.

Apart from his *Telegraph* article, his television appearance, his words to the Royal Fine Art Commission and his joining the deputation to Macmillan, John kept in the background during the Euston Arch campaign. He did not write letters to *The Times*, clamber about on scaffolding or (with the exception of Wyatt) lobby MPs. Yet when people looked back on the scandal of the Euston Arch and execrated Macmillan, Marples, British Railways and Haley, it was always John who was mentioned as the leader of the campaign to save it. Bernard Kaukas firmly believed that John had led the deputation to Macmillan. Bernard Levin also helped perpetuate this myth of John's central rôle, in his book about the 1960s, *The Pendulum Years* (1970). In, for him, a rare and perverse aberration of taste, Levin reviled, or affected to revile, the arch.

> At times [he wrote] the urge to preserve the past, with which the Sixties were obsessed, took on the proportions of mania. There was nothing

so ugly, so dirty, so useless, so lacking in any kind of aesthetic, historical or stylistic attraction that it was impossible to find a group of people willing to solicit funds for its removal to a permanent home. Often the name of John Betjeman was attached to appeals, and eventually Mr Eric Lyons, himself an architect, coined the phrase 'Betjemanic depressives' to stigmatize collectively those who would preserve at all costs everything from the past, be it a wrought-iron lamp-post due for replacement in Chelsea, a Victorian church in Essex complete with its 'blue-jowled and bloody' stained glass, or the celebrated Doric portico at Euston Station. This last created the greatest preservationist furore of the decade . . .

Levin said he found it difficult to believe that most of the protesters about the arch had ever set eyes on it.

Several of the journalists who wrote about Euston in 1968 also went in for blame-laying and scapegoat-hunting. The *Sunday Times* published a swingeing article by John Fielding on 22 September. He viewed the whole Euston saga as 'an acid reminder of how to throw away money'.

By failing to exploit a site in an area where office accommodation brings in almost £5 a square foot and freehold land sells for almost any price you like to pull out of a hat, the railways – and ultimately the taxpayers – have abandoned an asset potentially worth a good £40 million.

On 14 October 1968 – the day the new station was opened by the Queen – Michael Baily, the respected transport correspondent of *The Times*, contributed an article headed 'Lost opportunity'. He wrote: 'As a piece of urban planning in the capital of a country with severe traffic and transport problems it stands as a monument to ignorance and bureaucratic bungling.' The fault with BR's plans, Baily thought, was not that they were too ambitious but that they were not ambitious enough. 'If there is anywhere in London that deserves mile-high skyscrapers it is at the centre of the main railway terminals.' Workers could be brought right into their offices by trains 'originating in darkest Surrey', relieving buses and roads of congestion. Baily thought British Rail should be stripped of the property-developing function in which they had proved themselves so incompetent.

Both Fielding and Baily compared British Rail's performance with the rival Euston Centre rising near by (opened 1969). Fielding wrote:

Four hundred yards to the west of Euston [station] stands Joe Levy's 400 ft office tower at Euston Centre, an embarrassing indication that dealing with many of the same authorities over the same period of time as the railwaymen, private enterprise pulled off one of the biggest development coups of the century.

Why, he wondered, had there been planning permission for the Centre, but no planning permission for the station? A book that would have given him the answer (he and Baily had evidently not read it) was *The Property Boom* (1967) by Oliver Marriott, financial editor of *The Times* – a penetrating exposé of the commercial-property business since 1945. Marriott devoted a chapter to 'The Euston Centre: Joe Levy and Robert Clark'. He laid bare the way in which, at every turn, the LCC valuers had favoured the private property developers D. E. and J. Levy and Robert Clark. Because, in the early 1950s, Joe Levy had obtained outline planning permission from the LCC for a 120,000 square foot office block, he had the Council 'over a barrel'; also, the LCC 'needed a private developer who would fit in with its own plans'. A cosy relationship was established. The LCC made closing orders on houses and flats. Marriott concludes: 'Throughout the LCC was . . . exceedingly cooperative with Joe Levy. It was almost like having a fourth estate agent in the consortium.' And great secrecy was preserved. Only in 1960 did insiders wake up to the possibility that Stock Conversion (the Levy–Clark company) 'might be a vast iceberg'. Not until 1964 was something like the full story uncovered – by Judy Hillman of the *Evening Standard*. After George Brown put a ban on new offices, in November of that year, Joe Levy gleefully referred to his Euston Tower as 'Monopoly House'.

Oliver Marriott does not so much as mention the Euston Arch. But it is clear from his book that John, in his efforts to save the arch, was pitted not just against British Railways, but against the LCC with its bias in favour of Levy and Clark. 'If British Railways had been allowed to build its offices,' Bernard Kaukas said, 'that would have paid for the Doric arch to be moved anywhere you like.'

In October 1961, as if to rest him after his campaign to save the arch, John's former employers, the British Council, flew him to Australia for a five-week cultural tour. He was to sing for his supper by giving lectures. Before he left, though, there were some problems to sort out. He was dissatisfied with his current secretary, the Rev. Mr Jourdain, the latest in the long sequence of 'non-secular secs'. On 21 October John wrote to Penelope that he had had to get rid of him. 'He is very conscientious & pathetic but really too incapable to be able to deal with things in my absence & know what was important from what was not. He has got a better paid, if duller job with the Metal Box Company.' In his place John was taking on another part-time clergyman, the Rev. R. N. Timms of Brockham, Surrey, who would look after his affairs in his absence.

John was worried about his son Paul, who was jobless and staying with Gerard Irvine at 'St Philbert's' (St Cuthbert's Clergy House, Philbeach

Gardens, London). Paul had applied for a job as a trainee interior decorator with the leading designer David Hicks. He had desperately swotted up in homes-and-gardens magazines but had been turned down ('thank goodness', John wrote to Penelope, who was on a riding holiday in Spain).

John left London on a BOAC airliner on Sunday 29 October. In an article about the trip which he later wrote for *Vogue* he recalled: 'An official of the British Council in London asked me to lunch before I went, to warn me not to patronize the Australians. Such had not been my intention, but I can see what he meant. It is a mistake to expect a welcome simply because one comes from England.' He added: 'I read the *Penguin Book of Australian Verse* on my way out, which was a better guide to the people and scenery than any official brochure.'

Of the living poets represented in the Penguin book, there were two John decided he would try to meet while in Australia: Douglas Stewart and Judith Wright. John was going to Australia in quest of the Australian, and he found it in the exhilaration of Stewart's lines –

> Schute, Bell, Badgery, Lumby,
> How's your dad and how'd your mum be?
> What's the news, oh, far from here
> Under the blue sky burning clear
> Where your beautiful business runs
> Wild as a dingo, fresh as a brumby?

Judith Wright was even more ur-Australian than Stewart (who was born in New Zealand). She was born in 1915 at Thalgarrah Station near Armidale, New South Wales, into a pastoral family who had been pioneer settlers of the New England district. In 1960 she had published a prose history of her family, *The Generations of Men*. She was close to the land, a passionate conservationist. Sometimes the tone of her poetry is too elevated and self-consciously 'poetic' for most readers, the echo hollow. But in her best poems, her candour carries its own austere nobility.

John's journey was broken by a night in Singapore. He had told Penelope that he would be staying at the Raffles Hotel, but in fact wrote to her on 31 October from the Hotel de l'Europe, 'I spent last night here and I CAN ABSOLUTELY UNDERSTAND your passion for the gorgeous East.' He concluded: 'But all I long for is us again back at Wantage and in peace and though I've never been to Aussieland, my longing for home is so great I would gladly forgo the trip.' He added a drawing of himself and Penelope in bed at Wantage with Archie the teddy bear.

John was welcomed to Sydney by Norman Williams, the British Council's chief representative in Australia, and his wife Margery, a leading 'literary hostess', who was the same age as John. John reported to Penelope:

> Oi'm *loovin* Aussieland. This is a glorious time to be here, late spring with the most violent coloured trees & flowers & always, here in Sydney, glimpses of the sea & ships. The Jacaranda trees are out, bright purple flowers, no leaves, & as big as sycamores. Then there are weird palm like plants with flowers like exotic birds – cockatoos.

The Williamses introduced John to Douglas Stewart, one of the two poets he most wanted to meet. Stewart had become the grand panjandrum of Australian letters, and he put out the flags for John. In the *Vogue* article, John wrote: 'I went to a party given by Douglas Stewart, the poet, in a suburb of Sydney and recall a spider's web as big as a sheet between the eaves of the verandah of his bungalow and the ground. In the middle of it was a beautiful green spider as big as one's hand which everyone took for granted as a common sight.'

John's tour was to take in the capitals of the five states and Tasmania. His trip to Brisbane was made while he was still based in Sydney. On 17 November he wrote to Penelope:

> I did a long 600 miles through bush & scrub & terrific heat to Brisbane by car & came back, thank God, by air. Brisbane is all banana trees & parrots & bright flowers & koala bears & little white wooden bungalows built on stilts. It is a warm, welcoming & tropic city. J.L. Pearson's Cathedral is his finest work I've seen all in the lovely pale yellow & pink local stone. I met a gecko – a lizard with a frill round its neck – on the road & we picked it up – put it on a fence where it lay stock still disguised as a piece of bark.
>
> Brisbane is very high & the RC Archbishop & ours are both very old & great friends & Catholics of both denominations get on well together there – unlike Sydney which is low & Irish.

From Brisbane John made a detour to the wild country near Mount Tamborine, where Judith Wright, the other poet he wanted to meet, lived with her husband J. P. McKinney and their daughter Meredith. 'Nor shall I forget standing in the rain forests below Mt Tamborine near Brisbane with Judith Wright, the poet,' John wrote in *Vogue*. 'We heard cicadas loud as jet engines outside London Airport. They stopped suddenly and in the hush one could almost hear the jungle growing in the steamy depths below us where parasite climbed on parasite and strange and huge flowers burst from the greenness and the crack of the stock-whip bird increased the strangeness.'

By mid-November John was back in Sydney, where he was *the* social catch of the season. His daughter writes: 'One well-known Sydney lady, having failed to get him to dinner, dared not admit her failure in the eyes of the city and printed in the paper an account of a dinner she never gave.' Then he was off to Canberra, where he stayed with the Governor-General of Australia, Lord De L'Isle and Dudley VC and his wife Jacqueline, who, like Penelope, was the daughter of a field-marshal (in her case Lord Gort VC). Three years younger than John, De L'Isle was a descendant of the poet Sir Philip Sidney and the owner of one of John's favourite houses in England, Penshurst Place in Kent. On 23 November John moved on to Melbourne, from which city he wrote to Penelope: 'Canberra, as I told you, is like Welwyn set down in a basin of the hills round Urbino. Melbourne where I am now is, in its old parks, like Paris if none of the houses were more than two or three storeys high.'

What John needed most when he came home to Wantage on 9 December was a good rest – almost a period of convalescence. But he still found time to write an article on Australian architecture, which appeared in the *Daily Telegraph* on 18 December, barely more than a week after his return. The article showed that, while he had concentrated on the cities, he had also pressed the organizers of his tour to let him see small towns in the country.

> The average country town is at a crossroads, with a bank on one corner built in a solid-looking classic style, broad-eaved and with decorative details which, even if incorrect, are elegant and strangely Australian. There may be a town hall and post office in variants of this style and always on one or more corners an hotel, two storeys high, with verandahs of richly patterned cast iron.

John admired the houses' gardens, where hibiscus of every colour and lantana grew and mesembryanthemums cascaded 'in sheets of crimson'. But the *Telegraph* article was also a chance to release some of the bile that had built up during the long, taxing journey – 'Thus if it were not for the hoardings, the sky signs, the cats' cradles of wires, the plethora of poles, the brash shop fronts, and the over-abundance of hideous petrol stations which disfigure the more prosperous towns, Australia would have, as it does in many parts, the pleasantest architecture in the world.'

What had entranced John most in Australia was the prodigality of Nature. 'First there was the light, with its dazzling clearness everywhere. Next there was the brilliant colour of flowers, trees, rocks, birds, reptiles and insects.' In Australia he recaptured some of the exaltation he had felt as a youth, swooping down the Cornish hills on his bicycle in the search for wild flowers.

The gum-trees of Australia are of every shape and colour. Some look like British elms, others like oak or ash. There are hundreds of varieties of mimosa, or wattle, whose flowers vary from pale gold to deepest orange. The scarlet of the flame-tree flares on the mountain sides. The millions of flowers which appear everywhere after the rain give an impression of luxuriance, like the tropics one reads about in *The Swiss Family Robinson*. There are trees of vast height, and some of the palms and pines look like the fossilized plants in coal . . . In Canberra, how odd it was to see pink parrots flying about the trim suburban avenues and find snakes slithering over the municipally mown grass between the footwalk and the road, which is seductively called 'the nature strip' in Australia. How pleasantly embarrassing, too, to be sitting in a drawing-room making polite conversation and suddenly to burst into giggles caught from the maniac laughter of the kookaburra birds on the lawn outside.

John's liking for Australia was reciprocated. The official British Council report on his visit was eulogistic.

Because of his unique qualities Mr Betjeman was an ideal visitor for Australia. He aroused in his audiences and acquaintances that pleasant sensation of nostalgia for 'Home' which is a feature of the old Australian character . . . The professorial and academic architects he met were amazed by his knowledge of Australian architectural history, and by the clarity of the canons of taste he applied to Australian buildings . . . His poetry was a major factor in his popularity in Australia . . . A very successful tour. Press and public alike were convinced of the sincerity of Mr Betjeman's liking for Australia. The visit will remain a yardstick by which Australians will measure the success of other Council visitors.

John 'recycled' his impressions of Australia in a number of articles during the 1960s. In 1964 he was roped in to contribute an article ('Beneath the Wattle Tree') to a three-page section of the *Daily Express* designed to encourage emigration to Australia and supported by a large advertisement for Consolidated Gold Fields Ltd of London EC2. On the strength of his single trip, John was billed as one of the 'important writers who know Australia well'. Among his fellow contributors was Neville Cardus, the writer on cricket and music, who assured prospective immigrants that 'Nearly every Australian girl can play the piano reasonably well – no, not "pop" music, but Beethoven. The Australian girls are unique. Good-lookers as a rule . . .' John offered the more rarefied temptations of 'diamond light', the bell-bird's chimes and 'vast Gothic cathedrals in honey-coloured local stone or variegated brick'. In 1968 he returned to these topics in an article for the *Daily Telegraph Magazine*, headed 'John Betjeman's Kangaroo Island: Old-Fashioned Betjemanesque Pleasures'.

Besides spawning the somewhat repetitive articles (in every one of them, Canberra was compared to Welwyn), the Australian tour of 1961 served as a thorough reconnaissance for John's four Australian television films ten years later – rather as his excursions to suburban London cinemas as a film critic in the 1930s gave him a framework for his celebrated *Metroland* film of 1972. In 1961, with his verse autobiography published, he was already beginning to transform himself from Bright Young Thing and *enfant terrible* into Grand Old Man. The arduous legwork he put in then, at fifty-five, might have proved too punishing at sixty-five, when the onset of Parkinson's Disease, which would reduce him to an invalid in his last years, first became apparent.

Australia was briefly to present itself as a possible solution to the next crisis to confront the preservationists, the fate of the Coal Exchange. Despite the lessons of the Euston Arch débâcle, it turned out that in conservation forewarned is not always adequately forearmed. The case of the Coal Exchange was one of the first taken up by the Victorian Society, which was aware of the Corporation of London's designs on the Exchange two years before British Railways' threat to the Euston Arch came to its notice. The forewarning enabled the society to make trouble for the developers in Parliament, at the Guildhall and in the press. Even so, it only won a reprieve for the building. The Exchange was demolished a year after the Euston Arch, in 1962. The aesthetic and historical arguments were urged as eloquently as John and his allies knew how; the developers opposed them with the unanswerable argument of big money.

If anything, the scandal of the Exchange was greater than that of the arch, though its fate never roused such a public outcry. The building in Lower Thames Street, London, near the Billingsgate fish market (soon itself to disappear) was begun in 1847. The architect was James Bunning, and it was opened by the Prince Consort in 1849. The exterior was not unlike that of a Regency church, its rounded portico crowned with a two-storey turret. This gave no indication of the interior. Walking through the portico, the visitor found himself in a large domed court, fifty feet in diameter and almost wholly constructed of cast iron. The circular court was surrounded by tiers of small offices reached by galleries. The principal iron supports were moulded with a cable motif derived from the ropes used in the coal mines and by the colliers that carried the coal by sea to London. The three galleries and the dome were decorated with arabesques and paintings by Frederick Sang of colliers, collieries, tree ferns, coal miners and towns associated with the industry. Curved iron ribs formed the dome. Originally the spaces between the ribs had been filled with ground glass and the eye of the dome with amber glass, but that had been shattered by bomb blasts in the war. The rotunda was the earliest example in England of a public building constructed with extensive use of cast iron. In that, it anticipated the Crystal Palace, built two years later. There was no equivalent surviving cast-iron monument of such an early date in the country.

John was already concerned about the future of the building before the Victorian Society was founded in 1957. He learned that the Corporation of the City of London had plans to demolish it, ostensibly as part of a road-widening scheme. He thought that the real reason was to clear the site so that part of it could be sold or redeveloped. In March 1956, writing to the secretary of the Council for the Care of Churches, he raised – lightly enough – the question of the threatened Exchange. 'Darling Miss Scott, Indeed we must keep up the fight but I am told that [Anthony] Eden wants to show himself as a strong man here at any rate, even if he can't in Cyprus. If we do save it, you and I might go away to the south of France together.' In September of the same year he contrived to deliver the annual speech of the Society for the Protection of Ancient Buildings in the Coal Exchange.

In October 1958, John was defending the building in a letter to *The Times*: 'Its round porch and tower are a fine feature as street architecture, its side elevations are original and thoughtfully designed, its domed entrance hall leads one naturally to the really splendid glass and cast-iron round the galleried hall of the Exchange itself.' Not everyone agreed. Another correspondent wrote a few days later: 'We must not be sentimental about buildings of this type: it seems incredible that Mr Betjeman deems it more important to keep the Coal Exchange standing until "the last possible moment" than to solve the City's vital problem of traffic congestion.'

The Victorian Society tried to persuade the City Corporation to adopt an alternative scheme which would save the Exchange. The campaign dragged on, and in 1959 the society's attention was diverted for months on end to the urgent case of the Euston Arch. By November 1960 champions of the Exchange felt there was now 'no hope of retaining it on its present site', though the London County Council might keep the dismantled iron frame for re-erection elsewhere. However, on 2 February 1961, as a result of representations, the Court of Common Council gave the Exchange a temporary reprieve.

On 8 February the defenders of the Coal Exchange held a press conference. John, speaking for the Victorian Society, said that while his society realized the importance of widening Lower Thames Street it felt – and here the Georgian Group was in agreement – that if any building must go the authorities should level their first attack at 'the much less attractive rear façade of the Custom House opposite'. He urged the Corporation of London to seek an alternative use for the Coal Exchange – 'this airy and top-lit galleried building' – suggesting that it might house the Corporation's own collection of paintings and sculpture which had been removed from Guildhall art gallery before the war.

The day after the press conference, John's old friend Tom Driberg raised the matter in Parliament. In some ways Driberg was, just as Woodrow Wyatt had been in the case of the Euston Arch, an unfortunate choice. Conservatives, who might by definition have favoured conservation, regarded him as an extreme left-winger verging on Communism. Others, in that less enlightened age, were put off by his open homosexuality. On the other hand, Driberg was a clever and articulate aesthete: and there might be some Labour support for saving a building that commemorated the coal industry.

Driberg told the House that 'that noble galleried rotunda' could be preserved where it was, and as it was. 'If the Minister can bring that about, I am sure that Londoners of the future will bless his name.' Sir Keith Joseph, Parliamentary Secretary to the Ministry of Housing and Local Government, rose to reply, offering no more than a sop to the conservationists: he still hoped that somebody might pay to move and re-erect the building. With this end in view, he would see 'whether it is possible to keep this building up until the very last moment, at least to maximize the opportunity for sympathizers to preserve it'. (This would seem to be a direct echo of John's letter to *The Times*.)

In March 1961 a committee was appointed to organize the Coal Exchange campaign, and rapidly came up with three alternative schemes for saving the Exchange. It was agreed that a deputation would wait on the Minister of Housing. Keith Joseph received the deputation, on 17 April, and the different schemes were all put to him. On 29 May Joseph's private secretary wrote to the Victorian Society to say that the City was now examining the three schemes. For the next six months the society again allowed the Coal Exchange issue to go cold while battle proceeded over the Euston Arch.

At last, in March 1962, the Corporation decided to pull down the Exchange. Demolition would begin as soon as practicable after 27 July. On 26 July, at the eleventh hour, the Victorian Society received an enthusiastic approach from Eric Westbrook, director of the National Gallery of Victoria, Melbourne, and Roy Grounds, architect of the new Cultural Centre being built in Melbourne. The two men expressed their wish to acquire the rotunda for re-erection as the nucleus of the new centre. They asked for rough estimates for dismantling it and shipping it to Melbourne.

The society accordingly asked the Corporation for a deferment of demolition to allow a chance to obtain the necessary information.

But this proposal succeeded only in postponing the end. At a meeting on 3 December the Victorian Society decided that the cause was lost. Demolition followed. Two cast-iron griffins from the Exchange were erected on Victoria Embankment in 1963 to mark the City boundary – in its way, as ironic a gesture as Valori's presentation of the Euston Arch model to the Victorian Society.

For years afterwards there were bitter post-mortems. In 1973 the *City Press* ran a story under the headline 'Why did the Corporation pull the Coal Exchange down?'

> Over ten years ago the Coal Exchange in Lower Thames Street was demolished. Jane Fawcett, secretary of the Victorian Society, is still asking the question why, since nothing has been done to the site – a windswept plot of vacant land . . . It now appears that far from using the site for the road-widening scheme there may well be a mammoth office block built there instead. The City Corporation say that there has been a road actually over a third of the site for the past five years, and that the City's Planning Committee have approved an office development application from Fitzroy Robinson and Partners for the other two thirds of the site . . . Mrs Fawcett told City Press she disagreed with this first claim: 'As far as I know the pavement has been narrowed but the site has not been eaten into.' . . .
>
> *The big question still remains, ten years later – should the City have gone ahead with demolition? Why couldn't Common Council wait until the building had been resited, since it has not exactly sprung into action now that the building has gone? And why is the City considering using the site for a purpose different from that given as the reason for demolition? After ten years of red tape, these questions will probably never be answered.*

John's suspicions about the Corporation's ulterior plans had proved well founded. In 1977 Jennifer Freeman wrote in *Built Environment*:

> Remember the Coal Exchange in Lower Thames Street? Fifteen years ago J. B. Bunning's cast-iron masterpiece was demolished by its owner, the City Corporation, the greatest architectural loss of that authority's post-war rampage . . . Recently completed in its stead stands the (pseudonymously) named St Mary's House, 85,000 sq ft of offices designed by Fitzroy, Robinson and Partners for the Legal and General Assurance Society. It is an irregular, eight-storey block with tinted glass windows, finished in grey polished granite and arranged round a central car park. After so long a hiatus the City Corporation must eagerly anticipate the reinstatement of a substantial ratepayer.
>
> Conservationists may bitterly reflect that the rates foregone while the site lay vacant must far exceed the £125,000 refused to restore the building in

1962. Lower Thames Street is now transformed into a major east–west artery which pedestrians cross at their peril, for there are no crossings and few subways. The Coal Exchange could easily have been retained. At the narrowest place the Exchange stood 43 ft across the street from Billingsgate Market. Further west on the Southern Route, for example at Blackfriars Underpass, the highway is only some 40 ft wide. Pedestrians could have been accommodated by insetting the pavement into the entrance vestibule and providing a subway to link with the proposed riverside walk. An ideal tenant for the Coal Exchange might have been the London Metal Exchange which has needed new headquarters for several years.

Why did John and his friends fail to save the Coal Exchange? The tragedy of its loss cannot be attributed entirely to the City's greed, duplicity and philistinism. To use legal language, there was perhaps 'contributory negligence' by John and the Victorian Society. He was a great catalyst in any controversy or campaign; but he lacked 'follow-through' and staying power. He wrote striking letters to the newspapers. His appearances on television fascinated. He was astute at smelling out his opponents' motives. But he was no organizer. He could get the public's attention but could not keep it. As his friend Philip Harding (whose office in the brand-new *Times* building overlooked Upper Thames Street in 1962) was fond of saying, 'Brag is a good dog; *but Holdfast is a better.*' Months went by with no discussion of the case at Victorian Society meetings, and with no public campaigning. The Corporation was not kept wincing in the pillory. Part of the trouble was that the society had too few officers and not enough troops. Then again, the crisis over the Euston Arch distracted it from the Coal Exchange: the small force was fighting on two fronts at once, and one was neglected. Peter Fleetwood-Hesketh's rearguard action was tenacious, but it came too late. The real villain of the piece was Keith Joseph, whose silky politeness lulled the preservationists into false confidence, and who then struck with no warning or quarter given. The architect of Thatcherism was in training for his profession.

The loss of the Coal Exchange was a blow to John's vanity as well as to the English architectural heritage. In both the Euston Arch and the Coal Exchange campaigns he was the front man; both ended in failure. John was now on his mettle to achieve a success. All that he had learned from the defeats of 1961 and 1962 was brought into play in the campaign of 1963 – the Battle of Bedford Park.

28

A Natural Showman

Throughout the 1960s, John worked on a television *ABC of Churches* with the BBC producer Kenneth Savidge, who was based at Bristol. The two had first got to know each other in radio work when Savidge was a Religious Broadcasting assistant. Savidge graduated from radio to television. By then, the Rev. Martin Willson had already filmed the first of the *ABC of Churches* (Aldbourne, Wiltshire). Savidge was given the job of making the rest, and he and John made three *ABC* films a year. They reconnoitred in the spring and filmed in the summer. 'B' was inevitably Blisland, Cornwall, one of John's favourite churches. 'U', no less predictably, was Uffington: the film began with John bowing three times into the eye of the White Horse.

The *ABC* series was made with the BBC's Outside Broadcast Unit (OBU).

> Although it was somewhat more cumbersome than film [Ken Savidge said] (with film you had a crew of six people, while OBU could be up to twenty-five), you did have the advantage of four or five cameras all working at once and you could do long 'takes'. You could do a take in which John walked down an aisle and talked about details of bench-ends, and actually slot them in, which you can't do with a single camera.

Savidge thought that John was a television 'natural': 'I don't know what it means, except that I recognize it when I see it. It's nothing to do with technique . . . the great thing about John was that he wanted you to *share* his love and enthusiasm. He wasn't without vanity, but it didn't show on screen.' He added: 'Crews loved working with John. They virtually queued up to do so.' John was friendly and remembered their names. Often he joined them in a pub for the lunch break, paying for the drinks. 'He was always sneaking off to the pub with them,' Savidge told Candida. 'I remember losing him completely in the village of Edington – eventually I found him an hour later in the pub with the drivers.'

The one person in the BBC who never quite understood John was

Frank Sheratt. His title was West Region Programme Executive, though John always called him 'The Accountant'. 'Fancy a grown man like that going around with a teddy bear!' Sheratt said to Savidge.

> He was a quiet, kindly Lancastrian [Savidge recalls]. JB liked to imagine him sitting at a high desk, with pince-nez, writing with a quill pen. Once, particularly dissatisfied with a contract, John threatened to ditch the BBC and go and work for 'those commercial people down next to the crematorium' (a reference to Television West and Wales, now Harlech Television). That little difficulty was surmounted – though John did some work for TWW – but poor Mr Sheratt was completely nonplussed when John presented one set of expenses, which went something like this:

> > Taxi from Cloth Fair to Heathrow £1 7s 6d
> > Morning papers 1s 10d
> > Coffee in Forte's 4d
> > Tip to waitress £5

In May 1962 Maria Aitken, a granddaughter of John's wartime boss Lord Rugby and later a well-known actress, wrote to John from Sherborne School for Girls, asking him to talk to the school's literary society. He agreed to do so, telling her that he expected to be in Sherborne some time between 25 and 29 May. 'With a very nice Old Harrovian called Jonathan Stedall and his Secretary, Miss Diana Gray, I am making a reconnaissance of the town for a series of films on towns in the West Country which I am making for the commercial television.' The films were made for the short-lived TWW. When the company closed down, John took part in a filmed tribute to it, entitled *Come to an End,* in which he said, 'TWW – or Tellywelly as I call it – was a good firm to work for . . . They found for me a young producer, Jonathan Stedall, who had just started with them. We liked the same jokes and we had the same point of view and we worked out our programmes unhampered by accountants and officialdom.' Stedall, who was twenty-three in 1962, later wrote of John: 'For me he was, in a way, like the father I never had – but without the complications.' John gave the talk at Sherborne School for Girls. He dined first with (Dame) Diana Reader Harris, whom Maria Aitken had temptingly described as 'the most beautiful headmistress in England'. Stedall thought her name was 'Rita Harris', and John ever afterwards referred to her as that.

By 1962 John had twenty-five years' experience of television work. He ranked as one of the leading pioneers of the medium, with Compton Mackenzie, Mortimer Wheeler, Gilbert Harding, Malcolm Muggeridge, David Attenborough and A. J. P. Taylor. He had perfected his television technique. In front of the camera he seemed to be able to cast off all self-consciousness. He talked, not in carefully honed passages of prose, but as one might chat to a friend, with jerky inconsequence, asides and second thoughts. In Devizes, he said:

> I think a church is a very good place from which to start on a tour of this too little regarded Wiltshire assize town of Devizes. And, by the way, always look down alleys if you want to find the real history of a town. I mean, look at those half-timbered houses. Built before brick was used and when stone was so rare it was only used for castles and churches. I should think that's fifteenth century. Late fifteenth.

In 1951 John had agreed with the pioneer television producer Mary Adams that there was 'not enough silence in television'. He practised what he preached. Reaching the covered market in the film on Devizes, he says, 'There's no need for me to talk here. Just have a look round.' After the camera has had time to forage round the market, John interrupts the silence with an afterthought:

> Oh, and I forgot this. The Bear 'otel in the marketplace, a relic of coaching days. Look at that ironwork. About 1800, I should think. And then follow along to the older part. Sir Thomas Lawrence, the portrait painter, was born here; his father was the innkeeper. I like that great fat lettering across the front . . .

In the films on Bath and Clevedon, he deployed another of his talents, mimicry of voices. In Bath he conducted an imaginary conversation with a heartless developer. 'Today's building', he said in the developer's estuary twang, 'must express itself honestly and sincerely, as in this feature, which might be termed the *vital buttock* of the construction . . .' In a small Clevedon hotel, in winter, he imagined what the permanent residents were thinking or saying.

In June 1963 John was paid 200 guineas to take part in a *Monitor* programme about Philip Larkin, produced by Patrick Garland. He interviewed Larkin in Hull, and rather took command. In a Hull graveyard, he harangued him about the social classes of those buried there, where they might have lived, and what he himself felt about death. Larkin submitted with a good grace: John was older, more famous and much more used to the television camera – though Alan Bennett, reviewing Andrew Motion's biography of Larkin in 1993, wrote: 'He was interviewed, or at any rate was talked at, by Betjeman, and typically, of course, it's Larkin who comes out of it as the better performer.' Larkin was flattered by John's ability to reel off Larkin poems from memory. But after the filming Larkin wrote to

Garland with wry good humour, suggesting that he retitle the film *To Hull with John Betjeman*. 'The only question was what kind of a film could be made out of the inexplicable scraps you found you had brought back with you . . . I can see it taking shape: Betjeman ("Uncle Abel") shows me my father's grave: "Ay, 'e wor a reet skipper, was your dad – a great seaman – a great gentleman . . ." ' When the film was transmitted, Larkin wrote to Garland: 'I was sorry that our remarks about death had been excised. The whole programme had a rather funereal tone . . . ' and reported that he had received an abusive letter from 'a dotty old lady from Edinburgh objecting to the "grey sludge of my mind" '.

In 1965 John wrote a television play with Stewart Farrer, *Pity About the Abbey*. The plot was that Westminster Abbey was sold to Texas to make way for traffic improvements and offices; Farrer added some 'love interest'.

> ARCHITECT: Something had to be sacrificed. The new Treasury
>   building replaces . . . the Abbey!
> DEVELOPER: Good. Pity about the Abbey, though.
> ARCHITECT: Mr Page, no one regrets having to make this
>   decision more than I do, but . . .

The developer's daughter (half the love interest, with a blonde beehive hairdo) comes in and looks at the architect's model.

> DAUGHTER: But what have you done with the Abbey?
> DEVELOPER: I've got rid of it. Why?
> DAUGHTER: But you *can't*!

John was still in demand for panel games. He took part in several sessions of *Call My Bluff*, in which he guessed the meanings of recherché words with such old friends as the giggling Arthur Marshall and the stuttering Patrick Campbell. Anthony Burgess wrote that the game 'was based on the complacent acceptance of ignorance by the ignorant, so long as it was the higher ignorance'. Robert Robinson chaired *Call My Bluff*. He also presented the literary quiz *Take It or Leave It*, which was often produced by the young Melvyn Bragg. Extracts from famous authors were read out without attribution and the panellists had to say who the writer was. 'Betjeman was a regular participant,' Robinson recalled, 'and always referred to the programme as *Money for Jam*: he didn't feel it necessary to say more than, "I say, it's awfully good," or if the passage in question featured names like Serge or Alexandrovna he might opine that it was "certainly Russian".'

On 2 January 1967 John wrote to David Attenborough (then Controller of BBC2 Television): 'I have been having a very jolly time filming the

Edgware Road with Julian Jebb. In its way it was as thrilling and dangerous and mysterious as those jungles you used to explore and where centi-
pedes rushed out to bite your ankles.' Jebb, who was a grandson of Hilaire
Belloc, was a sensitive, amusing, slightly fey character who had joined
BBC TV in 1967, researching and producing features for the Arts Features
department. The film was transmitted on 31 January 1968 as *Contrast: Marble
Arch to Edgware – A Lament by John Betjeman*.

In the same year the BBC had a sudden windfall from colour television
licence fees. It spent some of it on a series called *Bird's-Eye View*, a three-
year project in which England was filmed from a helicopter. The production was entrusted to Edward Mirzoeff, a young film-maker with an ironic
but sympathetic approach to his subjects.

> One of the first things that came to mind [Mirzoeff recalls] was that we had
> to bring in writers; it was quite important that, given the nature of the view
> from above, the remote view from the helicopter, you had to personalize,
> and John was suggested as one of the possible writers. I had never met him;
> I knew of him, of course. He came to Kensington House [BBC offices in
> west London] and we met in the bar and talked about it. He was charming
> and thought it a lot of fun as an idea. He actually found it quite hard to say
> no to almost any proposal we made eventually – not that he would *do* things,
> he would just say yes and afterwards you found that saying yes didn't neces-
> sarily mean that he was going to do it at all. That's how we first met and we
> made thirteen films in the helicopter series of which John wrote three and
> I directed two of those three.

The first *Bird's-Eye View* programme, 'The Englishman's Home', was
savaged by Sean Day-Lewis in the *Daily Telegraph*:

> Mr Betjeman was invited to air his prejudices and he did so predictably, and
> with more illogicality than usual, in a poetic manner that at best sounded
> like tongue-in-cheek parody of his own verse. He rhymed with reverence
> about everything up to the 1920s, even the post-1918 Sussex bungalow sub-
> urbs, and was acid about all building since 1945. His apparent view was that
> an eighteenth-century masterpiece like Castle Howard and a high rise
> twentieth-century block of flats are genuine alternatives.

John may not have seen these words, as he had written to Mirzoeff asking
him not to send him reviews. 'I only notice the bad ones, and they give
me terrible persecution mania.'

John agreed to go up in the helicopter for another programme, 'Beside
the Seaside'. In one scene, the helicopter hovered above a Butlin's holiday
camp. John excelled himself in the verse commentary for this section. An
old man and two children are seen on the roller-coaster.

The twins inveigle grandpa
On the switchback by a trick
But grandpa has the laugh on them –
For both the twins are sick.

John was paid £750 for the *Bird's-Eye View* series.

In 1968 and 1969 he made another film with Julian Jebb, *Tennyson: A Beginning and an End*. Jebb summed up the filming on the Isle of Wight in his diary for 17 September 1969. 'We have been an exceptionally happy and united crew. The atmosphere has been extraordinarily gay and we have a whole bag of private jokes and references which have grown up during the film. This is partly John's genius for getting on with people, which really consists in paying careful attention to everyone and having a very good memory.'

When Tristram and Georgia Powell published Jebb's diary in 1993, the sound-recordist Andrew Barr contributed to the book a memory of John during the making of the Tennyson film.

> Whose film was it, Julian's or John Betjeman's? Certainly Julian was passionate about some moments that had to be included, and to us he was a serious film-maker. Yet a fledgling sound-recordist had to fear if the extraordinary scenes were to be realized. John Betjeman was frequently to be positioned a long way from the camera, requiring the use of the then unreliable radio microphone; the first evening, he stood in a gale on top of Tennyson Down reciting 'Sunset and Evening Star'. It was only a whiff of what was to come. Then a long scene was played with the [future] Poet Laureate up to his knees in the North Sea. It looked idyllic, but loud and quite unrecognizable explosions declared that a bombing range had been chosen for this idyll. Even the radio microphone would not do. Julian was unrepentant. Briefly belligerent, he would walk off demanding a miracle without delay on all such occasions.

For now, there was harmony between John and Jebb. Two years later, it was to be irretrievably disrupted.

John enjoyed a much more sustained friendship with Barry Humphries. He knew Humphries long before the Australian comic became famous in Britain in the late 1970s as Dame Edna Everage, 'housewife superstar' – a *monstre sacré* with 'natural wistaria' hair, diamanté-studded butterfly spectacles, basilisk eyes, twitching scarlet lips, a rich falsetto voice and sublimely over-the-top costumes. He first heard his name in the British Council office at Sydney on his 1961 trip to Australia. Somebody there had two records Humphries had made, *Wild Life in Suburbia* (1958) and *Wild Life in Suburbia: Volume Two* (1959). John played them over to himself dozens of times. Even more than the monologues by Edna Everage, the aggressively genteel Melbourne housewife, he enjoyed the Pooter-like musings of Humphries's other creation, Sandy Stone, an elderly, decent, childless man of the suburbs with a battleaxe wife called Beryl.

John made a flattering reference to Humphries in one of his Australian press conferences of 1961. A friend sent Humphries a newspaper cutting of the compliment. Humphries discovered John's Cloth Fair address and wrote to him in ink, making several drafts of the letter before he sent it. At the time the Australian was living in Grove Terrace, Highgate Road – the very row of Georgian houses in which John once said he would have liked to live as a small child, rather than in the ugly Parliament Hill Mansions near by. Humphries received a prompt reply, in an envelope bearing a Manx stamp.

> The letter within [Humphries wrote], inscribed with a fountain pen in Arts and Crafts calligraphy, contained an invitation to lunch the following week . . . The poet greeted me effusively and we went up two flights of narrow stairs to his small flat with its William Morris wallpapers, beetling book-shelves and, over the fireplace, a faded Arcadian improvisation in water-colour by Conder, an almost forgotten artist of the 1890s who had always interested me.
>
> John dispensed bubbly in pewter tankards with boyish exclamations such as 'I am as rich as Croesus' and 'You are a great genius', at which the other luncheon guests – two members of the high Anglican clergy – exchanged glances that were appropriately reverential and sceptical.

The two men had an uncanny – as Dame Edna would say, 'spooky' – amount in common; Humphries was almost an Australian *Doppelgänger* of John. Both were born (Humphries in 1934) in city suburbs and into the upper-middle class, with nannies. Both their fathers supplied the luxury Art Deco market – Humphries senior with houses, Betjemann *père* with fur-nishings. Each was fascinated by 'decadence', particularly by Oscar Wilde, and read and collected neglected writers of the 1890s. Both were also much taken by neglected artists – John by Tuke and Julius Olsson, Humphries by little-known Australian Impressionists. Another trait John and Humphries shared was a love of the music-hall, also pre-eminently an art of the 1890s. They both enjoyed dated slang, such as the 'Devil if I understand!' of John's poem about an old poet at the Café Royal. In one of his monologues, Sandy Stone referred to a car jaunt as a 'spin' – the same expression used by John's 'Retired Postal Clerk'. Although John and Humphries loathed parroted jargon, both revelled in brand names. Edna Everage evoked the Melbourne of her childhood by creating a poetry of them –

The Melbourne of my girlhood was a fine Rexona Town.
Her smile was bright with Kolynos and Persil white her gown,
Her Bedgood shoes with Nugget shone, she scorned inferior brands,
And in her Lux-white gloves there slept her soft Palmolive hands . . .

John wrote of Elaine in 'Middlesex':

> Well cut Windsmoor flapping lightly,
>   Jacqmar scarf of mauve and green
> Hiding hair which, Friday nightly,
>   Delicately drowns in Drene;
> Fair Elaine the bobby-soxer,
> Fresh-complexioned with Innoxa . . .

Humphries could have had a career as a poet, just as John could have done as an actor. John's influence on Humphries's verse is obvious, and is meant to be.

Both men recognized the virtues of suburbia as well as such cosy absurdities as Sandy's Cries of London table-mats and Edna's mulgawood serviette rings. Humphries sees himself as 'sinking artesian wells into the suburban desert . . . I'm in the boredom-alleviation business, aren't I?' Both rejected the label of 'satirist' – partly, perhaps, because they did not want to seem merely part of the trendy Sixties 'satire movement' – but accepted there was an element of caricature in their work, characterized by Humphries as 'lying to get at the truth'. Both were obsessively interested in taste, particularly in notions of 'bad taste'. John wrote *Ghastly Good Taste* when he was twenty-seven; Humphries wrote a book on Australian kitsch.

Striking as it is, however, the comparison between John and Humphries cannot be carried too far. They differed in significant ways. Humphries was more extreme than John, more shocking. They were drinking companions in the 1960s; but, while John liked his drink, Humphries became for a time an alcoholic. A more central difference from John was Humphries's imperviousness to religion. For a time he was a Sunday-school teacher in Melbourne. 'I felt I was a terrible hypocrite,' he recalls, 'mouthing the teachings of the Church of England to these indifferent brats, and at the same time writing agnostic and frankly anti-clerical verses for the school magazine. The rapture of an authentic spiritual experience has always eluded me.' John was assailed by doubts, but he lived and died in the Church of England.

In 1961 Cliff Hocking of Melbourne, who was beginning his career as a theatrical impresario, came to Humphries with the idea of a one-man show featuring Edna Everage and Sandy Stone. Humphries liked the idea, and he and his wife Rosalind set sail for Australia. Elizabeth Cavendish and John came to see them off. On 30 July 1962 in a church hall in central Melbourne, Edna, dressed in a Jackie Kennedy pillbox hat with veil, a red coat and pearls, opened *A Nice Night's Entertainment*. John had written a blurb for the programme. 'Barry Humphries', he predicted, 'is one who, I have no hesitation in saying, will become internationally famous, because he is an artist with words, imagination and mimicry who belongs to the great tradition of music hall and theatre.'

The show was a success, and in May 1963 Peter Cook, who was running the Establishment Club in Soho, London, asked Humphries to fill in for the American Lenny Bruce, at £100 a week. John turned up at the Establishment Club to support his protégé on his opening night. In her autobiography *My Gorgeous Life* (1989), Dame Edna described the scene: 'That evening the little tables in the club were packed with celebrities, and kind, supportive Peter [Cook] pointed some of them out to me as we nibbled our steaks in the corner. That jolly little balding man with the wavy upper lip was John Betjeman, the famous poet, who apparently adored me.'

There was some poetic licence in this account: Peter Cook was in fact still in America, and Humphries was glad he was not in the club to witness his humiliation. Humphries's punchlines fell flat, and Peter Cook (who no doubt heard the full story from staff or punters) later said that, in the annals of the Establishment, no turn went down worse. 'The stoniest of stony silences,' Cook said. '*Nobody* found Barry remotely amusing. It was dreadful. Must have been dreadful for him. There were about three or four people who thought this is very very funny. Mainly John Betjeman, John Osborne, and (later) me. I felt ashamed of my fellow-Londoners for not appreciating him.' The reviews were bad, and Nick Luard, the club's business manager, told him they would have to cut his season short.

John and Humphries met often, sometimes giving each other rare books or pictures as presents. They would go to art exhibitions together, or to Abbott and Holder's shop in Barnes to look at watercolours and drawings.

> On a summer afternoon [Humphries remembered] we would sit under the enormous weeping beech in the garden, and Eric Holder would bring out bundles of paintings and drawings and spread them on the grass for our amusement.
>
> 'Art never lets you down,' said John, as if most other things did.
>
> One day we chose about six pictures between us, all very fairly priced . . . John bought a big seascape by Laura Knight, a breezy watercolour by Robert Anning Bell (given to me after John's death) and a nude boy on a rock in Cornwall by Henry Scott Tuke, who specialized in such subjects and

was patronized by Edwardian schoolmasters and clergymen with Greek inclinations and more recently collected by Sir Elton John.

When the pictures were spread out on the lawn, John and Humphries would walk along them, up and down, 'as if inspecting troops'. 'My purchases were quite modest at that time,' Humphries says. 'I might come away with a Phil May sketch.' (Though the Victorian cartoonist – 'Film A' as he was once mistranscribed by a secretary, to John's amusement – was British, he worked in Australia for a while.) 'But John would buy much more expensive things. I had to be very careful not to admire anything too much as I would at once be given it.'

John did everything he could to champion and promote Barry Humphries. He constantly played the Sandy and Edna records to his friends, not all of whom were captivated. When Humphries first met Osbert Lancaster, the cartoonist said that he did not know any Australian comedians, 'but there's one that John Betjeman insists on playing who is a terrible bore'. Humphries did not dare to admit it was he. During the early Sixties John was invited by the BBC to make a programme about his special loves. He suggested Humphries as one of his enthusiasms and the Corporation tentatively approached the Australian to recite one of his monologues. The BBC soon backed out, thinking that Humphries's act would not be to the taste of their viewers. 'And John Betjeman was so embarrassed about this,' Humphries recalled. 'He felt so responsible – though of course I didn't hold him responsible. So he sent me this beautiful vellum-bound 1890s book which must have cost him at least double his fee. It was the visitors' book of Amaryllis Hacon, the wife of Llewellyn Hacon, the lawyer who funded the Vale Press. And it had all these signatures in it – Beardsley, Wilde, Conder, Shannon, Ricketts . . . It arrived by special delivery. He sent it just because he was disappointed that the BBC had erased me from the programme.'

For Barry Humphries, 1970 was the worst year of his life. His television series was cancelled. His marriage to Rosalind Tong was dissolved. He broke with his Australian impresario, Cliff Hocking. The Australian authorities served writs on him for unpaid taxes. He returned to Australia, 'ill and mad'. Mixing anti-depressant drugs and several glasses of schnapps, he was arrested in Melbourne as drunk and disorderly. His lawyer got him off most of the charges by emphasizing his 'depression'; but two days later – his medication doubled – Humphries was mugged and left in a Melbourne gutter. A passing car dumped him off at St Vincent's Hospital. 'I must have spent many months in the Dymphna Ward of St Vincent's

Hospital,' Humphries wrote. 'John Betjeman wrote me a long and comforting letter containing much information about the life and good works of St Dymphna herself.'*

Days after he had gone along to the Establishment Club in May 1963 to support Humphries, John was being conscripted for his next great conservation campaign, on behalf of Bedford Park. He had long been interested in this estate. In May 1952 Peter Clarke and Tom Greeves, with Greeves's wife Eleanor, visited their friend Derick Behrens, who was a neighbour of John's in Wantage. Behrens, an atomic scientist at Harwell, had been at King's College, Cambridge, with Clarke and Greeves. He had heard how his two friends had met John in Cambridge before the war. He took his guests to The Mead for tea. 'We sat around John Betjeman, on the lawn, in an adoring circle,' Eleanor Greeves recalls. 'His long-suffering wife went off to feed the ducks.'

In 1951 Tom and Eleanor had moved to Bedford Park. It is an estate of arty villas, many of them designed by Norman Shaw, near Turnham Green Underground Station in London. Bedford Park interested John because it was the first 'garden suburb' and the prototype of all the decorative suburbia he both celebrated and satirized. The 'Queen Anne' front elevation of each house was embellished with a brick panel containing a sunflower motif – one of the emblems of the Aesthetic Movement led by J. M. Whistler and Oscar Wilde. The style owed less to Queen Anne's reign than to English vernacular tradition – with some Renaissance flourishes and Dutch gabling. The foundation stone of a church was laid in 1879 and in 1880 the Tabard Inn was opened, with tiled friezes by William Morris's pupil William De Morgan and other tiles by Walter Crane. The inn sign was painted by T. M. Rooke, a pupil of Edward Burne-Jones and friend of John Ruskin. Rooke lived in Bedford Park from 1879 to 1942. Among other early residents were the young W. B. Yeats.

The visit of Peter Clarke and the Greeveses to Wantage in 1952 reminded John of the charms of Bedford Park. Six months later he wrote to Clarke, 'I am now thinking of little else than Bedford Park. I am going to try to get "Patmac's", who now own the Tabard Inn, to allow me to redecorate it in the Norman Shaw style.' In 1955 Patmac's indeed commissioned an architect to renovate the Tabard's interior, but not at all as John

---

* In the 1970s, Barry Humphries found sobriety and success. See Chapter 33, ' ". . . As I Lose Hold" '.

would have wished. Greeves, as one of the pub's regulars, heard of the plan and telephoned the Society for the Protection of Ancient Buildings. He was told: 'You should get hold of John Betjeman.' He did so. Horrified by the news, John telephoned the architect, then rang Greeves to give him a lifelike imitation of the architect's reply, which was not conciliatory. The next day, Greeves was at the Tabard.

> Somebody said, 'Look, there's the architect. Why don't you go and talk to him?' So I did. He was just responsible for that particular pub. I said, 'Can you explain to me what you're doing?' He looked at me rather narrowly and said, 'Now look 'ere: for thirty years we've been doing up pubs. There's nothing you can tell us about it.'
>
> I said, 'Oh. Well perhaps you could answer one or two questions: for example, what are you going to do with that fireplace?' It was the one with the Walter Crane tiles.
>
> 'Oh, we're 'aving that out.'
>
> 'Oh,' I said, 'what are you going to put in its place?'
>
> 'Well, I thought a nice piece of Tudor brickwork.'
>
> I said, 'Do you know who designed that fireplace?'
>
> 'No.'
>
> I said, 'He was a better architect than you or I will ever be.'
>
> 'Oh, oo's that?'
>
> 'Norman Shaw.' Then he looked at me and he said, 'You're not Mr *Betjeman*, are you?' Of course, they'd been having a very persistent Mr Betjeman on the telephone.

John's protests had their effect. Although the Tabard was redecorated, the more drastic plans were abandoned and the De Morgan and Crane tiles left in place.

John again mentioned the Tabard in an article headed 'Suburbs Common or Garden' in the *Daily Telegraph* of 11 August 1960. This time the inn was described as having been a place 'where men could play the clavichord to ladies in tussore dresses, and where supporters of William Morris could learn of early Socialism'. (When John set his 1965 poem 'Narcissus' in Bedford Park, the clavichord became a spinet – 'clavichord' does not rhyme with 'suffragette'.) In the *Telegraph* article John called Bedford Park 'the most significant suburb built in the last century, probably the most significant in the Western world'.

By the date of John's article, only a few of Bedford Park's buildings had come to grief. But in 1962 Tom Greeves was outraged when Acton Council demolished The Bramptons, a large house in Bedford Road, and built an old-people's home on the site, in yellow brick. He wondered whether a group could be formed to protect Bedford Park. 'So I sounded out people in the pub, but I didn't get much response. Even Peter Clarke wasn't very encouraging.' In February 1963 Greeves saw an article in the *Acton Gazette*. The piece was headed 'A BETJEMAN BROADSIDE: It's sounded in defence of Bedford Park'. It told how a leading Acton Conservative, Harry Taylor, aged eighty-two, had 'declared war on Town Hall progress planners'. With the battle-cry 'Forward the "John Betjeman Brigade"!' Taylor declared: 'It is about time the Bedford Park people started a protection society . . .' Greeves was slightly put out by Taylor's headline-grabbing initiative on his own pet subject, but the two men met, and lost no time in planning the launch of the Bedford Park Society.

In May a committee was formed. Greeves and Taylor persuaded Arnold Walker to be chairman. He was just finishing his term as the last Mayor of the borough of Brentford and Chiswick, which in 1964 was amalgamated with Hounslow. It was Walker's idea to ask John Betjeman to be the society's patron. Not all the committee thought this a good idea. 'To some of them', Greeves remembered, 'Betjeman was a figure of fun.' But Walker got his way, and John replied from Cloth Fair on 15 May:

> Dear Mr Mayor,
>   Full willingly and with a sense of honour, will I be a patron of the Bedford Park Society. As you know, the best way to protect it against Clore and Cotton's* agents is to get the paper of the society printed at once and write on it a letter of protest to the Middlesex County Council planning officer with a copy to the Secretary of the Royal Fine Art Commission.
>   With best wishes,
>   John Betjeman
> God bless you for encouraging so excellent and vital a society. Afraid I am away such a lot I cannot do more than give advice.

Later in 1963 John telephoned Tom Greeves to ask if he would help him make a television film about Bedford Park. Greeves had the job of showing the cameraman which streets and houses to include. When the film was made, John dubbed a commentary on to it.

Almost eighty people attended the first public meeting of the Bedford Park Society in May 1963. They agreed that the main aim was to get buildings listed. Through the Victorian Society, Greeves got an introduction to Anthony Dale, chief investigating officer on the listing committee of the then Ministry of Housing and Local Government. Greeves showed Dale

---

* Charles Clore and Jack Cotton were leading property developers in the Sixties.

Count Gleichen's statue of Alfred the Great at Wantage

In 1960, John saved Candida's friend Anne Baring from being expelled from St Mary's, Wantage, for painting the figure red

Candida Betjeman (later Lycett Green) in 1960

John with Penelope in 1960 after he was appointed CBE

Campaigning to save Lewisham town hall, 23 August 1961: John with thirteen-year-old William Norton

John with Veronica ('Ron') Sharley at the wedding of her sister Diana to Eric Kendrick on 7 September 1968

Penelope in the garden at Wantage

The wedding of Candida Betjeman and Rupert Lycett Green at Wantage Church on 25 May 1963

Philip Larkin and John making a BBC *Monitor* television film in Hull in 1964

Above: Realizing a schoolboy dream: John as a temporary train driver

Left: John with Mervyn Stockwood in the open-air pulpit of Christ Church, North Brixton

Princess Margaret with Lady Elizabeth
Cavendish

Princess Margaret presents the Duff Cooper
Prize to John in 1958 for *Collected Poems*

Mervyn Stockwood, John and Lady Elizabeth Cavendish in holiday mood

With Osbert Lancaster in *Time with Betjeman*

At No. 29 Radnor Walk with Bevis Hillier in 1982. By now, the poet's face was 'frozen' by his Parkinson's Disease

John with Lady Elizabeth Cavendish at Trebetherick, Cornwall, during the filming of *Time with Betjeman*

On 24 June 1983 John named British Rail's main-line electric locomotive No. 86229 after himself in a ceremony at St Pancras station; (*right*) Sir Peter Parker, chairman of British Rail, and (*to his left*) Jim O'Brien, general manager of the London Midland region

his map of Bedford Park and the many photographs he had taken. Dale asked Greeves which buildings he thought should be listed. He replied: 'Well, if you're going to list Bedford Park you cannot pick and choose – it must all be saved.' Dale was astonished. 'You can't expect me to list *all* these houses,' he said. 'They're not worth it! Architecturally, they're just not good enough. And look at the lay-out. I mean, there isn't one. Compare it with Hampstead Garden Suburb [which had recently been listed].' Greeves had not expected this kind of rebuff. He consulted Nikolaus Pevsner, who was also on the listing committee. 'This is awful,' said Greeves. 'Yes, it *is* awful,' Pevsner agreed. 'I will see what I can do.' But in committee Pevsner's proposal that a large number of the Bedford Park houses should be listed was vehemently opposed, and scuttled, by that philistine in aesthete's clothing Sir John Summerson, who had already virtually drafted the death warrant of the Euston Arch in his *Times* article of 1960. On 16 October 1963 Pevsner wrote to Greeves:

> Dear Tom,
>   This is, alas, to let you know that I lost the battle over Bedford Park. The treatment was fair. Everybody had a chance of speaking, and in the end it was put to the vote. I am, of course, very distressed.
>   Yours sincerely,
>   Nikolaus Pevsner

The great setback of 1963 was followed by another in 1964: the death of Harry Taylor. Fortunately, new blood was coming into the society to replace the old. During the 1960s a number of young people moved into Bedford Park – among them Mark Glazebrook, an Arts Council officer, with his then wife Elizabeth. Tom Greeves, with not entirely mock crustiness, called these new arrivals 'the trendies'. Bedford Park was suddenly 'in'. In 1965 Father Jack Jenner arrived in Bedford Park as the new vicar of St Michael and All Angels Church. His first concern was for the church, whose roof was in need of repair. He decided that a festival should be held, partly to raise money, partly to raise consciousness of Bedford Park's history and quality. A committee was formed. John Betjeman, approached by Jenner, agreed to be patron of the festival as well as of the society.

To launch the campaign to restore the church roof, a party was held on the vicarage lawn on 19 July 1966. John was the guest of honour. The Bishop of Kensington and the Mayors of Ealing and Hounslow were also present. John made a speech. 'We are standing right in the centre of the world's first garden suburb,' he said. He praised Norman Shaw's church: 'The chapel is a miracle of how to get atmosphere in a small place.' Those in John's audience who had read his *First and Last Loves* (1952) might have noticed that the speech marked a volte-face: in the book he had said the church lacked mystery.

After the speech, Mark Glazebrook's wife Elizabeth, in the costume of a Victorian maid, served tea and tea-cakes. 'The dress wasn't of a very saucy nature,' she recalls. 'It was quite decorous – a long black dress with a small white apron and a white mob cap.' John sat down next to Glazebrook on a bench. 'You must be a happy man,' John said. 'Not only do you have a beautiful wife dressed up as a Victorian maid. (How did you manage to get her to do it?) You also have a Bedford Park house by Norman Shaw, with a shell porch.' Glazebrook later commented: 'Little did he know that we were just in the throes of getting divorced. In fact, I think it was the Victorian costume that put the lid on it for me. She's a very good *ex*-wife. My life was in ruins – I was out of a job, too. But it was a lovely idyll.' Glazebrook further points out that his house, which could be seen over the vicarage garden wall, was by E. J. May, not Norman Shaw.

Mark Glazebrook was thirty in 1966 and John was twice that age, but there was no generation gap. Glazebrook had much of John's charm, wit, artistic interests and helpless susceptibility to jokes. As usually happened when John made a new friend, he both volunteered and invited confidences. He told Glazebrook that he felt he should never have married Penelope Chetwode. 'The reason he had done – and of course I know that things change in old men's memories from reality and I know nothing about it – but what he *said* was that he got married because he thought that if one had carnal knowledge of someone, one had to marry them. It was only later that he discovered that you didn't have to – it wasn't the law or a religious obligation. That was his excuse, it seemed to me – he'd made this marriage that didn't work out entirely right. What marriage does?'

In turn, John soon found out what was bothering Glazebrook. Under questioning which from anybody else might have seemed intrusive, Glazebrook spilled out his feelings of insecurity.

> The reason why you felt a sort of love for Betjeman [he recalled] was that he understood what people who had had a privileged background sensed in the age of the common man. He had a very soft spot for slightly hopeless but charming aristocrats and middle-class people like my family, with good values. You got the feeling that it was important to *him* that your grandfather had founded the Royal Cornish Yachting Club and your uncle had played squash at Marlborough and your father was director of the Midland Bank in its heyday. He made you feel less of an endangered species.

For about a year before the festival, the Victorian Society had been trying to save No. 1 Marlborough Crescent, one of the finest houses, but it was demolished because it was not listed. During the campaign to save it, Arthur Grogan of the Greater London Council Historic Buildings Division had come to investigate. Greeves showed him round the district, and although Grogan was unable to save the Marlborough Crescent building, he became interested in Bedford Park. By luck he was transferred to the listing committee of the Ministry of Housing and Local Government just before the first festival. Greeves telephoned him and said, 'You must come and see the exhibition, I've got these photographs.' Grogan came to the show (John was also there – he brought Lady Elizabeth Cavendish), and said, 'It's scandalous that this place has not been listed.' By that time Port Sunlight, Lord Lever's 'ideal village' for the workers at his soap factory, had been listed as well as Hampstead Garden Suburb. 'I've only just arrived in the job, and there's a lot of hostility towards Bedford Park,' Grogan said. 'But I'll do my best.' The next day he was seen in Bedford Park with a notebook.

In July 1967 a 'summit' meeting was held in the Greeves' house in Newton Grove: two representatives of the GLC, two from Ealing Council, two from Hounslow Council and Arthur Grogan from the Ministry. 'Grogan was the last to arrive,' Greeves recalled. 'We sat round a table and waited for him to appear. We were all discussing what could be done.' When he arrived, Grogan kept them in suspense. He went out to the kitchen with Eleanor Greeves to help her bring in coffee on trays. As he came into the room, carrying a tray, he said: 'We're going to list 356 houses. Is that what you wanted?'

Grogan had brought a plan with him. He indicated the houses which the Ministry had decided to list, provisionally, as Grade II. Greeves said of Grogan: 'He looks a mild sort of person, but he's not. I've since asked him how he got round the committee, but he's rather reticent and doesn't like to give away any secrets.' The second festival, in 1968, was a celebration. John wrote one of his less sophisticated poems for the programme. Beginning 'The dogs do bark in Bedford Park' (a pastiche of an old nursery rhyme), it was printed as 'A message from our patron'.

In 1975 Bedford Park celebrated the centenary of its founding and John made a second television programme about the suburb. Again he asked Tom Greeves for help. On the day of the filming, Greeves was to pick him up at Cloth Fair and was also to collect some books that John said he wanted to give him. When Greeves arrived at Cloth Fair he found that John had already left. John had told the cleaning woman that he wanted to go by Underground. He had left sandwiches and wine for Greeves, and the books – nine large volumes of offprints of Maurice B. Adams's illustrations to the *Building News*. 'It was an incredibly generous present,' Greeves said.

Most of the credit for winning the Battle of Bedford Park must go to Harry Taylor, Tom Greeves and Arthur Grogan. Without these three men Bedford Park today might be as devastated as Fitzjohn's Avenue, Hampstead, of which the red-brick houses by Norman Shaw and E. J. May, which were a largely unspoilt sequence in the mid-1960s, have been shockingly gouged into by later developments. But John's contribution to the victory was not peripheral. He was already fighting to save the suburb in the 1950s, before anyone else. His *Daily Telegraph* article of 1960 gave the Bedford Park Society its battle-cry. His poem 'Narcissus' (1965), though affectionately satirical, was the best evocation of the suburb's early days and 'atmosphere' since Yeats and Chesterton had described it.

By agreeing to be patron of the society, John threw the weight of his public fame (never higher than after the publication of *Summoned by Bells* in 1960) behind the campaign, even at the cost of opposing his old friend John Summerson and linking arms with his old enemy Nikolaus Pevsner. He attended the festivals and wrote a poem for one of the programmes. And in two television appearances he kept Bedford Park in the public eye. The almost total victory that he helped to win could not compensate for the ruin of the Euston Arch and the Coal Exchange; but it re-nerved John's confidence as a gladiator of conservation. From now on, no letter of complaint to the press, about historic buildings, seemed valid without his signature.

29

High and Low

IN 1965 JOCK MURRAY decided it was time to persuade John to publish a further 'slim volume' of his poems – a chaser to the runaway success of *Collected Poems* in 1958. The usual process began, by which secretaries rummaged through desk drawers and magazine editors were plagued for lists of the Betjeman poems they had published in the last few years. In January 1966, with John's agreement, Murray sent Lord Birkenhead the poems he had so far managed to marshal.

Birkenhead had been at Oxford with John, who respected his judgement. He had written an introduction to the *Collected Poems*. On 10 January he wrote back to Murray that he would read the new poems with great interest, adding, 'The next step is to overcome [John's] reluctance about their publication. I will try to get hold of Elizabeth Cavendish some time soon and have a talk with her as to how this could best be done, as I know she is very keen on their coming out.'

The letter is revealing. In John's lifetime, most of the public would have been surprised to learn that he was reluctant to go into print. Their impression of him was of a man constantly invading their homes on television or sounding off in newspapers and magazines – hardly a shrinking violet. What few of them can have guessed was how acutely sensitive he was to unfavourable reviews of his work. His poetry meant so much to him – he told Candida, 'I know nothing in the world, not even love, quite as fulfilling as completing a poem to one's satisfaction' – that an attack on it had almost the force of a physical wound. Birkenhead's letter also makes clear the recognition by John's friends that the best way of getting him to do something was to have a quiet word with Lady Elizabeth – rather as a courtier wanting a favour from Louis XIV would approach Madame de Maintenon.

The title gave some trouble. John's first suggestion was *Evensong*, which seemed unsatisfactory to Murray on two counts: first, that it bore no relation to many of the poems in the book; and second, that John seemed to be implying that this was a farewell or near-farewell performance and that not many more golden eggs were to be expected from this goose. It is not clear from the surviving correspondence whether the title finally adopted, *High and Low*, was suggested by John, by Murray or by somebody else. While, like *Evensong*, it had obvious religious connotations, it was less specific, more comprehensive. It could refer to the contours of landscape or to John's mercurial spirits as well as to Church of England rites.

As usual, Tom Driberg was asked to suggest amendments to poems. Murray wanted to pay him a £25 'advisory fee', but John said, 'Double it' – because (Murray told his staff in a memo) 'JB said that Tom Driberg was hard up and he valued his advice.' Birkenhead was also full of suggestions, mainly about John's unseasonal references to flowers. In the poem 'Cornish Cliffs' John referred to primroses and gorse flowering at the same time. 'This could certainly not happen where I live,' Birkenhead wrote from Oxfordshire. 'It is possible that they might briefly coincide in the Cornish climate, but I am doubtful about this.'

By the end of October, John's friends had received their complimentary copies. Maurice Bowra wrote to him on the 29th:

> When I think how few of our friends have fulfilled their first promise or how little one has oneself done from first hopes your achievement in poetry stands up solid and splendid and encouraging and defiant. The old boy [Ernest Betjemann] must be pleased – he was after all an artist, and the worms won't have taken that from him.

Of the thirty-four poems in the new book, nearly half had not appeared in print before, though a few were of some vintage. ('In Willesden Churchyard' was first printed in *Vogue* in 1957.) There was a more strongly autobiographical element than in any previous Betjeman collection. In 'Tregardock' he made bitter reference to 'journalism full of hate'. 'A Bay in Anglesey' was written while staying with his friend the Marquess of Anglesey at Plas Newydd. Two poems, one easily decodable, the other less so, alluded to Lady Elizabeth: 'A Lament for Moira McCavendish' and 'The Cockney Amorist'. John's *saeva indignatio* gave passion to 'Matlock Bath', 'Inexpensive Progress' ('O age without a soul') and 'Harvest Hymn', the poem which infuriated Britain's farmers when it was published as a letter in the *Farmers' Weekly*. Based on a favourite hymn, the poem begins:

> We spray the fields and scatter
> The poison on the ground
> So that no wicked wild flowers
> Upon our farm be found.
> We like whatever helps us
> To line our purse with pence;

> The twenty-four-hour broiler-house
> And neat electric fence.

Contrary to John's fears, most of the reviews were excellent. Several of the critics noticed an improvement and a greater adventurousness in his technique – among them, Cyril Connolly ('he is more than ever expert in the traditional metres which he affects'). Two leading critics repudiated the view that John was merely nostalgic and cosy. John Gross wrote in *The Observer*: 'In fact he is a serious, not to say an impassioned writer, who uses objects and landmarks to conjure up the eternal moment, the sudden stab of terror, intimate feelings and buried memories.' John Carey declared in the *New Statesman* that 'what his poetry constantly implies is raw passion . . . He fronts the world's bullies with quivering rage.'

Only one of the many articles about the book really got under John's skin. This was a skit in *Punch* by Basil Boothroyd, a veteran contributor to that magazine. Under a cartoon by Leslie Illingworth, he pictured John with the controversial journalist and television star Malcolm Muggeridge, engaged in a dialogue in Willesden cemetery. John's half of the conversation consisted entirely of quotations from *High and Low*.

> *The scene is Willesden cemetery. JOHN BETJEMAN and MALCOLM*
> *MUGGERIDGE saunter among the graves.*
> MUGG: We should come here more often. One of life's few remaining pleasures is contemplating the inestimable blessing of release.
> (*He stops to read a headstone.*)
> Who's this fortunate guy?
> BETJ: 'Where is Anne Channel who loved this place the best, With her tense blue eyes and her shopping-bag falling apart . . . ?'
> MUGG: Not here, my dear John. I'm not unaware that you had another book of poems out last week, but this enviable plot has nothing to do with the deceased ladies in your life. It appears to be occupied by a gentleman called William Trundle. Nineteen-twenty-two. He should be about ready to move over. (*Laughs uncontrollably.*)
> BETJ: 'The heart in me's dead, like your sweetest of daughters, And I would that my spirit were lost on the air.'
> MUGG: I recognize the quotation, old boy. That's your girl-friend Moira McCavendish. I see her as the Joan Hunter Dunn of Erin, distasteful though the concept may be. On the whole I prefer your moving obituary of the golf-club secretary. My only feeling—
> BETJ: 'The flag that hung half-mast today
> Seemed animate with being,
> As if—'
> MUGG: My personal feeling—

BETJ: 'As if it knew for whom it flew
   And will no more be seeing.'

MUGG: Yes. Did these weary old eyes deceive me, by the way, or did I read
   in your foreword that the ineffable Tom Driberg had kindly corrected
   your grammar, and punctuation? I only ask because any politician is naturally a figure of farce, and I couldn't help thinking it an odd choice.
   However, putting that aside, I fancy I detect a distressing streak of anti-
   death sentiment here, and I regard it as a great mistake. (*Laughs with
   sudden gusto*) . . .

Perhaps the reason John detested this article was that he saw it as cattily
'outing' his close friendship with Elizabeth; he may also have resented the
snipe against Driberg. The article earned Boothroyd his lasting enmity.

High and Low sold well. On 8 December Murray sent John a copy of
the second printing. 'Already it is going at a tremendous speed,' he wrote,
'and the third printing is in train . . .' By then the book was fifth in the
Evening News's list of non-fiction bestsellers. John agreed to an interview
with Graham Lord of the *Sunday Express*, a clever journalist who in a
number of newspaper profiles became a sort of vaudeville commentator
on the poet's later years. He talked to Lord about the poems. 'My themes
are that you're all alone, that you fall in love, that you've got to die.' He
confessed to feeling insecure about the future: would he still be able to
afford vodka in ten years' time? At lunch in a pub near Cloth Fair, Lord
saw another side of John's character.

> Over steak-and-kidney pie . . . young men nod and murmur 'That's John
> Betjeman' as he walks out to a neighbouring bank with quick short steps to
> cash a cheque.
>
> He returns affronted, almost sulky. He had to wait in a long queue of
> market porters paying in great piles of money. Indignant, he sets off after
> lunch to change to another bank.

In that moment of petulance, Lord saw John's 'for public consumption'
persona lifted; his evident vulnerability endeared John to him still more.

A few months later John met a man who saw even more of his vulnerability, and of Penelope's. On a fine July day in 1967, he was returning to
The Mead after morning service in Wantage Church, his summer suit
creased, his boater rakishly askew. As he neared the house, he saw a lean,
dark-haired young man standing at the front door, holding a large parcel.
'I thought,' John later told his visitor, '"What's that Cornishman doing,
knocking at my front door? And what's that parcel under his arm?"'

Though he was born in Cheltenham and grew up in Ilfracombe in

Devon, the stranger, John Nankivell, *was* Cornish by ancestry. The surname means 'Valley of the wild horses' in the old Cornish language. He
turned to face John. 'I was wondering, Mr Betjeman . . . I've got some of
my drawings here and I was wondering if you'd look at them and tell me
what you think of them.'

'We-e-ll . . . we-e-ll . . .' John looked uncertain, but after some hesitation invited Nankivell in. The artist recalls:

> The Mead was cool and white-walled, much smaller than I had imagined.
> A homely kitchen, with a large dresser, crowded with colourful plates. The
> passage walls were hung with luminous Pre-Raphaelite paintings. We passed
> the sitting-room, full of flowery patterned sofas and dominated by a high,
> black lacquer Chinese cabinet, surmounted by two bronze Thai dragons.
>
> I was led upstairs to a large, long, low room, converted from several
> bedrooms into a library, not without strain to the rolling floor, I felt. Dark
> pink-red walls and deep, tall shelving held thousands of inviting books: art,
> architecture, poetry and other literature. We sat in two comfortable old arm-
> chairs. He looked intently at my drawings, which were of Ilfracombe. I knew
> that he was enthusiastic about the place, from his book *First and Last Loves*; he
> admired the high Victorian resort as much as I did.

John was impressed by the drawings. Though they depicted Ilfracombe's
buildings with careful detail, there was something about the perspective –
a hardly perceptible distortion – that saved them from being drily academic;
it was as if the buildings were reflected in a lake with a slight shiver across
its surface. 'We got on as well as I had always hoped and imagined,'
Nankivell writes, 'sharing, it seemed, the same love of wayward and hybrid
architecture – "rogue", he called it – with such architects as Teulon, White
and Burges and their polychromatic brickwork, turrets, towers and grotesque carving. We talked and talked.'

Nankivell was working as a painter, decorator and signwriter, having
recently abandoned a career as a schoolmaster teaching art. When they met
on that July day in 1967, he was twenty-six, John Betjeman sixty. The
encounter was not unlike one of Max Beerbohm's cartoons of the Old Self
confronting the Young Self. Both Johns had strange, trisyllabic surnames
which needed explaining to people (inevitably, Nankivell was nicknamed
'Nanki-Poo' by student wags). In each case, there was a strong link with
Cornwall. Both were brilliant creators with a touch of eccentricity; and John
Betjeman, the writer, was as capable an amateur artist as John Nankivell, the
artist, was a skilful amateur writer. Both loved Victorian architecture. Both
rebelled against authority and, when young, suffered social slights which
rankled in later years. And both were susceptible to women.

John Betjeman was so taken with Nankivell that he invited him to breakfast at The Mead the next day, the Monday.

It was then that I met for the first time the formidable and terrifying Honourable Mrs Betjeman and an even frostier daughter, Candida. They, fully knowing John Betjeman's weakness when faced with his 'fans', were understandably suspicious of me, this interloper into their family life. 'I spend my life protecting John from people like you,' Penelope told me years later, 'and somehow you slipped through the net – thank God!' Yet for a while it was a delicate situation, somewhat softened by Penelope's quick appreciation of my drawings, and by the growing warmth and support of John, who seemed genuinely interested in my then vague future.

John Betjeman had come to hate driving, particularly after his car suddenly broke down in Trafalgar Square. Nankivell became his unofficial chauffeur.

Sometimes, when he was invited out to dinner, our departure would be delayed when he discovered buttons missing on his jacket or, more often, his waistcoats. I would have to sit beside him on the sofa or bed, frantically sewing before we could set off and somewhat worried lest I stick a large needle into his stomach.

One morning, arriving at The Mead early to collect him and Penelope to set off south to the opening of the restored Crofton Beam Engine down on the Kennet and Avon Canal, I found a great scene in progress. John, always nervous and highly strung before such events, especially when he had to speak, was desperate to set off, being terrified of a last-minute rush. But Penelope would not start, because she was expecting a long overdue visit from 'the Bendix man': her huge washing-machine stood silent and malevolent amid mounds of linen in the laundry room.

John got more and more agitated, eventually becoming beside himself and yelling 'Plymouth!', one of his nicknames for her. When eventually the unfortunate man arrived, he was quickly abandoned to his task – but not before he'd suffered from the frustrations of both of them.

Nankivell repaid John's kindness by giving him several of his architectural drawings: John particularly liked one of Cranmore Tower, an Italianate folly above Shepton Mallet. But John also found a way of boosting Nankivell's income by commissioning and paying for drawings as wedding presents or as gifts for his godchildren; and in 1967 he arranged for an exhibition of the drawings of Ilfracombe to be staged at Exeter University. Nankivell was half delighted and half embarrassed when John volunteered to come down and open the show. In 1968 the two men made a short television film about the Ilfracombe drawings, with the BBC producer Michael

Croucher. It lasted about eight minutes. The camera panned over the drawings and John gave an extempore commentary.

In 1970 Penelope left for India for a year and let The Mead to
an American psychologist and his family for fifteen guineas a week. 'She is
going with three people called Elizabeth, whose surnames are Simpson
[*sic*], Cuthbert and Chatwyn [*sic*],' John wrote to Harry Jarvis, 'and she is
taking John Nankivell to do some drawings. It is costing the earth, but let
us hope it will repay at any rate part of itself.' Elizabeth Chatwin was the
wife of Bruce Chatwin, the future travel writer and novelist. He was
originally to have been part of the group going to India but he reneged,
telling his wife in 1970, 'Penelope seems to be very demanding and I'm
afraid that eccentricity has an uncommon tendency to develop into ego-
mania. This is perfectly all right as long as you don't have to travel with it.'

John Nankivell remembers their departure on that epic journey.
Penelope had bought two Morris J4 vans:

> We were all loaded up: Elizabeth Simson with masses and masses of shoes;
> me with beautiful boxes with things like silver hair brushes which the others
> thought very freaky; and Penelope with her saddles and tack and God knows
> what. And one lovely night in September with the Wantage bells ringing
> madly – they were ringing specially for us – we set off. Virtually all
> Penelope's friends turned out around The Mead to wave us goodbye.

John Nankivell made a masterly series of drawings on the tour of India
in 1970–71. John Betjeman and Penelope both attended the private view of
an exhibition of them at Hartnoll & Eyre's gallery in London. Nankivell was
valued by John as a creative artist, a friend, a driver and one of the young
men – others were Mark Girouard, Simon Jenkins, Gavin Stamp, Glynn
Boyd Harte, David Watkin and myself – who shared his appetite for 'rogue'
architecture and his distaste for the New Brutalism. But, like Chatwin later
on, Nankivell also became a great friend of Penelope. In the years of John's
and Penelope's widening separation, he was able to act as an ambassador
between their courts, an Ariel traversing continents, materializing with
Penelope in Chelsea, Simla, or with John in Chelsea, London, and welcomed by each of them.

John's activities as a preservationist had not fallen off in the course of
the Sixties. Between 1958 and 1963, as we have seen, he took part in three
great campaigns to save nineteenth-century buildings: the Euston Arch,
the Coal Exchange and Bedford Park – two defeats and a victory. He still
found time to protest at the axing of railway lines; at the taking over of
Ince Blundell Pantheon, near Liverpool, by an order of nuns which

refused public access to the sculpture collections housed there since 1811; and at the deterioration of the Great Barn at Avebury, Wiltshire. With financial help from John's friend Bryan Guinness (Lord Moyne) the barn was turned into a rural-life museum. Brian Edwards, who worked in the museum as a volunteer and has written about the Avebury campaign, thinks it was the beginning of the popular preservation movement which was celebrated in the Kinks' pop song of 1967, 'The Village Green Preservation Society'. The interest was no longer just in stately homes built and owned by aristocrats. 'It was "Save the schoolhouse"; "Save the park"; "Save the buses",' Edwards says. It went with the fashion for rural communes, organic food and real ale. The Wiltshire Folk Life Society was founded in 1975.

John was in the news again in December 1963: 'SUPERMARKETS RUIN OUR TOWNS: MR BETJEMAN'S ATTACK'. On 2 December about 350 leaders of Lincolnshire opinion met in Lincoln for a conference on Lincolnshire past, present and future. The conference 'began with an assault by Mr John Betjeman against supermarkets, which were "wrecking the West Country"'.

> Two habits of thought were helping to spoil our towns. One was the idea that nothing mattered except money. The other was the modern point of view that there was always another side to the argument.
>
> Mr Betjeman said: 'You know that on the wireless you are never allowed to express an opinion unless someone else disagrees with you. It comes of allowing ourselves to be dominated by the Civil Service, which likes to gather power to itself on its way up from prefect to knight to nobleman. It does not mind what decision is made so long as it makes the decision.'
>
> If amenities would be destroyed by the widening of a road, the civil servant would say, 'I would be the first to tell you that we should not broaden the street at all, but there are other considerations.' Mr Betjeman pounded the table. 'Well, there aren't,' he said. Supermarkets could be sited on the outskirts of towns.

On 31 August 1964 John mounted another of his favourite hobby-horses in a letter headed 'PYLONS ON THE MARCH'. He would never allow his name to be taken in vain without retaliating; and three days earlier, a Joseph Wilby of Chiswick had mentioned him slightingly in a *Times* letter. If one engaged in research, Wilby was sure, one would find men of the seventeenth and eighteenth centuries 'campaigning against the building of those monstrosities, the windmills, which mar the Sussex landscape'. And he was 'more than sure that the John Betjemans of the twenty-first and twenty-second centuries will still be campaigning for the preservation of the pylons which carried that ancient form of power to the homes of their forebears'. John snapped back:

> One of your correspondents advocating the case of the Minister of Power for putting up pylons regardless of public opinion brings my name into a letter likening pylons to windmills.
>
> May I point out the falsity of this analogy? Windmills could never be put underground. Windmills never marched in straight lines from a central generating station. Windmills were hand made and not all of a pattern . . .
>
> It is sentimental to glorify pylons. We all really know why pylons are to be allowed to industrialize and change the character of downs and modest agricultural landscape . . . The reason is money.

Just as John was not too proud to court his 'enemies', such as Maxwell Fry and Pevsner, to persuade them to join his campaigns, so he was not afraid to pillory his friends if their actions threatened the landmarks he cared for. Sir William Holford had signed several of John's gang-bang letters, but no quarter was shown him when, in November 1964, John thought his plans for the precincts of St Paul's would block the Cathedral and destroy the famous skyline. 'What is to happen to the churches, livery halls and historic buildings which give the City character and are at present at ground level?' John asked. 'Are they to disappear along with the old alleys with their little shops where we used to walk in our lunch hours? It looks to me as though the City will become a second-rate New York.'

John admired all the Scott family of architects and in 1944 had written to Sir Giles Gilbert Scott (designer of the red telephone kiosks), asking this time if he would let him write a chronicle of the family over the past century and a half. (Scott replied, 'I am much interested in your proposal', but the book never materialized.) So John was prepared to do battle when, in September 1966, British Rail announced their intention to redevelop both the King's Cross and St Pancras termini. J. M. Richards, as *The Times*'s architectural correspondent, assessed both buildings on 3 September. They were, he thought, of first-rate quality. With Lewis Cubitt's King's Cross (1851), character was derived from function; the station was 'one of the forerunners of modern architecture', a work of 'heroic engineering'. St Pancras was different: its designer was 'a highly conscious artist'. It was a contribution to the London street scene and in particular to the skyline. Though the earlier station would be 'a very great loss', St Pancras would be the greater. 'It is unique, and it would mean a loss of visual richness and excitement.'

After this, John might have felt that he did not need to reiterate the case for the defence; but over St Pancras he encountered, for the first and last time in his campaigning career, an adversary able to turn on him his own weapons of irony, ridicule and provocative flippancy. Sir Edward Playfair, a suave alumnus of Eton and King's, Cambridge, had served with the Inland Revenue and the Treasury. He had become Permanent Under-Secretary of State for War and Permanent Secretary at the Ministry of Defence. Then he had moved from the Civil Service into industry, as chairman of International Computers and Tabulators. Like John Maynard Keynes, he was a finance man with an arts bent: he had served with John on the Royal Fine Art Commission and was a future chairman of the National Gallery. The usual philistine or mercenary opponents of conservation, who spoke of buildings outliving their usefulness or standing in the way of commercial progress, John could swat easily enough. But when Playfair's letter appeared at the top of the *Times*'s correspondence page on 6 September 1966, John recognized a superior foe who would need to be tackled with greater finesse.

No one could make the case for St Pancras better than your Architectural Correspondent [Playfair wrote] . . . Could you find space for one who positively loathes the building? My reason for asking it is that (morally at least) the conservationists have it all their own way.

They are the experts and the men of feeling; those who do not share their views (as your Correspondent implies) are ignorant followers of an obsolete fashion.

In fact, of course, his reaction and mine are both subjective, though his is much better informed. St Pancras gives a lift to his spirit: mine droops at its sight and I have never passed it without hoping . . . that it would soon be demolished. As a critic, I do not count against your Correspondent; as voters, ratepayers, passers-by, and railway-travellers we are equal. Haters of St Pancras should register their feelings as emphatically as its lovers do.

Not enough is said about the virtues of demolition. [The present taste is for] the national junk-yard, the museum with far too many walls, plans distorted to accommodate the fashionable, the obsolete and the unusable, and restrictions placed on today's achievements in favour of the dead.

Anyway, what fun it would be. Think of our delenda list, starting with Elizabethan vulgarities . . . and rising to a climax in modern times, with St Pancras at its head, advancing through Waterhouse (*opera omnia*) towards that arch-delendum the Ministry of Defence. It is a pity that we destructionists are so passive: we need an anti-Betjeman to lead us.

John could not let this pass; but instead of rehearsing all the pro-St Pancras arguments, as he would have done with a stolider opponent, he brushed Playfair aside with disdainful brevity.

Sir Edward Playfair wrote amusingly to you in your issue of September 6 and in his last line refers not very flatteringly to me.

I have heard of him as a senior civil servant who resigned to take up more constructive work in the computer industry. But now he seems to have taken on a new job on behalf of the demolitionists and to have developed into an unashamed developer. Surely in human reason they have devoured enough already?

In 1969 Betjeman the preservationist was affectionately satirized by the cartoonist Trog (Wally Fawkes) in his 'Flook' comic strip in the *Daily Mail*. The artist caught brilliantly both John's appearance and his way of talking – which by then, the height of the Swinging Sixties, was as much a period piece as some of the buildings he was trying to save.

The big campaign of 1969, however, was not an attempt to save a build-ing, but a protest against the proposal for a new airport at Wing, Buckinghamshire. The name might be apt, but, John told the Roskill Commission at Aylesbury on 16 July, 'only Stansted would be a worse choice than Wing . . . for London's third airport. The scenery here in north Bucks is the sort that Henry James described as "unmitigated England".' (The main front-page news was the lift-off of Apollo 11, the day before, on its way to the moon.) John would probably have protested about the proposed airport of his own volition; but he was goaded on by his friend Lady Pamela Berry, whose house at Oving, Buckinghamshire, was near the proposed site. She wrote to him: 'I can't begin to tell you how thrilled we are that you have agreed to come and address us on the subject of the air-port menace . . . Everyone is wildly excited about your appearance . . .' John wrote a poem for the Wing Airport Resistance Association (Wara), conjuring up a picture of a bulldozed Vale of Aylesbury. It was a variation on William Cowper's 'The Poplar Field' (1784), which begins:

> The poplars are fell'd, farewell to the shade
> And the whispering sound of the cool colonnade . . .

Early in 1970 Candida accompanied John to a large meeting of protest-ers at Oving, and he recited his poem.

> . . .
> The birds are all killed and the flowers are all dead
> And the businessman's aeroplane booms overhead;
> With chemical sprays we have poisoned the soil,
> And the scent in our nostrils is diesel and oil.
> The roads are all widened, the lanes are all straight

So that rising executives won't have to wait.
For who'd use a footpath to Quainton or Brill
When a jet can convey him as far as Brazil?

The Wing Airport scheme never took off. Stansted, with no Lady Pamela Berry and no Betjeman poem to defend it, was not so lucky.

The more caught up he became in controversies, the more John seemed to value the rather escapist friendship he had recently started with Mary Wilson, wife of the Prime Minister, Harold Wilson. The two first met in 1967 through the Earl of Drogheda, chairman of the Royal Opera House and later of the *Financial Times*.

> Lord Drogheda used to invite me to join his party at Covent Garden [Lady Wilson recalls]. I had admired John Betjeman for a very long time and had seen him on the television, and I thought, 'That's the man I would like to meet!' I saw the guest list of the party when I got to Covent Garden and I said to Garrett Drogheda, 'Is John Betjeman *really* coming?' And he said, 'Yes.' I said, 'Oh how marvellous, I've always wanted to meet him.' So he said, with his characteristic rather cool manner, 'Oh well, I must change the table plan, then,' which he did. I sat next to John and we had a lot of conversation. We wrote to each other soon afterwards; and so began a friendship.

Mary Wilson wrote to John on 10 November 1967: 'I did so enjoy meeting you and it would be delightful if you could come to tea and a proper talk.' She enclosed two of her own poems, a carol and 'After the Bomb'. John replied that he liked both the poems, but thought the carol the better of the two. 'It is so *good* like you are, really good.'

In a regular feature headed 'Mrs Wilson's Diary' (based on the long-running radio serial *Mrs Dale's Diary*), *Private Eye* portrayed Mary Wilson – 'Gladys' – as a cosy *Hausfrau* with strictly domestic horizons. This travesty related to Harold Wilson's reputation as a tough little nugget from oop north who was partial to HP Sauce – a condiment mocked by John himself in his poem 'Lake District'. Mrs Wilson was not *grande dame*, but she was an attractive, kind and sensible woman, the sort that had always appealed to John. Cynics thought that he was sucking up to her in the hope of ingratiating himself with the Prime Minister; and it was through Wilson, in 1969, that he received his knighthood. Perhaps John was a little over-gushing in his praise of her poems; but it is clear that he felt genuine affection for Mary Wilson and that he was able to ask her advice or confide in her when he was depressed.

She would go to tea with him, or he with her. He 'found the lift at Number 10 Downing Street very erotic', Lady Wilson told Candida

Lycett Green. 'It was lined with red suede and always took a very long time to reach its destinations.' He told her 'how he imagined all the things that had happened in it'. Apart from dinners at the Garrick Club, they kept their friendship private; there was no knowing what a malicious gossip columnist might insinuate if their innocent companionship was observed. As a result, some of their meetings had almost the air of lovers' trysts.

When they met in each other's homes, they would often spend the whole afternoon reciting and talking about poetry. 'Now how many people', Lady Wilson asked in 1982, 'would know enough poetry to talk about it as he did and know every poem that you mentioned? We had lovely quoting sessions, back and forth, and then we'd rush to the reference book to make quite sure whether we were right or not. And he liked me to read to him, which I always found rather embarrassing, because he reads things so much better than I do. I used to read to him – and then he'd go to sleep. Very soothing.' The poets they read were mostly John's old favourites.

What Mary Wilson found especially sympathetic in John was his admission that he was afraid of things. 'Most people wouldn't say, "That's very frightening" – but he does, which is very endearing. He suffers terrific guilt, too. I'm a great guilt-feeler as well; and what John really dislikes are the guilt-*givers*. We've talked a lot about that.' Because Mary understood John's melancholy side, she became, as Candida writes, 'a gentle support which he knew he could always turn to'. 'I . . . knew when he was worried about something,' she told Candida. 'He had this habit of putting his hand to his mouth and biting his knuckles.' The friendship existed almost in isolation. In spite of their deepening rapport, neither found the other's friends very congenial. John once took Mary to dinner with John Osborne and Jill Bennett, 'but it didn't work'. And John was not interested in politics.

John encouraged Mary to read him her poems, and he in turn sent her early drafts of some of his poems. The Wilsons owned a painting of stormy seas by Julius Olsson RA. John bought an Olsson of a sunlit scene and wrote a poem about it. He sent the poem to Mary, with a note: 'What about this? I've just made it up. I got the picture from a dealer in Falmouth, Peter Jackson. It's not as big as yours and it's bright sunlight and in a very 1920s frame with "dull gold".'

In February 1968, Mary read John a poem she had written about Fulbourn in Cambridgeshire, where she had lived from the age of five to ten. She had total recall of that time, she told him, but did not remember much of Diss, where she had been born. 'Oh, Diss is a wonderful place,' John replied. 'Why don't we go there?' They planned the train journey they would make, and that evening John wrote the poem later published as 'A Mind's Journey to Diss' – 'a mind's journey' because they had not yet made it.

> Dear Mary,
> Yes, it will be bliss
> To go with you by train to Diss,
> Your walking shoes upon your feet . . .

When the poem was printed in *A Nip in the Air* (1974), one critic unkindly wondered where else Mrs Wilson might have worn her walking shoes, if not on her feet. Others teased John about the intimate tone of the lines. Robert Nye – never a Betjeman fan – wrote in *The Times*: 'Can our Poet Laureate really be asking the wife of our Prime Minister to accompany him on a railway trip to Diss, Norfolk, for an unspecified purpose? Diss is the Latin for hell, of course, but that is no excuse. The poem . . . ends with a line to make the stuffed owl hoot: *Dear Mary Wilson, this is Diss*. It is all rather splendid and I await the denial from Downing Street.' The visit had in fact been made eighteen months after John's poem was written.

The friendship between John and Mary lasted until his death; but their correspondence petered out, because in his last years of illness she very often visited him at Radnor Walk, Chelsea, so there was no need to write. In all, he wrote her seventy-five letters. Some were from Cloth Fair and Radnor Walk. He always sent her letters and postcards when on his travels – in Australia, Romania, Spain, Italy, Biarritz and Iceland. Frequently he wrote from Cornwall: the correspondence shows just how often he was there with Elizabeth from the late 1960s onwards. Sometimes the tone was rapturous.

> The hot smell of Nivea Cream on Brummy [Birmingham] limbs tanning in glorious June weather here, is more potent than thyme. The sea pinks are just over . . . The elders are creamy green, the sea is emerald with purple shadows . . . The blackbirds are in full song and the thrushes. A goshawk has been seen here . . .

But then there are days when depression engulfs him:

> I did like getting your telephone call. Sometimes in Cornwall I feel trapped. I do now . . . I think we live in a Press state, run by gloom-casters – those school bullies who give the ITN TV news.

In Cornwall, John and Elizabeth were near the Isles of Scilly, which the Wilsons regarded as their real home. (When Harold Wilson resigned as Prime Minister in 1976, John relayed to Mary a remark a taxi driver had made to him: 'He's all right. He can go to the Sicilies.') In March 1970 John and Elizabeth took a helicopter trip to Tresco to visit the gardens there. (The Wilsons were in London.) John wrote to Mary:

> We walked up the granite quay and through the gate after we had crossed that mysterious football pitch and there was that high shorn avenue up to Neptune and the peacocks in full splendour two thirds of the way up. The camellias are out, the scented heathers and the bushes that smell of curry and Eliz who knows all about shrubs and flowers was in heaven at all this sunlit beauty and so was I . . . It was for me a marvellous day and everywhere I thought of you and almost saw your ghost on the shore and down by the quay and in the little lanes back to the airport. I couldn't imagine you in Tresco Gardens. But I saw you going across to Bryher. God! it was wonderful. It must keep you all sane and brave as you seem to have it as a hide-out. But I wouldn't like to live there for ever – certainly not on Tresco. Personalities are too strong. Like the Irish, the Cornish say what they think you want to hear, not what they mean . . .

In spite of these reservations, John was to return to the Isles of Scilly, ten years later. This time, Mary Wilson would be there to greet him.

30

The Church of England Ramblers

⊶⊷

PENELOPE WAS IN India when John wrote to her on 18 June 1971; the monsoon, he imagined, had started. He speculated that the cholera and riots in Bengal had delayed the mails, but he had received thirteen pages of her 'fascinatin doiary', photocopied for him by Jock Murray. Unfortunately John would miss Penelope's homecoming. On 14 September he was to fly to Australia again, this time with a BBC film unit. On 7 July he wrote again with the melancholy news that Maurice Bowra had died of a heart attack the Sunday before. 'Very sad for me. Not for him. He had a strong belief in the next life & in personal survival & often talked to me about it. He said we would meet our friends . . . Oh God! you and I will miss him!' The next day Ann Fleming drove John to Oxford to attend the private funeral with John Sparrow. Bowra's death reminded John of his own mortality: more than anyone, he had been the moulder of his youthful self.

The 1971 tour of Australia was to be altogether a more organized visit than the one of ten years before. The British Embassy and consulates and the British Council were sent his itinerary. The airlines gave him the red-carpet treatment all the way. For John, at sixty-five, a little cosseting and ceremony were welcome. In 1961 he had still been a young man pretending to be old. Now he was an old man trying to recapture his youth.

Not that the new trip was devoid of fun. John was delighted that the producer in charge was Margaret McCall. She was the kind of dominant, vivacious woman he responded best to – the film crew called her 'Big Marge' (she was five foot eight inches tall). She made programmes on Robert Graves, Lawrence Durrell and Graham Sutherland. Durrell's biographer writes that the novelist 'was powerfully attracted to her'. She accompanied him on his travels, but refused to be booked into the Shelbourne Hotel in Dublin as 'Mrs Durrell' and the two split up because 'she would not have him on his terms'.

In some ways, she thought, John and Robert Graves were similar. 'They both had this very fey quality which went well beyond intellect. Graves used to show me where the fairies lived underneath the trees – and mean it. John *almost* did that.' But in other ways John was quite different from the arts celebrities she had filmed before.

> John was a natural. The camera liked him. A natural is not easy to find; and that's why I got into the habit, with the others, of trying to question them about something they did not know I was going to question them about, to make them *think* – they were not natural otherwise. But it was a very bad thing to do with John. He liked to be forewarned of the questions. Where we were going to; what we were going to see; what he was going to say.

Julian Jebb, who had got on well with John before, was also directing part of the series.

The film-makers had Lady Elizabeth Cavendish to contend with as well as John. He had insisted that it be written into his contract that the BBC should pay for her to accompany him on the tour. Margaret McCall remembered:

> The first time I was introduced to this enormous and very healthy-looking lady, John said, 'Oh, look at poor Feeble! Look at those little wrists! You know, she can't carry anything' – all this caper. I liked her very much: and without her John, being a little boy, couldn't have gone through with it. She took care of him, completely. She told him what to do and what not to do. She cooked terrible dinners – pieces of dried toast. And, after we came back, when John wanted to give Philip [her husband] a book about Greece, she didn't want him to give it away. She ruled John's life.

To make the long outward journey less gruelling for John, 'stopovers' were arranged at Teheran and Bangkok. In Teheran McCall noticed for the first time his 'chameleon' nature. 'His fear I always remember and – the other side of the coin – he would be very much braver than we were.'

> When we got to Teheran, John was terrified, with all these native people around, coming out of a crowded station. He was quivering and didn't know what to do. Got him into a taxi, drove through the very busy streets and got him into a crash where people were out drawing their guns rapidly – and he loved it! Loved it and it was very dangerous.
>
> We stayed at a very nice hotel there. That was my first introduction to really good caviar. John and I sat outside on the lawns having caviar and Feeble went around, as she would – very adventurous lady – seeing what

Teheran was like. Came back and swept John and me up and said, 'We've got to go into all the bazaars.' And the only way to get there . . . there weren't any taxis, the way you do it in Teheran is to jump on the back of an empty cart and go as far as you want and jump off. And to see John – little fat John – doing that! He *did* it – and again there was no fear – and enjoyed it, loved it. And this has always been incredible to me, that he had this double nature: this fear that went right through his life, maybe cowardice, maybe not cowardice, it doesn't matter, but sensitivity; and, then, suddenly pushing forward where nobody else would dare to tread.

Margaret McCall had decided to begin filming in the north of Australia and then to move southwards, ending in Tasmania, where Julian Jebb would be allowed to make the last film. John and the team drove to a desert place in Queensland called Charters Towers, almost in the outback.

I hadn't worked with John that much [Margaret McCall said] and I still, at this stage, thought that the best way of doing it was not to tell him exactly what was going to happen, so that you would get, not the set answer, but the look of trying to find his own answer. Spontaneity, more expression. Of course he was such a professional, I didn't need to do that.

On this first opening, out he came with Feeble to this goldrush town of Charters Towers – it was right off the tourist beat – and met me at what were the ruins of something or other. And he wouldn't come out of the car, he was so terrified. He was jittery – 'I don't know what all this is about; I can't do it.' And Julian Jebb – later John gave him hell but they were still friends at that point – told him, 'Now John, just remember how you've started so many programmes. "Now, where am I?" are your opening words, and after that you are going to be quite calm.' It was like a hypnotist. The crew were waiting around, the lighting people and so on. And finally he emerged from the car and started, 'Now, where am I?' and off he went.

In 1971 John was for the first time showing signs of infirmity. In fact these were the first symptoms of the Parkinson's Disease which blighted his last years and enforced the old-mannishness he had sometimes adopted as a pose. 'It was a lot of work for one man,' said Margaret McCall, 'and, what I've never forgiven myself for, I never knew he had Parkinson's Disease. Sometimes I used to see him walking like an old man and I'd think, "Why does he do this to me?"' It was now clear that walking any distance really did tax him. In the rest of the first film he travelled by train and by tram – his favourite means of transport. The train ran from Melbourne to Bendigo, following the pioneer trail to gold. 'You see the real country from [the train],' John commented as he rode through 'Australian Impressionist' scenery, 'not those awful petrol advertisements which ruin the roads.' The former copywriter of Shell petrol posters might have felt a twinge of guilt as he delivered that line.

The second film, entitled 'Pomp and Circumstance', blended Melbourne and Sydney. The film ended inside the Anzac Memorial in Sydney, with the sculptures of the Manxman Reyner Hoff. 'Inside, emotion: the idea here was to give an impression of the horror of war. A naked Anzac soldier lies stretched on a shield and sword . . . Incised in the pavement are these words: "DON'T SPEAK: CONTEMPLATE." ' John told Julian Jebb that he thought that would be a good motto for a television film-maker: as far as possible, architecture, landscape and works of art should be allowed to speak for themselves, not be cluttered with gratuitous commentary.

There was so much to see and show in Australia that the unit decided there would have to be four films, not three as John had originally envisaged. The third film was based in Brisbane and Sydney. 'Nobody told me that Brisbane is so beautiful a city,' John said in his commentary. He dreaded making the final, Tasmanian sequences because Julian Jebb was to direct them, and Jebb had 'got across' him. Margaret McCall remembered:

Julian Jebb – 'JJ' we called him – was putting on an act and John said he didn't do his job properly – didn't get the reference books John wanted, and so on. And with Feeble's backing John got up a great hatred against poor Julian, who was a very sensitive little creature. I had told Julian before we left London that he could have the last film to direct, which was Hobart, Tasmania. But, to make matters worse, the crew were very fond of me and not at all fond of Julian, because Julian threw his weight around. He'd say to an experienced cameraman, 'We can't use you unless I see what work you've done' – can you imagine what the reaction to that was? And he danced a jig when we came off the 'plane; and John of all people didn't want to be obvious. Julian was pretending to be something he wasn't. He wasn't all that sincere, he was playing a game.

So when the time came for Hobart . . . What I had been used to doing with John was knocking on his door and sometimes he was running round *tout nudité*, giggling away; and Feeble was pretending that she was horror-struck when she wasn't. So come Hobart, little Julian goes and knocks on his door, the door opens and John shouts 'GO AWAY! GO AWAY! GET OUT OF IT!' and bangs the door. So I found Julian walking by the river, ready to commit suicide. John's door was still closed so I went and saw Feeble. '*What*', I said, 'is going on? I promised JJ that he could do this, and I see no reason why he shouldn't. He's been okay as far as I'm concerned.' And she, being a magistrate, which made her very fair, went over to my side: 'Right, then he must do it.' And I went up in her estimation because I stood up against her, and against John too, of course. And John immediately gave in. He did what madam said he would do. I think the whole episode was caused not just by his dislike of Julian; it was also that he had got used to working with me.

Jebb was allowed to make the Tasmanian film. John, exhausted by the months of filming, was not at his most tractable, but McCall, as producer of the series, was present all the time and was able to cushion him against Jebb's occasional bumptiousness. '*And* I had to edit Julian's footage severely,' she said. 'But Julian did get some unusual shots.' The best of these, 'which started the Tasmanian film, was John in the rain forest with an English umbrella over him. It was such a lovely contrast. Julian had little brilliances like that.'

John and Elizabeth did not arrive back in England until December. Julian Jebb was home by 6 December, on which day he telephoned his great friend Frances Partridge, the Bloomsbury survivor, writer and diarist. A week later, he was meant to join her at a party at the Reform Club, 'but after one or two telephone calls [Partridge wrote] I realized he was in dire distress, and drove round to see him'.

> I think he was suffering from sheer understandable exhaustion after his Australian tour. But he had the desperate person's desire to press to extremes, to tell me he was 'ill', feeling suicidal. His use of 'ill' I've long ago noticed is an emergency exit whether for himself or others; but I was saddened by his haunted expression, and large tragic eyes, and tried to give sensible advice while dreading being too much of a hospital nurse or schoolmistress.

That year, Frances Partridge spent Christmas with the David Cecils at Cranborne, Dorset. On Christmas Eve they all went to dinner with 'the Trees, Andrew Devonshire's handsome sister and her flashy husband (who appeared in a bright cherry-coloured velvet evening suit, bulky and genial)'. Partridge added: 'Elizabeth Cavendish, Betjeman's "Feeble", was also there. David [Cecil] has twigged that there were difficulties in Australia. I was interested that the forceful Feeble said she had been knocked out for three weeks by the thirty-four-hour flight home.' If Elizabeth and Jebb, respectively twenty and twenty-eight years younger than John, and fitter than he, were exhausted, how much more so must he have been.

The Australia films were shown on British television ten months later. 'Oi'm glad you liked the Aussieland films,' John wrote to Penelope. Before the public screening, a private one was organized in June 1972 for the Prince of Wales, who loved Australia, and for Princess Margaret, who was about to go there for the first time. After the film show there was a dinner. Among those invited was (Sir) John Drummond, who had persuaded the Australian Broadcasting Corporation to put up some money to help the BBC make the films. He wrote:

> The other guests were Lord Snowdon, Elizabeth's mother, the Dowager Duchess of Devonshire, the writer and diarist James Lees-Milne and his formidable wife Alvilde, Patrick Garland, who like me had Australian connections, and his then girlfriend, Jenny Agutter. We dined in a top-floor room at Rules in Maiden Lane, chosen by John – perhaps not entirely tactfully, because Edward VII used to entertain his girlfriends there. At one moment four of us trooped in procession through the crowded restaurant to the gents. I could sense people saying to each other, 'The Prince of Wales, Lord Snowdon, John Betjeman, and who's that with them?' 'He must be the private detective,' I heard a woman say. The evening culminated in a spectacular row between Princess Margaret and Lord Snowdon, after which he refused to leave and she had to be driven back to Kensington Palace in Patrick Garland's Mini. In fact we all trooped back and were there until two in the morning, since the Princess never seemed to tire. James Lees-Milne wrote of the occasion in his diary, but better than that was the letter he wrote to John Betjeman, in which he said he found Princess Margaret 'very very very frightening but beautiful and succulent like Belgian buns'.

It was in 1972 that John enjoyed the last of a series of foreign holidays under the auspices of Mervyn Stockwood. Stockwood had become a controversial figure. In November 1958 Edward Heath, as Chief Whip of the Conservative Government, arrived at No. 10 Downing Street for his morning meeting with Harold Macmillan.

'You look annoyed,' said the Prime Minister to the future Prime Minister.

'I *am* annoyed. You've made a Commie a bishop.'

Maintaining his reputation for unflappability, Macmillan looked only mildly surprised. Heath explained that Mervyn Stockwood, who had just been appointed to the Southwark see, was a red-hot radical and an outspoken critic of the Government.

Even a Labour prime minister might have thought twice before advancing Stockwood to the important see of Southwark. (And indeed, in 1974 a quarrel between Stockwood and Harold Wilson denied Stockwood the Archbishopric of York.) His capacity to provoke had not lessened since John had first met him at Cyril Tomkinson's table in Bristol in 1939. Yet his beautiful resonant voice, his urbanity, wit, hard work and flair for making himself agreeable to people in high places, had all helped to propel him upwards in the church hierarchy, first as Vicar of St Matthew

Moorfields, Bristol, next as an honorary canon of Bristol Cathedral and then, from 1955 to 1959, as Vicar of the University Church, Cambridge.

John and Stockwood had never lost touch, but Stockwood's Cambridge appointment, in particular, brought them together. Bishop Stockwood recalled:

> Simon Phipps [much later Bishop of Lincoln] was chaplain of Trinity then. He had grown up with the royal family – his father was a Gentleman Usher to the Queen. He was a close friend of Princess Margaret and was one of her advisers in the 'Townsend affair'. And Lady Elizabeth Cavendish was the Princess's lady-in-waiting . . . John was Elizabeth's friend . . . you can see the whole set-up. Simon was a very dearly beloved friend of mine.

The friends Stockwood helped to bring together were mainly bachelors. Two who became lasting friends of John and Elizabeth were Raymond Leppard, then a fellow of Trinity and lecturer in music, and the Rev. Harry Williams, Dean of Chapel at Trinity. In his earlier years, Williams had been regarded as a conservative theologian; but now he was making a name as a revolutionary preacher, in sermons later gathered in his book *The True Wilderness*. Penelope thought it disgraceful that he, a priest, abetted John – as she saw it – in his unfaithfulness to her. Williams was outwardly a plump, worldly cleric with a sly wit much appreciated at high table and by John. But in a much later autobiography, *Some Day I'll Find You*, he described a searing mental breakdown and wrote with brave candour about his homosexuality and affairs with men.

The Stockwood–Williams circle in Cambridge also included Simon Stuart, the younger brother of Lord Castle Stewart; Lord Rossmore, a Trinity undergraduate with whom Stockwood stayed on fishing holidays in Ireland; Julian Grenfell (later Lord Grenfell) of King's, president of the Cambridge Union in 1959; Graham Storey of Trinity Hall, the editor of Dickens's letters; and David Cobbold (now Lord Cobbold) of Knebworth, the Victorian Gothic house where Dickens had taken part in amateur theatricals. There were also three future suffragans of Stockwood's: John Robinson, a Trinity lecturer in divinity who was to shock the theological world in 1963 with his bestseller *Honest to God*; David Sheppard, an undergraduate at Trinity Hall, a future England cricket captain and Bishop of Liverpool; and Hugh Montefiore, Dean of Gonville and Caius College, who later provoked headlines and a rebuke from the Archbishop of Canterbury by suggesting that Christ might have been homosexual. Though an Oxford man, Ned Sherrin, the television director and impresario, became one of the group after meeting Stockwood in a television debate on censorship. John and Elizabeth fitted into this coterie, with its Church of England beliefs, its jokes, *bon vivant* tastes, spattering of titles and mixture of muscular Christianity and campness.

Once Stockwood was installed as bishop, John accompanied him on journeys which were part episcopal progress, part 'church-crawl'.

> I had two marvellous church-crawls with Elizabeth and John [Stockwood recalled]. We did about ten churches each time, starting early in the morning, about seven o'clock, and ending late in the evening. Preferably, churches with clergy who were quite the most dotty in the diocese. John would say, 'Take me to a church, the odder and madder the better.' He loved laughing at the Church of England.

Stockwood was an enthusiastic ecumenist. Intellectually, John saw the point of ecumenism; emotionally, he was less committed, since he felt resentful about what he felt was Penelope's apostasy. But both John and Beverley Nichols were, as Stockwood put it, 'fixtures' at an annual party which John called 'the Ecumenical'.

> When I went to Southwark first [Stockwood said] it was in the hard days of no dealings between the Roman Catholic Archbishop of Southwark and us Anglicans. But then, as the thaw gradually came under John XXIII, the Archbishop [Cyril Cowderoy] and I became very close friends. I always had lunch with him on St George's Day and he always came to me the last week of December, near St Thomas's Day, because it was the day he was made a bishop and I was made a priest. We used to have this wonderful party, always with John and Beverley – and many others besides. And I suppose this went on for twenty years. The first time the Archbishop was very nervous about the whole thing; I remember [Lord] Hailsham and [Lord] Longford were there. But then it became so much less formal, we used to have glorious parties.

The guests were waited on by Stockwood's cook–chauffeur, a Christian Arab called Munir (known as El Fhatah), a former barman at the Panorama Hotel, Jerusalem, whom the Bishop had brought to England. Besides John, Elizabeth and Nichols, they often included John Robinson, Hugh Montefiore, David Sheppard, Tom Driberg, Norman Hartnell, the Queen's dressmaker; Barbara Cartland, the romantic novelist; Frankie Howerd, the comedian; Eric Crabtree, a leading London hairdresser of John's generation; Ned Sherrin and his friend Caryl Brahms; and leading clergy of the Roman Catholic Church, the Orthodox Church and the Church of England. 'Mervyn's Palestinian cook cooked as badly as he drove the bishop's car,' Sherrin wrote, 'but the friendly nature of the feast made up for burnt chicken and sausages.'

John and Elizabeth went on holidays with Mervyn Stockwood, Harry Williams and others of their set. Osbert Lancaster, who twice met a group of them – once on a Greek island and again among the royal tombs of the Escorial – christened them 'the Church of England Ramblers Association'. The name stuck, and Williams mystified some readers when, in 1972, he dedicated his book *True Resurrection* to members and honorary members of the association: it was thought that a celestial metaphor was intended. There were fourteen Ramblers in all, but they were never all present. Because of John's antipathy to 'abroad', Elizabeth sometimes left him in England when off with the Ramblers. In 1962 she went to the Middle East with Stockwood and Williams.

In April 1966 John was induced to accompany Elizabeth and Williams to Apulia and Sicily. On 1 May he wrote to William Plomer:

> I came back from Sicily – wild irises, Greek temples, shepherds and sheep bells and at Syracuse Cathedral the first Mass of Easter when the gong-like bells rang out and the lights suddenly filled that Greek Doric temple of Athens with Christian walls between the columns and all in honey-coloured stone like the wine – I suddenly realized what I saw with my eyes and heard – that BC and AD become one with the Resurrection and it didn't matter whether one was R[oman] C[atholic] or C[hurch] of E[ngland].

Simon Stuart was rich. His mother was a daughter of the financier Solomon Guggenheim, who had himself married a Rothschild. Stuart had a villa at Ancona, Italy, at which Elizabeth, John and Harry Williams stayed in August 1966. He was host both to them and to an undergraduate reading-party. 'I am very surprised I like abroad so much,' John wrote to Penelope on 22 August. 'This place is a paradise of olive trees, little hills . . . among the farms and little walled towns and shrines of our lady and smells of sage.' Stuart was a master at Haberdashers' Aske's School. As he did for most of his friends, John soon devised a nickname for him.

> John called me 'bad Simon' [Stuart wrote] to distinguish me from 'good Simon' – Simon Phipps . . . mostly I think because I had affairs with boys (though not in his company). Thence I became 'Wicked' or 'The Wicked' – which I always suspected carried more affection than was offered to 'The Good'. I always enjoyed his euphemism for 'queer' – 'I say, he was a bit unmarried, don't you think?' . . . A. L. Rowse told me years before I met him that JB was utterly tormented by boys – but I never saw anything to substantiate that, unless I adduce his declining to give a lecture at Haberdashers' – which he could have regarded as a torment with no possible reward.

Stuart regarded himself as only an honorary Rambler, but he was with John, Elizabeth and others of the Association on three holidays abroad: Umbria in 1966, Biarritz in 1970 and the French Pyrenees, followed by Barcelona, in 1971.

> John was terrified of having to talk to foreigners [he wrote]. Once in a church in the Pyrenees a Frenchman approached him: he peremptorily summoned 'Feeble, Feeeeble, FEEBULL!' to come and defend him from the unbearable. And when I told him a young German would be a co-guest at dinner, he said, deeply anxious: 'Will I have to speak a foreign language?' Yet it wasn't ordinary xenophobia – in Umbria he was very happy chatting to the not-much-educated couple who looked after us, in pidgin Italian, and gave them a charming water-colour he did of the house. In the Pyrenees we stayed in a small hotel where Monsieur was a top chef, and when he walked through the dining-room, JB and Harry warmly exclaimed '*Artiste!*' and ordered the top vintage on the wine-list. On that occasion, Elizabeth and I went into a titled huddle and discovered we both thought it wicked to spend so much on a bottle of drink – a puritanism from which the bourgeoisie was delightedly free.

Graham Storey was with the Ramblers on the visit to Italy in 1966. He remembered 'how mercilessly we all teased John about his goggling admiration for the Italian boys we saw'.

On 8 February 1968, John wrote to his Oxford friend Lionel Perry, who now lived in Co. Donegal, to tell him that he, Elizabeth, Harry Williams and Simon Stuart were going to Lerwick for a fortnight before Easter on 30 March – 'Shetland is very bracing and beauteous.' In the event, Stuart did not join the other three on that trip. Harry Williams remembered the holiday with special clarity, because on it he received what he considered a 'divine imperative'. He had left for the Shetlands in a state of tension, hoping for a respite from a question that was troubling him. He was nearly fifty and was wondering whether to leave Cambridge and become a monk in the Community of the Resurrection at Mirfield, Yorkshire.

On Easter Sunday Williams thought he had better go to church, 'partly out of a sense of duty and partly not to upset John, for whom at that time . . . attendance at the Holy Communion on Sunday was a bit of a neurotic compulsion; all the more so, therefore, on Easter Sunday'. The three of them went to the small episcopal church in Lerwick for the eight o'clock morning service. It was here that Williams, as he later put it, met his doom. The priest read the usual Prayer Book epistle for Easter Sunday 'and a sentence of it burnt itself into me like fire: "Ye died, and your life is hid with Christ in God." The words overpowered me. It was like being struck fiercely in the face.' From that moment, Williams knew that he was being invited 'to die somehow to an old life in order to find a truer identity in the encompassing mystery of which I had been so long aware'. In practical terms this meant leaving Cambridge and asking if Mirfield would give him a try.

A few days after returning to Cambridge, Harry Williams wrote to the Superior of Mirfield asking to become an aspirant. He told a few intimate friends, and was taken aback to find that 'Elizabeth Cavendish was totally opposed to what I had done.' In the spring of 1969 he stayed with her and John in Cornwall. After the first calming week there, he felt at dinner that something was in the air. 'I was right. Elizabeth told me straight out that she thought I was making the most catastrophic mistake in going to Mirfield and said she was going to spend the evening telling me why.' Williams remembered how her mother, the Dowager Duchess, had told him one evening in Derbyshire that Elizabeth had a rough tongue but a kind heart. He had witnessed 'the most passionate quarrels' between mother and daughter, by the end of which the two would be shouting at each other things like 'If that's what you mean, then for God's sake say so!' But the quarrels left no trace. 'Sitting that evening at Trebetherick I remembered those occasions, fastened my seat belt, and prepared for the worst. John's face, meanwhile, was a mixture of concern, anxiety, amusement and reassurance. He remained silent most of the time, but every now and then he interjected a sort of miniature scherzo which sounded irresistibly funny.' Williams proceeds to write what is in effect a delicious one-act play, a double act by John and Elizabeth in which the characters of both, and their interplay, are revealed.

'First of all,' said Elizabeth, 'you enjoy conviviality. You get a great deal of pleasure out of parties and dinners. There's nothing wrong in that, and it's just silly to cut yourself away from it. It's a much more important side of your life than you imagine, and you'll feel the loss of it desperately.'

At this point John interjected the first of his scherzos. Sounding like the Walrus in Alice in Wonderland he said gravely: 'I suppose you reach a state where a *petit beurre* tastes delicious.'

'And then,' Elizabeth went on, 'what about your holiday travels? You've often said they're the best part of your life. Certainly they liven you up. Won't you be more than half-dead without them?'

'Oh, those ceramic tiles at Caltagirone. I shall never forget them,' said John.

I had no secrets from Elizabeth. She knew all about me, and she continued: 'And young people, the undergraduates and those you've been able to make permanent friends of like Simon and James and William and that young man – what's he called? – who works at Rota's, and those amusing young Fellows, what's the name of the one who's such a good mimic, you know, the one who's a scientist? And that lovely old man who kissed me when I came to the Ladies' Night, the Russian, Susie, no, Bessy, something – won't you be cutting yourself off from your life-blood if you can't see them?'

'I thought that young man in front of us in church on Sunday was very handsome. Do you think he noticed us?' said John.

'What I'm getting at is this,' said Elizabeth. 'What you say and write is of enormous help to hundreds of people. I know because I've met a lot of them. It's not conventional parson's stuff. You get to the heart of things. But this depends upon your imagination. And imagination needs to be fed. It's parties and travel and young men, however much it sometimes hurts, and interesting people, which feed your imagination. It'll dry up without that sort of stimulus. And we shall all be the losers. And for what? I'm going to have my say. For a fit, for what is probably no more than a passing fit, a fit of – yes, I'm going to say it – a fit of conceit. Yes, I don't care what you think, of conceit, spiritual conceit. I don't know the technical name for it, but I'm sure it exists. Is it "accident" or something like that? And it won't work because you're simply not like that. You're not the stuff from which stained-glass windows are made.'

'Kempe's windows in Wakefield Cathedral are rather good,' said John.

'I'm sorry,' said Elizabeth, 'but I've got to say what I think. I think you're being madly silly, utterly insane, criminally stupid.'

She paused and I said, 'But I've done it now. I've resigned from Trinity.'

'Yes, I know,' she said. 'But there are dozens of other things you could do which would keep you in circulation. One thing you must promise me – if when you go to Mirfield it doesn't work, you must be humble enough to admit it frankly and leave. I mean this with all my heart – you mustn't be wasted. People need terribly what you have to give them.'

'I would like a glass of port,' said John.

The dialogue shows how unfeeble 'Feeble' could be when she chose. It also shows how John usually wanted to avoid confrontations and dissipate tension. Williams went to Mirfield and stayed there, though with many revivifying sorties to London.

In Williams's last years at Trinity College, Prince Charles was an undergraduate there. Williams was the first person Charles met in January 1966 when visiting the college for the first time with his father; and the Prince's biographer, Jonathan Dimbleby, writes that Williams was 'to exert much influence over his undergraduate life' and that, after Charles came up in the

autumn of 1967, he was 'a frequent guest at the Dean's table'. John was sometimes there, too. At the end of the Lent term each year, the undergraduates
got up a revue, with many satirical references to the dons. In 1969 Charles,
who was an addict of *The Goon Show*, was in the cast. To the tune of 'Lily
the Pink', the actors sang:

> Let's get drunk, get drunk, get drunk
> For Harry the monk, the monk, the monk.

Charles's presence meant that the song was published the next morning in
the *Daily Telegraph* and other national newspapers. A letter John sent Mary
Wilson suggests that he may have had a hand in the squib's composition.

In May John and Elizabeth attended Williams's fiftieth birthday party at
the Savoy (Williams was by no means ascetic). On 1 July John and Williams
were both present at Charles's investiture as Prince of Wales, an event stage-
managed by Lord Snowdon at Caernarvon Castle. At Charles's request,
John wrote a ballad to commemorate the occasion. He began it by describing the evening on which Charles asked him to write the poem – an
evening spent with the Prince, Harry Williams, Elizabeth and two of
Charles's Trinity friends, William Hastings Bass (later Earl of Huntingdon)
and Edward Woods, younger son of the then Dean of Windsor.

> The moon was in the Cambridge sky
>   And bathed Great Court in silver light
> When Hastings-Bass and Woods and I
>   And quiet Elizabeth, tall and white,
> With that sure clarity of mind
> Which comes to those who've truly dined,
>   Reluctant rose to say good-night;
> And all of us were bathed the while
> In the large moon of Harry's smile . . .

In 1970, Simon Stuart took a house in Biarritz and invited out John,
Elizabeth, Harry Williams and Joe Bain, who had been a colleague of
Stuart's when he taught at Stowe. Queen Victoria had spent her winters in
the Belle Epoque town; the Ramblers were there in high summer. John
wrote to Stuart from Cloth Fair on 20 August 1970:

> That was the best holiday I could imagine. Sitting here in my city room pity-
> ing myself (9.30 a.m.) I think if I were at Biarritz now I would be just about
> waking up & shuffling over the floor to the hall & out on to the terrace &
> I would hear Harry's laugh & you would get up & fetch me a boiled egg &
> coffee & the others would have finished except for poor Elizabeth who,
> white & quiet & inarticulate, would not yet have appeared.

The witty, 'Wicked' Simon Stuart remained a favourite of John's. Sometimes, John stayed with him at his Sussex house, which had the Betjemanesque name Windyridge. Stuart wrote:

> Perhaps it was when my marriage was approaching [in 1973, at forty-three, Stuart married Deborah Jane Mounsey and they had three children] that he volunteered that he didn't think he could face the whole ordeal of husband and fatherhood all over again. I recognized a world of anguish there, but didn't take warning. Actually that ended our association – meeting my fiancée he embarked on making a fuss of her; but Feeble put paid to that, by cutting her then and subsequently. Harry glossed, 'She can't bear women,' but I think it carried some snobbery too.

John's last trip to the Continent with the Ramblers was in Lent 1972. Mervyn Stockwood had been loaned a house at Moraira in Spain. Hugh Montefiore and his wife Elisabeth joined Stockwood, John, Lady Elizabeth and Lord Rossmore (Montefiore supervised him in the New Testament in Cambridge), who was recovering from his broken engagement to a pop star. Rossmore was a keen photographer and his black-and-white photographs evoke the sunlit days in Moraira: the wrought-iron and marble table on the verandah, loaded with bottles of gin, martini and wine, with local wines in wicker-cased bottles under the table; Mervyn Stockwood pouring champagne (wearing a three-piece suit – he found it difficult to 'go casual'); Elizabeth Cavendish in pullover and slacks; John carrying a pottery wine flask back from the local shop; the company lolling on the verandah, drinking and laughing. 'I have memories of a very happy house party,' Bishop Montefiore wrote, 'and the countryside was looking idyllic with all the almond blossom out. I remember John Betjeman laughing uproariously when seated on a model steam railway when we took a journey; and also his delight in the delicious *gambas* served with an apéritif before meals. It was here that Betjeman wrote his moving poem "The Costa Blanca".' The poem, consisting of two sonnets, is about an English couple who have a house built in Spain. In the first sonnet the wife describes what tempts them to Spain ('Skies without a stain! / Eric and I at almond-blossom time / Came here and fell in love with it . . . Good-bye democracy and smoke and grime . . .'); in the second sonnet, the husband, five years on, pours out their regrets about the move, and their yearning for their 'Esher lawn'.

> That Dago caught the wife and me all right!
> Here on this tideless, tourist-littered sea
> We're stuck. You'd hate it too if you were me:
> There's no piped water on the bloody site.

Our savings gone, we climb the stony path
Back to the house with scorpions in the bath.

The two sonnets might be taken to represent the two sides of John's ambivalent feelings about 'abroad'.

His fascination for Esher lawns, however, lasted much longer. In *The Secret Glory* – the novel which profoundly influenced John in his teens – Arthur Machen indicated the rich material awaiting the writer who would choose the suburbs as his subject, 'who has the insight to see behind those Venetian blinds and white curtains, who has the word that can give him entrance through the polished door by the encaustic porch!'. What was needed, Machen considered, was a writer 'able to tell the London suburbs the truth about themselves in their own tongue'. In his later years, Machen moved into the suburbs, to Amersham, Buckinghamshire, where John visited him and heard stories of Oscar Wilde, whom Machen had known. Amersham was in that region of suburbs known, from its penetration by the Metropolitan Line of the London Underground railway, as 'Metroland' – a name made popular in the Twenties and Thirties by property developers promoting their villas in Neasden, Wembley, Chorleywood and other dormitory towns along the Line. (Evelyn Waugh borrowed the name for Lady Metroland in *Decline and Fall*, 1928.)

In one of his film criticisms of 1934, John deplored the lack of good films about London. 'The possibilities of London have never yet been explored,' he wrote. 'There are the corrugated lanes of Finsbury Park, the clatter round the Peckham High Road, the quiet squares of Clerkenwell and Islington, the rutty roads of some half-finished bit of Metroland, all waiting to be photographed and immortalized as René Clair has immortalized Paris.'

In 1972 John got the chance to practise what he and Machen had preached. In that year he made the television film *Metro-land*, directed by Edward Mirzoeff – by common consent the best of all John's television appearances, a classic of television art. Mirzoeff had seen John's potential in making the helicopter *Bird's-Eye View* films in the late Sixties, but before any filming could begin, the idea had to be sold to the BBC. Mirzoeff got John to write a letter to Robin Scott, the Controller of BBC2, who gave the project his blessing.

What parts of London should be filmed for the programme? To debate this question, Mirzoeff and the film editor Ted Roberts took John to lunch at one of his favourite restaurants, Wheeler's in Old Compton Street, Soho. It was Roberts who came up with the idea of making the Metropolitan

Line the 'spine' of the programme. He pointed out that St John's Wood, near the beginning of the Line, could be regarded as the historical beginning of suburbia. Mirzoeff was enthusiastic. As for John, Roberts was preaching to the converted: no fewer than three of the poems in John's collection of poems *A Few Late Chrysanthemums* (1954) were about the Metropolitan Line.

The film begins with a careering, speeded-up ride along the Metropolitan Line, past hedgerows, under bridges and through stations, to the music of 'Tiger Rag'. In the carriage, as fields flash past, John is reading a 1910 copy of the *News of the World*. Then he looks out of the carriage window and sees, in black and white, the view from the Metropolitan Line in 1910, rushing past. John was a friend of Michael Robbins, then managing director of the London Underground. At an early stage of the research for *Metro-land*, John wrote to him to tell him what was planned and to ask for his approval and co-operation. Robbins wrote back that he thought it 'a lovely idea' and that he would be delighted to help. 'Extraordinarily enough,' he added, 'by some strange coincidence we discovered some film in the cupboard this week that might possibly have some relevance.' This was the film made from the Metropolitan Line in 1910. Mirzoeff thought it a 'stroke of genius' on Ted Roberts's part 'to use the moment where John gazes out of the window in the train and to see outside the window the old black-and-white footage'.

When the film reaches Wembley, John indulges in an autobiographical flashback. In 1924, at eighteen, he had visited the British Empire Exhibition with his father. He had preferred the Imperial pavilions of India, Sierra Leone and Fiji 'With their sun-tanned sentinels of Empire outside', to the Palaces of Industry and Engineering 'Which were too much like my father's factory'. He had had to wait in the Palace of Arts 'While my father saw the living models in Pears' Palace of Beauty'. (One might have thought that, at eighteen, John was old enough to accompany his father into the Palace of Beauty – but he seems to want to convey the idea that he was still a large-eyed child at the Wembley Exhibition; perhaps, too, he wants to present his father as coarse, a dirty old man, and himself as a refined young one.) John's commentary continues:

> Oh bygone Wembley, where's the pleasure now?
> The temples stare, the Empire passes by . . .

> But still people kept on coming to Wembley.
> The show-houses of the newly built estates.
> A younger, brighter, homelier Metro-land:

'Rusholme', 'Rustles', 'Rustlings', 'Rusty Tiles',
'Rose Hatch', 'Rose Hill', 'Rose Lea', 'Rose Mount', 'Rose Roof',
Each one is slightly different from the next,
A bastion of individual taste . . .

This suburban idyll is followed by one of the best lines in the film, 'Roses are blooming in Metro-land' (after the haunting First World War song 'Roses are blooming in Picardy'). Frank Delaney noted in his *Betjeman Country* (1982) that the rose house-names had gone. 'On Oakington Avenue [Wembley] no more "Rusholme", "Rustles" or "Rustlings" – only numbers, the new egalitarian snobbery . . .' But in fact, Mirzoeff reveals, 'Those houses never had those names – we made them up from a book of house names John brought into the cutting-room.'

On to Harrow Weald and Grims Dyke, the half-timbered mansion which Norman Shaw built for W. S. Gilbert, the lyricist of the Savoy Operas. John regarded it as 'a prototype of all suburban homes in southern England'. The BBC research team had learned that a meeting of the Byron Luncheon Club was to be held there and addressed by the historian Elizabeth Cooper. Eddie Mirzoeff 'did a recce' at an earlier meeting and realized he would be able to make striking picturesque capital out of the Tory ladies' hats.

> Elizabeth Cooper was the local historian [he said]. She was blonde and rather chubby and pretty and John strongly took to her; she very much took to him, too. The idea was originally to use her speech to give us facts about whatever was being shown; but it became clear that the fun was not so much in that as in the faces and the hats. I knew they were going to look like that because of my preliminary recce.
>
> We could not film John at the lecture – he would have been talking while Elizabeth Cooper was talking; and he'd have been looking down at the ladies and they'd have been craning upwards to look at him. So we filmed him separately, arriving at the top of the stairs and looking as if he saw them, when in fact they weren't there. That was one of the more ludicrous events – my standing there and saying, 'Pretend I'm a woman wearing a strange hat, John. Try and smile! Go on, think of a curious sort of hat on my head.' Poor man.

The stratagem worked. There is an almost Hitchcockian suspense as John climbs the oak staircase, beckoning us on. 'If I go up there I'll see – goodness knows what. Let's go and look.' Then he appears to burst into the hall of hatted ladies and his face breaks into a smile of bemused delight.

The next part of the film was meant to be a tour of the architectural glories of Moor Park Golf Club, a great house of the early eighteenth century. To Baroque music, John would talk amusingly about the Venetian *trompe l'oeil* allegories of gods and cupids; he might also try his hand at a stroke or two on the course. That was what eventually happened; but not before a storm in a tea caddy had been played out.

The plan was [Eddie Mirzoeff recalled], we would film inside the clubhouse first of all – do all the architectural stuff, get that out of the way. It was a massive lighting job. John was due to come to Moor Park station. He liked to come to the locations by Underground, not by car; he thought it was in the spirit of the film to come on the Metropolitan Line – sort of 'method acting'. So we arranged to meet him at the station. The team were at the golf club much earlier to sort out the lighting and other problems.

He was late. We were sitting there waiting. There was no sign of him. We didn't know what had happened. Christine Whittaker, one of our young researchers, had been sent to collect him. Time went by and eventually we saw a Mini appear with John in it. It drew up and we all lined up outside Moor Park Golf Club waiting to greet him good morning. He came out of the door looking like a thundercloud, saying, 'I know I'm only the *artiste* and therefore the least important person in this team . . .'

I thought, 'Oh God, something's gone wrong'; turned round and noticed that everybody had disappeared, edging away and leaving me to face this . . . this major difficulty. What had happened, Christine quickly explained, was that Moor Park station – we hadn't realized – had two exits. She was at the main exit, he went to the other exit. He stood there and waited and waited and waited and thought we'd forgotten all about him; and finally, when Christine went exploring and found him, he was in this terrible temper. What could we do? Clearly he was in no state to start talking about architecture. I think somebody went and got some gin and tonic. I had to make a quick decision, and I decided we'd do the easy bit first. I knew that John played golf quite well. He played it down in Cornwall and enjoyed it. So I said 'Let's do the golf bit first – change everything around.'

If you look quite carefully at the piece he does just before he hits the golf ball – he says the nearness of golf to London is the attraction of Moor Park Golf Club – he's very, very serious. It's an absolutely dead straight face, there isn't the flicker of a smile. He's still fuming at the fact that he hasn't been picked up on time. There's this turbulence. And we say, well, can we do the drive off? (It was going to be quite a big sequence, his playing golf.) And he does this grandiose swing and completely misses, this first take. And you had this marvellous moment when he suddenly broke up laughing and the cameraman went on filming, and all the tension disappeared, just like that. It was the most magic moment in the film, I think.

As Chorleywood comes into view ('Where in '89 the railway came') John says: 'This is, I think, essential Metro-land.' He knew what he wanted to show there: The Orchard, the family home which C. F. A. Voysey had built for himself and his wife in 1900. 'I think it was the parent of thousands of simple English houses,' John says, perhaps forgetting that he has already brought a similar paternity suit against Norman Shaw's Grims Dyke. He makes full play of the fact that he, speaking in 1972, had known the architect and his wife who had lived in that house built in Victoria's reign. In his affectionate tour of the house, John shows his genius for television commentary. It is neither literary prose nor verse, but a series of effortless impromptus which yet manage not to be inconsequential:

> Voysey liked to design every detail in his house. For instance, that knocker, Voysey. A typical curious-shaped handle, Voysey. And this handle or iron hinge with what seems to be his signature tune, the heart. It's there at the end of the hinge, it's here round the letterbox, it's also round the keyhole and it seems to be on the key. That's a Voysey key, and in the house he did everything down to the knives and forks.

There was genuine improvisation in this intimate patter; John had veered right away from the scenario that had been agreed with Mirzoeff.

Also in Chorleywood, and a contrast to the arty-crafty restraint of The Orchard, was the Art Deco glare and blare of the Wurlitzer organ removed from the Empire Cinema, Leicester Square and erected in the suburban house of Len Rawle. This was the scene of one of the film's worst crises.

> We had planned to film at Len Rawle's house the whole day [Mirzoeff said]. It was a difficult thing to film. Mr Rawle has this extraordinary Wurlitzer which he plays in the living room and which you have to crawl behind to get inside. John arrived at ten o'clock, again by the Metropolitan Line at Chorleywood; and he announced to a totally astonished film unit that he was going to leave by 10.45 – the first mention of this. Some time later we found that he had double-booked himself with another film crew for another film the same morning. He was making a pair of films with Jonathan Stedall – *London on Sunday* and *London in the Country*, two half-hour films that Ted Roberts actually cut as well. With his usual inability to say no to anybody or anything, John had arranged to be at Cloth Fair with Jonathan Stedall and a film crew at half-past eleven, and he'd sort of thought that would be all right – in spite of the fact that we had made it absolutely clear that this would be a full day. He literally walked in at ten saying 'Well, I've got exactly three-quarters of an hour. I must be away at 10.45.' The extremely equable and placid cameraman, John McGlashan – 'The Bishop'

as John called him, he really was a bishop in some obscure church – threw a fit at that point. He said to me, as if it were my fault, 'I just cannot be expected to work in this way. How do you think I can do this in three-quarters of an hour? There's no possibility whatsoever of being able to film the sequence with Sir John not here.' I said to John, 'You can't do this. It's absolutely not on.' And he got into a tizz, as he quite often did. You could see he was getting upset – because he was guilt-ridden, as usual. And tempers got extremely frayed.

In the end what Mirzoeff managed to do was to film John walking in from outside and standing by in one shot while Len Rawle played the organ. 'A wide shot and a close-up: that was it. 10.45 came and off he went.' For the rest of the day Len Rawle played the organ and smiled happily at the open space where John should have been. By sleight-of-hand editing it was made to seem as if John were there, enjoying and responding to the playing.

In the film's last scene, John is leaning on a fence at Verney Junction. The ghost station was named after the Buckinghamshire family whose nearby seat, Claydon House, had been a country refuge for Florence Nightingale. John turns to camera: 'The houses of Metro-land never got as far as Verney Junction. Grass triumphs. And I must say I'm rather glad.'

Most of John's work on the film was done, not on location, but in the cutting-room. To some extent he enjoyed the process and the craftsmanship of editing. He liked coming in to Document Films, Ted Roberts's editing studio in Soho.

> A mythology grew around it [Eddie Mirzoeff said], as it grew around a lot of the things John was interested in. On his way up Wardour Street he would always pass a music publisher – gone now – called Peters Editions (with the two words on the shop sign very close together); and he'd say, 'Look, there's Peter Sedition, the well-known anarchist.' And there was a man called Ben Henry OBE, whose name he got obsessed by. Henry lived on the floor below Document. Nobody ever met him, but John would see the sign on the door and ask, 'And how is Ben Henry OBE and his kiddiz and his little wife?' The fantasies grew. It was a nice friendly small film-editing place, and he felt at home there. He wrote all his films – everything, not only mine but everybody else's too – in the cutting-room.

John's commentary was always written to the cut footage in the end. He would sit at a Steenbeck editing machine, which he had learned how to work, and would go backwards and forwards on it with reams of paper. Mirzoeff recalled: 'He'd write in his tiny spidery hand, which he couldn't read and nobody else could read, many many pages of iambic verse and of prose – just throwing papers on the floor one after another.'

If John was up against a 'writer's block', as often happened, he would go off to another room at Document. His favourite, because it was the only one where he could be certain of being on his own, was a tea cupboard, which he called 'the composition cell'. He would sit there trying to get the verse right. Then he would come back and say, 'What about this?' Ted Roberts, who had a talent for pastiche, would be sitting trying to write the same kind of verse. He would hand it to John and say, 'What about this?' And John would usually say, 'That's much better than mine, let's throw away mine.' Then Mirzoeff would tactfully chip in, 'No, John, but perhaps it's edging you towards what you want to say.'

> There was an extraordinary rapport between John Betjeman and Ted Roberts [Mirzoeff said]. John would write a line of verse and Ted would cap it with another rhyming line, which was usually pretty obscene. And they would shriek with laughter . . . It was absolutely magical. Those were great days. At other times, I must say, it wasn't like that at all. John's idea was that anything was better than writing – *anything*. Always, coming in to look at the assembled film, he would say, 'Oh, it doesn't need words at all; let's go and have a drink.' And we'd say, 'No, it really does need words, John.' 'Oh *dear*.'

It usually took John three to four weeks to write the commentary for a fifty-minute film. He came in most days, sometimes staying the whole day, sometimes going after an hour – 'It's no good, I'm not in the mood.' He arrived mid-morning or after lunch.

> Quite often he brought friends [Mirzoeff recalled] – people he was fond of or just people he was seeing that day. 'Let's go to the cutting-room and see the film' – which meant that no work was done. My face would fall when I saw him walk in with people. There were exceptions, such as his friend Margie Geddes.* He was particularly close to her and trusted her judgement. He was always convinced that the film was no good, frightful, a disaster. We would show sequences to Margie Geddes and she would say, 'But this is wonderful, John,' and he would be temporarily lifted by that. So we were quite pleased to see her. She helped to shore up this lack of confidence that John always had. It wasn't just about working; I was struck in the early days by the genuine sense he had, that this was a temporary phenomenon, that he was in vogue and therefore able to scratch a living, but that it wouldn't last and that he would unquestionably end in the workhouse. He used to say that regularly as a joke – but it was one of those things that you knew *wasn't* a joke. He had a terror that suddenly one day it would all go away. Coupled

---

* Sister of the Addis brothers of Heddon Court school. See Chapter 8, 'With the Bright Young People'.

with the fear of death, which was very manifest, was the fear of poverty. He lived by his wits, he felt; one day, quite soon, people were going to see through it. And as a result he was always susceptible to adverse criticism. He hated the faintest whiff of anybody disliking anything. He was terrified by what the critics would say about his television programmes. Hours were spent in the cutting-room writing the scathing reviews that he was sure were going to be written about *Metro-land*. Instead of writing the commentary, he was writing these stinking reviews. They were put in sealed envelopes to be opened after the actual reviews had been published. The reviewer he feared most was the son of one of his friends – Sean Day-Lewis, son of Cecil Day Lewis, John's predecessor as Poet Laureate. Sean would invariably pull apart a Betjeman programme, saying it was bitty, had no structure, had nothing going for it. John was paranoid about what Sean was going to say. And Sean's reviews were quite vitriolic, actually. John had this constant sense of uncertainty. The impression of the man on television and the man himself were two different things. He was by no means the person that the world thought it saw.

Often John tried to dispel his depression with drink, and Mirzoeff had to ban alcohol in the cutting-room. In the early sessions John would arrive holding a bottle of burgundy and a bottle of whisky in his string bag. He was usually holding his teddy bear Archie, too, and Archie's companion Jumbo came occasionally. One day John arrived and said, 'Jumbo is very depressed indeed,' meaning that he himself was depressed. 'How can we cheer him up?' Ted said. 'Let's give him a ride.' He put Jumbo on the flat plate rewind machine that went round and round – and Jumbo went round as if on a merry-go-round. After a while John said, 'Jumbo *is* enjoying himself,' and Mirzoeff knew that everything was going to be all right. 'It was ludicrous, really; but it was rather touching.'

When the commentary had been finally worked out, and Gina Hobson had managed to type John's near-illegible notes, a day was set for recording the commentary right through. Eddie Mirzoeff arrived at Document at about nine o'clock in the morning. Ted Roberts was already there, with a very serious expression on his face. 'I think you'd better have a word with John immediately,' he said.

Mirzoeff thought: 'Oh, God, what's happened now?' He walked over and said, 'Hello, John, how are you?'

He said: 'A-a-a-a-a-ll r-i-i-i-i-ght.'

Mirzoeff thought: 'Why is he sounding so slow?'

He sounded terribly slow and slurred and sleepy. We clearly had a major problem. We thought that something awful had happened, and we asked him could he remember the name of his doctor. Eventually we found the name of his doctor [John Allison] in his address book and we rang him and said, 'Sir John sounds terribly funny; can you possibly have a word with him?' He spoke on the phone to his doctor. Finally, we spoke again, we got handed the telephone, and we said to the doctor, 'What's the matter?' And he said, 'He's perfectly all right; no problem at all. The only thing is that he was clearly feeling very nervous about recording the commentary, had some difficulty in sleeping, and took a sleeping pill at about a quarter to six this morning. So actually he's fast asleep.' Great! What do we do? The doctor said, 'Well, there's only one thing to do, and that's to put him to bed immediately.'

I said, 'We're in a Soho commentary-recording theatre.'

He said: 'I don't care where you are, put him to bed *now*.' He said, 'He'll be all right in a few hours.'

We turned to the dubbing mixer and said, 'What are we going do? Is there a bed?' and the man said, 'Yes. Curiously enough we often work quite late here and there is a camp bed.' We suggested to John that he might like to lie down on this bed, and he thought, yes, that was quite a good idea; and somehow or other a blanket was produced, and we tucked him into this bed, said Good-night, switched the light off and tiptoed out. I stood outside in absolute despair. I asked the people who ran the place whether they had a rate for sleeping as opposed to a rate for commentary recording, because we didn't want to pay the full rate. Anyway, we went away, came back about lunch-time – and he'd gone.

He'd left a message: 'JUST GONE FOR A DOZEN OYSTERS AND HALF A BOTTLE OF BUBBLY. BE BACK BY TWO.' He'd gone to Wheeler's. He came back full of beans, perfectly all right. We started recording that afternoon – and it was brilliant.

On 23 February 1973 a private showing of the film was held for John and his friends at Colour Film Services, off Portman Square, London. Among those present were Lady Diana Cooper, her son Lord Norwich, Barry Humphries and John's old aunt Queenie Avril. 'We all went and had champagne in the Portman Hotel opposite,' Mirzoeff said, 'not a piece of architecture that John approved of, but the champagne was all right and Barry Humphries paid for it.'

When the film was screened on 26 February 1973, it was recognized not only as a high point in television history, but as a benediction on suburbia. John and Mirzoeff liked best an *Evening Standard* review by Simon Jenkins which took flight in Betjemanesque verse:

> Panorama's breath is bated,
> World in Action holds its hand.

For at 10.10 on the TV
Betjeman's gone to Metro-land . . .
For an hour he held enraptured
Pinner, Moor Park, Chorley Wood.
'Well I'm blowed,' they said, 'He likes us.
'Knew one day that someone should.'

31

'A Heavy Crown'

L ORD MOTTISTONE, JOHN'S co-landlord at Cloth Fair, died in 1963. He had become Surveyor to the Fabric of St Paul's Cathedral, a post in which Paul Paget – his partner in business and in life – immediately succeeded him. For a time, Paget was desolated; but in 1971, to everyone's amazement, he married. Winifred Hector, John's friend at Bart's Hospital, remembered: 'When we heard the news at Bart's, we said: "*MARRIED?!*"' The architect's bride was the author Verily Anderson, widow of Captain Donald Anderson, a man much older than herself who had served in the Indian Army under Penelope's father and had been chief press officer for the 1951 Festival of Britain. By an almost Dickensian coincidence, John already knew Verily. Her maiden name was Bruce and she was of that Bruce family which had looked after John's Heddon Court pupil Kenric Rice when Rice's parents went to China and 'advertised' him in *The Times*. Kenric had been 'like a brother' to her; and, through him, John had met the Bruces in the late 1920s, including Verily and her father, the Rev. Rosslyn Bruce, whose life she wrote as *The Last of the Eccentrics* (1972).

Something that recommended Verily to John was that she was a close friend of his friend, the entertainer Joyce Grenfell. He and Grenfell had been in touch since the 1940s, when he suggested for her monologues 'a lady who speaks in a rosy soft voice and loves all "lovely" things and no sudden noises or vulgarity. She will probably wear homespun and a necklace of painted cotton reels.' Verily remembered Grenfell's saying, 'I had to do a television programme with John Betjeman the other day; I always think he's rather unsavoury – well, really, *savoury*, more.' (She disapproved of his drinking and smoking.) But gradually the two had become friends, their sense of humour overcoming all differences.

On a hot summer's day in 1971 Verily and Paul went to see John in Cloth Fair, to ask him to be their best man. 'I had on a thin white summer dress,' Verily recalls. 'Paul and I thought it was very funny that we were getting married at a total age of 127. We didn't take it very seriously, and naturally we thought we'd get some awful crack from John. But he came towards me, his arms spread in an embrace, and said, "*All in white!*" ' Verily and Paul were married in August, in St Bartholomew the Great, with John as best man and Joyce Grenfell as 'a rather mature bridesmaid'. The bride wore a white spotted dress from Grenfell's wardrobe. Grenfell was taller and thinner than Verily but, as she said, 'Your width takes up the length.'

After the wedding, Paul and Verily moved into the splendour of Templewood, the shooting box the Partners had designed for Paul's uncle Samuel Hoare. On the façade were sphinxes from the demolished Nuthall temple and Ionic columns from the old Bank of England. John and Elizabeth were already familiar with the house, as they had stayed there with Paget in 1969.

In 1972, Verily's son Eddie, having been expelled from school, was working as Lord Leicester's gamekeeper on the estate at Holkham Hall. There he fell seriously ill with a quinsy – acute inflammation of the tonsils. He was brought to Templewood to recover.

> I was lying in Paul's dressing-room in some distress [he recalls] – agonizing pain. And I was just beginning to get better when John Betjeman came to stay. He came in to see me and said, 'How does it feel to have quinsies?' He was rather amused by the word, it was like something from Edward Lear to him, I think. I said: 'It's like having hat pins driven into your ears.' And then perhaps six months later I went into St Bart's to have my tonsils out. I was rather old for the operation, I was about twenty. The reason it had been delayed was that Verily thought that I had a wonderful career as a treble for ever, so she didn't want my tonsils interfered with. Anyway, I now had them ripped out and John Betjeman came to see me. All of the nurses were a-twitter that the Poet Laureate was coming to see me. And when he did arrive, he made up a poem about me, which began –
>
> > Eddie lies upon Bart's bed,
> > In to have his hat-pins out;
> > Now that horrid quinsy's dead,
> > Ed can sing and dance and shout.

When Paul and Verily were in London, John often had breakfast with them. He would look down from his window at No. 43 Cloth Fair and Verily would raise her frying-pan in the window of No. 45 to signal he was to come across. Sometimes he dined with the couple, too. In return, Verily benefited from John's architectural knowledge. 'He used to take us on wonderful shuffles round the City,' she recalled. 'And one day I asked him: "Where did you learn all these amazing ins and outs?" He said:

"There's not one word I have told you that I did not learn from either John or Paul" – because they'd been there forty years.' The answer was calculated to please, and did; but it was not strictly true. John had known and loved the City for forty years before he met the Partners. By 1973, however, its charms for him were palling. 'The hellish noise of articulated lorries coming in from Europe in the small hours' was one gripe. John also hated the New Brutalist buildings going up in the City, 'eggbox' architecture. In his poem 'Monody on the Death of Aldersgate Street Station', he wrote:

> Snow falls in the buffet of Aldersgate station,
>   Toiling and doomed from Moorgate Street puffs the train,
> For us of the steam and the gas-light, the lost generation,
>   The new white cliffs of the City are built in vain.

To add to John's misery, Paul Paget sold his five Cloth Fair houses for £90,000 to the Landmark Trust, a charity whose chairman, Sir John Smith, had married a sister of Verily's second cousin, the Duke of Grafton. The Trust raised rents so that a woman John was fond of had to leave and the cloth shop closed down. The houses were turned into holiday homes with a high rental. By 1973 Parkinson's Disease was visibly undermining John's health. He often lost his balance. Penelope, who saw him at Christmas 1972, was concerned enough to write to Elizabeth Cavendish, suggesting that the two of them might take turns in looking after him. She was prepared to stay at Cloth Fair when necessary. She addressed directly the issue of John's relationship with Elizabeth.

Naturally I was jealous when he first got fond of you, many years ago now. But over the years I have realized that from HIS point of view at any rate it has been a wonderful thing for him, as you are literary and I am not really, and you have provided the sort of companionship he needs and never really gets from me. I simply cannot get him to slow down now, can you? I mean I suggested, and Jock Murray thought it an excellent idea, that when he reached retiring age he should put a notice in the papers saying he could no longer afford a secretary and could therefore answer no more letters except from personal friends. Correspondence is KILLING him. And he should give up all, or nearly all, committee work so that he can have more time to relax and read. But WHO CAN MAKE HIM?? He has recently gone on to the board of governors of the King Edward's School in Oxford. WHY? Why give himself one more completely unnecessary chore at his age? Is there NO-ONE who can persuade him to cut down to what really interests him and to hell with the rest?

The tribute to Elizabeth was handsome, and deserved; but clearly, too, there was an angry implied reproach: in effect, 'If you are meant to be looking after my husband, why is he being allowed to ruin his health by overwork?' Elizabeth diplomatically replied that she was touched by such a generous letter, and suggested Penelope get in touch with his doctor, John Allison, about his health. Allison was fairly reassuring; but Penelope was still worried about making a proposed trip to India, in case John's condition (at that stage considered 'a prematurely early failing of his leg muscles') should worsen. Elizabeth urged her to go and said she could cope.

In April 1973 John moved to No. 29 Radnor Walk, Chelsea, a few doors from Elizabeth's house in the same road.* To Penelope who, from whatever motive, had tried to dissuade him from moving, he wrote on 24 March 1973: 'I am getting very windy about the move to 29 Radnor Walk . . . as all you say about Cloth Fair is true. The views from the house are beautiful, the rooms are beautiful and so are the books . . .' But the die was cast and on 27 April he sent her his first letter from Radnor Walk.

The decline in John's health made it much harder for him to do well in the office to which he had only recently been appointed – of Poet Laureate. Newspaper columnists had tipped him as a future laureate ever since the success of *Collected Poems* in 1958. In June 1960 his chances of gaining the laurel when the aged John Masefield should die were enhanced by his winning the Queen's Gold Medal for Poetry. It was Masefield who had suggested to King George V, in 1933, that the medal be instituted; and it was Masefield who recommended that John should receive it. The medal came as the culmination of a series of honours for John: the Duff Cooper Memorial Prize in 1958; the William Foyle Poetry Prize in 1959; and the CBE in the New Year's Honours list in 1960. Reporting the award of the Queen's Gold Medal, the Londoner's Diary of the *Evening Standard* suggested that 'it points [towards] what becomes a more and more accepted prediction: that Mr Betjeman will himself become the next Poet Laureate'. In 1962 John added further to his qualifications for a court place when he presented a masque to the Queen on the opening of the Festival of the City of London. Those who took part in the 'Entertainment' included Sir John Gielgud and the pop singer Tommy Steele.

John Masefield died on 12 May 1967. By Christmas that year the new Laureate had still not been appointed. On Christmas Eve the *Sunday Express* published an interview with John by Graham Lord.

* See Chapter 32, 'Radnor Walk'.

If Poets Laureate were chosen simply for their popularity [Lord wrote] there is little doubt that John Betjeman would get the job as John Masefield's successor.

Not only do his verses sell better than any other living British poet. His appearances on television have also given him a fireside fan club, a vast suburbia of Betjemaniacs, all enamoured of his mild eccentricity, his quietly humorous niceness.

Before the interview, John had said he would not talk about the poet laureateship – 'That wouldn't be right. I hate any form of competition and treating the candidates like a lot of racehorses.'

But somehow we got round to it [Lord wrote]. He is a kindly man. With a smile, he explained to his secretary: 'This chap has a sort of innocence. You think you've got to help him in his work or he'll get the sack.'

So, for the sake of my job, we talked about the Poet Laureateship.

When Masefield died, Betjeman's wife Penelope told me that even if he were offered the job he'd turn it down. Was that still true?

'I wouldn't refuse it,' he said. 'That would be very arrogant. But I wouldn't like it. I'd get so many more of these letters and manuscripts.

'But anyway, I don't think I would be chosen. If it's to be an honour then why choose only one poet? And if it's to be political verse, which was superbly done by Dryden, or State verse – superbly done by Tennyson – then it should be the sort of person who enjoys writing occasional verse. A sort of A. P. Herbert.

'And if it's to be an honour for poetry then it's invidious that there should be only one Poet Laureate.'

Should it be a post held in rotation?

'I think that's quite a good idea. But it all smacks of Arts Council and I don't like it very much.'

Graham Lord's article was headed 'The man who'd rather not be Poet Laureate'. Some of John's friends were beginning to suspect that he didn't want to be Poet Laureate in much the same way as the tar baby didn't want to be thrown into the tar. But this time it was not to be. On 2 January 1968 it was announced that C. Day Lewis had been appointed.

It was from John, however, not from Day Lewis, that Prince Charles requested a poem on his investiture as Prince of Wales at Caernarvon Castle in 1969. As we have seen, the Prince and the poet met at a dinner-party given by Harry Williams. Prince Charles recalled: 'I thought it was the greatest possible fun, and John Betjeman was extremely enjoyable. We had one of those marvellous evenings afterwards: he told all sorts of stories and I think he read some poems. It impressed me enormously, and I remember thinking what fun he was, how amusing – he made me laugh a great deal.'

As Prince Charles left the party, he said to John, 'I want a poem out of you on my Investiture in Wales.' He slightly raised his hand. 'And that', he added, 'is a command.' Remembering from his Oxford days how King Richard II had urged John Gower to write him a poem, and how Gower had proudly described the bestowing of the commission in his *Confessio Amantis* (completed 1390), John in 'A Ballad of the Investiture 1969' described how the charge had been laid on him. He cast the poem in the form of a 'rhyming letter', detailing the journey from Euston to Wales, then the rapt moments of the ceremony in which the Queen crowned her son. The poem ended:

> You knelt a boy, you rose a man.
> And thus your lonelier life began.

In the same year as the Caernarvon ceremony, John was knighted. He received over a thousand letters of congratulation, from both friends and strangers. Angus Wilson wrote:

> That your *Herald* review set my books on the right road would alone suffice – but seriously, it is the greatest pleasure to me as to thousands and thousands of others who have attended your adolescent dances, your beach cricket, and wept with you at the Café Royal and the Cadogan Hotel. Long years of rhododendrons and pony clubs to you.

On 22 May 1972 Cecil Day Lewis died at Lemmons, Hadley Wood, Hertfordshire, the home of Kingsley Amis. He had been staying there with his wife, the actress Jill Balcon, while she made a television play at Elstree Studios. (The last poem Lewis wrote was 'To All – Lemmons'.) John attended the memorial service: he was photographed with the grieving Jill Balcon on his arm. Reporting the death on the front page of *The Times*, Philip Howard, later literary editor of the newspaper, wrote: 'The Laureateship has always been a heavy crown. It carries, besides the burden of writing ceremonial verse to order, a fee of £70 a year, with £27 "in lieu of a butt of sack".' Two days later, Geoffrey Handley-Taylor, author of books on the laureates Masefield and Day Lewis, wrote in to correct Howard: it was an old journalistic misconception that the Laureate was expected to write ceremonial verse. Even in Victoria's reign, he pointed out, Prince Albert had confirmed that the Poet Laureate was not required to write official odes on great occasions. The principal duty of the Laureate now was to recommend to the sovereign each year the name of the poet who should receive the Queen's Gold Medal for poetry – as Masefield had recommended John in 1960.

On 24 May *The Times* published an article headed 'W. H. Auden is favourite to become the new Poet Laureate'. But Auden had become an American citizen in 1946, so he would have to become a British citizen again to qualify. Auden himself soon scotched any such plan. Other candidates being mentioned were John Betjeman, Roy Fuller (then Professor of Poetry at Oxford), Stephen Spender, Philip Larkin, Ted Hughes and William Plomer. Spender effectively ruled himself out with the words: 'If I had to write about a public event, I would want to write about the bombing of Haiphong, which I am sure would not be very suitable.' Larkin was thought to have dished his chances by publishing a poem that began, 'They fuck you up, your mum and dad,' a sentiment unlikely to be endorsed by the Queen.

At the beginning of October the Prime Minister Edward Heath wrote to tell John that he was recommending to the Queen that she should consider appointing him poet laureate. On 9 October, when John was on holiday in Trebetherick, his secretary in London was telephoned from No. 10 Downing Street with the news that the appointment was confirmed: 'Summoned by Telephone Bell' as the *Guardian* later put it. 'I was surprised and humbled when I heard that I was to be appointed,' John told John Winder of *The Times*. 'Then I was very pleased. I love poetry and hope that my brother poets, many of them much better poets than I, will not be jealous.' He said he was pleased to be in the succession of Wordsworth, Tennyson and Bridges, 'but not quite so pleased to be the successor of Alfred Austin. I am sure he wrote some good poetry. I have been reading his work looking for it.' Philip Larkin told Winder he thought it 'an enormously appropriate appointment', and added: 'In the eyes of a great many people, from the royals down to the humblest television watchers, he has become identified with so much of the nation's cultural heritage.'

The Times had also sent Tim Devlin to interview John in Cornwall. 'I don't think I am very good,' he told him, 'and if I thought I was any good I wouldn't be any good.' He added that he was interested in former laureates. 'Henry James Pye, in the late eighteenth century, who was lampooned in the Four-and-Twenty Blackbirds nursery rhyme, was a very good poet. He wrote a very good poem called "Faringdon Hill" but he was laughed at.' Asked if becoming Laureate might sound the death knell of his talent, John said, 'I should think it would have . . . had I not been in Australia for three months. That has restored my confidence, because the Australians took me for what I was without dipping into my past.'

Devlin commented: 'If there has been any failure, it is his portrayers who have failed him. We have always been blinded by his eccentricity and have portrayed him as a lovable uncle from a Trollope novel preserving the past, but not so much as the serious poet he has always striven to be.'

David Holloway, the *Telegraph*'s literary editor, was less welcoming. There could be no doubt, he wrote, that the Queen had made the most popular choice. 'But it must be said that if the office of Poet Laureate should be given to the best poet in the land, then Sir John Betjeman would not be the first choice.' Holloway thought that if a vote had been taken among published poets, the laurel would have gone to Roy Fuller, 'a better poet than Sir John, though less of a public figure'. However, Holloway fairly noted that John was one of the few poets of the day who had written 'royal' poems, citing 'Death of King George V' (1936). And he conceded that John was also appropriate in that, 'in a secular age [he] is a genuinely religious poet . . .'.

Interviewed by Dennis Barker of the *Guardian*, John said he would write only when moved and otherwise 'remain a silent thrush'. He added: 'Isn't that a beautiful remark? I just made it up.' Perhaps he was remembering Horatio Bottomley's gibe about Robert Bridges – 'the dumb Laureate'. John spoke truer than he knew. It was over a year before he wrote any 'official' poem; and whatever Prince Albert might have said in Victoria's reign, journalists persisted in suggesting that it was the Laureate's duty to write poems on 'royal' occasions.

The first big test of John's skills as laureate was Princess Anne's wedding to Captain Mark Phillips on 14 November 1973. By the end of October he was already panicking. At a wake after W. H. Auden's memorial service in Oxford, he told Philip Larkin that he wanted 'to pack in the Laureateship'. Candida records that he became so worried about it that in the end his doctor decided to take action. 'He rang up [Sir] Rennie Maudslay, an old patient of his, who was Keeper of the Privy Purse, and asked him to ask the Queen to speak to JB. She confirmed to him that it was indeed not a *duty* to write something every time there was a Royal occasion. But somehow the *public* expected it of him . . .'

On 12 November the headline above Philip Howard's article in *The Times* was 'Awesome machinery of a royal wedding is moving inexorably into top gear'. The couple had met as Olympic riders – their courtship might have been the perfect subject for a Betjeman poem if John had been able to allow himself even the mildest levity or satire in his Laureate poems. Instead, he 'recycled' the pavement/enslavement rhyme which he had first used in serenading Mary Shand in Bath. He wrote:

> Hundreds of birds in the air
> And millions of leaves on the pavement,
> And Westminster bells ringing on
> To palace and people outside –
> And all for the words 'I will'
> To love's most willing enslavement.
> All of our people rejoice
> With venturous bridegroom and bride.
>
> Trumpets blare at the entrance,
> Multitudes crane and sway.
> Glow, white lily in London,
> You are high in our hearts today!

John admitted to Tim Devlin in *The Times* that this was 'one of the most laborious things he had ever written' and 'not the best poem he had ever penned'. Being Poet Laureate had not affected his talent, he told Devlin. 'But what would have been a death knell to my talent would have been writing about Princess Anne if I had had to write anything horsey.'

Michael Leapman, the *Times* diarist, began what became a long campaign of denigration of John's laureate work, with an item about the wedding poem.

> *The Incorporated Linguist* has asked its readers to translate this gem into a language of their choice. No prizes. To show the way it is done, they persuaded one T. Lindkvist to translate it into Swedish and then, ignoring the original, to translate the Swedish back into English. Some may think the result just as good as the original:
>
> > Bedded with leaves is the ground,
> > And bird-flights wheel high among buildings.
> > Then shall the bell-metal peal . . .

In December 1974, Cyril Connolly died and John contributed an article about him to the *Sunday Times*. A remark in the piece caused one of John's old dragons, Geoffrey Grigson – the dreaded 'Griggers' – to rear up with a letter of furious expostulation in the next week's *Sunday Times*.

> I have no wish to quarrel over the passing of Cyril Connolly. *Requiescat in pace*. But a statement in John Betjeman's tribute to him seems to me so disgraceful as to demand a protest.
>
> He explained that Connolly was cut off from the London literary life of the Thirties because temperamentally he was 'neither Left Wing nor homosexual'. No such double passport to that 'life' was ever required. As far as Connolly was concerned, some writers who are now taken to denigrate the

Thirties were repelled by what they took to be Connolly's mixture of social and aesthetic attitudes. In matters of value they saw him as a late and provincial acolyte of much that they rejected.

However, the disgracefulness of Betjeman's remark resides in that collocation of Left Wing and homosexual, that repetition of a smear. It ill fits the man who earlier this week was laying a wreath on the Abbey stone of W. H. Auden [who had died in September 1973].

John left this letter unanswered.

In November 1974, the first fruits of his laureateship were published by John Murray in a new collection, *A Nip in the Air*. As the poet's seventieth birthday was less than two years ahead, the implication of the title was obvious. In sending the book to friends, John offered the quip that the book was 'not about a Japanese aviator' or joked, 'I hope the Japanese ambassador won't be offended.' As usual, John had first thought of off-putting titles. In May Jock Murray had firmly steered him away from *Penultimate Poems* and *Last Words*.

Up to and during August, there was much debate between Jock Murray and John as to which poems should be included in the new book and which omitted. The poem originally entitled 'The Mistress' began:

> Isn't she lovely, the mistress,
> With her wide apart grey green eyes.
> And her drooping lips and when she smiles
> The glance of amused surprise . . .

The poem was inspired by an elegant woman John admired at the Grosvenor Chapel in South Audley Street, where he and Elizabeth regularly worshipped after he moved to Radnor Walk. John did not know her name. She was in fact Joan Price, the beauty editor of *Harper's Bazaar* (later *Harper's & Queen*). John and Jock agreed that the poem should go in, but under the more decorous title 'Lenten Thoughts of a High Anglican'. When it was published in the *Daily Express* as a 'trailer', *Private Eye* lampooned it –

> Lovely lady in the pew,
> Goodness, what a scorcher – phew!
> What I wouldn't give to do
> Unmentionable things to you.
>
> If old God is still up there
> I'm sure he wouldn't really care.
> I'm sure he'd say, 'A little lech
> Never really harmed old Betj.'

The main sticking-point, in choosing the poems to go into *A Nip in the Air*, was over John's poem about the journey to Diss with Mary Wilson.* Elizabeth Cavendish wanted it omitted. She argued that it might lead to the taunting of John in the press; but was she, perhaps, just a little bit jealous of his friendship with the Prime Minister's wife? Jock Murray, Tom Driberg and John Sparrow were all in favour of its retention, and the poem stayed in.

In August 1974 John wrote to Mary Wilson: 'I have been having a terrible time in the newspapers – misrepresented, lied about, often with the best intentions, and made so nervous I hardly dare put pen to paper.' In an interview with Graham Lord published in the *Sunday Express* three days earlier, he had been defensive about his poem on Princess Anne's wedding. ('It was an unhappy squib, but I can't think why people were so rude about it.') But gradually, reassured by such friends as Mary Wilson and Jock Murray, he steeled himself to a new assertiveness. By publication day, 18 November, he was even prepared to make a defiant case for the Princess Anne poem in a *Daily Express* profile by Peter Grosvenor headed 'Betjeman is back – with a nip for his critics'.

> 'It was criticized by silly asses who don't understand poetry and expected some heroic verses on the Princess. You know the sort of thing . . .'
> He began to extemporize:–
>
> > *Thou art the spirit of equestrian pride,*
> > *Thou ridest gracefully through the countryside . . .*
>
> Then he rolled his eyes heavenwards in horror. 'Anyone can write rubbishy rolling couplets like that. And that's what some of them wanted. Well, they didn't get it.'

The reviews of *A Nip in the Air* were more consistently good than those of any other of John's books. 'Betjeman at his best' was the heading of Elizabeth Jennings's review in *The Scotsman*. 'There is not a bad poem in this large collection,' she wrote. In *The Listener*, John Bayley said: 'The eye for life is as sharp as ever, and the rhythms as crisp as a Worcester apple.' Clive James suggested in the *New Statesman* that 'he can be called light-minded only by the thick-witted'. A number of the reviewers commented on John's increasing preoccupation with death. T. C. Worsley, who had been at school with him at Marlborough, complained in the *Financial Times* that for his generation the poems spoke less of nostalgia

---

* See Chapter 29, '*High and Low*'.

than of mortality. Only a few of the reviews were openly hostile, and sales were excellent.

On 26 April 1976, under the heading 'Idle muse', the *Times* Diary attacked John with a new malevolence: 'Francis Kinson, who writes for our Business News section on Saturdays, is upset by the Poet Laureate's failure to produce a poem for the Queen's fiftieth birthday – or indeed for any royal occasion since his appointment in 1972 except Princess Anne's wedding.' He had therefore penned 'Lines to a Laureate'. One stanza demanded 'Did God, who moulded Blake, mould thee?' and the last stanza ran:

> Rest on thy laurels, laureate,
> Priest of the social shibboleth
> Conserve thy Muse inviolate,
> For yawns thou'd better'st save thy breath.

In May 1976 Prince Charles wrote to John from a 'creaking, tossing ship in the middle of the English Channel' in his capacity as chairman of the King George Jubilee Trust, which was to administer a charitable appeal to coincide with the Queen's Silver Jubilee in 1977. 'I am determined that it should be as much of a success as possible . . .' he wrote. 'It would be marvellous if you could find the time to construct one of your masterpieces of scansion for the Queen's Jubilee . . . I would be enormously grateful, personally, if you felt able to conjure up your muse! . . . I am sure you will agree that a Silver Jubilee is something to be remembered with suitable splendour.' It was only seven years since Charles had been pleased by John's lines on his investiture as Prince of Wales. He did not realize the extent to which Parkinson's Disease had depleted his powers. In July the *Times* Diary belatedly caught up with the news that John was to collaborate with Malcolm Williamson, Master of the Queen's Music, to write a 'Jubilee hymn' to mark the Queen's Silver Jubilee. 'For Sir John,' it suggested, 'the enterprise will help appease his critics, who complain that he has not written sufficient royal verse since becoming Laureate, and that he takes his duties unseriously.'

John Nankivell remembers how he and his then girlfriend, Bess Cuthbert, helped to get John over the 'trauma' of writing the Silver Jubilee poem by spending an afternoon with him concocting amusing doggerel.

> Every time something like this turned up he'd get really upset about it. He knew how ridiculed many of the previous laureates had been when they produced official verse. He'd hate the thought of it and he'd despair: he was going to make a mess of it; it would be rubbished by everyone; and he'd be regarded as the usual disastrous laureate who's a waste of space.

John managed to send his 'Jubilee Hymn' to Prince Charles in the month the Prince requested it, though his letter enclosing the poem was inadvertently put on a 'B' pile in the Prince's private office so that he did not see it until several days after it had arrived at Buckingham Palace. Only with the publication of Jonathan Dimbleby's biography of Prince Charles, in 1994, was Charles's reaction to the poem made public. 'When he finally read it, he was aghast, though he noted with uncharacteristic understatement that "this poem is not exactly what I was expecting".' Dimbleby added:

> Doubtless conceived 'in humble duty', Betjeman's five stanzas were lacklustre to the point of pastiche, without that verve which had rightly earned him a reputation as a great contemporary poet. The Prince was so dismayed that he contemplated asking the Poet Laureate to try again, but since the Queen had already given her approval to a modified version of the same poem to be put to music by Malcolm Williamson . . . he decided reluctantly not to press the matter.

On 6 February 1977, the Jubilee Hymn, set to Williamson's music, was performed for the first time at the Royal Albert Hall. It was received with loud, long applause from an audience of 5,500. However, on the next day *The Times* quoted Nicholas Fairbairn, Conservative MP for Kinross and West Perthshire, who described the hymn as 'absolutely pathetic . . . the most banal, ninth-rate piece of child's verse. It has none of the mystery of poetry about it.'

In October James Lees-Milne went to see his doctor, John Allison, who was also John's physician.

> He talked about John B., in his indiscreet fashion, because we are both such friends. I respect his confidence accordingly. Says J's health is much affected by his happiness and unhappiness. The fact that Paul came over from USA and was nice to his father has helped to make him better. Allison says J.B. suffers terrible guilt over Paul. Why on earth? That now he suffers badly from press persecution; references to 'our ageing laureate', and such-like wounding phrases, notably *The Times* in its boring Diary on the middle page. J.B. complained to me about this. If I saw such criticism I would at once write to Rees-Mogg [the newspaper's editor] in protest. I would always champion J.B. in any and every instance.

Even though in April 1981 he had a stroke, John still wanted to write a poem to celebrate the marriage of Prince Charles to Lady Diana Spencer on 29 July. *The Times* of 27 July reported that 'Sir John, aged 75, will not be able to attend the service. A friend said: "He is not very well. The poem is his personal gift."'

The poem ended:

> A dozen years ago I wrote these lines:
> 'You knelt a boy, you rose a man
> And thus your lonelier life began.'
> The scene is changed, the outlook cleared,
> The loneliness has disappeared;
> And all of those assembled there
> Are joyful in the love you share.

Perhaps because of the general awareness that John was ill, this poem attracted less harsh criticism than his earlier exercises in royalism. There were even some compliments.

Paul Johnson has written: 'Even the best of the twentieth-century Laureates, John Betjeman, seemed to lose all his talent once the laurel was nailed to his brow.' Why did John fail so miserably in the rôle in which almost everybody thought he would excel? It was partly that his health was failing – as Penelope said, 'he has gorn orf'. His near-reverence for the Queen as the head of the Church of England inhibited his usual sense of humour. And the whole idea of 'writing poetry to order' (however much the Queen might assure him that this was not required of him) went against the grain. He had always jibbed against authority, and to have anybody, from the *Times* diarist upwards, suggesting what he should write was anathema to him. He could not be himself. Interviewing him in 1974, Graham Lord had reported: '"One knows poetry can't be written to order," he says, pointing towards the heavens. "One just waits for something to come through from The Management upstairs and The Management can be very capricious."'

Beyond that, all that can be said in mitigation is that John was not as dreadful a laureate as Alfred Austin, who wrote:

> Spring is here! Winter is over!
> The cuckoo-flower gets mauver and mauver.

The honour of the laurel belonged to the classical world. John Sparrow, the classicist, applied to John's tenure a famous Latin tag, Tacitus' words on the Roman emperor Galba: 'Omnium concensu, capax imperii, nisi imperasset' (In the opinion of all, he was worthy to rule – had he not ruled).

32

Radnor Walk

⸻◈⸻

AFTER THE SUCCESS of *Metro-land*, Eddie Mirzoeff was encouraged by Robin Scott, the Controller of BBC2, to make another Betjeman film for television. Mirzoeff looked for a subject which would involve John to the same degree but would take him and the viewer into a different world. It seemed to him that John's relationship with the Church of England was like his relationship with suburbia – 'something he was passionate about, had written about and saw in a way that was unique to him'. And, like the pleasures of suburbia, the life of the Church of England had not been touched on much before, on television. The idea appealed to John.

Mirzoeff suggested that, just as the Metropolitan Line had been the 'spine' of *Metro-land*, giving the film shape and coherence, a single diocese should be chosen as a focus for the Church of England film. The question was, which diocese? Ted Roberts thought Salisbury would be an ideal choice – 'The architecture is so stunning, everybody's idea of what a cathedral should look like; and it's set in the heart of Wessex.' But John wanted Southwark, which for him had two great advantages: it was conveniently near his London home and the Bishop was his friend Mervyn Stockwood. In March 1973 John, Elizabeth Cavendish and Mirzoeff dined with Stockwood in Southwark.

> It was positively the most unpleasant evening I can remember – *ever* [Mirzoeff recalls] – battling through on behalf of the BBC. I was not at all taken by his personality, and still less taken by the set-up he had there, of young Arab boys going round looking after him, in a number of different ways.
>
> Betjeman obviously was a great chum of his, but could see, absolutely see, halfway through the evening, that it was a total disaster. And there was no question about it: the following morning, well, I was furious, because of the way Mervyn Stockwood had behaved, which I thought was very, very rude, actually. He was so arrogant and *de haut en bas*; he more or less ignored me. He was really *horrible*.

John wrote Mirzoeff an apologetic letter after the Stockwood dinner ('Feeble and I thought he had been fasting during Lent and lost his propor-

tion'). But John was still urging that 'Southwark is the right place for a celebration.' Then Ted Roberts, who had edited *Metro-land* and was to edit the
new film too, suggested the diocese of Norwich. He was himself Norwich-
born and bred, and his parents still lived there. 'I was afraid that everybody
would think I just wanted to promote my home team, so to speak,' he recalls.
'But I think it was a good idea, because in East Anglia you have the most
dense collection of medieval churches in Christendom. So there was a visual
richness.' And the diocese of Norfolk had one other great recommendation.
In Holt lived Billa Harrod. Not only was she very close to John; she had
written the Shell Guide to Norfolk for him, was much involved in helping
to save redundant churches, and was a friend of the Bishop of Norwich,
Maurice Wood. 'She loved having John to stay,' Mirzoeff says.

John had been reading *Walsingham Way*, a book by his friend Colin
Stephenson. It had convinced him that the Shrine of Our Lady of
Walsingham could not be ignored in the film. 'The pilgrimage was of
European fame before the Reformation and though I don't much like relic
worship myself, things do get an extra quality when they have been revered
for centuries by thousands.' What he wanted at all costs to avoid was 'solemnity and conscious do-goodery and taking ourselves too seriously'. The
film would be given shape by the progression of the Sacraments. A letter
was even sent to Norgate Bros, undertakers, of Horstead, with a view to
having a grave dug in the churchyard there; but eventually Mirzoeff decided
that the subject of death was too daunting for John, and abandoned the
sequence. After some debate, the title *A Passion for Churches* was agreed to.

The Norfolk pilgrimage had a poignancy for John. He was revisiting the
county where, in early childhood, he and his father had been friends,
before they quarrelled. In his poem 'Norfolk' he had written –

> How did the Devil come? When first attack?
> These Norfolk lanes recall lost innocence . . .

He particularly remembered his father when, with Mirzoeff, he 'did a
recce' on the River Bure and they met a Mr Cook whose parents-in-law
had known the Betjemanns. Filming began on 8 April, and the first scene
was at Belaugh on the Bure. Mirzoeff asked John how he first came to
appreciate churches. John replied that he thought it was the outline of
Belaugh church tower against the sky, when his father took him sailing and
rowing on the Bure, that had given him 'a passion for churches; so that
every church I've been past since, I've wanted to stop and look in'. For the
first scene in the film, Mirzoeff asked John to repeat this explanation while
rowing a dinghy on the Bure. Disaster followed.

John *could* row [Mirzoeff recalled] – in the same way as he could play golf – but not as well as when he was younger. And in one of the tapes he was rowing, facing backwards, as one does, and he hit the bank. Instead of going straight down the middle of the river, he edged towards the side; and there was this extraordinary sight of him toppling, terribly terribly slowly, in the boat, with his legs in the air. It was one of those awful moments – both extremely funny and, obviously, very concerning, because you don't want poor old Sir John to drown in the River Bure.

We rushed him into – it so happened – the near-by rectory. We knocked at the door and said, 'We have a poet here, he's soaking wet. Could you possibly take him in and dry his clothes?' And this intensely filthy, disreputable old rector with egg stains all down his front and clothes which hadn't been dry-cleaned for twenty-five years, had us in. A charming man, clearly a sort of throw-back to the nineteenth century. He wrapped up Sir John in a dressing-gown and dried his trousers.

John emerged from the rectory dried out and unscathed. But it was an ominous start; and the incident showed up his growing infirmity. Those of the crew who had worked with him on *Metro-land* two years earlier noticed the decline in his strength and his difficulty in walking. 'He needed to be wrapped up very well,' Mirzoeff remembers, 'and he came out with one of those Puffa jackets, which Billa or somebody had insisted he wore. I said, "No, it looks terrible, we can't have you walking around like that in the film." He said, "Well, I need something." And we were in Swaffham and we went in a gents' outfitters and he bought a terrible blue plastic mac. In the film, it trails behind him like a gown. He called it "my Swaffham". There were a lot of jokes of that kind.'

After the boating upset at Belaugh, the filming went well. The weeks of research had suggested many vignettes of Church of England life. In the church at Trunch, with its magnificent carved wood font-cover, baby Cherry Ann Schamp was baptized. The Sacrament of marriage was filmed at Lyng Church, where the bride's father, Canon Townshend, was priest. The young bridegroom was Nigel McCulloch, who was to become Bishop of Manchester.

We bought Nigel and Celia McCulloch a BBC wedding present [Eddie Mirzoeff recalls]. I asked the secretary to buy it, and she got a coffee-maker. And I said, 'John, this is from all of us and you've got to write a little poem to go with it.' He put it off and put it off; and finally we could put it off no longer. He was being given a special journey on a steam train, round the inner London railway that has Olympia on it. And, as Olympia is near where we then worked, at Kensington House, I telephoned John and said, 'I'm coming to Olympia and I want you to write something down.' And there he was with the bosses of British Rail. I rushed up – 'Hello, John! You've *got* to write something.' The British Rail bosses looked on in surprise. And he wrote:

> Nigel and Celia, may you be
> Fonder of coffee than of tea.

That was his moving epithalamium! He was there at the wedding, in the congregation. And we gave Nigel and Celia all the material that we shot – the parts that were not used in the film. By the way, we found out later that neither of them likes coffee, so the gift was a dead loss.

Ted Roberts and others who had worked with John on *Metro-land*, noticed that he had lost some of his élan. 'We felt that the spark that was there in *Metro-land* had started to wane,' Roberts says. But there was one piece to camera in the Norfolk film as inspired as any *coup de théâtre* in *Metro-land*. He was keen to show the 'sculptured gold' work of his old friend Sir Ninian Comper in Wymondham Abbey and in Lound Church. At Lound, he paused while descanting on Comper's gilding, turned to look direct into the camera, and said:

> I knew Comper. He died a few years ago and he looked rather like that advertisement for Colonel Sanders' Kentucky Chicken. Little white pointed beard; and he spoke in a very lah-di-dah manner – 'my wark, doncha know, in that charch'. And his wark in this charch is really marvellous.

'The Colonel Sanders comparison, the personal memory, the acting – John had put none of these into the rehearsal,' Mirzoeff says.

But, with all the caricatures and jokes, John was intent on conveying to the viewer the spiritual essence of the Church of England. For him, this was most tellingly illustrated by the Vicar of Flordon, Bill Fair, saying Offices in an empty church. Father Fair was Irish. 'We have done tose tings which we ought not to have done,' he declared. For John, he had the simplicity of the Celtic saints.

> It doesn't matter that there's no one there.
> It doesn't matter when they do not come.
> The villagers know the parson is praying for them in their church.

When filming *Metro-land*, John and the crew had spent only one night away from home. With *A Passion for Churches*, they were on location for weeks at a time. 'There was a lot of socializing in pubs at lunchtime,' Mirzoeff says. 'John was absolutely lovely with the crew around him, telling them stories – all the old stuff, stories of his youth, of his days as a prep-school master, that sort of thing. All the jokes he loved about film paraphernalia. (We had the same recordist as we had on *Metro-land*, Simon Wilson.) But in the evening it was slightly different, for various reasons. One of them was that Penelope came up and stayed for several days.'

Penelope's arrival on the scene was a complication that no one had bargained for, and not everyone welcomed. She stayed with John both at Holt and in Norwich. Like the Pipers, the Harrods had remained loyal to her and did not approve of John's liaison with Elizabeth Cavendish. Learning that he would be away from Elizabeth and safely *chez* Harrod or in a Norwich hotel, Penelope gatecrashed the party. Her presence unsettled John, stirring more feelings of guilt to add to those he felt about his father.

> For me [Mirzoeff recalls] the most memorable thing that happened, in personal terms, was that after Penelope left the Maid's Head Hotel, the big old hotel in Norwich, just John and I were left alone. All the others had gone out . . . And we had the most extraordinary talk, the only time I had a talk like that with him. Extremely personal. It started with his talking about Penelope. Then he talked about Paul – 'the Powlie', as he called him – and his desperate sadness at what he felt was his failure to build bridges, to keep him alongside. He'd gone, left for Canada or somewhere as a musician. There was no contact. And John was feeling guilt, terrible terrible guilt.
>
> So I said to him, 'Why don't you *write* to him? Why don't you write and say what you feel? Why don't you say that you have this affection for him which you have failed to communicate?' He said: 'I can't do it.' I said: 'Come on, you can.' I went on and on about this, though it wasn't my business at all. He said he would write, but I don't think he did. This long talk brought us very close together. I never felt closer to him, as a human being, than I did that night. One felt one broke through the jokes and the performance to the real person – who was, on that occasion, a very sad, unfulfilled, guilt-ridden person. It made you feel very warm towards him.

Mirzoeff also remembers how generous John was:

> [The novelist] Elizabeth Jane Howard [at that time Kingsley Amis's wife] was sent out by the *Radio Times* to write an article about the filming. She stayed several days. She was very grand – she would only talk to John and she wouldn't talk to any of us. But she insisted on taking him into various antique shops and saying, 'That's absolutely wonderful, John, you must buy it.' So he would be carrying round these paintings and things that she made him buy. The moment she left, he gave them to us. I've still got a lovely painting that he gave me. We all did rather well.

John told Howard that he loved making films for television; but at the end of the article she observed, 'He has a proper aversion to being hectored, bullied and made to do things, and somewhere, very deeply hidden, one suspects a streak of that ruthlessness essential for the self-protection of any working artist'. That John possessed such a faculty, Eddie Mirzoeff was to be made painfully aware in the editing of the film.

After the filming, he drove John back to London. 'John had been in the best of form, extremely alive and cheerful,' he recalled. 'But the closer to London, the more tense he got. By the time we reached the suburbs, he had got into a state of abject terror. It was all to do with having been away from Elizabeth, the likelihood of being late, and what was going to happen when we turned up in Radnor Walk – maybe having to confess that Penelope had been with him. It was extraordinary to see this transformation.'

The editing went much less smoothly than the filming. 'For me,' Mirzoeff says, 'it was just another film; and Ted is a standard C of E chap. But for John, this was a subject terribly close to the core of his being. It mattered to him; it mattered enormously; and he therefore found it quite difficult. He was very, very uncertain about how it was going to be received, and whether we could show certain sequences, get away with them – sequences which seemed to us totally harmless.' He was worried, for example, by the apparent Romishness of the Walsingham scenes; and it upset him that the Mass – to him the most holy of the Sacraments – had to be omitted from the film altogether.

At times, John seemed to be suffering from acute writer's block. He reached a stage when he could not write anything. 'There were a lot of very short days,' Ted Roberts remembers. 'He'd say, "Well, I think we're doing quite well. I'm going home now, and I'll be back at eleven tomorrow." And you'd had half an hour, you know. Eddie was tearing his hair out.' Mirzoeff tried to be sympathetic about John's anxieties. 'So many things were too close to the bone. He kept saying to me, "This is very very important to me. I can't treat this easily."' But time was getting short, and one essential part of the commentary remained unwritten. Mirzoeff needed from John some words to link the brass of Sir Simon and Lady Margaret Felbrigg, at Felbrigg Church, to the wedding of Nigel and Celia McCulloch at Lyng. Surely this should not be a difficult transition – from medieval marriage to modern marriage.

It was the last thing [Mirzoeff recalls]. We'd done the front of the film and we'd done the end of the film. We'd added this and we'd added that. Gradually, as with a jigsaw, we were filling in the last bits, and we'd got stuck with this hole. We were due to record the commentary the next day. There was no way we could put it off any longer. But John just couldn't do it. In the past, Ted and I had between us done a lot of drafts for him, saying 'roughly this?' and so on. And I was saying this to him now: 'Come on,

John, it's not difficult; why can't you say this?' – when, suddenly, he snapped, like *that*. And I have never seen it before or, thank God, since; but it was terrifying, because he literally yelled, he lost his temper in a way that you can't imagine the lovable teddy bear figure of the jolly Poet Laureate doing. He felt he was being pushed too far and he felt I was asking more than he could give.

He said: 'I'm an old man and I can't do this sort of thing to order. I'm nearly seventy and I'm not being treated as I should be.' He went on and on. It was absolutely frightening to see this temper, and embarrassing. One just sat there and there was this anger which was obviously an accumulation of frustration, but it was serious anger. One couldn't go on. So when all this had come out, I finally said, 'Well, I'm going to go. I can't deal with this.'

Mirzoeff went into another cutting-room, and for two or three days Ted Roberts acted as an intermediary. In the end, John overcame his block and made a fine, poetical link between the Felbrigg brass and the Lyng wedding. After a while he and Mirzoeff got back on speaking terms, though Mirzoeff called him 'Sir John' for some time afterwards. Mirzoeff made another film with him, but feels that they never quite recovered their old relaxed relationship.

The film was transmitted on BBC2 on 7 December 1974 at 10.05 p.m., clashing with *Match of the Day* on BBC1 at 10.10. The day before, Osbert Lancaster previewed it in the *Times Literary Supplement*. Under the Old Pals' Act, he wrote that 'In this medium, *A Passion for Churches* is, I think, Sir John's masterpiece to date.' But most of the other critics, while praising the film, saw in it a falling-off from the near-perfection of *Metro-land*. Chris Dunkley observed in the *Financial Times*: 'It takes the mind of a poet, and an unusual poet at that, to see the middle classes as worthy of considerable notice and, having done so, to make this clear to the audience.'

The filming of *A Passion for Churches* had coincided with John's move from Cloth Fair to Radnor Walk. Penelope too had moved. In his sombre fiftieth-birthday letter of 1956, John had told her that he left it to her whether and when to sell The Mead. By 1972 the logic of selling it had become irresistible. In February John wrote to a friend to say that Penelope had decided to sell the house. 'It is impossible to let so large a place or to keep the vandals out, or pay for the upkeep out of income.'

John's move to the house Elizabeth had bought for him at No. 29 Radnor Walk, Chelsea, just a few doors away from her own house at No. 19, ratified the love affair which had now lasted for over twenty years. There was also a more practical reason for moving to Chelsea. In the two years since 1971,

John's health had noticeably declined. The debilitating effects of Parkinson's Disease had begun to appear, in the shuffling gait which Lord Longford wrongly took to be part of an 'old man' act. John now needed, if not twenty-four-hour care, a watchful eye kept on him. Whatever she may have been to him in the earlier years of their relationship, in the Seventies Elizabeth also became something of a nurse to him, almost a nanny.

Like Old Church Street, where he had spent some of the less happy years of his childhood, Radnor Walk led off the King's Road. If a competition had been held to design a setting into which John would not fit, Chelsea in the Seventies could well have been the winner. His peculiar dislike of dogs has been noted. In Radnor Walk he had to pick his way through deposits of dogs' mess, a sort of pedestrian slalom. The Thames stank: he mentioned it as 'awful' in a letter of 1974 to Patrick Cullinan. The noise of the lorries at Cloth Fair was replaced by that of sports-car engines being gunned and motor-bikes revving up in the small hours as young bloods left the Arethusa Club with their 'birds'; and there was usually a hubbub at the Chelsea Potter pub on the corner of Radnor Walk. (The Chelsea Pottery, whose fine glazed earthenwares are today collected as 'antiques', was *in* the Walk, a few doors from Elizabeth's house.) If John wanted to do some shopping, he had to brave the Hieronymus Bosch pageant of the King's Road – a bald old-timer shuffling with his string bag past druggy young people with harlequin clothes and mad haircuts (dyed Mohicans in the Punk era).

The move to Radnor Walk was a turning-point in his relations both with Elizabeth Cavendish and with Penelope. In the daytime he worked at No. 29 – the house ostensibly his – mainly dictating letters about poetry and threatened buildings, to a succession of secretaries. But he spent the nights at Elizabeth's house down the road, No. 19. Up to this time the London gossip columnists had not been able to pin a 'relationship' on John and Elizabeth. Now they closed in like hounds on a fox breaking cover. The two separate houses in Radnor Walk could not quite be reckoned a 'love nest'; but on 21 August 1974 the *Daily Express* printed an insinuating story headed 'Old friend Lady Elizabeth comforts Betjeman', with a photograph of the couple together several years earlier. John knew that the paragraph would distress Penelope. As late as 1972 – just after The Mead was sold – she had still been able to talk, in a television interview, as if she and John were together.

After the gossip paragraph appeared, John wrote to her:

I did not like all that probing and prying in the *Express*, I felt very sorry for you, what business is it of theirs, fuck them. It is absolutely lovely here in

London in August because the dog messes on the pavement dry up much quicker. I laugh a lot when I think about your labour camp but what the *Sunday Express* ought to have said was that you are a very distinguished Indologist in your own right which is what you have always wanted to be and it has only recently been broken to me by John Allison, my doctor, and by Elizabeth that I had to be moved here last year because I was not fit to be left alone in the City with no-one else in the house. I am really much better now but will never be able to walk fast and far or keep up with the grand-kiddiz. But you will be doing that as you are a much better person in all respects than yours truly.

Penelope replied from *her* new house – on stationery which she had had printed, in red, 'No telephone thank God'. After The Mead was sold, she had had some thoughts of living in a convent. 'We all wondered whether the nuns would drive her mad first, or she them,' Mollie Baring said. But instead Penelope had moved to a glorified cottage on the Welsh border, at Cusop, near Hay-on-Wye, Herefordshire. She called it 'New House', but John always referred to it as 'Little Redoubt' (or 'LR'), and to Hay-on-Wye as 'Kulu-on-Wye', after the part of India on which Penelope had written her book of 1972. Penelope did eventually invest in a telephone; but it was one of the few mod cons at New House. She had the fanciful idea that it might still be possible for her to lure John away from Elizabeth and per-suade him to live with her at Cusop. She put a bed in a downstairs room so that he would not have to toil up the stairs. He came to stay, but was appalled by the Spartan accommodation, inadequately heated by the tem-peramental boiler which Penelope called 'The Crem'.

A few months before the exposé about Elizabeth and himself appeared in the *Daily Express,* John had written Billa Harrod a letter to thank her for her hospitality to him and Eddie Mirzoeff when they were 'doing a recce' for the television film about Norfolk churches. In it he tried to set down what he felt about his 'Two loves I have . . .' dilemma, while evidently bear-ing in mind that Billa was decidedly in Penelope's camp rather than Elizabeth's.

> Your kindest action to me in our long and loving friendship was to speak to me so kindly and clearly of Penelope. I love her. *But I cannot live with her for long without quarrelling.* I sensed her anguish when we went to the cinema last night with Emily [Villiers-Stuart]. I cannot bear to hurt her. She kissed me on the cheek when she got out of the taxi last night and I went back to Radnor Walk.
>
> You said being loved is a great burden. I have lived so long apart from Penelope, that Elizabeth now loves me more than anyone else in the world.

I cannot hurt *her* either, any more than I can Penelope. I depend on Elizabeth for food and for my body and mind. She is v much part of me too.

Both P and E feel threatened. Fear steps in and with it hatred and anger. It is difficult. I *think* Penelope would be wounded if we separated, though she says that is what she wants to do. I don't want to, but may have to because she will precipitate it in rage at E and all Cavendishes. I can understand her rage and misery. She won't believe how much I love her. I think she needs to be given her rights and dignity. She is okay at Kulu-on-Wye and insecure in London with me in the enemy's camp. I must buy, if it ruins me, a camp for her in London where she can entertain her friends with me.

In all this awful storm of misery, the one thing I cling to is my love for Penelope *and* for Elizabeth who has given up marriage and a family life with her own children, out of love for me.

I think, but am not sure, that P is more defenceless than E and must therefore be propped up by a London base as well as Kulu-on-Wye. Radnor Walk would never do. It is too near the enemy, though P has tried to be friendly with E.

Ora pro nobis [pray for us] . . .

Penelope gave her view of the situation in a letter of 1975 to Lord Kinross.

But for E, I could never have gone back to India so often. I am so grateful to her in so many ways & would love to be friends & share John – as Jock Murray says that some men need two wives! – but she refuses to see me & John gets terrible guilt whenever he goes to stay either in Kulu-on-Wye or at . . . Candida's & starts fussing about his train back to London almost before his arrival . . . It's the old story of a middle-aged woman without children being unfulfilled (a psychological FACT) & clinging to her man in a completely possessive way.

Penelope had offered John a divorce, even though she was a Roman Catholic. Whether from religious scruples or from fear of adverse publicity, he declined the offer. And he never did buy her a London house or flat. Possibly he could not afford to; more probably, he preferred to keep his two loves a healthy distance apart. It was true that Penelope had tried to make friends with Elizabeth, and been politely repulsed. Magda Rogers, who was John's secretary from 1974 to 1977, remembers that Penelope had to make an appointment to see John. 'Elizabeth was very definite about not seeing Penelope,' Jonathan Stedall recalls, 'and I can quite see why she did that. It was not out of animosity. She knew that Penelope was a very powerful personality and would kind of take over.'

Stedall saw a lot of John, Elizabeth *and* Penelope in the 1970s. Elizabeth liked Stedall: Magda parodied her attitude towards him as '*Dear* little

Jonathan!' When he stayed at No. 29 Radnor Walk, he was absorbed into the ménage at No. 19, too. He remembers Princess Margaret's visits.

> She wasn't a very relaxing person to be with. She made it difficult, because part of the time she was very matey – one of us – and then she'd become the little Princess. Quite a few times I was at dinner at No. 19 and she'd turn up at about 11.00 when we were all about to go to bed, and she'd want scrambled egg. And there was this kind of etiquette that you don't go to bed until she leaves – and she had bugger all to do.

At dinner parties, Stedall met Elizabeth's circle of friends. 'They tended to be gay men,' he said. He remembered that the playwright Peter Shaffer was also a frequent guest at No. 19. It was one of the cases that Elizabeth Cavendish heard as a magistrate that gave him the plot of his play *Equus*, first presented at the Old Vic Theatre in July 1973. John and Elizabeth often saw Jeremy Fry, who was to have been best man to Antony Armstrong-Jones at his wedding to Princess Margaret in 1960, but had been hastily replaced by Roger Gilliat when a past homosexual 'indiscretion' came to light. A great friend of Fry's – the two went on many holidays together – was the play- and film-director Tony Richardson, predominantly gay, even though he had two daughters by Vanessa Redgrave during their five-year marriage. He, too, was in John and Elizabeth's circle.

Through Rupert and Candida, John became a friend of Terence Stamp, the star of *Far from the Madding Crowd* (1966). A central figure of the Swinging Sixties, Stamp was the boyfriend of another, the model Jean Shrimpton. When Stamp wanted to move into a set of rooms in Albany, Piccadilly, John was asked for a testimonial. He wrote to Colonel A. L. Chetwynd-Talbot, the secretary of Albany: 'I can assure you that he is honourable, quiet, sober and a keen vegetarian. In addition to this he is honest, good company and entertaining as well as a most distinguished actor.' Stamp's application was successful.

James Lees-Milne was the homosexual man whom John and Elizabeth saw most often. His incomparable diaries are a window into the couple's life and a mournful periodic bulletin on John's declining health. He was also a friend of Penelope, whom he had known since the early 1930s, before her marriage to John. Unlike some of John's friends – the Pipers and Harrods, for example – who were dismayed by John's abandoning Penelope and taking up with Lady Elizabeth, Lees-Milne was happier to meet a John discreetly escorted by Lady Elizabeth than a John resoundingly accompanied by Penelope.

For the last fifteen years of John's life, the diaries are a kind of Greek chorus. The entry for 11 March 1972 reads:

> Penelope telephones to say they are leaving Wantage and she doesn't know where she is going to live. Says John will never tear himself away from London and will die there in harness; that he hates going away for week-ends and so seldom goes to Wantage (I did not tell her that he is staying with us next weekend *and* with Elizabeth); and he would rather she took a small house right away, possibly in the Welsh Marches where he could retire for weeks on end. It is extraordinary how people deceive themselves. Poor Penelope, surely she must realize that John does not want to live with her at all. And surely she must know that on the contrary he goes off weekend after weekend at a time. I suppose it is pride which makes women cling to delusions of this sort, rather than face the ugly truth. Yet she is eminently sensible, and cherishes her independence.

On 6 May 1973, when Elizabeth Cavendish rang him to ask if she and John might stay on the 19th, Lees-Milne wrote in his diary: 'How I love that dearest man, and dearest woman.' Bath was a convenient staging-post for the couple on their way to Cornwall. With Lees-Milne, his wife Alvilde and their old housekeeper Miss Barrett they watched *Metro-land* on the television. Lees-Milne was shocked at how old John had become, though he thought he looked worse in the film, made some months before.

On 20 May the two couples had lunch at Cerney House, near Cirencester, with Quentin Craig. Alvilde drove Elizabeth there, and Lees-Milne took John, who was in a confiding mood.

> He told me Penelope, although she had wanted to marry him, probably was never in love with him; that she is quite impossible to live with; that he does not know if his son is alive or dead, for his last letter was returned from the dead-letter office in New York. He is worried over lack of money. His secretary costs him £50 a week and he does not earn enough to cover this item of expense. The demands made on him now he is Laureate bring no financial return, and much work. Showed us a letter he has just received from the Duke of Kent who offers his services in preventing London being totally transformed. John must go and see him. Another letter, from [Edward] Heath, asking him to translate a Portuguese poem into English to be put to music by Arthur Bliss and played to the Portuguese President on his visit to the Queen. And so it goes on . . . As we drove past Malmesbury John said, nodding to a signpost, 'In that village I had my first experience of sex with the son of the Vicar. It was in a punt on the river. I was quite spent. That night the brother came into my room, but I was too shocked by what I had done with the other, during the afternoon, and so lost a second opportunity.'

He was then fifteen. We agreed that no subsequent escapades have eclipsed those early schoolday ones.

In December, Lees-Milne was dining with Rosamond Lehmann at an Italian restaurant opposite Buckingham Palace mews, when someone tapped on the window. It was Osbert Lancaster, who was beckoned to join them. He had walked from the Beefsteak Club where he had sat next to Cyril Connolly. Alvilde, who dined that evening with John and Elizabeth, later told Lees-Milne that 'Cyril wanted to dine with them but Elizabeth sent him away because she only had three cutlets.' Was Elizabeth being mean and inhospitable? Couldn't she have rustled up some other dish for Connolly, like the scrambled eggs that were there when Princess Margaret asked for them? Quite possibly her motive in turning Connolly away was to avoid taxing John, who would need to be on top form in conversation with the critic.

In March 1974, the *Illustrated London News* published an interview with John by Wilfred De'Ath, better known as a television producer than as a journalist. De'Ath asked him, didn't his Christian belief provide an adequate shield against his malaise of the soul?

> 'Well, sometimes it does and sometimes it doesn't, you know. I've had long moments of thinking Christianity isn't true, but on the whole I'm convinced that it is . . . In my youth I was attracted to the Quakers and I used to go to their meetings, but I think that was chiefly to avoid going to confession. I was much troubled by sex as a young man – I suppose most young men are. With me a sense of sin was always inextricably involved with sex and in my book masturbation was as bad as, if not worse than, murder . . . and I hated having to confess it.'

That August, John stayed with Rupert and Candida. In 1970–1, while Penelope was away in India with John Nankivell and the three Elizabeths, he had visited his daughter and her husband more often at their home in Chepstow Villas, Notting Hill. There were grandchildren now: Lucy, Imogen and Endellion (named after the saint of one of John's favourite Cornish churches) were born in the Sixties, David and John in the Seventies. 'He enjoyed his grandchildren's company,' Candida writes, 'but only when they were quiet. (He hated noise, and yelling children were one of his worst nightmares.) He would open his mouth hugely and his eyes would twinkle when he saw them. He always brought stacks of presents.' He also took the children on outings.

In the late summer of 1974 the Lycett Greens had just moved to Blacklands, near Calne in Wiltshire beside the River Marden. The large

Georgian house was in a bad state of repair: the top two floors had been gutted by fire. 'It had had a lot of money lavished on it and the grounds in the nineteenth century,' Candida writes, 'and none since.' On 5 August John wrote to Mollie Baring: 'Darling Mollie, I am writing this on the terrace in the sun looking south to the downs at Wibz's new abode. Rupert is working the motor mower, the children rush about; only the downs and expensive-looking horses are still. It will make the most beautiful house and garden and has affinities with Ardington.'

In November 1975 John stayed with Penelope again at the Little Redoubt. They visited Lady Chetwynd at her '1870-ish fantasy palace of tiles and iron and coloured marbles and steep gables' at Barmouth. John wrote to Penelope on 1 December: 'I love you as much as I ever did and this visit was like old times. I saw a very good telly last night on hell. It was a film. It said hell is now and is separation from God. Quite true.' This letter was a harbinger of the mental torment he suffered in the next year. On 17 March 1976 he wrote to Harry Jarvis, 'I have a very strong feeling that this earth is going to crack beneath me and I will sink into fire through mattresses of chicken-wire, telephone cables and sewage pipes which compose the ground under our feet in Radnor. On Monday the whole of it was bathed in an ominous violet pink light.' It did not help that, on his morning constitutional, peering into the window of the King's Road boutique called Sex, he saw his name in the list of 'Hates' on a T-shirt which Bernard Rhodes, Malcolm McLaren and Vivienne Westwood had designed for the shop. The shirt was intended to be a manifesto and a 'poem', as well as an article of clothing. John was fourth in the long list of Hates on the front of the shirt, after Television, Mick Jagger and the Liberal Party. The 'Loves' which appeared on the back included Christine Keeler, the Society for Cutting Up Men, Ronnie Biggs and Rubber.

On 11 April 1976 John went to Romania for just over a week with Elizabeth Cavendish, Jonathan Stedall and Stedall's cameraman, John McGlashan. They were making a 'recce' for Stedall's television film *The Long Search*, about the Orthodox Church in Romania. Stedall recalls:

> We went to monasteries quite a lot, and convents, and had the best wine and the best food. At one monastery we had quite a lot to drink. Then we had to stand at the end for grace, and Elizabeth got the giggles. She is a terrific one for getting the giggles. She told me that when she went to Holland with Princess Margaret they had to listen to a very poker-faced man delivering a speech about dams. And he told that story about the boy putting his finger in the dyke; and both the Princess and Elizabeth had to control giggles.

Patrick Kinross died on 4 June of cancer of the intestine. On 8 June, James Lees-Milne was at Radnor Walk again: 'Since Patrick was to have dined with me this evening, Feeble and John Betj. had me to dine with them. JB very unhappy over P's death.' Kinross's funeral was on 11 June, at Paddington Green Church. John gave the address. James Lees-Milne found it hard to control his emotion. He wrote in his diary: 'Paddy [Leigh Fermor] read one lesson with his difficult voice. John Betjeman's address from the pulpit most beautiful. His excellent, calm, quiet, professional delivery. He likewise very moved . . .' But Lees-Milne also wrote: 'Oh dear. Dreadful to watch JB's painful ascent to and descent from the high pulpit. Osbert [Lancaster] there looking a million [years old].'

Privately and publicly, John's seventieth birthday, on 28 August 1976, was celebrated in style. Rupert and Candida held a party for him at Blacklands. Jonathan Stedall made a television film of *Summoned by Bells*, in which John retraced his early life. Even though Stedall was the producer, John did not enjoy it. He told James Fox, who contributed a birthday article about him to the *Radio Times*: 'Doing this thing has been the most devastating experience. I had no idea the kind of draining effect it has on one . . . It did upset me most surprisingly. I felt as though I were undressing in public and showing my parts.' He wrote to Penelope on 8 September, 'I had to go back to the very earliest places I can remember and see Ernie's grave in Highgate Cemetery and a passport photograph of Bess and remember nursery things. It was like being the bath water and running down with it as part of the London drains. And then suddenly the BBC girded its loins and started a sort of fiesta so that I find myself not myself but a public figure and quite inhuman.'

Five days after John's seventieth birthday, James and Alvilde Lees-Milne drove to Hay-on-Wye. Afterwards they called on Penelope at Cusop, without pre-warning, bringing a picnic lunch with them.

> She was busily cooking in the kitchen [Lees-Milne wrote]. Received us as though we had been with her all the morning, went on cooking, talking, talking without cease, treating us with her extraordinary detached, candid manner. Is a round little tub with close-cropped grey hair, wearing a brown one-piece garment, trousers, the legs very tight, also the behind, which is enormous. From the behind a thick hair was dangling like a tail, of which she was totally unconscious. She is very worried about John. Thinks his health is impaired by what she calls his 'dichotomy', i.e., his divided allegiance to her and Feeble. She says F. is very possessive and John is afraid of her, which isn't true. Thinks John is killing himself with drink and drugs which his doctor plies him with. This is far more likely. It was distressing to

see how old he has become, for in the film given on his seventieth birthday he walked like Charlie Chaplin, as though his legs did not belong to him. Very sad film, for he did not speak throughout. A background recitation in his voice taken from *Summoned by Bells*. At the very end he broke into that delicious smile, made a joke and came alive.

In 1977 John made one last film with Eddie Mirzoeff, to mark the Queen's Silver Jubilee in that year. Mirzoeff was producing a helicopter series called *The Queen's Realm*, of Scotland and Wales and England, using nothing but library footage. He gave all the helicopter footage to Ted Roberts and asked him to work out what could be done with it. Eventually the two men decided that it might be a good idea to do something based on the seasons, particularly as one of the helicopter films was *Around the Seasons*. The words would be an anthology of English poetry. Mirzoeff first approached Geoffrey Grigson, whom he regarded as an anthologist of genius. On the telephone, Grigson sounded enthusiastic; but when Mirzoeff sent him the scripts of the helicopter films (of which some were written by John) saying 'You'll get a sense of what we've done,' Grigson sent back a curt note, 'I'm afraid I can't take on this project.' Mirzoeff thinks he was put off by the discovery that John was involved. So Mirzoeff went back to John and said, 'Look, if we do lots of the work, could you possibly try and tie it all together?' John agreed to help.

Mirzoeff formed a small team, including his wife, and they 'just read day and night, looking for seasonal stuff'. They would say to John, 'We've found these ten poems, John. What do you reckon?' John also came up with a few things the rest of the team would never have thought of, such as a Hilaire Belloc poem about electricity and a passage from Elizabeth Barrett Browning.

> The main question was [Mirzoeff recalls] should we use John to read the poems, or actors? John was now getting on. Also, I thought it would be misleading to have him reading – people would think they were all poems by him. So in the end he read his own bits and voices read the other bits – Michael Hordern, Richard Pasco, Prunella Scales. And that did not go down well in Radnor Walk, let me tell you. Lady Elizabeth had done her best to stop John being taxed by the work; but when we got these actors, she felt he had been marginalized. They had not been very keen on his working in the first place, but once he actually did get involved they wanted to maximize the impact of it. It was silly, because the thing was hugely successful.

In the late 1970s, John also made his last films with Ken Savidge, *Betjeman's Belfast* and *Betjeman's Dublin*. His old friend, after a time as a consultant in Pakistan and 'a rather unhappy period in the foreign relations department of the BBC', had asked to be a producer again. He was told, 'If you are determined to work at the coal face, it will have to be in Northern Ireland.' So Savidge moved to Ulster.

> And, knowing John's delight in many of the buildings of Belfast, I thought it would be a good idea to do thirty minutes on them. But at first – not from him, but from Elizabeth – there was great resistance. 'Oh, he will be kidnapped, he will be assassinated!' We got over that and in any case he had connections there, for example with the Dufferins at Clandeboye. So we embarked on this. He was most hospitably received. The BBC really pushed the boat out.

Though clearly in decline, John was still capable of animated contributions to chat shows. As with *Desert Island Discs* on radio, he was the only person invited to appear three times on Michael Parkinson's television shows – once with the camp *Carry On* comedian Kenneth Williams and the actress Maggie Smith and once with the Lancashire singer Gracie Fields, whom he had first seen forty years before in the otherwise deserted theatre at Alexandra Palace. Williams and Maggie Smith decided they would recite John's 'Death in Leamington' in his presence. Williams wrote in his diary: 'To TV studios for the "Parkinson Show". I was introduced to Sir John Betjeman and he was a great delight. One of the most lovable and kindly gentle people I've ever met.'

Anyone watching the third Parkinson programme of 1977 would have thought John on top form. He recited his poem 'A Russell Flint' (about 'Freckly Jill') to the music of Jim Parker, played live. And he gave fluent answers to Parkinson's questions.

> PARKINSON: When exactly did you last write a poem or try to write a poem in recent weeks?
>
> JOHN: About three days ago I was trying to do one on Peterborough Cathedral, a beautiful building which has got in it a chapel called St Sprite and I imagine that's the Holy Spirit, and it's such a nice name for a chapel, I thought I'd try and do a thing about the Sprite in Peterborough Cathedral. I got the first words out and have now lorst them.
>
> PARKINSON: You've lost them? Mislaid them?
>
> JOHN: Mislaid them.
>
> PARKINSON: Can't you remember them?
>
> JOHN: No.
>
> PARKINSON: So what are you going to do?
>
> JOHN: Hope I'll find them again.

John told Parkinson, 'I started as a journalist, as you did – and it teaches one to write things simply and not like government department forms.'

PARKINSON: Advertising slogans and phrases have always been a part of your poetry, haven't they? You've always stuck them in there. What's the fascination you have?

JOHN: I think sitting in the Underground and seeing things like:

> Whatever her Party, the smart young thing,
> It's certain she'll vote for a Bravington ring.

PARKINSON: And Virol.

JOHN: 'Anaemic girls need it'. And Iron Jelloids! Mazawattee tea! I think they're most beautiful names.

Candida was watching the programme. She later wrote: 'Although there was jollity in his air and the audience laughed at almost everything he said, I could detect a fear in his eyes. He told me afterwards it had been one of the most frightening experiences of his life. He was terrified that he was going to be asked difficult questions.' He need not have worried. 'Is your poetry *relevant*, do you think?' Parkinson asked. '*No*, thank God.'

In the non-trendy sense of 'relevant', John mattered as much as ever – not least in architectural conservation. As early as 1958, *The Times*, reviewing his *Collected Poems*, had said of him: 'He has established a personal regency over contemporary taste.' By 1970 he had become something more practical – a sort of ombudsman for conservationists throughout the country. The *Times* Diary reported in October 1970: '[He] gets some 50 letters daily on threatened buildings, redundant churches, old market places, Victorian town halls, etc, and most generate three or four letters at least. "I was made to be a writer, and I'm being turned into a Post Office."'

He was not only called upon to sign letters of protest; he was also in demand as a witness at public hearings. In March 1971 he told an inquiry at Bristol that the city 'would suffer at the hands of commercial enterprise' if the Grand Hotel Company were allowed to build a £1 million hotel on the slopes of the Avon Gorge. He described Brunel's 1829 suspension bridge across the gorge as 'an effortless conquest of space' and pointed out that Brunel had been inspired by the setting. John was brought into the campaign by Penelope's cousin Lord Methuen, whose action group had secured the services of a fiery young barrister, Paul Chadd (later QC).

The inquiry was held on 17 May. John's old *Architectural Review* colleague James Richards also attended. But Paul Chadd considered John his star witness.

I gave lunch to him and Lady Elizabeth Cavendish before the hearing [he says]. My impression was that he was diffident; despondent, too. He said, '*They always win*,' and it made me quite sad. So it gave me great pleasure to ring him up later and say, 'We've won.' He was nervous, uncomfortable in the witness box; but he created the Betjeman atmosphere. Everybody liked him. Even the tough counsel on the other side was courteous to him. 'My wife enjoys your television programmes very much,' he said, in a rather patronizing and I suppose 'sexist' way. James Richards was analytical; but John gave the *flavour*. The combination was ideal. One of the things John said was that he was worried about the effect of the hotel windows at night. The bridge is the only thing illuminated there – it *would* have made a big difference.

Although the Avon Gorge development was stopped, the Bristol hearing was not quite the end of the matter. On 29 May 1971 a news report appeared in *The Times* under the headline 'SIR JOHN BETJEMAN'S EVIDENCE "INACCURATE"'. William Huntley, for the developers, said that the project's opponents had made 'gross misrepresentations' about it and had circulated 'despicable posters which showed the hotel the wrong size'. Huntley added: 'A statement made by Sir John Betjeman that the hotel would urbanize the Gorge was grossly inaccurate. Sir John came here post-haste from Cornwall to give evidence, without seeing the plans.'

A threat to Southend pier, in February 1974, touched John more personally. It would cost £1.5 million to repair the pier over ten years, *The Times* reported; total demolition would cost £800,000, only partly offset by the income from scrap. It happened that the foremost authority on English piers, Cyril Bainbridge, was then night news editor of *The Times*. On 16 February he contributed an article headed 'How far to the end of the longest pier in the world?' On 22 February John wrote, 'I am one of millions who have used Southend Pier as the nearest place to London for real sea-air, recreation and complete change of scene . . . In winter or summer the pier is a delight with its tram-way, once of toast-rack type, running for a mile and a third into a wide prospect of sea and sky. There is all the advantage at the end of the pier of being right out to sea and no feeling of sea-sickness.' He hoped the preservation of the pier would be considered 'not merely of local interest but . . . of national importance'. The pier was saved.*

John's most significant campaign of 1974 was in defence of Holy Trinity Church, Sloane Street, London – the church on which he had written a

---

* On John's visit to Southend pier with Simon Jenkins, see Chapter 33, '". . . As I Lose Hold"'.

poem in the 1930s. As Dr Gavin Stamp has written, this was an important case, as it exposed the vulnerability of historic churches under historic-building legislation: if they were in use, no protection was guaranteed, no matter how fine they were. John wrote: 'Holy Trinity is a celebration of the Arts and Crafts movement. It only lacks a bishop's throne to be the Cathedral of West London.' It was full of stained glass and metalwork by such artists as Sir Edward Burne-Jones, F. W. Pomeroy and Hamo Thornycroft.

In June 1971 Lord Cadogan and the Cadogan Estate announced plans to demolish the church and redevelop the site (which had been provided by an earlier Lord Cadogan). John condemned these as 'the height of irresponsibility'. The Greater London Council and the Victorian Society also vehemently opposed the scheme. Three years later, still campaigning against the demolition plans, John contacted Stamp. He knew him because Stamp had approached him in 1973, via Gerard Irvine, asking if he would write a short introduction to a book of architectural fantasies Stamp had drawn, *The Architect's Calendar*. John admired Stamp's drawings, which might have been the work of an accomplished 'black-and-white' artist of *c*.1904. He now asked him to make drawings of Holy Trinity which he would offer to the parish to sell, to generate both income and publicity – knowing that the offer would be declined. *A Plea for Holy Trinity Sloane Street* was published in 1974 with an ironic foreword by John. Both men made sure that the booklet generated a great deal of unwelcome publicity for the parish and Lord Cadogan.

'That did the trick,' Stamp concludes; though he also credits John with strengthening the campaign by a second poem he wrote about Holy Trinity, published in the *Sunday Times* on 15 September 1974, above a photograph of the chancel screen and one of Pomeroy's bronze angels –

> Bishop, archdeacon, rector, wardens, mayor
>   Guardians of Chelsea's noblest house of prayer.
> You your church's vastiness deplore
>   'Should we not sell and give it to the poor?'
> Recall, despite your practical suggestion,
>   Which the disciple was who asked that question.

This was written the year after John was publicly criticized for his poem about Princess Anne's wedding. The stab of satire proved how effective he could still be when he chose his own subject and his emotions were engaged.

Gavin Stamp feels that the Holy Trinity campaign had a number of valuable long-term consequences.

There was no more talk of redevelopment after this although as Peyton Skipwith says in his guide to the church (2002), Holy Trinity remained generally closed and was 'as though in a state of parochial sulks' for the following two decades. The hand of the Victorian Society in fighting for the best nineteenth-century churches was strengthened; it eventually became possible for Historic Buildings grants to go to churches in use and the C of E tightened up its own mechanisms for protecting churches while public attention was focused on the ecclesiastical exemption . . .

In 2002 Peyton Skipwith dedicated his fine guide to Holy Trinity: 'IN MEMORIAM J. D. Sedding, George 5th Earl Cadogan and Sir John Betjeman, architect, patron and preserver, respectively, of the Church of The Holy Trinity, Upper Chelsea'. The tribute to John was just. When he passed that church, towards the end of his life, he knew that, but for him, it might well not be standing.

John was girding himself for a greater campaign, nearer his heart. In February 1975 he had written to me that there was much he wanted to talk about under three headings, one of which was 'Liverpool Street station and Hotel and Broad Street station', a topic which 'must be confidential for the moment'. In August – the day after the Government announced that two bays of the Liverpool Street train sheds of 1872 were to be listed as Grade II – John and others wrote to *The Times* to oppose British Rail's plans to redevelop Liverpool Street and Broad Street and the Great Eastern Hotel.

British Rail were claiming that, because of the future operating requirements of the station, all the existing buildings at Liverpool Street must be demolished and replaced by a brand new station. Allegedly to pay for the new station, they were proposing 'a vast commercial development', consisting of 840,000 square feet of lettable office space, a shopping centre, and a new 300-bed hotel, at a total cost of £120 million. John and his allies counter-claimed that this total redevelopment was unnecessary; the station could be brought up to date by adapting the existing buildings. 'Liverpool Street's trainsheds, with their breathtaking fan-vaulting and aisle-and-transept form, can be described as a cast-iron citadel of the railway age . . .' John wrote. 'The Great Eastern Hotel . . . contains some of the most spectacular Victorian and Edwardian interiors in London.'

Eventually a compromise was reached. Bernard Kaukas, who was chief architect of British Rail at the time, recalls:

It was not true that the big commercial development was necessary to pay for the new station – something the preservationists constantly claimed. British Rail had no remit from the Government to use the money for that. It was true that the Government pressed on us the idea of commercial development. I think I did eventually get John to see that it wasn't British Rail architects who said, 'Let's pull down all this muck and put up something new.' We were servants of the Government. Early on, I realized that all that the preservationists really cared about was the western train shed; they didn't worry much about the offices. And we *did* compromise – we very quickly decided that the western train shed should remain.

In a letter to *The Times* (16 January 1980), the Archbishop of Canterbury, Donald Coggan, with Henry Moore and Lord Alexander of Tunis, fired a salvo in what was to be John's last great conservation battle. They complained that the proposed tower of the European Ferries office block, opposite the Tate Gallery on the south bank of the Thames, would be nearly twice as high as Big Ben – 'so colossal that it is known as "The Green Giant", being clad in green glass, or by local campaigners as "The Incredible Hulk of the South Bank".' A front-page *Times* news report on 14 January had named John among the tower's opponents. Four days later, Lord Duncan-Sandys, president of the Civic Trust, was quoted as saying that the block would be 'the thin end of the wedge', leading to 'a forest of giants'. (The tower was to be 500 feet high and 260 feet wide.) But in the same issue of the paper, the developers' architect, E. L. Howard, making the case for the building, said that the Archbishop and his co-signatories had complained of 'a lack of publicity' but, in reality, the developers had taken pains to ensure publicity. There had been two public exhibitions, 'one of them within 100 yards of the Archbishop's London residence'. The Archbishop and the other correspondents had described the building as clad in green glass. 'This is not so,' Howard wrote. 'It is clad in a light tinted glass giving an appearance of transparency . . .'

On 7 June a *Times* news report appeared, headed 'Green giant objectors fear failure'. The protesters expected the 'giant' to win when Michael Heseltine, Secretary of State for the Environment, announced that he would make his decision within the next four weeks. On 18 July 1980, however, Heseltine rejected the 'green giant' scheme for the South Bank. He made the announcement 'to a visibly surprised audience at the Royal Institute of British Architects' annual conference in Newcastle-upon-Tyne'.

The vanquishing of the 'green giant' symbolized the way a preservationist David could defeat a Goliath of a developer. It had been a model campaign: the protest by a formidable group of people, rather than one person; the branding of the building as the 'green giant', a picturesque smear-phrase that fitted easily into newspaper headlines; the mention of 'opposite the Tate Gallery', as though the nation's art heritage were somehow imperilled; Duncan-Sandys's prophecy of a 'thin end of the wedge' (exactly the tactic John had used in the Letcombe Bassett fight); speeches in Parliament; the keeping up of a constant din of protest until the Government capitulated. John did not intervene directly with a letter, but he allowed his name to be brandished, and his influence was felt behind the scenes. He had been at Magdalen with Duncan-Sandys; as a Chelsea resident he was in touch with the Chelsea Society; the Archbishop was a friend and consulted him on architectural questions.

33

'. . . As I Lose Hold'

IN 1970 JOHN was asked if he would give a reading of Kipling at the Royal Court Theatre, Chelsea. He was flattered to be invited, and liked the idea of appearing on stage, but was dubious about presenting a programme of Kipling. 'Imperialism' was then notably out of favour, and in any case he preferred Newbolt. He replied: 'I will do Kipling, if I can also do T. E. Brown.' The Royal Court's response was 'Who?', but after John had spent an evening explaining his enthusiasm for the Manx poet, his suggestion was accepted. He said that he would read the Kipling works, but that somebody with a Manx accent, or who could 'do a Manx accent', must be found for the Brown poems. His old Oxford friend Douglas Cleverdon, now at the BBC, suggested that the man for the job was William Bealby-Wright, who had grown up on the Isle of Man, with a Manx mother. Although Bealby-Wright's normal way of speaking was British upper-middle class, he could do a Manx accent very convincingly. The Royal Court programme was a success; later, John and Bealby-Wright made a long-playing record of Brown's poetry and prose, *Manxman*.

Through the show and the recording, John became a friend of Bealby-Wright and his wife Susan Baker, often visiting them and their young children at their house on Parliament Hill, Highgate, the land of his own earliest memories. The couple were both members of a group called the Barrow Poets, which read poetry and played music in pubs. 'Eventually,' Susan Baker recalled, 'the performances in pubs got so packed out that even the landlord couldn't get to the Gents.' People came and went in the group, but by the end of the Sixties it had solidified into six members: Susan Baker and William Bealby-Wright, with Cicely Smith, Heather Black, Gerard Benson and the composer–oboist–pianist Jim Parker.

Born in 1934, Jim Parker had grown up in wartime Hartlepool. His great value to the Barrow Poets was that he could look at a poem and write incidental music in character with it. A splinter-group of the Barrow Poets, known as Doggerel Bank (Baker, Bealby-Wright, Parker) recorded *Silver Faces* (1973) and *Mr Skillercorn Dances* (1975) for a company in Wardour

Street, London, called Charisma. It was owned by an enterprising if slightly fly man, Tony Stratton-Smith, who had previously run reggae groups and edited *The Football Year Book*. The producer of the Doggerel Bank records was Hugh Murphy, described by Susan Baker as 'a boy with long hair and one earring, very working-class . . . an interesting person'.

Baker and Bealby-Wright invited Murphy to stay; he said at dinner one day, 'I'd love to produce John Betjeman poems.' Murphy admired John for reasons quite other than those which made the poet the darling of the Women's Institutes. 'To me – even though it was in the midst of the Sixties when I discovered it – Betjeman's time was roughly the same sort of time in history as mine. When he was young it was the Twenties, and the Twenties were incredibly exciting as well . . . There was a parallel.' Murphy wanted the poems to have a musical accompaniment. Susan Baker told him: 'We know John Betjeman very well. I'll introduce you to him, but only if you promise to use Jim Parker as composer.' When Murphy returned to England, he took the idea to Tony Stratton-Smith, who liked it. John had just become Poet Laureate.

Susan Baker telephoned John to invite him to dinner, broaching the idea of a musical record. John was doubtful about the plan – 'I always thought poetry was its own music,' he said – but he accepted the invitation. During the next few weeks he, Jim Parker and Murphy worked out which poems should be chosen. It was Murphy who thought of the title *Banana Blush*, from John's early poem 'The Flight from Bootle', which begins:

> Lonely in the Regent Palace,
> Sipping her 'Banana Blush',
> Lilian lost sight of Alice
> In the honey-coloured rush.

The recordings were made in a studio in Willesden. John was usually driven there by Hugh Murphy. Each morning Murphy would pick him up in Radnor Walk and strap him into the passenger seat of his Volkswagen Beetle. 'And I'd take different routes each day . . . And he'd point out things, all the time. I was passing Kensal Rise. He'd tell me who was buried there. He'd be looking up, he'd see the tops of buildings and remember what they used to be. I had a running commentary by John Betjeman. I didn't really appreciate it at the time.'

Instrumentally, Parker used 'a sort of Thirties dance band. We tried to get the atmosphere of the Thirties – a kind of innocence.' John read his words in a glass box in the studio. 'I brought him in, he knew where to stop,' Parker says. Parker adopted an old music-hall device for getting round the problem of John's not speaking in strict tempo. 'I used what are called "till ready" bars, because otherwise I would have had to write the music to fit exactly the time he was going to take, out of tempo, to get to a certain point. Sometimes one can do that; but if there's a rhythm going, one can't. So I had this sort of "till ready" system. "Till ready" was a thing used in music-hall – you know, you'd get this *RROOM*-boom-boom-boom, *RROOM*-boom-boom-boom, and eventually, after several goes and a few jokes they'd come in. "Till ready" is exactly what it is: you play till they're ready to start the song. It was the same idea, really, except that I was waiting for John to finish rather than waiting for him to come in. If John was falling behind we'd play the repeat bar a few times.'

Tony Stratton-Smith's confidence in the enterprise was justified. The record was generally well reviewed and sold well too. On 22 March 1974 John wrote to Parker: 'I must write to tell you, albeit on a typewriter for the sake of legibility, how entranced I am with your brilliant and sympathetic music to my verses. They [*sic*] give the poems a new dimension . . .' At the same time, John was mildly worried that his becoming a pop artist might give offence at the Palace. To forestall any criticism he wrote to Major Sir Rennie Maudslay, Keeper of the Privy Purse and Treasurer to the Queen:

> I committed a lapse of taste last month and I will not be surprised if I am dismissed from my honourable office. A respectable and literary pop group called the Barrow Poets wanted me to recite some of my verse to music. This I did and was pleased with what little of the result I heard. However, the publicity of the pop world is so appalling that I was not prepared for it. They called the pop record 'Betjeman's Banana Blush'. They've had a T-shirt made for me to wear which I've refused to do. It had on it, in white letters, this frightful title. Well, I have made my confession, reverend father. It is up to you to give me my penance, counsel and absolution, if you can.

The courtier replied: 'I can echo the admonition from *Hamlet*, "O shame, where is thy blush?" But as this is your first offence I am prepared to offer you a more gentle reproach from *Henry V* – "Put off your maiden blushes."' John played down the record's merits in an interview with Graham Lord of the *Sunday Express*. 'The cover is the most appalling yellow and pink,' he told him, 'and it has a photo of me completely bald and sitting on a chair giggling. As for one of the pictures on the back, one friend saw it and wrote to me, "Dear Dracula".'

The Parker settings for *Banana Blush* became popular in live performances too. The Nash Ensemble gave one at the Royal Festival Hall in June

1974. John attended and made a short speech: 'Thank you very much for coming. And thank you for finding your way through all this concrete.' He wrote to Jim Parker on 6 June: 'I loved the music. I loved the acting and the audience. I even grew quite fond of the Festival Hall and this all because of Nash Ensemble and you. Many thanks.'

In spite of some arguments over money, Jim Parker agreed to co-operate with Tony Stratton-Smith in making a second Betjeman record. John was enthusiastic. Parker thought that this time some sort of theme should link the poems chosen: perhaps they could be poems about women? John agreed. The title was to be *Late Flowering Love*, a squeamish adaptation of one of the poems' titles, 'Late Flowering Lust'. Parker did not want to make a second record with a Thirties band sound. He decided to use a consort of viols, combining it with a Fifties style of band, because a lot of the poems were post-war and would benefit from the 'big band' sound.

Two years later, in 1977, Tony Stratton-Smith thought of another reason to make a Betjeman record. John was the Poet Laureate and 1977 was the year of the Queen's Silver Jubilee. As the 'special selling point' of the record, he wanted John to write a poem for the jubilee and asked Parker to get Malcolm Williamson, the Master of the Queen's Music, to set it to music to issue on a jubilee record. 'That did not come about,' Parker says. 'We ended up with a record that had very little royal about it except the cover and John's poem on the Death of George V. It was more a celebration of Betjeman than the Queen.'

The record was issued as *Sir John Betjeman's Britain*. As a concession to the jubilee idea, the second side was about London. One of the poems John read was 'South London Sketch, 1944', which contains the lines

> Where the waters of the Wandle do
> Lugubriously flow.

As a break from recording, John and Parker went off to have a look at the River Wandle. 'It's just down in Wandsworth – dark brown, treacly, absolutely filthy,' Parker says. The two men stood on a small bridge and looked down. 'It really *is* "lugubrious", isn't it?' John said.

As before, it was often Hugh Murphy who drove John to and from Willesden. When they returned to Radnor Walk, John would usually offer him a malt whisky. 'And he enjoyed just sitting there and watching me drink it,' Murphy said. John was rather smitten by the young producer. '[He] has long, gold hair and one earring,' he told *The Observer*, 'but he's a wonderful fella.' And Murphy said of John: 'I got the chance of meeting somebody who brought his time with him . . . It wasn't quite a falling in love; but in a way it was *like* falling in love, because it's a big experience.' One day, John came to Murphy's office in Knightsbridge. 'We had a lovely girl there called Judy London, who was thin and very good-looking – long red hair and freckles. And he fell in love with her like you wouldn't believe. I took him home and he said, "Who was that beautiful girl? Those freckles!" She reminded him of a girl whom he wrote about.' That girl, of course, was 'Freckly Jill'.

In 1981 Parker found an excuse to make another record with John, which was to be the last. The film-maker Charles Wallace had made a television programme and a short cinema film based on the earlier records, using the tracks he liked best. He wanted to make another Betjeman film, so he egged Parker on to persuade John to record some new arrangements. Wallace suggested the poems he would like to be recorded, among them 'Death in Leamington', 'Slough', 'Exeter' and 'The 'Varsity Students' Rag'. John agreed and the record was eventually issued as *Sir John Betjeman's 'Varsity Rag*. (The inside record sleeve bore a drawing of John by Julia Whatley, perhaps the best caricature ever made of him.)

'John was very happy to do the record,' Parker recalls, 'because he was doing very little at that time. It gave him something to get on with.' But Parkinson's Disease and a stroke had enfeebled him. 'He was frail and I have to say he does sound a lot frailer. He was visibly tired. With *'Varsity Rag* we recorded the voice first. That meant John didn't have to come into the studio at set times any more. He came in totally at his leisure, with nobody waiting around, so he didn't have to rush to finish, he was just on his own. We took as many takes as we needed, and the poems were recorded in bits. I wrote the music round what he recorded. With the poem "'Varsity Rag" he did, for once, actually say it in time.'

Jim Parker continued to visit John at Radnor Walk. He admired the way Lady Elizabeth Cavendish looked after him. One evening Parker was having a drink with John and Jonathan Stedall, the television film-maker. The telephone rang and Stedall answered it. Cupping his hand over the receiver he whispered to John: 'Elizabeth is coming round and she's bringing Little Friend.'

'Oh *no!*' John said. Turning to Jim Parker he asked, 'Will you stay as well? Princess Margaret is coming to supper.' Parker did stay and helped keep the Princess entertained in John's small dining-room.

The records came out during years when John's reputation, as Laureate, was at low ebb. The presentation of some of his best earlier poems, in such an appetizing form, helped revive his popularity. A lot of people who might not have read the poems listened to the records. Parker modestly disclaims any responsibility for rehabilitating John. 'But the records did turn up on an awful lot of desert islands.'

Another man to have a rejuvenating effect on John was the *Evening Standard* columnist Simon Jenkins. They paired up in 1971, as a direct result of the census of that year. Every ten years since 1841 (except for 1941) a census has been held in Great Britain, and in recent decades, it has usually provoked a public row. The British do not take kindly to being asked personal questions or to being categorized and put on file. The dispute over the 1971 census also prompted an article by Simon Jenkins, who took a line different from all the other columnists. At twenty-seven, Jenkins – a future editor of both the *Standard* and *The Times* – had made a name as a writer on London architecture; it was in this year that his book *A City at Risk* was published. On 20 April Jenkins wrote in the *Standard*:

> The great census rumpus has at least served one useful purpose. It has brought under the spotlight one of London's most long-standing scandals – the use of Somerset House.
>
> Last week, while the Registrar-General, Michael Reed, did battle in his room with the Press, pressure groups and assorted MPs, I sloped off to wander round the block of offices in his command.
>
> The home of the Inland Revenue, the Registry of Births, Marriages and Deaths and the Probate Registry, Somerset House is no mere civil service building. It is one of the most magnificent palaces in London, on one of the best sites and dominating the finest view. It is quite absurd that it should be used for offices which are totally inaccessible to the public.

Jenkins suggested that Somerset House should be opened up, as soon as possible, to house one of the great national art collections, preferably the 'disgracefully neglected' British art collection at the Tate Gallery. One telling point that he neglected to make was that Somerset House had, after all, been the original home of the Royal Academy. But John Betjeman made it in a letter he wrote to the *Standard* in Jenkins's support. John added: 'What could be one of the finest eighteenth-century squares, not just in the United Kingdom but in Europe, is at present a private car park for tax collectors and registrars in the very heart of London.' In two years, under further pressure from a caucus led by John and Jenkins, the registry had been ejected and the rooms hung with Turner paintings. Later, much more of the building was turned into galleries.

Less than a year after Jenkins's article on Somerset House appeared, John and Jenkins had lunch together in Covent Garden. They met at Boulestin, the grand old subterranean restaurant founded by X. Marcel Boulestin in the 1920s. What began as a brief stroll back to the car afterwards had by teatime extended into 'an Odyssey of London sights and characters', as Jenkins recorded in an article of 27 April, 'A walk through Betjeman's London'.

> His knowledge is encyclopaedic. A woman once approached him and said, 'Mr Betjeman, I saw something perfectly horrible the other day. I know you'll love it.'
>
> Yet his judgments are always exhaustively researched and scrupulously fair. And as far as the 19th century is concerned, he could write a complete vade-mecum to the London offices of Victorian architects.

Jenkins remembers his friendship with John as a series of these architectural tours. Most of them began with lunch in the main dining-room of the Charing Cross Hotel, later named the Betjeman Room. After one such lunch, they took a taxi to Southwark. Jenkins recalls the trip mainly for an episode which showed John's insecurity.

> He always had a real horror of Irish drunks [Jenkins recalled in 1990]. We were walking through Borough Market and I remember he wanted to go to Southwark Cathedral, and there were three Irish drunks on a bench in the little Close of the Cathedral. And he simply wouldn't go past them. I said, 'John, they're really harmless old boys,' but he said, 'Oh, no, I won't go' – it was as if there were a bull in the Close. And I noticed whenever I was walking with him anywhere, he had an absolute horror of drunks. He thought they'd attack him. I often wondered whether he'd had that experience. But of course he was a very sensitive chap.
>
> Once we went to St Paul's Cathedral and he wanted to show me one of the monuments in the crypt. We walked to the Cathedral, to the steps down to the crypt. It must have been about 5.45 and the crypt was closing at 6.00. And the verger on duty said, 'I'm sorry, gentlemen, it's closed.'
>
> And I said, 'Look, it's closing at 6.00. It's now 5.45.'
>
> 'Well, no people are admitted after 5.45.'
>
> 'We're just going to see one thing down there. Our money's as good as anyone else's. Please can we go down?'
>
> 'No, it's an absolute rule.'
>
> And Betjeman simply flew off the handle. He went completely mad. He shouted: 'Listen, I was a night watchman on this Cathedral in the war. I'm a Friend of this Cathedral. I'm a friend of the Dean. How dare you not let me into the crypt? It's outrageous. *Do you know who I am?*'
>
> And the hapless verger, who was a really unpleasant character, suddenly realized who he was and said, 'Oh, Sir John, I'm most awfully sorry, I do beg your pardon; please, please come down.'

In 1973 John said to Jenkins, 'We must do Middlesex.' They decided to explore the churches within two miles of Terminal One at Heathrow

Airport. The area had been left surprisingly undeveloped. The airport's swift expansion after the Second World War had imposed a freeze on the land around it, partly with an eye to future acquisition, partly because it was assumed that nobody would want to live in houses so near a runway. Farms, manors, churches, fields, lanes all stayed as they were, locked in the past. Trunk roads and motorways cut separate paths, leaving old byways undisturbed.

'We got in a car and we simply tottered round all these little churches,' Jenkins said. 'Within two miles of Terminal One is a circle of these great old Middlesex churches, all of which you could visit if your plane was delayed a couple of hours. And John Betjeman knew them all.' The car stopped at the southern edge of the perimeter road at Heathrow, and the two men got out. John stood surrounded by a seemingly endless wasteland of aircraft hangars, restricted areas, sparking-plug factories and deserted petrol stations. 'Ah,' he said with deep satisfaction, 'rural Middlesex, rural Middlesex – one of the very best counties.' The fuel crisis of 1973 had made that corner of the Home Counties more tolerable than usual. Traffic was much reduced, and it was possible to imagine what the old village of Heathrow must have been like before the coming of the airport.

They reached the old village of Harmondsworth, whose showpiece was its great tithe barn, known since the Middle Ages but largely undiscovered.

> 'It's really a cathedral,' says Betjeman, approaching it across the muddy farmyard in which it still serves its original purpose. 'The biggest and noblest medieval barn in the whole of England. Built, I'd say, at the end of the 14th century.' He rubs its vast walls as a tailor might feel fine silk. 'Pudding stone, they used to call it in this part of Middlesex. Isn't it beautiful.'
>
> Getting inside entailed crawling under locked doors and up through the bales of hay inside. Betjeman burrowed up through the hay like a mole to admire the magnificent nave and roof supported on vast oak columns with huge wooden vaults.
>
> He carried that hay round with him on his suit for the rest of the day with great pride. He would gaze at it and murmur, reverently, 'Harmondsworth hay.'

These were the last days of John's agility. 'He was already *supposed* to be crippled,' Jenkins observed in 1990.

John was '*extremely* unsteady', he remembered, by 1976, the year of a memorable jaunt the two made to Southend. On 22 July, Jenkins wrote to John to propose that he 'receive' a cheque from the Southend Society, of which he was patron, representing money raised for the Architectural

Heritage Fund. 'An additional reason for my writing, however,' Jenkins went on, 'is that I would love to make one of our erstwhile expeditions out of it.'

John was enthusiastic. Jenkins duly arrived in Chelsea in a taxi to take him to Fenchurch Street station. 'Despite the weather he fervently refused to take more than a flimsy plastic mac and his flat cap. Gone are the days of the black overcoat and pork-pie hat. A day out at Southend called for more proletarian garb.' Jenkins found that John was 'totally obsessed' with a visit he had made as a boy to the church in the forecourt of Fenchurch Street station. By now, the church was only a crypt beneath a modern development. 'But there – you can still see the trees in the old churchyard,' John said, pointing to 'a thoroughly squalid patch of open space beneath an office block'. Jenkins thought: how wonderful to be able to invest any pattern of the City streets with their pre-war glory.

But Fenchurch Street was not much changed; and the ticket clerk gave satisfaction by asking, 'Single, day return, or will you be staying the night?' This prompted one of John's musings-aloud. 'Staying the night! Could it be at the Royal Hotel? Done in I'm sure. Or perhaps the Palace – Oh what a night that might once have been!' Jenkins noticed how John adopted his characteristic pose of 'standing, feet firmly on the ground, hand on some rail or baluster and eyes peering skyward in search of joy'.

By the time they reached Southend, there was a steady, relentless drizzle, but John liked that: 'It keeps Southend just for us, no people around.' He got off the train with his cloth cap pulled down on his head and the plastic mac round his shoulders. In an old airline bag he was carrying an embossed volume of the Southend poet Robert Buchanan. In 1990 Jenkins recalled an unfortunate incident just after their arrival.

> Betjeman had a very delicate flashpoint – I knew that from our encounter with the verger at St Paul's. When we got off the train at Southend, the station was totally deserted except for a mother and child waiting on the platform. We got off the train, and Betjeman was, frankly, acting. 'Ah! Wonderful place, Southend!' you see. Well, that station was ghastly. He went up to this woman and said, 'Isn't it marvellous, living in Southend, my dear? You are so lucky, living in Southend.' Anyway, she thought this man was completely crackers, and turned away and covered up her child. Betjeman was furious. He expected her to say, 'Oh, Sir John, how grateful I am . . .' but clearly she had no idea who he was. And that got him into a really bad mood.

After lunch, they strolled down Royal Terrace. 'You could get a house there for £10,000,' John said, 'but it would need a lot spent on it. £10,000 – it's worth ten times that. Look at the view, always changing. Let's find

Buchanan's grave – here it must be, what a marvellous spot. Palace Hotel, like Broderick's in Scarborough, only better. And St Erkenwald's, like a great ship there.' His slow walk speeded up occasionally, then slowed again. 'Who lives in Southend? Discriminating people. I would live here – and travel up to Fenchurch Street.'

It was time for the official part of the day. Because of John's infirmity Jenkins had ordered cars to take them from one part of Southend to another. He had also arranged, because he knew John liked to be made a fuss of, a reception by civic dignitaries and a good showing by the local press. 'But what he really wanted to do was to see the pier. Unfortunately, the pier had just burned down, there had been this terrible fire. And the dignitaries said, "We're awfully sorry, Sir John, but the pier train is out of action, because of the fire." It was pouring with rain, it was a really ghastly day. He said: "We'll walk." And dammit, he did. No stick – he just strode out the length of that wretched pier. I was slightly miffed, because I had actually got all these cars to take him a hundred yards here and a hundred yards there. It was all a bit of a show on his part.' At a ceremony in the Westcliff Hotel, John read out long extracts from Robert Buchanan – 'an appalling poet', in Jenkins's view. The Buchanan volume was presented to the local conservation society and John duly received the cheque from the society for the Architectural Heritage Fund.

They returned to Fenchurch Street in the evening, both exhausted – John from showing off all day and walking too far, Jenkins from watching over his capricious companion. Southend pier, in spite of two severe fires, survives. And one of the two miniature locomotives that carries visitors to the end of the pier and back is named *The Sir John Betjeman*.

In 1977 John made a new friend – the bookseller Reg Read, who served him as librarian, companion and court jester. Infiltrating and absorbed into the ménage at No. 29 Radnor Walk, and to some extent into that at No. 19, Read had an intimate view of John's day-to-day life for eight years, until the poet's death. Introduced by a mutual friend from Cloth Fair, Read went along to Radnor Walk:

> We took to each other absolutely. He plied me with bubbly; later on, I continually got blamed by Lady Elizabeth for his drinking too much. We had a wow of a morning. I commented about his books – how the sets had been broken up. Volume I was on the top shelf, Volume III on the bottom shelf and so on. Chaos! He said, 'What are you doing tomorrow?' I said, 'Why?' He said, 'Well, you're criticizing my books; you might as well come and put them in order.' So I became his librarian. If he felt very grand, he'd say, 'librarian and literary companion'.

The next day, Read began putting the books in order; but before he could make much headway John had a new idea. 'He said: "I think they should be *catalogued*." (I think it was: anything to keep our friendship going.) He said: "You can go upstairs into the parlour. There's a typewriter up there." We had great fun. Because of the amount of materials tucked away, he didn't always remember where things were; so he'd get great pleasure when I took a book downstairs, perhaps an 1890s poet – "Oooh, isn't it lovely!" ' Not all Read's discoveries pleased John.

> I had a desk in the study with him, and in the bookcase above my desk there was a fair quantity of books by Evelyn Waugh. Many were presentation copies, signed by Waugh to John or Penelope, or both of them. And in my excitement at finding these I said, 'Oh, *look*!' He was furious, because he considered – rightly or wrongly – that Evelyn Waugh had been responsible for the breakdown of his marriage. 'He was cruel,' he was this, he was that – John went berserk. Then he said, 'Let's have some more bubbly,' and the matter was dropped. I was surprised those books stayed where they were; because one day I happened to say, 'What a lovely collection of Nikolaus Pevsner you've got.' My *God*!
>
> '*Don't mention his name!*' John maintained that Pevsner never went to the buildings. He said that he used to gather up any university undergraduates and put them on bicycles and send them off to gather information. 'Well,' John said, 'they don't know anything. They probably don't even go to the places; they can tell him anything they like.' Of course, this was nonsense; but he just couldn't stand Pevsner. He made me put all the Pevsners into boxes and take them down to the cellar. 'Put them in the darkest corner you can find,' he said.

Read, who owned bookshops in Highgate, Islington and Charing Cross Road, was bisexual: he had left his wife to live with another man, a fellow bookseller with a shop in Cecil Court. He felt about his wife much as John felt about Penelope: 'I loved her, and we get on; but I can't live with her. Twenty-four hours and I'm nearly up the wall!' John quizzed Read about his sex-life and played along with the camper side of his nature. Read remembers: 'I went to a Chelsea café one morning with John and his then secretary, Elizabeth Moore. It was the time of Wimbledon and there was quite a lot of the Wimbledon set in there. We went to this restaurant about 11.00 in the morning and it was filling up with people having coffee. And John, in a voice which could be heard across the room, said "Look at that waiter's bum! It's like two apples. Reg! Invite him over – then maybe I might be able to brush against him with my hand." ' John had a taste for the scatological. 'He loved smutty stories,' Read says. 'And naughty postcards.' Jonathan Stedall also remembers John's Rabelaisian streak. 'He got very irritated if journalists who rang up asked him to spell his name. He would shout into the telephone: "B for bugger; E for entrails; T for turd; J for jockstrap"' and so on. It was almost as if he was now living the life he had foreseen in the lines –

> I made hay while the sun shone.
>   My work sold.
> Now, if the harvest is over
>   And the world cold,
> Give me the bonus of laughter
>   As I lose hold.

Read did not get on particularly well with Lady Elizabeth Cavendish, and relations were not improved by an unfortunate incident. John suggested that Read should sort out the papers above the wardrobe in his bedroom at No. 19. Read remembers:

There wasn't anything very exciting there. So, as one does, one moved from one room to another. And there in the adjoining room was a big cupboard full of clothes. Above it was a mass of boxes. Standing on a chair I got to reach these boxes. They were full of bundles of letters. And I had just started to undo the first bundle when I realized these were love letters from Elizabeth to John and from John to Elizabeth. Something said to me I mustn't look at these things, but before I could put them back and get myself off the chair, up comes a *tank engine* – Lady Elizabeth, of course. And there was I standing on the chair with these letters in my hand. She hauled me down. 'How *dare* you! These are *private*' – and she grabbed the letters. I mean, her reaction was quite understandable; but I had acted in all innocence. Lady Elizabeth already thought me a 'bad influence'; now she must have thought me some kind of spy.

I said to John, 'I think I've upset Elizabeth. I was looking through your papers and I happened on some love letters.' He almost laughed; and I even wondered if he had intended me to find them.

By contrast, Read made great friends with Penelope on her rare visits to Radnor Walk. He was invited to stay at Cusop. 'Much of the conversation was about how unreasonable John was regarding the temperature of the house. But it *was* cold!'

John still managed to entertain his friends in style. But beyond the jokes and the conversational patball, there are hints of inner misery. Reg Read often found him in tears. 'Many an afternoon he would sit in the large chair and he'd weep. The tears would be flowing down his face: he thought that Jesus was going to cast him into hell because of what he'd done to Penelope.' When Harry Williams was staying, he was able to comfort John, telling him that the marriage to Penelope had been a mistake and that he was destined to be with Elizabeth. John's physical condition worsened; and he became more and more disaffected with Chelsea. All his hatred of Chelsea boiled over in his poem 'Chelsea 1977'.

> The street is bathed in winter sunset pink,
> The air is redolent of kitchen sink,
> Between the dog-mess heaps I pick my way
> To watch the dying embers of the day
> Glow over Chelsea, crimson load on load
> All Brangwynesque across the long King's Road.
> Deep in myself I feel a sense of doom,
> Fearful of death I trudge towards the tomb.
> The earth beneath my feet is hardly soil
> But outstretched chicken-netting coil on coil
> Covering cables, sewage-pipes and wires
> While underneath burn hell's eternal fires.
> Snap! crackle! pop! the kiddiz know the sound
> And Satan stokes his furnace underground.

John made no fewer than six drafts of the poem; he later made a present of them to Read. The penultimate version which – unlike all the earlier drafts – was typewritten, ended with ten lines which were deleted from the poem when it was finally published. They expressed John's longing to escape from Chelsea and cross the river to the diocese of Southwark, ruled by his friend Mervyn Stockwood.

One source of misery, at least, was removed in 1977. The only thing that had detracted from John's enjoyment of his seventieth-birthday celebrations in 1976 was that no greeting arrived from his son. 'Not a bleep from Paul, who is still hung up in his subconscious . . .,' John had written to Penelope. But in the summer of 1977 the long alienation of father and son ended when Paul brought to England a beautiful girlfriend, Linda Shelton. John was greatly taken with her. He wrote to Candida's mother-in-law, Lady Grimthorpe, 'Our son Paul appeared this summer with a smashingly pretty and humorous girl from Missouri. They lightened life and warmed the cockles of my heart. They stayed at Blacklands.' (In May 1979 Penelope and John received a telegraph: 'Linda and I are getting married on Saturday May 19th at the Advent Lutheran Church on 93rd Street and Broadway, New York. Please be there in spirit although we do not expect you there in body. Paul and Linda.' The young Betjemans were to have three children, Thomas, Timothy and Lily.)

James Lees-Milne still saw a lot of John and Elizabeth. He had been concerned when the couple stayed with him just before Christmas 1976, *en route* for Cornwall. He wrote of John:

> He has aged alarmingly. Can hardly move. Passed the shuffling stage. Has to be guided along. With difficulty was able to enter our front door and collapse on an upright chair. There he sat till dinner, and ambled to the kitchen. Getting him upstairs and down the following morning a slow and laborious process. Talked after dinner about religion, and discussed how few practising Christians today really believed implicitly, whereas those of our grandparents' generation did believe without question, not all of course, but the majority. John said he *hoped*. Hope was greater than charity. All we could do was to hope.

In the second half of 1977, Jock Murray gave John lunch at the Charing Cross Hotel. 'John was putting on his "helpless" act,' Murray recalled. 'He said, "Oh, Jock, my fork is wobbling so much, I can't get the food to my mouth." I said, "Maybe not, John; but I notice you don't seem to be having so much trouble with the *wine glass*."' In November 1977 John stayed with Penelope again at Cusop and she consented to worship with him at Hereford Cathedral. The Roman Catholic Church had relaxed its rule forbidding its members to attend Anglican services. 'I have never felt so happy and fulfilled,' John wrote to Penelope; '. . . the happiness still steals over me like radiant heat.' Penelope had not yet acquired a telephone. John wanted to work out a system by which she would make regular calls to him at stated times. 'I very much like talking to you on the telephone. It is like those daily letters Woad and Mrs Woad [Penelope's parents] wrote to each other.'

On 16 March 1978, James Lees-Milne attended a meeting of the Royal Society of Literature at which John took the chair. This ordeal may have contributed to the heart attack that John suffered a few days later. Candida was driving home from London to Wiltshire when she heard on the car radio that her father had been rushed into the Royal Brompton Hospital.

> My own heart came up into my mouth [she wrote] and I continued round the roundabout in the rain and sped at over a hundred miles an hour back to London. I kept him alive in my mind. I could do nothing but say the Lord's Prayer constantly. As I drove up the Fulham Road I saw thirty or forty press men outside the Royal Brompton Hospital. It was raining even harder. I still kept JB alive in my head. I did not ask them any questions. I parked the car and walked into the hospital with my head down and eyes on the ground. I didn't ask the porter if my father was dead. I still kept him alive. I asked what ward he was in and went up to the fourth floor saying the Lord's

Prayer all the way up in the lift. He was alive. I sat by his bed and held his hand. He had the softest hands I had ever felt on a man, and when I looked back, I realized it was because he had never done a stroke of manual work in his life.

Slowly he regained his strength. On 28 November the Lees-Milnes dined with him and Elizabeth at No. 19 Radnor Walk, which was 'more topsy-turvy than usual, the builders in process of installing a heating system'. Lees-Milne found the heat 'asphyxiating', but John said he could never, himself, be too warm. Some of the talk was about the Jeremy Thorpe case: the Liberal leader had been charged, with others, with conspiracy to murder Norman Scott, his former lover. (All the defendants were later acquitted.) 'John said that in no circumstances was he ever shocked by sex cases. A[lvilde] said, not even when children are seduced? Never, John answered.'

In July 1979 Lees-Milne invited John and Elizabeth to dine at his club, Brooks's, with himself, Alvilde and the young historian Michael Bloch, for whom the diarist had conceived a platonic passion.

> I think A[lvilde] liked M[ichael] [Lees-Milne wrote], though she finds him looking, as she says, unhealthy. After dinner, M. and John had a long talk about Uranian [homosexual] verse, and liked one another. I worry about John, who is worse. Finds walking a great effort. E. leads him by the arm, making encouraging noises as one would to a recalcitrant horse. He has both sleeves of his shirt, without links, hanging over his hands. This, and his staggering gait, make him seem drunk after dinner. I felt sad. A. and I drove away, having put John in his car, and leaving Michael on the pavement.

A month later, the Lees-Milnes lunched with Penelope at Cusop. James noted that she 'talked of John as if he were still hers. Deplored his addiction to drugs: he takes every medicine which is going, and they conflict with one another'.

The Betjemans were together again for Penelope's seventieth birthday on St Valentine's Day, 1980 ('*the* day in my life,' John assured her); but two days later John and Elizabeth were guests of the Queen Mother at Royal Lodge, Windsor Great Park – 'surely a change in the tradition of royalty never to countenance domestic irregularities,' Lees-Milne noted. He added:

> John was given a bedroom next to the Queen Mother's and not next to E's. Nevertheless she went to say goodnight to him and tuck him up. She told the policeman on duty, who apparently sits all night on a chair outside the QM's bedroom, to see if John needed anything during the night, which this kind man did.

Sir Roy Strong, then director of the Victoria & Albert Museum, and his wife, the theatre designer Julia Trevelyan Oman, were also at Royal Lodge that weekend. Strong heard of an incident involving a group of the Queen Mother's guests – among them Elizabeth Cavendish and Sir Frederick Ashton, founder choreographer to the Royal Ballet.

> The story came to me direct from Fred Ashton [Strong writes]. He recalled how the bathroom door at Royal Lodge was suddenly flung open and Lady Eliz said 'And here is Sir Frederick's bathroom.' Fred was sat on the loo completely pole-axed and said, 'Thank goodness I had a dressing-gown on.' The moment was dissolved to mirth by Liz Cav. screaming with laughter.
>
> We went four times to Royal Lodge for Qu. Eliz's 'Arts' weekend – I didn't write them all up in my diary. Latterly, it was Ted Hughes. J.B. got dropped when he became too difficult to cope with – he drank so heavily that it was [Sir] Martin Gilliat's task to carry him upstairs somehow, undress him & put him to bed.

In 1980 John and Elizabeth visited the Scillies again. Arriving by helicopter, they were greeted by Mary Wilson with a bouquet of flowers, and stayed in a house owned by Prince Charles. Also, John was still up for trips to the English seaside, though not always with his partner's blessing. Reg Read remembers something of a showdown with Elizabeth Cavendish in 1980.

> One morning John came into his office at No. 29 – into his den – and said, 'Oh, Reg, what are we going to do? The Lung of London is going to be demolished! Southend pier.' So he sits himself down and I said, 'Explain.' He says, 'Oh, look!' and he showed me a cutting to the effect that Southend Council had agreed to a development which would mean that the whole of the pier would come down. So out came the bottles.

Reg had the idea of getting a protest by John on to the television by taking him to Southend. Within half an hour everything was fixed. But when John told Elizabeth of their plans, she was furious. Reg later tried to persuade her to join them on the trip, but again 'She hit the ceiling.' He recalls the day of departure.

> . . . I was waiting by the door of No. 29 to get a cab, and Lady Elizabeth realized that we were going. You could tell from where we were at No. 29 that she was yelling. So I went down to her house and said, 'Sorry, Lady Elizabeth, but I did ask you to come with us. Why don't you? There's still time.' '*No!*' She was so angry she could hardly speak. The cab came along and we all piled in, and there was Lady Elizabeth in the middle of the road, making frenzied gestures.

The visit was well covered on television and in the newspapers; and the pier was saved.

On 21 July 1980 Lees-Milne went to tea with Michael Bloch at the Oxford and Cambridge Club and found that he had also asked the writer Lady Caroline Blackwood, daughter of John's Oxford friend Basil Dufferin. 'Chain-smoking, churchyard cough, beautiful blue staring eyes, raddled complexion,' the diarist noted. 'A difficult girl. No come-back, no return of the ball.' He went on to drinks with John and Elizabeth. When Elizabeth left the two men to attend a meeting, Lees-Milne talked about his encounter with Caroline Blackwood. John told him of his unrequited love for Dufferin. In return, Lees-Milne described his passionate embraces, at Eton, with Tom Mitford – 'lips to lips, body pressed to body, each feeling the opposite fibre of the other'.

> J's eyes stood out with excitement. And then? he asked. And then, I said, when Tom left Eton it was all over. He never again had any truck with me, and turned exclusively to women. J's eyes filled with tears.

The eyes of a character obviously based on John fill with tears in a novel by Anthony Burgess published that same year. The book was *Earthly Powers*, which has perhaps the most arresting first sentence in modern literature – 'It was the afternoon of my eighty-first birthday, and I was in bed with my catamite when Ali announced that the archbishop had come to see me.' Burgess, an inveterate umbrage-taker, was envious of John's knighthood. In the novel – which kind friends soon drew to John's attention – he portrayed, with maximum malice, a Poet Laureate, Dawson Wignall. (Did Burgess, who knew so much, know that Dawson was the maiden name of John's mother?) Wignall is contemptuously described: 'a round, duckdownheaded, hamsterteethed children's book illustration of a benign humanoid who held the office John Dryden had once held'. Vulnerable himself, Burgess was adept at detecting other people's vulnerabilities. Over thirty years earlier, in *Scott-King's Modern Europe*, Evelyn Waugh had satirized John's fantasies about schoolgirl prefects. Burgess went further, making explicit the charges of perversion and fetishism and garnishing the attack with a parody of John's verse – clever, funny and lethal.

John, whose earthly powers were failing, was at the stage of life at which one assesses what one has achieved and what one has failed to achieve. When he asked, 'Mirror, mirror, on the wall . . . ?' there leered back at him the effigy which Burgess had created to stick pins in. He brooded over it. Not only was it mortifying in itself, a public humiliation; it was upsetting, too, to be made aware that there was anyone who despised and disliked him enough to mount such an attack. The rave reviews for Burgess's book did nothing to salve the wounds.

As John's *Angst* intensified, his secretary Elizabeth Moore and Reg Read encouraged people he liked to visit him. 'He was sometimes embarrassed,' Read says, 'because he lost control of his body, pooped his pants. So it had to be friends who knew him well.' Barry Humphries, for whom the 1970s had brought the triumph John had predicted, was always welcome. So were Margie Geddes, Kingsley Amis, Mary Wilson, Alan Ross, editor of the *London Magazine*, the broadcaster Robert Robinson, who had compèred television quiz shows in which John had taken part, and Richard Boston, editor of the magazines *Vole* and *Quarto*.

As John lapsed into illness and Barry Humphries increasingly went on tours abroad, the two men saw less of each other. When Humphries did visit John, he thought he was 'very much in the grip of alcohol. There was a lot of booze: champagne in pewter tankards in the morning; drinks before lunch; drinks at lunch; drinks after lunch; drinks in the evening. It all built up – and he was mixing it with anti-depressant pills. Most people didn't notice because of the fun of it all. It looked like merriment, generosity, enjoyment, celebration – but the truth was, he was pissed.'

For John, the most welcome visitor of all was Osbert Lancaster. 'I have a strong memory of Osbert and John at Radnor Walk, with Osbert sitting on the sofa,' Jonathan Stedall says. 'There is that thing about somebody you know really well, that you can sit in silence together. I had the feeling of a real closeness there – more than, I would say, with Jock Murray.' In August 1980 John said to Read, 'Oh Reg, we must go to Covent Garden for lunch. Shall we ask Osbert?'

> So a telephone call was put through to Osbert. He turned up. We got down to Covent Garden. There was a huge queue. I took one look and said, 'I'll see what I can do.' So I did a great act of 'I've got the Poet Laureate with me' – did a queue-jump. The waiter made it a condition that I must get him John Betjeman's signature. We got down to eating. Osbert decided to leave – which had happened before. So poor old John was landed with the bill. We made our way to the front of the house to go, and the waiter comes charging up about his autograph.
>
> The waiter says: 'I hope you don't mind me saying so: you might be the Poet Laureate but I think the poem you wrote for the Queen Mother's eightieth birthday was bloody awful!'
>
> John went the colour of your shirt [white] with rage. I said, 'Come on, John'; but he turned to the waiter and said, 'Have you ever tried to write poetry?' He said, 'You don't realize how difficult it is to write poetry to order.'

I grabbed him by the arm. I said, 'Come along, come along. I'll get a cab.' He was *shaking*, in the lobby. I got him out into the road and I said, 'Now, John, I'll go and get a cab down at the court – Bow Street. You stand there. Don't move.' I left him clutching a bollard. And I hadn't been gone more than thirty seconds before, 'Reg! Reg!' I thought, 'Oh God, are we going through that manure process again? Has he messed himself?' So I went back. I said, 'Oh for goodness sake, John! How can I get a taxi unless you . . . what is the matter?'

'Just look over there,' he said.

I followed his gaze to a row of neatly stacked black high-powered motor-cycles, glistening in the sun.

'We don't need a taxi,' he said. 'We'll go home on one of them. *Just think of all that power between your legs!*' He was laughing, the whole situation was defused.

Reg Read had to steer John through another crisis in September 1980, over the publication of *Church Poems*, a selection illustrated by John Piper. There had been a temporary falling-out between John and Piper, because Piper's son Edward was now the designer of the Shell Guides. John Betjeman hated his designs, and said so; John and Myfanwy Piper took offence and their son's side. As so often, Jock Murray's gentle, wise and humorous diplomacy came into play. He jollied the two men out of their antagonism. The two Johns' collaborating on *Church Poems* set the seal on reconciliation. But that volume itself then landed Murray in hot water. John was outraged to find that lines had been cut and other changes made without his knowledge. Murray had to recall the faulty copies and print a corrected edition the following March.

In April 1981 John went to stay with Elizabeth at Moor View, near Chatsworth. On Easter Sunday he lingered in bed. Elizabeth told him to hurry up or they would be late for church; but she soon found that he could not speak or move his right arm. He had suffered a stroke and was admitted to the Royal Hallamshire Hospital in Sheffield. He stayed there over a month and was attended by the neurologist Dr Cyril Davies-Jones, to Candida's eye 'extraordinarily good-looking'. Penelope and Elizabeth played Box and Cox in visiting hours. 'I hope your hozzie smells nice,' Sandy Stone (alias Barry Humphries) wrote from Melbourne on 29 May.

John was out of hospital by the time of his seventy-fifth birthday, 28 August 1981. To mark that anniversary, the Celandine Press published *A Garland for the Laureate*: verses by over twenty poets in an edition of 350 copies. On the title-page was a woodcut by Miriam Macgregor of a garland of wild flowers. Among the poets represented were Kingsley Amis,

Roy Fuller, Ted Hughes, Elizabeth Jennings, Stephen Spender, R. S. Thomas and Laurence Whistler. Even the old enemy John Wain contributed. The book was not ready for August, but was presented to John as a surprise in November. Many of the poets came to Radnor Walk for the ceremony, bringing bottles of champagne and smoked salmon sandwiches. On 4 December, John wrote to John Pringle of the Celandine Press, whose idea the book had been, 'The wild flowers in the Garland are innocently beautiful and make me think of the Christian names of the nurses who attended me at the Royal Hallamshire.'

Lees-Milne saw John again in March 1982. At Radnor Walk for dinner, he was shocked by his condition.

> When I arrived, he was sitting in his usual chair under the window, his belly swollen and prominent. Not his usual self, but quieter than usual. No guffaws of laughter, and when amused he gave a funny little half-snigger, half-grunt as though it were painful for him to laugh outright. But I tried to cheer him . . . J. said he (John) was only interested in young men. Wanted to go to bed with them. This did make him laugh outright. I said, 'We must get used to the fact that this is impossible now.'

Lees-Milne again dined with John and Elizabeth on 15 June.

> Noticeable declension since my last visit. J. barely spoke. Must have had another little stroke by the slipped look of his face on right-hand side. Enormous blown-up stomach. Movement from his chair to dinner table most painful. Was told not to help. Nice friendly old Anglican monk [Harry Williams] staying. While Elizabeth supported J.'s shoulders the monk gently kicked J's feet. Thus they dragged him, bent sideways like a telephone pole half blown over, to the table. I sat beside him. Tried to tease him into amusement. Barely succeeded. Yet yesterday, he was televised sitting in his chair. I said, 'I suppose you were talking about yourself as usual?' He laughed in the old way. He said, 'No, I was catty.' Strange reaction . . . Left feeling very sad. Cannot believe he will survive the year.

In October 1982 John Murray published a selection of poems by John which (with two exceptions) had never appeared in book form before. I had found them among his papers at the University of Victoria, British Columbia; and he had given the choice his approval. The verses, dedicated to Elizabeth, appeared under the title *Uncollected Poems*. Kingsley Amis said, 'Perhaps they should have stayed that way,' and John suggested the alternative title *Barrel Scrapings*. Most of the reviews were of the kind that Jock Murray diplomatically described as 'unhelpful', though the selection contained poems as good as '1940', 'Interior Decorator' and 'The Retired Postal

Clerk'; and in 2001 the verses were subsumed into a new edition of the *Collected Poems*.

John confounded James Lees-Milne's prediction that he would not survive 1982. 'By 1983,' Candida writes, 'he often looked sad and haunted behind his long, clear gaze. He would spend each morning at number 29, sitting at his Swedish-made pine table opposite his gentle secretary, Elizabeth Moore, whom he always called "Dorinda" and who lived on the other side of the street.' Candida felt that, in a way, the letters that still poured in 'anchored' her father, gave a structure to his day. But 'his dictated replies got shorter and shorter. Sometimes Elizabeth Moore would write them herself and say that JB was not feeling well and could not do this or that.'

One thing John did consent to do was to attend a lunch in his honour at Fishmongers' Hall on 7 April 1983, under Pietro Annigoni's exquisite portrait of the Queen. It was his second-to-last public appearance. John Mallet, who was keeper of the Ceramics Department at the Victoria & Albert Museum, presided over the event, and recorded it in his diary. After the lunch:

> we wheeled him through the Hall looking at things, though I have an idea his eyesight is pretty bad and he couldn't see much. But he seemed to enjoy it for a time and when he looked like tiring I hustled his wheel chair down into the lift and John Gough drove him home. I hope the old boy enjoyed himself; I think he did. Several times he threw back his head and opened his mouth in a loud, boyish clap of laughter.

34

His Last Bow

———◦◦◦———

IN 1981 AND 1982 – the last period when John was articulate – Jonathan Stedall made a series of seven television programmes with and about him, entitled *Time with Betjeman*. It was akin to the retrospective exhibition of a painter; instead of paintings, extracts from his earlier television films were shown. Though they ranged from one of John's earliest surviving televised broadcasts – at Exeter College, Oxford, in 1954 – to 1982 in Radnor Walk and Cornwall, they were not in chronological sequence, nor grouped under themes. Stedall made each episode a gallimaufry, a kind of lucky dip. At one moment one was watching the youngish, vital John mounting a diatribe against modern office blocks; at the next, the John of 1982 was slumped in an armchair, talking with old friends or haltingly answering Stedall's questions about his life and beliefs. For the viewer, the effect was 'Through all the changing scenes of life'; for John himself, it must have seemed more like the cliché about near-drowning – 'The whole of my life flashed before me.' To somebody already familiar with his television work – a Betjemaven, so to speak – the main interest of the series was to see the poet in the Eighties, his state of body and mind. Never, before or since, has there been so intimate a delving into a writer's life so near its end. Philip Larkin observed:

> The current television series, 'Time with Betjeman', allows us to study his face. Like most old faces, it has collapsed somewhat, but is still watchful, the eyes moving from speaker to speaker, faintly apprehensive.
>
> When he himself says something, there is a hint of the old nostril-lifting irony, the corners of the mouth turning down crookedly; then suddenly comes the uproarious back-of-the-pit horse-laugh wide open, all teeth and creases. And above it the extraordinarily powerful skull, like a Roman bust, or a phrenologist's model waiting to be marked into thirty-three sections and labelled with Superior Sentiments and Reflective Faculties. Impossible to characterize such features: the top half is authoritative, perhaps a famous headmaster, but lower down is the schoolboy: furtive, volatile, ready to burst out laughing, never entirely at ease.

In the first two episodes, Stedall intercuts the extracts with film of John in 1982 talking to John Osborne, Eddie Mirzoeff, Candida Lycett Green and Barry Humphries. John has not lost his wit. In episode three, he and Stedall join John and Myfanwy Piper in Harefield Church, Middlesex – a church the artist had first visited with John in the late 1930s.

STEDALL: Do vicars have good taste, in general?
JOHN: The holier the man, the worse the taste.

And again:

PIPER: Why do you suppose we all like churches so much?
JOHN: Because they're there, whatever happens.

The next episode shows John at Radnor Walk discussing religion with Harry Williams and Stedall.

STEDALL: Do you go to church, John?
JOHN: Yes. I used to think it was boring when I was at school – but much nicer than the other boys! Now I can't do without it: I think it fulfils something.
WILLIAMS: When I first knew you, years and years ago, the sort of churches you preferred were definitely Anglo-Catholic; but I think that now you are much more drawn to what I would call ordinary Church of England, that is to say, a sort of church which is averagely Anglican and what you used to call 'middle stump'. I think you feel at home. Am I right in that?
JOHN: Absolutely.

Stedall then shows an extract from *A Passion for Churches*, including John's inspired lines of verse commentary:

What would you be, you wide East Anglian sky,
Without church towers to recognize you by?

In Radnor Walk again, Stedall reminds John that in a radio broadcast on Tennyson about ten years ago, he had said: 'He held a very vague faith such as mine.' Would John stand by that? Williams interrupted:

I detect beneath the surface of your poetry . . . a view of life not as bloody but as terrifying, as full of horror.

John agrees with this. 'I'm frightened a lot of the time. Who isn't?'

STEDALL: Love of life, too. I suppose the two can coexist?
WILLIAMS: That's the doubt and the faith. It's expressed in his poetry. I

533

mean, the way he loves life – that's the faith. And when he feels the terror and horror – that's the doubt.

STEDALL: What do you fear most, John?

JOHN: Pain . . . I remember hearing somebody say, 'Of course as a Christian I'm bound to believe in eternal life; but I prefer the idea of extinction.' That was a very good man, said that. And I thought it was really the most awful thing you could say. And now I find it's true.

Episode six takes the cameras into Murray's offices at No. 50 Albemarle Street, where John, Stedall, Jock Murray and John Sparrow are discussing corrections to the proofs of John's *Uncollected Poems* (1982).

STEDALL: Jock, do you think that John's involvement with radio and television has been important in making him much more widely known and appreciated?

MURRAY: Very important . . . John can correct me if I'm not right, but I should have thought that it has stimulated him to create things that he would never have created.

John agrees. Asked which living poets he admires, he nominates 'old Philip' (Larkin) and mischievously quotes, without a stumble, the whole poem beginning, 'They fuck you up, your mum and dad . . .' Sparrow is asked what are the outstanding qualities of John's poetry. He dodges the question, but the four men identify what they consider John's main subjects – among them, churches, architecture, death and the fear of the unknown.

JOHN: Fear . . . I'm very timid and by nature a masochist.

STEDALL: But a lot of your poems are very funny . . .

JOHN: Death frightens me. Desperately frightens me.

Sparrow reads John's poem 'A Child Ill' aloud. Stedall asks John if it was about Paul. In his reply, John comes close to acknowledging that he has mismanaged his relationship with his son: 'It wasn't that Paul was ill. I thought he *might* be ill. One is always afraid of losing people. I made the mistake, probably, of thinking my son belonged to me, which he doesn't.' Again John is questioned about contemporary poets.

STEDALL: Auden you knew. And you like his verse?

JOHN: I liked him even more than his verse.

There follows what for many is the *pièce de résistance* of all seven episodes. Stedall had driven John back to Uffington while Penelope was trekking in India. Now the film is played over to Penelope in a studio, with John beside her; and she contradicts almost everything he says on screen. Showing John Garrard's Farm, in pouring rain, Stedall says: 'Your two children were born here before the war, weren't they?'

JOHN: Yes.
PENELOPE: Neither of them. One in London, one in Dublin. [She might have added that Candida was born *during* the war.]

On screen, John tells Stedall, 'the house was run for horses'.

STEDALL: Did you ever ride?
JOHN: No.
PENELOPE: He did. I took him out, yes. This is *all* wrong!
STEDALL: Was he any good?
PENELOPE: No. I'll tell you. Robert Heber Percy bought a very old grey cob to take Lord Berners out riding on, Gerald Berners. It was a fleabitten grey. And I borrowed it for John. I took him out on the downs one day, and it was so lame in every leg . . . it could hardly hobble along. We went up on the downs, beyond White Horse Hill. We got into a huge field full of little bullocks, sort of yearling bullocks. And you know how inquisitive they are. They all rushed round us and started chasing John, who set spurs to this old grey who galloped off up the hill and John shouting, 'You've brought me here to kill me! You've brought me here to kill me!' And I laughed so much I nearly fell orf.

In episode seven, John is filmed in his wheelchair in Cornwall with Stedall in attendance. And here comes the most famous exchange of the entire series.

STEDALL: Do you have any regrets, John?
JOHN: Yes. I haven't had enough sex.

There is more talk about death.

STEDALL: Do you remember that thing that your friend Harry Williams said, that death is like letting go?
JOHN: Yes. That's a very good description of it. Letting go.
STEDALL: Have you minded getting old, John?
JOHN: Yes. Because I don't feel so well. Growing old is the most disillusioning thing we have to go through. It isn't easier to be alive now we're old. Now *I'm* old.
STEDALL: Can you explain, John? Why is it disillusioning?
JOHN: I think it's because . . . I'm very worried about this *Guinness* thing [a 'Guinness' label on his windcheater].
STEDALL: I've cut mine off.

JOHN: I wish I'd cut mine off. I don't like advertising.
STEDALL: Are you changing the subject?
JOHN: No. Well, I suppose I am, yes.

Stedall ends his series where he first met John, in his cottage in Cornwall. Trebetherick is in sunshine and the two men sit in the garden. The noise of a delivery van is heard. John says: 'Mother's Pride.' Stedall asks if he was ever interested in the news.

JOHN: No, never. As an undergraduate, I became very 'Left' in order to annoy my father and mother . . .
STEDALL: Was your father very right-wing?
JOHN: No. I think he was a very nice man and I'm only beginning to see that now he's dead. A very nice man and a very funny man and good-humoured. I'm peevish. But he wasn't [though] he used to get into bad tempers.

Aware that Stedall's film was probably his last chance to say things 'on the record', John used the opportunity to make his peace with his father, in effect apologizing for his misjudgement of him and explicit hatred of him. There is the sense of a resolution.

STEDALL: John, do you think your father really resented your becoming a poet, as opposed to going into the family business?
JOHN: No. I think he was secretly rather pleased. Yes, he *was* pleased.
STEDALL: Was there a bit of a poet in him?

In answer to this last question, John quoted the lines Ernest had given him to start him off on a poem about Frank Bramley's painting in the Tate Gallery, 'Hopeless Dawn', repeating:

He was a nice man. I'm beginning to see that now – too late. But I expect in Eternity he knows I'm fond of him – which I certainly *wasn't* at one time. Fear . . . 'Perfect love casteth out fear.' I had great fear of him. He was a large man, deaf . . . my mother was very kind, could always be got round.

A bread delivery van is heard on its return journey.

JOHN: That's nice, that's Mother's Pride come back. There it is, they've had a loaf. You can find nowhere that's quite silent . . . People are afraid of silence, but nothing is silent. All the time there's something bubbling up.
STEDALL: John, is there anything that you feel quite unshakable about in your convictions, whatever anyone else says?
JOHN: No. No, I don't think there is anything. I don't think I'd ever lay down the law . . . I *hope* 'The Management' is benign and in charge of us. I do very much hope that.

STEDALL: Hope rather than belief?

JOHN: Yes, certainly hope. Hope's my chief virtue.

He gazes at the lawn, trees and flowers at the end of the garden. 'Lovely here,' he murmurs.

STEDALL: Finished?

JOHN: Yes.

Some people thought it was a mistake to make a series of films of John in his enfeebled state. In 1994 the novelist, biographer, columnist and critic A. N. Wilson wrote, perhaps characteristically:

> During the sad period of Sir John Betjeman's decrepitude, a man in a cap called Jonathan Stedall had the idea of pushing him around in a wheelchair and asking him a lot of damn-fool questions.
>
> You could not be sure, even in these circumstances, whether Sir John was not playing to the gallery (interrupting the barrage of questions to listen to a passing Mother's Pride van for example). But in the years that have passed one imagined Stedall (a BBC producer) repenting of having put Sir John through all this.
>
> Not a bit of it. We turned on the telly on Sunday night (*Time Enough! or Not Enough Time!* BBC2) to find Stedall squatting beside the wheelchair while Betjeman, in the last stages of Parkinson's disease, wandered in his speech. I have often wondered in geriatric wards, or when visiting old friends in the final stage, that those who devote themselves to caring for the old seem positively to enjoy the aspects of the work which most of us would find most distressing. Dark thoughts about such matters are precisely the kind out of which Betjeman made poetry . . .

Stedall himself has said that he regrets not filming John a year or two earlier. But, while acknowledging that in 1982 John not only had difficulty with his speech but could not always hold on to a line of thought, he feels that there was one advantage to leaving the filming so late. Through infirmity, John's defences were down. 'He was almost totally unselfconscious in front of the camera. The performer in him was largely laid aside . . . He became more transparent, more truly what he was in essence.'

The doctor who diagnosed the Parkinson's Disease was John's friend Jill Parker. He had first met her in 1964 at a dinner party given by Frank Tait, Elizabeth Cavendish's next-door neighbour in Radnor Walk. Jill, who was then thirty-nine years old, was the daughter of Sir Ernest Rowe-Dutton, a Treasury official who had retired in 1951 as a director of the International Monetary Fund. In 1943, when she went up to Oxford to read medicine, she had dark hair and 'a long equine face like a Chardin'.

She was a *femme fatale*: her string of boyfriends included John Godley (later Lord Kilbracken) and Kenneth Tynan, to whom she was briefly engaged. At Oxford she also encountered the dashingly handsome Peter Parker, who played Hamlet, as Tynan snidely put it, 'as if he badly wanted to be king'. They were married in 1951. Six years later Jill joined a National Health Service practice in Palace Gardens Terrace, London, with a patient list of four thousand in a catchment of Kensington and Notting Hill Gate. It was run from the white-stuccoed early-Victorian house in which Max Beerbohm had been born.

Jill Parker made an immediate hit with John at Frank Tait's dinner-party in 1964, and their friendship was reinforced when not long afterwards John met Peter Parker at a dinner-party held by Elizabeth Cavendish in Radnor Walk. John became a friend of the Parker family, visiting them at their country home, a medieval farmhouse at Minster Lovell, Oxfordshire. So when his private doctor Dr John Allison, died in 1978, it was natural that John should put his faith entirely in Jill's practice. 'I think Lady Elizabeth didn't really want me to be his GP,' Jill said. 'She wanted him to have one of the royal doctors. And when I became his doctor, she thought that I wasn't being sufficiently professional. He would insist on starting with a glass of claret. I would try to ask him what was the matter, but she would come upstairs and find us in fits of laughter over something. *Both* in fits, you see. But I mean it was the only way to talk to him about whatever medically needed to be done.'

Jill diagnosed Parkinson's Disease, but thought John was fortunate in that, although he had the typical difficulty in walking which British doctors call a 'festinant gait' and the French *la marche aux petits pas*, he suffered only a little of the tremor associated with out-and-out Parkinson's. She prescribed L-dopa drugs for him. Jill's mother, Lady Rowe-Dutton, who had had the same illness, had been greatly helped by Dr Kevin Zilkha of the National Hospital for Nervous Diseases – 'the Hospital for Nervous Wrecks', as John called it. So Jill sent John to him. 'As with any doctor he ever went to, Kevin fell for him, and John was very well looked after. He never really got . . . I mean, Parkinson's can be soul-destroying. It held up his walk, but not more than that, I would say. It was certainly not the cause of his death.'

Some of the patients at the Palace Gardens Terrace practice were private; most were National Health. John thought it almost *sans-culotte* to be a National Health patient. It did not occur to him that he should make an appointment.

He just rang up one day [Jill recalled] and said, 'I've got to see you now. It's an *emergency*. It's really terrible – and I'm coming in a taxi.' And he put the phone down . . . He came in and sat in the surgery waiting-room . . . I think he had Archie with him. And of course everybody in the surgery recognized him and was frightfully impressed and amazed. And I cheated slightly, because I wasn't going to keep him waiting through *too* many patients. And anyway, if it was an emergency . . . And then he came in and sat down. He said: 'I don't know what to do. I've been too wicked – over Penelope and Elizabeth. Do you think I'll go to hell?' This was the emergency! . . . I said: 'I shouldn't think so. I don't think you'll go to hell. You just feel guilty because you're a guilty sort of person.'

John called Palace Gardens Terrace 'the little toy surgery', because he was often seen, not by Jill, but by one or other of the practice's two young partners, Dr Christopher Calman and Dr Gregory Scott. It was Calman who treated him for a phobia about crossing the cracks between the paving-stones on the pavement of Radnor Walk. In April 1977, not long afterwards, Jill Parker took the homosexual Scott to Radnor Walk to meet the poet for the first time. Scott wrote up the red-letter day in his diary.

As a result of being told [about the paving-stones episode] I was aware . . . that he suffered from considerable feelings of anxiety or Angst as he refers to it. Oddly, an article about him in a reference book written in 1963 refers to his fear of death, something that assails him more than ever. John [Stevenson – Scott's lover] sees this attitude, the High Anglican afraid to meet his maker, as typical of Betjeman's generation, a feeling perhaps shared by W. H. Auden and Tom Driberg.

At John's house, Scott and Jill Parker found him and John Byrne, a bookseller, reading poetry.

The poems were by one of the Uranian poets, a Rev. Davidson who had been a Cambridgeshire cleric.[*] When I showed recognition of this school of poetry, Betjeman was obviously pleased and was amused when I later pointed out that they were also known as 'the bathing shed school of poetry'. Glancing through the book, I quickly realized that the poems were fine examples of the pederastic school of poetry at its most overripe stage. The poems were all about moonstruck friendships where pubescent boys expressed undying love for each other. Suddenly, on prompting from Betjeman and John Byrne, I found myself reading one of them. After each verse, Betjeman encouraged me – 'Go on! Go on!' The poem was luckily

---

[*] John Byrne has told the author that the poet read was not in fact Davidson, but the Rev. E. E. Bradford.

not too provocative and in fact each verse finished with a twee refrain about eating Banbury buns on the beach!

While we sat sipping burgundy, Betjeman encouraged John Byrne to read more of John Davidson's Uranian poems. In fact several more were read to the point where it became a little embarrassing, particularly since it so firmly underlined Betjeman's pederastic interests. Jill laughed heartily as yet another poem was recited, but commented afterwards on Byrne's tactlessness.

Eventually Byrne left, and Jill and Scott were able to address John's medical problems.

By this time [Scott continues] Betjeman was seated beside me . . . Jill says that his cardio-vascular system is OK and that his apparent infirmity is all due to his Parkinson's Disease. He has seen a neurologist [Kevin Zilkha] about this and is on L-Dopa but it doesn't seem to help much. The three features of Parkinson's Disease are rigidity, tremor and bradymysesia. He doesn't seem at all disabled by the first two of these – perhaps they are controlled by the L-Dopa – but the third symptom disables him almost totally. Obviously prone to depression and anxiety, he can hardly bear his present immobility. He bemoaned the fact that he will probably never be able to get on a bus again and asked plaintively 'Am I going downhill? Do you think this is it? Am I going to die?' This may sound self-pitying, but in fact such comments were interspersed with witty utterances and his old sparkle and charm still pervade his whole behaviour. He also bemoaned the fact that his creative powers have totally disappeared.

'I haven't written a poem for years. Will I ever write one again?' Jill strenuously contradicted him, but he is obviously in such a restricted state mentally and physically that lack of creative impetus is hardly surprising.

John told Scott that he was delightful and that he would be happy to die in his arms.

While Jill Parker and the 'toy surgery' boys were ministering to John's body, Peter Parker was doing wonders for his ego. In 1976 Parker was appointed chairman of British Rail. (He was knighted in 1978.) He wanted British Rail to 'draw inspiration from the entrepreneurial past, from our great days, and [so] help us to correct an imperfect present . . .'. In John Betjeman – already well known to the public as a nostalgic railway-lover – he saw the ideal instrument for such a policy. He was fond of John, and genuinely wanted to do him honour; but he also hoped, as he recalled in 1990, that John would help to 'energize' his plans for British Rail. (Was there also some hope of gagging John's public criticism of British Rail's developments and demolitions if British Rail honoured him, stopping his gob with sweets?)

In July 1977 Peter Parker joined Jill late at a dinner-party and found John there too. John told him how lucky he was to work with railway people, the best sorts in the world. 'You know, I carry a book by a railwayman around with me most days,' he added. He pulled from his pocket a small book: Parker noticed that the soft black cover had become 'curved to the pear-drop shape of the Betjeman hip'. The book was *Joy to Know*, a collection of 'prayers and thoughts' by Walter Sinkinson, a retired signalman. Technically, few of the poems were much higher than parish-magazine standard. What attracted John was the serene certainty of Sinkinson's faith; he also enjoyed the touches of railway lore that enlivened the imagery. The next day, Parker found out who Sinkinson was and wrote to him to say how much John Betjeman enjoyed his work. He also asked one of his lieutenants, Bernard Kaukas, to keep in touch with the signalman.

In 1977, Peter Parker appointed Bernard Kaukas to be director of environment for British Rail. It was a newly created post. Like 'ecology', 'environment' was 'in': the Ministry of Works had become the Department of the Environment in 1970. A warm-hearted and genial, if sometimes peppery, man, Kaukas had previously been chief architect of British Rail and development director for the BR Property Board. One of the first things Parker asked him to do, as director of environment, was to think of some way of honouring John Betjeman. 'We must move quickly: he's not at all well,' Parker said. Kaukas had already known John for some years.

In 1976 William McAlpine (later Sir William) invited Kaukas on a trip to 'circumnavigate' London in a private train on 6 May. Accepting, Kaukas suggested that McAlpine might care to invite John Betjeman too. John accepted the invitation, and the 'McAlpine Special' left Kensington Olympia at 10.50 a.m. on 6 May, four classic carriages rolling behind a modern diesel engine. John's natural attitude to British Rail architects was antagonism: there was nothing they could put up that would placate him for what they were pulling down. But after the McAlpine Special jaunt he regarded Bernard Kaukas as a friend.

When Peter Parker asked Kaukas to think of a way of honouring John, Kaukas replied that as John was Poet Laureate, the honour had to be something lasting. Eventually it was decided to rename the restaurant at the Charing Cross Hotel after him. John had described it as 'the best proportioned Victorian hotel dining-room in London' – it had been one of his haunts when he was young. The renamed Betjeman Restaurant was opened on 24 January 1978, after John had been treated to a special saloon trip to four London termini. The train arrived at Charing Cross on time. When Parker went over to thank the staff, he said to one of the railwaymen: 'Does

Sir John know everything, or is it an amateurish knowledge?' The man was 'quite awed'. He said: 'Oh no, he knows everything. He's really serious.'

'*What* does he know?'

'He knew my father had built some warehouses along the line.'

Under the chandeliers of the restaurant about forty guests assembled to hear Peter Parker give an address. The purpose of the celebration, he said, was to name the room after 'Sir John Betjeman, Railwayman Extraordinary – and one of our greatest and toughest customers'. Betjeman's genius, he said, was 'an infinite capacity for taking trains'. During the reception, Parker noticed Bernard Kaukas with Walter Sinkinson and his wife in a corner at the back. The Sinkinsons had been invited down to meet John, although John had not been told they were coming. 'But, inexplicably, there was no surprise at all,' Parker wrote. 'Bernard brought Walter through the crowd, and before he could introduce him, in the midst of all that chatter and excitement, John stared a moment and said quietly, "You must be Walter Sinkinson."'

In March 1978 Peter Parker went into the Middlesex Hospital for an operation on his leg; and John, overcoming his fear of hospitals and his hatred of 'hospital smell', visited him. He brought with him a copy of his children's book *Archie and the Strict Baptists*, which Murray had recently published with illustrations by Phillida Gili, some of them loosely based on John's originals. On the flyleaf John wrote:

> For Peter's convalescence. Middlesex 1978
> A Dog Lover's Poem
> Big and barking and smelly is my landlady's dog
> It has tits all over it and turds the size of a log
> I know I must try to like it for it's ever so fond of me
> And must never attempt to strike it if it thinks I'm the trunk of a tree.

This rhyme (which soon found its way into a newspaper gossip column) was the final recrudescence of John's lifelong canophobia.

John made his last public appearance in June 1983. Three years before, James O'Brien, deputy general manager of the London Midland Region, had written to Peter Parker asking if he would invite John Betjeman to allow his name to be used on a locomotive, with a naming ceremony at St Pancras station if John were well enough. John would thus become British Rail's third 'living loco': the first two were Harold Macmillan, the former Prime Minister, and Lord Olivier, the actor. Parker at once agreed, but in fact the naming ceremony did not take place until 24 June 1983.

Accompanying John, as the wheelchair was manoeuvred alongside the train, were Elizabeth Cavendish and both of his children – Paul was over from America with his wife. There was also a buzzing throng of railway enthusiasts with notebooks and cameras; after the ceremony they were going to ride on the *Sir John Betjeman* to Bedford and back, at £10 a ticket. Peter Parker made one of his polished speeches. He spoke of John's campaigns to save the railway buildings heritage; of the famous lost battle over the Euston Arch that ironically became the rallying-point to fight on; of 'the frays (I put the word no higher)' which had developed since then, and the courtesy and understanding British Rail had received from Sir John, which were very much appreciated. The power of John's arguments, he added, had been responsible for the Board's decision, seven years before, to create an Environment department with a special remit to examine carefully its building heritage policy.

With some help, John pulled a cord to draw aside the curtain covering the gleaming 'SIR JOHN BETJEMAN' plaque on the locomotive. The crowd cheered. He tried to speak to them, but failed.

> When we got to the train [Parker recalled] at first he said he wasn't going to say anything; but when people began applauding he said he wanted to say something, and a thin little ribbon of a mike was pushed in front of him. But no one could hear a word. He did speak, and of course he did not realize that his whisper wasn't catching anything. So we had, I'd say, sixty seconds when he was speaking and none of us could hear. It was a very still moment. He was looking round as if he were wondering what was happening.

The *Sir John Betjeman* electric locomotive 86229 left for Bedford, pulling carriages with railway enthusiasts at every window. John was not on board. He was going off to a private luncheon in 'the Mess' at Euston House, headquarters of the London Midland Region. As James O'Brien (by now general manager) wheeled him from the dais, John said: 'Does it all have to end?'

Two weeks after the locomotive-naming ceremony, James Lees-Milne did 'what I would never do for anyone else' – drove to London to dine with John and Elizabeth, returning to Badminton the same evening. He arrived at Radnor Walk at eight o'clock.

> After all I need not have come. Feeble sweetly welcoming and cooked delicious roast chicken breast, and provided strawberries and cream. John slumped in his arm chair by the window, watching Coronation Street when I arrived, at an angle to the screen, two feet from it. Made signs of recognition. Spoke little. Mouth down at both sides. Difficult to elicit interest or response, yet I think fairly pleased to see me. Did not move to the table. Feeble put a board across arms of chair and gave him his helping, tied a bib,

gave him a spoon. He toyed with his helping. Just like a baby. His trousers totally loose, not tied to body by belt or braces.

Other old friends continued to visit John. Kingsley Amis wrote in his memoirs:

At the end, John was finally incapacitated by Parkinson's Disease, and that incomparably expressive face became set into a mute unchanging mask. I went and read poems to him, some of them by his much-admired Newbolt, not 'Drake's Drum' but later pieces like 'The Nightjar'. His stare remained as blank as before but I know the words reached him.

In September 1983 John had another heart attack. Lees-Milne again visited him and Elizabeth at Radnor Walk on 13 October.

JB sitting in his old armchair between window and fireplace looking different again since that bad heart attack. Totally bald, egg-shaped and dead white. A silent Buddha. Did not speak at all except to ask me, 'How's the Dame?' Eliz. says he rarely speaks now. Likes to be read to. No explanation for the heart attack. Might have another tomorrow, or in two years' time.

Lees-Milne saw John for the last time on 1 February 1984: 'In evening went to see John Betj. at Radnor Walk. Worse than ever. Very tragic. Sitting in his chair like a sack, his head lolling to one side. Feeble went up, kissed him and said she would set him straight. Promptly the head fell to the other side. Did not recognize me. I left feeling very sad.'

In April 1984, Penelope wrote to Jessie Sharley: 'I went to see John when I returned to London at the end of March and he smiled and said Yes several times when I asked him questions but otherwise he never speaks at all now and just sits in a chair with Archie and has a trained nurse in attendance . . .'

In May, John went to Cornwall with Elizabeth and his nurses, Carole and Vicky. 'Please relax . . . and don't drink any WHISKY,' Penelope wrote to him. Candida came down to Trebetherick and read him Evelyn Waugh's *The Ordeal of Gilbert Pinfold*. 'He was utterly happy in Trebetherick,' she later wrote. 'I could see it in his eyes.' John was due to return to London by ambulance on 19 May. Candida is sure that he heard of this arrangement and that he decided he wanted to die at Treen. Elizabeth read to him on the evening of the 18th and Carole watched over him that night. He died peacefully at 8.30 a.m. Elizabeth later wrote to Billa Harrod:

I truly think those last months he was more serene and at peace than I have ever known him . . . He died on the most beautiful sunny morning with the sun streaming into the room and the French windows open and the lovely smell of the garden everywhere. Carole was holding one of his hands and me the other and Vicky was just gently stroking his head and he had old Archie and Jumbo in each arm and Stanley the cat asleep on his tummy. He was completely conscious right up to that last moment. We none of us moved for nearly an hour afterwards and the sense of total peace was something I shall never forget.

Elizabeth telephoned Candida, who rang her mother in Herefordshire. Candida went into the garden at Blacklands and picked all the parrot tulips she had planted the autumn before, put them in the back of her car and drove down to Cornwall. That day John's death was a main item on the television news programmes. In the pubs, people talked about him, though it was Cup Final day. On 20 May most of the Sunday newspapers ran long and affectionate obituaries. *The Observer*'s headline was: 'Betjeman the people's poet dies'. On another page, Kingsley Amis, under the heading 'Frightfully good, old Betjeman', added an appreciation of his friend: 'In our century he has few equals and no superiors.' The *Sunday Times* published an essay by John Piper. The *Sunday Express* called John 'the man who took verse into the best-seller lists'. On the Monday, Philip Larkin wrote the obituary in the *Daily Telegraph*: 'Truly he has created, as Wordsworth said all great and original writers must, the taste by which he was relished.' The *Times*, too, judged John 'a true original'. Even the *New York Times* gave space to the news on its front page.

The funeral took place in St Enodoc Church in Cornwall on 22 May. It was a day of driving rain. The *Guardian* reporter, John Ezard, wrote of 'a horizontal monsoon and an umbrella-splintering wind'. The sand was so wet that the two gravediggers were worried that their work would collapse. Mourners were drenched as they struggled on foot towards the church's witch-hat spire. Penelope, Paul, Candida and Elizabeth were there, with Jock Murray, Billa Harrod and James Lees-Milne. The congregation of more than a hundred sang John's favourite hymns – 'The Church's One Foundation' and 'Dear Lord and Father of Mankind'. Lees-Milne wrote of the coffin-bearers: 'They, poor things, dripped throughout service on to the floor, and I felt them shivering.' He stood in the porch with others while the simple coffin was carried out into the torrential rain. It was buried beside the lych gate. Barely twenty yards away, fresh flowers had been placed on the grave of John's mother.

The service was a delicate operation, as Penelope and Elizabeth did not speak to each other. After the ceremony, there were two distinct wakes. Lees-Milne, who had telephoned Elizabeth, not Penelope, to ask if he would be welcome at the service, walked back across the field, with Lady Anne Tree, to the cottage, where a fire was burning.

Given toasted sandwiches and a glass of whisky. The others went to a neigh-bouring house for luncheon with Penelope whom I did not see to talk to. And Billa. Silent embrace in the rain. Poignancy of sitting on John's little deathbed with Archie, teddy bear, and Jumbo propped against pillow. Anyway I have paid my respects to the best man who ever lived and the most loveable.

Lees-Milne was, of course, a partisan mourner, one of John's oldest sur-viving friends. But John Ezard noticed how a group of what, in cliché terms, would have been called 'hard-bitten journalists', who had been allowed to stand under the lych gate with their notebooks and cameras, were affected by the rainswept ceremony. 'The scale of the place was so intimate and Betjemanesque that as they peered out they made an ashamed discovery. It is possible, even when rainwater is streaming down people's faces, to tell that they are also crying.'

The memorial service was held at Westminster Abbey on 24 June. In the congregation were most of John's surviving friends, and many people who had never known him but had applied for tickets to pay their respects. Three formidable diarists were present and recorded the occasion: Anthony Powell, James Lees-Milne and Peter Parker (not to be confused with the former chairman of British Rail), who was writing the biog-raphy of John's old friend Joe Ackerley, the novelist and literary editor. All three were given seats at good vantage points. Parker observed the arrivals.

We bobbed up and down as, unseen from where we sat, assorted royalty filed in to the strains of 'Nimrod'. The family, led by Candida Lycett Green in a beautiful grey outfit with pillbox hat and veil, trotted round the back to take their seats. Lady Betjeman was also in grey, her bosom resting down by her belt, her face like a disgruntled pekinese. Strings of children. Last of all, in shuffled an old man in a grubby raincoat, his thin hair brushed forward Caesar-style, held in place by a hairnet.

Powell contrasted the extravagant honour being done to John with his own memory of the scruffy joker of the 1920s.

Service a tremendous affair, the Archbishop of Canterbury [Robert Runcie] in charge; Prince of Wales reading the Lesson (which he did well), perfectly right for the Poet Laureate. The address by a cleric named Harry Williams, who emphasized how much Betjeman loathed the smoothness of business executives. (Williams himself gave an unrivalled example of ecclesiastical smoothness, and for ingratiating himself in other ways Betjeman too unequalled.) After a polite reference to Penelope Betjeman as wife, he spoke of 'thirty years' help and support from another', tho'

Elizabeth Cavendish was not mentioned by name. Finally, in obeisance to the Prince of Wales, adding how much Betjeman would have agreed with 'certain recent remarks about architecture'. One could not help indulging in rather banal reflections about the seedy unkempt (but never in the least unambitious) Betjeman of early days, snobbish objections to him at Oxford, Chetwodes' opposition to the marriage, crowned at the last by all this boasted pomp and show. It was a remarkable feat.

James Lees-Milne, too, reflected 'how amazed JB would have been had he known forty, fifty years ago when I first knew him, of this national hero's apotheosis, which is what it was'.

Before service opened we listened to John's favourite tunes, from *In a Monastery Garden* to Elgar and school songs he loved. Immediately long procession of twenty-five to thirty clergymen I would guess – dear old Gerard Irvine prancing among them – followed by Archbishop of Canterbury in white mitre. Feeble to whom I blew a kiss in a stall five away from mine was lunching with him afterwards. Billa [Harrod] very shocked. 'Most unbecoming in the Archbishop entertaining not the widow but the concubine.'

A memorial service was also held at Magdalen College, Oxford, and a Requiem Mass at Pusey House, where John had worshipped as an undergraduate. Penelope wrote to Father Ursell, the principal of Pusey House:

I will come with a friend (who is driving me to Oxford as I have no car & it is too far for my bike or pony cart) to the Requiem Mass . . . I would much rather just join the general congregation & not go in a front pew. I do hope you don't mind but the whole thing is very traumatic & I feel BOGUS. As I am sure you know J. B. settled with Elizabeth Cavendish for the last ten or twelve years & altho' I saw him occasionally & we were on good terms, E. did not like us meeting & she looked after him thro'out the Parkinson period. Of course I told J.B. I would divorce him if he wanted to marry E, but he IMPLORED me not to.

I have got to be in a front pew in W[estminster] A[bbey] as I am John's official widow but I can't face it at Pusey House as well.

Penelope died in April 1986, leading a Himalayan trek above Simla, where she had fallen in love with Sir John Marshall in 1931. She was cremated on a funeral pyre in the Hindu fashion.

Ten years later, on 11 November 1996, John's family and friends came to Westminster Abbey again for the dedication of a monument to his memory in Poets' Corner. It was an eighteenth-century stone cartouche which had been found in the triforium, still in its original crate. John Betjeman's extended family had grown: there were great-grandchildren now. His friends were depleted: Osbert Lancaster, among others, had died since 1984. Patrick Leigh Fermor, another classic writer of the 'Murray stable', gave the address. In this tabernacle of English antiquity, and to a congregation whose freshest memory of John was as a sad old man in a wheelchair, Leigh Fermor was able to conjure an image of the poet as he had first known him, in 1931, when John had given a lecture to his school, King's, Canterbury.

> He was twenty-five and nothing about this slim, dinner-jacketed figure, with his dark, rather floppy hair, his chalky pallor and his vivid and mobile mouth, in the least resembled any of our previous lecturers. His large dark eyes looked rather forlorn . . . His discourse was light, spontaneous, urgent and convincing, and it began with a eulogy of the spare and uncluttered lines of the Parthenon and this led on, astonishing as it may sound today, to a eulogy of the spare, uncluttered lines of the modern architecture of Le Corbusier and the Bauhaus School . . . and the merits of ferro-concrete and the simplicity of tubular steel furniture were rapturously extolled. Conversely, not an aspidistra, not an antimacassar was spared, and the slide of a half-timbered Victorian villa was dismissed with a pitying wave – 'and that's a tribute to Anne Hathaway, I suppose'. Wonderful jokes welled up in improvised asides and when, as if by mistake, the simple joke of a slide of Mickey Mouse playing a ukelele dropped on to the screen for a split second, it brought the house down. We reeled away in a state of gaseous exhilaration and the result would have been the same, whatever his theme.

This resurrection of the springtime Betjeman – in some ways the antithesis of his later public persona – was as telling as the celebrated coda of Lytton Strachey's *Queen Victoria*, in which the mind of the dying Queen flits back constantly to images of the young Prince Albert. Mary Wilson unveiled the monument. Leigh Fermor revealed how the antique stone had been discovered a few years before.

> It was blank then [he said] but it is inscribed now with his name, and raised forever on the flank of a pillar, like a hatchment. He would have liked the uprush of the clustered piers overhead and the interlock of the cloisters over there . . . Not many steps away sails the great vaulting of Henry VII's chapel; John always gloried in the thought that fan tracery was England's one original contribution to architecture; it only exists in the British Isles, like grouse. He would rejoice in his surroundings, and we all of us rejoice with him, for he has bestowed great gifts on us . . .

JOHN
BETJEMAN
1906-1984
Poet Laureate

Epilogue

SOMEBODY WITH A taste for the epigrammatic might suggest: 'John Betjeman's life was lived wholly within the twentieth century; but all his interests lay outside it.' (Love affairs excepted, of course.) He was famous for liking and preserving Victorian architecture. He wrote in a style that Tennyson would not have found outlandish. He was a man of religion in an age of irreligion.

It is a tenable debating case; but the arguments against it are stronger. Betjeman was a Bright Young Thing in the 1920s. He wrote with a post-Freudian freedom about sex, from 'Get on the bed there and start' in 'Clash went the Billiard Balls' to 'Late-Flowering Lust' and the sympathetic treatment of homosexuality in 'Monody on the Death of a Platonist Bank Clerk', published before homosexuality between consenting adults in private was made legal in Britain. He was a pioneer of the new medium of television. And, despite all his huffing and puffing about the 'infernal combustion engine', he helped, with the Shell Guides, to encourage people to explore Britain's heritage by motor-car.

In the long run, more cars meant dangerous pollution; but Betjeman has been claimed as an ecological trail-blazer. Michael Foot wrote in 1970: 'How many of the anti-pollutionists or community-preservers of the 1970s may look for their inspiration to early Betjeman? . . . He anticipated and, maybe, excited the modern outcry against the desecration of England in general and London in particular . . .' Betjeman's hymn for ecologists, 'We spray the fields and scatter / The poison on the ground', was published in 1966, the same year as Rebecca West's *The Birds Fall Down* and three years after Rachel Carson's *Silent Spring*.

He was able to conjure and capture the *Zeitgeist* of every decade he lived through (except the Eighties, when he was too ill); as examples, the Twenties children's party in 'Indoor Games near Newbury' and the caustic send-up of a young Sixties blade in 'Executive'. Betjeman may have felt culturally *dépaysé* from the late Fifties onwards, but his *Summoned by Bells* (1960) has plausibly been hailed as the first clarion of the Swinging Sixties, heralding the 'Let it all hang out' philosophy of the decade. A much less benign view of that book is taken by Andrew Sanders, Professor of English Studies at Durham University. In *The Short Oxford History of English Literature* (2000 edition) he writes:

> Although Betjeman claimed in his gushy, blank-verse autobiography *Summoned by Bells* to have presented a volume of his schoolboy poems to 'the American master, Mr Eliot', his later verse never revealed much of a response to Eliot's metrical, intellectual and lexical novelty.

That is rather like demanding: Why did Ronald Firbank never take up kick-boxing?

Sanders is rebuking Betjeman for not being 'modern'. In the sense in which professors of English Studies use the word (experimental; mimicking the 'fragmentation' of twentieth-century society), Betjeman was not modern; yet in another sense of the word he was more modern than Eliot himself. His friend Richard Ingrams wrote in 1984: 'He was never, as some opponents held, an obsolete fuddy-duddy . . . More so than many of today's poets he wrote about the modern world.' Though Betjeman is eternally associated with 'nostalgia', we learn far more about the world he lived in, from his poetry, than we learn about the world Eliot lived in, from Eliot's. If only in that respect, Betjeman is the more modern of the two.

In 1971, in attempting – as Auden had done before him – the difficult task of introducing Betjeman's poetry to American readers, Philip Larkin wrote: 'The quickest way to start a punch-up between two British literary critics is to ask them what they think of the poems of Sir John Betjeman.' The 'critical response' to him had always been polarized: Betjephiles versus Betjephobes. In October 1958 the critic A. Alvarez – himself a modernist poet – returned to England from America, where he had been lecturer in creative writing at Princeton. He found the English literary scene becalmed – a calm, he wrote, that was 'disastrously shattered' on 1 December that year by the publication of Betjeman's *Collected Poems*. He felt that its success showed 'that the revolution called "modern poetry", on which all our critical standards are founded, never took place for a huge proportion of the English poetry-reading public'. At the time Alvarez wrote his article, 33,400 copies of Betjeman's *Collected Poems* had been sold in two and a half months. 'This', he wrote, 'is almost certainly a good many more than the *Collected Poems* of T. S. Eliot sold in as many years.'

Alvarez's attack showed the main gripes and grievances of the Betjephobes, who tended to be left-wing disciples of Eliot. In their view, Betjeman was 'light' (frivolous) and snobbish, and was writing from and for the upper-middle class. Above all, he was considered a poetic reactionary, a foe of modernism. As a friend of Eliot, the last thing he wanted was to be pushed into the ring of a literary prize-fight with such a heavyweight. But, like it or not, his poetry is the antithesis of Eliot's. His poems are of great clarity. Eliot had written that 'Poets in our civilization, as it exists at present, must be *difficult*.' His critics accused him of being obscure.

In 1978, when Murray published a selection by John Guest entitled *The Best of Betjeman*, it was reviewed in the *New Statesman* by the poet and critic Ian Hamilton. He began by admitting that in the late Fifties hostility towards Betjeman was almost a 'knee-jerk reaction' by young writers such as himself.

> Needless to say, it wasn't *just* his popularity that stuck in the throats of the more steely critics of the day. He was despised for this, of course, but what really riled the hatchet men (or so they said) was that he'd somehow done the dirty on Poetry by dishing out a sugared substitute for the real thing. The real thing at that time was meant to be difficult, 'committed', and prosodically experimental. Betjeman's stuff was simple, idly snobbish and trippingly traditional in metre. It was also lots of other things: insular, ingratiating, churchy, smug and so on. He was thought by many to be the arch-enemy of What Needed to be Done in poetry. I seem to remember vaguely accepting that this was the case, without having read much Betjeman beyond the odd anthology piece. After all, the indictment sounded pretty well conclusive: popular, rhymes and scans, goes on about tennis clubs and subalterns . . . a clear case, it seemed, of What Needed to be Done In.

If anybody – including the then still living Betjeman – imagined that this paragraph was to be the prelude to a breast-beating *mea culpa*, he was disappointed. Hamilton was repelled by Betjeman's inverting phrases for the sake of the rhyme, and in his review impudently rewrote two Betjeman stanzas, wreaking havoc with their metre and rhyme in order to invert the inversions.

Betjeman's fame as a television 'eccentric' was harmful to his reputation as a poet. Alan Bennett and John Wells did lifelike comic impressions of him. (Bennett's 'Betjeman' gazed moonily after a departing London bus and murmured: 'I wonder where it's orf to. Newington Butts? Whipp's Crorss?') Alan Pryce-Jones quipped: 'It was John's fate to be sent down in his youth, and sent up in his old age.' In 1982 the writer and librarian Alan Bell contributed to *The Times* a profile of Betjeman which (to Bell's irritation) a sub-editor headed: 'By Appointment: Teddy Bear to the Nation'.

The label stuck. The 'cuddly' image still further exasperated the modernists. After the poet's death in May 1984 the critics, who had had few enough inhibitions about putting the boot in while he was alive, felt free to say whatever they wanted. The publication, late that year, of my book *John Betjeman: A Life in Pictures*, provoked a snarling poem by Gavin Ewart, which was less a squib against Betjeman than against the cult of Betjeman.

Geoffrey Grigson was another longstanding Betjephobe. Betjeman was still alive when he dismissed him as 'the lowbrow's middle-brow' in *The Private Art: A Poetry Notebook* (1982). Grigson wielded his famous 'billhook' with greater ferocity a few months after Betjeman's death, in *Recollections* (1984).

> How many have asked what [Betjeman] really stood for; if he was indeed quite real, and if he was not, on second thoughts, some kind of changeling found under a castor oil plant in the suburbs?
>
> Often the insults have been more insulting, and even bitter and scornful. What were his life's keepings? Wasn't it odd to make verse – skilfully to be sure – into a parody of verse, using forms and metres, even rhythms, adapted from hymn books both to mock those who enjoy them and think them to be the eternal essence of poetry, and to make them enjoy being mocked? 'Culture' without difficulties, 'culture' easily come by, without problems . . .
>
> Indignation asks . . . what have we expected the 'modern' poet to be? Serious.

Grigson ended his essay:

> Do I believe, as I have been told, that after some . . . pinprick Betjeman climbed from his house at Uffington and cursed me from the backside of the White Horse? Why not? John Betjeman showed himself a kindly and forgiving man; but I detested and still detest his verses, or most of them.

In May 1985, a year after Betjeman's death, Anthony Thwaite assembled a group of poets to give their views on him in a BBC Radio 3 discussion. Thwaite himself had never been enthusiastic about Betjeman's poetry; and in the programme the dice were a little loaded against the dead poet. Donald Davie admitted that 'He is infernally difficult to get any sort of critical callipers on.' But the Northern Irish poet Tom Paulin was unambiguously hostile.

> He represents that anti-intellectual antiquarian strand that there is in English culture. For me, he goes with a children's book I once read about a character called Molesworth, who tends to find things like old ear-trumpets in Hull. It's the kind of whimsy which, after a while, becomes terrible and frightening and surreal and bizarre, because of its enormous, trivializing stupidity.

On the same programme, however, Kingsley Amis defended his old friend from the charge of 'cosiness'.

I remember distinctly the first poem that sank in, which was 'Croydon' in his first collection. I had naturally taken him to be what so many people already thought him to be and so many people still think of him as – a light, entertaining, extremely funny versifier. But then, you see, I paid especial attention to 'Croydon', because I grew up near there.

> In a house like that
>   Your Uncle Dick was born;
> Satchel on back he walked to Whitgift
>   Every weekday morn.

Notice the 'morn' there: I thought, 'This is sly fun going on.' It's like an affectionate little postcard – a suburban scene. But then we see that it isn't just that and it ends with saying

> the steps are dusty that still lead up to
> Your Uncle Dick's front door.

> Pear and apple in Croydon gardens
>   Bud and blossom and fall,
> But your Uncle Dick has left his Croydon
>   Once for all.

And I remember thinking, 'My God, I hadn't bargained for that.' It's a very characteristic Betjeman thing, of course: it's that horrible dig in the ribs. Very often the message is, it seems, in the midst of life we're in death. It's not always that way but in the midst of ordinary, boring, amusing, vaguely entertaining life there's something unexpected done with incredible speed and incredible concentration.

Both during Betjeman's life and after it, his greatest cheerleader was Kingsley Amis's best friend, Philip Larkin. While the Betjephobes reviled Betjeman for not being 'modern', Larkin made that very quality the key-stone of his defence of him. Reviewing the *Collected Poems* in the maga-zine *Listen* in 1959, he wrote:

The chief significance of Betjeman as a poet is that he is a writer of talent and intelligence for whom the modern poetic revolution has simply not taken place. For him there has been no symbolism, no objective correlative, no T. S. Eliot or Ezra Pound, no rediscovery of myth or language as gesture, no *Seven Types* or *Some Versions*, no works of criticism with titles like *Communication as Discipline* or *Implicit and Explicit Image-Obliquity in Sir Lewis Morris*. He has been carried through by properties and techniques common to all but his immediate predecessors: a belief that poetry is an emotional business, rather than an intellectual and moral one, a belief in metre and rhyme as a means of enhancing emotion, a belief that a poem's meaning should be communicated directly and not by symbol.

In 1983, in his review of Patrick Taylor-Martin's study of Betjeman, Larkin made the case for the humorous poems which had earned the poet a reputation as 'just a funny man'.

> The trouble with the Plain Man's evaluation of Betjeman, putting one's money on the 'serious' poems and trying to forget the rest ('bad poems by his own standards, and not even very good light verse'), is that it misses the primitive, farcical, even Dionysian element in his work that expresses an essential side of his personality that may even power the rest. Mr Taylor-Martin's struggle with Captain Webb ('the nonconformist industrial setting is fondly described') ignores the sheer thumping silliness ('The *gas* was on in the Institute, The *flare* was up in the *gym*') that is the whole intoxicating point.

This was an amplification of a comment Larkin had made in a conversation with Neil Powell: 'I think it's significant that a lot of Betjeman's poems are funny – quite often there are things that you can only say as jokes. He is rather like the fool that speaks the truth through jokes, though that's a horribly literary way of putting it.'

Academe had set its face against Betjeman; but in the 1980s both a future Oxford don and an Oxford professor broke the ostracism and acknowledged Betjeman's genius. When the poet Craig Raine reviewed Patrick Taylor-Martin's book in 1983, he was poetry editor at Faber & Faber, Eliot's publishers. Subsequently a fellow in English at New College, Oxford, he has written a book entitled *In Defence of T. S. Eliot* and, though he defends him on the charge of having been an anti-Semite rather than a bad poet, he *is* an admirer of Eliot's poetry. So his praise for Betjeman in 1983 showed that a regard for Eliot and an enthusiasm for Betjeman need not be mutually exclusive, as Philip Larkin had implied they were in *All What Jazz*, in which he asserted that poetry had been ruined by Eliot, art by Picasso and jazz by Charlie Parker. Raine wrote:

> It is useless to approach [Betjeman's poetry] in the Arnoldian spirit of high seriousness. Betjeman is not interested in the noble application of ideas to life. He is interested in the thing itself – life – and he succeeds marvellously, without recourse to the Grand Style . . .
>
> You can scarcely understand Betjeman's poetry until you have grasped that he writes 'badly' in order to write well. It is a brilliant device and one which has disorientated his critics.

The Oxford professor who championed Betjeman was John Bayley. His review of the first volume of this biography, published in 1988, contained perhaps the most sympathetic appreciation ever of the emotional appeal of Betjeman's poetry.

Betjeman was probably the most sociable and conversable poet of this century, but his poetry is best discovered on one's own, and read in private. I remember doing that, as an undergraduate, and the world revealed was as magical as that of Auden had been at school. It was not Betjeman's fashionably social and ecclesiastical world. Like Auden's minefields and pitheads and scars where kestrels hover, through which one tiptoed in a state of heightened and excited awareness, it was a plangent but impersonal world of suburban joy and beauty, Odeons flashing fire, electric trains swinging low down the line through resin-scented fir-trees; Uncle Dick dying; sardine games in furry cupboards; the six o'clock news and a lime-juice and gin. It was pure romance, the light that never was on sea or land, the something ever more about to be, the familiar made wondrous and strange.

And sex, and love, as in all romance. They were immanent in the scent of the woods, the packet of Weights squashed in the grey sand of Surrey, the Edwardian plantations of Upper Lambourn making the swelling downland, far surrounding, seem their own. Most moving of all, the end of 'Love in a Valley' (from *Continual Dew*, 1937):

> Portable Lieutenant! They carry you to China
> And me to lonely shopping in a brilliant arcade;
> Firm hand, fond hand, switch the giddy engine!
> So for us a last time is bright light made.

It made me shed ecstatic tears. The complex mastery in it is in fact very great: the history and locality; the contemporary mechanics and outmoded slang; all rushed along with seeming effortlessness by the brilliant transformation of Meredith's metre, in which exultation is not replaced by loneliness and sadness, but mingled in with it. A total newness and lack of self-consciousness finds paradoxical expression in Victorian music, thus confounding the modernist pundits who maintained that new verse needs totally new form.

On what Larkin called Eliot's 'fatal phrase' about the desirability of poetry's being difficult, Betjeman commented: 'It's easy to be difficult.' And on the notion of modernism as an unshackling of poetry from wearisome conventions: 'There is a difference between liberty and taking liberties.' But he was not a pathological or doctrinaire anti-modernist. He was much more tolerant towards the modernists than they were towards him. Rather as he accepted that some Christians were temperamentally more drawn to 'Low' worship than to 'High', he understood the appeal of the looser genres to some of his friends. What he objected to in modern-ism was what he principally disliked about Roman Catholicism: its author-itarian stance, its insistence that all should follow its diktats or be pariahs.

I have suggested that 'His was the desolation of the Romantic whose vision of the world is eroded by the world's reality.'* His fear of death and hell – expressed in a number of his poems, and witnessed at its most extreme by Reg Read – originated in his indoctrination by his 'hateful' Calvinist nurse, Maud. His guilt-feelings intensified as he broke with Penelope and lived with Lady Elizabeth Cavendish. (His was a classic instance of 'the love of two women'. It was not a case of 'How happy could I be with either, / Were t'other dear charmer away!' Rather, he found in each woman qualities which he missed when with the other – for exam-ples, Penelope's scholar's brain and Elizabeth's ministering attentiveness.) Betjeman had faith, but the faith was assailed by doubts.

His guilt was not just religious. He felt guilt at not living up to his father's expectation that he would enter the family firm as 'the fourth generation'. His whole life could plausibly be interpreted as a Hamlet-like appeasement of his father's ghost – one long refutation of Ernest Betjemann's prophecy that his son would turn out a ne'er-do-well, 'Bone-lazy like my eldest brother Jack'; one long yearning for the benediction, 'This is my beloved son, in whom I am well pleased.' With Betjeman, art came before ambition; but still he craved the glittering prizes, emblems of success. This tendency showed up early, when he was at the Dragon School. The boys were asked to draw a strip-cartoon, illustrating 'how you would rescue and revive a drowning person'. Betjeman won the competition and his drawing was printed in the school magazine. In the last frame of the cartoon, the three brave rescuers are shown. On the left lapel of each is pinned a medal as large as a dinner plate. This 'going for a gong' trait continued in adult life. Betjeman made light of his accolade; but it was something he had set his heart on. What might Ernest Betjemann have felt if he had been able to wit-ness the memorial service of Sir John Betjeman, with the Prince of Wales reading 'Let us now praise famous men'?

As the balance-scales of reputation are adjusted – Eliot down a bit, Betjeman up – it is natural to wonder: what will be Betjeman's eventual place in English literature? Craig Raine thinks Betjeman 'succeeds marvel-lously' in presenting 'life', but all the same Raine's essay is in the nature of an affectionate put-down: 'he writes "badly" in order to write well'. And then there is the Grigsonian view that the poems are piffling and detestable.

---

* See Chapter 10, 'Marriage'.

A biographer has to be on his guard against making exorbitant claims for his subject. Setting aside, for a moment, the rôle Larkin assigns Betjeman – of valiant heresiarch against modernism – I believe Betjeman's poetry will last and will still be read with enjoyment in hundreds of years' time. He is a pre-eminent poet of places – in Harold Acton's words, 'the genius of the *genius loci*'. His skill in conveying places' character is hardly surpassed in English literature. Wordsworth has it in *The Prelude*; but often poets ostensibly dealing with places – Gray in his *Elegy* or T. S. Eliot in *Four Quartets* – are more interested in telling us their thoughts in or about Stoke Poges or Little Gidding than in evoking those places themselves, as Betjeman would do. If England stays much the same, it will be delightedly recognized in Betjeman's poems; if ruined, it will survive in them.

Some of his admirers think his reputation will rest on his 'serious' poems, such as 'Death in Leamington'. In accord with Larkin, I think it is more likely to rest on his humour – the humour which even sidles into 'Death in Leamington' ('Oh! Chintzy, chintzy cheeriness, / Half dead and half alive!'). Poets greater than Betjeman have written on love and death; but in (say) satire of the English middle classes in the Fifties, he is incomparable; those poems have a historical, as well as literary, value. And, just as humour invades the 'serious' poems, so the humorous ones are not all exclusively funny.

John Betjeman was happy to be compared to William Cowper, George Crabbe and Winthrop Mackworth Praed, all of whom he admired; but his range was greater than theirs, and they did not have the twentieth century to grapple with. He was, at the least, the very model of a major minor poet; and of course he was more besides – architectural historian, conservationist and television star, an authenticated National Treasure, archetype of the species. If he had not written a line of verse he would deserve a place in the national pantheon. Like Dr Johnson and Oscar Wilde, he imprinted and impressed his personality on his age. As a result, the word 'Betjemanesque' – apparently first used by John Edward Bowle in his Marlborough diary in 1924 – entered the language. It joined bowdlerize, boycott, banting, Bradshaw, Belisha beacon, Biro, Benedictine, Bewick's swan, buddleia and Byronic in the *Oxford English Dictionary*. In 1961 Cummings could draw Betjeman alongside President Kennedy as one of the six men best known to Britons. That fame was temporal. Betjemania is over; but the Betjemanesque survives, and will survive.

Select Bibliography

Books by Betjeman with autobiographical content

Collected Poems, John Murray, London 2003 edn.
First and Last Loves, John Murray, London 1952
Ghastly Good Taste, Anthony Blond, London 1970 edn.
An Oxford University Chest, John Miles, London 1938
Summoned by Bells, John Murray, London 1960

Betjeman's letters

John Betjeman Letters, ed. Candida Lycett Green, vol. i: *1926 to 1951*, Methuen, London 1994
John Betjeman Letters, ed. Candida Lycett Green, vol. ii: *1951 to 1984*, Methuen, London 1995

Books with contributions by Betjeman of autobiographical interest

T. S. Eliot, ed. Tambimuttu and Richard March, Frank & Cass, London 1965 edn.
The Future of the Past: Attitudes to Conservation 1174–1974, ed. Jane Fawcett, Thames & Hudson, London 1976
Hugh Gaitskell 1906–63, ed. W. T. Rodgers, Thames & Hudson, London 1964
Little Innocents, ed. Alan Pryce-Jones, Cobden-Sanderson, London 1932
My Oxford, ed. Ann Thwaite, Robson, London 1977
(with David Vaisey) *Victorian and Edwardian Oxford from Old Photographs*, Batsford, London 1971

Bibliographies

A Bibliographical Companion to BETJEMAN, compiled by Peter Gammond with John Heald, The Betjeman Society, Canterbury 1997
Sir John Betjeman 1906–1984: A checklist of writings by and about him, compiled by Peter Gammond and John Heald, The Betjeman Society, Guildford 2005

The bibliography on which Dr William Peterson of the University of Maryland has been working for many years, is eagerly awaited.

Books about John Betjeman

Jocelyn Brooke, *Ronald Firbank and John Betjeman*, Longmans, Green & Co., London 1962

Frank Delaney, *Betjeman Country*, Hodder & Stoughton, London 1983

Bevis Hillier, *John Betjeman: A Life in Pictures*, John Murray/Herbert Press, London 1984

John Press, *John Betjeman*, British Council, London 1974

Lance Sieveking, *John Betjeman and Dorset* (pamphlet), Dorset Natural History and Archaeological Society, Dorchester 1963

Derek Stanford, *John Betjeman: A Study*, Neville Spearman, London 1961

Patrick Taylor-Martin, *John Betjeman: His Life and Work*, Allen Lane, London 1983

Other relevant books

The Letters of Kingsley Amis, ed. Zachary Leader, HarperCollins, London 2000

Kingsley Amis, *Memoirs*, Hutchinson, London 1991

Beaton in the Sixties: More Unexpurgated Diaries, ed. Hugo Vickers, Weidenfeld & Nicolson, London 2003

The Unexpurgated Beaton Diaries, ed. Hugo Vickers, Phoenix, London 2003 edn.

Alan Bennett, *Writing Home*, Faber, London 1998 edn.

Anthony Blond, *Jew Made in England*, Timewell Press, London 2004

Wilfred Blunt, *Married to a Single Life*, Michael Russell, Salisbury 1983

Wilfred Blunt, *Slow on the Feather: Further Autobiography 1935–1959*, Michael Russell, Salisbury 1986

C. M. Bowra, *Memories 1898–1939*, Weidenfeld & Nicolson, London 1966

Anita Brookner, *Romanticism and its Discontents*, Viking, London 2000

The Diaries of Sir Robert Bruce Lockhart, ed. Kenneth Young, Macmillan, London 1973

Anthony Burgess, *Earthly Powers*, Hutchinson, London 1980

John Carey, *The Intellectuals and the Masses: Pride and Prejudice among the Literary Intelligentsia 1880–1939*, Faber, London 1992

Humphrey Carpenter, *W. H. Auden: A Biography*, Allen & Unwin, London 1981

Miranda Carter, *Anthony Blunt: His Lives*, Macmillan, London 2001

Helen Cathcart, *Princess Margaret*, W. H. Allen, London 1974

Bruce Chatwin, *On the Black Hill*, Vintage, London 1998 edn.

Kenneth Clark, *Another Part of the Wood*, John Murray, London 1974

The Ossie Clark Diaries, ed. Lady Henrietta Rous, Bloomsbury, London 1998

Peter Coleman, *The Real Barry Humphries*, Robson, London 1990

John Cooney, *Charles McQuaid: Ruler of Catholic Ireland*, The O'Brien Press, Dublin 1999

Lord Drogheda, *Double Harness*, Weidenfeld & Nicolson, London 1978

John Drummond, *Tainted by Experience: A Life in the Arts*, Faber, London 2000

Dame Edna Everage (Barry Humphries), *My Gorgeous Life: An Adventure*, Macmillan, London 1989

Duncan Fallowell, *20th Century Characters*, Vintage, London 1994

Robert Fisk, *In Time of War: Ireland, Ulster and the Price of Neutrality 1939–1945*, Deutsch, London 1983

Peter and Leni Gillman, *'Collar the Lot': How Britain Interned and Expelled its Wartime Refugees*, Quartet, London 1980

William Glenton, *Tony's Room: The Secret Love Story of Princess Margaret*, Bernard Geis Associates/Pocket Books, New York 1965

Richard Percival Graves, *Richard Hughes: A Biography*, London 1994

Geoffrey Grigson, *Recollections Mainly of Artists and Writers*, Hogarth Press, London 1984

Selina Hastings, *Evelyn Waugh: A Biography*, Sinclair-Stevenson, London 1994

Mark Haworth-Booth, *E. McKnight Kauffer: A Designer and his Public*, Gordon Fraser Gallery, London 1979

Christopher Hollis, *The Seven Ages: Their Exits and their Entrances*, Heinemann, London 1974

Michael Holroyd, *Lytton Strachey: The Years of Achievement 1910–1932*, London 1968

Alistair Horne, *Macmillan 1957–1986* (vol. ii of the official biography), Macmillan, London 1988

Barry Humphries, *More Please*, Viking, London 1992

Barry Humphries, *My Life as Me*, Michael Joseph, London 2002

Richard Ingrams and John Piper, *Piper's Places: John Piper in England and Wales*. Chatto & Windus, London 1983

A Dedicated Fan: Julian Jebb 1934–84, ed. Tristram and Georgia Powell, Peralta Press, London 1993

John Lahr, *Dame Edna Everage and the Rise of Western Civilization*, Bloomsbury, London 1991

John Lahr, *Prick Up your Ears*, Allen Lane, London 1978

Osbert Lancaster, *All Done from Memory*, John Murray, London 1967

Osbert Lancaster, *With an Eye to the Future*, John Murray 1967

Philip Larkin, *Further Requirements*, ed. Anthony Thwaite, Faber, London 2002 edn.

Philip Larkin, *Required Writing*, Faber, London 1983

James Lees-Milne, *Ancient as the Hills: Diaries 1973–1974*, John Murray, London 2000 edn.

James Lees-Milne, *Through Wood and Dale: Diaries 1975–1978*, John Murray, London 1999 edn.

James Lees-Milne, *Deep Romantic Chasm: Diaries 1979–1981*, ed. Michael Bloch, John Murray, London 2003 edn.

James Lees-Milne, *Holy Dread: Diaries 1982–1984*, ed. Michael Bloch, John Murray, London 2003 edn.

Bernard Levin, *The Pendulum Years: Britain in the Sixties*, Cape, London 1970

C. S. Lewis, *Collected Letters: Books, Broadcasts and the War*, ed. Walter Hooper, HarperCollins, London 2004

Robert Lusty, *Bound to Be Read*, Cape, London 1975

Louis MacNeice, *The Strings Are False*, ed. E. R. Dodds, Faber, London 1965

J. P. W. Mallalieu, *On Larkhill*, Alison & Busby, London 1983

Patrick Marnham, *The 'Private Eye' Story*, Deutsch, London 1982

Oliver Marriott, *The Property Boom*, Hamish Hamilton, London 1967

Penelope Middleboe, *Edith Olivier from her Journals 1924–48*, Weidenfeld & Nicolson, London 1989

Caroline Moorehead, *Sidney Bernstein: A Biography*, Cape, London 1984

Timothy Mowl, *Stylistic Cold Wars: Betjeman versus Pevsner*, John Murray, London 2000

Harold Nicolson, *Diaries and Letters 1939–1945*, ed. Nigel Nicolson, Collins, London 1967

David O'Donoghue, *Hitler's Irish Voices: The Story of German Radio's Irish Service*, Beyond the Pale, Belfast 1998

John Osborne, *Almost a Gentleman: An Autobiography*, vol. ii: *1955–1966*, Faber, London 1991 edn.

John Osborne, *Inadmissible Evidence*, Faber, London 1965

Peter Parker, *Ackerley: A Life of J. R. Ackerley*, Constable, London 1989

(Sir) Peter Parker, *For Starters: The Business of Life*, Cape, London 1989

Anthony Powell, *To Keep the Ball Rolling: Infants of the Spring*, Heinemann, London 1976

Anthony Powell, *To Keep the Ball Rolling: Messengers of Day*, Heinemann, London 1978

Anthony Powell, *To Keep the Ball Rolling: Faces in My Time*, Heinemann, London 1980

Anthony Powell, *To Keep the Ball Rolling: The Strangers All Are Gone*, Heinemann, London 1982

Anthony Powell, *Journals 1982–1986*, Heinemann, London 1995

Anthony Powell, *Journals 1987–1989*, Heinemann, London 1996

Anthony Powell, *Journals 1990–1992*, Heinemann, London 1997

Craig Raine, *Haydn and the Valve Trumpet*, Picador, London 2000 edn.

Stephen Regan (ed.), *Philip Larkin: Contemporary Critical Essays*, Palgrave Macmillan, Basingstoke, Hampshire 1997

J. M. Richards, *Memoirs of an Unjust Fella*, Weidenfeld & Nicolson, London 1980

Cecil Roberts, *The Bright Twenties*, Hodder & Stoughton, London 1970

Cecil Roberts, *The Pleasant Years*, Hodder & Stoughton, London 1974

Robert Robinson, *Skip All That*, Century, London 1996

J. D. Scott and Richard Hughes, *The Administration of War Production* (History of the Second World War, United Kingdom Civil Series), Longmans, Green & Co., London 1955

Nicholas Shakespeare, *Bruce Chatwin*, The Harvill Press/Cape, London 1999

Lance Sieveking, *The Eye of the Beholder*, Hulton Press, London 1957

Randall Stevenson, *The Last of England?* (vol. xii, 1960–2000. *The Oxford English Literary History*), Oxford University Press, Oxford 2004

John Sutherland, *Reading the Decades*, BBC, London 2002

Laura Thompson, *Life in a Cold Climate*, Review, London 2003

The Diaries of Evelyn Waugh, ed. Michael Davie, Weidenfeld & Nicolson, London 1976

The Letters of Evelyn Waugh, ed. Mark Amory, Weidenfeld & Nicolson, London 1980

Evelyn Waugh, *A Little Learning*, Chapman & Hall, London 1964

Trevor West, *Horace Plunkett, Co-Operation and Politics: An Irish Biography*, Colin Smythe/Catholic University of America Press, Washington DC, 1986

Terry Whalen, *Philip Larkin and English Poetry*, Palgrave Macmillan, Basingstoke, Hampshire 1986

Harry Williams, *Some Day I'll Find You*, Mitchell Beazley, London 1982

Mary Wilson, *New Poems*, Hutchinson, London 1979

Derek Wood, *Attack Warning Red: The Royal Observer Corps and the Defence of Britain 1925 to 1975*, Macdonald & Jane's, London 1976

Derek Wood with Derek Dempster, *The Narrow Margin: The Battle of Britain and the Rise of Air Power*, Arrow, London 1969 edn.

The Journals of Woodrow Wyatt, ed. Sarah Curtis, Macmillan, London 1999 edn.

Index

Betjemann, Eleanor (*née* Smith; JB's great-great-grandmother), 3

Betjemann, Ernest Edward (JB's father): rows with wife, 1–2; character and qualities, 4, 6; marriage and homes, 4–5; visits JB in Cornwall, 5; deafness, 17, 20, 30–1, 78; death, funeral and memorial tablet, 20, 149, 163–4; JB's relations with, 29–33, 77–8, 81–2, 87–8, 115–16, 130, 489, 536, 557; manages business, 29–31; motor car, 30; JB's poem on, 33; disapproves of JB's correspondence with Lord Alfred Douglas, 46; supports JB at Oxford, 51–3; praises JB's undergraduate poem, 64; and JB's failing exams at Oxford, 74; portrayed in JB's play, 77; in Ireland, 80–1; and JB's job prospects, 83, 87, 557; visits Plunkett, 88; house in Cornwall, 115, 116, 164; JB sends copy of *Mount Zion* to, 130; and JB's prospective marriage, 141; attends JB's wedding, 144; and JB's experience at death, 163; second wife and family appear at funeral, 163–4; contributes article to Shell Guide to Cornwall, 178; JB visits grave, 502

Betjemann, G. & Co. (cabinet makers), 2–3, 29; business liquidated, 164

Betjeman, George (JB's great-grandfather), 2–3

Betjemann, George (JB's great-great-grandfather), 3, 327

Betjemann, George (JB's great-uncle), 3

Betjemann, Gilbert H. (musician), 3–4

Betjemann, Hannah (*née* Thompson; JB's grandmother), 3–4

Betjemann, Harriott Lucy (JB's great-aunt), 3

Betjemann, Henry (JB's cousin), 3

Betjeman, Sir John: family name and origins, 2–4; birth, 5; childhood and upbringing, 6–10, 17–18; early schooling, 9, 11–15, 17; exhibitionism, 11; at Marlborough College, 14, 34–44, 49; juvenile verse, 14–16; holidays in Cornwall, 17–20; poetic models, 17; works for Shell-Mex, 17–19, 110, 194, 431; early interest in architecture, 18–19, 26–8, 31; burial in St Enodoc's churchyard, 20; golfing, 20, 44, 467; attends Dragon School, Oxford, 21–7; amateur dramatics, 25–6, 43, 64; book-buying, 28, 290; churchgoing, 28–9, 380, 533; relations with parents, 29–33, 77–8, 81–2, 87–8, 115–16, 130, 536; rejects father's factory work, 31–2; practical ineptitude, 32; appearance, 34, 43–4, 57, 70, 244–5; writes for *Spectator*, 36, 39, 340–2, 344–8, 370; contributes to school magazines, 40–3; debating at school, 42; mimicry, 44, 54, 420; homosexual inclinations, 46–7, 72–3, 114, 117, 387, 458, 499, 539–40; early romances, 48–9; at

Oxford (Magdalen Colllege), 50–61; religious beliefs and practices, 53, 58, 65–6, 114; vendettas, 55–7, 148, 278; motoring, 61, 230, 305, 317; snobbishness in friendships, 61, 71–2; contributes to and edits *Cherwell*, 63, 77, 79; expelled from OUDS, 64–5; supposed relations with Auden, 72; fails Divinity examination at Oxford, 74; rusticated and takes up temporary teaching post, 74, 76; fined for speeding, 78; leaves Oxford for good, 78–9; studies Welsh, 78; first visits to Ireland, 80–2; as private secretary to Plunkett, 83–5; becomes Quaker, 86, 176, 205, 229; jaundice, 86, 88; Plunkett dismisses, 88–9, 113; teaches at Heddon Court preparatory school, 89, 90–8; adopts left-wing views, 90; drawings, 96; as assistant editor and contributor on *Architectural Review*, 97, 100–10, 128, 131, 146, 296; attitude to Modernism, 103, 111–12, 267, 291, 351, 551–2, 555–7; interest in girls, 114; proposes to Lady Mary Erskine, 114; revisits Ireland, 115, 117–21; dislike of abroad, 116–17, 459; attempts novel-writing, 120; engagement to Camilla Russell, 121–3; as press attaché in wartime Dublin, 121, 199, 218–28; meets Penelope, 123, 137, 188; ends romance with Camilla, 124; kite-flying, 124; in love with Penelope, 126; contributes to *London Mercury*, 127–8; uses full Christian names of friends, 134; courtship and engagement difficulties, 137–43; nicknames for Penelope, 137; fantasies over masterful women, 139; marriage, 144; earnings, 146, 235, 337, 423; as film critic of *Evening Standard*, 149, 161–70; moves to Uffington, 149; affairs, 150; bell-ringing, 151–2, 241; marriage relations, 151, 153, 162, 186, 249, 252–3, 257–8, 262, 365, 385–6, 398, 432, 499; dislikes Farmer John Wheeler, 157–8, 194, 248, 259, 323, 358; visits Rome, 157; melancholy moods, 161, 163, 194, 447–8, 522–3; and father's death, 163–4; records views on bad taste, 168–9; appears in Ashcombe film, 171–2; leaves *Evening Standard*, 171–3; in Ministry of Information Films Division, 173, 205–8; diary, 174–5; anti-fascist views, 175–6; edits and contributes to Shell Guides, 176–7, 180, 182–3, 275, 550; feud with Pevsner, 180, 358–60; Myfanwy Piper's assessment of, 183; mocking behaviour, 184; relations with children, 187–9, 252, 313, 534; sensitivity to adverse criticism, 191, 422, 435, 471; money worries, 194–5; writes handyman hints for *Daily Express*, 195; edits *Decoration*, 196–7; seeks house in